ICSE Exams 2026

AF819950

All in One HISTORY & CIVICS

Class 10

Author
Kamlesh Kumar Prasad

arihant
SUCCESS AND NOTHING LESS

arihant
SUCCESS AND NOTHING LESS

ARIHANT PRAKASHAN
(School Division Series)

卐 *ADMINISTRATIVE & PRODUCTION OFFICES*

Regd. Office
'Ramchhaya' 4577/15, Agarwal Road, Darya Ganj, New Delhi -110002
Tele: 011- 47630600, 43518550; Fax: 011- 23280316

卐 *Head Office*
Kalindi, TP Nagar, Meerut (UP) - 250002, Tel: 0121-7156203, 7156204

卐 *SALES & SUPPORT OFFICES*
Agra, Ahmedabad, Bengaluru, Bareilly, Chennai, Delhi, Guwahati, Hyderabad, Jaipur, Jhansi, Kolkata, Lucknow, Nagpur & Pune.

PO No : TXT-XX-XXXXXXX-X-XX

Published By Arihant Publications (India) Ltd.

For further information about the books published by Arihant, log on to www.arihantbooks.com or e-mail at info@arihantbooks.com

Follow us on

卐 *PRICE* ₹330.00

PRODUCTION TEAM

Publishing Managers
Mahendra Singh Rawat & Keshav Mohan

Cover Designer
Salman Shaikh

Inner Designer
Ankit Tyagi

Project Head
Shivam Gupta

Page Layouting
Sundar Bisht

Proof Reader
Priya Kumari

Index *cum* Study Planner

CIVICS

HISTORY

		Studied	Revised	Exam ready
2. The Rise of Nationalism and the Indian National Congress	**99-111**			
Meaning of Nationalism	99-101	☐	☐	☐
Foundation of the Indian National Congress	102-103	☐	☐	☐
Chapter Practice	104-110	☐	☐	☐
Chapter Assessment	111	☐	☐	☐
3. First Phase of the Indian National Movement (1885-1907)	**112-125**			
The Early Nationalists (or Moderates)	112-113	☐	☐	☐
Demands of the Early Nationalists	113	☐	☐	☐
Methods of the Early Nationalists	113-114	☐	☐	☐
Prominent Early Nationalist Leaders	114-116	☐	☐	☐
Chapter Practice	118-124	☐	☐	☐
Chapter Assessment	125	☐	☐	☐
4. Second Phase of the Indian National Movement (1905-1916)	**126-139**			
Partition of Bengal	126-127	☐	☐	☐
The Assertive Nationalists or Radicals	127-128	☐	☐	☐
Prominent Assertive Nationalist Leaders	128-129	☐	☐	☐
Chapter Practice	131-138	☐	☐	☐
Chapter Assessment	139	☐	☐	☐
5. The Muslim League and Lucknow Pact	**140-155**			
Factors/Events Leading to the Formation of the Muslim League	140-143	☐	☐	☐
Formation of Muslim League	143-144	☐	☐	☐
The Lucknow Pact	145-146	☐	☐	☐
Chapter Practice	148-154	☐	☐	☐
Chapter Assessment	155	☐	☐	☐
6. Mahatma Gandhi and the National Movement (1915-1947)	**156-177**			
Mahatma Gandhi	156	☐	☐	☐
Non-Cooperation Movement	157-159	☐	☐	☐
Civil Disobedience Movement	159-162	☐	☐	☐
Events Leading to Quit India Movement	162	☐	☐	☐
Quit India Movement	162-164	☐	☐	☐
Chapter Practice	166-177	☐	☐	☐
Chapter Assessment	177	☐	☐	☐
7. Forward Bloc and Indian National Army (INA)	**178-187**			
Formation of Forward Bloc	178-179	☐	☐	☐
Formation of the Indian National Army (INA)	179-181	☐	☐	☐
Chapter Practice	182-186	☐	☐	☐
Chapter Assessment	187	☐	☐	☐

One Book- Endless Features

to Help you Succeed

Chapter Outlines

At the start of each chapter, all the topics of the chapter have been listed, so that students may know what they are going to study.

CHAPTER
01

The Union Legislature

SYLLABUS

Meaning of the Federal Setup in India (I) Lok Sabha-term, composition, qualifications for membership, • Parliamentary procedures : A brief idea of sessions, quorum, question hour, adjournment and no-confidence motion. Speaker-election and functions. (II) Rajya Sabha-composition, qualifications for membership, election, term, Presiding officer.
Powers and Functions of Union Parliament • Legislative, financial, judicial, electoral, amendment of the Constitution, control over executive. • Exclusive powers of the two Houses.

Quick Revision

At the end of each chapter, Quick Revision is given. It contains crux of the chapter in pointer form that provides the quick revision of the whole chapter.

QUiCK Revision

- Indian Constitution adopted both unitary and federal feature, therefore the Indian political structure is known as Quasi-Federal.
- Federal government means distribution of power between Centre and States by the Constitution itself and both operate in their respective jurisdictions independently.
- Lok Sabha is the House of the People and it is the popular House of the Parliament. The members are directly elected by the people. At present, the Lok Sabha consists of 543 members. Out of these, 530 are from States, 13 from Union Territories.
- The normal tenure of the Lok Sabha is 5 years, but it may be dissolved earlier by the President.

Complete Theory in Each Chapter

Each chapter has Complete, Easy to Understand and Simplified theory covering latest syllabus. Theory is developed in such a way that it suitable for all types of learners.

Federal Set-up in India

The Constitution of India provides for a federal system of government in the country. The Federal government means distribution of power between Centre and States by the Constitution itself and both operate in their respective **jurisdictions**[1] independently. However, the Central Government is more powerful than the States.

Check Your LEARNING...

1. Name the two sets of authority under the Federal Setup in India.
2. Which level of government is powerful in Unitary system?
3. Which judicial body has the authority to protect the supremacy of the Constitution?
4. Division of powers between States and Centre is mentioned in which part of Constitution ?

Check Your Learning

A set of 3-5 Questions given in between the text, helps students to remain connected with the text while studying. They can instantly assess themselves for their understanding.

One Book- Endless Features

to Help you Succeed

Chapter Practice

Chapter Practice have all types of questions that are asked in the examinations such as Multiple Choice Questions, Short Questions and Structured Questions.

Chapter Practice

Section-I

Multiple Choice Questions

1. The Lok Sabha session which is conducted in the months of November and December is the ....
   (a) Summer Session
   (b) Monsoon Session
   (c) Winter Session
   (d) Budget Session

Ans. (c) Winter Session

2. Under what circumstances may the term of the Lok Sabha be extended by one year at a time?
   (a) When the government resigns.
   (b) Proclamation of a National Emergency.
   (c) Economic instability.
   (d) Rajya Sabha declares by ¼ majority.

7. The Rajya Sabha is called a Permanent house because 1/3 members retire every ....
   (a) two years (b) one year
   (c) three years (d) six years

Ans. (a) two years

8. Which of these is considered to be an exclusive power of the Rajya Sabha?
   (a) It can approve an Ordinary Bill.
   (b) It can make amendments to the Constitution.
   (c) It can empower the Parliament to make laws on the State list.
   (d) It can make laws on subjects in the Union List.

Ans. (c) It can empower the Parliament to make laws on the State list.

9. Who elect the members of the Rajya Sabha? [Specimen Paper Semester-II 2022]

Sample Question Papers

To make students practice of examination in real sense, there are 5 Sample Question Papers at the end. All these Sample Questions Papers are exactly prepared on the latest syllabus & pattern of examination.

Chapter Assessment

It is the Assessment exercise for the complete chapter. With this exercise, students can access their understanding of the chapter and can prepare for it accordingly.

Chapter Assessment

Section-I

Multiple Choice Questions

1. The right of the members to ask questions in the House is known as ....
   (a) Interpellation (b) Interjection
   (c) Defection (d) Prorogation
2. Who elect the Speaker of the Lok Sabha?
   (a) The President
   (b) Only the members of the ruling party
   (c) The Chairman of the Rajya Sabha
   (d) The members of the Lok Sabha.
3. The creation of a new All India Services is an exclusive power of the ....
   (a) President (b) Lok Sabha
   (c) Rajya Sabha (d) Supreme Court
4. Complete the given table.

Term of Lok Sabha	5 years
Term of Rajya Sabha	?

Section-II

Very Short Answer Questions

1. What is meant by Unitary Government?
2. Why is the Lok Sabha called Lower House and Rajya Sabha called Upper House?
3. Mention any one qualification to be a member of Rajya Sabha.
4. Name the body which elects the members of the Rajya Sabha.
5. Write any two unique features of the Rajya Sabha.
6. How does the session of the Parliament end?
7. What options are available to the President when a money bill is sent to him?

Structured Questions

1. With reference to the Rajya Sabha and Lok Sabha, answer the following questions.
   (i) Mention any three powers of the Lok Sabha.
   (ii) Differentiate between the powers of the Lok Sabha and the Rajya Sabha.
   (iii) As the Upper House of the Parliament, how does the Rajya Sabha enjoy its powers?
   (iv) Mention any three powers of Speaker of the Lok Sabha.
2. In the view of the power and control of the Indian Parliament explain the importance of
   (i) Question Hour
   (ii) No-Confidence Motion
   (iii) Zero Hour

SAMPLE QUESTION PAPER 1

A HIGHLY SIMULATED Sample Question Paper for ICSE Class X

History & Civics (Solved)

General Instructions

1. Answers to this paper must be written on the paper provided separately.
2. You will not be allowed to write during the first 15 minutes.This time is to be spent in reading the question paper.
3. The time given at the head of this Paper is the time allowed for writing the answers.
4. Attempt all questions from Part I (Compulsory).
5. A total of five questions are to be attempted from Part II, tw.o out of three questions from Section A and three out of five questions from Section B.
6. The intended marks for questions or parts of questions are given in brackets ( ).

Time : 2 Hrs **Max. Marks : 80**

Part - I (30 Marks)

Attempt all questions from this Part

Question 1

(i) In case the President wishes to resign, to whom he has to address his resignation? (1)
   (a) Prime Minister (b) Council of Ministers
   (c) Vice-President (d) Chief-Justice of India

Latest Course Structure

There will be one paper of two hours duration carrying 80 marks and an Internal Assessment of 20 marks.

SECTION A : CIVICS

1. The Union Legislature

Meaning of the federal setup in India.

(i) Lok Sabha - Term, composition, qualifications for membership. Parliamentary procedures: a brief idea of sessions, quorum, question hour, adjournment and no-confidence motion. Speaker – election and functions.

(ii) Rajya Sabha – Composition, qualifications for membership, election, term, Presiding Officer.

Powers and functions of Union Parliament – (legislative, financial, judicial, electoral, amendment of the Constitution, control over executive). Exclusive powers of the two Houses.

2. The Union Executive

(i) The President: Qualifications for election, composition of Electoral College, reason for indirect election, term of office, procedure for impeachment.
Powers (executive, legislative, financial, judicial, discretionary and emergency)

(ii) The Vice-President: Qualifications for election, term of office and powers.

(iii) Prime Minister and Council of Ministers: Appointment, formation of Council of Ministers, tenure, functions - policy making, administrative, legislative, financial, emergency. Position and powers of the Prime Minister. Collective and individual responsibility of the members of the Cabinet. Distinction between the Council of Ministers and the Cabinet.

3. The Judiciary

(i) The Supreme Court: Composition, qualifications of judges, appointment, independence of judiciary from the control of executive and legislature; Jurisdiction and functions: Original, Appellate, Advisory, Revisory, Judicial Review and Court of Record. Enforcement of Fundamental Rights and Writs.

(ii) The High Courts: Composition, qualifications of judges, appointment; Jurisdiction and functions: Original, Appellate, Revisory, Judicial Review and Court of Record. Enforcement of Fundamental Rights and Writs.

(iii) Subordinate Courts: Distinction between Court of the District Judge and Sessions Court.

Lok Adalats: Meaning and advantages.

SECTION B : HISTORY

1. The Indian National Movement (1857 – 1917)

(i) The First War of Independence, 1857
Only the causes (political, socio-religious, economic and military) and consequences will be tested. [The events, however, need to be mentioned in order to maintain continuity and for a more comprehensive understanding.]

(ii) Factors leading to the growth of Nationalism – economic exploitation, repressive colonial policies, socio-religious reform movements (brief mention of contribution of Raja Ram Mohan Roy and Jyotiba Phule) and role of the Press.

Foundation of the Indian National Congress - the Indian National Association (Surendranath Banerjee) and the East India Association (Dadabhai Naoroji) as precursors. Immediate objectives of the Indian National Congress - the first two sessions and their Presidents should be mentioned.

(iii) First Phase of the Indian National Movement (1885-1907) - Objectives and methods of struggle of the Early Nationalists. Any two contributions of Dadabhai Naoroji, Surendranath Banerjee and Gopal Krishna Gokhale.

Second Phase of the Indian National Movement (1905-1916) - Brief mention of the causes of the Partition of Bengal and its perspective by the Nationalists. Brief mention of Surat Split of 1907; objectives and methods of struggle of the Radicals. Any two contributions of Bal Gangadhar Tilak, Bipin Chandra Pal and Lala Lajpat Rai. The Muslim League; Factors leading to the formation of the Muslim League and its objectives. Brief mention of the significance of the Lucknow Pact - 1916.

2. Mass Phase of the National Movement (1915-1947)

(i) Mahatma Gandhi:- Non-Cooperation Movement : causes (Khilafat Movement, Rowlatt Act, Jallianwala Bagh Tragedy), programme and suspension – Chauri Chaura incident and impact of the Movement; the Civil Disobedience Movement: causes (reaction to the Simon Commission, Declaration of Poorna Swaraj at the Lahore Session of 1929), Dandi March, programme and impact of the Movement, Gandhi-Irwin Pact and the Second Round Table Conference; the Quit India Movement: causes (failure of the Cripps Mission, Japanese threat), Quit India Resolution and the significance of the Movement.

(ii) Forward Bloc (objectives) and INA (objectives and contribution of Subhas Chandra Bose).

(iii) Independence and Partition of India – Cabinet Mission Plan (clauses only); Mountbatten Plan (clauses and its acceptance); and the Indian Independence Act of 1947 (clauses only).

3. The Contemporary World

(i) The First World War :
Causes (Nationalism and Imperialism, Armament Race, division of Europe and Sarajevo crisis) and Results (Treaty of Versailles, territorial rearrangements, formation of League of Nations).

(ii) Rise of Dictatorships :

Causes for the rise of Fascism in Italy and the rise of Nazism in Germany. A comparative study of Mussolini's Fascist and Hitler's Nazi ideologies.

(iii) The Second World War :

Causes (Dissatisfaction with the Treaty of Versailles, Rise of Fascism and Nazism, Policy of Appeasement, Japanese invasion of China, Failure of League of Nations and Hitler's invasion of Poland). Brief mention of the attack on Pearl Harbour and bombing of Hiroshima and Nagasaki. Consequences (Defeat of Axis Powers, Formation of the United Nations and Cold War).

(iv) United Nations
(a) The objectives of the U.N. :
The composition and functions of the General Assembly, the Security Council and the International Court of Justice.
(b) Major agencies of the United Nations:
NICEF, WHO and UNESCO - functions only.

(v) Non-Aligned Movement : Brief meaning; objectives; Panchsheel; role of Jawaharlal Nehru; Names of the architects of NAM.

List of Important Topics

from each chapter

On the basis of analysis of last 6 Years' Board Examination Papers, we have identified Important Topics from each chapter.

Civics

Chapter 1: **The Union Legislature**

- Union Legislature in India

  (Average Marks in last 5 Yrs; 2023- 14 Marks, 2020- 24 Marks, 2019- 3 Marks, 2017- 5 Marks)

Chapter 2: **The Union Executive : The President and Vice-President**

- The President of India

  (Average Marks in last 5 Yrs; 2023- 10 Marks, 2020- 11 Marks, 2018-3 Marks, 2017-1 Mark)

- Vice-President of India

  (Average Marks in last 5 Yrs; 2023- 10 Marks, 2020- 1 Mark)

Chapter 3: **The Prime Minister and Council of Ministers**

- The Prime Minister

  (Average Marks in last 5 Yrs; 2020- 1 Mark, 2019- 10 Marks)

- The Council of Ministers

  (Average Marks in last 5 Yrs; 2020- 1 Mark, 2019- 2 Marks, 2018-1 Mark, 2017- 12 Marks)

Chapter 4: **The Supreme Court**

- Composition of Supreme Court

  (Average Marks in last 5 Yrs; 2019- 1 Mark)

- Jurisdiction and Powers of Supreme Court

  (Average Marks in last 5 Yrs; 2023- 10 Marks, 2020- 11 Marks, 2019- 2 Marks)

Chapter 5: **The High Courts and Subordinate Courts**

- The High Court

  (Average Marks in last 5 Yrs; 2023- 1 Mark, 2018-1 Mark, 2017- 1 Mark)

- Subordinate Courts

  (Average Marks in last 5 Yrs; 2019- 1 Mark, 2018-1 Mark)

- Lok Adalat

  (Average Marks in last 5 Yrs; 2020- 1 Mark, 2018-1 Mark, 2017- 1 Mark)

History

Chapter 1 & 2: The First War of Independence and the Rise of Nationalism and the Indian National Congress

- Beginning of Revolt of 1857
  (Average Marks in last 5 Yrs; 2023- 13 Marks, 2020- 10 Marks, 2019- 1 Mark, 2018 - 10 Marks)
- Growth of Nationalism
  (Average Marks in last 5 Yrs; 2023- 12 Marks, 2019- 1 Mark, 2017- 11 Marks)
- Indian National Congress
  (Average Marks in last 5 Yrs; 2023- 1 Mark, 2018-1 Mark)

Chapter 3: First Phase of the Indian National Movement (1885-1907)

- Early Nationalists (Moderates)
  (Average Marks in last 5 Yrs; 2023- 4 Marks, 2020- 1 Mark, 2019- 1 Mark)
- Assertive Nationalism (Radicals)
  (Average Marks in last 5 Yrs; 2023- 3 Marks, 2020- 4 Marks, 2019- 11 Marks, 2018- 1 Mark)

Chapter 4 & 5: Second Phase of the Indian National Movement (1905-1916) and the Muslim League and Lucknow Pact

- Partition & Anti-Partition Movement
  (Average Marks in last 5 Yrs; 2023- 3 Marks, 2020- 1 Mark)
- Formation of Muslim League
  (Average Marks in last 5 Yrs; 2023- 1 Mark, 2018- 1 Mark)

Chapter 6: Mahatma Gandhi and the National Movement

- Non-Cooperation Movement
  (Average Marks in last 5 Yrs; 2023- 7 Marks, 2020- 4 Marks, 2019- 10 Marks, 2017- 4 Marks)
- Civil Disobedience Movement
  (Average Marks in last 5 Yrs; 2023- 3 Marks, 2018-2 Marks, 2017-2 Marks)
- Quit India Movement
  (Average Marks in last 5 Yrs; 2023- 1 Mark, 2018-10 Marks)

Chapter 7 & 8: Forward Bloc and Indian National Army and Independence and Partition of India

- Forward Bloc & INA
  (Average Marks in last 5 Yrs; 2023-2 Marks, 2020- 2 Marks, 2018-10 Marks, 2017-2 Marks)
- Independence & Partition of India
  (Average Marks in last 5 Yrs; 2023- 4 Marks, 2020- 10 Marks, 2019- 2 Marks)
- Indian Independence Act (1947)
  (Average Marks in last 5 Yrs; 2019- 2 Marks, 2018-2 Marks)

Chapter 9 & 10: The First World War and Rise of Dictatorships : Fascism and Nazism

- First World War
  (Average Marks in last 5 Yrs; 2023- 7 Marks, 2020- 1 Mark, 2019- 2 Marks, 2018- 3 Marks, 2017- 7 Marks)
- Rise of Disctatorships
  (Average Marks in last 5 Yrs; 2023- 4 Marks, 2018-2 Marks)

Chapter 11: The Second World War

- Causes and Consequences
  (Average Marks in last 5 Yrs; 2023- 1 Mark, 2020- 8 Marks, 2019-14 Marks, 2018 - 2 Marks, 2017- 5 Marks)

Chapter 12: The United Nations and its Major Agencies

- United Nations (Establishment)
  (Average Marks in last 5 Yrs; 2023- 2 Marks, 2020- 5 Marks, 2017- 3 Marks)
- Organs of United Nations
  (Average Marks in last 5 Yrs; 2023- 6 Marks, 2019- 2 Marks, 2018-6 Marks, 2017- 3 Marks)
- Specialised Agencies of UN
  (Average Marks in last 5 Yrs; 2023- 4 Marks, 2020- 2 Marks, 2019- 3 Marks, 2018- 4 Marks, 2017- 2 Marks)

Chapter 13: The Non-Aligned Movement

- Non - Aligned Movement
  (Average Marks in last 5 Yrs; 2023- 1 Mark, 2020- 4 Marks, 2019- 4 Marks)

All in one®

Civics

CHAPTER 01

The Union Legislature

SYLLABUS

Meaning of the Federal Setup in India (i) Lok Sabha-term, composition, qualifications for membership, • Parliamentary procedures : A brief idea of sessions, quorum, question hour, adjournment and no-confidence motion. Speaker-election and functions. (ii) Rajya Sabha-composition, qualifications for membership, election, term, Presiding officer.

Powers and Functions of Union Parliament • Legislative, financial, judicial, electoral, amendment of the Constitution, control over executive. • Exclusive powers of the two Houses.

The legislature is the law-making body of a political unit. This law-making is usually done by the national government that has power to enact, amend and repeal (cancel) the policies. In Indian democratic political system, the union legislature is called **Parliament** and the set up is known as parliamentary form of government.

Federal Set-up in India

The Constitution of India provides for a federal system of government in the country. The Federal government means distribution of power between Centre and States by the Constitution itself and both operate in their respective **jurisdictions**[1] independently. However, the Central Government is more powerful than the States.

Initially, the Constitution provided for a two-tier government i.e. the Union Government and the State Governments. The third level of federalism was added later in the form of Panchayats and Municipalities. The Indian model of federalism is called a **quasi-federal system** as it contains major features of both a federation and union.

Federal Features of the Constitution of India

- **Dual Government** The Constitution establishes double set of government, i.e. union at the Centre and the States at the **periphery.**[2] Both the levels of government have their own jurisdiction with respect to law- making, monetary independence and administration. This type of arrangement is constitutionally guaranteed. The fundamentals of the Constitution can't be changed by any level of the government because consent of both levels of government is essential for this.
- **Division of Powers** The Constitution divided the powers between the Centre and States in terms of lists, i.e. Union List, State List and Concurrent List in the 7th Schedule.
- **Independent Judiciary** There is an independent judiciary headed by Supreme Court, for the purpose of protecting the supremacy of the Constitution and to settle down the disputes between the Centre and the States.
- **Bicameralism** The Constitution of India provides for a **bicameral legislature**[3] to protect the interests of the states against the undue interference of the centre.

1 **Jurisdiction** The official power to make legal decisions and judgements.

2 **Periphery** The outer limits or edge of an area or object.

3 **Bicameral legislature** In government, bicameralism is the practice of having two parliamentary chambers, i.e. the Lok Sabha and the Rajya Sabha.

Unitary Features of the Constitution of India

Besides the federal features, the Constitution of India also provides some unitary features. In Unitary government, the centre is powerful and regional governments derive their authority from national government. The unitary features of Constitution of India are

- **Single Constitution** There is a single Constitution for the Union and States in India. Both the Union and the States must operate within this single frame.
- **Strong Centre** The Indian Constitution guarantees more powers with the Union List i.e. more power is vested with the Central Government as per the 7th Schedule. The Centre has overriding authority over the laws made by the State Government mentioned in the Concurrent List subjects.
- **Emergency Provisions** The Constitution of India provides for emergency power, which enables the federal government to acquire the strength of unitary system in emergencies. When an emergency is imposed then the Centre acquires control over the states which undermines the autonomy of the states.
- **Flexibility of the Constitution** The Indian Constitution is rigid as well as flexible. There are certain provisions in the Indian Constitution which can be easily amended either by a simple majority or by a two-thirds (2/3rd) majority in the Parliament.
- **Single Citizenship** There is single citizenship in India. This helps in increasing the feeling of nationality amidst the regional and cultural differences.
- **Integrated Judiciary** India has an integrated judiciary, which means that the Supreme Court controls the judicial administration in the country.
- **Unequal Representation of States in Rajya Sabha** The representation of states in the Rajya Sabha (Upper House) is based on the states' population. It means that the states with more population will send more representatives as compared to states with less population. In an ideal federal structure, equal representation is provided to all states.
- **Existence of Union Territories** These are administrative units which are directly governed by the Union Government that clearly demarcates them from states of the Indian Union.

Check Your LEARNING...

1. Name the two sets of authority under the Federal Setup in India.
2. Which level of government is powerful in Unitary system?
3. Which judicial body has the authority to protect the supremacy of the Constitution?
4. Division of powers between States and Centre is mentioned in which part of Constitution ?

The Union Legislature in India

According to the Constitution, the Parliament or Union Legislature of India consists of three bodies i.e. the President, the Council of States also called **Rajya Sabha** and the House of the People also called **Lok Sabha**. The Hindi names, Rajya Sabha and Lok Sabha were adopted in 1954 by the Parliament. The Rajya Sabha is the Upper House and it represents the States and Union Territories of the India while the Lok Sabha is the Lower House and it represents the people of India as a whole.

Lok Sabha

It is the popular House of the Parliament. The members of Lok Sabha are directly elected by the people of India through the Universal Adult Franchise with secret Ballot.

Qualifications for Membership

To be a member of Lok Sabha, the candidate

- must be a citizen of India.
- must have attained the age of 25 years.
- must have his/her name in the electoral rolls in any part of the country.
- must not hold any office of profit under the Government of India.
- must be of sound mind.
- must not be punished under any law.
- must possess the ability to meet his/her financial commitments.

Term

The normal duration of the Lok Sabha is 5 years, but it may be dissolved earlier by the President on the advice of the Prime Minister. During the proclamation of an emergency, the term of Parliament may be extended to 1 year at a time. The new Lok Sabha must be elected within 6 months once the emergency is declared.

Composition

The maximum strength of Lok Sabha according to the Constitution of India was 552. Out of this, 530 members can be elected by the people from different states, while 20 members can be elected from the Union Territories and 2 members to be nominated by the President from the Anglo-Indian Community. However, as per the **104th Constitutional Amendment Act** passed in January 2020, the nomination of Anglo-Indian Community to Lok Sabha and certain State Assemblies is not extended further. This reservation was provided for the period of 70 years which was expired in January 2020.

At present, the Lok Sabha consists of 543 members. Out of these, 530 are from states and 13 are from Union Territories. The allotment of members is made to the various states on the basis of population of a particular state.

Vacation of Seats

A seat in the Parliament will become vacant in the following situations

- If a member resign by writing to the Speaker.
- If a member is absent for 60 consecutive days of proceeding of the House, without prior permission of the Speaker.
- If a member is subject to any disqualification mentioned in the Constitution or any law enacted by the Parliament.
- If a member stands disqualified under the **Anti-Defection Law**[4].

Speaker of the Lok Sabha

The **presiding**[5] officer of the Lok Sabha is the Speaker. He/she holds the office from the date of election immediately before the first meeting of the Lok Sabha. The Speaker is eligible for re-election. He/she may resign from office by writing to the Deputy Speaker. The Speaker is the true guardian of the Lower House as he/she is responsible for ensuring the smooth functioning of the House.

Election of the Speaker

The Speaker of Lok Sabha is elected from its members by a simple majority of its members present in the house. Usually, a member belonging to ruling party becomes the Speaker. The Speaker is elected for a term of five years.

Deputy Speaker

The Deputy Speaker is the vice- presiding officer of the Lok Sabha. He/she acts as the presiding officer in case of leave or absence caused by death or illness of the Speaker of Lok Sabha. Deputy Speaker is also elected in the same manner as Speaker. The Speaker and Deputy Speaker normally hold office during the life of the House, but they may also leave office earlier.

The Deputy Speaker has a right to speak in the House, take part in its deliberations and vote as a member, but he/she can do all this only when the Speaker is presiding. Generally, the Deputy Speaker is chosen from the members of the opposition.

Powers and Functions of the Speaker

- The Speaker presides over the meetings of the House, except when a resolution for his/her removal is being considered.
- He/She has the final power to maintain order in the House and to interpret its rules of procedure.
- He/She can ask a member to withdraw from the House for disorderly behaviour or may even suspend a member from the service of the House on a motion for gross disorderly behaviour.
- He/She communicates the decision of the Lok Sabha to the concerned authorities.
- He/She decides whether a Bill is a Money Bill or not. All the Bills that are passed by Lok Sabha are signed by the speaker before they are sent to Rajya Sabha for its consideration.
- He/She presides over a joint sitting of the two Houses of Parliament.
- He/She appoints the Chairman of all Parliamentary Committees.
- He/She nominates personnel for parliamentary delegations to other countries.
- Each House of the Parliament shall have a separate secretariat staff. The secretariat is under the control of the Speaker.

Rajya Sabha

The Rajya Sabha is also called the Council of States. It represents the federation of states of the Indian Union.

Election of Members

The Parliament has prescribed that the members of Rajya Sabha are indirectly elected by members of an Electoral College for that territory. They are elected on the basis of proportional representation by means of the single transferable vote.

4 **Anti Defection Law** According to this law, a member of the House belonging to one political party would be disqualified from his membership if he joins another political party.

5 **Preside** Be in the position of authority in a meeting.

Qualifications for Membership

To be a member of Rajya Sabha, the candidate

- must be a citizen of India.
- must not be less than 30 years of age.
- must not be a proclaimed criminal and he/she must be of sound mind.
- must not hold any office of profit under the government.
- must have his name on electoral rolls in some part of the country.
- must have such other qualifications as may be prescribed by the Parliament from time-to-time.
- must be parliamentary Elector in the state from which he/she is seeking election. He must subscribe an oath or affirmation before some person authorised by the Election Commission, according to the form set out by the 3rd Schedule of the Constitution.

Term

The Rajya Sabha never dissolves because it is a permanent House. But one-third (1/3rd) of its members are retired on the expiration of every second year, in accordance with provisions made by Parliament. Each member of Rajya Sabha is elected for a term of 6 years.

Composition

The maximum strength of the Rajya Sabha according to Article 80 of the Constitution of India is 250, out of which 12 members are nominated by the President of India and the remaining 238 are those who represent the States and the Union Territories. The 12 nominated members are distinguished people in the fields of Literature, Science, Art and Social Service.

The allotment of seats to the states is made on the basis of the population of a particular state. The states with large population have more representatives in the Rajya Sabha and the states with small populations have less members in Rajya Sabha. At present, there are 245 members in the Rajya Sabha of which 233 are members of States and Union Territories of Delhi and Puducherry and 12 are nominated by the President.

Presiding Officers

The Constitution stipulates (specify) that the **Vice-President of India** is the ex-officio Chairman of the Rajya Sabha. He presides over its meetings. The Chairman may be removed only if he/she is removed from the office of the Vice-President.

Rajya Sabha also has a Deputy Chairman which is elected from its members. In the absence of Chairman, the Deputy Chairman performs his functions and duties. The Deputy Chairman may be removed from his/her office by a resolution of the Rajya Sabha. This resolution must be passed by the majority of the current members of the Rajya Sabha and after 14 days prior notice has been given to move the resolution.

Check Your LEARNING...

1. What do you mean by Upper House of the Parliament?
2. Who acts as the Presiding officer in case of leave or absence caused by death or illness of the Speaker ?
3. How many member of Rajya Sabha retired every second year?
4. Who is the ex-officio Chairman of the Rajya Sabha?

Parliamentary Procedures

Under the parliamentary procedures, the role of both the Houses are to allow the formation of various laws and orders which would help in better functioning of the country.

Some parliamentary proceedings are

Sessions of the Parliament

There are usually three sessions of the Parliament in a year which are

(i) The Budget Session (February to May)
(ii) The Autumn or Monsoon Session (July to September)
(iii) The Winter Session (November to December)

The President of India **summons**[6] each House of the Parliament time-to-time for meetings. The Constitution States that each House shall meet at least twice a year and there should not be a gap of more than 6 months between two consecutive sittings of the Parliament.

Quorum for the Session

Quorum is the minimum number of members required to be present in the House before it can organise any business. It is one-tenth (1/10th) of the total number of members in each House including the presiding officers. Thus, to conduct a sitting of Lok Sabha, there should be at least 55 members present while to conduct a sitting of Rajya Sabha, there should be at least 25 members present.

6 **Summons** Issuing an order to the parliamentarians for conducting sessions or meeting of Lok Sabha and Rajya Sabha.

Question Hour

It is one of the important device of the members of Parliament to seek information about the matter of public importance. The first hour of every parliamentary sitting is allotted for the question hour. However, in 2014 the question hour was shifted in Rajya Sabha from 11 am to 12 noon. It is regulated according to Parliamentary rules.

There are three types of questions which are

(i) **Starred Question** It is one which is distinguished by an **asterisk.**[7] The member is expected to give an oral answer for this question. Answer to this question may be followed by supplementary questions by the members.

(ii) **Unstarred Question** It is one which is not distinguished by an asterisk. It requires a written answer and hence, supplementary questions cannot follow.

(iii) **Short Notice Question** It is one which is asked by giving a notice of less than 10 days. It is answered orally. It is related to a matter of urgent importance.

Zero Hour

It is an informal device as it is not mentioned in the rules of procedure. It is available to the Members of the Parliament to raise all types of questions and matters without any prior notice.

Zero hour begins at 12 o'clock immediately after the question hour and lasts until the agenda for the day is taken up. In other words, the time gap between the question hour and the agenda is known as zero hour.

Motions of the Parliament

The term motion means any proposal made for the purpose of **eliciting**[8] a decision of the House.

The motions in the Parliament are

(i) **Adjournment Motion** It is introduced in the Parliament to draw attention of the House to a definite matter of urgent public importance. It needs the support of 50 members to be admitted. As it interrupts the normal business of the House, it is regarded as an extraordinary device.

(ii) **No-Confidence Motion** It is a proposal that expressed lack of confidence in the Ministry or the Government. The Lok Sabha can remove the Government from office by passing the no-confidence motion. It means that the Government stays in office as long as it enjoys confidence of the majority of members of the Lok Sabha. It can be moved against the entire Council of Ministers. It needs the support of 50 members to be admitted. It has to be taken up for discussion within the 10 days from the day on which it is granted.

End of the Session

There are three types of procedure which ends the session

(i) **Adjournment** It is a postponement of the sitting of the House. The Speaker has the power to adjourn the House **sine-die**[9]. Once the House is adjourned sine-die, he/she is empowered to call it again.

(ii) **Prorogation** It means the termination of a session of the Houses by an order made by the President.

(iii) **Dissolution** It means end of the term of the Lok Sabha either by an order made by the President or on the expiration of the period of 5 years from the date of its first meeting.

Guillotine

On the last of the allotted days at the appointed time, the Speaker puts every necessary question to dispose off all the outstanding matters in connection with the demands for grants. This is known as guillotine.

Powers and Functions of the Union Parliament

In the parliamentary form of government, the executive power is in the hands of the group of members of the Parliament. Some important powers of the Parliament are

Legislative Powers

- The Parliament has exclusive power to make laws on all 97 subjects of **Union List** such as foreign affairs, atomic energy, defence, banking, etc.
- The Parliament can legislate the 61 subjects of State List only when
  - There is emergency in the country or President Rule or a State emergency.
  - If two or more States ask for making a law. But this law will be applicable to States which have so requested.
  - If State List become the national importance or it requires to fulfil international commitments.

7 **Asterisk** It is a symbol (*) used for distinguishing the starred question in Question Hour.

8 **Elicit** Evoke or draw out from someone.

9 **Sine-die** It means without assigning a day for a further meeting or hearing.

- The Parliament along with State Assemblies make laws on the 47 subjects of **Concurrent List** such as forest, criminal law, electricity, etc. If there is a conflict between the Union and States, then Union law will prevail and law made by State Assembly will become null and void.
- The Parliament also makes law on **Residuary Subjects**. All subjects which are not mentioned in either Union List, State List or Concurrent List come under it like the computer software.
- The President has power to promulgate (circulate) an **ordinance**[10] at a time when the Parliament is not in session. All ordinance must be put up before the Parliament. These ordinances have the same force and effect as an Act of Parliament, but are temporary in nature. Ordinance ceases to operate after 6 weeks from the re-assembly of Parliament, unless they are approved by the Houses.
- The Parliament become the legislature in the State when emergency is declared in that state. During this period, the Parliament assumes all the powers including the financial powers of the State Government.
- The Parliament may alter the name or boundary of the state. It can also form a new state by merging or separating a part of territory of a state.

Financial Powers

- No money can be spent or no tax can be imposed by the government without the approval of the Parliament.
- The Parliament passes the **Union budget** which contains the estimates of receipts and expenditure of the government for the financial year.
- The salaries and allowances of ministers and Members of Parliament are determined by the Parliament.
- A **Money Bill** can be introduced only in the Lok Sabha. The Rajya Sabha have to sent back the money bill within 14 days to the Lok Sabha. The Lok Sabha may accept or reject the recommendations of the Rajya Sabha.

Judicial Powers

- The Parliament has the power to elect and impeach the President. For the **impeachment of the President**, the charges must be placed before one House and supported by two-third (2/3rd) of the majority. These charges are investigated by second House and if accepted by a similar majority in second House, the President stands impeached.
- The Parliament can remove the Judges of the Supreme Court, the High Court, the Chief Election Commissioner, Comptroller and Auditor General of India, if they are found guilty of violating the provisions of the Constitution.
- The Parliament has the power to make laws about the jurisdiction and composition of the Supreme Court. It also creates a common High Court for two or more states.
- The Parliament can give punishment to a person for obstructing the work of it or showing disrespect to any of its House.

Electoral Powers

- The Parliament along with Legislative Assemblies of state elects the President.
- Both Houses of the Parliament elect the Vice-President of India.
- The Lok Sabha elects the Speaker and Deputy Speaker from its own members while the Rajya Sabha elects its Deputy Chairman.

Powers for Amendment of the Constitution

Both the Houses of the Parliament can amend the Constitution. However, a bill for amendment can be initiated in either House of Parliament by a majority of total membership as well as by two-third (2/3rd) majority of members present in voting. In some cases, amendments need ratification from half of the Legislative Assemblies of the states.

Powers to Control the Executive

- **Interpellation or Inquiry** The Parliament can ask questions to the government about its policies and performance.
- **Adjournment Motion** The Parliament can bring Adjournment motion to bring matters of urgent public importance.
- **Vote of No-Confidence** If a government does not follow the provisions of the Constitution, the Parliament can pass a vote of no-confidence to the government. In such a case, whole ministry or government has to resign.
- **Monetary Control** The Parliament can bring out motion during the budget session to disapprove any monetary policy of the government. It also examines the report of Comptroller and Auditor-General (CAG).

10 **Ordinance** An authoritative order.

- **Censure Motion** The Parliament can bring Censure motion over the policies of the government by the opposition party members.

Exclusive or Special Powers of the Lok Sabha

- Only the Lok Sabha can vote on the demands for grants in the budget.
- The Council of Ministers is collectively responsible only to the Lok Sabha. Thus, the Lok Sabha alone can vote a minister out of office.
- Only the Lok Sabha can introduce a motion of no-confidence against the government.
- Only the Lok Sabha has the power to pass a resolution for the discontinuance of the national emergency.
- The Speaker of the Lok Sabha presides over the joint sitting of the Houses.
- If a **deadlock**[11] occurs between both the Houses over an Ordinary Bill, the Bill of the Lok Sabha normally prevails, as its strength is more as compare to the Rajya Sabha.

Exclusive or Special Powers of the Rajya Sabha

- The Parliament can assume temporary power to legislate on State List subjects (Article 249) only if Rajya Sabha passes a resolution, which is supported by two-third (2/3rd) majority of its members present and voting.
- The All-India Services can be established only if the Rajya Sabha pass a resolution for it, which is supported by two-third (2/3rd) majority of its members present and voting.
- During the emergency, if the Lok Sabha is dissolved then Rajya Sabha becomes *de-facto* (effective) and *de-jure* (legal) because Rajya Sabha is a permanent body.

Joint Sitting

Generally, the Speaker of Lok Sabha presides over a joint sitting. If Speaker is absent then Deputy Speaker presides over it. Joint sitting of both Houses are possible in the following cases

- If after a bill passed by one House (originating House) transmitted to other.
- If the House rejects the Bill, the President may call for a joint sitting of the two Houses.
- If the originating House does not accept the amendments.
- If the other House takes no action on the Bill for 6 months from the date of reception of the Bill, then the President can summon a joint sitting.

Check Your LEARNING...

1. Name any two process by which Parliament controls the executive.
2. What is an starred question ?
3. Which motion is passed to remove the Government from office?
4. Which type of bill can only be introduced in Lok Sabha?
5. Write any one exclusive power of the Rajya Sabha.

11 **Deadlock** A situation, typically one including opposing parties in which no progress can be made.

QUiCK Revision

- Indian Constitution adopted both unitary and federal feature, therefore the Indian political structure is known as Quasi-Federal.
- Federal government means distribution of power between Centre and States by the Constitution itself and both operate in their respective jurisdictions independently.
- Lok Sabha is the House of the People and it is the popular House of the Parliament. The members are directly elected by the people. At present, the Lok Sabha consists of 543 members. Out of these, 530 are from States, 13 from Union Territories.
- The normal tenure of the Lok Sabha is 5 years, but it may be dissolved earlier by the President.
- The presiding officer of the Lok Sabha is the Speaker, who is elected by the members from amongst themselves. A Deputy Speaker is also elected in the same manner as the Speaker. The Speaker and Deputy Speaker normally hold office during the life of the House.
- Lok Sabha has many special powers, such as Money Bill can be introduced only in Lok Sabha. Rajya Sabha cannot reject and amend it. The Union Budget is discussed in both Houses but vote on demand for grant can take place in Lok Sabha only. If a deadlock occurs between the both Houses over a ordinary bill, the will of the Lok Sabha normally prevails.
- A Speaker decides whether a Bill is a Money Bill or not. He/she presides over joint sitting of the two Houses of the Parliament. The Deputy Speaker presides the Lok Sabha only in absence of the Speaker and exercises all the power of Speaker in the process.
- Rajya Sabha is called the Council of States. Its maximum strength is 250, out of this 12 members are nominated by the President from the fields of Literature, Science, Art and Social Services.
- The Rajya Sabha is not dissolved because it is a permanent body. But one-third (1/3rd) of its members retire on the expiration of every second year. The members of the Rajya Sabha are elected for a term of 6 years.
- The Constitution stipulates that Vice-President of India is Ex-officio Chairman of the Rajya Sabha. A Deputy Chairman of the Council of States is to be chosen by the members from among themselves.
- There are three types of procedure, which ends the session, which are Adjournment, Prorogation and Dissolution.
- The Parliament of India consists of the President, the Rajya Sabha (Upper House) and the Lok Sabha (Lower House).
- The Parliament has legislative power to regulate the laws. The Parliament has exclusive power to make laws on all Union List. In case of emergency, it make laws on State List and if there is some conflict in Concurrent List, then Union Legislature laws will prevail.
- There are usually three sessions in a year i.e. the Budget Session (February to May), the Autumn or Monsoon Session (July to September) and the Winter Session (November to December).
- The Constitution only says that, there should not be a gap of more than 6 months between two consecutive sittings of the Parliament.
- Quorum is the minimum number of members required to be present in the House before it can transact (organise) any business.
- The Parliament may alter the name or boundary of state. It can also form a new state by merging or separating a part of territory or a state. The Parliament can remove the Judges of the Supreme Court, the High Court, the Election Commissioner and CAG etc.
- The Parliament has power to create and abolish the Legislative Council in a state.

Chapter Practice

Section-I

Multiple Choice Questions

1. The Lok Sabha session which is conducted in the months of November and December is the ....
   (a) Summer Session
   (b) Monsoon Session
   (c) Winter Session
   (d) Budget Session

Ans. (c) Winter Session

2. Under what circumstances may the term of the Lok Sabha be extended by one year at a time?
   (a) When the government resigns.
   (b) Proclamation of a National Emergency.
   (c) Economic instability.
   (d) Rajya Sabha declares by ¼ majority.

Ans. (b) Proclamation of a National Emergency.

3. Which of these statements regarding the Speaker is false?
   (a) He/She is the presiding officer of the Lok Sabha.
   (b) Elected from among the members of the Lok Sabha.
   (c) Elected when the newly elected house meets for the first time..
   (d) The members of both the houses vote to choose the Speaker.

Ans. (d) The members of both the houses vote to choose the Speaker.

4. How many members of the Rajya Sabha retire once every two years? **[Specimen Paper Semester-II 2022]**
   (a) One-sixth
   (b) One-fourth
   (c) Two-third
   (d) One-third

Ans. (d) One-third

5. Which of these denotes the correct composition of the Rajya Sabha? **[Specimen Paper Semester-I 2022]**
   (a) 232 elected + 2 nominated
   (b) 238 elected + 12 nominated
   (c) 238 elected + 2 nominated
   (d) 250 elected + 12 nominated

Ans. (b) 238 elected + 12 nominated

6. Which of these is not a qualification required to be a member of the Rajya Sabha?
   (a) Should be a citizen of India.
   (b) Should not be an insolvent.
   (c) Should be at least 30 years of age.
   (d) Should be a graduate from any university in India.

Ans. (d) Should be a graduate from any university in India.

7. The Rajya Sabha is called a Permanent house because 1/3 members retire every ....
   (a) two years (b) one year
   (c) three years (d) six years

Ans. (a) two years

8. Which of these is considered to be an exclusive power of the Rajya Sabha?
   (a) It can approve an Ordinary Bill.
   (b) It can make amendments to the Constitution.
   (c) It can empower the Parliament to make laws on the State list.
   (d) It can make laws on subjects in the Union List.

Ans. (c) It can empower the Parliament to make laws on the State list.

9. Who elect the members of the Rajya Sabha? **[Specimen Paper Semester-II 2022]**
   (a) The members of the Lok Sabha
   (b) The members of the Vidhan Sabha
   (c) The members of the Vidhan Parishad
   (d) The citizens of India

Ans. (b) The members of the Vidhan Sabha

10. What is the quorum of the Indian Parliament?
   (a) 1/3 (b) 1/2
   (c) 1/10 (d) 1/4

Ans. (c) 1/10

11. Assuming the powers of the State which is under an emergency is a .... power of the Parliament.
   (a) Financial (b) Emergency
   (c) Legislative (d) Executive

Ans. (c) Legislative

12. The .... motion allows the house to take up a definite matter of urgent importance.
   (a) No-Confidence (b) Adjournment
   (c) Censure (d) Prorogation

Ans. (b) Adjournment

13. Who determines the salaries and allowances of Members of Parliament and Ministers?
   (a) The President
   (b) The Parliament
   (c) The Chairman of UPSC
   (d) The Finance Minister

Ans. (b) The Parliament

14. If the strength of the House is 350 members, the quorum will be ....
   (a) 36 members (b) 40 members
   (c) 60 members (d) 35 members

Ans. (d) 35 members

15. An ordinance has to be approved by the Parliament within ....weeks. [2023]
(a) two (b) three
(c) six (d) eight

Ans. (c) six

16. Which of the following statements about Ordinances is false?
(a) Promulgated by the President.
(b) Issued when the Parliament is not in session.
(c) Has to be approved within six months from the re-assembly of the Parliament.
(d) Has to be approved by both the houses of the Parliament.

Ans. (c) Has to be approved within six months from the re-assembly of the Parliament.

17. In case of a conflict between the Centre and the State with reference to a subject in the Concurrent List.
(a) Each follow their own law.
(b) The State law will prevail.
(c) The President is empowered to decide.
(d) The Union law will prevail

Ans. (d) The Union law will prevail.

18. Who is empowered to promulgate an ordinance when the Parliament is not in session?
(a) The Vice-President (b) The President
(c) The Prime Minister
(d) The Attorney General of India

Ans. (b) The President

19. Which of the following procedures authorises the Executive to draw funds from the consolidated Fund until the Budget is passed by the Parliament?
(a) Vote on Account (b) Veto
(c) Prorogation (d) Supplementary Grants

Ans. (a) Vote on Account

20. Complete the given analogy.
Election of Lok Sabha member : Citizens of India
Election of Rajya Sabha member : ?
(a) Members of the Legislative Assembly
(b) Member of the Legislative Council
(c) Members of the Lok Sabha
(d) Member of the Cabinet

Ans. (a) Members of the Legislative Assembly

21. Complete the given analogy.
Lok Sabha : Speaker :: Rajya Sabha :?
(a) Vice-President (b) Prime Minister
(c) President (d) Chief Justice of India

Ans. (a) Vice-President

22. Complete the given analogy.
Union List : Foreign Affairs :: Concurrent List : ?
(a) Atomic Energy (b) Defence
(c) Criminal Law (d) Banking

Ans. (c) Criminal Law

23. Replace the underline word to correct the statement.
A system of government in which power is divided between a Central authority and various constituent unit of the country is called Communalism.
(a) Totalitarianism (b) Federalism
(c) Socialism (d) Liberalism

Ans. (b) Federalism

24. Replace the underline word to correct the statement.
To bring matters of urgent public importance, the Parliament can bring Censure Motion.
(a) Adjournment Motion (b) Vote of no-confidence
(c) Interpellation (d) Monetary Control

Ans. (a) Adjournment Motion

25. Complete the following table.

Lok Sabha members from States	530
Lok Sabha members from Union Territories	?

(a) 25 (b) 22
(c) 20 (d) 30

Ans. (c) 20

26. Complete the given table.

Lok Sabha	550 members
Rajya Sabha	?

(a) 250 members (b) 545 members
(c) 500 members (d) 350 members

Ans. (a) 250 members

27. Which of the following statement is incorrect with respect to the exclusive powers of the Rajya Sabha?
(i) During the emergency, if the Lok Sabha is dissolved then Rajya Sabha becomes effective and legal.
(ii) The establishment of All-India Services also depends on the Rajya Sabha.
(iii) Money bill can only be introduced in Rajya Sabha.
(iv) Rajya Sabha has the power to pass a resolution for the discontinuance of the national emergency.

Codes
(a) Only (i) (b) Both (i) and (ii)
(c) Both (iii) and (iv) (d) Only (iv)

Ans. (c) Both (iii) and (iv)

28. When can the Parliament not legislate on subjects included in the State List? [Specimen Paper Semester-II 2022]
(i) When the State is ruled by a coalition.
(ii) During the proclamation of an emergency.
(iii) When the Rajya Sabha passes a resolution by two-thirds majority.

(iv) When two or more States are of the opinion the Parliament should legislate on the subject.

Codes

(a) Both (i) and (ii)
(b) Both (i) and (iii)
(c) Both (iii) and (iv)
(d) Both (ii) and (iv)

Ans. (b) Both (i) and (iii)

29. Which of the following aspect is correct with respect to the exclusive powers of the Lok Sabha?

(i) The Speaker of the Lok Sabha presides over the joint sitting of the Houses.
(ii) Lok Sabha has the power to vote on the demands for grants in the Budget.
(iii) Lok Sabha alone can vote a minister out of office.
(iv) Ordinary bill can only be introduced in Lok Sabha.

Codes

(a) Both (i) and (ii)
(b) Only (iii)
(c) (i), (ii) and (iii)
(d) Only (iv)

Ans. (c) (i), (ii) and (iii)

30. Match the following.

List-1	List-2
A. Power to remove the Judges of the Courts	1. Financial power of the Parliament.
B. Alter the name or boundary of the State	2. Judicial power of the Parliament.
C. Passing of Budget	3. Legislative power of the Parliament.
D. Electoral Vice-President	4. Electoral power of the Parliament

Codes

	A	B	C	D
(a)	1	2	3	4
(b)	2	3	1	4
(c)	3	2	1	4
(d)	2	1	3	4

Ans. (b)

31. Match the following.

List-1 (Position)	List-2 (Election Procedure)
A. Speaker of Lok Sabha	1. Chosen by the members of Rajya Sabha from among themselves.
B. Member of Lok Sabha	2. Indirectly elected by members of an electoral college for that territory.
C. Member of Rajya Sabha	3. Directly elected by the people of India through Universal Adult Franchise.
D. Deputy Chairman of Rajya Sabha	4. Elected by the Lok Sabha members by simple majority in the House.

Codes

	A	B	C	D
(a)	2	1	4	3
(b)	4	3	2	1
(c)	3	2	1	4
(d)	2	4	3	1

Ans. (b)

Passage Based Questions

32. Read the passage given below and answer the following questions.

The Legislature is the law-making body of a political unit. This law-making is usually done by the national government that has power to enact, amend and repeal (cancel) the policies. In Indian democratic political system, the Union Legislature is called Parliament and the set up is known as Parliamentary form of government.

According to the Constitution, the Parliament of Indian consists of three bodies i.e. the President, the Council of States also called Rajya Sabha and the House of the People also called Lok Sabha. Both Hindi names Rajya Sabha and Lok Sabha were adopted in 1954 by the Parliament. The Rajya Sabha is the Upper House and the Lok Sabha is the Lower House. The former represents the States and Union Territories of the India while the later represents the people of India as a whole.

(i) The Legislature is the .... body of a political unit.

(a) Judicial
(b) Vigilance
(c) Law-making
(d) Both (a) and (c)

Ans. (c) Law-making

(ii) In which Prime Minister's tenure both Hindi names Rajya Sabha and Lok Sabha were adopted by the Parliament?

(a) Indira Gandhi
(b) Lal Bahadur Shastri
(b) Jawaharlal Nehru
(d) Morarji Desai

Ans. (c) Jawaharlal Nehru

(iii) Which House of the Parliament represents the States and Union Territories of India?

(a) Rajya Sabha
(b) Lok Sabha
(b) Both (a) and (b)
(d) Rajya Sabha represents UTs and Lok Sabha represents States

Ans. (a) Rajya Sabha

(iv) In India, Laws are enacted by

(a) State Assemblies
(b) Lok Sabha
(b) Rajya Sabha
(d) All of these

Ans. (d) All of these

Section-II

Short Questions

1. What do you understand by the Parliament?

Ans. The Parliament is the law-making body of a political unit, usually a national government that has power to enact, amend and repeal the public policy.

2. Name the law-making body of the Union Government. **[2012]**

Ans. The law-making body of the Union Government is the Parliament or Union Legislature.

3. Name the three components of the Indian Parliament. [2011]

Ans. Three components of the Indian Parliament are
(i) The President
(ii) The Lok Sabha
(iii) The Rajya Sabha

4. Name the two Houses of the Indian Parliament. [2020]

Ans. The two Houses of the Indian Parliament are Lok Sabha and Rajya Sabha.

5. When were the Hindi names of Council of States and House of the People adopted?

Ans. The Hindi names of Council of States and House of the People have been adopted by the Parliament in 1954. After this, the Council of States is called Rajya Sabha and House of People is called Lok Sabha.

6. What is the meaning of federal government?

Ans. The federal government means distribution of power between Centre and States by the Constitution itself and both operate in their respective jurisdiction independently.

7. Name the two types of authority in a federal set-up in India. [2013]

Ans. The two types of authority in a federal set-up in India are the Union and the State.

8. Mention any one federal feature of the Constitution of India.

Or State any one federal feature of the Indian Constitution. [2017]

Ans. One of the federal features of the Constitution is that it divided the powers between the Centre and States in terms of lists, i.e. Union List, State List and Concurrent List.

9. What do you mean by bicameral legislature?

Ans. Bicameralism is the practice of having two legislative of parliamentary chambers. The relationship between the two chambers of a bicameral legislature can vary. In some cases, they have equal power and in others, one chamber is clearly superior to the other.

10. What is meant by the Lok Sabha?

Ans. The Lok Sabha is called the House of the people. It is the popular House of the Parliament. Its members are directly elected by the people.

11. Mention one advantage of the Lok Sabha. [2008]

Ans. The Lok Sabha is called House of the People which means it is mirror and voice of the citizens and the members of it are directly elected by the people of the nation.

12. What is the normal term of office of the Lok Sabha? [2019, 2016]

Ans. The normal term of office of the Lok Sabha is 5 years.

13. An adult Indian citizen holding an office of profit under the State Government wishes to contest for election to the Lok Sabha. If he/she eligible? Give a reason to justify your answer. [2006]

Ans. No, he/she is not eligible because according to the law, to be a member of Lok Sabha, he/she cannot hold an office of profit under the State Government or any offices.

14. What is the strength of the Rajya Sabha at present?

Ans. At present, there are 245 members in the Rajya Sabha. Of these, 12 members are nominated by the President and rest are elected by their respective State Assembly and Union Territories.

15. Mr. Gurudev was nominated by the President to the Rajya Sabha. Mention any one criterion on which the President would nominated him. And how many such members can the President nominate to the Rajya Sabha? [2010]

Ans. The one criterion on which the President would nominate a member in the Rajya Sabha is that the Legislative Assembly of the state concerned, passed a resolution by two-third (2/3rd) majority of those present and voting. There are 12 members which President can nominate to the Rajya Sabha.

16. Who is the Chairman of the Rajya Sabha? [2015]

Or Who is the ex-officio Chairman of the Rajya Sabha? [2006]

Ans. Vice-President of India is the ex-officio Chairman of the Rajya Sabha.

17. Who presides over the meeting of the Rajya Sabha in the absence of the Vice -President of India?[2016]

Ans. Deputy Chairperson presides over the meeting of the Rajya Sabha in the absence of the Vice-President of India.

18. In what manner the Deputy Chairman of the Rajya Sabha is removed?

Ans. The Deputy Chairman of the Rajya Sabha may be removed from his/her office by a resolution passed by Rajya Sabha.

19. What is meant by the term 'quorum'? [2018]

Ans. The quorum refers to the required number of members needed to be present in both the Houses of Parliament for passing a bill.

20. What is the maximum gap allowed between two Parliamentary sessions? [2018]

Ans. The maximum gap allowed between two Parliamentary sessions is 6 months.

21. What is the required quorum to hold the meetings of the Lok Sabha? [2015]

Ans. At least one-tenth (1/10th) of total strength of each of the House is required to hold the meetings of the Lok Sabha.

22. What is meant by prorogation?

Ans. The prorogation means the termination of a session of the House by an order made by the President.

23. What happens if a vote of no-confidence is passed against a minister in the Lok Sabha? [2015]

Ans. If a vote of no-confidence is passed, then all the Council of Ministers have to resign in the Lok Sabha.

24. What is meant by the term question hour in the context of parliamentary procedures in India?

Or State the meaning of the term Question Hour. [2019]

Ans. Question hour is one of the important devices of the Member of Parliament to seek information about a matter of public importance.

25. What is a starred question?

Ans. A starred question is distinguished by an asterisk. It requires an oral answer and hence supplementary questions can follow.

26. What is the language of the Parliament?

Ans. Constitution of India declares Hindi and English as the languages for conducting the business of the Houses.

27. How is the Speaker of the Lok Sabha elected? [2020]

Ans. The Speaker of the Lok Sabha is elected from amongst its own members.

28. How do the officers of the Lok Sabha leave the office? Mention any one.

Ans. The officers (Speaker and Deputy Speaker) of the Lok Sabha leave the office, when they are removed from office by a resolution passed by a majority of all the current members of the House.

29. Who presides over the joint sessions of the two Houses of the Parliament ? [2017]

Ans. The Speaker of the Lok Sabha presides over the joint sessions of the two Houses of the Parliament.

30. When can the Speaker of the Lok Sabha cast his vote? [2017]

Ans. The Speaker of the Lok Sabha does not cast his vote in the House, except when there are equal votes on both sides, i.e. the treasury benches and the opposition.

31. State the minimum number of times the Lok Sabha must meet in a year. [2014]

Ans. The Lok Sabha meets 3 times in a year during Budget Session, Autumn or Monsoon Session and Winter Session.

32. State any one subject wherein the Lok Sabha and the Rajya Sabha enjoy co-equal powers in legislation of laws. [2016]

Ans. Introduction and passage of constitutional amendment bill is the subject wherein the Lok Sabha and Rajya Sabha enjoy co-equal powers in legislation of laws.

33. Mention any one situation when both the Houses of Parliament meet for a joint session. [2010]

Or Mention the occasion on which the President addresses a joint session of Parliament? [2012]

Ans. When an Ordinary bill is passed by originating House and second House rejects it, then, President may call for a joint sitting (session) of the two Houses.

34. Mention any one circumstance when the Parliament can make laws on a state subject. [2011]

Ans. When the State List is of national importance or it requires to fulfil international commitments, the Parliament can make laws on a state subject.

35. What is meant by 'Residuary Power' of the Parliament? [2016]

Ans. Parliament has exclusive power to make any law with respect to any matter not enumerated in the three lists i.e. Union List, State List and Concurrent List. This power of legislation is known as 'Residuary Power.'

Structured Questions

1. The Constitution of India provides for a federal system of government in the country. In this context, explain the following questions.
   (i) What do you understand by federal government?
   (ii) What are the types of government?
   (iii) What are the unitary features of the Indian Constitution?
   (iv) What are the federal features of the Indian Constitution?

Ans. (i) The Federal government means distribution of power between Centre and States by the Constitution itself and both the levels of government have their own jurisdiction with respect to law-making, monetary independence and administration. This type of arrangement is constitutionally guaranteed. The fundamentals of the Constitution can't be changed by any level of the government because consent of both levels of government is essential for this.

(ii) According to political scientists, there are two types of government i.e. Unitary and Federal

Unitary Government In Unitary government, the centre is powerful and regional governments derive their authority from national government.

Federal Government In Federal government, powers are distributed between Centre and States by the Constitution itself and both operate in their respective jurisdictions independently.

(iii) The Unitary features of the Indian Constitution are

- **Single Constitution** There is a single constitution for the Union and the States in India. Both the Union and the States must operate within this single frame.

- **Strong Centre** The Indian Constitution guarantees more powers with the Union list i.e. more power is vested with the Central Government as per the 7th Schedule. The Centre has overriding authority over the laws made by the State Government mentioned in the Concurrent List subjects.
- **Emergency Provisions** The Constitution of India provides for emergency power, which enables the Federal government to acquire the strength of unitary system in emergencies. When an emergency is imposed then the Centre acquires control over the states which undermines the autonomy of the states.

(iv) The Federal features of the Indian Constitution are
- **Dual Government** The Constitution establishes double set of government i.e. Union at the Centre and the States at the periphery. Both the levels of government have their own jurisdiction with respect to law-making, monetary independence and administration. This type of arrangement is constitutionally guaranteed.
- **Division of Powers** The Constitution divided the powers between the Centre and States in terms of lists i.e. Union List, State List and Concurrent List in the 7th schedule.
- **Independent Judiciary** There is an independent judiciary headed by the Supreme Court, for the purpose of protecting the supremacy of the Constitution and to settle down the disputes between the Centre and the States.

2. With reference to the Indian Parliament, explain the following. **[2014]**
(i) The tenure of the members of the Lok Sabha and the Rajya Sabha.
(ii) The composition of the Lok Sabha.
(iii) Explain any two situations for the vacation of seats of Parliament.
(iv) Mention the qualifications required for the membership of Lok Sabha.

Ans. (i) **Tenure of the Members of Lok Sabha** The Constitution has provided for a fixed term of 5 years. However, it can be dissolved earlier by President or can be extended for 1 year during emergency by the Parliament.

Tenure of the Members of Rajya Sabha The Rajya Sabha is not dissolved because it is a permanent body. But its one-third (1/3rd) members retire on the expiration of every second year. The term of each member of the Rajya Sabha is for a period of 6 years.

(ii) The maximum strength of Lok Sabha according to the Constitution of India was 552. Out of this, 530 members can be elected by the people from different states, while 20 members can be elected from the Union Territories and 2 members to be nominated by the President from the Anglo-Indian Community. However, as per the 104th Constitutional Amendment Act passed in January 2020, the nomination of Anglo-Indian Community to Lok Sabha and certain State Assemblies is not extended further.

(iii) A seat in the Parliament will become vacant in the following circumstances
(i) If a member resign by writing to the Speaker.
(ii) If a member is absent for 60 consecutive days of proceeding of the House, without prior permission of the Speaker.

(iv) The qualifications required for the membership of the Lok Sabha are
- The candidate must be a citizen of India.
- The candidate must have attained the age of 25 years.
- The candidate must have his/her name in the electoral rolls in any part of the country.
- The candidate must not hold any office of profit under the Government of India.
- The candidate must be of sound mind.

3. The Parliament is the body of people's representatives who have supreme power in a democracy. With reference to the Union Legislature answer the following. **[2019]**
(i) How are the members of the Rajya Sabha elected? Why is it called a Permanent House?
(ii) Mention the qualifications required for the membership of Rajya Sabha.
(iii) State any two financial and any two legislative powers of the Indian Parliament.
(iv) Write any two Judicial powers of the Indian Parliament.

Ans. (i) The members of the Rajya Sabha are elected indirectly by the members of the State Legislative Assemblies with the system of proportional representation by means of a 'Single Transferable Vote'.

The Rajya Sabha is called a Permanent House as each of its members is elected for a period of 6 years and 1/3rd of the total members retire after every two years. The Vice-President is the ex-officio Chairman of the Rajya Sabha.

(ii) The qualifications required for the membership of the Rajya Sabha are
- The candidate should be a citizen of India.
- The candidate should not be less than 30 years of age.
- The candidate should have such other qualifications as may be prescribed by the Parliament from time-to-time.
- The candidate must be parliamentary Elector in the State from which he/she is seeking election.

- The candidate must make and subscribe before some person authorized in that behalf by the Election Commission an oath or affirmation asserting his allegiance to the Constitution of India.

(iii) The financial powers of the Indian Parliament are

(a) No money can be spent or no tax can be imposed by the Government without the approval of the Parliament.

(b) The Parliament passes the budget which contains the estimates of receipts and expenditure of the government for the financial year.

The legislative powers of the Indian Parliament are

(a) The Parliament has exclusive power to make laws on all 97 subjects of Union List such as foreign affairs, atomic energy, defence, banking, etc.

(b) The Parliament along with State Assemblies make laws on the 47 subjects of Concurrent List such as forest, criminal law, electricity, etc. If there is a conflict between the Union and States, then Union law will prevail and law made by State Assembly will become null and void.

(iv) The judicial powers of the Indian Parliament are

(a) The Parliament has the power to elect and impeach the President. For the impeachment of the President, the charges must be placed before one House and supported by two-third (2/3rd) of the majority. These charges are investigated by second House and if accepted by a similar majority in second House, the President stands impeached.

(b) The Parliament can remove the Judges of the Supreme Court, the High Court, the Chief Election Commissioner, Comptroller and Auditor General of India, if they are found guilty of violating the provisions of the Constitution.

4. With reference to the Union Parliament, state the following questions.

(i) Give three reasons to justify, why the Lok Sabha is considered to be more powerful than the Rajya Sabha.

(ii) Three functions of the Speaker of the Lok Sabha.

(iii) Write a brief note on the Speaker of the Rajya Sabha.

(iv) Write a brief note on the Deputy Speaker of the Lok Sabha.

Ans. (i) Following are the three important reasons which justifies the powerful status enjoyed by the Lok Sabha

(a) Money bill can be introduced only in the Lok Sabha and not in the Rajya Sabha. The Rajya Sabha cannot amend or reject the money bill, it should return the bill to the Lok Sabha within the period of 14 days. The final power to decide whether a bill is money bill or not is also vested with the Presiding officer of the Lok Sabha i.e. Speaker.

(b) Rajya Sabha can only discuss the budget but cannot vote on the demand for grants.

(c) The resolution for the discontinuance of the National Emergency can be passed only by the Lok Sabha and not by the Rajya Sabha.

(ii) The three functions of the Speaker of the Lok Sabha are

(a) The Speaker presides over the meetings of the House, except when a resolution for his/her removal is being considered.

(b) The Speaker has the final power to maintain order in the House and to interpret its rules of procedure.

(c) The Speaker can ask a member to withdraw from the House for disorderly behavior or may even suspend a member from the service of the House on a motion for gross disorderly behavior.

(iii) The Presiding officer of the Lok Sabha is the Speaker. The Speaker of the Lok Sabha is elected from its members by a simple majority of its members present in the House. Usually, a member belonging to a party becomes the Speaker. He/she is elected for a term of five years. He/she holds the office from the date of election immediately before the first meeting of the Lok Sabha. The Speaker is eligible for re-election. He/she may resign from office by writing to the Deputy Speaker. The Speaker is the true guardian of the Lower House as he/she is responsible for ensuring the smooth functioning of the House.

(iv) The Deputy Speaker of the Lok Sabha is the Vice-presiding officer of the Lok Sabha, the lower house of the Parliament of India. He/she acts as the presiding officer in case of leave or absence caused by death or illness of the Speaker of Lok Sabha. Deputy Speaker is also elected in the same manner as the Speaker. He/she normally hold office during the life of the House, but may leave office earlier.

5. With reference to the parliamentary Procedures, answer the following questions.

(i) How many sessions are held in the Parliament?

(ii) How can a session be ended?

(iii) Mention any three motions of the Parliament.

(iv) What is Question Hour?

Ans. (i) A session of the Parliament begins with an official summon from the head of the state i.e. the President of India.

There are three sessions of the Parliament which are

(a) The Budget Session (February to May)

(b) The Autumn or Monsoon Session (July to September)

(c) The Winter Session (November to December)

(ii) There are three types of procedure which ends the session. These are

(a) **Adjournment** It is the postponement of the sitting of the House. The Speaker has the power to adjourn the House sine-die. Once the House is adjourned sine-die, he/she is empowered to call it again.

(b) **Prorogation** It means the termination of a session of the Houses by an order made by the President.

(c) **Dissolution** It means end of the life of the Lok Sabha either by an order made by the President or on the expiration of the period of 5 years from the date of its first meeting.

(iii) The three motions passed in the Parliament are

(a) **Adjournment Motion** It is introduced in the Parliament to draw attention of the House to a definite matter of urgent public importance. It needs the support of 50 members to be admitted.

(b) **No-Confidence Motion** The Lok Sabha can remove the government from office by passing the no-confidence motion. It means that the government stays in office so long as it enjoys the confidence of the majority of members of the Lok Sabha. It needs the support of 50 members to be admitted.

(c) **Censure Motion** It can be introduced against an individual minister or a group of ministers. It is moved for censuring the Council of Ministers for specific policies and actions.

(iv) Question Hour is one of the important device of the Members of Parliament to seek information about the matter of public importance. The first hour of every Parliamentary sitting is allotted for the question hour. However, in 2014 the question hour was shifted in Rajya Sabha from 11 am to 12 noon. It is regulated according to Parliamentary rules.

6. With reference to the Union Legislature, answer the following questions. **[2020]**

(i) Explain any three legislative powers of the Union Parliament.

(ii) State any three exclusive powers of the Lok Sabha that is not enjoyed by other House.

(iii) List any four functions of the Speaker of the Lok Sabha.

Ans. (i) The legislative powers of the Union Parliament are

(a) The Parliament has exclusive power to make laws on all subjects mentioned in the Union List such as foreign affairs, atomic energy, defence, banking, etc.

(b) The Parliament along with State Assemblies make laws on certain subjects of Concurrent List such as Forest, Criminal Law, electricity, etc. If there is a conflict between the Union and States, then Union Law will prevail and laws made by the State Assembly will become null and void.

(c) The Parliament makes law on residuary subjects. All subjects that are not mentioned in Union List, State List or Concurrent List come under it.

(ii) Following are the three exclusive powers of the Lok Sabha that are not enjoyed by the other House.

(a) Money bill can be introduced only in the Lok Sabha and not in the Rajya Sabha. The Rajya Sabha cannot amend or reject the money bill but it has to return the bill to the Lok Sabha within the period of 14 days. The final power to decide whether a bill is money bill or not is also vested with the Presiding officer of the Lok Sabha i.e. Speaker.

(b) Rajya Sabha can only discuss the budget but cannot vote on the demand for grants.

(c) The resolution for the discontinuance of the National Emergency can be passed only by the Lok Sabha and not by the Rajya Sabha.

(iii) Refer to chapter theory page no. 5

7. The powers and functions of the Indian Parliament are wide ranging. In this context, answer the following questions. **[2017]**

(i) Explain three ways by which the Legislature exercises control over the Executive.

(ii) Mention any three special powers of the Rajya Sabha that is usually not enjoyed by the other House.

(iii) Mention any two judicial powers and two electoral powers of the Indian Parliament.

Ans. (i) The three ways by which the Legislature exercises control over the Executive are

(a) **Interpellation or Inquiry** The Parliament can ask questions to the government about its policies and performance.

(b) **Adjournment Motion** The Parliament can bring adjournment motion to bring matters of urgent public importance.

(c) **Vote of No-Confidence** If a government does not follow the provisions of the Constitution, the Parliament can pass a vote of no-confidence to the government. In such a case, whole ministry or government has to resign.

(ii) The special powers of Rajya Sabha are

(a) The Parliament can assume temporary power to legislate on State List subjects (Article 249) only if Rajya Sabha passes a resolution, which is supported by two-third (2/3rd) majority of its members present and voting.

(b) The All-India Services can be established only if the Rajya Sabha pass a resolution for it which is supported by two-third (2/3rd) majority of its members present and voting.

(c) During the emergency, if the Lok Sabha is dissolved then Rajya Sabha becomes *de-facto* (effective) and *de-jure* (legal) because Rajya Sabha is a permanent body.

(iii) The judicial powers of the Indian Parliament are

(a) The Parliament has the power to make laws about the jurisdiction and composition of the Supreme Court. It also creates a common High Court for two or more states.

(b) The Parliament can give punishment to a person for obstructing the work of it or showing disrespect to any of its House.

The electoral powers of the Indian Parliament are

- The Parliament along with Legislative Assemblies of state elects the President.
- Both Houses of the Parliament elect the Vice-President of India.

8. The Union Legislature comprises the President and two houses of the Parliament. With reference to the Parliament, answer the following questions. [2023]

(i) Mr Raj wants to be a member of the Lok Sabha. Mention any three qualifications required to contest elections for the Lok Sabha.

(ii) Mention any three legislative powers of the Union Parliament.

(iii) The Parliament controls the Executive. Mention any four ways in which it exercises its control.

Ans. (i) The Constitution mentions the qualifications for the membership of the Lok Sabha.

The conditions for the citizens are that, he/she

(a) should be an Indian citizen.

(b) should be at least 25 years of age.

(c) should not be of unsound mind.

(ii) Refer to chapter theory page no. 7.

(iii) Refer to chapter theory page no. 8.

Chapter Assessment

Section-I

Multiple Choice Questions

1. The right of the members to ask questions in the House is known as ....

   (a) Interpellation (b) Interjection
   (c) Defection (d) Prorogation

2. Who elect the Speaker of the Lok Sabha?

   (a) The President
   (b) Only the members of the ruling party
   (c) The Chairman of the Rajya Sabha
   (d) The members of the Lok Sabha.

3. The creation of a new All India Services is an exclusive power of the ....

   (a) President (b) Lok Sabha
   (c) Rajya Sabha (d) Supreme Court

4. Complete the given table.

Term of Lok Sabha	5 years
Term of Rajya Sabha	?

Section-II

Very Short Answer Questions

1. What is meant by Unitary Government?
2. Why is the Lok Sabha called Lower House and Rajya Sabha called Upper House?
3. Mention any one qualification to be a member of Rajya Sabha.
4. Name the body which elects the members of the Rajya Sabha.
5. Write any two unique features of the Rajya Sabha.
6. How does the session of the Parliament end?
7. What options are available to the President when a money bill is sent to him?

Structured Questions

1. With reference to the Rajya Sabha and Lok Sabha, answer the following questions.

   (i) Mention any three powers of the Lok Sabha.
   (ii) Differentiate between the powers of the Lok Sabha and the Rajya Sabha.
   (iii) As the Upper House of the Parliament, how does the Rajya Sabha enjoy its powers?
   (iv) Mention any three powers of Speaker of the Lok Sabha.

2. In the view of the power and control of the Indian Parliament explain the importance of

   (i) Question Hour
   (ii) No-Confidence Motion
   (iii) Zero Hour

CHAPTER

02

The Union Executive : The President and the Vice-President

SYLLABUS

The President Qualifications for election, composition of Electoral College, reason for indirect election, term of office, procedure for impeachment.
• Powers (executive, legislative, financial, judicial, discretionary and emergency)
The Vice-President Qualifications for election, term of office and powers.

The President

According to the Constitution, the executive authority of the Indian Union is vested in the President of India. The President is the head of the State and the Supreme Commander of the Defence Forces of India. He/she is the first citizen of India and acts as the symbol of unity, **integrity**[1] and **solidarity**[2] of the nation.

All executive actions of the state are taken in his name. As per the 42nd Amendment Act, the powers of the President have to be exercised with the advice of Prime Minister and Council of Ministers.

Qualifications for Election

To be eligible for election of the President, a person

- must be a citizen of India.
- must have completed 35 years of age.
- must be qualified for election as a member of the Lok Sabha.
- must not hold any office of profit under the Union Government or any State Government or any local authority or any other public authority.

Election

The manner and procedure of election of the President of India is mentioned in Article 55 of the Indian Constitution. The President is elected indirectly by members of **electoral college**[3].

The President's election is held in accordance with the system of **proportional representation**[4] by means of the single transferable vote and the voting is done by secret ballot.

1 **Integrity** The quality of being honest and fair.

2 **Solidarity** A feeling of unity between people who have the same interests, goals, etc.

3 **Electoral College** A body of electors, who elect the President and Vice-President of India.

4 **Proportional Representation** It is an electoral system in which parties gain seats in proportion to the number of votes cast for them.

The nomination of a candidate for election to the office of the President must be subscribed by at least 50 electors as **proposers**[5] and 50 electors as **seconders**[6].

Initially, this requirement was 10 proposers and 10 seconders. The ordinance of June, 1997 increased the number of proposers and seconders, that later became an Act of Parliament on 29th August, 1997.

As per this **ordinance**[7], now every candidate has to make a security deposit of ₹ 15000 in the Reserve Bank of India. The security deposit is liable to be forfeited in case the candidate fails to secure one-sixth (1/6th) of the votes polled.

According to the Constitution, all doubts and disputes arising out in relation to the election of a President shall be inquired and decided by the Supreme Court.

Single Transferable Vote (STV) System

It is an electoral system of proportional representation in which a person's vote can be transferred to a second or further competing candidate (according to the voter's stated order of preference), if the candidate of first choice is eliminated during a succession of counts or has more votes than are needed for election.

Composition of the Electoral College

The Electoral College includes

- The elected members of both the Houses of the Parliament.
- The elected members of the Legislative Assemblies of the states.
- The elected members of the Legislative Assemblies of Union Territories of Delhi and Puducherry.

Reasons for Indirect Election

The framers of the Constitution chose the method of indirect election to the office of the President due to the following reasons

- If the President is elected directly, he could become a rival centre of power to the Council of Ministers. Thus, this would be against the parliamentary system with ministerial responsibility.
- An indirect election protects the President to become a nominee of the ruling party at the centre.
- The process of indirect election give a clear role to the states as the Electoral College included the elected members of the State Legislative Assemblies.

Oath of Office

The President has to take an oath in the presence of the Chief Justice of India or in his/her absence, the senior-most judge of the Supreme Court.

In his/her oath, the President swears

- to faithfully execute functions of the office.
- to preserve, protect and defend the Constitution and the law.
- to devote himself to the service and well-being of the people of India.

Term of Office

The President's term of office is 5 years. The President's term can be terminated earlier by the following ways

- The resignation in writing addressed to the Vice-President of India.
- The removal for violation of the Constitution, by the process of impeachment.
- Due to his/her death.
- When he/she becomes disqualified to hold office or when his/her election is declared void.

Procedure for Impeachment

The President can be removed from the office by a process of impeachment for violation of the Constitution of India. Following is the impeachment procedure of the President

- Firstly, a **14 days notice** signed by not less than 1/4th of the total number of members of the house and preferring the charges, should be given to the President.
- Secondly, a resolution containing the charges has to be passed by a majority of not less than 2/3rd of the total membership of the House.
- Any House of Parliament may submit the charge of violation of the Constitution before the other House. After that the other House investigate the charges.
- During the investigation, the President shall have the right to defend himself/herself.
- After investigating the charges by the other house, it has to pass a resolution by 2/3rd majority, that the charges have been proved.

Check Your LEARNING...

1. Who deals with the disputes related to the elections of President of India?
2. 'The election to the office of the President is held indirectly by the Electoral College.' Who are the members of this college?
3. To whom does the President send his resignation?
4. In which situation does the office of the President fell vacant?

5 **Proposer** A person who suggests someone for a position or as a member of an organisation.

6 **Seconder** A seconder is someone who supports the proposer and his proposed candidate.

7 **Ordinance** It is an order of the President when both Houses of the Parliament are not in session. The ordinance should be laid down before both the Houses reassemble.

Powers and Functions of the President

Executive Powers of the President

Head of the Union As the head of the Union, the President performs and enjoys the following powers

- All executive actions of the Government of India are formally taken in his/her name.
- He/She can make rules specifying the manner in which the orders and other instruments made and executed in his/her name, shall be authenticated.
- He/She can seek any information relating to the administration of affairs of the Union and proposal for legislation from the Prime Minister.

Appointment of Officials of the Union The President of India appoints some important officials of the government. These include

- The Prime Minister and other ministers.
- The Attorney General of India.
- The Comptroller and Auditor General of India, the Chief Election Commissioner, the Chairman and members of the Union Public Service Commission, the Governors of States, the Chairman and members of Finance Commission, the Election Commission of India, etc.
- The commissions to investigate into the conditions of SCs, STs and OBCs.

Control over States The President has the power of direction, co-ordination and control of certain functions relating to State Governments. These include

- He is empowered to send directives to Governors in some executive matters.
- He can direct any Governor to ensure that the State Government complies with the laws made by the Union Government.
- The President is also directly responsible for the administration of Union Territories like Delhi, etc.

Administrator of Union Territories and Scheduled Areas The President directly administers the Union Territories through administrators appointed by him/her. He/She can declare any area as scheduled area and has powers with respect to the administration of scheduled and tribal areas.

Legislative Powers of the President

- **Address to the Parliament** The President can address both Houses of the Parliament at the beginning of the first session after each general election and the first session of each year, i.e. the Budget Session.
- **Send Message to the Houses** The President can send messages to the Houses of the Parliament, with respect to a bill pending in the Parliament or any other matter.
- **Summon or Prorogue[8] of the Parliament** The President can summon or prorogue the Parliament and dissolve the Lok Sabha. He/She can also summon a joint sitting of both the Houses of the Parliament.
- **Nomination of Members** The President nominates 12 members to the Rajya Sabha which have special knowledge or practical experience in respect of matters such as art, literature, science and social service.
- **Power Related to Bills** The President's prior recommendation or permission is needed to introduce certain types of bills in the Parliament. When a bill is passed by the Parliament, it is sent to the President for his/her assent. No bill can become a law without the assent and the signature of the President.
  - The President then can
  - give his/her assent to the bill, or
  - withhold his/her assent to the bill, or
  - direct the Governor to return the bill (if it is not a money bill) for reconsideration of the State Legislature.

  When a bill is passed by a State Legislature and is presented to the Governor, he/she may reserve it for the consideration of the President.
- **Promulgate Ordinance** When the Parliament is not in session, the President can promulgate ordinance. The ordinance must be approved by the Parliament within 6 weeks from the day when both Houses of the Parliament reassemble.

  The President can also withdraw an ordinance at any time. The ordinance lapses, if it is not approved by the Parliament.
- **Formation of New States** Without the recommendation of the President a bill for the formation of new states or alteration of areas of the existing states cannot be introduced.

Financial Powers of the President

- It is the responsibility of the President to introduce the annual budget every year in the Parliament. The Finance Minister on behalf of the President presents the Annual Budget before Parliament.
- Under constitutional provision, it is the duty of the President to appoint a Finance Commission after every five years, to recommend the revenues sharing between the Centre and the States.

8 **Prorogue** Discontinue a session without dissolving it.

- The President is authorised to withdraw money from Contingency Fund of India to meet certain emergency requirement.
- A money bill can only be introduced after the President's recommendation.
- No demand for grant can be made except on the recommendation of the President.

Judicial Powers of the President

- The President appoints the Chief Justice and the Judges of Supreme Court and High Courts.
- No criminal suit can be initiated against him during his tenure of office. The President is not answerable before any court of law for the exercise of the powers and duties of his office.
- The President can grant pardon, **reprieve**[9], **respite**[10] and remission (cancellation) of punishment or commute (reduce) the sentence of any person, convicted of any offence. This can be done in the following cases
  - In all cases where the punishment or sentence is by a court martial.
  - In all cases where the punishment or sentence is for an offence against union law.
  - In all cases where the sentence is a sentence of death.

Discretionary Powers of the President

The President has no discretionary powers according to the Constitution, but he/she has some situational discretionary powers. These are

- The President appoints the Prime Minister when no party has a clear majority in the Lok Sabha appointment of a Prime Minister when the Prime Minister in the office dies suddenly and there is no obvious successor.
- He/She dismiss the Council of Ministers when it cannot prove the confidence of the Lok Sabha.
- He/She dissolve the Lok Sabha if the Council of Ministers has lost its majority.

Emergency Powers

The President has certain extraordinary powers to deal with emergency situations. It is of three types which are

(i) National Emergency (Article 352)
(ii) President's Rule (Articles 356 and 365)
(iii) Financial Emergency (Article 360)

(i) National Emergency

The President has the power to make a proclamation of emergency, if there is a threat to the security of India or any part of it, by war, **external aggression**[11] or **armed rebellion**[12]. The President can declare such an emergency only on the basis of a written request by the Cabinet of Ministers headed by the Prime Minister.

Duration

The proclamation of National must be laid before both the Houses of the Parliament and approved by them within 1 month from the date of its issue, otherwise the proclamation ceases to be operative.

Every such resolution must be passed by a special majority i.e. not less than 2/3rd of the members present and voting. It will terminate at the end of 6 months from the date of the resolution unless Parliament passes a fresh resolution for its continuation.

The duration of a National Emergency can be extended by 6 months at a time. However, no such Emergency proclamation shall remain in force for more than three years.

Effects

- **Effects on Centre-State Relations** During the proclamation of National Emergency, the normal ties of the Centre-State relations undergo a basic change. This can be understood under the following heads
  - **Executive** The centre acquires the power to give directions to states on any matter.
  - **Legislative** The Parliament becomes empowered to make laws on any subject mentioned in the State List. The President can issue ordinances on state subjects also, if the Parliament is not in session.
  - **Financial** The President can modify the constitutional distribution of revenues between the Union and the States.
- **Effects on Lok Sabha and State Assembly** When National Emergency is in operation, the life of Lok Sabha may be extended beyond the normal tenure for one year at a time. On the other hand, this extension can't be extended beyond a period of 6 months after the Emergency. Similarly, the Parliament may extend the tenure of a State Legislative Assembly by one year during a National Emergency. It is subject to a maximum period of 6 months after the Emergency has ceased to operate.

---

9 **Reprieve** A cancellation or postponement of a punishment.
10 **Respite** To grant a temporary period of relief in prison sentence.
11 **External Aggression** An act of war against the republic of India.
12 **Armed Rebellion** An effort by many people supported by arms, armour, etc to change the government or leader of a country.

- **Effects on Fundamental Rights** The six fundamental rights under Article 19 are automatically suspended during National Emergency. The right to move the court for the enforcement of fundamental rights are also suspended except Articles 20 and 21. Article 20 states that no person shall be punished for the same offence more than once, whereas Article 21 states that no person shall be deprived of his life or personal liberty except according to the procedure established by law.
- **Effects on Finance** During National Emergency, the centre can suspend the financial provisions of the Constitution. Some matters such as the salaries of MPs and the distribution of revenues between the Centre and the States may also be changed.

(ii) President's Rule (Articles 356 and 365)

This is also called State Emergency or Constitutional Emergency. The Constitution authorise the President to make a proclamation of this Emergency in the following two situations

(i) If the President is satisfied that the government of a state cannot be carried on according to the provisions of the Constitution.

(ii) If the State fails to comply with or give effect to any of the directions given by the centre in the exercise of its executive power.

If any of these two conditions are proved, then the President may assume all the functions of the state.

Duration and Parliament's Approval

After the proclamation of this Emergency, it must be ratified from the Parliament within 2 months, after which, it remains operational for 6 months. This Emergency can be extended beyond a year, if it must fulfil two conditions

(i) If the proclaimation of National Emergency is in operation in the nation or in any part of the country.

(ii) If the Election Commission certifies that holding elections to the Legislative Assembly of the state (concerned) is difficult.

However, no such emergency shall remain for more than 3 years.

Effects

- State administration is directly controlled by the President with the Governor acting according to the instructions issued by the Union Government.
- The President may either dissolve the Vidhan Sabha and dismiss the Council of Ministers or keep them suspended.
- The President may authorise expenditure from the State Consolidated Fund, when the Lok Sabha is not in session.
- The President may also suspend the provision of the Constitution relating to the authority of the state.
- During State Emergency, the Union Parliament can pass laws on all subjects of the State List. The Budget can also be presented and passed by the Parliament.

(iii) Financial Emergency

Article 360 of the Constitution of India deals with Financial Emergency. The President can declare this Emergency if he/she feels.

- that a situation has arisen whereby the financial stability of the country is threatened.
- that credit of India or of any part of its territory is threatened.

Duration

Financial Emergency shall ordinarily remain in force for a period of 2 months, unless before the expiry of that period, it is approved by resolutions of Parliament. If approved, it operates for 6 months and can be extended by 6 months at a time. It can remain in operation for a maximum period of 3 years. Financial Emergency has never been declared since the declaration of the Constitution.

Effects

- The President may appoint a finance commission to suggest suitable measures to get out of the financial crisis and restore financial stability.
- The President can ask the states to reserve all money bills passed by the State Legislature for his/her consideration.
- The President can issue directions for the reduction of salaries and allowances of all or any class of persons who serve in relation to the affairs of the Union, including the Judges of the Supreme Court and the High Court.
- The President may issue certain directions to the states in regard to the utilisation of funds in the manner he thinks as reliable.

Diplomatic Powers of the President

- The President of India represents India in international conferences. The President has the power of appointing Indian ambassadors to other countries.
- All international treaties and agreements are concluded on behalf of the President, however, they are subject to satisfaction of the Parliament.

- The President receives ambassadors, diplomatic envoys and high commissioners from other nations.

Military Powers of the President

- The President is the Supreme Commander of the Indian Armed Forces.
- He/She can declare war or conclude peace on the advice of the Council of Ministers.
- He/She appoints the Chiefs of the Army, the Navy and the Air Force.

Veto Power of the President

A bill passed by the Parliament can become an act only if it receives the assent of the President. The Veto power enjoyed by the President of India regarding the bill are of three categories. These are

(i) **Pocket Veto** In this case, the President neither ratifies nor reject or return the bill, but simply keeps the bill pending for an indefinite period.

(ii) **Absolute Veto** It refers to the power of the President to withhold his/her assent to a bill passed by the Parliament. The bill then ends and does not become an act.

(iii) **Suspensive Veto** The President exercise this veto when he/she returns a bill for reconsideration of the Parliament. However, if the bill is passed again with or without amendments and presented to the President again, then he/she is obligatory to give assent to the bill.

Limitation of the President

The limitation of the President is that according to the 42nd Constitutional Amendment, it is necessary for the President to exercise his/her functions in accordance with the advice of the Council of Ministers, which is headed by the Prime Minister.

Check Your LEARNING...

1. Who summons the sessions of the Parliament?
2. What is the duration of Constitutional Emergency?
3. Which Aritcle deals with the Financial Emergency?
4. For how long the duration of Lok Sabha can be extended during National Emergency?

The Vice-President

According to the **Article 63** of Indian Constitution, there should be a Vice-President for India, who occupies the second highest office in the country.

Qualifications for Election

To be eligible for election as Vice-President, a person

- must be a citizen of India.
- must have completed 35 years of age.
- must be qualified for the election as a member of the Rajya Sabha.
- must not hold any office of profit under the Union Government or any State Government or any local authority or any other public authority.
- must not be a member of either House of the Parliament or a House of the State Legislature. If any such person is elected Vice-President, he/she is deemed to have vacated his/her seat in that House on the date on which he/she enters upon his/her office as Vice-President.

Election

The nomination of a candidate for election to the office of Vice-President must be subscribed by at least 20 electors as proposers and 20 electors as seconders.

Every candidate has to make a security deposit of ₹ 15000 in the Reserve Bank of India. The Vice-President of the Indian Union is elected jointly by both the Houses of the Parliament.

Composition of the Electoral College

Like the President, Vice-President is also elected indirectly by an electoral college in accordance with the **system of proportional representation** by means of single transferable vote. This electoral college consist of both elected and nominated members of the Parliament but it does not include the members of the State Legislative Assemblies.

Oath or Affirmation

Before entering upon his/her office, the oath to the office of the Vice-President is administered by the President or some person appointed on behalf of him/her. The Vice-President swears

- to bear true faith and allegiance to the Constitution of India.
- to faithfully discharge the duties of his/her office.

Term

The term of the office of the Vice-President is 5 years. It may terminate earlier by resignation (addressed to the President). The Vice-President can hold office beyond his/her term until his/her successor assumes the charge. He/She may be elected for any number of terms.

The Vice-President may be removed for the violation of the Constitution by the process of impeachment.

Powers and Functions

The powers and functions of the Vice-President are of two types

(i) **As an Ex-officio Chairman of the Rajya Sabha** The Vice-President acts as an ex-officio Chairman of the Rajya Sabha. In this capacity, his/her powers and functions are similar to those of the Speaker of the Lok Sabha. He conducts the business of the House by maintaining the discipline and decorum in the House. He has the power to take action against those who violate the rules of Rajya Sabha.

(ii) **Vice-President as President** The Vice-President acts as the President when a vacancy occurs in the office of the President due to his/her resignation or removal or his/her death or otherwise. He/She can act as the President only for a maximum period of 6 months. When the sitting President is unable to discharge his/her functions in this case also, the Vice-President acts as the President until the President resumes his/her office. It only happens due to absence or illness or any other cause. While acting as the President or discharging the functions of the President, he/she does not perform the duties of the office of the Chairman of Rajya Sabha. During this period, those duties are performed by the Deputy Chairman of the Rajya Sabha.

Check Your LEARNING...

1. What qualifications are required for the office of the Vice-President? Mention any one of them.
2. How is the Vice-President removed from the office?
3. Under what circumstances can the Vice-President take over the office of the President?
4. How long can the Vice-President officiate as President?

QUiCK Revision

- The President of India is the Head of the Union. He/she is the first citizen of India and acts as the symbol of unity, integrity and solidarity of the nation.
- The President's election is held in accordance with the system of proportional representation by means of the single transferable vote and the voting is by secret ballot.
- The President is elected by the members of the electoral college.
- The President takes an oath in the presence of the Chief Justice of India or in his/her absence, in the presence of the senior-most Judge of the Supreme Court.
- The term of the President's office is 5 years from the date on which he/she enters upon the office. The term of the office of the President may terminate earlier also like he can be removed from the office by the process of impeachment for violation of the Constitution.
- The Constitution stipulates that all doubts arising out of or in connection with the election of a President shall be inquired into and decided by the Supreme Court of India.
- The President can seek any information relating to the administration of affairs of the union and proposals for legislation from the Prime Minister.
- The President appoints important officers of the Government, such as Prime Minister, Attorney General of India, Chief Election Commissioners, members of Finance Commission, etc.
- The President can promulgate ordinance, when the Parliament is not in session. Such ordinance must be approved by the Parliament within 6 weeks from its re-assembly. President can also withdraw an ordinance at any time.
- The budget is laid before the Parliament in the name of the President. A money bill is introduced only on his/her recommendation.
- In addition to normal power, the President has certain extraordinary powers to deal with Emergency. It is of three types i.e. National Emergency, President's Rule and Financial Emergency.
- The National Emergency is imposed due to war, external aggression or armed rebellion. It implies that the security of India or any part of it is threatened by war or external aggression or armed rebellion.
- When government of a State cannot be carried on in accordance with the provisions of the constitution, either on the report of the Governor or otherwise, then the President proclaims Emergency. It is called President's Rule or Constitutional Emergency.
- If a state fails to comply with or give effect to any directions given by the union in the exercise of its executive power, then President's rule can be proclaimed.
- The President can declare Financial Emergency if he/she is satisfied that a situation has arisen whereby the financial stability or credit of India or of any part of its territory is threatened.
- The 44th Constitutional Amendment Act of 1978 authorised the President to require the Council of Ministers to reconsider such advice either general or otherwise.
- The Constitution of India provides for the office of Vice-President of India. He occupies the second highest office in the country. Like the President, Vice-President is also elected indirectly by an electoral college.
- Election disputes are decided by the Supreme Court and same principles apply in case of the Vice-President as in the case of the President.
- The oath of the office to the Vice-President is administered by the President or some person appointed on the behalf of him/her.
- The Vice-President acts as the ex-officio Chairman of the Rajya Sabha. In this capacity his/her powers and functions are similar to those of the Speaker of the Lok Sabha.
- The Vice-President acts as the President when a vacancy occurs in the office of the President, only for a maximum period of 6 months.

Chapter Practice

Section-I

Multiple Choice Questions

1. .... is the minimum age for the eligibility to be a Presidential candidate.
   (a) 28 years (b) 30 years
   (c) 35 years (d) 45 yeras

Ans. (c) 35 years

2. The President of India is elected by
   (a) only the members of Rajya Sabha.
   (b) only the members of Lok Sabha.
   (c) members of Legislative Assembly.
   (d) the elected members of Rajya Sabha, Lok Sabha and State Legislative Assembly.

Ans. (d) the elected members of Rajya Sabha, Lok Sabha and State Legislative Assembly.

3. The President's term of office is ....
   (a) 3 years (b) 5 years (c) 6 years (d) 7 years

Ans. (b) 5 years

4. The impeachment of the President can be initiated in ....
   (a) Lok Sabha
   (b) Rajya Sabha
   (c) either House of the Parliament
   (d) joint session of the both Houses

Ans. (c) either House of the Parliament

5. Who appoints the Comptroller and Auditor General of India?
   (a) The Prime Minister
   (b) The Finance Minister
   (c) The President
   (d) Speaker of the Lok Sabha

Ans. (c) The President

6. The President can nominate how many members of the Rajya Sabha?
   (a) 10 (b) 12 (c) 14 (d) 15

Ans. (b) 12

7. Which article related to National Emergency?
   (a) A-352 (b) A-365 (c) A-356 (d) A-360

Ans. (a) A-352

8. Which article deals with the Vice-President?
   (a) Article 53 (b) Article 63
   (c) Article 55 (d) Article 65

Ans. (b) Article 63

9. The term of the office of Vice-President is
   (a) 3 years (b) 4 years (c) 5 years (d) 6 years

Ans. (c) 5 years

10. The Vice-President acts as the President only for maximum period of
    (a) 6 months (b) 10 months
    (c) 12 months (d) 15 months

Ans. (a) 6 months

11. Complete the given analogy.
    Executive Powers : Control over States : : Legislative Powers : ?
    (a) Address to the Parliament
    (b) Head of the Union
    (c) Appointment of Official of the Union
    (d) Administrator of UTs

Ans. (a) Address to the Parliament

12. Complete the given analogy.
    National Emergency : Article 352 :: Financial Emergency : ?
    (a) Article 356 (b) Article 360
    (c) Article 365 (d) Article 368

Ans. (b) Article 360

13. Replace the underline word to correct the statement.
    <u>The Vice-President</u> has the power to make a 'proclamation of Emergency'.
    (a) The Prime Minister (b) The Council of Ministers
    (c) The President (d) The Attorney General

Ans. (c) The President

14. Replace the underline word to correct the statement.
    The ex-officio Chairman of the Rajya Sabha is <u>Prime Minister</u>.
    (a) The President (b) Vice-President
    (c) Chief Justice of India (d) The Speaker

Ans. (b) Vice-President

15. Complete the following table.

President	50 electors
Vice-President	?

    (a) 10 electors (b) 20 electors
    (c) 30 electors (d) 40 electors

Ans. (b) 20 electors

16. The President exercises his power on the advice of the
    (i) Prime Minister (ii) Council of Ministers
    (iii) Vice-President (iv) Speaker

    Codes
    (a) Only (i) (b) Both (i) and (ii)
    (c) Only (iii) (d) Both (i) and (iv)

Ans. (b) Both (i) and (ii)

17. Which of the following is/are the power of the President?
(i) Address to the Parliament.
(ii) Summon of the Parliament.
(iii) Send message to the House.
(iv) Formation of New States.

Codes
(a) Only (i) (b) Only (ii)
(c) Both (i) and (ii) (d) All of these

Ans. (d) All of these

18. Which of the following is the effect of National Emergency?
(i) Centre aquire the power on states.
(ii) Distribution Legislative powers between Union and State gets suspended.
(iii) Constitutional distribution of revenues between the Union and States.

Codes
(a) Only (i) (b) Both (i) and (ii)
(c) Both (ii) and (iii) (d) All of these

Ans. (d) All of these

19. Match the following.

	List - I		List - II
A.	Vice-President	1.	Article 63
B.	Election of President	2.	Article 55
C.	Financial Emergency	3.	Article 360
D.	National Emergency	4.	Article 352

Codes

	A	B	C	D		A	B	C	D
(a)	1	2	3	4	(b)	4	3	2	1
(c)	3	4	1	2	(d)	2	3	1	4	3

Ans. (a)

20. Match the following.

	President's Power		Related Field
A.	Financial Powers	1.	International treaties
B.	Diplomatic Powers	2.	Introduction of money bill often President's recommendation
C.	Judicial Powers	3.	Head of the Union
D.	Executive Powers	4.	Appoints Chief Justice

Codes

	A	B	C	D		A	B	C	D
(a)	1	2	3	4	(b)	2	1	4	3
(c)	3	1	4	2	(d)	4	3	2	1

Ans. (b)

Section-II

Very Short Questions

1. In whom the executive power of the Union is implicit?

Ans. The Constitution implicit the executive power of the Union in the President of India. He/she exercises the power either directly or indirectly through officer's subordinate to him/her.

2. Who acts as the symbol of unity, integrity and solidarity of the nation?

Ans. The President of India acts as the symbol of unity, integrity and solidarity of the nation. He/she is the head of the India and he/she is the first citizen of India.

3. State any one qualification necessary for the election of the President of India. **[2015]**

Ans. One qualification necessary for election of the President is that the President should not hold any office of profit under the Union Government or any State Government or any local/public authority.

4. State the composition of the electoral college in the election of the Vice-President of India. **[2014]**

Ans. Following is the composition of the electoral college for the election of Vice-President of India
- It include both elected and nominated members of the Parliament.
- It does not include members of the State Legislative Assemblies.

5. What do you understand by Single Transferable Vote?

Ans. The Single Transferable Vote (STV) is an electoral system of proportional representation in which a person's vote can be transferred to the second or further competing candidate.

6. State any one reason, for why the President is elected indirectly. **[2018, 2013]**

Ans. The framers of the Constitution choose the method of indirect election to the office of the President because if elected directly, he could become a rival centre of power to the Council of Ministers.

7. The President is to take oath in the presence of whom?

Ans. The President is to take oath in the presence of the Chief Justice of India or in his/her absence the senior-most Judge of the Supreme Court.

8. When and how can the President of India be removed from the office? **[2006]**

Or Name the official procedure by which the President can be removed. **[2016]**

Ans. The official procedure of removing President is the process of impeachment which can be initiated by either House of the Parliament for violation of the Constitution.

9. Who settles the disputes arising in connection with the election of the President of India? **[2012]**

Ans. The Supreme Court of India settles all the disputes arising in connection with the election of the President of India.

10. Which Amendment Act has taken away the Supreme Court's power to settle disputes in connection with the election of the President of India?

Ans. The 39th Constitutional Amendment Act has taken away the power of Supreme Court to settle disputes in connection with the election of the President of India.

11. Who appoints the Prime Minister of India?

Ans. The Prime Minister of India is appointed by the President of India.

12. On whose advice can the President appoint the Council of Ministers?

Ans. The Council of Ministers are appointed by the President on the advice of the Prime Minister.

13. The Finance Commission of India is appointed by whom?

Ans. The President of India appoints the Finance Commission of India.

14. As the administrator of scheduled area, the President performs how many functions? Mention.

Ans. As the administrator of scheduled area, the President performs one function i.e. the President can declare any area as scheduled area and has powers with respect to the administration of scheduled and tribal areas.

15. Mention any one important occasion when the President addresses a joint session of the Parliament. **[2016]**

Ans. The President can address a joint session of both the Houses of the Parliament at the commencement of the first session after each general elections and at the first session of the each year i.e. the Budget Session.

16. When does the President appoints the Presiding officer of the Houses?

Ans. The President can appoint any member of both the Houses of the Parliament, as the Presiding officers when the Presiding officers of the Houses fall vacant.

17. What happens, when the bill is again passed by the State Legislature and is then presented to the Governor for his/her assent?

Ans. If the bill is passed again with or without amendments, by the State Legislature, the Governor must give his assent to it.

18. What is an ordinance? When can it be passed? **[2014]**

Or What is an ordinance? **[2018, 2007]**

Ans. Ordinances are short-term laws that are promulgated by the President of India on the recommendation of the Union Cabinet when the Parliament is not in session.

19. Who has the power to promulgate an ordinance at the centre ? When can it be promulgated? **[2015]**

Ans. An ordinance is promulgated by the President when the Parliament is not in session. These ordinance must be approved by the Parliament within 6 weeks from the date on which both the Houses of the Parliament reassemble.

20. Who is the Supreme Commander of the Armed Forces of India?

Ans. The President of India is the Supreme Commander of Armed Forces of India.

21. When can the President use his discretionary power to appoint the Prime Minister? **[2017]**

Ans. One circumstance when the President can appoint the Prime Minister using his discretionary power is that when no party has a clear majority in the Lok Sabha and there is a hung Parliament or when the Prime Minister in the office dies suddenly.

22. Write any one circumstance when the President can declare a National Emergency.

Ans. Under Article 352, the President can proclaim a National Emergency, only if he is satisfied that the security of the nation is threatened due to war or external aggression or due to armed rebellion.

23. What is the impact of National Emergency over the State Legislature?

Ans. When National Emergency is proclaimed, then the State Legislature will not be suspended, but the distribution of legislative powers between Union and State gets suspended.

24. What is the effect of National Emergency over the Fundamental Rights?

Ans. During the National Emergency, Article 19 of the Fundamental Rights will automatically get suspended on the grounds of war or external aggression.

25. Under what circumstance does the President's rule be continued beyond the period of 1 year?

Ans. The continuance of the President's rule beyond 1 year is possible only if the proclamation of Emergency under Article 352 is in operation.

26. Mention the circumstance when the President can declare Financial Emergency.

Ans. If the President is satisfied that the situation has arisen whereby the financial stability of the country is threatened. He can declare Financial Emergency.

27. What is Veto Power?

Ans. Veto power is enjoyed by the President over bills passed by the Parliament. It means he/she can withhold his/her assent to the bills.

28. Through which amendment, the President is bounded by the advice of Council of Ministers?

Ans. The 42nd Constitutional Amendment Act of 1976, made the President bounded by the advice of Council of Ministers headed by the Prime Minister.

29. State the reason why the President cannot dissolve the Rajya Sabha.

Ans. The President cannot dissolve the Rajya Sabha because it is a permanent House of the Parliament.

30. State the body that decides the major policies of the government.

Ans. The President decides the major policies of the government.

31. Who is the Vice-President?

Ans. The Constitution of India, under Article 63, provides that there should be a Vice-President. The Vice-President occupies second highest office in the country.

32. Mr Konar was not found eligible for the election as the Vice-President of India even though he had the qualifications of being a citizen of India and not being a member of the Parliament and the State Legislature. On what grounds was he disqualified? Give one reason. **[2009]**

Ans. Mr Konar holds the office of profit under the Union Government or any State Government or any local public authority. On the basis of this ground he was disqualified.

33. Who decides the election disputes of the Vice-President?

Ans. Election disputes related to the office of the Vice-President and the President, are decided by the Supreme Court of India.

34. Who administers the oath to the office of the Vice-President?

Ans. The oath to the office of the Vice-President is administered by the President or some person appointed on this behalf by him/her.

35. When can the Vice-President cast his/her vote in the Rajya Sabha? **[2013]**

Ans. Generally, the Vice-President, acts as the ex-officio Chairman of the Rajya Sabha, cannot cast a vote. But when there is a tie then he/she can cast a vote to clear the majority.

36. Mention any one difference between the election of the President and the Vice-President of India.

Ans. One difference between the election of the President and the Vice-President of India is that for the election to the office of the President, the members of the State Legislature Assemblies participate, but it does not happens for the election of the Vice-President.

Structured Questions

1. The President is the Executive Head of the Union of India. In this regard, answer the following questions.

(i) Mention any two qualifications for the election of the President.

(ii) Explain the impeachment procedure of the President.

(iii) What is the manner of the election of the President?

(iv) Which oath does the President of India subscribe before entering upon his office?

Ans. (i) Two qualifications for the election of the President are

(a) He/she must be a citizen of India.

(b) He/she must have completed 35 years of age.

(ii) The impeachment procedure of the President is

- Firstly, a 14 days notice signed by not less than 1/4th of the total number of members of the house and preferring the charges, should be given to the President.
- Secondly, a resolution containing the charges has to be passed by a majority of not less than 2/3rd of the total membership of the House.
- Any House of Parliament may submit the charge of violation of the Constitution before the other House. After that the other House investigate the charges. During the investigation, the President shall have the right to defend himself/herself.
- After investigating the charges by the other house, it has to pass a resolution by 2/3rd majority, that the charges have been proved.

(iii) The manner and procedure of election of the President of India is mentioned in Article 55 of the Indian Constitution. The President is elected indirectly by members of electoral college.

The President's election is held in accordance with the system of proportional representation by means of the single transferable vote and the voting is done by secret ballot. The nomination of a candidate for election to the office of the President must be subscribed by at least 50 electors as proposers and 50 electors as seconders.

(iv) The President before entering upon his office make and subscribe to an oath or affirmation. In his oath, the President swears

- to faithfully execute the office.
- to preserve, protect and defend the Constitution and law.
- to devote himself to the service and well-being of the people of India.

2. The President of India is elected indirectly, despite it, he is the head of the Union. With reference to this, answer the following questions.

(i) What is meant by proportional representation?

(ii) What are the conditions required for getting nominal to the post of the President?

(iii) Write any two appointments made by the President. **[2015]**

(iv) Why does the framers of the Constitution choose the method of the indirect election to the post of the President?

Ans. (i) Proportional representation is a concept in which the number of seats won by a party or a group of candidates are proportionate to the number of votes received.

(ii) The conditions required for getting nominal to the post of the President are
- The nomination of a candidate for the election to the office of the President must be subscribed by at least 50 electors as proposers and 50 electors as seconders.
- The President is the constitutional Head of the Union Government.

(iii) Two appointments by the President of India are

(a) Comptroller and Auditor General of India (CAG).

(b) Attorney General of India.

(iv) The framers of the Constitution choose the method of the indirect election to the post of the President because
- if the President is elected directly, he could become a rival centre of power to the Council of Ministers.Thus, this would be against the Parliamentary system with ministerial responsibility.
- an indirect election protects the President to become a nominee of the ruling party at the Centre.

3. The President of India is the constitutional Head of the Indian Republic. In this context, answer the following questions. **[2016]**

(i) How is the President elected?

(ii) Mention three types of Emergencies that the President is empowered to proclaim.

(iii) Explain briefly any four 'executive powers' of the President.

Ans. (i) Refer to chapter theory page no. 21-22.

(ii) Three types of Emergencies that the President is empowered to proclaim are

(a) **National Emergency** The President, if satisfied that the security of the nation is threatened by war or external aggression or armed rebellion, he can proclaim this emergency.

(b) **State Emergency or President's Rule** On receipt of a report from the Governor, if the President is satisfied that there is a breakdown of constitutional machinery in the state, he can proclaim this emergency.

(c) **Financial Emergency** If a situation has arisen whereby the financial stability or credit of the nation is threatened, the President can proclaim this emergency.

(iii) The executive powers of the President are

(a) As a Head of the Union Administration, all executive orders are issued in the name of the President.

(b) He makes appointments to key posts to run the government's administration such as the Prime Minister and the Council of Ministers, the Chief Justice and judges of Supreme Court and the High Courts etc.

(c) The administration of the Union Territories and the border areas is the responsibility of the President.

(d) He makes rules for more convenient transaction of business of the Union Government.

4. The President is the head of the State and exercises his / her power on the advice of the Prime Minister and Council of Ministers. With reference to this, answer the following questions **[2023]**

(i) What are the three types of emergencies that can be proclaimed by the President ?

(ii) Mention any three legislative powers of the President.

(iii) Give any two reasons to justify the need for indirect election of the President.

What is the composition of the Electoral College which elects the President ?

Ans. (i) Refer to Structured Question 3(ii).

(ii) Legislative powers of the President are as follows

(a) He can address both the Houses of the Parliament at the first session of the year and after the general election.

(b) He has the power to send message to either House of the Parliament.

(c) He has the power to nominate 12 members of the Rajya Sabha and 2 members of the Lok Sabha.

(iii) The reasons that were given for adopting the method of indirect election for Presidential election are

(a) The power resided in the Council of Ministers, headed by the Prime Minister and the Union Parliament and not in the President as such. Therefore, it would be not be appropriate if the President is to be elected directly by the people and is not given any real power.

(b) At tremendous loss of time, energy and money would be involved in a direct Presidential election.

The President is elected indirectly by the members of an Electoral College consisting of

(a) the elected members of both Houses of Parliament.

(b) the elected members of the Legislative Assemblies of the States and those of the National Capital Territory of Delhi and the Union Territory of Puducherry.

5. The executive power of the Indian Union is vested in the President of India. In this context, answer the following questions.
[Specimen Paper Semester-II 2022]

(i) Give any two reasons for the indirect election of the President.

(ii) What is the duration of National Emergency?

(iii) Mention any three legislative powers of the President.

(iv) Name the three kinds of emergencies that can be proclaimed by the President.

Ans. (i) Two reasons for the indirect election of the President are

(a) An indirect election protects the President to become a nominee of the ruling party at the centre.

(b) If the President is elected directly, he could become a rival centre of power to the Council of Ministers. Thus, this would be against the parliamentary system with ministerial responsibility.

(ii) The proclamation of National must be laid before both the Houses of the Parliament and approved by them within 1 month from the date of its issue, otherwise the proclamation ceases to be operative. Every such resolution must be passed by a special majority i.e. not less than 2/3rd of the members present and voting. It will terminate at the end of 6 months from the date of the resolution unless Parliament passes a fresh resolution for its continuation. The duration of a National Emergency can be extended by 6 months at a time. However, no such Emergency proclamation shall remain in force for more than three years.

(iii) Refer to Structured Question 4 (ii)

(iv) Refer to Structured Question 3 (ii).

6. The President of India proclaims the Emergency powers with respect to it, answer the following questions.

(i) Mention any three effects of the National Emergency.

(ii) What is the duration of President's rule?

(iii) Duration of Financial Emergency.

(iv) Mention any two effects of the Financial Emergency.

Ans. (i) The effects of the National Emergency are

(a) **Effects on Lok Sabha and State Assembly** When National Emergency is in operation, the life of Lok Sabha may be extended beyond the normal tenure for one year at a time.

(b) **Effects on Fundamental Rights** The six fundamental rights under Article 19 are automatically suspended during National Emergency.

(c) **Effects on Finance** During National Emergency, the centre can suspend the financial provisions of the Constitution. Some matters such as the salaries of MPs and the distribution of revenues between the Centre and the States may also be changed.

(ii) After the proclamation of President's Rule, it must be ratified from the Parliament within 2 months, after which, it remains operational for 6 months. This emergency can be extended beyond a year, if it must fulfil two conditions

(a) If the proclamation of National Emergency is in operation in the nation or in any part of the country.

(b) If the Election Commission certifies that holding elections to the Legislative Assembly of the state (concerned) is difficult.

However, no such Emergency shall remain for more than 3 years.

(iii) Refer to chapter theory page no. 25.

(iv) The effects of the Financial Emergency are

(a) The President may appoint a finance commission to suggest suitable measures to get out of the financial crisis and restore financial stability.

(b) The President can ask the states to reserve all money bills passed by the State Legislature for his/her consideration.

7. With respect to the President of India, as the executive head, answer the following questions

(i) State the oath or affirmation to the office of the President.

(ii) Mention any three appointment powers of the President.

(iii) With respect to the bills, what is the veto power of the President?

(iv) Explain in brief about the military powers of President.

Ans. (i) Refer to chapter theory page no. 22.

(ii) The appointment powers of the President are

(a) The President of India appoints the Prime Minister and other ministers.

(b) The President appoints the Attorney General of India, the Comptroller and Auditor General of India, the Chief Election Commissioner, the Chairman and members of the Union Public Service Commission, the Governors of States, the Chairman and members of Finance Commission, the Election Commission of India, etc.

(c) The President appoints the Commissions to investigate into the conditions of SCs, STs and OBCs.

(iii) The Veto power enjoyed by the President of India is regarding assent to the bill passed by the Parliament.

The Veto power are of three categories

(a) **Pocket Veto** In this case, the President neither ratifies nor reject or return the bill, but simply keeps the bill pending for an indefinite period.

(b) **Absolute Veto** It refers to the power of the President to withhold his/her assent to a bill passed by the Parliament. The bill then ends and does not become an act.

(c) **Suspensive Veto** The President exercise this veto when he/she returns a bill for reconsideration of the Parliament. However, if the bill is passed again with or without amendments and presented to the President again, then he/she is obligatory to give assent to the bill.

(iv) The military powers of the President are

- The President is the Supreme Commander of the Indian Armed Forces.
- He/She can declare war or conclude peace on the advice of the Council of Ministers.
- He/She appoints the Chiefs of the Army, the Navy and the Air Force.

8. The President of India is the Head of the Indian Republic. In this context, answer the following questions. **[2012]**

(i) Besides being a citizen of India, state three other qualifications required for a person to be eligible to the President of India.

(ii) Mention three legislative powers.

(iii) Under what circumstances can the President of India declare an Emergency in the country?

Ans. (i) Other qualifications required to be eligible to be the President of India besides being a citizen of India are

- He/She must have completed the age of 35 years.
- He/She should be qualified for election as a member of the Lok Sabha.
- He/She should not hold any office of profit under the Government of India or Government of any State or under any local authority.

(ii) Refer to chapter theory page no. 23.

(iii) Under following circumstances the President can declare an Emergency in the country.

- When the President is satisfied of an imminent danger of such external aggression or armed rebellion.
- When the President is satisfied that the Government of a State cannot be carried on in accordance with the provisions of the Constitution.
- When a State fails to comply with or give effect to any of the directions given by the Union in the exercise of its executive power.
- When the President is satisfied that a situation has arisen whereby the financial stability or credit of India or of any part of its territory is threatened.

9. The President of India is a nominal and constitutional head of the nation. In this context, answer the following questions. **[2010]**

(i) Why is the President of India referred as a nominal head of the state? State two examples of his legislative powers that suggest his nominal status. **[3]**

(ii) Mention the circumstances when the President can declare a National Emergency. **[3]**

(iii) Explain two discretionary powers of the President. **[4]**

Ans. (i) According to constitutional provisions, the President exercises his powers on the advice of the Prime Minister and the Council of Ministers, thus he is referred to as the nominal head of the state.

Two legislative powers of the President that suggest his nominal status are

- The ordinance power of the President is subjected to ratification by the Parliament. If not ratified, the ordinance ceases.
- The nomination of members in Lok Sabha and Rajya Sabha is also done by the President on the advice of Prime Minister and the Council of Ministers. So, he has a sort of a nominal status.

(ii) Refer to chapter theory page no. 24.

(iii) Refer to chapter theory page no. 24.

10. The President and the Vice-President are part of the Union Executive. In this context, answer the following questions. **[2018]**

(i) State any three qualifications required for a candidate to be elected as the Vice-President of India.

(ii) State the three functions of the Vice-President.

(iii) Explain briefly any two legislative and any two executive powers of the President.

Ans. (i) Three qualifications required for a candidate to be elected as the Vice-President of India are

(a) He/She must be a citizen of India.

(b) He/She should have completed 35 years of age.

(c) He/She should be qualified for the election as a member of the Rajya Sabha.

(ii) Three functions of the Vice-President are

(a) The Vice-President acts as an ex-officio Chairman of the Rajya Sabha.

(b) The Vice-President acts as the President when a vacancy occurs in the office of the President due to his/her removal or his/her death or otherwise.

(c) When the sitting President is unable to discharge his/her functions, the Vice-President acts as the President until the President resumes his/her office.

(iii) The legislative powers of the President are

(a) **Nomination of Members** The President nominates 12 members to the Rajya Sabha which have special knowledge or practical experience in respect of matters such as art, literature, science and social service.

(b) **Prior Recommendation** The President's prior recommendation or permission is needed to introduce certain types of bills in the Parliament.

The executive powers of the President are

(a) All executive actions of the Government of India are formally taken in his/her name.

(b) He/she can make rules specifying the manner in which the orders and other instruments made and executed in his/her name, shall be authenticated.

11. The office of the Vice-President is the second highest office of our country. In this regard, answer the following questions:

(i) Mention any three qualifications for the office of the Vice-President.

(ii) When does the Vice-President act as the President?

(iii) Discuss the term of the office of the Vice-President.

(iv) Discuss in brief, the removal process of Vice-President.

Ans. (i) Refer to chapter theory on page no. 26.

(ii) The Vice-President acts as the President under the following circumstances.

- When a vacancy occurs in the office of the President due to his/her removal, or death or otherwise. He/she can act as President only for a maximum period of 6 months.
- When the sitting President is unable to discharge his/her functions, the Vice-President acts as the President untill the President resumes his/her office. It only happens in case of absence or illness or any other cause.

(iii) Refer to chapter theory page no. 26.

(iv) The removal process of the Vice-President is

- He can resign from his office at any time by addressing the resignation letter to the president.
- He can also be removed from the office on the violation of the Constitution by the process of impeachment.

12. According to Article 63 of our Constitution, there shall be a Vice-President of India. In this context, state

(i) composition of electoral College.

(ii) oath of affirmation

(iii) The term of office of the Vice President of India and his functions.

Ans. (i) Like the President, the Vice-President of India is elected indirectly by an Electoral college, through the system of proportional representation by means of Single Transferable Vote. This electoral college consists of both the elected as well as the nominated Members of the Parliament. However, it does not include the Members of the State Legislative Assemblies.

(ii) Before entering upon his/her office, the oath to the office of the Vice-President is administered by the President or some person appointed on behalf of him/her. The Vice-President swears

- to bear true faith and allegiance to the Constitution of India.
- to faithfully discharge the duties of his/her office.

(iii) The term of the office of the Vice-President is 5 years. It may terminate earlier by resignation. The Vice-President can hold office beyond his/her term untill his/her successor assumes the charge. He/she is also eligible for re-election to that office for any number of terms.

The functions of the Vice-President are

- **As an ex-officio Chairman of the Rajya Sabha** The Vice-President acts as an ex-officio Chairman of the Rajya Sabha. He conducts the business of the House by maintaining the discipline and decorum in the House. He has the power to take action against those who violate the rules of Rajya Sabha.
- **Vice-President as President** The Vice-President acts as the President when a vacancy occurs in the office of the President due to his/her resignation or removal or his/her death or otherwise. He/she can act as the President only for a maximum period of 6 months.

Chapter Assessment

Section-I

Multiple Choice Questions

1. .... is regarded as the head of the Indian state.
   (a) The Prime Minister (b) The President
   (c) Attorney (d) Chief Justice of India
2. Who has the power to declare an area as a scheduled area?
   (a) The Chief Minister (b) The Governor
   (c) The Prime Minister (d) The President
3. Replace the underline word to correct the statement.
   The Speaker may dissolve the Vidhan Sabha and discuss the Council of Ministers.
   (a) The Prime Minister (b) The Chief Minister
   (c) The President (d) The Vice-President
4. Complete the given analogy.
   Presidents Oath : Chief Justice of India : :
   Vice-President's Oath : : ?
   (a) The Prime Minister (b) The Speaker
   (c) The President (d) Attornery General

Section-II

Very Short Questions

1. Who elects the President of India?
2. To whom does the President send his resignation?
3. Who administers the Union Territory?
4. What options are open to the President when an ordinary bill is sent to him/her for his/her assent?
5. What are the circumstances for the National Emergency?
6. Mention any one effect of the President's Rule.
7. Mention any one reason, why the President election is indirect?
8. Mention the process for the impeachment of the President.
9. Mention two important functions of the Vice-President.
10. Who is the ex-officio chairperson of the Rajya sabha?

Structured Questions

1. The President is the Executive Head of the State or Union. With reference to it, answer the following questions.
   (i) Write any three powers of the President.
   (ii) What all Veto powers are enjoyed by the President?
   (iii) When can the President proclaim the Financial Emergency?
   (iv) What are the limitations of the President?
2. The second head of the Union is the Vice-President of India. With reference to it, answer the following questions.
   (i) What is the manner for the election of the Vice-President?
   (ii) Mention any two powers of the Vice-President.
   (iii) What are the qualifications for the office of the Vice-President? Describe in brief the removal process of Vice-President of India.

CHAPTER

03

Prime Minister and Council of Ministers

SYLLABUS

Prime Minister and Council of Ministers Appointment, formation of Council of Ministers, tenure, functions-policy making, administrative, legislative, financial, emergency. • Position and powers of the Prime Minister. • Collective and individual responsibility of the members of the Cabinet. • Distinction between the Council of Ministers and the Cabinet.

Prime Minister

Article 74 of the Constitution of India provide that there shall be a Council of Ministers, with the Prime Minister at the head, to aid and advise the President. The President shall exercise his/her functions according to their advice. In parliamentary form of government, the President is the nominal executive authority (*de jure* executive) and Prime Minister is the real executive authority (*de facto* executive).

Appointment

The Prime Minister (PM) is appointed by the President, who according to **convention**[1], invites the leader of the majority party or group in the Lok Sabha to form the government. The members of the majority group or party elect their leader in the Lok Sabha to be appointed as the Prime Minister.

The President may use his discretionary power to appoint the Prime Minister, when no single party or group secures the majority in the House. However, the President has to appoint the person who can prove his majority in the House, by the support of some smaller groups or parties.

Oath

Before entering upon the office of Prime Minister, the President administers the oath of office and secrecy to the Prime Minister which are

- To bear true faith and **allegiance**[2] to the Constitution of India.
- To uphold the sovereignty and integrity of India.
- To faithfully and honestly discharge the duties of his/her office.
- To do right to all manner of people according to the Constitution and the law, without the fear or favour, affection or ill-will.

Term

The full term of the Prime Minister is 5 years which correspond to the normal term of the Lok Sabha. However, the Prime Minister remain in power as long as he enjoys the confidence of the Lok Sabha as he/she can be dismissed by the President, if he/she fails to enjoy the majority support of the Lok Sabha. The Prime Minister may also resign by writing to the President. There are no term limits on the office of the Prime Minister.

1 **Convention** A way in which something is done.
2 **Allegiance** Loyalty or commitment

Position and Powers of the Prime Minister

In Relation to the Council of Ministers

- The Prime Minister is the head of the Cabinet. He/She recommend the persons to be appointed as ministers, to the President.
- The Prime Minister **allocates**[3] and **reshuffles**[4] various portfolios among the ministers.
- The Prime Minister can advise the President to dismiss a minister in case of difference of opinion.
- The Prime Minister presided the meeting of Council of Ministers and influences its decisions.
- The Prime Minister bring about end to the Council of Ministers by resigning from the office.
- The Prime Minister is the Chief Coordinator between various ministers on policy issues.

In Relation to the President

- The Prime Minister is the principal advisor to the President.
- The Prime Minister chooses the ministers and on his advice the President appoints them.
- The Prime Minister acts as a link between the President and the Council of Ministers as it communicates all the decisions of the Council of Ministers to the President on administration of the Union.
- The Prime Minister **furnishes**[5] all the administrative affairs of the union, when the President may call for.
- The Prime Minister advises the President with regard to the appointment of important officials, such as CAG, members of UPSC, ECs, etc.

In Relation to the Parliament

- The Prime Minister is the leader of the Lok Sabha as he is the leader of majority party in the Parliament.
- The Prime Minister advises the President with regard to summoning and proroguing (discontinuing) the sessions of the Parliament.
- The Prime Minister can recommend **dissolution**[6] of the Lok Sabha to the President at any time.
- The Prime Minister is the leader of the Lower House in the Parliament and the Chief Spokesperson of the government in the Parliament. He/She announces government policies on the floor of the House.
- Whenever an unwanted situation arises in the Parliament, the matter generally ends with the intervention of the Prime Minister.

As the Leader of the Nation

- The Prime Minister represents the nation. He/She decides the kind of relation India would have with other countries.
- He/She tries to protect the interest of the country in international forums.
- He/She is the ex-officio Chairman of the NITI (National Institution for Transforming India) Aayog that replaces Planning Commission of India.
- He/She is also the ex-officio Chairman of Atomic Energy Commission.

Check Your LEARNING...

1. What does Article 74 of the Constitution relate to?
2. In relation to the President, state any one power enjoyed by the Prime Minister.
3. How is the Prime Minister a link between the Cabinet and the President?
4. Write any one function of the Prime Minister in relation to the Parliament.

Council of Ministers

The Union Council of Ministers exercises executive authority in the Republic of India. They are collectively responsible to the Lok Sabha.

They are led by the Prime Minister. A smaller executive body of the council called the Union Cabinet is the supreme decision-making body in India. Only the Prime Minister and ministers with the rank of 'Cabinet Ministers' are the members of Union Cabinet as per Article 352.

Formation

The Constitution originally does not specify the number of the Council of Ministers. However, the Constitution (91st Amendment Act, 2003) mentioned the size of the Council of Ministers to 15% of the strength of the Lok Sabha or the State Legislatures. In the case of smaller states, the maximum number of ministers allowed is 12.

3 **Allocate** Distribute for a particular purpose .
4 **Reshuffle** Interchange the positions of government ministers.
5 **Furnish** To provide something necessary or desire.
6 **Dissolution** The action of formally ending or dismissing an assembly.

Composition

The Council of Ministers consists of three categories of ministers, namely

(i) **Cabinet Ministers** They are the senior ministers. They head the important ministers of the government such as Home, Defence, Railway and Finance, etc. They attend all the meetings and also play an important role in deciding the policies. A Cabinet Minister can be incharge of one ministry or sometimes more than one ministry.

(ii) **The Ministers of State** They are the junior or second category ministers. They may either be given independent charge of ministries or departments or may be attached to the Cabinet Ministers. They do not participate in the Cabinet meetings, but they are sometimes invited to the Cabinet meetings to discuss matters related to their departments.

In case of independent charge, they perform the same functions and exercise the same powers in relation to their ministries or departments as Cabinet Ministers perform.

(iii) **Deputy Ministers** They are responsible to assist the Cabinet Ministers and the Council of Ministers in performing their administrative, political and parliamentary duties. They are not the members of Cabinet and they never take part in Cabinet discussions.

Appointment

Council of Ministers are appointed by the President on the advice of the Prime Minister. Generally, the Members of Parliament (either the Lok Sabha or the Rajya Sabha) are appointed as ministers. A person who is not a member of either houses can also be appointed as a minister. But he/she must become a member (either through election or nomination) of either House of the Parliament within 6 months, otherwise he/she ceases to be a minister.

Oath

Before entering upon the office, the President administers the oath and secrecy of office to the minister. A minister swears in the same manner as that of the Prime Minister.

Tenure

Generally, the maximum term for which a ministry can remain in office is 5 years i.e. one full term of the Lok Sabha. However, the ministers shall hold the office during the pleasure of the President or as long as the Prime Minister does not resign.

The Prime Minister can, at any time demand a resignation from any minister and recommend to the President to do so. Thus, the tenure of the ministry or a minister is not fixed.

Salaries and Allowances

The salaries and allowances of ministers are determined by Parliament from time-to-time. The ministers get the salaries and allowances that are payable to a Member of Parliament. Additionally, the ministers get sumptuary allowance, free accommodation, travelling allowances, medical facilities, etc.

Powers and Functions

Administrative Powers

- **Policy Making** The Council of Ministers is mainly a policy formulating body. It formulates both external and domestic policies of the government on important matters such as defence, economic policy, security needs and important reforms, etc.
- **Implementation of Policies** When the policy decision on any subject is taken by the Cabinet, then, the Minister of State and the Deputy Minister of the concerned ministry **scrutinise**[7] the policies properly and forward it to the civil servants to implement the decision.
- **Co-ordinate the Activities of the Various Departments** The Cabinet has the power to co-ordinate the activities of various departments of the Central Government as these departments are involved in fulfilling the purposes of the government policies.
- **Appointments** All major appointments are made by the President with the advise of the Council of Ministers, such as appointment of Judges of Supreme Court and High Courts, Governor of States, Chief Election Commissioner and other dignitaries.

Legislative Powers

- **Power of Initiating Bills** Almost 95% of the bills in the legislature are initiated by the Cabinet. These are called **official bills**. These bills are given priority and preference over private bills. Important bills are introduced by the Cabinet, are regulated through the various stages of legislation and get passed by the Parliament with party support.
- **President's Address** The President addresses the Parliament after every general election and at the beginning of each session of the Parliament. But the President only reads out the address which is drafted by the Cabinet.

7 **Scrutinise** Examine or inspect closely and thoroughly.

- **Amendment to the Constitution** Without the approval of the Cabinet, the amendment to the Constitution is not possible.
- **Issuing of Ordinance** The Council of Ministers advises the President to issue an ordinance when the Parliament is not in session.
- **Summoning the Parliament** Generally, the President summons the Parliament, but it is initiated by the Ministry of Parliamentary Affairs.
- **Source of Information** The ministers alongwith the secretaries of the concerned departments answer the questions put to them by the members of the Lok Sabha and provide information to the public through their representatives.

Financial Powers

- **Budget** The Annual Budget is prepared at the instance of the Cabinet. The proposals for taxes and expenditures are made by the Cabinet. It is the duty of the Finance Minister to present the Budget in the Parliament and expected it to be passed.
- **Introduction of Money Bills** The money bills can only be introduced in the Lok Sabha and only by the ministers.
- **Taxes** The Finance Ministry proposes the imposition of taxes or suggest reduction or abolition of taxes.

Emergency Powers

The President can declare a proclamation of National Emergency under Article 352. However, after 44th Amendment Act, such proclamation can only be made after the written recommendation of the Council of Ministers.

Responsibility of the Members of the Cabinet

There are mainly two types of responsibilities of the members of the Cabinet. These are

(i) **Collective Responsibility** Article 75 of the Constitution clearly state that the Council of Ministers is collectively responsible to the Lok Sabha. This means that all the ministers are jointly responsible to the Lok Sabha for all their acts of omission and commission. The decisions taken in the Cabinet are equally applicable to all the ministers. They work as a team and swim and sink together.

When the Lok Sabha passes a no-confidence motion against the Council of Ministers, all the ministers have to resign including those ministers who are from the Rajya Sabha. The Council of Ministers can also advise the President to dissolve the Lok Sabha on the basis that the House does not represent the views of electorate faithfully and call for fresh elections.

(ii) **Individual Responsibility** Article 75 of the Constitution also contains the principle of individual responsibility. It states that the ministers holds the office during the pleasure of the President, which means that the President can remove a minister even at a time when the Council of Ministers enjoys the confidence of the Lok Sabha. However, the President removes a minister only on the advice of the Prime Minister.

Distinction Between the Council of Ministers and the Cabinet

Basis	Council of Ministers	Cabinet
Members	It includes three categories of ministers i.e. Cabinet Ministers, Ministers of State and Deputy Ministers.	It is a smaller body consisting of senior ministers who holds important portfolios such as Finance, Defence, etc.
Collective Function	It has no collective function, so that it does not meet as a body to transact government business.	It has collective function so that it meets as a body to transact government business.
Supremacy of the Cabinet	Its functions are determined by the Cabinet.	It directs the Council of Ministers by taking policy decisions which are binding on all the ministers.
Implementation	It implements the decisions taken by the Cabinet.	It supervises the implementation of its decisions by the Council of Ministers.
Responsibility	It is collectively responsible to the Lower House (Lok Sabha) of the Parliament.	It enforces the collective responsibility of the Council of Ministers to the Lok Sabha.

Check Your LEARNING...

1. How long can a minister stay in office?
2. How does the Council of Ministers control the financial stability?
3. What role does the Council of Ministers play with regard to emergency? State any one.
4. Under what circumstances does a minister own individual responsibility?

QUiCK Revision

- The Constitution of India facilitates that there shall be a Council of Ministers with the Prime Minister at the head, to aid and advise the President, who shall in the exercise of his/her functions, act in accordance with such advice. The Prime Minister shall be appointed by the President of India.
- The President has to appoint the leader of majority party in the Lok Sabha as the Prime Minister.
- When no party has a clear majority in the Lok Sabha, then the President may appoint the Prime Minister.
- The term of the Prime Minister is not fixed and he/she holds office as the pleasure of the President.
- The President appoints only those persons as ministers who are recommended by the Prime Minister.
- The Prime Minister can advise the President to dismiss a minister in case of difference of opinion.
- The Prime Minister brings about the collapse of the Council of Ministers by resigning from the office.
- The Prime Minister communicates to the President with respect to the administration of affairs of the Union and proposals for legislation.
- The Prime Minister can recommend dissolution of the Lok Sabha to the President at any time.
- Generally, the Members of Parliament are appointed as ministers. A person who is not a member of either Houses can be appointed as a Minister, but he/she must become a member within 6 months.
- The Council of Ministers consists of three categories of ministers namely; Cabinet Ministers, the Ministers of State and Deputy Ministers.
- The Cabinet Ministers head the important ministries of the government such as Home, Defence, Finance, External Affairs and so on.
- The Ministers of State may either be given independent charge of ministries or departments or may be attached to Cabinet Ministers.
- The Deputy Ministers are not the members of the Cabinet and do not attend Cabinet meetings.
- The Cabinet formulates the legislative programme for each sessions of the Parliament through its power of initiating bills.
- Article 75 of the Constitution clearly states that the Council of Ministers are collectively responsible to the Lok Sabha and individually responsible to the President.

Chapter Practice

Section-I

Multiple Choice Questions

1. The Prime Minister is appointed by
(a) President (b) the Vice-President
(c) the Council of Minister (d) majority party

Ans. (a) President

2. The .... is considered to be the leader of the Lok Sabha.
(a) President (b) Speaker
(c) Vice-President (d) Prime Minister

Ans. (d) Prime Minister

3. A person who is not a member of either House can also be appointed as a minister, but he must become the member of either Houses of Parliament within
(a) 6 months (b) 10 months
(c) 12 months (d) 15 months

Ans. (a) 6 months

4. Who advises the President with regard to appointment of CAG?
(a) Council of Ministers
(b) The Vice-President
(c) The Prime Minister
(d) Speaker of the Lok Sabha

Ans. (c) The Prime Minister

5. The .... is the ex-officio Chairman of the NITI Aayog.
(a) President (b) Governor
(c) Prime Minister (d) Council of Ministers

Ans. (c) Prime Minister

6. Only those persons appointed as Council of Ministers by the President who are recommended by ....
(a) the Vice-President (b) the Speaker
(c) the Prime Minister (d) None of these

Ans. (c) the Prime Minister

7. What is the maximum allowed size of the Council of Ministers?
(a) 15% of the strength of the Lok Sabha.
(b) 12% of the strength of the Lok Sabha.
(c) Cannot exceed 10% of the strength of the Lok Sabha.
(d) No such upper limit.

Ans. (a) 15% of the strength of the Lok Sabha.

8. A Council of Minister is removed by the
(a) President (b) Speaker
(c) Prime Minister (d) Vice-President

Ans. (a) President

9. The salaries and allowance of ministers are determined by
(a) the Prime Minister
(b) the President
(c) Parliament
(d) Council of Ministers

Ans. (c) Parliament

10. The junior category of ministers who assist senior ministers are **[2023]**
(a) Cabinet Ministers (b) Ministers of State
(c) Deputy Ministers (d) Council of Ministers

Ans. (c) Deputy Ministers

11. Almost .... per cent of the bills initiated in the legislature are done by the Cabinet.
(a) 80 (b) 90
(c) 95 (d) 100

Ans. (c)95

12. Which article state that the Council of Ministers is collectively responsible to the Lok Sabha ?
(a) Article 75 (b) Article-74
(c) Article 352 (d) Article-360

Ans. (a) Article 75

13. Complete the given analogy.
Vice-President : Chairman of Rajya Sabha : : ? : Leader of the House
(a) The Speaker
(b) The President
(c) The Prime Minister
(d) None of the above

Ans. (c) The Prime Minister

14. Replace the underlined word to correct the statement.
The Prime Minister can recommended dissolution of the Lok Sabha to <u>the Speaker</u> any time.
(a) the Council of Minister
(b) the President
(c) the Vice-President
(d) None of the above

Ans. (b) the President

15. Replace the underlined word to correct the statement.
The Speaker presided the meeting of Council of Ministers by resigning from the office.
(a) The President (b) The Prime Minister
(c) The Vice-President (d) None of these

Ans. (b) The Prime Minister

16. Which of the following is/are features of Cabinet Ministers?
(i) They hold important portfolios like-Home, Defence etc.
(ii) They attend all the Cabinet meeting.
(iii) They determine the policy and programmes

Codes
(a) Only (i) (b) Both (ii) and (iii)
(c) Both (i) and (ii) (d) All of these

Ans. (d) All of these

17. Match the following.

List - I	List-II
A. Cabinet Ministers	1. Head in the important ministeries
B. Ministers of States	2. Don't attend Cabinet meeting
C. Deputy Ministers	3. Independent charge

Codes

	A	B	C		A	B	C
(a)	1	2	3	(b)	3	2	1
(c)	1	3	2	(d)	2	1	3

Ans. (c)

Passage Based Question

19. Read the passage given below and answer the questions that follow.
The Union Council of Ministers exercises executive authority in the Republic of India. It consists of senior ministers, called Cabinet Ministers, Junior Ministers called Ministers of State and Deputy Ministers.
A smaller executive body, called the Union Cabinet is the supreme decision-making body in India. Only the Prime Minister and ministers of the rank of 'Cabinet Ministers' are members of Union Cabinet as per Article 352.
The Constitution originally does not specify the number of the Council of Ministers. However, the Constitution (91st Amendment Act, 2003) put a ceiling on the size of the Council of Ministers to 15% of the strength of the Lok Sabha or the State Legislatures. The Constitution does not classify the members of the Council of Ministers into different ranks. The Council of Ministers is also called the Cabinet.

(i) All the Union Ministers are appointed by
(a) President
(b) Speaker of Lok Sabha
(c) Vice President
(d) Prime Minister

Ans. (a) President

(ii) What is the maximum number of ministers allowed in smaller states?
(a) 12 (b) 11
(c) 13 (d) 10

Ans. (a) 12

(iii) Independent charges of ministries are provided to which category of ministers?
(a) Cabinet Ministers
(b) The Minister of State
(c) Deputy Minister
(d) All of the above

Ans. (b) The Minister of State

(iv) The Council of the Ministers doesn't include
(a) Minister of State (b) Deputy Minister
(c) Cabinet Secretary (d) All of these

Ans. (c) Cabinet Secretary

Section-II

Very Short Answer Questions

1. Which article of the Constitution facilitates that there shall be a Council of Ministers with the Prime Minister at the head?

Ans. Article 74 of the Constitution facilitates that there shall be a Council of Ministers with the Prime Minister at the head.

2. Who is the real executive of the government?

Ans. In the parliamentary system of the government, the President is the nominal executive and Prime Minister is the real executive of the government.

3. Does our Constitution contain any specific procedure for the appointment of the Prime Minister?

Ans. No, the Constitution does not contain any specific procedure for the selection and appointment of the Prime Minister. But Article 75 says that the Prime Minister shall be appointed by the President of India.

4. What is the term of the office of the Prime Minister? **[2006]**

Ans. The term of the office of a Prime Minister is 5 years. However, the President may dismiss him before, if the Prime Minister losses the majority support of the Lok Sabha.

5. Mention any one way by which the authority of the Prime Minister can be checked. **[2014]**

Ans. The authority of Prime Minister can be checked by the members of opposition party in the Parliament.

6. The Prime Minister is Chairman of which organisations?

Ans. The Prime Minister is the Chairman of NITI Aayog, National Development Council, National Integration Council, Inter-State Council and National Water Resources Council.

7. State any one administrative function of the Cabinet. **[2018]**

Ans. Cabinet takes decisions on important matters such as defence, finances, foreign affairs, etc. It also formulates and decides the domestic and international policies of the Government.

8. Mention the different categories of ministers in the Union Council of Ministers. **[2013]**

Ans. The different categories of ministers in the Union Council of Ministers are

- The Cabinet Ministers
- The Ministers of State
- The Deputy Ministers

9. State ant two legislative powers of the Cabinet. **[2023]**

Ans. The two legislative powers of the Cabinet are as follows

(i) All major policies, decisions or amendments are moved by the Cabinet in the Parliament. These legislative proposals are called official bills.

(ii) The ministers along with the secretaries of the concerned departments answer the questions of the members of the Parliament.

10. What do you mean by the Ministers of State?

Ans. The Ministers of State are those ministers who may either be given independent charge of ministries or departments or may be attached to the Cabinet Ministers.

11. Who are the Deputy Ministers?

Ans. The Deputy Ministers are those ministers who are not given independent charge of ministries/ departments. They are attached to the Cabinet or Ministers of State to assist them in their administrative, political and parliamentary duties.

12. How are the ministers appointed?

Or By whom and on whose advice are the Council of Ministers appointed? **[2016]**

Ans. The Council of Ministers are appointed by the President on the advice of the Prime Minister.

13. Under what condition can a non-Member of Parliament be made a minister? **[2017]**

Ans. If a person who is not a Member of Parliament appointed as a minister, he/she must become a member (either through election or nomination) of either House of Parliament, within 6 months, otherwise he/she ceases to be a Minister.

14. What is the oath of secrecy of a minister?

Ans. In the Minister's oath of secrecy, he/she swears that he/she will not directly or indirectly communicate or reveal to any person(s), any matter that is brought under his/her consideration or becomes known to him/her as a Union Minister.

15. Who administers the oath of office to the Council of Ministers? **[2018]**

Ans. The President of India administers the oath of office to the Council of Ministers.

16. Which body formulates the foreign policy of India? **[2012]**

Ans. The Cabinet formulates the foreign policy of India, but the Prime Minister plays an important role in shaping the foreign policy of the country.

17. When does the President address the Parliament?

Ans. The President addresses the Parliament when the session is going to start and also addresses the Parliament after every General Election.

18. Which article of the Constitution deals with the word Cabinet?

Ans. Article 352 of the Constitution deals with the word Cabinet. It was inserted by the 44th Constitutional Amendment Act, 1978.

19. Explain the term collective responsibility. **[2013]**

Or What is meant by 'collective responsibility' of the Cabinet? **[2017]**

Ans. The collective responsibility of the Cabinet means that all the ministers own collective responsibility to the Lok Sabha for all their acts of omission and commission. They work as a team and swim or sink together.

20. What happens if a vote of no-confidence is passed against a minister in the Lok Sabha? **[2015]**

Ans. When the Lok Sabha passes a no-confidence motion against the Council of Ministers, then all ministers have to resign including those ministers who are from the Rajya Sabha.

21. What is understood by the term 'individual responsibility' in a parliamentary democracy? **[2014]**

Ans. The term 'individual responsibility' implies that each Minister is responsible for personal lapses, breach of oath of Secrecy, departure from the official policy or for the failures of his department.

22. State one point of difference between the Cabinet and the Council of Ministers with reference to their responsibility to the government. **[2010]**

Ans. The Cabinet supervises the implementation of decisions by the Council of Ministers whereas the Council of Ministers implements the decisions taken by the Cabinet.

Structured Questions

1. In the parliamentary form of government, the President is the nominal executive head and Prime Minister is the real executive head. In respect to this, answer the following questions.

(i) What are the conventions regarding the appointment of the Prime Minister?

(ii) Mention any three swears of the oath to the office of the Prime Minister.

(iii) Discuss about the financial powers of Council of Ministers.

(iv) Discuss in brief about the term of the office of the Prime Minister.

Ans. (i) The conventions regarding the appointment of the Prime Minister are

- The President has to appoint a leader of the majority party in the Lok Sabha as the Prime Minister.
- When no political party has a clear majority in the Lok Sabha, then the President may exercise his/her personal discretion in the selection of the Prime Minister.

(ii) Before entering upon the office of the Prime Minister, the President administers the oath of the office and secrecy to the Prime Minister. The Prime Minister swears

(a) to bear true faith and allegiance to the Constitution of India.

(b) to uphold the sovereignty and integrity of India.

(c) to faithfully and honestly discharge the duties of his/her office.

(iii) The financial powers of Council of Ministers are

- **Budget** The Annual Budget is prepared at the instance of the Cabinet. The proposals for taxes and expenditures are made by the Cabinet. It is the duty of the Finance Minister to present the Budget in the Parliament and expected it to be passed.
- **Taxes** The Finance Ministry proposes the imposition of taxes or suggest reduction or abolition of taxes.

(iv) The full term of the Prime Minister is 5 years which correspond to the normal term of the Lok Sabha. However, the Prime Minister remain in powers as long as he enjoys the confidence of the Lok Sabha as fails to enjoy the majority support of the Lok Sabha. The Prime Minister may also resign by writing to the President. There are no term limits on the office of the Prime Minister.

2. The head of the Council of Ministers in the country is the Prime Minister, who is the real executive head of the government. In this context explain the following questions. **[2013]**

(i) The appointment of the Prime Minister.

(ii) His relationship with the Council of Ministers.

(iii) Explain Prime Minister's relations with the President.

Ans. (i) The Prime Minister is appointed by the President. According to the convention, the President invites the leader of the majority party or group in the Lok Sabha to form the Government. The members of the majority party elect their leader to be appointed as the Prime Minister.

(ii) The Prime Minister is related to the Council of Ministers in the following ways

- The Prime Minister is the head of the Cabinet. He/She recommend the persons to be appointed ministers, to the President.
- The Prime Minister allocates and reshuffles various portfolios among the ministers.
- The Prime Minister can advise the President to dismiss a minister in case of difference of opinion.
- The Prime Minister presided the meeting of Council of Ministers and influences its decisions.
- The Prime Minister brings about the end to the Council of Ministers by resigning from the office.
- The Prime Minister is the Chief Coordinator between various ministers on policy issues.

(iii) The Prime Minister is related to the President in the following ways

- The Prime Minister is the principal advisor to the President.
- The Prime Minister chooses the ministers and on his advice the President appoints them.
- The Prime Minister acts as a link between the President and the Council of Ministers as it communicates all the decisions of the Council of Ministers to the President on administration on of the Union.
- The Prime Minister furnishes all the administrative affairs of the union, when the President may call for.
- The Prime Minister advises the President with regard to the appointment of important officials, such as CAG, members of UPSC, ECs, etc.

3. The Union Executive which consists of the President, Prime Minister and the Council of Ministers is a powerful body in a Parliamentary democracy. In this context answer the following questions. **[2017]**

(i) State the position of the Prime Minister and state any two of his powers in relation to the President.

(ii) Mention the three categories of Ministers in order of their rank and status.

(iii) Mention any four legislative powers of the Cabinet.

Ans. (i) The Prime Minister with the backing of the majority party or groups in the Parliament is the real executive head of the nation.

The powers of the Prime Minister in relation to the President are

(a) The President summons and prorogues the Parliament on the advice of the Prime Minister.

(b) The President appoints the Council of Ministers on the advice of the Prime Minister.

(ii) The three categories of minister in order of their rank and status are

(a) **Cabinet Ministers** They are the senior ministers. They head the important ministers of the government such as Home, Defence, Railway and Finance, etc. They attend all the meetings and also play an important role in deciding the policies.

(b) **The Ministers of State** They are the junior ministers. They may either be given independent charge of ministries or departments or may be attached to the Cabinet Ministers. They do not participate in the cabinet meetings, but they are sometimes invited to the cabinet meetings to discuss matters related to their departments.

(c) **Deputy Ministers** They are responsible to assist the Cabinet Ministers and the Council of Ministers in performing their administrative, political and parliamentary duties. They are not the members of Cabinet and they never take part in Cabinet discussions.

(iii) The legislative powers of the Cabinet are

(a) **Power of Initiating Bills** Almost 95% of the bills initiated in the legislature are initiated by the Cabinet. These are called official bills. These bills are given priority and preference over private bills. Important bills are introduced by the Cabinet, are piloted through the various stages of legislation and get passed by the Parliament with party support.

(b) **President's Address** The President addresses the Parliament after every general election and at the beginning of each session of the Parliament. But the President only reads out the address which is drafted by the Cabinet.

(c) **Amendment to the Constitution** Without the approval of the Cabinet, the amendment to the Constitution is not possible.

(d) **Issuing of Ordinance** The Council of Ministers advises the President to issue an ordinance when the Parliament is not in session.

4. The makers of our Constitution adopted the Parliamentary and the Cabinet form of government. With reference to this, answer the following questions. **[2015]**

(i) (a) Who is the head of the Union Council of Ministers?

(b) What is meant by the collective and individual responsibility of the members of the Cabinet?

(ii) Explain briefly the position and powers of the Prime Minister in relation to the Cabinet.

(iii) Distinguish between the Cabinet and the Council of Ministers.

Ans. (i) (a) The Prime Minister is the head of the Union Council of Ministers.

(b) **Collective Responsibility** Article 75 of the Constitution clearly states that the Council of Ministers is collectively responsible to the Lok Sabha. This means that all the ministers own joint responsibility to the Lok Sabha for all their acts of omission and commision. They work as a team and swim or sink together.

Individual Responsibility Article 75 of the Constitution also contains the principle of individual responsibility. It states that the Ministers hold office during the pleasure of the President, which means, the President can remove a Minister even at a time when the Council of Ministers enjoys the confidence of the Lok Sabha.

(ii) Refer to chapter theory on page no. 38.

(iii) The differences between the Council of Ministers and Cabinet are

Basis	Council of Ministers	Cabinet
Members	It includes three categories of ministers i.e. Cabinet Ministers, Ministers of State and Deputy Ministers.	It is a smaller body consisting of senior ministers who holds important part folios such as Finance, Defence, etc.
Collective Function	It has no collective function, so that it does not meet as a body to transact government business.	It has collective function so that it meets as a body to transact government business.
Implementation	It implements the decisions taken by the Cabinet.	It supervises the implementation of its decisions by the Council of Ministers.
Responsibility	It is collectively responsible to the Lower House (Lok Sabha) of the Parliament.	It enforces the collective responsibility of the Council of Ministers to the Lok Sabha.

5. The Council of Ministers headed by the Prime Minister, is the most powerful institution in the Indian Polity. In this context, answer the following. **[2019]**

(i) State briefly the position of the Prime Minister in the Parliamentary system of Government. State any two powers of the Prime Minister as a leader of the nation.

(ii) Distinguish between the Council of Ministers and the Cabinet.

(iii) Write any four functions of the Cabinet.

Ans. (i) The Prime Minister, with the backing of the majority party or groups in the Parliament, is the real executive head of the nation (i.e. *de-facto* head).

The powers of the Prime Minister as a leader of the nation are

(a) The Prime Minister decides the kind of relation India would have with other countries.

(b) He/She tries to protect the interest of the country in international forums.

(ii) Refer to chapter theory page no. 40.

(iii) The functions of the Cabinet are

(a) All major appointments to various key posts which are made by the President are advised by the Cabinet.

(b) The Cabinet being the senior leaders' /ministers' group co-ordinates the functioning of various ministries for smooth implementation of government policies.

(c) All major policies, decisions or amendments are moved by the Cabinet in the Parliament. These legislative proposals are called official bills.

(d) The ministers along with the secretaries of the concerned departments answer the questions of the Members of the Parliament.

6. The Cabinet holds a pivotal position in the working of the Indian Parliamentary Government. In this context, discuss the following questions.

(i) The formation of the Cabinet.

(ii) Emergency power of the Cabinet.

(iii) Any three administrative powers of the Cabinet.

(iv) Discuss any two legislative powers of the Cabinet.

Ans. (i) The formation of the Cabinet include

- It consists of 15 to 20 ministers, hence it is a smaller body.
- It has collective functions so that it meets as a body to transact the government business.
- The Cabinet consists of the most experienced and senior leaders of the ruling party.

(ii) The Emergency power of the Cabinet is that according to 44th Amendment Act, the procalamation of Emergency can only be made by the President after the written recommendation of the Council of Ministers.

(iii) The administrative powers of the Cabinet are

(a) **Policy Making** The Council of Ministers is mainly a policy formulating body. It formulates both external and domestic policies of the government on important matters such as defence, economic policy, security needs and important reforms, etc.

(b) **Implementation of Policies** When the policy decision on any subject is taken by the Cabinet, then, the Minister of State and the Deputy Minister of the concerned ministry **scrutinise** the policies properly and forward it to the civil servants to implement the decision.

(c) **Co-ordinate the Activities of the Various Departments** The Cabinet has the power to co-ordinate the activities of various departments of the Central Government as these departments are involved in fulfilling the purposes of the government policies.

(iv) The legislative powers of the Cabinet are

(a) **Amendment to the Constitution** Without the approval of the Cabinet, the amendment to the Constitution is not possible.

(b) **Issuing of Ordinance** The Council of Ministers advises the President to issue an ordinance when the Parliament is not in the session.

Chapter Assessment

Section-I

Multiple Choice Questions

1. Who administers the oath to the Prime Minister?
   (a) The CJI (b) The President
   (c) The Speaker (d) The Vice-President
2. The ...... is Chairman of Atomic Energy Commission.
   (a) Prime Minister (b) President
   (c) CDS (d) Vice-President
3. Which Act provide Central Council of Ministers not to exceed 15% of the total strength?
   (a) 90th Constitutional Amendment Act, 2003
   (b) 91st Constitutional Amendment Act, 2003
   (c) 92nd Constitutional Amendment Act, 2003
   (d) 93rd Constitutional Amendment Act, 2003
4. Which of the following is/are true about Council of Ministers?
   (i) They shall hold the office during the pleasure of the President.
   (ii) They are collectively responsible to Rajya Sabha.
   (iii) Their salaries are determined by the Parliament.
   Codes
   (a) Only (i) (b) Only (ii)
   (c) Both (ii) and (iii) (d) All of these
5. Replace the underlined word to correct the statement.
   The President enforces the collective responsibility of the Council of Ministers of the Lok Sabha.
   (a) The Cabinet (b) The Prime Minister
   (c) The Vice-President (d) The Speaker

Section-II

Very Short Questions

1. Who is the chief spokesperson of the Union Government?
2. What is the term of the office of the Council of Ministers?
3. Who administers the oath to the Prime Minister? Mention any one of his swear.
4. Who appoints the Council of Ministers?
5. Under what circumstances, can the President use his discretionary power in appointing Prime Minister?
6. Whom does the President call upon to form the government after the election of the Lok Sabha?
7. What happens if the Prime Minister losses the confidence of the Parliament?
8. By whom and on whose advice is the Union Council of Ministers appointed?
9. What is the principle of collective responsibility?
10. Mention any two ways in which the Constitution ensures the pre-eminent position of the Prime Minister in relationship to the Council of Ministers.

Structured Questions

1. The Prime Minister is the head of the government and also the head of the Council of Ministers.
   In relation to this, answer the following questions.
   (i) What are the powers and functions of the Prime Minister in relation to the Parliament?
   (ii) What are the financial and emergency powers of the Council of Ministers?
   (iii) What are the other powers of the Prime Minister, except in relation to the President, Council of Ministers and the Parliament?
   (iv) The 'Council of Ministers are collectively responsible to the Lower House of the Parliament' how?
2. In relation to the powers and functions of the Council of Ministers, answer the following questions in terms of
   (i) Power of initiating bills
   (ii) Appointments
   (iii) Budget and introduction of Money Bills

CHAPTER

04

The Supreme Court

SYLLABUS

The Supreme Court • Composition, qualifications of judges, appointment, independence of judiciary from the control of executive and legislature. • Jurisdictions and functions : Original, Appellate, Advisory, Revisory, Judicial Review and Court of Record. • Enforcement of Fundamental Rights and Writs

The Judiciary

It is the system of courts that interprets and applies the law in the name of the state. It also provides a mechanism for the resolution of disputes. It plays a crucial role in the functioning of India's democracy. The Indian Constitution provides a **Single Integrated Judicial System**[1] of courts for the Union and the States. The single integrated system means that

- At the head of the entire judicial system is the Supreme Court which not only supervises, but also exercises control over the functioning of other courts.
- There is no distinct set of laws and a single civil and criminal judicial system operates throughout the country.
- All the cases from the subordinate courts come to the High Courts first and then finally to the Supreme Court.

Need for a Single Independent Judiciary

India has opted for single integrated judicial system which is independent of the remaining two organs of the government i.e. of the Executive and Legislature.

The need for an independent judiciary is

- In a representative democracy, administration of justice assumes special significance in view of rights of people. Thus, the independence of judiciary is essential to protect any violation of the rights of people.
- In a federal set-up, there is a Constitutional division of powers between the Executive, Legislature and Judiciary. Thus, an independent and impartial judiciary is essential for a federal governance.
- It is an essential for ensuring human rights and protecting democracy.

The Supreme Court

The Supreme Court of India is the Supreme Judicial body of India and the highest court of the Republic of India under the Constitution. It was **inaugurated**[2] on 28th January, 1950 and succeeded the Federal Court of India which was established under the Government of India Act, 1935. The seat of Supreme Court is in Delhi.

1 **Single Integrated Judicial System** It means Supreme Court is the apex court. Below it, there are High Courts in each state and below High Courts are Sub-ordinate District Courts.

2 **Inaugurated** An inauguration is a formal ceremony to mark the beginning of a major public leader's team of office.

Composition

The Supreme Court consists of 34 Judges in which there is 1 Chief Justice and 33 other Judges. Originally the strength was fixed to 8 (1 Chief Justice and 7 other Judges). The strength of the Supreme Court to 33 Judges, excluding the Chief Justice was increased by the Supreme Court (Number of Judges) Amendment Act, 2019.

Qualifications of Judges

A person to be appointed as a Judge of the Supreme Court should

- be a citizen of India.
- have been the Judge of a High Court or of two or more such courts in succession for at least five years.
- have been an advocate of a High Court or of two or more such courts in succession for at least ten years.
- be a distinguished jurist in the opinion of the President.

Appointment of Judges

The President of India appoints the Judges of the Supreme Court through the following procedure

- When the President appoints the Chief Justice, he/she may consult with Judges of the Supreme Court and the High Court.
- When the President appoints other Judges of the Supreme Court, he/she consults with the Chief Justice of India. Usually, the seniormost Judge of the Supreme Court is appointed as the Chief Justice of India.

Appointment of Acting Chief Justice

The President can appoint a Judge of the Supreme Court (Article 126) as an acting Chief Justice of India when

- the office of Chief Justice is vacant.
- the Chief Justice is temporarily absent.
- the Chief Justice is unable to perform the duties of his/her office.

Appointment of Ad hoc Judges

Under Article 127, when there is a lack of Quorum of the permanent Judges to hold or continue any session of the Supreme Court, the Chief Justice can appoint a Judge of High Court as an Ad hoc Judge of the Supreme Court for a temporary period. It can be done after consultation with the Chief Justice of High Court concerned and with the consent of the President. The Judge so appointed should be qualified for appointment as the Judge of the Supreme Court.

Term of Office

The Constitution of India has not provided the fixed term for the Judge of the Supreme Court. However, it has made the following provisions in this respect

- He/She holds office until the age of 65 years.
- He/She can resign from his/her office by writing to the President.
- He/She can be removed from the office by the President on the recommendation of the Parliament.

Impeachment of a Judge

The Judge of the Supreme Court can be removed only on the grounds of proved misbehaviour and incapacity [Article 124(4)]. A Judge may be removed from his office in the following manner which is commonly known as impeachment.

- A motion of the removal is addressed to the President which is signed by atleast 100 members of the Lok Sabha or 50 members of the Rajya Sabha and then it is delivered to the Speaker or the Chairman.
- The motion is to be investigated by a committee of three Judges i.e. two Judges of the Supreme Court and a distinguished jurist.
- If the committee finds the Judge guilty of misbehaviour or that he suffers incapacity, the motion along with the report of the committee is taken up for consideration in the House where the motion is pending.
- If the motion is passed in each House by majority of the total membership of that House and by a majority of not less than two-thirds of the House present and voting, the motion is presented to the President.
- The Judge will be removed after the President gives his order of removal on the said address.

In 1993, Justice V Rama Swami became the first Judge of the Supreme Court against whom an impeachment motion was passed.

Independence of Judiciary from the Control of Executive and Legislature

The Constitution of India has made some provisions to safeguard and ensure the independence of judiciary from the control of Executive and Legislature. These provisions are

- **Appointment of Judges** The Judges of the Supreme Court are appointed by the President after consulting the other judges of the Supreme Court and the High Court. Thus, it reduces the interference of Executive and political considerations.

- **Security of Tenure** The Judges of the Supreme Court are removed by the President only in the manner and on the grounds mentioned in the Constitution.
- **Salaries and Emoluments** The salaries and other emoluments of the Judges cannot be changed to their disadvantage during their term of office, except in case of Financial Emergency. The salaries, allowances and pensions of the Judges are charged on the Consolidated Fund of India. Thus, they are non-votable by the Parliament.
- **Conduct of Judges** The Constitution of India provides that the conduct of the Judges of the Supreme Court is not subject to discussion in the Parliament or in the State Legislature.
- **Ban on Practice after Retirement** After retirement, a Judge of the Supreme Court shall not plead or act in any court or before any authority within the territory of India.
- **Power to Punish for its Contempt** The Supreme Court can punish for the contempt (disrespect) of court, if a person/authority makes an attempt to lower its authority and dignity.
- **Freedom to Recruit its Staff** The Chief Justice of India can recruit officers and servants of the Supreme Court without any interference from the Executive.
- **Freedom to Announce Decisions and Decrees** The Judges have complete freedom to announce their decisions and discuss in the court chambers.
- **Full Control over its Procedure of Work** The Supreme Court is free to decide its own procedure of work. The Constitution declares Delhi as the seat of the Supreme Court. But, it also authorised the Chief Justice of India to appoint other place or places as seat of the Supreme Court.

Check Your LEARNING...

1. What system of courts is provided by the Indian Constitution?
2. Name the highest court of India.
3. In which year did the federal court of India establish?
4. Who was the first Judge of Supreme Court against whom an impeachment motion was passed?

Jurisdictions and Functions of the Supreme Court

Original Jurisdiction

It means the power to hear and determine a dispute in the first instance. It happens in those cases, which cannot be transferred in any court other than the Supreme Court.

These cases include

Centre-State or Inter-State Disputes The Supreme Court has original jurisdiction over the case of a dispute between

- the Union Government and one or more states
- two or more states
- the Union and State Governments on one side and one or more states on the other side

- **Transfer of Cases** The Supreme Court has the power under original jurisdiction to transfer the cases to itself from a lower court, if the cases involve questions of law or Constitutional validity of the union laws.
- **Protection of Fundamental Rights** The Supreme Court has the jurisdiction in the cases that involve violation of the Fundamental Rights of individuals. For the enforcement of these rights, the Supreme Court can issue several writs.

Interpretation of the Constitution

- The Supreme Court has original jurisdiction in all the cases in which interpretation of the Constitution is required. The cases which involve questions of law or are of great importance can be transferred by the Supreme Court from one or more High Courts to itself.

Appellate Jurisdiction

The appellate jurisdiction of the Supreme Court extends to constitutional, civil and criminal cases. Any matter that involves important points of law and needs interpretation of the Constitution can be brought to the Supreme Court. The cases related to appellate jurisdiction that can be appealed in the Supreme Court are

- **Constitutional Cases** In constitutional cases, an appeal can be made to the Supreme Court against the judgement of the High Court, if the High Court certifies that the case involves an important question of law and requires the interpretation of the Constitution. On the basis of the certificate, the party in the case can appeal to the Supreme Court on the ground that the question has been wrongly decided.
- **Civil Cases** In these cases, an appeal can be made to the Supreme Court against the judgement of High Court, if the High Court certifies
  - that the case involves an important question of law of general importance.
  - that the question needs to be decided by the Supreme Court.
  - However, if the High Court refuses to give a certificate, the Supreme Court can grant special leave to appeal in suitable cases.

- **Criminal Cases** In these cases, an appeal can be made to the Supreme Court, if the High Court
  - has reversed an order of **acquittal**[3] and sentenced the accused to death.
  - has taken any case from any subordinate court and convicted the accused person and sentenced him/her to death.
  - certifies that the case involves an important question of law and interpretation of the Constitution.

Appeal by Special Leave Under Article 136, The Supreme Court is authorised to grant special leave to appeal against any judgement of any court or tribunal in the country (except military tribunal and court martial). This provision contains the four aspects as under

(i) It is a discretionary power and hence, cannot be claimed as a matter of right.
(ii) It can be granted in any judgement whether final or **interlocutory**[4] meeting.
(iii) It may be related to any matter i.e. constitutional, civil, criminal, income tax, labour, revenue advocates, etc.
(iv) It can be granted against the judgement of any court or tribunal and not necessarily against a High Court (except a Military Court).

Advisory Jurisdiction

Under Article 143, the Constitution of India authorises the President to seek the opinion of the Supreme Court on two categories of matters. These are

(i) On any question of law or fact of public importance which has arisen or which is likely to arise. The advice in this case is not binding on the President who may or may not accept it.
(ii) On any dispute arising out of any pre-Constitution treaty, agreement, engagement, sanad (Indian Government Charter, Warrant or diploma) or other similar instruments.

Revisory Jurisdiction

The Supreme Court has power to review its own judgement or order with a view to remove any mistake or error that might have occur in the judgement or orders under Article 137.

Writ Jurisdiction/Enforcement of Fundamental Rights

The Constitution has constituted the Supreme Court as the guarantor and defender of the Fundamental Rights of the citizens.

The Supreme Court is empowered to issue writs for the enforcement of the Fundamental Rights of an aggrieved citizen.

Writs are a written order from the Supreme Court or High Court that commands constitutional remedies for Indian citizens against the violation of their Fundamental Rights. Article 32 of the Indian Constitution deals with the constitutional remedies. There are five types of writs

(i) ***Habeas Corpus*** It literally means *you shall have the body*. It is a court order to a person or agency holding someone in custody (such as a warden) to deliver the imprisoned individual to the court and to show a valid reason for that person's detention.
(ii) ***Mandamus*** It means we *command*. It is a command issued by the court to a public official asking any public body, an inferior court, a tribunal, etc to perform its official duties.
(iii) ***Prohibition*** It means to *forbid*. It is issued by the higher court to a lower court or tribunal to prevent the later from exceeding its jurisdiction.
(iv) ***Certiorari*** It means to be *certified* or to be *informed*. It is issued by a higher court to a lower court or tribunal, to transfer a case to itself or to terminate the order.
(v) ***Quo-Warranto*** It means *by what authority* or *warrant*. It is issued by the court to enquire into legality of claim of a person to a public office.

Function of Judicial Review

The Supreme Court is the sole interpreter of the Constitution. It has the power to review any laws passed by the Union or State Legislature. If any law passed by the legislature is against the spirit of the Constitution or contravenes any provision of the Constitution, the Supreme Court can declare such law as null and void.

A legislative enactment or an executive order can be challenged in the Supreme Court on the following three grounds

(i) If it **infringes**[5] the Fundamental Rights.
(ii) If it is outside the competent authority which has framed it.
(iii) If it is against the constitutional provisions.

3 **Acquittal** The judgement of a court that a person charged with a crime is not guilty.
4 **Interlocutory** A decree or judgement given provisionally during the course of a legal action.
5 **Infringe** Actively break the terms of a law, agreement, etc.

If some legislative enactments and executive orders are found to be violative of the Constitution, then these can be declared as illegal, unconstitutional and invalid (null and void) by the Supreme Court.

Judicial review is necessary for the following reasons

- The Constitution is a written Constitution. So, whenever the question of interpretation arises, the Supreme Court helps to sort it out.
- To uphold the principle of supremacy of the Constitution.
- To maintain federal **equilibrium** between the Centre and the State.
- To protect the Fundamental Rights of citizens.
- The legislature may not possess the wisdom experience and impartiality, which are needed to explain meaning of the law. This function can be best performed by the Supreme Court.

Functions as a Court of Record

- The judgements, proceedings and acts of the Supreme Court are recorded for perpetual memory and testimony. These records cannot be questioned when produced before any court. The judgements are in nature of precedents i.e. the High Courts and other courts are bound to give a similar decision in a similar case.
- The Supreme Court has power to punish for the **contempt**[6] of court, either with simple imprisonment for a term of 6 months or fine upto ₹ 2000 or with both.

Administrative and Supervisory Functions

- The Supreme Court makes rules regarding the conduct of advocates and other persons appearing before it.
- The Chief Justice of India appoints officers and staff of the Supreme Court.
- The recommendation of the Chief Justice of India to transfer Judges of the High Courts are binding on the government, if it was made after consulting at least 4 seniormost Judges of the Supreme Court.

Check Your LEARNING...

1. What is the meaning of mandamus?
2. Who is considered as a sole interpreter of the Constitution?
3. Who appoints officers and staff of the Supreme Court?
4. What is judicial review?

QUiCK Revision

- The Indian Constitution has provided for a single integrated system of courts for the Union and the State.
- The Supreme Court is placed at the apex of the entire judicial system in India that was inaugurated on 28th January, 1950.
- The Supreme Court consists of 34 Judges including 1 is Chief Justice and 33 other Judges.
- The President of India appoints the Judges of the Supreme Court and the Chief Justice of India with the consultation of the Cabinet.
- The President can also appoint a Judge of the Supreme Court as an acting Chief Justice of India.
- When there is a lack of quorum of the permanent Judge to hold or continue any session of the Supreme Court, the Chief Justice of India can appoint a Judge of a High Court as an Ad hoc Judge of the Supreme Court.
- The Constitution of India has not provided for the fix term of the Judge.
- The Judges of the Supreme Court can be removed from the office by an order of the President.
- The salaries, allowances and pensions of the Judges of the Supreme Court are charged on the Consolidated Fund of India.
- After retirement, a Judge of the Supreme Court shall not plead or act in any court or before any authority within the territory of India.
- The Parliament has no authority to curtail the jurisdiction and powers of the Supreme Court.
- Under its original jurisdiction, the Supreme Court decides the disputes between the Centre and the States.
- The Supreme Court acts as the guarantor and defender of the Fundamental Rights of the citizens through its power to issue writs. These writs are Habeas Corpus, Mandamus, Certiorari, Prohibition and Quo-warranto.
- The Supreme Court enjoys the appellate jurisdiction in matter of constitutional, civil, criminal and appeal by special leave.
- The Constitution of India authorises the President to seek the opinion of the Supreme Court.
- The Supreme Court has power to punish for contempt of court.
- Judicial review power of the Supreme Court is to examine the constitutionality of legislative enactments and executive orders of both the Centre and the States.
- If the legislative enactments and executive orders of both the Centre and the State Governments are found to be violative of the Constitution, then these can be declare as null and void by the Supreme Court.
- The judgements, proceedings and acts of the Supreme Court are ordered for perpetual memory and testimony.
- The Chief Justice of India appoints officers and staff of the Supreme Court.

6 **Contempt** An act of deliberate, disoberate, disobedience, or disregard for the laws, regulation or decorum of a public authority, such as a court or legislative body.

Chapter Practice

Section-I

Multiple Choice Questions

1. Which of the following is the highest judicial authority in India whose decisions are binding on all Courts?
(a) Supreme Court (b) Parliament
(c) Law Minister (d) Lok Sabha

Ans. (a) Supreme Court

2. The Supreme Court of India first inaugurated in
(a) 1947 (b) 1949 (c) 1950 (d) 1954

Ans. (c) 1950

3. The Supreme Court consists of how many Judges?
(a) 30 (b) 31 (c) 34 (d) 36

Ans. (c) 34

4. Originally the strength of the Judges of the Supreme Court was fixed to
(a) 6 (b) 8 (c) 10 (d) 12

Ans. (b) 8

5. When the Supreme Court reviews any judgement made by it to remove an error, it falls under .... jurisdiction. **[2023]**
(a) Advisory (b) Revisory
(c) Original (d) Appellate

Ans. (b) Revisory

6. Who is appointed as the Chief Justice of India?
(a) The President appoints the Chief Justice of India on his sole discretion.
(b) The seniormost Judge of the Supreme Court is appointed as the Chief Justice of India.
(c) The panel of Judges of Supreme Court elect a Chief Justice of India from amongst themselves.
(d) The Chief Justice of India is elected by the voting of Lok Sabha members.

Ans. (b) The seniormost Judge of the Supreme Court is appointed as the Chief Justice of India.

7. Which among the following is not a criteria for being eligible to be a Judge of the Supreme Court?
(a) Judge of one High Court or more (continuously), for at least five years.
(b) An advocate of Supreme Court for at least ten years.
(c) A distinguished jurist in the opinion of the President.
(d) Above 40 years of age.

Ans. (d) Above 40 years of age.

8. The Judges of the Supreme Court holds office until the age of
(a) 60 years (b) 62 years (c) 65 years (d) 70 years

Ans. (c) 65 years

9. Which statement is not correct regarding the tenure of Judges of the Supreme Court?
(a) A Judge of the Supreme Court can remain in office till the age of 65 years.
(b) Judge of the Supreme Court gives his resignation letter to the Chief Justice.
(c) On the recommendation of Parliament, he can be removed by the President.
(d) A Supreme Court Judge can be removed only in the condition of misconduct.

Ans. (b) Judge of the Supreme Court gives his resignation letter to the Chief Justice.

10. Who was the first justice of the Supreme Court against whom an impeachment motion was passed?
(a) V Rama Swami (b) Soumitra Sen
(c) Indira Banerjee (d) S Abdul Nazeer

Ans. (a) V Rama Swami

11. Which article give the power to High Court to issues orders, directions and writs?
(a) 226 (b) 32 (c) 126 (d) 124

Ans. (a) 226

12. Which of the following is directly related to the appellate jurisdiction of the Supreme Court of India?
(a) Adjudication of disputes between states.
(b) Appeals made in civil, criminal and constitutional cases.
(c) Appeals made in constitutional cases.
(d) Adjudication of disputes between the Union and the States.

Ans. (b) Appeals made in civil, criminal and constitutional cases.

13. Judicial review in India is based on
(a) convention (b) rule of Law
(c) due process of Law
(d) procedure established by Law

Ans. (d) procedure established by Law

14. Complete the given analogy.
Mandamus : we command : : Prohibition : ?
(a) forbid (b) to be certified
(c) warrant (d) shall have the body

Ans. (a) Forbid

15. Replace the underlined word to correct the statement.
A Judge of the Supreme Court can be removed from his office by an order of the <u>Prime Minister</u>.
(a) Speaker (b) President
(c) Vice-President (d) All of these

Ans. (b) President

16. Complete the following table.

Article - 126	Acting Chief Justice
Article - 124 (4)	?

(a) Qualification of Judges
(b) Ad hoc Judges
(c) Impeachment of Judge
(d) Term of the office of Judge

Ans. (c) Impeachment of Judge

17. Which is true about the qualification of the Judge?

(i) He/She should be citizen of India.
(ii) He/She should have been the Judge of a High Court.
(iii) He/She should be a distinguished jurist in the opinion of the President.

Codes

(a) Only (i) (b) Only (ii)
(c) Both (ii) and (iii) (d) All of these

Ans. (d) All of these

18. When the acting Chief Justice is appointed?

(i) The office of the Chief Justice is vacant.
(ii) The Chief Justice is temporarily absent.
(iii) The Chief Justice is unable to perform the duties of his/her office.

Codes

(a) Only (i) (b) Only (ii)
(c) Both (i) and (iii) (d) All of these

Ans. (d) All of these

19. Match the following.

List-I (Writ)	**List-II** (Literal Meaning)
A. Habeas corpus	1. We command
B. Mandamus	2. To be certified
C. Prohibitions	3. You shall have the body
D Certiorari	4. To forbid

Codes

	A	B	C	D		A	B	C	D
(a)	1	2	3	4	(b)	4	3	2	1
(c)	3	1	4	2	(d)	2	4	1	3

Ans. (c)

Passage Based Questions

20. Read the passage given and answer the questions that follow.

The Constitution has not fixed the tenure of a Judge of the Supreme Court. He holds office until he attains the age of 65 years. Any question regarding his age is to be determined by such authority and in such manner as provided by Parliament. He can resign his office by writing to the President. He can be removed from his office by the President on the recommendation of the Parliament.

(i) Which constitutional post of the Republic of India is being addressed in the official resignation of the justice of a Supreme Court?

(a) President (b) Vice-President
(c) Chief Justice (d) None of these

Ans. (a) President

(ii) Who is authorised by the Constitution to decide the matter related to maximum age of retirement of Judges of Supreme Court?

(a) Rajya Sabha (b) Parliament
(c) Council of Ministers (d) Vice-President

Ans. (b) Parliament

(iii) President can be removed from his office on

(a) recommendation of the President.
(b) recommendation of Council of Ministers.
(c) recommendation of the Judges of the Supreme Court.
(d) None of the above

Ans. (d) None of the above

(iv) The President can declare a Judge an exclusive Chief Justice of the Supreme Court of India when

(a) post of Chief Justice is vacant.
(b) Chief Justice is unable to discharge his duties.
(c) Chief Justice is absent.
(d) All of the above

Ans. (d) All of the above

21. Read the passage given and answer the questions that follow.

A Judge of the Supreme Cout can be removed from his office by an order of the President. The President can issue the removal order only after an address by Parliament has been presented to him in the same session for such removal.

The address must be supported by a special majority of each House of Parliament (i.e. a majority of the total membership of that House and a majority of not less than two-thirds of the members of that House present and voting).

The grounds of removal are proved misbehaviour or incapacity. The Judges Enquiry Act (1968) regulates the procedure relating to the removal of a Judge of the Supreme Court by the process of impeachment. No Judge of the Supreme Court has been impeached so far. Impeachment motions of Justice V Rama Swami (1991-1993) and the Justice Dipak Misra (2017-18) were defeated in the Parliament.

(i) A Judge of the Supreme Court may resign from his office by writing to

(a) the President (b) the Prime Minister
(c) the Law Minister (d) the Attorney General

Ans. (a) the President

(ii) Which Article is associated with the impeachment of the Judge of the Supreme Court?

(a) 124 (b) 124(4)
(c) 126 (d) 127

Ans. (b) 124(4)

(iii) A motion addressed to the President signed by at least 100 members of the Lok Sabha or .... members of the Rajya Sabha.
(a) 40 (b) 50 (c) 60 (d) 70

Ans. (b) 50

(iv) In which of the following cases, an appeal can be made to the Supreme Court against the judgement of High Court?
(a) Criminal cases (b) Civil cases
(c) Constitutional cases (d) All of these

Ans. (d) All of these

Picture Based Question

22. Look at the picture given below and answer the questions that follow

(i) Identify the judicial body from the given options
(a) Supreme Court of India (b) District Court
(c) High Court (d) Lok Adalat

Ans.(a) Supreme Court of India

(ii) What is the necessity of this judicial body in a federal state like India?
(a) To interpret the Constitution
(b) To protect the Fundamental Rights
(c) For ensuring human rights and protecting democracy
(d) All of the above

Ans.(d) All of the above

(iii) Who determines the strength of this judicial body?
(a) Rajya Sabha (b) Parliament
(c) President (d) None of the above

Ans.(b) Parliament

(iv) Which of the following is/are the essential qualifications for the Judge of this judicial body?
(a) An advocate of a High Court or of two or more such courts for at least ten years.
(b) He/She should have completed 35 years of age.
(c) He/She should be a citizen of India.
(d) Both (a) and (c)

Ans. (d) Both (a) and (c)

Section-II

Very Short Questions

1. What is meant by a single integrated judicial system, as provided in the Indian Constitution? **[2014]**

Ans. A single integrated judicial system means the Supreme Court is the apex court and entire judicial system is below it.

2. Which body is the head of the entire court system in India?

Ans. The head of the entire court system in India is the Supreme Court and it not only supervises, but also exercises control over the functioning of other courts.

3. By which act the Supreme Court was set-up?

Ans. The Government of India Act, 1935 facilitated the succession of the Federal Court as the Supreme Court of India.

4. When does an Ad hoc Judge get appointed?

Ans. When there is a lack of quorum of the permanent Judges to hold or continue any session of the Supreme Court, an Ad hoc Judge is appointed.

5. What is the tenure of a judge of the Supreme Court? **[2012]**

Ans. The Constitution of India has not provided for a fix term of the Judges of the Supreme Court. However, they hold the office until the age of 65 years.

6. When can the President issue the removal order of the Judges of the Supreme Court?

Ans. The President can issue the removal order only after an address by the Parliament has been presented to him/her in the same session.

7. Mention any two ways in which the Constitution ensures the independence of the Judiciary from the Executive. **[2023]**

Ans. The independence of the Judiciary is ensured through the following
(i) The salaries and other emoluments of the Judges cannot be changed to their disadvantage during their term of office, except in case of financial emergency.
(ii) The Judges have complete freedom to announce their decisions and discuss in the court chambers.

8. Who has power to punish for the contempt of Supreme Court?

Ans. The Supreme Court has the power to punish any person for its contempt. Thus, its actions and decisions cannot be criticised and opposed by anybody.

9. Who can increase the number of Judges of the Supreme Court? **[2011]**

Ans. The Parliament can increase the number of Judges of the Supreme Court.

10. Under what circumstances can the salaries and allowances of the Judges of the Supreme Court be reduced? **[2008]**

Ans. Under the Financial Emergency, the salaries and allowances of the Judges of the Supreme Court can be reduced.

11. Which body has the final authority to interpret the Constitution of India? [2006]

Ans. The Supreme Court has the final authority to interpret the Constitution of India.

12. Mention any one matter which is outside the original jurisdiction of the Supreme Court.

Ans. One matter which does not extend to the original jurisdiction is the dispute arising out of a treaty or agreement which is in operation.

13. Which body is the guarantor and defender of the Fundamental Rights of the citizens?

Ans. The Supreme Court acts as the guarantor and defender of the Fundamental Rights of the citizens.

14. Name the courts that are empowered to issue writs for the enforcement of Fundamental Rights. [2013]

Ans. The Supreme Court and the High Courts are empowered to issue writs for the enforcement of the Fundamental Rights.

15. Which jurisdiction is enforced, when the Fundamental Rights of the citizens are infringed?

Ans. Writ jurisdiction is enforced when the Fundamental Rights of a citizen are infringed.

16. Why is the Supreme Court said to be the guardian of the Constitution? [2010]

Ans. The Supreme Court is said to be the guardian of the Constitution because if any Fundamental Right of any citizen is violated, then he/she can seek the protection of the Supreme Court.

17. If the President of India considers that a question of law may be referred to the Supreme Court, under which jurisdiction will the Supreme Court express its opinion on the matter? [2007]

Ans. If the President of India considers that a question of law may be referred to the Supreme Court, it will come under the advisory jurisdiction and under it, the Supreme Court expreses its opinion on the matter.

18. What is meant by the term judicial review? [2010]

Ans. Judicial review means the Supreme Court examine the constitutionality of legislative enactments and executive orders of both the Central and the State government.

19. Name any two writs issued by the Supreme Court. [2018]

Ans. Two writs issued by the Supreme Court are Certiorari and Quo-warranto.

20. Who has the power to enlarge the jurisdiction and powers of the Supreme Court in respect to the Union List and other matters?

Ans. The Parliament has power to enlarge the jurisdiction and power of the Supreme Court in respect to the matters in the Union List and in other matters by a special agreement of the Centre and the States.

Structured Questions

1. The country's judicial system has the Supreme Court at its apex. In this context, discuss the following. [2013]
   (i) Explain the manner of appointment of Judges.
   (ii) Explain the term of office and removal of Judges.
   (iii) Explain its power of judicial review.

Ans. (i) The President of India appoints the Judges of the Supreme Court through the following procedure

- When the President appoints the Chief Justice, he/she may consult with Judges of the Supreme Court and the High Court.
- When the President appoints other Judges of the Supreme Court, he/she consults with the Chief Justice of India. Usually, the seniormost Judge of the Supreme Court is appointed as the Chief Justice of India.

(ii) The Constitution of India has not provided the fixed term for the Judge of the Supreme Court. However, it has made the following provisions for term and removal of Judges.

- A Judge holds office until the age of 65 years.
- He/She can resign from his/her office by writing to the President.
- He/She can be removed from the office by the President on the recommendation of the Parliament on the ground of proved misbehaviour and incapacity.

(iii) According to the power of Judicial Review, the Supreme Court has the power to review any laws passed by the Union or State Legislature. If any law passed by the legislature is against the spirit of the Constitution or contravenes any provision of the Constitution, the Supreme Court can declare such law as null and void. A legislative enactment or an executive order can be challenged in the Supreme Court on the following three grounds

(i) If it infringes the Fundamental Rights.
(ii) If it is outside the competent authority which has framed it.
(iii) If it is against the constitutional provisions.

2. The Supreme Court is the apex court of India. In relation to this, answer the following questions.
   (i) Explain the Supreme Court in short.
   (ii) What is meant by the writ jurisdiction of the Supreme Court?
   (iii) Mention the administrative and supervisory functions.
   (iv) Explain in brief about the 'Habeas Corpus' writ of Supreme Court.

Ans. (i) The Supreme Court is the highest court in India. It was inaugurated on 28th January, 1950 and succeeded the Federal Court of India which was established under the Government of India Act, 1935. The Supreme Court consists of 34 Judges in which there is 1 Chief Justice and 33 other Judges.

Originally the strength was fixed to 8 (1 Chief Justice and 7 other Judges). The strength of the Supreme Court to 33 Judges, excluding the Chief Justice was increased by the Supreme Court (Number of Judges) Amendment Act, 2017.

(ii) The Constitution has constituted the Supreme Court as the guarantor and defender of the Fundamental Rights of the citizens. The Supreme Court in empowered to issue writs for the enforcement of the Fundamental Rights of aggrieved citizens. These writs are of five types

- Habeas corpus
- Mandamus
- Prohibition
- Quo-Warranto
- Certiorari

(iii) The administrative and supervisory functions of the Supreme Court are

- The Supreme Court makes rules regarding the conduct of advocates and other persons appearing before it.
- The Chief Justice of India appoints of officers and staff of the Supreme Court.
- The recommendation of the Chief Justice of India to transfer Judges of the High Courts are binding on the government, if it was made after consulting at least 4 seniormost Judges of the Supreme Court.

(iv) A writ of Habeas Corpus which literally means 'you shall have the body' is a court order to a person or agency holding someone in custody (such as warden) to deliver the imprisoned individual to the court and to show a valid reason for that person's detention.

3. The Supreme Court is the apex court of our country. In this context, explain the following. **[2011]**

(i) The composition of the Supreme Court of India.

(ii) The meaning of independent judiciary and the need to do so.

(iii) The manner in which the Constitution seeks to maintain the independence of the judiciary. (Any two points)

Ans. (i) The following points explain the composition of the Supreme Court of India.

- Originally, the strength of the Supreme Court was fixed at 8 (1 Chief Justice and 7 other Judges).
- The Parliament has increased the number of other Judges progressively to 10 in 1956, 13 in 1960, 17 in 1977 and 25 in 1986.
- In February 2009, the Judges are increased to 31 and in 2019, it increased to 33 excluding 1 Chief Justice. 31 Judges sit in the Supreme Court.

(ii) The meaning of independent of Judiciary is that the Judiciary is free to work without the influence of other forms of government i.e. Executive and Legislature.

The need for an independent judiciary is

- In a representative democracy, administration of justice assumes special significance in view of rights of people. Thus, the independence of judiciary is essential to protect any violation of the rights of people.
- In a federal set-up, there is a constitutional division of powers between the Executive, Legislature and Judiciary. Thus, an independent and impartial judiciary is essential for a federal governance.
- It is an essential for ensuring human rights and protecting democracy.

(iii) Refer to chapter theory page no. 50-51.

4. The Supreme Court is the apex court in the entire judicial set-up in India. In this context, answer the following questions. **[2010]**

(i) What is meant by the term single integrated judicial system?

(ii) Explain the impeachment procedure for the removal of the Judges of the Supreme Court.

(iii) In the extensive jurisdiction of the Supreme Court states the difference between the original jurisdiction and appellate jurisdiction. Mention two functions that come under original jurisdiction.

Ans. (i) Refer to chapter theory page no. 49.

(ii) The impeachment procedure for the removal of the Judges of the Supreme Court is

- A motion of the removal is addressed to the President which is signed by atleast 100 members of the Lok Sabha or 50 members of the Rajya Sabha and then it is delivered to the Speaker or the Chairman.
- The motion is to be investigated by a committee of three Judges i.e. two Judges of the Supreme Court and a distinguished jurist.
- If the committee finds the Judge guilty of misbehaviour or that he suffers incapacity, the motion along with the report of the committee is taken up for consideration in the House, where the motion is pending.
- If the motion is passed in each House by majority of the total membership of that House and by a majority of not less than two-thirds of the House present and voting, the motion is presented to the President.
- The Judge will be removed after the President gives his order of removal on the said address.

(iii) Original jurisdiction means the power to hear and determine the dispute between the Union and the State or more States. On the other hand, appellate jurisdiction means anyone can appeal for hearing the case of the High Court.

The appellate jurisdiction are of four types; constitutional matters, civil matters, criminal matters and appeal by special leave. Functions that comes under the original jurisdiction are

(a) As the original Federal Court, the Supreme Court decides the dispute between
- the Centre and one or more States.
- two or more States.
- the Government of India and any State or States on one side and one or more States on the other side.

(b) The Supreme Court has also the exclusive and original jurisdiction to inquire into and decides all doubts and disputes in connection with the election of the President and the Vice-President of India.

5. With reference to the powers and functions of the Supreme Court, answer the following questions.

(i) What is meant by judicial review and original jurisdiction?

(ii) What is appellate jurisdiction? Mention any two types of cases over which the Supreme Court has appellate jurisdiction.

(iii) Why is the judiciary kept independent from the control of the Executive and Legislature? **[2015]**

(iv) What is the procedure for the removal of the Supreme Court Judge?

Ans. (i) The judicial review means that the Supreme court upholds the principle of supremacy of the Constitution. It also maintains federal equilibrium between Centre and State.

The original jurisdiction means the authority of the Constitution in a dispute between the Union Government and one or more State comes under original jurisdiction.

(ii) Appellate jurisdiction means the power of granting special leave to appeal against the judgement delivered by a High Court.

The Supreme Court enjoys a wide appellate jurisdiction which can be understood through the following two cases over which the Supreme Court has appellate jurisdiction

(a) **Constitutional Cases** In these cases an appeal can be made to the Supreme Court against the judgement of a High Court. If the High Court certifies that the case involves a substantial question of law regarding interpretation of the Constitution.

(b) **Civil Cases** In these cases, an appeal can be made to the Supreme Court against any judgement of the High Court, if the High Court certifies that the case involves a substantial question of law of general importance.

(iii) Refer to chapter theory page no. 50 and 51.

(iv) Refer to chapter theory page no. 50.

6. With reference to the Judiciary, answer the following questions.

(i) How does the President appoint an acting Chief Justice and Ad hoc Judge of the Supreme Court?

(ii) The Constitution has made various provisions to safeguard and ensure the independent and impartial functioning of the Supreme Court. Mention any three.

(iii) State the aspects of the appeal by special leave power of the Supreme Court.

And. (i) The President appoint acting Chief Justice and Ad hoc Judges in the following ways

- **Appointment of Acting Chief Justice** The President can appoint a Judge of the Supreme Court (Article 126) as an acting Chief Justice of India when
  - The office of Chief Justice is vacant.
  - The Chief Justice is temporarily absent.
  - The Chief Justice is unable to perform the duties of his/her office.
- **Appointment of Ad hoc Judges** Under Article 127, when there is a lack of Quorum of the permanent Judges to hold or continue any session of the Supreme Court the Chief Justice can appoint a Judge of High Court as an Ad hoc Judge of the Supreme Court for a temporary period. It can be done after consultation with the Chief Justice of High Court concerned and with the consent of the President. The Judge so appointed should be qualified for appointment as the Judge of the Supreme Court.

(ii) The three provisions to safeguard and ensure the independency of the Supreme Court are

(a) **Ban on Practice after Retirement** After retirement, a Judge of the Supreme Court shall not plead or act in any court or before any authority within the territory of India. This ensures that they do not favour any one in the future.

(b) **Freedom to Recruit its Staff** The Chief Justice of India can recruit officers and servants of the Supreme Court without any interference from the Executive.

(c) **Power to Punish for its Contempt** The Supreme Court has right to punish any person for its contempt. Its actions and decisions cannot be criticised and opposed by anybody.

(iii) The Supreme Court is authorised to grant special leave to appeal against the any judgement of any court or tribunal in the country (except military tribunal and court martial). This provision contains the four aspects as under

(a) It is a discretionary power and hence, cannot be claimed as a matter of right.

(b) It can be granted in any judgement whether final or interlocutory meeting.

(c) It may be related to any matter i.e. constitutional, civil, criminal, income tax, labour, revenue advocates, etc.

(d) It can be granted against the judgement of any court or tribunal and not necessarily against a High Court (except a military court).

8. Our judicial system has a Supreme Court at its Apex, followed by the High Court and other Subordinate Courts. In the light of this statement, explain the following. **[2018]**

(i) Any three types of cases in which the Supreme Court exercises its original jurisdiction.

(ii) Any three ways by which the Constitution ensures the Independence of the judiciary.

(iii) 'Advisory' and 'Revisory' jurisdiction of the Supreme Court.

Ans. (i) Refer to chapter theory page no. 51.

(ii) Three ways by which the Constitution ensures the independence of the judiciary are

- Clear division of powers among Legislature, Executive and Judiciary.
- The jurisdiction of courts at different level is clearly mentioned.
- The Judges of the Supreme Court and High Courts have fixed tenure.

(iii) **Advisory Jurisdiction** Under Article 143, the President can seek advice from the Supreme Court on any question of law or fact of public importance which has arisen or which is likely to arise. The advice is not binding on the President who may or may not accept it.

Revisory Jurisdiction The Supreme Court has a power to review its own judgement or order to remove any mistake or error that might have occur in the judgement or orders.

9. The Supreme Court has an extensive jurisdiction. In the light of this statement answer the following questions. **[2016]**

(i) What are the qualifications of the Judges of the Supreme Court?

(ii) (a) Explain the composition of the Supreme Court.

(b) How are the Judges of the Supreme Court appointed?

(iii) Explain the cases in which the Supreme Court enjoys original jurisdiction.

Ans. (i) Refer to chapter theory page no. 50.

(ii) (a) Refer to structured question no. 3 (i).

(b) Refer to chapter theory page no. 50.

(iii) Refer to chapter theory page no. 51.

Chapter Assessment

Section-I

Multiple Choice Questions

1. Where did India get its concept of single order of court?
   (a) Government of India Act, 1935
   (b) Government of India Act, 1919
   (c) Pitts India Act, 1773
   (d) None of the above
2. Article 126 of the Indian Constitution deals with the ....
   (a) Acting Chief Justice
   (b) Ad hoc Judges
   (c) Impeachment of the Judge
   (d) None of the above
3. Judicial review is necessary for
   (a) To uphold the principle of supremacy.
   (b) To protect the Fundamental Right of citizens.
   (c) To maintain federal Equilibrium between the Centre . and State.
   (d) All of the above

Section-II

Very Short Questions

1. After how many years of practice as an advocate in the High Court, a person will be qualified to be a Judge of the Supreme Court?
2. Who appoints an Ad hoc Judge of the Supreme Court?
3. What is the term of office of a Judge of the Supreme Court?
4. What do you mean by 'prohibition of practice' after retirement of a Judge?
5. What are the civil cases in the appellate jurisdiction?
6. What is the 'revisory jurisdiction' of the Supreme Court?
7. The court of record is one of the powers of the Supreme Court. Mention its implications.

Structured Questions

1. Under our Constitution the judiciary is a single integrated system of courts for the Union and the States with the Supreme Court at the apex. In this context, answer the following questions.
   (i) Why has India opted for Single Integrated Judicial set-up?
   (ii) Mention the appointment procedures of Judges including Chief Justice of India and Ad hoc Judges.
   (iii) Mention any two provisions of the independence of judiciary.
   (iv) Explain the composition of Supreme Court.
2. Jurisdiction is the power that a court of law exercises to carry out judgements and enforce laws. In this context, answer the following questions.
   (i) What is the original jurisdiction of the Supreme Court?
   (ii) What is the appellate jurisdiction of the Supreme Court? Mention the extention of criminal cases.
   (iii) What is judicial review? Why there is a need for judicial review in Indian judicial system?
3. Supreme Court plays a vital role in the judicial system of India. In this regard, answer the following questions.
   (i) Under which jurisdiction, the Supreme Court enforces Fundamental Rights? Mention any three.
   (ii) Which principles are laid down in the power of appeal by special leave of the Supreme Court?
   (iii) What is the power of the Supreme Court as a Court of Record?
   (iv) Explain the process of appointment of Ad-hoc Judge.

CHAPTER 05

The High Courts and Subordinate Courts

SYLLABUS

The High Courts Composition, qualifications of Judges, appointment.
- Jurisdiction and functions : Original, Appellate, Revisory, Judicial Review and Court of Record.
- Enforcement of Fundamental Rights and Writs

Subordinate Courts Distinction between Court of the District Judge and Sessions Court.
- Lok Adalats : Meaning and advantages

The High Courts

The Constitution of India states that there should be High Court for each state, but the 7th Constitutional Amendment Act, 1956 authorised the Parliament to establish a common High Court for two or more States and a Union Territory. At present, there are 25 High Courts in India, including those having jurisdiction of more than one state. Delhi is the only Union Territory that has High Court of its own. The other Union Territories fall under the jurisdiction of different state High Courts, while Goa and Daman and Diu have a Judicial Commissioner.

Composition

Every High Court consists of a Chief Justice and such other Judges who are appointed by the President of India from time-to-time. The Constitution does not specify the strength of a High Court so that, the President of India determines the strength of High Courts which is depended upon the workload of these courts. The composition of High Court also includes the appointment of additional judges for temporary periods i.e. not exceeding two years for clearance of work in the High Court.

Qualifications of Judges

According to the Constitution, to be qualified for appointment as a Judge of a High Court, a person

- should be a citizen of India.
- should have held a judicial office in the territory of India for 10 years.
- should have been an advocate of a High Court for 10 years.
- should not be over 62 years.

The Constitution does not describe the minimum age for appointment as a Judge of a High Court.

Appointment of Judges

The Judges of the High Court are appointed by the President. The Chief Justice of a High Court is appointed by the President after consultation with Chief Justice of India and the Governor of that state.

For appointment of other Judges, the Chief Justice of concerned High Court is also consulted. In case of a concerned High Court for two or more states, the Governors of all the concerned states are consulted by the President. The President can appoint any Judge of the High Court as the acting Chief Justice of the High Court, when the Chief Justice is unable to perform his duties.

Oath

The Governor of a state administers the following oath of office to the High Court Judges

- To bear true faith and allegiance to the Constitution of India.
- To perform the duty without fear, or favour, affection or ill-will.
- To uphold the Constitution and the law of the land.

Term

All the Judges of the High Courts are independent in carrying out their work from the government side. A Judge enjoys the security of the tenure and can remain in office till he has attained the age of 62 years. He/She can only be removed from his/her office by an order of the President.

Removal of Judges

The President can issue the removal order of a Judge only after an address by the Parliament has been presented to him/her in the same session for such removal. The address must be supported by a special majority of each House of the Parliament and by a two-third majority of these present and voting in both the Houses.

Finally, the President passes an order for removing the Judge. This procedure is called the **impeachment** of a Judge. It is noted here that the removal procedure of a Judge of the High Court by the process of impeachment is same as the Supreme Court i.e. on the grounds of proved misbehaviour or incapacity.

Justice Soumitra Sen of the Calcutta High Court became the first Judge of High Court in India's history against whom an impeachment motion was passed in the Rajya Sabha in August 2011.

Transfer of Judges

The President can transfer a Judge from one High Court to another after the fulfilment of the following conditions

- Orders for transfer can be issued only after consulting the Chief Justice of India.
- The Chief Justice of India must make recommendation only after consulting 4 seniormost Judges of the Supreme Court and the Chief Justice of the 2 High Courts (1 from which the Judge is being transferred and the other receiving him).
- When a Judge has been transferred, he/she shall be entitled to compensatory allowance in addition to his/her salary.

Salaries and Allowances of Judges

The salaries, allowances, privileges, leaves and pensions of a Judge of a High Court are determined from time-to-time by the Parliament. The Judges of High Courts are also paid **sumptuary**[1] allowance. They are provided with free accommodations and other facilities such as medical, car, telephone etc.

Ban on Practice after Retirement

The retired permanent Judges of a High Court are prohibited from pleading or acting in any court or before any authority in India except the Supreme Court and the other High Courts where he has not served as a Judge.

Check Your LEARNING...

1. By whom the Judges of a High Court are appointed?
2. What is the maximum age of retirement of a High Court Judge?
3. What is the term of the Judge of the High Court?
4. Who decides the salaries and allowances of High Court Judge?

Jurisdictions and Functions of High Courts

High Court has extensive and effective powers like Supreme Court. It is the highest court of appeal in the state. It is the protector of the Fundamental Rights of the citizens as well as the interpreter of the Constitution.

Original Jurisdiction

It means that High Court has power to hear disputes in the first instance, not by way of appeal. High Court has original jurisdiction in the following cases

- Disputes relating to the election of Members of the Parliament and State Legislatures.
- Cases regarding **revenue**[2] matter or an act ordered or done regarding revenue collection.
- Cases regarding enforcement of Fundamental Rights of citizens.

1 **Sumptuary** Relating to or denoting laws that limit private expenditure on food and personal items.
2 **Revenue** A State's annual income from which public expenses are met.

- Cases ordered to be transferred from a Subordinate Court, involving the **interpretation**[3] of the Constitution.
- Cases regarding matter of admirality, will, marriage, divorce, company laws and contempt of court.

Appellate Jurisdiction

The appellate jurisdiction of a High Court is wider than its original jurisdiction. It means that a High Court has power to hear appeals against the judgments of Subordinate Courts functioning in its territorial jurisdiction. It has appellate jurisdiction in both **civil and criminal cases.**

Civil Cases

Only those civil cases which are decided by the District Courts, Additional District Courts and other Subordinate Courts under the jurisdiction of the High Court concerned, can be brought to the High Court by an appeal.

Appeals that can be brought to High Courts are

- In matters concerning land revenue.
- In matters where evident injustice has been committed by any tribunal.

Criminal Cases

Appeal related to criminal cases that can be brought to High Courts are

- Appeals against a Sessions Judge or an additional Session Judge, where the sentence is of imprisonment exceeding 7 years.
- Appeals against the death sentence awarded by a Sessions Court or an additional Sessions Court.
- Appeals from the judgements of the Assistant Sessions Judge, Metropolitian Magistrate or other Magistrates, where the sentence of imprisonment exceeds 4 years.
- Appeals against the state, when the order of acquittal (declaration of innocence) is passed by a Sessions Judge.

Supervisory Jurisdiction

A High Court has the power of superintendence over all the courts and tribunals functioning in its territorial jurisdiction (except military courts or tribunals). Thus, it may

- call for returns from them.
- make an issue, general rules and prescribe forms for regulating the practice and proceedings of them.
- prescribe forms in which books, entries and accounts are to be kept by them.
- settle the fees payable to the sheriff, clerks, officers and legal practitioners of them.

Advisory Jurisdiction

The High Courts can advice the Governor in any case related to governmental department and legislature, if he/she seeks the advice of the High Court on constitutional as well as on other matters of law.

But its advice is not binding on the agency seeking such advice.

Revisory Jurisdiction

A High Court can call for the record of a case which has been decided by a Subordinate Court. Therefore, a High Court can review the case and take appropriate action on it. The revisory jurisdiction is applicable in the following cases

- Injustice or an error of law evident on the record.
- Violation of the principles of natural justice.
- **Arbitrary**[4] authority leading to wrong judgements.
- **Flagrant**[5] error in procedure.

As a Court of Record

The High Court has following two powers as a Court of Record.

(i) The judgements, proceedings and acts of the High Courts are recorded for **perpetual**[6] memory and testimony.

(ii) A High Court has power to punish for contempt of court, either with simple imprisonment or with fine or both.

Power of Judicial Review

The High Court examines the constitutionality of legislative enactment and executive orders of both the Centre and the State Governments. If the enactments and orders are found to be violative of the Constitution, they can be declared as illegal, unconstitutional and invalid (null and void) by the High Court.

3 **Interpretation** The action of explaining the meaning of something.
4 **Arbitrary** Based on random choice or personal whim, rather than any reason or system.
5 **Flagrant** An action considered as wrong or immoral.
6 **Perpetual** Never ending or changing.

The enactments and executive orders can be challenged in a High Court on the following three grounds

(i) If it violates the Fundamental Rights.
(ii) If it is outside the competence of the authority which has framed it.
(iii) If it is against to the constitutional provisions.

Enforcement of Fundamental Rights and Writs

The Constitution of India empowers High Court under Article 226 to issue writs including Habeas Corpus, Mandamus, Certiorari, Prohibition and Quo-Warranto for the enforcement of the Fundamental Rights of the citizens and for any other purposes like enforcement of an ordinary legal right. The power of writ jurisdiction can be exercise by a High Court not only within its territory, but also outside its jurisdiction, if causes of action arises within its territorial jurisdiction.

The power of writ jurisdiction of a High Court is wider than that of the Supreme Court. This is because, the Supreme Court issue writs only for the enforcement of Fundamental Rights and not for the case where the breach of an ordinary legal right is alleged.

Control Over Subordinate Courts

A High Court has an administrative control over the Subordinate Courts in the following ways

- High Court is consulted by the Governor in the matters of appointment, posting and promotion of District Judges and in the appointments of persons to the judicial service of the state.
- High Court deals with the matters of posting, promotion, grant leave, transfer and discipline of the members of the judicial service of the state. Its law is binding on all Subordinated Courts, functioning within its territorial jurisdiction.

Check Your LEARNING...

1. The powers of High Courts are similar to which other Court of India?
2. Who is the protector of the Fundemental Rights of the citizens of a state?
3. Which jurisdiction of High Court is wider than original jurisdiction of Supreme Court?
4. How many writs are mentioned in Indian Constitution?

Subordinate Courts

In every state, besides the High Court there are number of judicial courts to administer justice. These courts are known as Subordinate Courts and function under the complete control and supervision of the High Court.

Structure and Composition

In India, the organisation and structure of the Subordinate Courts is generally uniform. For judicial administration purpose, every state is divided into a number of districts, each under the jurisdiction of a District Judge.

Qualifications of District Judge

To be appointed as a District Judge a person

- should not already be in the service of the Central or the State Government.
- should have been an advocate or a pleader for 7 years.
- should be recommended by the High Court for appointment.

Appointment

The District Judges are appointed by the Governor in consultation with the Judges of the High Court of the concerned state. All other Judges are appointed through competitive examinations held by State Public Service Commission. The District Judges exercise administrative control over all Civil Courts in the district.

Types of Subordinate Courts

Every district has Civil Courts, Criminal Courts and Courts of Revenue.

Civil Courts

The cases related to land, property and money transactions, arbitration, guardianship, marriage, divorce and cases involving a will, etc are exercised under jurisdiction of Civil Courts.

These Courts are graded in the following manner

- **Court of District Judge** This court decides both civil and criminal cases and is the highest court of the district. When a Judge decides civil cases, he is called as **District Judge** and when he decides criminal cases, he is called **Sessions Judge**. The District Judge exercises both judicial and administrative powers. He also has supervisory district powers over all the Subordinate Courts in the district.

- **Court of Civil Judge** This court comes next to the District Court. It deals with the cases involving an amount of ₹ 5000.
- **Munsiff's Court** This court hears cases involving amount less than ₹2000. Appeal against its decisions can be made to the Civil Judge.
- **Small Court** This court deals with cases of nominal money value. The juniormost Judges head these courts. There is no appeal against its decisions.

Criminal Courts

It exercises jurisdiction in cases related to murder, robbery, theft, assault etc. Criminal Courts are broadly classified as

- **Session Court** It is the highest Criminal Court of the district. It deals with cases concerning robbery, dacoity and murder. It can award sentence up to life imprisonment or death sentence. But it is mandatory, that a death sentence must be confirmed by the High Court before its execution irrespective of whether an appeal is made to the High Court or not.
- **Court of Chief Metropolitan Magistrate** It deals with less serious offences and can award fine authorised by law and sentence up to 7 years imprisonment.
- **Court of First Class Magistrate** It can award sentence up to 3 years imprisonment or fine of ₹5000 or both.
- **Court of Second Class Magistrate** It can award sentence not more than 1 year or impose a fine of ₹5000 or both.
- **Court of Third Class Magistrate** It can award sentence up to 1 month of simple imprisonment or a fine up to ₹50 or both. It deals with criminal cases involving simple individual quarrels or rioting.

Difference between Court of the District Judge and Sessions Court

Court of the District Judge	Sessions Court
It is the highest Civil Court of the district.	It is the highest Criminal Court of the district.
It is presided by a District Judge.	It is presided by a Sessions Judge.
The District Judge and the additional District Judges are appointed by the Governor in consultation with the Chief Justice of the High Court of the concerned state.	The Sessions Judge and the Additional Sessions Judges are appointed by the Governor in consultation with Chief Justice of concerned High Court.
Civil cases related to land, property, money, transactions, arbitration, guardianship, marriage, divorce and will are decided by the District Judges.	The cases such as murders, theft, dacoity, pick-pocketing, etc are decided by the Sessions Judges.

Courts of Revenue

These courts deal with cases relating to the maintenance of land records and assessment and collection of land revenue.

The types of revenue courts are

- **The Board of Revenue** This is the highest revenue court in the district. Under this, the Courts of Commissioners, Collectors, Tehsildars and Assistant Tehsildars (Naib) are included. The Board of Revenue hears the final appeal against all the lower revenue courts under it.
- **Commissioner's Court** This court deals with assessment and collection of revenues of all districts in particular division.
- **Collector's Court** This court deals with the assessment and collection of revenues of the district. It also hears first appeals against the decision of the Tehsildar.
- **Tehsildar's Court** It deals with the collection of the revenue and property taxes as assessed by the Naib Tehsildars.
- **Naib Tehsildar's Court** This is the lowest court. It hears cases of farmers relating to the assessment of the land revenue and property taxes from the farmers.

Lok Adalats

It is a system of alternative dispute resolution developed in India. It roughly means **People's Court.** The idea of Lok Adalat was mainly advocated by **Justice PN Bhagwati** (Former CJI). The first Lok Adalat was held at **Junagarh**, in Gujarat, on 14th March, 1982.

The Lok Adalat accept the cases pending in the regular courts within their jurisdiction which could be settled by conciliation (agreement) and compromise. The Lok Adalat is presided over by a sitting or retired judicial officer as the Chairman, with two other members, usually a lawyer and a social worker.

Types of Lok Adalats

- **National Lok Adalats** These Lok Adalats are held at regular intervals. Civil cases, matrimonial cases, MACT (Motor Accident Claims Tribunals) cases and petty offence cases are mainly referred to National Lok Adalats.
- **Permanent Lok Adalats** These are organised under Section 22-B of the Legal Services Authorities Act, 1987. These Lok Adalats include a Chairman and two members for providing

compulsory pre-litigative mechanism for conciliation and settlement of cases relating to Public Utility Services like transport, postal, telegraph, etc. The decision of the Permanent Lok Adalat is final and binding on all the parties in a particular case.

- **Mobile Lok Adalats** These Lok Adalats are organised in various parts of the country which travel from one location to another to resolve disputes.

Working of Lok Adalats

The Lok Adalat resolves disputes related to matters which are not very complicated in nature. The Judges of these courts are actually counsellors. These adalats are assisted by Legal Aid Committee and Social Action Group, which advise the people about legal matters and help them to solve the cases by mutual participation.

A dispute is referred to the Lok Adalat only when both the parties are agreed to get their dispute resolved through the Lok Adalat.

Advantages of Lok Adalats

- It delivers fast and inexpensive justice.
- It reduces the workload of other courts enabling them to deal with more serious matters.
- It promotes social justice by providing legal aid to weaker sections of the society.
- It works in the spirit of compromise and understanding, where both the parties feel satisfied.

Scope of Lok Adalats

Lok Adalats are becoming popular as the government departments have began to hold Lok Adalats for solving hundreds of cases in a single day. It is required that Lok Adalats are organised more frequently and their jurisdiction must expand as many cases are pending in different courts in India.

The Lok Adalats can play important role in the settlement of family feuds, disputes between the neighbours and minor cases of assault and injury.

Family Court

The Family Courts Act, 1984, provides for setting up of Family Courts in cities having population over 10 lakh. It aims at promoting conciliation in and securing speedy settlement of disputes relating to marriage and family affairs.

Check Your LEARNING...

1. Who appoints District Judge?
2. What sentence can be awarded by a court of first class Magistrate?
3. Name any one type of Revenue Court.
4. What is the other name of Lok Adalat?

QUiCK Revision

- The Constitution of India provides for a High Court for each state, but the 7th Constitutional Amendment Act, authorised the Parliament to establish a common High Court for two or more States and a Union Territory . At present, there are 25 High Courts in India. Delhi is the only Union Territory that has High Court of its own.
- Every High Court consists of a Chief Justice and such other Judges who are appointed by the President of India . The Constitution of India does not describe the minimum age for the appointment of a Judge of the High Court.
- For the appointment of Judges of a common High Court for two or more states, the Governors of all the states concerned are consulted by the President.
- The Constitution has not fixed the tenure of a Judge of the High Court. A Judge of the High Court can be removed from his/her office by an order of the President. The High Court has original jurisdiction, it means that it has power to hear disputes in the first instance, not by way of appeal.
- The appellate jurisdiction means that a High Court has power to hear appeals against the judgements of Subordinate Courts functioning in its jurisdictions.
- A High Court has the power of superintendence over all the courts and tribunals functioning in its territorial jurisdiction (except military courts or tribunals).
- A High Court can advice Governor, any government department and legislature, if they seek its advice on any matter of law.
- A High Court examines the constitutionality of legislative enactments and executive orders of both the Centre and the State Governments.
- The Constitution of India empowers High Court in Article 226 to issue writs including Habeas Corpus, Mandamus, Certiorari, Prohibitions and Quo-warranto for enforcement of the Fundamental Rights of the citizens and for any other purpose.
- The state judiciary consists of a High Court and a hierarchy of Subordinate Courts also known as lower courts. Every district has a Civil Court , Criminal Court and Revenue Court.
- The District Judge is the highest judicial authority in the district. The Lok Adalat is a system of alternative dispute resolution developed in India. It roughly means People's Court.
- The Lok Adalats settle family feuds, disputes between the neighbours and minor cases of assault and injury by setting the disputes through compromise.

Chapter Practice

Section-I

Multiple Choice Questions

1. The Act which authorised the Parliament to establish a common High Court is ....
(a) 7th Amendment Act, 1956
(b) 6th Amendment Act, 1956
(c) 8th Amendment Act, 1960
(d) 9th Amendment Act, 1960

Ans. (a) 7th Amendment Act, 1956

2. In which year, 7th constitutional amendment authorised the Parliament to establish a common High Court for two or more states?
(a) 1952 (b) 1954
(c) 1956 (d) 1960

Ans. (c) 1956

3. Name a Union Territory which has a High Court of its own?
(a) Andaman and Nicobar (b) Delhi
(c) Puducherry (d) Lakshadweep

Ans. (b) Delhi

4. The Judge of the High Court can hold office till the age of
(a) 60 years (b) 62 years
(c) 65 years (d) 70 years

Ans. (b) 62 years

5. Who was the first Judge of High Court against whom the impeachment motion was passed in Rajya Sabha?
(a) Justice Soumitra Sen
(b) MK Basu
(c) H. Benerjee Biswas
(d) Pradeep Kumar

Ans. (a) Justice Soumitra Sen

6. Who has the right to transfer a Judge of High Court?
(a) The Governor (b) The Chief Minister
(c) The President (d) Legislative Assembly

Ans. (c) The President

7. Which Article of the Indian Constitution empowers the High Court to issue writs?
(a) A-226 (b) A-368 (c) A-322 (d) A-324

Ans. (a) A-226

8. A person to be appointed as a District Judge
(a) should have been an advocate or a pleader for 9 years.
(b) should already be in the service.
(c) should be recommended by the High Court for appointment.
(d) All of the above

Ans. (c) should be recommended by the High Court for appointment.

9. Which type of cases are exercised under Civil Court?
(a) Marriage (b) Divorce
(c) Arbitration (d) All of these

Ans. (d) All of these

10. The additional Sessions Judges are appointed by
(a) Judge of High Court (b) Governor
(c) Chief Minister (d) President

Ans. (b) Governor

11. The Judges of which court are counsellors?
(a) Lok Adalat (b) Criminal Courts
(c) Civil Court (d) Small Court

Ans. (a) Lok Adalat

12. Family Court was established in
(a) 1985 (b) 1984 (c) 1983 (d) 1982

Ans. (b) 1984

13. Complete the given analogy.
Court of Civil Judge : ₹ 5000 : : Munsiff's Court : ?
(a) ₹ 2000 (b) ₹ 3000
(c) ₹ 4000 (d) ₹ 6000

Ans. (a) ₹ 2000

14. Court of District Judge : Civil Cases: : Sessions Court : .... Cases **[2023]**
(a) Advisory (b) Criminal
(c) Constitutional (d) Appellate

Ans. (b) Criminal

15. Replace the underlined word to correct the statement. The salaries and allowances of a Judge of a High Court determined by <u>Legislative Council.</u>
(a) the Governor (b) the Parliament
(c) the Chief Minister (d) the President

Ans. (b) the Parliament

16. Replace the underlined word to correct the statement. The Chief Justice of High Court is appointed by <u>the Governor</u>.
(a) President
(b) Vice-President
(c) Chief Justice of India
(d) Chief Minister

Ans. (a) President

17. Complete the following table.

Judge of High Court	The President
Judge of District Court	?

(a) Chief Minister (b) Governor
(c) The Prime Minister (d) The Vice-President

Ans. (b) Governor

18. Qualifications for appointment as a Judge
(i) be a citizen of India.
(ii) have held a judicial office for at least 10 years.
(iii) have been an advocate of a High Court or Courts for at least 10 years.

Codes
(a) Only (i) (b) Only (ii)
(c) Both (ii) and (iii) (d) All of these

Ans. (d) All of these

19. The revisory jurisdiction is applicable in the case of
(i) violation of the principles of natural justice.
(ii) arbitrary authority leading to wrong judgements.
(iii) injustice or an error of law apparent on the face of the record.

Codes
(a) Only (i) (b) Only (ii)
(c) Both (i) and (ii) (d) All of these

Ans. (d) All of these

20. Match the following.

A. The Board of Revenue	1. Hears first appeal against the decision of Tehsildar.
B. Commissioner's Court	2. Deals with assessments and collection of revenues of all district.
C. Collector's Court	3. Collection of revenue and property taxes as assessed by the Naib Tehsildar.
D. Tehsildar's Court	4. Highest revenue court in district.

Codes

	A	B	C	D		A	B	C	D
(b)	1	2	3	4	(b)	2	3	4	1
(c)	4	2	1	3	(d)	3	4	2	1

Ans. (c)

Passage Based Questions

21. Read the passage given below and answer the questions that follow.

There is no court fee payable when a matter is filed in a Lok Adalat. If a matter pending in the court of law is referred to the Lok Adalat and is settled subsequently, the court fee originally paid in the court on the complaints/petition is also refunded back to the parties. The persons deciding the cases in the Lok Adalats are called the members of the Lok Adalats, they have the role of statutory conciliators only and do not have any judicial role, therefore they can only persuade the parties to come to a conclusion for setting the dispute outside the court in the Lok Adalat and shall not pressurise or coerce any of the parties to compromise or settle cases or matters either directly or indirectly.

The Lok Adalat shall not decide the matter so referred at its own instance, instead the same would be decided on the basis of the compromise or settlement between the parties. The members shall assist the parties in an independent and impartial manner in their attempt to reach amicable settlement of their dispute.

(i) Which court means 'People's Court'?
(a) Civil Court (b) High Court
(c) Supreme Court (d) Lok Adalat

Ans. (d) Lok Adalat

(ii) The Lok Adalat was mainly advocated by
(a) CJI PN Bhagwati (b) CJI RS Pathak
(c) CJI Ajit Nath Ray (d) CJI Sarv Mitra Sikri

Ans. (a) CJI PN Bhagwati

(iii) In which year the first Lok Adalat was held ?
(a) 1985 (b) 1982
(c) 1990 (d) 1995

Ans. (b) 1982

(iv) The Lok Adalat can play important role in the settlement of
(a) family feuds
(b) disputes between neighbours
(c) minor case of assault and injury
(d) All of the above

Ans. (d) All of the above

22. Read the passage given below and answer the questions that follow.

The High Courts of India are the principal civil courts of original jurisdiction in each State and Union Territory. However, a High Court exercises its original civil and criminal jurisdiction only, if the Subordinate Courts are not authorised by law to try such matters for lack of pecuniary, territorial jurisdiction. High Courts may also enjoy original jurisdiction in certain matters, if so designated specially in a State or Union Law.

Basically, the work of most High Courts primarily consists of appeals from lower courts and writ petitions in terms of Articles 226 and 227 of the Constitution. Writ jurisdiction is also an original jurisdiction of a High Court.

Each state is divided into judicial districts presided over by a District and Sessions Judge. He is known as District Judge when he presides over a civil case, and Session's Judge when he presides over a criminal case. He is the highest judicial authority below a High Court Judge. Below him, there are courts of civil jurisdiction, known by different names in different states.

(i) The first High Court was established in
(a) Chennai (b) Kolkata
(c) Guwahati (d) Delhi

Ans. (b) Kolkata

(ii) The High Court has the jurisdiction under Article 226 for the enforcement of
(a) Civil Rights (b) Sanctioning Rights
(c) Fundamental Rights (d) Child Rights

Ans. (c) Fundamental Rights

(iii) Ladakh is under the jurisdiction of which High Court?
(a) Himachal Pradesh
(b) Jammu and Kashmir
(c) Delhi
(d) Uttarakhand

Ans. (b) Jammu and Kashmir

(iv) What is the maximum fine, a court of second class Magistrate can impose on a person?
(a) ₹ 5000 (b) ₹ 4000
(c) ₹ 1000 (d) ₹ 3000

Ans. (c) ₹ 1000

Section-II

Very Short Questions

1. By which Constitutional Amendment Act the Parliament has the authority to establish a common High Court?

Ans. The 7th Constitutional Amendment Act, 1956, authorised the Parliament to establish a Common High Court for two or more States and a Union Territory.

2. Who determines the strength of the High Court?

Ans. The President determines the strength of the High Court which depends upon the workload of the High Court.

3. State one other qualification required to become a Judge of the High Court, apart from Indian citizenship. **[2017]**

Ans. Apart from Indian citizenship, other qualification is that a person should have held a judicial office in the territory of India for 10 years.

4. The President is consulted by whom for appointing the Chief Justice of High Courts?

Ans. The Chief Justice of High Court is appointed by the President after consultation with the Chief Justice of India and the Governor of that State.

5. Who administers the oath of office to the High Court Judges? **[2011]**

Ans. The Governor of a state administers the oath of office to the High Court Judges.

6. Mention the process of removal of a Judge of the High Court.

Ans. A Judge of the High Court can be removed from his/her office by the President on the recommendation made by the Parliament.

7. What is the 'appellate jurisdiction' of the High Court? **[2014]**

Ans. The appellate jurisdiction of the High Court refers that the High Court has power to hear appeals against the judgements of Subordinate Courts functioning in its territorial jurisdiction.

8. Mention any one civil matter of appellate jurisdiction.

Ans. A civil matter of appellate jurisdiction is the case where a serious injustice has been committed by any tribunal. In such cases, the High Court may cancel the order of the tribunals.

9. Mention any one supervisory jurisdiction of the High Court.

Ans. One of the supervisory jurisdiction of the High Court is that the High Court may prescribe forms in which books, entries and accounts are to be kept by them.

10. What is meant by every High Court is a 'Court of Record'? **[2007]**

Ans. A 'Court of Record' means that the High Court has power to record its judgements, proceedings and acts for perpetual memory and testimony.

11. What is meant by the term 'Judicial Review' of the High Court? **[2016]**

Ans. Judicial Review is the power of the High Court to examine the constitutionality of legislative enactments and executive orders of both the Central and State Government.

12. Mention any one ground of Judicial Review power where the enactments and executive orders can be challenged.

Ans. The enactments and executive order can be challenged in a High Court on the ground of infringing the Fundamental Rights.

13. Which Article of the Constitution empowers the High Court to issue writs?

Ans. Article 226 of the Constitution empowers the High Court to issue writ.

14. Name the courts that are empowered to issue writs for the enforcement of Fundamental Rights. **[2020, 2013]**

Ans. The Supreme Court and the High Court are empowered to issue writ for the enforcement of Fundamental Rights.

15. How does the High Court protect the Fundamental Rights of individuals?

Ans. The High Court protects the Fundamental Rights of individuals by issuing writ including Habeas Corpus, Mandamus, Certiorari, Prohibitions and Quo-Warranto.

16. Name the writ issued by the High Court which provides a remedy to the person who has been unlawfully detained in prison. **[2008]**

Ans. The writ of Habeas Corpus is issued by the High Court which provides a remedy to the person who has been unlawfully detained in prison.

17. What do you understand by the Subordinate Court?

Ans. The Subordinate Courts are those courts that function below and under the High Court at district and lower levels.

18. What are the powers of the District Judge?

Ans. The District Judge exercises both judicial and administrative powers. He/She also has supervisory powers over all the Subordinate Courts in the district.

19. Mention the three types of courts that a district usually have. **[2010]**

Ans. The three types of courts that a district usually have are

(i) Civil Courts (ii) Criminal Courts
(iii) Courts of Revenue

20. Name the highest court dealing with civil cases at the district level.

Or Name the highest Civil Court in a district. **[2016]**

Ans. The Court of District Judge that deals with the civil cases is the highest court at the District level.

21. Which is the highest Criminal Court in a district? **[2013]**

Or Which is the highest court dealing with the criminal cases at the district level? **[2009]**

Or Name the highest Criminal Court in a district? **[2018]**

Ans. The Sessions Court is the highest Criminal Court in a district, which deals with criminal cases at the district level.

22. Mention any one power of the Sessions Judge.

Ans. The Sessions Judge has the power to impose any sentence including life imprisonment and capital punishment. However, a capital punishment passed by him is subject to confirmation by the High Court.

23. At the lowest level of a State, who are the head of the judicial system.

Ans. At the lowest level, the Court of Munsiff on the civil side and the Court of Judicial Magistrate on the criminal side are the head of the judicial system.

24. What is meant by Lok Adalat? **[2018, 2016, 2006]**

Ans. Lok Adalat is the people's court to provide aid and justice to those, who are not in a position to engage lawyers or bear expenses of legal proceedings.

25. What is the composition of Lok Adalat?

Ans. The Lok Adalat is presided over by a sitting or retired judicial officer as the Chairman, with two other members, usually a lawyer and a social worker.

26. Which kind of cases are dealt by the Lok Adalat?

Ans. The Lok Adalat can deal with all civil cases, matrimonial disputes, land disputes, partition disputes, labour disputes and compoundable criminal cases.

27. State one advantage of a Lok Adalat. **[2015]**

Or Mention one reason to state that the Lok Adalat has its own advantage. **[2017]**

Ans. An advantage of the Lok Adalat is that it encourages the settlement of disputes through compromise between two parties.

28. Mention one reason why the system of Lok Adalat has become popular. **[2011]**

Ans. The Lok Adalat system has become so popular because various government department have began to hold Lok Adalat for solving hundreds of cases in a single day.

Structured Questions

1. With reference to the judiciary.

(i) Discuss the qualifications needed for a person to be appointed as a Chief Justice of a High Court.

(ii) State the term of office of the Judges of the High Court. Explain when and how the Judges can be removed from office?

(iii) Name the types of courts at the District level. Explain the different categories of cases that fall under the jurisdiction of each.

(iv) Write in short about the composition of High Courts in india.

Ans. (i) According to the Constitution, to be qualified for appointment as a Chief Justice of High Court, a person

- should be a citizen of India.
- should have held a judicial office in the territory of India for 10 years.
- should have been an advocate of a High Court for 10 years.
- should not be over 62 years.

(ii) A Judge enjoys the security of the tenure and can remain in office till he has attained the age of 62 years.

A Judge can only be removed from his/her office by an order of the President. The President can issue the removal order of a Judge only after an address by the Parliament has been presented to him/her in the same session for such removal.

The address must be supported by a special majority of each House of the Parliament and by a two-third majority of these present and voting in both the Houses. Finally, the President passes an order for removing the Judge. This procedure is called the **impeachment** of a Judge.

(iii) There are three types of courts at the District level which are

(a) **The Civil Courts** The Civil Courts hear cases of land, property, money transactions, marriage, divorce, will and guardianship.

(b) **The Criminal Courts** In these courts serious cases of murder, robbery and dacoities are tried.

(c) **Court of Revenue** These courts deal with cases relating to the maintenance of land records and assessment and collection of land revenue.

(iv) Every High Court consists of 1 Chief Justice and other Judges who are appointed by the President of India from time to time. The Constitution does not specify the strength of a High Court, so that the President of India determines the strength of High Courts which is depended upon the workload of these Courts.

2. India has a single integrated judicial system that is independent and supreme. With reference to the judiciary, answer the following. **[2019]**

(i) (a) Who appoints the Judges of the High Court?

(b) State any two qualifications required for a person to be appointed as a High Court judge.

(ii) Explain briefly the term Court of Record with reference to the High Court.

(iii) List any four writs that the High Court can issue for the enforcement of Fundamental Rights.

Ans. (i) (a) The Judges of the High Court are appointed by the President of India. The Chief Justice of a High Court is appointed by the President after consultation with Chief Justice of India and the Governor of that state.

(b) Two qualifications required for a person to be appointed as a judge of a High Court are

(a) He/she should be a citizen of India.

(b) He/she has held a judicial office within Indian Territory for at least 10 years.

(ii) The High Court is considered as a Court of Record. It means

- The judgements, proceedings and acts of the High Court are recorded for perpetual memory and testimony.
- These records are admitted to be of value as evidence and cannot be questioned when produced before any court. They are recognised as legal precedents and legal references.
- It has the power to punish for contempt of court.

(iii) All the High Courts are empowered to issued writs in cases related to enforcement of Fundamental Rights. A writ is an order from a judicial authority asking a person to perform some act or refrain from performing an act. The writs that are issued are Habeas Corpus, Mandamus, Prohibition, Quo-Warranto and Certiorari. The writ jurisdiction of a High Court is much wider than the Supreme Court. The High Court can issue writs only for enforcing Fundamental Rights.

3. With the reference to the power of the High Court. Answer the following questions.

(i) What is the Criminal appellate jurisdiction of the High Courts?

(ii) Mention the supervisory jurisdiction.

(iii) What are the powers related to the exercises of the Subordinate Courts?

(iv) What do you mean by Power of Judicial Review of High Court?

Ans. (i) The appellate jurisdiction refers that a High Court has power to hear appeals against the judgement of Subordinate Courts functioning in its territorial jurisdiction. It has appellate jurisdiction in both civil and criminal matters. The appeal related to criminal matters are

- Appeals against a Sessions Judge or an additional Session Judge, where the sentence is of imprisonment exceeding 7 years.
- Appeals against the death sentence awarded by a Sessions Court or an additional Sessions Court.

(ii) A High Court has the power of superintendence or supervisory jurisdiction over all the courts and tribunals functioning in its territorial jurisdiction (except military courts or tribunals). Thus, it may

- call for returns from them.
- make an issue, general rules and prescribe forms for regulating the practice and proceedings of them.
- prescribe forms in which books, entries and accounts are to be kept by them.
- settle the fees payable to the sheriff, clerks, officers and legal practitioners of them.

(iii) The powers related to the exercises of the Subordinate Courts are

- High Court is consulted by the Governor in the matters of appointment, posting and promotion of District Judges and in the appointments of persons to the judicial service of the state.
- High Court deals with the matters of posting, promotion, grant leave, transfer and discipline of the members of the judicial service of the state.
- Its law is binding on all Subordinated Courts, functioning within its territorial jurisdiction.

(iv) Refer to chapter theory on page no. 64-65.

4. The Constitution of India provides for a High Court for each State. With reference to the High Courts and Subordinate Courts, answer the following questions **[2023]**

(i) Who appoints the judges of the High Court ? Mention any two qualifications required for a person to be appointed as a judge of a High Court.

(ii) Mention any three cases that come under the Original Jurisdiction of the High Court.

(iii) What are Lok Adalats ? Mention any three advantages of the Lok Adalats.

Ans. (i) Refer to Structured Question 2(i).

(ii) Cases in which the High Court has the authority to hear and decide at first instance comes under the Original Jurisdiction of the High Court. These are as follows

(a) Settle disputes relating to State revenue and its collection.

(b) Cases regarding wills, divorce, marriage, company law and contempt of court to interpret the Constitution.

(c) Enjoys Original Jurisdiction for the enforcement of the Fundamental Rights.

(iii) Lok Adalat means people's court. These courts provide quick and inexpensive justice to those, who are not in a position to bear the cost of legal proceedings.

Three advantages of Lok Adalats are as follows

(i) Lok Adalats work on the spirit of compromise and understanding. As a result, both the parties feel satisfied.

(ii) Lok Adalats deliver fast and inexpensive justice.

(iii) Lok Adalats reduce the workload of other courts.

5. With reference to our judiciary, discuss the following questions.

(i) Norms governing the transfer of a Judge.

(ii) What do we mean when we refer to the High Court as a 'Court of Record'?

(iii) Name the writs that the High Courts are empowered to issue.

(iv) What is meant by the advisory jurisdiction of the High Court? **[2015]**

Ans. (i) The President can transfer a Judge from one High Court to another after the fulfilment of the following norms

- Orders for transfer can be issued only after consulting the Chief Justice of India.
- The Chief Justice of India must make recommendation only after consulting 4 seniormost Judges of the Supreme Court and the Chief Justice of the 2 High Courts (1 from which the Judge is being transferred and the other receiving him).
- When a Judge has been transferred, he/she shall be entitled to compensatory allowance in addition to his/her salary.

(ii) Refer to chapter theory on page no. 64.

(iii) The Constitution of India empowers in Article 226 that a High Court can issue writs including Habeas Corpus, Mandamus, Certiorari, Prohibition and Quo-Warranto. These writs are issued for enforcement of the Fundamental Rights of the citizens and advisory for any other purpose.

(iv) According to the advisory jurisdiction, the High Court can advice the Governor in any cases related to the governmental departments and legislature if he/she seeks the advice of High Court on constitutional as well as on other matters of law. But its advice is not binding on the agency seeking such advice.

6. The Subordinate Courts are so called because of their subordination to the High Court. With reference to this answer the following questions.

(i) Mention the qualifications needed for a person to be appointed as a District Judge.

(ii) Who administers the appointment of District Judge? What role does he play?

(iii) Difference between Court of the District Judge and Sessions Judge.

(iv) Mention functions of any two Revenue Courts.

Ans. (i) Refer to chapter theory page no. 65.

(ii) The appointment of District Judge in a state is made by Governor of the state in consultation with the Chief Justice of the concerned High Court of the state.

The District Judge is the highest authority in the district. He/She posses original as well as appellate jurisdiction in both civil as well as criminal matters.

In addition to this, District Judge exercises both the judicial and administrative powers.

(iii) The differences between Court of the District Judge and Sessions Court are

Court of the District Judge	Sessions Court
It is the highest Civil Court of the district.	It is the highest Criminal Court of the district.
It is presided by a District Judge.	It is presided by a Sessions Judge.
The District Judge and the additional District Judges are appointed by the Governor in consultation with the Chief Justice of the High Court of the concerned state.	The Sessions Judge and the additional Sessions Judges are appointed by the Governor in consultation with Chief Justice of concerned High Court.

(iv) Functions of Revenue Courts are

(a) **Commissioners Court** It deals with the assessment and collection of revenues of all districts in particulars division.

(b) **Tehsildar's Court** It deals with the collection of the revenue and property taxes as assessed by the Niab Tehsildars.

7. Lok Adalat roughly means 'People's Court'. In this context, answer the following questions.

(i) (a) What is meaning of the Lok Adalat?

(b) Briefly explain the scope of Lok Adalat.

(ii) State any three advantages of the Lok Adalat. **[2012]**

(iii) Write any two functions of Lok Adalat. State any two types of Lok Adalts.

Ans. (i) (a) Refer to chapter theory page no. 66.

(b) Lok Adalats are becoming popular as the government departments have began to hold Lok Adalats for solving hundreds of cases in a single day. It is required that Lok Adalats are organised more frequently and their jurisdiction must expand as many cases are pending in different courts in India.

(ii) Refer to Structured Question 4(iii).

(iii) The functions of Lok Adalats are

(a) The Lok Adalat resolves disputes related to matters which are not very complicated in nature.

(b) The Judges of these courts are actually counsellors. These adalats are assisted by Legal Aid Committee and Social Action Group, which advise the people about legal matters and help them to solve the cases by mutual participation.

The types of Lok Adalats are

(a) **National Lok Adalats** These Lok Adalats are held at regular intervals. Civil cases, matrimonial cases, MACT (Motor Accident Claims Tribunals) cases and petty offence cases are mainly referred to National Lok Adalats.

(b) **Permanent Lok Adalats** These are organised under Section 22-B of the Legal Services Authorities Act, 1987. These Lok Adalats include a Chairman and two members for providing compulsory pre-litigative mechanism for conciliation and settlement of cases relating to Public Utility Services like transport, postal, telegraph, etc.

Chapter Assessment

Section-I

Multiple Choice Questions

1. Who administers the oath of Judge of the High Court?
   (a) The President
   (b) The Governor
   (c) The Chief Justice of India
   (d) The retired Judge of High Court
2. In India, the first impeachment motion was passed against the Judge of High Court in ....
   (a) 2007 (b) 2008
   (c) 2011 (d) 2017
3. Which one is advantage of Lok Adalat?
   (a) It delivers fast and inexpensive justice
   (b) It reduces workload of other courts
   (c) It promote social justice
   (d) All of the above
4. Replace the underlined word to correct the statement. Original Jurisdiction means that a High Court has power to hear appeals against the judgement of Subordinate Court.
   (a) Appellate Jurisdiction
   (b) Supervisory Jurisdiction
   (c) Advisory Jurisdiction
   (d) Revisory Jurisdictions
5. Complete the given analogy.
   Civil Court : Marriage :: Criminal Court : ?
   (a) Divorce
   (b) Money Transaction
   (c) Arbitration
   (d) Robbery

Section-II

Very Short Questions

1. What is the composition of High Court?
2. What is the maximum tenure of a High Court Judge?
3. To whom does the High Court Judge address his / her resignation?
4. What is the role of the Chief Justice of India in transfer of the High Court Judge?
5. Mention one difference between Mandamus and Prohibition writs.
6. Name one case in which Revisory Jurisdiction is applicable.
7. What is the criterion to reappoint a retired Judge for a temporary period in a High Court?
8. Who appoints and gives promotion to District judges?
9. Name one measure in which the independence of High Court is ensured.
10. By which act Lok Adalat was setup?

Structured Questions

1. With reference to the functions of High Court, explain briefly the following questions.
   (i) High Court's power of superintendence.
   (ii) High Court's power of issuing writs.
   (iii) High Courts control over lower courts.
   (iv) Revisory Jurisdiction of High Court
2. With reference to the Subordinate Courts, briefly describe the following questions.
   (i) The Court of a District Judge
   (ii) Munsiff 's Court
   (iii) Courts of Session Judge and Courts of Civil Judge
3. With reference to the lower courts under the jurisdiction of the High Court, answer the following questions.
   (i) At the level of a district, which courts hear the civil and criminal matters?
   (ii) What are the differences between the District Court and Sessions Court?
   (iii) Briefly explain Board of Revenue.
   (iv) Briefly explain Commissioner's Court.

All in One®

History

CHAPTER
01

The First War of Independence (1857)

SYLLABUS

The First War of Independence Only the causes (political, socio-religious, economic and military) and Consequences will be tested. (The events, however, need to be mentioned in order to maintain continuity and for a more comprehensive understanding).

The Revolt of 1857 was widely considered as the beginning of the India's struggle for independence. By 1856, people's dissatisfaction against the East India Company's economic exploitation and unjust administrative policy gained strength. This dissatisfaction led to a revolution which is known as the **Revolt of 1857** in history.

The war was led by millions of peasants, artisans, soldiers, rebels, etc which distressed the British empire. Some Indian nationalists, like VD Savarkar described it as 'a Planned War of National Independence' and 'as the First War of Indian Independence'.

Causes of the First War of Independence

According to some Anglo-Indian writers, the most important causes of Revolt of 1857 were the military grievances and greased cartridge affair. But modern historians think that these are not the most important causes.

The causes of the revolt arised in the last 100 years of British rule, from the Battle of Plassey (June, 1757) to the rebellion of Mangal Pandey (March, 1857).

The possible causes according to modern historians are

- The exploitation and administrative changes done by the British adversely affected all the sections of Indian society.
- In the Indian society, many changes took place like the power of ruling classes were dispossessed, the peasantry was deprived of its land rights and the artisans lost their livelihood.
- People belonging from middle and upper-classes of Indian society, especially in Northern parts of India, were annoyed because of not getting well-paid higher posts in the British administration. As the Indian rulers and zamindars had lost their authority, they were not able to provide patronage to priests and scholars, who also lost their livelihood.
- The Indian soldiers were also facing severe discrimination by the British officers, as they were getting low salaries, hard life and the ill-treatment.

Political Causes

1. Policy of Expansion and Annexation

After the Battle of Plassey June 1757, the East India Company tried to expand its territorial power. To achieve this aim, the British applied following four ways

(i) By Outright Wars

The British waged (fought) many wars in order to expand their territorial power and safeguard their economic and political interests in the country.

For example,

- By the Battle of Buxar (1764), the British captured Bengal, Bihar and Odisha.
- By the Anglo-Mysore Wars (1767 to 1799), they annexed most of the territories of the Mysore State.
- By third Anglo-Maratha War (1817-18), the British acquired the Peshwa's entire dominions and all the Maratha territory which lie North and South of the Narmada River.
- By the second Anglo-Sikh War, the British annexed the Punjab in 1849.
- From 1823 to 1856, the British further annexed Sindh, Assam, Arakan and Tenasserim and Pegu in Myanmar through wars.

(ii) By Subsidiary Alliance

Subsidiary Alliance was introduced by Lord Wellesley. It was actually an agreement between the British East India Company and the Indian Princely States through which these states lost their sovereignty to the British.

There were many conditions to accept the Alliance. If any Indian ruler wanted to accept the Subsidiary Alliance then it had to

- accept the British as the supreme power.
- surrender its foreign relations to the East India Company and agree that it would not enter into any alliance with any other power and would not wage wars.
- accept a British resident at their headquarters and agreed not to appoint any European in their service without consulting the British East India Company.
- agree to maintain British troops at their own cost.

The **Nawab of Awadh** (Oudh) in 1765 was the first to accept the Subsidiary Alliance on the conditions that the British Company would defend the frontiers of Awadh and the Nawab of Awadh would pay for the expenses of such defence.

The other states who accepted Subsidiary Alliance were the Nizam of Hyderabad, the ruler of Mysore, the Raja of Tanjore, the Sindhia, the Rajput states of Jodhpur, Jaipur, Macheri, Bundi and the ruler of Bharatpur.

(iii) By Doctrine of Lapse

According to this Doctrine, if a ruler died without a male heir to succeed him, then the state would be annexed to the British Empire. By applying the Doctrine of Lapse, Lord Dalhousie, the Governor-General of India annexed many Indian States like **Satara**, **Jhansi**, **Jaitpur**, **Sambalpur**, **Udaipur** and **Nagpur**.

(iv) By Imposing the Pretext of Misrule

Lord Dalhousie annexed Awadh to the British territory under the pretext (excuse) that state of Awadh was not properly governed. He justified annexation by saying 'it is for the good governance of the people'. However, the people of Awadh had to suffer many hardships due to this such as

- People of Awadh were forced to pay higher land revenue and additional taxes on food, houses and ferries.
- The annexation left many nobles, officials and soldiers of Awadh unemployed.
- The British also seized the estates of the taluqdars or zamindars.
- There were around 75000 soldiers in the company who were from Awadh. Their financial position got affected as they had to pay higher taxes on the land that their families had in Awadh.

Due to these hardships and the humiliation of the Nawab of Awadh, the people of Awadh joined the uprising in 1857.

2. Disrespect Shown to Bahadur Shah

Bahadur Shah Zafar was the Mughal ruler who received pension from the British and was under the protection of the company. Lord Dalhousie announced in 1849, that successors of Bahadur Shah Zafar would not be allowed to use the Red Fort as their palace. The Company also removed his name from the minted coins.

In 1856, Lord Canning announced that after the death of Bahadur Shah, his successors would not be allowed to attach imperial titles to their names and would be known as princes only. These policies of British dissatisfied Zeenat Mahal, wife of Bahadur Shah and also hurt the feelings of Muslims.

3. Disrespect Shown to Nana Sahib and Rani Laxmi Bai

Nana Sahib was the adopted son of Baji Rao II, the last Peshwa. After the death of Baji Rao, the British refused to recognise Nana Sahib as the ruler of Marathas and did not grant the pension to Nana Sahib.

Baji Rao-II Nana Sahib Rani Laxmi Bai

Nana Sahib was forced to live at Kanpur. This enraged the Marathas greatly. Nana Sahib travelled between Delhi and Lucknow to gather support for the movement.

There was a common legitimate practice of Indian kings to adopt an heir if the king had no son. But the Rani of Jhansi, **Laxmi Bai** was not allowed to adopt a son after the death of her husband, Raja Gangadhar Rao Newalkar. Due to this reason, Rani Laxmi Bai became bitter enemy of the British.

Disbanding the Armies of the Annexed States

The armies of all the states which were annexed by the British were disbanded. The soldiers of such disbanded armies lost their jobs and means of livelihood. They together with their families blamed the Company for their misfortune and were determined to take revenge.

Corrupt and Inefficient Administration

The British administration was corrupt and inefficient. The Britishers had a feeling of superiority as they treated Indians badly and always tried to humiliate them. The main aim of the Britishers was to enrich themselves at the cost of native people. This created bitterness among the Indians.

Distant Sovereignty of the British

The British Government was ruling India from England, which was a distance of thousands of miles. The earlier rulers like the Mughals came from thousands of miles in India, settled here and spent the collected revenues in the country only. But the British Government who ruled from England i.e. outside the country, was responsible for the draining of wealth of India and it did not utilise India's wealth for the welfare of Indian people. This act enraged the Indians.

Socio-Religious Causes

Changes in Social Customs

The British brought about several social reforms which affected the religious traditions of the Indians. These were

- The practice of *Sati* was made illegal and punishable by law (1829).
- Infanticide and polygamy were prohibited.
- Remarriage of widow was allowed through Widow Remarriage Act (1856).

Such reforms were strongly advocated by Indian reformers like Raja Ram Mohan Roy, Swami Dayanand Saraswati and others. But some people thought that the British introduced these reforms to fulfil their own interest.

Activities of Missionaries

The British Government indirectly supported some activities of the **missionaries**[1]. Earlier in 18th century, British had a friendly attitude towards Indian religions but from 19th century this attitude changed in 1813.

The British started to interfere in local religious and social customs so the numbers and activities of the Christian missionaries increased. As a result of this, Indians thought the missionaries would convert them to Christianity with government's support.

Suspicions about Modern Innovations

The introduction of railways and telegraphs by the British had created suspicion and fear in the minds of Indians. **Orthodox**[2] Indians felt humiliated to share seats in railway compartments with other backward classes.

Rumours were spread that telegraph poles were made to hang people who would oppose British rule in India. These modern innovations threatened the old social order and produced unrest in society.

Fears Generated by Western Education

In the 19th century, the British introduced Western education in India. They established different schools and the Christian missionaries played a significant role in it.

The Western education started at various places like in 1829, an English class was started by the Bengal Government in the Calcutta Madrasa, which was a Muslim institution. After this English classes were started in Banaras Sanskrit College.

1 **Missionary** A person who is sent to a foreign country to teach people about Christianity.
2 **Orthodox** Following closely the traditional beliefs and practices of religion.

The Western education reduced the importance of education taught by the *Pandits* and *Maulvis* who were responsible for the traditional education of India. Common people started thinking that the aim of Western education was not to promote Science and Literature, but to encourage the students to become Christians.

Taxation on Religious Places

The British Government introduced tax on temples and mosques. Earlier, these places were exempted from taxation in the reign of other rulers. This hurt the religious sentiments of the people.

Introduction of New Laws

The **Religious Disabilities Act** of 1850 was enacted which changed the Hindu Law of Property. According to this act, a person was required to convert from Hinduism to other religion to inherit his father's property. The orthodox Indians began to feel that this act was encouraging conversion to Christianity.

Racial Discrimination Policy

The British used a policy of racial discrimination with the Indians. They were very rude and arrogant towards the Indians. They considered the Muslims cruel and unfaithful. Thus, they usually insulted Indians and even rulers.

Oppression of the Poor

The British judicial system gave right to the rich British officials to oppress the poor, if they fail to pay their high rents, land revenue and interest on debt. Indian cultivators were the main victims of such cruelty. Thus, this kind of oppressive behaviour increased poverty rate in India and led to the uprising of 1857.

Check Your LEARNING...

1. Who participated in the First War of Independence in India?
2. The Battle of Plassey took place in which year?
3. Through which war the British acquired the Peshwa's entire dominions in India?
4. Explain how activities of missionaries created the negative impact on Indians.

Economic Causes

Exploitation of Economic Resources

The East India Company exploited the economic resources of India at the expense of the people of India in the following ways

- The Company purchased textiles, indigo, spices, tea, raw cotton, raw silk and foodgrains from India at cheaper rates and sold them abroad at extremely high prices.
- India was forced to export raw materials like raw cotton and raw silk, plantation products like indigo and tea and foodgrains, at cheaper rates.
- India was forced to buy the readymade British goods either duty-free or at nominal duty rates while high import duties were imposed on Indian products in England.

Collapse of Handicrafts and Cottage Industries

As a result of the British policy like heavy duties on Indian silk and cotton textiles and the competition with cheaper and machine made British products, Indian handicrafts and cottage industries collapsed. Thousands of craftsmen and artisans became jobless. By the middle of the 19th century, export of cotton and silk goods from India completely stopped.

When traditional patrons and buyers like Indian rulers and zamindars disappeared, the misery of the artisans further increased and the art of spinning and weaving became extinct. So, the manufacturers of silk and cotton goods began to look for other means of livelihood.

Drain of Wealth

The transfer of resources from India to England for which India did not get anything in return or get small part of return, was called the Drain of Wealth.

Before the Battle of Plassey (1757), the European traders used to buy Indian cotton and silk goods through gold. However, after gaining supremacy over Bengal, the British started to purchase raw material from the surplus revenues of Bengal and profits from duty-free inland-trade instead of gold.

This led to the draining of wealth, resources and raw materials of India by the hands of the British. This drain included the incomes, salaries and savings of Britishers, their expenditure in India on the purchase of military goods, interest on debts, etc.

Economic Decline of Peasantry

The peasants were dissatisfied with the revenue policy of the British. They had to bear the heavy burden of taxes to provide money for the trade and for the administrative and war expenditure of the Company.

The increased tax burden forced many peasants into indebtedness and sometimes they sold their lands and became unemployed.

The traditional zamindars who were sympathetic to the peasant class were replaced by merchants and moneylenders.

They forcefully collected rent from the peasants and often removed their tenants in case of non-payment.

Decline of Landed Aristocracy

During the British period, the landed aristocracy included the taluqdars and the hereditary landlords. According to **Inam Commission** (1852), their lands were seized if they failed to produce evidence like title–deeds by which they had right to own the land.

These seized lands were given to the highest bidders like merchants and moneylenders who had no concern for the tenants and exploited them badly. Thus, this led the landed aristocracy to poverty.

Inhuman Treatment of Indigo Cultivators

Indigo trade was highly profitable to the British but indigo cultivators were inhumanly treated by the British officials. The peasants were not allowed to plant other crops except indigo. If they plant other crops, the British planters used to destroy the crops and punish the peasants by seizing their cattle.

Unemployment

Many civil and military officers and other employees of the states lost their jobs due to Dalhousie's policy of annexation of the native states. The British took the policy to appoint only their countrymen to high posts and deprived the educated Indians. This resulted into bitterness amongst the Indians against the British.

Poverty and Famines

The poverty increased extremely in India due to corrupt administration of the British like economic exploitation, decay of indigenous industries, high taxation, the drain of wealth, etc. Besides these, India was hit by around twelve major and a number of minor famines between 1765 and 1857. These famines were the result of bad administration of the British along with natural calamities like drought etc and British government did nothing for the sake of the people.

Military Causes

Unjust Treatment to Indian Soldiers

The East India Company established the British Empire with the help of Indian soldiers but the British and Indian soldiers were not treated equally.

The Indian soldiers were treated in the following ways

- The British soldiers were paid eight times greater salary than the Indian soldiers.
- The Indian soldiers did not get the opportunity to get higher posts, as these were reserved for people of British origin. They could not rise above the rank of a Subedar. Thus, the future of the Indian soldiers were insecure without chances of promotions.
- The Indian soldiers were not allowed to wear caste or sectarian signs like turbans, beards and the British did not even care about the sentiments of these soldiers.

General Service Enlistment Act, 1856

The General Service Enlistment Act was passed in 1856, by the British Government.

According to this Act, Indian soldiers could be sent overseas on duty. This act hurt the religious sentiments of the Indian soldiers as crossing the sea was a religious **taboo**[3] for Indians.

Huge Strength of Indian Soldiers

In 1857, there were approximately 40,000 British and 2 lakh Indian soldiers in the army. The numerical strength of the Indian soldiers gave them courage to revolt against the British.

Poor Performance of British Army

The British army suffered disappointments in the First Afghan War (1838-42), in the Punjab Wars (1845-49) and in the Crimean War (1854-56). During Santhal rebellion (1855-56), Santhals of Bihar and Bengal drove away the rule of British temporarily from their area.

These events convinced the Indian soldiers that British could also be defeated and inspired them to declare war against the British.

Deprivation of Allowances

Indian sepoys were ill-treated and sent to areas away from their homes without any extra payment and additional *Bhatta* (Foreign Service Allowance).

Besides this, the Post Office Act of 1854, removed the privilege of free postage which was earlier given to sepoys.

Faulty Distribution of Troops

Delhi and Allahabad were strategically important places of the British but these places were handled alone by the Indian soldiers.

---

3 **Taboo** A cultural or religious custom that does not allow people to do, use or talk about a particular thing as people find it offensive or embarrassing.

On the other side, England was busy in several wars outside India. This gave a chance to Indian soldiers to eliminate the British from India.

The Immediate Cause

In 1856, it was decided by the higher authorities of the British to launch new 'Enfield rifle' in place of old fashioned musket (also known as 'Brown Bess rifle'). The loading process of the new Enfield rifle involved the use of mouth and biting off the top greased paper with the teeth.

A rumour was spread in Bengal regiments in January 1857, that the new Enfield rifles had the fat of cow or pig which was prohibited in both Hindu and Muslims religions.

After believing on this rumour, the Hindu and the Muslim soldiers refused to use these cartridges and started the Revolt of 1857.

Check Your LEARNING...

1. Surplus revenues of which region was used by the British to purchase raw material for the industries in England?
2. Why the peasants were dissatisfied with the Revenue Policy of the British?
3. In which year, Imam Commission was introduced ?
4. Mention any two military causes for the Revolt of 1857.

Beginning of the Revolt of 1857

The Revolt of 1857 first began at Barrackpore, when most of the Indian soldiers refused to use the grease cartridges. A Brahmin soldier of the 34th Native Infantry at Barrackpore, named **Mangal Pandey** led an attack on the military officer of 34th Native Infantry on 29th March, 1857.

After this incident, Mangal Pandey was arrested and hanged on 8th April, 1857. As a result of this, the uprising began in Meerut and spread in other parts of country like Delhi, Kanpur, Lucknow, Jhansi, etc.`

The events in these parts of country happened in the following ways

Meerut

- On 8th May, 1857 new cartridges were given to the Indian sepoys in Meerut. Some sepoys refused to touch the cartridge.
- On 10th May, the sepoys broke out in open rebellion, shot their officers and released their fellow sepoys from the prison.

Delhi

- On 12th May, 1857, Delhi was seized by the rebels. The rebels killed thousands of British soldiers and captured Delhi. The loss of Delhi was serious loss of prestige to the English.
- The British military officer Sir John Nicholson, captured Delhi with the help of the loyal Sikh soldiers. The Mughal Emperor **Bahadur Shah Zafar** was imprisoned with his two sons. His sons were shot dead in front of him and he was given life imprisonment and deported to Yangon in Myanmar where he died in the year 1862.

Lucknow

- On 30th May, 1857, the rebellion broke out at Lucknow which was led by **Begum Hazrat Mahal**, the wife of Nawab of Awadh.
- The British military officer Sir Henry Lawrence and many other British soldiers took refuge in the **residency**[4]. Later, the residency was attacked by the Indian rebels and Sir Henry Lawrence and many other British soldiers were killed.
- In November 1857, Sir Colin Campbell reached Lucknow and expelled Europeans. He defeated the Indian soldiers and recaptured Lucknow in March, 1858, but **guerilla activity**[5] continued till September of the same year.

Kanpur

- On 5th June, 1857, Kanpur was lost by the British. Here the war was led by **Nana Sahib**, the adopted son of Peshwa Baji Rao II. Nana Sahib was joined by his able and experienced Lieutenant **Tantia Tope**.
- On 27th June, 1857 General Sir Hugh Wheeler surrendered and some Europeans, men, women and children were killed by the rebels.
- The British defeated Nana Sahib in December, 1857. Nana Sahib fled to Nepal and Tantia Tope escaped and joined the Rani of Jhansi.

Central India (Jhansi and Gwalior)

- In Central India, Indian soldiers had two great leaders **Rani Laxmi Bai** of Jhansi and Tantia Tope. In the beginning of June, 1857, the British troops at Jhansi revolt against Rani Laxmi Bai, the widow of the late Raja Gangadhar Rao.
- On 3rd April, 1858, the British military officer Sir Hugh Rose captured Jhansi by assault due to which Rani and Tantia Tope marched towards Gwalior and occupied Gwalior. Sir Hugh Rose advanced towards Gwalior and defeated the Indian troops.

4 **Residency** The official house of somebody.
5 **Guerilla activity** The fight organised in an informal way and without official permission or approval.

- Rani died on 17th June, 1858 at Gwalior but Tantia Tope managed to escape. However in 1859, Tantia was betrayed by Gwalior Chief Man Singh and hanged on 18th April, 1859.

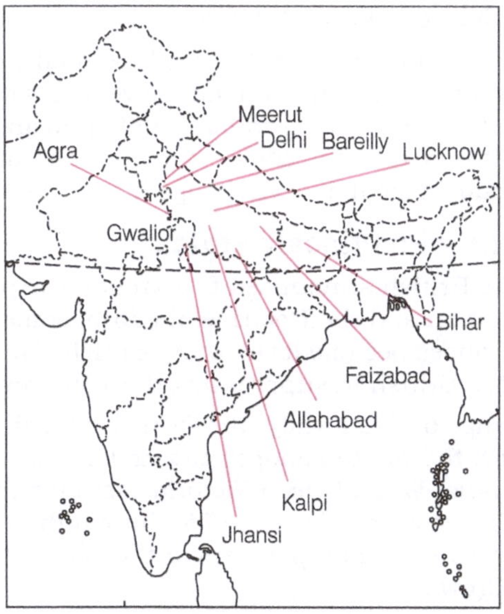

Centres of Revolt of 1857

Other Important Centres

- **Bareilly** At Bareilly, **Khan Bahadur Khan** Rohilla, a descendant of the former ruler of Rohilkhand had proclaimed himself the Nawab Nazim and led the movement.
- **Bihar** In Bihar, the movement was led by **Kunwar Singh**, a *zamindar* of Jagdishpur, who fought against the British.
- **Faizabad** In Faizabad, the revolt was led by **Maulvi Ahmadullah Shah**, a native of Madras. He encouraged the Muslim community against the British rule. Later, he was captured and put to death by the British.
- **Other Centers** Moreover Bengal, Rohilkhand, Bundelkhand, Central India and East Punjab also rose against the colonial power. However, by July 1858, the **rebellion**[6] had been almost completely suppressed by the British.

Consequences of the First War of Independence

The uprising of 1857 was suppressed completely, but this incident led far reaching effects on the socio-political life of India.

These effects or consequences of the revolt were

End of the Company's Rule

The most significant result of the Revolt of 1857 was that, the hundred years of Company's rule in India came to an end. Now, India was directly ruled by the Queen and the British Parliament. This was done by the **Government of India Act** of 1858. Its provisions were

- This act abolished the Board of Control and Court of Directors of the Company and the responsibility of the Government of India was passed on to a separate minister, who was known as the Secretary of state for India.
- The Governor General was made the Viceroy, who dealt with the Nawabs, the Rajas and other native Princes. Lord Canning was declared as the first Viceroy of India.
- The appointments to the Civil Services were to be made by open competition under the rule made by the Secretary of state.

Queen Victoria's Proclamation

The Queen's **proclamation**[7] regarding the transfer of governance from the East India Company to the British Crown was announced by **Lord Canning** on 1st November, 1858 at Allahabad. The proclamation promised the following

- Treat all subjects i.e. Indians and Europeans as equal (education and ability would be the basis of all appointments).
- Follow a policy of non-intervention in social and religious matters of Indians.
- A general pardon was granted to all those who laid down arms by 2nd January, 1859, except those who were found guilty of murder of British subjects.
- It promised that the British Crown would do, its best to develop the industries in India.
- To promote works of public utility in the country for the material as well as the moral progress of the people.

Abolition of Peshwaship and the Mughals

The war ended the Peshwaship and the Mughal rule. Nana Sahib, the last Peshwa who had fled to Nepal could not be traced. So, the office of the Peshwa was abolished.

After the revolt, Bahadur Shah was deported to Rangoon, where he died in 1862. Thus, the Mughal dynasty came to an end.

6 **Rebellion** An attempt by some of the people in a country to change their government.

7 **Proclamation** An official statement about something important that is made to the public.

Policy of Divide and Rule

After 1858, the British continued to follow the policy of 'Divide and Rule' in which they turned Hindus against the Muslims. This policy also separated people from their rulers for the special protections and concessions given to the rulers. The British also gave government services as attractions to create a split among educated Indians on religious basis. The policy of 'Divide and Rule' ultimately encouraged the partition of India.

Reorganisation of the Army

The Indian army was reorganised after the revolt in the following ways

- The proportion of the Europeans to Indians in the army was raised.
- Artillery and other effective weapons of war were placed exclusively under the charge of the Europeans.
- To curb nationalism, Indian soldiers of different communities, castes and religions were all mixed up and they were kept away in remote places.
- Indian soldiers were not provided newspapers, journals and nationalist publications to keep them separated from the life of the rest of the population.
- The positions of the European troops were kept in key geographical and military areas.
- The Indian sepoys faced discrimination on the basis of caste, region and religion in times of the recruitment process in the army.

Economic Exploitation

After the war, the economic exploitation of India by the British became more prominent. India became 'dumping ground of British manufacturers'.

The colonial power now started to misuse their political power for their economic interests. For example,

- India was used by the British as a colonial economy where raw materials were exported and finished goods were sold.
- The draining of wealth continued by high salaries, allowances of the Secretary of state and members of the Indian Council, the Civil servants and Military officers.
- The peasants were still under the grave condition. Against the oppressive policy of the British, the Indigo peasants of Bihar revolted in 1866-68.
- Indian rural artisan industries like handicrafts, cottage industries, etc collapsed.
- Heavy interests and dividends had to be paid by the Indians on the British capital invested in India. The British invested in railways, plantations, shipping, etc.

Rise of Nationalism in India

The war was a failure but it roused national feelings. It paved the way for the national movement and remained as a shining example of nationalism to the people. It served as the source of inspiration and also became a symbol of challenge for the Indians.

Relations with Princely States

When the British announced to abandon the policy of annexation and the Doctrine of Lapse, some of the Indian Princes became loyal to the British. They also helped the British in suppressing the 1857 revolt.

In exchange of this loyalty, the British rewarded them with the right to adopt heirs and continue their rule in India. When Queen Victoria assumed the title of the 'Empress of India' in 1876, these Indian Princes became junior partners or the agents of the British Crown.

Racial Antagonism

The British considered themselves racially superior over Indians. For this reason, they maintained a social distance from the Indian people. Thus, the good places in railway compartments, parks, hotels, clubs, etc were reserved for the Britishers or Europeans only. The British considered the Indians as unworthy of trust and subjected them to insults and humiliation.

Foreign Policy

The Foreign Policy of India was made to fulfill the interests of the British Government only. The two aims of the policy were

(i) To protect Indian Empire of the British.
(ii) To expand the British economic and commercial interests in Asia and Africa.

The cost of implementation of these policies was borne by the Indians. For example, during the times of war with Nepal and Burma (Myanmar), the Indian soldiers had to shed their blood and the Indian taxpayers had to meet the heavy cost of the war.

Check Your LEARNING...

1. When was Delhi seized by the rebels?
2. Who led the rebellion at Bareilly?
3. By which act the Company rule in India came to an end?
4. Where was the Queen Victoria's proclamation announced?
5. What do you mean by the policy of 'Divide and Rule'?

Time Line

Year	Important Events
Feb 26th, 1857	The Indian soldiers 34th Native Infantry at Barrackpore refused to use the grease cartridges.
23rd June, 1757	The Battle of Plassey
1856	General Service Enlistment Act
13th February, 1856	Lord Dalhousie annexed Awadh
29th March, 1857	Mangal Pandey refused to use cartridge of the Enfield rifle
8th April, 1857	Mangal Pandey was hanged
9th May, 1857	Resentment by 85 sepoys of the third Cavalry at Meerut.
10th May, 1857	The Indian sepoys at Meerut broke into war
11th-30th May, 1857	Outbreaks in Delhi, Ferozpur, Bombay, Bareilly, Aligarh, Etawah, Bulandshahar, Lucknow. The Mughal Emperor proclaimed as the Emperor of India.
12th May, 1857	Delhi was seized by the rebels
June, 1857	Uprising at Gwalior, Bharatpur, Jhansi, Allahabad, Faizabad.
21st September, 1857	Sir John Nicholson recaptured Delhi with the help of loyal Sikh soldiers
November, 1857	Defeat of the British at Kanpur.
March, 1858	Recapture of Lucknow by the British
17th June, 1858	Rani Laxmi Bai died at the battle field
1st November, 1858	Queen Victoria's proclamation was announced by Lord Canning
18th April, 1859	Tantia Tope was hanged
7th November, 1862	Bahadur Shah Zafar died

QUiCK Revision

- The main causes of the First War of Independence were political causes, economic causes, religious causes and military causes.
- Political causes were policy of annexation, the annexation of Awadh, disrespect shown to Bahadur Shah, disrespect shown to Nana Sahib and Rani Laxmi Bai, disbanding the armies of the annexed states, corrupt and inefficient administration and absentee sovereignty of the British.
- Social and religious causes were social reforms, activities of missionaries, suspicions about modern innovations, racial discrimination policy, oppression of the poor, fears generated by Western education, taxation on religious places and introduction of new laws.
- Economic causes were exploitation of economic resources of India, collapse of handicrafts and cottage industries, drain of wealth, economic decline of peasantry, decline of landed aristocracy, unemployment, poverty, famine and inhuman treatment of Indigo cultivators.
- Military causes were unjust treatment to Indian soldiers, General Services Enlistment Act, numerical strength of Indian soldiers in the army, poor performance of British troops, deprivation of allowances and faulty distribution of troops.
- The introduction of new Enfield rifle were regarded as the immediate cause of the uprising.
- In 1857, a new Enfield rifle was introduced in the army. A rumour spread that the cartridges were greased with fat of cows and pigs.
- The trouble first began at Barrackpore when a soldier named Mangal Pandey refused to use this cartridge.
- Within a month of Barrackpore incident, the revolt spread in Meerut, Delhi, Kanpur, Lucknow, Jhansi and other places.
- Other important centers of the revolt were Bareilly, Bihar, Faizabad, etc.
- Moreover, it spread in Bengal, Rohilkhand, Bundelkhand, Central India and East Punjab.
- By June, 1858, the revolt had been almost completely suppressed.
- The consequences of the war were end of the Company's rule, Queen Victoria's proclamation, religious freedom, abolition of Peshwaship and Mughals policy of Divide and Rule, reorganisation of the army, economic exploitation, rise of nationalism, relations with Princely States, racial antagonism and foreign policy.

Chapter Practice

Section-I

Multiple Choice Questions

1. The book 'The Indian War of Independence 1857' is written by ....
   (a) Veer Savarkar
   (b) Bal Gangadhar Tilak
   (c) Gopal Krishna Gokhale
   (d) Bankim Chandra Chatterjee

Ans. (a) Veer Savarkar

2. Which statement does not apply to the Subsidiary Alliance?
   (a) The kings virtually lost their powers.
   (b) It was introduced by Lord Dalhousie.
   (c) The kings had to maintain the British army at their cost.
   (d) They had a British resident in their court.

Ans. (b) It was introduced by Lord Dalhousie.

3. .... was denied pension under the Doctrine of Lapse.
   (a) Zeenat Mahal (b) Baji Rao II
   (c) Bahadhur Shah Zafar (d) Nana Saheb

Ans. (d) Nana Saheb

4. The General Service Enlistment Act implied that soldiers
   (a) would not be given promotions.
   (b) would have to travel overseas to fight.
   (c) would be given less salaries.
   (d) would not be given extra allowance.

Ans. (b) would have to travel overseas to fight.

5. Rani Laxmi Bai was the Queen of ....
   (a) Jhansi (b) Gwalior (c) Awadh (d) Bengal

Ans. (a) Jhansi

6. In 1857, the Hindu and Muslim soldiers refused to use the new cartridges because
   (a) they were greased with cow and pig fat.
   (b) they were paid less salaries.
   (c) they were forced to go abroad on duty.
   (d) they were ill fed.

Ans. (a) they were greased with cow and pig fat.

7. To which regiment did Mangal Pandey belong?
   (a) 34th Native Infantry
   (b) 7th Oudh Regiment
   (c) 19th Native Infantry
   (d) Madras Regiment

Ans. (a) 34th Native Infantry

8. Who was the Governor-General during the time of Sepoy Mutiny?
   (a) Lord Dalhousie (b) Lord Ripon
   (c) Lord Canning (d) Lord Reading

Ans. (c) Lord Canning

9. Who of the following was neither captured nor killed by the British?
   (a) Tantiya Tope (b) Nana Sahib
   (c) Mangal Pandey (d) Jhansi Laxmi Bai

Ans. (b) Nana Sahib

10. Complete the given analogy.
    1757 : The Battle of Plassey : : ? : Battle of Buxar
    (a) 1750 (b) 1764
    (c) 1857 (d) 1855

Ans. (b) 1764

11. Complete the given analogy.
    Huge Rose : Jhansi :: Captain Nicholson : ?
    (a) Meerut (b) Kanpur
    (c) Patna (d) Delhi

Ans. (d) Delhi

12. Complete the given analogy.
    1857 : First War of Independence :: 1858 : ?
    (a) End of the rule of British East India Company
    (b) Freedom from Europeans
    (c) Accession of Mughal Ruler on the throne
    (d) End of Racial Discriminational

Ans. (a) End of the rule of British East India Company

13. Replace the underlined word to correct the statement.
    The confiscation of lands during 1857 took place by the provisions of the <u>Doctrine of Lapse.</u>
    (a) Inam Commission
    (b) General Service Enlistment Act
    (c) Ryotwari System
    (d) Mahalwari System

Ans. (a) Inam Commission

14. Replace the underlined word to correct the statement.
    The date to start the uprising was set for <u>31st August, 1859.</u>
    (a) 31st May, 1857
    (b) 1st April, 1858
    (c) 3rd November, 1857
    (d) 4th June, 1858

Ans. (a) 31st May, 1857

15. Complete the following table.

Mughal Emperor of India during 1857	Bahadur Shah Zafar
Wife of Mughal Emperor Bahadur Shah Zafar	?

(a) Zeenat Mahal (b) Rani Laxmi Bai
(c) Begum Hazrat Mahal (d) None of these

Ans. (a) Zeenat Mahal

16. Which of the following is a political cause of uprising of 1857?
(i) Disrespect shown to Nana Sahib and Rani Laxmi Bai
(ii) Disbanding the Armies of the annexed states
(iii) Corrupt and Inefficient Administration
(iv) Absentee Sovereignty of the British

Codes
(a) Only (i) (b) Only (ii)
(c) Both (ii) and (iv) (d) All of these

Ans. (d) All of these

17. Which of the following is a socio-religious cause of the Revolt of 1857?
(i) Apprehensions about Modern Innovations
(ii) Fears generated by the Western Education
(iii) Introduction of New Laws
(iv) Racial Discrimination Policy

Codes
(a) Only (i) (b) Only (ii)
(c) Both (iii) and (iv) (d) All of these

Ans. (d) All of these

18. Which of the following was not the leader of 1867 revolt?
(i) Tantia Tope
(ii) Begum Hazrat Mahal
(iii) Rani Laxmi Bai
(iv) Subhash Chandra Bose

Codes
(a) Only (i) (b) Both (ii) and (iii)
(c) Only (iv) (d) All of these

Ans. (c) Only (iv)

19. Match the following.

List I		List II	
A.	1856	1.	General Service Enlistment Act
B.	13th February, 1856	2.	Lord Dalhousie annexed Awadh
C.	29th March, 1857	3.	Mangal Pandey refused to use cartridge of the Enfield rifle
D.	8th April, 1857	4.	Mangal Pandey was hanged

Codes

	A	B	C	D		A	B	C	D
(a)	1	2	3	4	(b)	2	1	4	3
(c)	3	4	1	2	(d)	4	3	2	1

Ans. (a)

20. Match the following.

List I		List II	
A.	17th June, 1858	1.	Queen Victoria's proclamation was announced by Lord Canning
B.	1st November, 1858	2.	Rani Laxmi Bai died at the battle field
C.	18th April, 1859	3.	Bahadur Shah Zafar died
D.	7th November, 1862	4.	Tantia Tope was hanged

Codes

	A	B	C	D		A	B	C	D
(a)	1	2	3	4	(b)	2	1	4	3
(c)	3	4	1	2	(d)	4	3	2	1

Ans. (b)

Picture Based Questions

21. Look at the picture given below and answer the questions that follow.

(i) Which of the following personalities is shown in the given picture?
(a) Tantia Tope (b) Akbar-II
(c) Bahadur Shah Zafar (d) Babur

Ans. (c) Bahadur Shah Zafar

(ii) He was the son of which Mughal ruler of India?
(a) Akbar (b) Jahangir (c) Humayun (d) Akbar-II

Ans. (d) Akbar-II

(iii) Who among the following captured Delhi when Bahadur Shah Zafar led the rebels during the 1857?
(a) Sir John Nicholson (b) Sir Henry Lawrence
(c) Lord William Bentinck (d) Sir Colin Campbell

Ans. (a) Sir John Nicholson

(iv) The last Mughal ruler of India died in which year?
(a) 1857 (b) 1858 (c) 1862 (d) 1899

Ans. (c) 1862

22. Look at the picture given below and answer the questions that follow.

(i) Which of the following personalities is shown in the given picture?
(a) Begum Hazrat Mahal (b) Queen Zeenat Mahal
(c) Queen Victoria (d) Rani Laxmi Bai

Ans. (c) Queen Victoria

(ii) In which year she gave a proclamation known as the 'Queen Victoria's proclamation'?
(a) 1899 (b) 1858 (c) 1845 (d) 1865

Ans. (b) 1858

(iii) What was the main objective of 'Queen Victoria's proclamation'?
(a) To disclaim any intention to annex Indian States.
(b) To place the Indian administration under the British Crown.
(c) To regulate East India Company's trade with India.
(d) Both (a) and (b)

Ans. (d) Both (a) and (b)

(iv) The Queen Victoria's proclamation was the result of which major event of India?
(a) Revolt by Indian Masses in 1857
(b) Annexation policy of the Lord Dalhousie
(c) Lapse policy
(d) Outright wars against Indian rulers

Ans. (a) Revolt by Indian Masses in 1857

Passage Based Questions

1. Read the passage given below and answer the questions that follow.

In the earlier periods i.e. before the Battle of Plassey (1757), the European traders used to buy Indian cotton and silk goods through gold. After gaining supremacy of Bengal, the British stopped bringing gold into India. Instead of gold, the British started to purchase raw material for their industries in England from the surplus revenues of Bengal and profits from duty-free inland- trade. It started the draining of wealth, resources and raw materials of India by hands of the British.

In comparison to Indians, the British officials were paid huge salaries, allowances which were sent back to England. This transfer of wealth from India to England, for which India got no proportionate economic return, is called the 'Drain of Wealth'. Besides salaries and allowances, the drain of wealth also includes savings of British officials, the British expenditure in India on the purchase of military goods, and unnecessary expenditure on the army, etc.

(i) Where did the Battle of Plassey took place?
(a) Bengal (b) Bihar
(c) Madhya Pradesh (d) Uttar Pradesh

Ans. (a) Bengal

(ii) The British started to purchase which of the following raw materials for their industries in England?
(a) Raw cotton (b) Raw Silk
(c) Indigo (d) All of these

Ans. (d) All of these

(iii) The Battle of Plassey was fought between .... and Nawab of Bengal.
(a) Dutch (b) British (c) Portuguese (d) French

Ans. (b) British

(iv) Which of the following was/were the significance of Battle of Plassey?
(a) It laid the foundation of British Empire in India.
(b) Ministry of supremacy was established by British in Bengal.
(c) The French settlement was captured in Bengal.
(d) All of the above

Ans. (d) All of the above

2. Read the passage given below and answer the questions that follow.

The nature of the revolt of 1857, can also be understood in the way that it was the First War of Independence because of the following reasons

The revolt of 1857, was the first mass uprising in which most of the sections of Indian society participated against the British which were considered as the common enemy.

The uprising is considered a bridge that led to rise of the modern Indian National Movement. The leaders who sacrificed their lives for the country like Laxmi Bai, Nana Saheb and Mangal Pandey, became a source of inspiration for the people of India to carry out further independence movement.

(i) Identify one positive aspect related to 1857 Revolt.
(a) Lack of Unity and Coordination
(b) First Mass Uprising
(c) All India Movement
(d) Lack of Military Strategy

Ans. (b) First Mass Uprising

(ii) Which of the following statements best explains the nature of the Revolt of 1857?
(a) It was the last effort of the old political order to regain power.
(b) It was a struggle of the common people against the Britishers.
(c) It was an effort to attain independence by the princely rulers.
(d) Both (a) and (c)

Ans. (d) Both (a) and (c)

(iii) How the Revolt of 1857, is considered a modern Indian National Movement? Identify the correct option.
(a) Because it was a major turning point in the history of modern India.
(b) Because it helped the Indians to become aware about their rights.
(c) Both (a) and (b)
(d) Because it helped in unification of India.

Ans. (c) Both (a) and (b)

(iv) Who was Nana Sahib?
(a) He was the adopted son of Baji Rao II, the last Peshwa.
(b) He was the brother of Rani Laxmi Bai.
(c) He was the last ruler of Jhansi.
(d) None of the above

Ans.(a) He was the adopted son of Baji Rao II, the last Peshwa.

3. Read the passage given below and answer the questions that follow

India's First War of Independence, better known as the Indian Rebellion of 1857, began on, 10th May, 1857. The first martyr of the revolt was Mangal Pandey and the war was the result of accumulation of many factors over time. The rebellion of 1857 is considered the first blow that came to shatter the British rule in India. Some epicenters of the revolt were Kanpur, Lucknow, Aligarh, Agra, Delhi and Jhansi. Due to all the epicenters being far from each other, there was a communication gap between the leaders of different parts of India. Due to the rebellion having no central leadership, it got limited to some parts of India only. Rebels did not have enough weapons and finance whereas British people had advanced weapons and enough finance.

(i) Identify the immediate cause of the above revolt.
(a) The General Service Enlistment Act.
(b) The inhuman treatment of indigo cultivators.
(c) The Subsidiary Alliance.
(d) The incident of greased cartridges.

Ans. (d) The incident of greased cartridges.

(ii) Which policy of expansion led to the annexation of Awadh?
(a) Subsidiary Alliance (b) Doctrine of Lapse
(c) Pretext of alleged misrule
(d) Outright wars

Ans. (a) Subsidiary Alliance

(iii) Which of these is a socio-religious cause of the revolt?
(a) Taxing religious places.
(b) Decay of cottage industries.
(c) Drain of wealth.
(d) Exploitation of economic resources.

Ans. (a) Taxing religious places.

(iv) The British showed total disregard towards the soldiers. In this context, which of the following statements is not true?
(a) They were deprived of allowances.
(b) They were forced to go overseas on duty.
(c) They were given the same salaries as that of the British soldiers.
(d) The chances of promotion were very bleak.

Ans. (c) They were given the same salaries as that of the British soldiers.

Section-II

Short Questions

1. State any two political causes responsible for the First War of Independence. **[2014]**

Ans. There were many political causes responsible for the First War of Independence. Two of them were
(i) Lord Dalhousie's, 'policy of annexation' and 'Doctrine of Lapse'.
(ii) British disrespect shown to Bahadur Shah II, the last Mughal Emperor.

2. Why did the Doctrine of Lapse become a political cause for the Revolt of 1857? **[2010]**

Ans. The Doctrine of Lapse became a political cause for the Revolt of 1857 because according to this Doctrine, heirs adopted without the consent of the Company, could inherit only the private property of the deceased ruler and not his territory, which would come under this Company's rule.

The prominent states, which became victims to this Doctrine were Jhansi, Satara, Jaipur, Sambalpur, Udaipur and Nagpur.

3. Name the three states annexed by the British using the Doctrine of Lapse.

Ans. The three states annexed by the British using the Doctrine of Lapse were Jhansi, Satara and Nagpur. This policy was resented by the local rulers and people.

4. Under which pretext and when was Awadh annexed to the Company's dominions?

Ans. Lord Dalhousie annexed Awadh to the Company's dominions on the pretext of alleged misrule on 13th February, 1856.

5. Which announcement of the British hurt the Mughals?

Ans. In 1856, Lord Canning announced that after the death of Bahadur Shah Zafar, his successors would not be allowed to attach imperial titles and dignities to their names. The successor of the emperor would not be allowed to use the Red Fort as their place. This announcement hurt the Mughals and the Muslim community.

6. What was Nana Sahib's grievance against the British? **[2012]**

Ans. Nana Sahib was the adopted son of the last Peshwa Baji Rao II. His grievance against the British was that they refused to grant him pension, which they were paying to Peshwa Baji Rao II.

7. Mention two economic factors, which became the causes of the First War of Independence, 1857.

Ans. The two economic factors which became the causes of the First War of Independence were

(i) Heavy taxation, forced evictions, discriminatory tariff policy against Indian products and destruction of traditional handicrafts that hit peasants and artisans.

(ii) India was forced to export raw materials like raw cotton and raw silk plantation products like indigo tea and foodgrains at cheaper rates.

8. What was the General Service Enlistment Act? **[2019, 2013]**

Ans. The British Parliament passed the General Service Enlistment Act in 1856. According to this Act, the Indian Soldiers in the East India Company could be sent overseas on duty. Indian soldiers feared sea voyage and considered it against their customs.

9. What was the impact of the defeat of the British in the First Afghan War on the Indian soldiers?

Ans. The defeat of the British in the First Afghan War increased the self-confidence of the Indian soldiers. After the war, they started believing that they could challenge the British in India also.

10. Mention any two reasons which encouraged the Indian soldiers to revolt.

Ans. The two reasons which encouraged the Indian soldiers to revolt were

(i) Numerical strength of Indian soldiers was approximately 2 lakhs against the 40,000 British soldiers.

(ii) The defeat of British Army in the Afghan War, Punjab War and the Crimean War inspired the Indian soldiers that they could also win against the mighty Britishers.

11. What was the immediate cause of the war of 1857? Where did the war have its beginning?

Ans. The immediate cause of the war of 1857, was the introduction of greased cartridge for the Enfield rifle of the soldiers. The rumour spread that these cartridges had fat of cows and pigs. The soldiers refused to use it and rose in revolt.

The war or revolt started in Meerut on 10th May, 1857.

12. Who was Mangal Pandey?

Ans. Mangal Pandey was a Brahmin sepoy in Barrackpore regiment of Bengal. He first protested against the greased cartridge, which was believed to have fat of cows and pigs. He was arrested and hanged on 8th April, 1857.

13. Mention any two repressive policies of Lord Lytton. **[2023]**

Ans. Two repressive colonial policies of Lord Lytton were

(i) **Vernacular Press Act (1878)** This Act forbade vernacular papers to publish any material that instigated Indians against the British.

(ii) **Indian Arms Act (1879)** This Act made it a criminal offence for Indians to carry arms without licence.

14. How did the Indian sepoys protest in Meerut?

Ans. On 8th May 1857, 85 Indian sepoys in Meerut refused to bite off cartridges of new Enfield rifle. They were sentenced for 10 years imprisonment. On 10th May, the other Indian sepoys broke into open war, killed the officers, attacked jail and released the prisoners. On the same day, these sepoys along with thousands of civilians marched towards Delhi.

15. Name the British officials who recaptured Delhi and Jhansi from the hands of revolutionaries in 1857.

Ans. Sir John Nicholson was the British officer, who recaptured Delhi with the help of loyal Sikh soldiers. After 4 months of fighting, the British succeeded in recapturing Delhi.

Sir Hugh Rose captured Jhansi on 3rd April, 1858. He defeated Rani Laxmi Bai and Tantia Tope.

16. Who was Khan Bahadur Khan Rohilla?

Ans. Khan Bahadur Khan Rohilla was a descendant of the ruler of Rohilkhand. He proclaimed himself the Nawab Nazim and took the leadership of 1857 uprising at Bareilly.

17. What was the immediate impact of the Revolt of 1857 on the East India Company?

Ans. The immediate impact of the Revolt of 1857 on the East India Company was the end of the Company's rule and India was put directly under the British Crown. This was done by the Government of India Act of 1858.

18. When, where and by whom was Queen Victoria's proclamation made public in India?

Ans. Queen Victoria's proclamation was made public on 1st November, 1858 at Allahabad.

It was made public by Lord Canning, the first Viceroy of India.

19. Mention any two assurances that were given to the Indian people by Queen Victoria in her proclamation of 1858.

Ans. The assurances given to Indian people by Queen Victoria's proclamation of 1858 were

(i) The British Government would follow a policy of non-intervention in social and religious matters of Indians.

(ii) The Government would treat all subjects i.e. Indians and Europeans, as equal. Education and ability would be the basis of all appointments.

20. What steps were taken by the proclamation of Queen Victoria regarding the Princely States?

Ans. According to the proclamation of Queen Victoria, following steps were taken regarding the Princely States

(i) The policy of annexation and the Doctrine of Lapse were abandoned. The Indian Princes were allowed the right of adoption.

(ii) The Indian Princes were assured that their territories would not be annexed to the British Empire and they would continue as rulers of their states.

21. Mention any two administrative changes that the British Government brought about regarding the East India Company's rule in India. **[2015]**

Ans. Two administrative changes that were brought by the British Government under the Government of India Act of 1858 were

(i) After the revolt of 1857, the governance of India was transferred from the East India Company to the British Crown.

(ii) By the act of 1858, the Crown was made directly responsible for the management of Indian affairs.

22. How was the army reorganised after the First War of Independence?

Ans. After the uprising of 1857, the Britishers reorganised the army. The proportion of British soldiers was increased. Even different castes and creeds were mixed to avoid any other further revolt.

23. Name the sections of the Indian society who were hostile to this revolt.

Ans. Some sections of Indian society like big merchants and moneylender classes whose main profits came from the British merchant class, were hostile to this revolt.

24. What impact did the uprising of 1857 have on the Mughal rule? **[2016]**

Ans. The impact of uprising of 1857 was that it ended the Mughal rule and the title of Mughal emperor was also abolished with the death of Bahadur Shah II in 1862.

Structured Questions

1. Explain the causes of the Great Revolt of 1857, with reference to the following. **[2020]**

(i) Any three political causes

(ii) Any three military causes

(iii) Any two economic causes

(iv) Any two social-religious causes

Ans. (i) The political causes of the Revolt of 1857 were

(a) The British Policy of effective control and gradual extinction of the native Indian states was one of the major grievances of the Indian rulers.

(b) The policy of 'Doctrine of Lapse', 'policy of annexation' the Subsidiary Alliance and by outright wars.

(c) The annexation of Awadh on the pretext of alleged misgovernance.

(ii) The military causes of the Revolt of 1857 were

(a) Ill treatment of the Indian soldiers and low salaries.

(b) General Service Enlistment Act, as per which, Indian soldiers could be sent overseas on duty.

(c) Larger proportion of Indian soldier in the Army.

(iii) The economic causes of the Revolt 1857 were

(a) Heavy taxation, forcibly evictions, discriminatory tariff policy against the Indian products and destruction of traditional handicrafts that hit peasants and artisans.

(b) The transfer of wealth from India to England for which India got no proportionate economic returns.

(iv) The socio-religious causes of the Revolt of 1857 were

(a) The practice of Sati was made illegal and punishable by law (1829).

(b) Remarriage of widow was allowed through Widow Remarriage Act (1856).

2. "Numerous causes were at work in causing the great upsurge of 1857" with reference to this, explain the following.

(i) Apprehension about Modern Innovations.

(ii) The introduction of the Enfield rifles.

(iii) The laws that interfered with the religious customs of the people and Racial Discrimination policy.

Ans. (i) The apprehension about modern innovations were

- The rapid spread of modern civilisation made people afraid and suspicious.
- People spread the rumours that the telegraph poles were erected for the purpose of hanging people, who opposed the British Rule in India.
- The orthodox Indians felt humiliated to know that in the railway compartments, Brahmins and people from the backward classes were made to sit side by side.

(ii) The introduction of Enfield rifles was the immediate cause of the revolt. In 1856, the British authorities decided to replace the old fashioned musket by the new 'Enfield rifles'. There was a rumour that the cartridges of these rifles were greased with the fat of cows and pigs.

The loading process of the Enfield rifles involved bringing the cartridge to the mouth and biting off the top greased paper with the mouth. Both the Hindu and Muslim sepoys refused to use the cartridges, as they felt that the English were defiling their religion.

(iii) The British introduced some laws which interfered with the religious custom of the people.

These were

- The laws allowing conversion from Hinduism to Christianity to inherit their ancestral property.
- Religious sentiments of the Indian were hurt by the official policy of taxing lands belonging to temples and mosques.

The British used Racial Discrimination Polity with the Indians in which they were very rude and arrogant towards the Indians. They considered the Muslims cruel and unfaithful. They usually insulted Indians and even rulers.

3. The Indian Nationalists described the Great Uprising of 1857 as the First War of Independence. With reference to this, answer the following questions. **[2023]**

(i) Mention any three policies used by the British to expand their political power in India.

(ii) The Revolt of 1857 is also known as the Sepoy Mutiny.
Mention any three military causes which led to the uprising.

(iii) Mention any four economic causes of the Revolt.

Ans. (i) The British used both battles and strategic policies to gain control over India. These are

(a) They used their financial strength to indebt local rulers and gradually surrendered their territories. Where this did not work, they used force and battles.

(b) The British official also adopted policies to annex territories.

(c) The expansion policies included the Subsidiary Alliance, Doctrine of Lapse.

(ii) Refer to Structured Question 1 (ii).

(iii) The most important reason for the popular discontent was the economic exploitation by the British. The economic exploitation took the following forms

(a) The East India Company made huge profits at the expenses of the people of India. The company purchased textiles, indigo, foodgrains and spices from India and sold them abroad at exorbitant prices.

(b) By buying and exporting Indian goods, the company encouraged their production in India. But gradually, the Indian textiles began to compete with the textiles manufactured in England. The British put pressure on the East India Company to forbid the sale of Indian textiles in England. The British Government then put restrictions on the import of Indian textiles besides imposing heavy import duties on such goods.

(c) People moved to cities to find employment, which was very difficult to get. Peasants were forced to pay tax in cash, which pushed them into the hands of the moneylenders, as tax was collected even during the famines.

(d) Indigo, tea, jute, cotton and opium were crops, which the British wanted the Indians to grow. If the peasants planted anything else, their crops were destroyed and cattle were carried off as a punishment.

4. Explain the important causes of the Revolt of 1857.

(i) Economic exploitation by the British.

(ii) The British policy of territorial expansion.

(iii) Interference in the social and religious life of Indians.

(iv) Activities of missionaries.

Ans. (i) Popular discontent against the British rule arose due to the policy of economic exploitation adopted by the colonial power. The company exploited the economic resources of India at the expense of the people of India. The company purchased textiles, indigo, spices and foodgrains from India at a cheap rate and sold them abroad at exorbitant prices. India became an economic colony of industrial England. While the raw materials were supplied to England at a very cheap rate, the finished goods were supplied to India at a very high rate. As a result, Indian handicrafts and cottage industries died out.

(ii) The British policy of territorial expansion was one of the main factors responsible for the Revolt of 1857. Under the Doctrine of Lapse, Jhansi, Satara and Nagpur were annexed. Under direct annexation policy, Sind and Punjab were captured. Under the policy of Subsidiary Alliance, a part of the ruler's territory was captured by the British if the ruler failed to pay for the maintenance of the British force. Again states like Awadh was captured on the pretext of misgovernance.

(iii) Interference in the social and religious life of Indians is another cause of the Revolt of 1857. In the 19th century, the Britishers introduced some reforms like the abolition of Sati, child marriage, female infanticide and polygamy. Some Indian social reformers like Ram Mohan Roy and Swami Dayanand Saraswati played a significant role in abolishing these social evils also.
But these reforms were not welcomed by all. The activity of Christian missionaries also generated fear and suspicion among the common men.

(iv) Activities of missionaries was also the cause of the Revolt of 1857. The British Government indirectly supported some activities of the missionaries by not objecting to their activities from the early 19th century, there was an increase in both the numbers and activities of the Christian Missionaries. Thus, Indians thought that with government's support, the missionaries would convert them to Christianity.

5. Describe the contribution of the following leaders to the Revolt of 1857.
(i) Rani Laxmi Bai
(ii) Nana Sahib
(iii) Bahadur Shah Zafar
(iv) Tantia Tope

Ans. (i) Rani Laxmi Bai was the Queen of Jhansi. After the annexation of Jhansi, she became a rebel and joined in the uprising of 1857. She was considered the bravest and best military leader of the rebels. She with the help of Tantia Tope occupied Gwalior. Sir Hugh Rose advanced towards Gwalior and defeated the Indian troops. Rani fought like a real hero and died in the battlefield. Her courage and military skill inspired her countrymen. She is still remembered by Indians for her great sacrifice.

(ii) Nana Sahib was the adopted son of Bazi Rao II. Being a brave and determined general, he declared himself as the Peshwa. He led the revolt in Kanpur and captured Kanpur fort. On 17th June, 1857 General Havelock recaptured Kanpur after defeating Nana Sahib. Nana Sahib fled to Nepal and nothing was heard of him after that.

(iii) Bahadur Shah Zafar was the last Mughal Emperor. He was forced to lead the revolt in Delhi. When Delhi was captured by the revolutionaries, he was declared the Emperor of India. But Sir John Nicholson with the help of Sikh soldiers from Punjab, attacked to Delhi. Bahadur Shah was captured and was found guilty of helping the rebels. As a punishment he was deported to Rangoon where he died in 1862. With him the mighty Mughal Empire came to an end.

(iv) Tantia Tope was an able and experienced Lieutenant in the army of Nana Sahib. After the defeat of Nana Sahib against the British, Tantia escaped and joined the Rani of Jhansi.
After the death of Rani Laxmi Bai, Tantia Tope managed to escape, but in 1859, betrayal by Gwalior Chief Man Singh, he fell in the hands of British. He was tried and hanged.

6. The events of the Revolt of 1857 were of great importance. In the context of the course of the revolt, explain the following.
(i) Events at Meerut
(ii) Events at Lucknow
(iii) Events at Kanpur and Delhi

Ans. (i) Refer to chapter theory page no. 84.
(ii) Refer to chapter theory page no. 84.
(iii) Refer to chapter theory page no. 84.

7. The First War of Independence led to several changes. With reference to this answer the following.
(i) The rights granted to the Indian Princes and Chiefs.
(ii) The reorganisation of the army.
(iii) The changes introduced in the administrative setup of the British territories.
(iv) The policy of 'Divide and Rule'.

Ans. (i) Several rights were granted to the Indian Princes and Chiefs as a result of the First War of Independence. The policy of annexation and the Doctrine of Lapse were abandoned. Some of the Indian Princes had remained loyal to the British and had helped them in suppressing the uprisings. All the treaties between the Princes and the company were decided to be respected. The British promised not to annex any territory and gave the Indian rulers the right to adopt heirs. The Indian Princes became junior partners of the British crown because they were promised that they would continue as rulers of their states.

(ii) Refer to chapter theory page no. 86.

(iii) The changes introduced in the administrative set-up of the British territories in India were
- In 1858, the British Parliament passed the Government of India Act. Due to this act, the responsibility to govern India was transferred to Queen and the British Parliament.
- This act abolished the Board of Control and Court of Directors of the Company and the responsibility of the Government of India was passed on to a separate Minister in the British Parliament. This Minister was known as the Secretary of State for India. He was to be helped by a council of 15 members, of which 9 should have worked in India for 10 years. The Governor-General was designated as the Viceroy.

(iv) Refer to chapter theory page no. 86.

8. The First War of Independence, 1857 led to several changes. With reference to this, explain the following.
(i) Religious Freedom
(ii) Rise of Nationalism in India
(iii) Economic Exploitation
(iv) Relation of Princely States with British.

Ans. (i) Refer to chapter theory page no. 81.
(ii) Refer to chapter theory page no. 86.
(iii) The economic exploitation after the First War of Independence was
- Agricultural India was made an economic colony to serve the interests of Industrial England.

- India was made to accept ready made British goods either duty free or at nominal duty rates, while Indian products were subjected to high import duties in England.
- The British capital invested in Indian markets especially in railway, shipping, oil exploration, tea and coffee plantations etc. was used to get huge profits and were sent to England.
- The export of raw materials and foodgrains deprived the country of its agricultural surplus and raised the prices of raw materials.

(iv) Refer to chapter theory page no. 86.

9. State the impact of Revolt of 1857 on

(i) The Mughal Empire
(ii) The East India Company
(iii) Hindu-Muslim Unity
(iv) Religious Interference

Ans. (i) The impact of Revolt of 1857 on the Mughal Empire was that Bahadur Shah Zafar was found guilty of helping the rebellious soldiers. As a punishment, he was sentenced to life imprisonment and deported to 'Rangoon' where he died in 1862. His two sons were shot dead in front of him. Thus, the mighty Mughal Empire came to an end as Lord Canning announced that after the death of Bahadur Shah, his successors would not be allowed to use the imperial titles and status. Rather they would be known as mere Princes.

(ii) The most significant result of the Revolt of 1857 was the end of the rule of the East India Company. In 1858, the British Parliament passed the Government of India Act, by which the responsibility to govern India was transferred to the British Crown and the British Parliament. This act abolished the Board of Directors of the Company and the responsibility of the Government of India was passed into a separate Minister in the British Parliament, who was known as the Secretary of State for India.

(iii) The Hindu-Muslim Unity played an important role in the Revolt of 1857. The Hindu as well as Muslim soldiers had enrolled in the British Army. Both had faced the common problems of the greased cartridges. These cartridge were bitten before they were loaded into the rifles.
It was believed that its grease was made of cow's and pig's fat. Both Muslims and Hindus united to protect their religious faith. They protested against British. Now the Hindu and Muslim had common enemy. It brought both the Hindu and Muslim sepoys together. They declared Bahadur Shah as their leader and marched together from Meerut to Delhi. This was the first time that both the Hindu-Muslim community fought for a common cause i.e. to end the British rule.

(iv) The interference of the British in Indian religions and culture was one of the prominent reason for the war of 1857. After the revolt of 1857, the British rulers declared that they would not interfere in the religious matters, customs and traditions of the Indians.

Picture Based Questions

1. Answer the following questions based on the picture given below.

(i) Identify the person in the picture.
(ii) Why he was not considered as the rightful heir to the throne?
(iii) Mention the role played by him in the Revolt of 1857.

Ans. (i) Nana Sahib is shown in the above picture. He was the adopted son of Peshwa Baji Rao II. Before his death in 1851, Baji Rao II gave all his property to Nana Sahib and declared him as his heir.

(ii) Nana Sahib was not considered as the rightful heir to the throne because he was not a biological son of Peshwa Baji Rao II. He was adopted son. After the death of Baji Rao II, the East India Company stopped the pension of Baji Rao II. So, they announced that this pension would not be given to Nana Sahib. Nana Sahib was greatly offended by both the termination of the pension and by the suspension of various titles and grants enjoyed by Baji Rao II.

(iii) When the Revolt of 1857 started, Nana Sahib led the revolt at Kanpur. Under him, the rebels fought so bravely that the British troops were compelled to surrender on 26th June, 1857.
On 17th July 1857, General Havelock succeeded in recapturing Kanpur after defeating Nana Sahib. But Nana Sahib was not the man to give in so easily. He fought back with the help of Tantia Tope.
Though they succeeded in recapturing Kanpur but could not hold it for long. They were defeated by General Campbell. Nana Sahib fled to Nepal and nothing was heard about him again.

2. Look at picture given below and answer the following questions.

(i) Identify the lady shown in the picture.

(ii) Name the state of which she was the ruler.

(iii) Why is she still remembered today?

Ans. (i) The lady shown in the picture is Rani Laxmi Bai. Laxmi Bai was born on 19th November, 1828 in the holy town of Varanasi into a Marathi Brahmin family. She was married in 1842.

(ii) Rani Laxmi Bai became the ruler of Jhansi after the death of her husband. She was married to Maharaja of Jhansi, Raja Gangadhar Rao Newalkar. Jhansi is situated in the North Central part of India.

(iii) Rani Laxmi Bai is still remembered for her bravery and role in the Revolt of 1857. The revolt began at Jhansi in June, 1857. Sir Hugh Rose laid siege to the fortress of Jhansi in March, 1858. Rani Laxmi Bai resisted, but Jhansi was captured by the British.

Rani escaped from the fortress on the night of 4th April, 1858 to join Tantia Tope. Under the leadership of the Rani, soldiers of Tantia Tope and her own soldiers occupied Gwalior. The ruler of Gwalior, Scindia fled and took refugee with the British at Agra. Sir Hugh Rose advanced towards Gwalior and defeated Indian troops. Rani Laxmi Bai died like a brave soldier, after putting up a tough fight on 17th June, 1858.

Chapter Assessment

Section-I

Multiple Choice Questions

1. Which of the following became the immediate cause of 1857 revolt?
   (a) Use of Enfield rifle
   (b) Use of Brown Bess rifle
   (c) Use of Baker rifle
   (d) Use of Armalite AR-30
2. At which of the following places was the revolt led by Kunwar Singh?
   (a) Meerut (b) Bihar
   (c) Bareilly (d) Gwalior
3. After the 1857 revolt the ratio of European to Indian troops was fixed at 1:2 for........ army and 2:5 for Madras and Bombay armies.
   (a) Bengal (b) Meerut
   (c) Lucknow (d) Gwalior
4. Complete the given analogy.
   SN Sen : Historian :: Mangal Pandey : ?
   (a) Writer
   (b) Novelist
   (c) Sepoy
   (d) Nawab of Bengal

Section-II

Short Questions

1. When did the First War of Independence takes place?
2. Which were the two Indian states brought under the British control using the Subsidiary Alliance?
3. Why did Rani Laxmi Bai become a bitter enemy of the British?
4. Explain how the British exploited resources of India with an example.
5. Which announcement of Lord Dalhousie of 1849, hurt the Mughals?
6. Name the soldier who first refused to use the cartridge used in the Enfield rifle. How was he punished?
7. 'Trade with England did not benefit Indian economy'. Explain it by giving two examples.
8. Mention two causes of discontent among the Indian soldiers of the British army which culminated into the uprising of 1857.

Structured Questions

1. Lord Dalhousie greatly extended the territories of the British India by introducing the 'Doctrine of Lapse'. In this context, answer the following questions.
   (i) What is meant by 'Doctrine of Lapse'?
   (ii) Mention why he annexed various states on the basis of this Doctrine?
   (iii) What were the consequences of the application of this Doctrine?
   (iv) Which states well annexed under the Doctrine of Lapse?
2. During the 19th century, the Britishers began to interfere with the local religious and social customs. In this context, briefly describe
   (i) Interference in social custom, like 'Sati' and the Widow Remarriage Act
   (ii) Resentment among the Hindu and Muslim priests.
   (iii) Introduction of New Laws.
3. With reference to the consequences of the Revolt of 1857, answer the following questions.
   (i) What were the promises made by the British Crown?
   (ii) State two administrative changes.
   (iii) What was the relation between the British Government and the Indian Princes?
   (iv) State religious changes.

CHAPTER

02

The Rise of Nationalism and the Indian National Congress

SYLLABUS

Factors leading to Growth of Nationalism Economic exploitation, repressive colonial policies, socio-religious reform movements (brief mention of contribution of Raja Ram Mohan Roy and Jyotiba Phule) and role of the Press.

Foundation of the Indian National Congress The Indian National Association (Surendranath Banerjee) and the East India Association (Dadabhai Naoroji) as precursors.
• Immediate objective of the Indian National Congress–the first two sessions and their Presidents.

The idea of nationalism started to originate in India from the second half of the 19th century. Nationalism in India was inspired by the French Revolution of 1789. The ideas of liberty and democratic rights given by the French Revolution inspired people. The memory of the Revolt of 1857 also inspired Indians to go ahead with their struggle for freedom.

Meaning of Nationalism

Nationalism is a feeling of togetherness and common consciousness based on political, historical, religious, cultural, psychological and other factors in a state. It is a strong sentiment, a feeling of love and pride for one's own country. It is fundamental for a nation's progress and unity.

Factors Leading to the Growth of Nationalism in India

British Policy of Economic Exploitation

The British followed the exploitative economic policies in India. These policies were

- The British collected land revenue but never cared for the welfare of the peasants. Many of them were forced to grow jute and cotton for the supply of raw materials to the factories in England.
- The British changed the land law. Before the British Raj, a moneylender could not charge very high interest for money. No land could be transferred to him, if the peasant failed to pay back his loan. But under the new land law, a moneylender could demand high interest rate and could also get the land transferred to his name, if the peasant failed to pay back. As a result, the peasant class suffered immensely.
- The British economic policy brought about industrial stagnation of India. Goods manufactured in England were dumped into India and sold at higher prices.
- Heavy duties were imposed on goods exported to England from India.
- The policy ruined the cottage industries of India and **artisans**[1] and handicraftsmen were deprived of their livelihood.
- A new social class- working class which was the result of the growth of modern industries suffered at the hands of English factory owners. As these factories were located in cities, their political awakening became more significant.

Repressive Colonial Policies

The British colonial power followed a repressive policy against Indians. Viceroys like **Lord Lytton**

1 **Artisans** A person who does skilled works.

(1876-1880) and **Lord Curzon** (1899-1905) took many repressive policies due to which the Indians were resented and nationalism grow among them. These were

- **Vernacular Press Act** It is also known as **Gagging Act**. Lord Lytton passed the Vernacular Press Act on 14th March, 1878 to suppress the freedom of the native press. This act provided the government with extensive rights to censor reports published in **vernacular**[2] papers, which would arouse dissatisfaction against the government. This law was not applicable to English newspapers. This law was repealed by Lord Ripon in 1882.
- **Grand Delhi Durbar** In 1877, when India was faced by a severe famine, Lord Lytton organised a Grand Delhi Durbar to proclaim Queen Victoria as the Empress of India without thinking about the welfare of famine gripped Indians. This angered the Indian masses.
- **The Indian Arms Act, 1878** Lord Lytton passed the Indian Arms Act in 1878 which compelled the Indians to acquire a licence to keep, sell or purchase arms. The offenders were to be punished both with punishment and a fine. But, this law was not applicable for the English, Anglo-Indians and government servants of certain categories.
- **New Law for Civil Service Examination** The British reduced the maximum age limit for the Indian Civil Service Examination from 21 to 19 years. This make it difficult for the Indians to compete for it.
- **Ilbert Bill** The Ilbert Bill of 1883 abolished judicial disqualification on the basis of racial distinction. Earlier Indian judges were racially discriminated for sentencing Europeans. This bill allowed the trail of Europeans by Indian Judges for criminal offences. The law provoked a strong criticism among the educated Indians. Ultimately, the government withdraw the bill.

Development of Transport and Means of Communications

The British built a network of roads and railways and means of communication in order to promote their own commercial interest. The means of transport and communication connected the vast country and gave Indians a sense of oneness which further led to growth of nationalism. As a result, regional feelings began to disappear and people started to believe that they belonged to one country. Thus, the means of transport made it possible to mobilise public opinion on a national scale and development of modern postal and telegraph system brought a radical change in social, intellectual and political life.

Influence of Western Education

The influence of Western education also led to growth of nationalism in India. The British introduced Western education in India to serve their own administrative and political ends. They wanted trained clerks for their administration. However, Western education had broadened the views of Indians.

It gave the opportunity to the Indians to study the work of Voltaire, Rousseau, Locke, Bentham, Marx, Engels, Thomas Paine, etc. Indians became aware of the ideals of French Revolution and American War of Independence.

The English language played a role of **lingua franca**[3] in India. In all parts of India, educated Indians could communicate with one another through English language. Further, Western education encouraged vernacular languages and literary works in them.

Socio-Religious Reform Movement

The second half of the 19th century witnessed the rise of many religious and social reformers in India. Reformers like Raja Ram Mohan Roy, Swami Dyananda Saraswati, Swami Vivekananda and Jyotiba Phule played an important role in the growth of nationalism through their reform movements.

Raja Ram Mohan Roy

He was the first great socio-religious reformer of the 19th century. He is known as the **Father of Indian Renaissance.** He wanted to remove the religious and social evils which were popular in India at that period.

Raja Ram Mohan Roy

2 **Vernacular** The language spoken in a particular area or by a particular group.

3 **Lingua franca** A language that is adopted as a common language between speakers whose native languages are different.

His contribution in the socio-religious reform movement was

- In 1809, Raja Ram Mohan Roy wrote 'Gift to Monotheist' in Persian preaching worship of a single God.
- He started the 'Atmiya Sabha' in 1814 which was against idol worship and meaningless rituals.
- In 1828, he founded the Brahmo Sabha, which was later renamed **Brahmo Samaj.** It opposed idol worship and supported Monotheism or the worship of one supreme God.
- He also opposed blind faith, superstition, untouchability, **polygamy**[4], child marriage, **female infanticide**[5] and rigid caste system.
- He started a Bengali weekly called 'Samvad Kaumudi' and a paper in Persian called 'Mirat-ul-Akbar'.
- It was due his constant effort that abolition of Sati became a law in 1829 and was passed by Lord Bentinck.
- He also favoured widow remarriage (which was legalised in 1856) and inter-caste marriage.
- He laid the foundation of an English school, the Hindu college and the Vedanta college.

Jyotiba Phule

He was an activist, thinker, social reformer who belonged to a low caste family from Maharashtra. He fought a long struggled life against caste discrimination and Brahmanical supremacy.

Jyotiba Phule

His contribution in the socio-religious reform movement was

- Jyotiba Phule and his wife established the first girls school at Poona in 1851.
- In 1854, he started a private orphanage for the widows and established a school for untouchables.
- In 1873, he founded the **Satya Shodhak Samaj** to fight against the caste system and with the aim to secure social justice for the weaker sections of society.
- He was the first leader who started the widow remarriage movement in Maharashtra.
- He wrote the famous book 'Gulamgiri' in which he described the hardships of lower castes.

Other Social Reformers

The contribution of other reformers like Swami Vivekananda and Swami Dyananda Saraswati were

- The **Ramkrishna Mission** was established by Swami Vivekananda in 1897 at Belur, West Bengal for serving human beings irrespective of caste, creed and religion.
- **Swami Dyananda Saraswati** raised the slogan 'India for the Indians' and he founded 'Arya Samaj' at Bombay in 1875 which allows and encourages converts to Hinduism.

Role of the Press

- The Indian Press has played a notable role in mobilising public opinion, organising political movements and promoting nationalism.
- Many newspapers like, The Amrit Bazar Patrika, The Hindu, The Patriot, The Mahratta, The Kesari and The Indian Mirror, etc were published from different parts of the country. They criticised the unjust policies of the colonial government and played a significant role to reuse patriotic sentiments among masses.
- Indian Press became the primary medium of popular public education and also the mirror of Indian nationalism.
- The Indian Press played an important role in exchanging of views among different social groups from different parts of the country.

Check Your LEARNING...

1. Who passed the Vernacular Press Act?
2. In which year the Indian Arms Act was passed?
3. Who is known as the 'Father of Indian Renaissance'?
4. Where was the first girls school established in colonial India?

4 **Polygamy** The practice or custom of having more than one wife or husband.

5 **Female Infanticide** The crime of killing a baby girl.

Foundation of the Indian National Congress

The second half of the 19th century witnessed the formation of various political associations or organisations which were the result of growing nationalism and political consciousness. The associations were considered as a based for the formation of the Congress.

The earliest political organisation formed in India was the **Landholder's Society** founded in 1838 by Dwarakanath Tagore of Bengal. Its aim was to safeguard the interests of the landlords of Bengal, Bihar and Orissa. The **Bengal British India Society** was formed in 1843 to protect the interests of general public. Later in 1851, these two organisations were merged to form the 'British India Association of Bengal.' Many other organisations were formed in different parts of India like Bombay Presidency Association (1871), Madras Native Association, Poona Sarvajanik Sabha (1870) and Indian League (1875).

Some of the significant associations among these were

East India Association (1866)

The 'East India Association' was founded by **Dadabhai Naoroji** (also called as 'The Grand Old Man of India') in London in 1866. Dadabhai thought that India's poverty was due to the imperfect economic policies of the British. The association had its branches in Bombay, Calcutta and Madras.

The main objectives of this association were

- Through this association, Dadabhai wanted to inform the British about the grievances of Indian people and suggested remedial measures.
- The association demanded the withdrawal of the Vernacular Press Act and abolition of cotton duties.

Indian National Association (1876)

The Indian National Association was founded in 1876 by **Surendranath Banerjee**. This was the first organised political association, comprised of lawyers, professionals and educated middle class as its members. The association also had branches outside Bengal.

The main objectives of this association were

- To create public opinion on political matters
- To promote friendly relations between Hindus and Muslims.
- This association tried to evolve a common political programme.
- It demanded changes in the Indian Civil Service Examination, cancellation of the Arms Act, the Vernacular Press Act and protection of the rights of tenants against landlords and British planters.

Indian National Conference (1883)

Surendranath Banerjee called for the "All India National Conference" at Calcutta in 1883. This was the first political organisation of an All-India character and its conference was attended by representatives from all over India. It offered a base to the Indian National Congress. It merged with the Indian National Congress in December, 1886 as both have same objectives.

Formation of the Indian National Congress (INC)

Allan Octavian Hume, a retired British member of Indian Civil Service wanted to set up an organisation that would draw the government's attention to the administrative drawbacks and would suggest the remedial measures. Thus, in 1884, Hume laid the foundation of the Indian National Union.

The first session of this association was to be held in Pune on 25th December, 1885 but plague broke out in Pune. So, the conference was shifted to Bombay. Further, the session was held at Gokuldas Tejpal Sanskrit college from 28th to 31st December, 1885. This session was presided by **WC Bonnerjee** and 72 delegates attended this session.

The name of this association was changed to Indian National Congress on the suggestion of Dadabhai Naoroji. Thus, on 28th December, the Indian National Congress was founded as an organisation of educated persons such as teachers, professors, lawyers, medical men and businessmen.

Initially, it was a non-political association which tried to get some concessions from the British. But gradually, the Congress attracted wide membership and became the main organisation to launch the freedom movement in India.

Objectives of the Indian National Congress

The main objectives of the Congress as enumerated by the WC Bonnerjee in inaugural session were

- Promotion of close relations between nationalist workers from different parts of the country.
- Development and consolidation of a feeling of national unity, irrespective of caste, religion or province.
- Formulation of popular demands and their presentation before the government.

- To train and organise the public opinion in the country.

Initially, the relation between the British Government and Congress was friendly as the aim of the Congress was to achieve self-government within the British Empire. Viceroy Lord Dufferin thought that the foundation of the Congress would act as a **safety valve** for popular discontent. However, gradually the British Government started to distrust the Congress for its growing popularity and changing demands.

Sessions of the Congress

The Congress held its sessions annually in different cities to rouse public opinion in favour of its aim.

The first two sessions of the Congress were

(i) The **first session** of the Congress was held at Bombay in 1885, which was presided by WC Bonnerjee.

(ii) The **second session** of the Congress was held at Calcutta in 1886, which was presided by Dadabhai Naoroji.

Check Your LEARNING...

1. In which year the landholder's society was founded?
2. Where was the East India Association founded?
3. Who was the founder of the Indian Association?
4. Where was the first session of Indian National Congress held?
5. Who presided the second session of the Indian National Congress?

Time Line

Year	Important Events
1829	Abolition of Sati by William Bentinck.
1838	The Landholder's Society
1843	The Bengal British Indian Society
1852	Madras Native Association
1866	East India Association,
1870	Poona Sarvajanik Sabha
1875	The Indian League
1876	Indian Association of Calcutta
1877	Delhi Durbar by Lord Lytton
1878	Vernacular Press Act, the Indian Arms Act
1882	Vernacular Press Act was repealed by Lord Ripon
1883	Ilbert Bill
1885	Foundation of Indian National Congress
1943	Bengal Famine

QUiCK Revision

- From the second half of the 19th century, the ideal of nationalism started.
- Nationalism is a feeling of love and pride for one's own country.
- Different factors were responsible for the rise and growth of national movement. These were British policy of economic exploitation, repressive colonial policies, development of transport and the means of communication and influence of Western education, etc.
- The Britishers applied repressive policies by introducing Vernacular Press Act, Indian Arms Act, New Law for Civil Service Examination, Ilbert Bill, etc. But they were compelled by the agitation of Indians to amend some bills.
- Development of transport and communication connected the Indian masses and Western education influenced the thinking of people.
- The second half of the 19th century witnessed the rise of many socio-religious reformers like Raja Ram Mohan Roy, Jyotiba Phule, Swami Vivekananda, Swami Dyananda Saraswati, etc in India.
- Due to British administrative and economic policies, new urban middle class grew.
- The emergence of Indian Press was very significant during early 19th century. Different newspapers and writings of Indian authors helped to change the minds of Indians and made them realise the repressive role of the colonial power.
- Different political associations grew at that time among which East India Association and Indian Association of Calcutta were important.
- In 1884, AO Hume founded Indian National Union. On 28th December, 1885, the Indian National Congress was founded.
- The first session of the Indian National Congress was held in Bombay in 1885 and it was presided by WC Bonnerjee.
- The second session was held in Calcutta in 1886 under the Presidentship of Dadabhai Naoroji.

Chapter Practice

Section-I

Multiple Choice Questions

1. Who of the following repealed the Vernacular Press Act, 1878?
(a) Lord Lytton (b) Lord Dufferin
(c) William Bentinck (d) Lord Ripon

Ans. (d) Lord Ripon

2. The law passed by Lytton reduced the age limit for appearing for Civil Service Examination from 21 to?
(a) 20 years (b) 18 years
(c) 17 years (d) 19 years

Ans. (d) 19 years

3. Ilbert Bill was passed in the year
(a) 1883 (b) 1885
(c) 1878 (d) 1877

Ans. (a) 1883

4. The 'Father of Indian Renaissance' was famously referred to ....
(a) Jyotiba Phule (b) AO Hume
(c) Raja Ram Mohan Roy (d) Dadabhai Naoroji

Ans. (c) Raja Ram Mohan Roy

5. Who founded the Vedanta college?
(a) Dyananda Saraswati (b) Jyotiba Phule
(c) Raja Ram Mohan Roy (d) Swami Vivekananda

Ans. (c) Raja Ram Mohan Roy

6. Who among the following was famous for widow remarriage movement in Maharashtra?
(a) Raja Ram Mohan Roy (b) Dyananda Saraswati
(c) Dadabhai Naoroji (d) Jyotiba Phule

Ans. (d) Jyotiba Phule

7. The main objective of the Assertive Nationalists was .... **[2023]**
(a) constitutional agitation
(b) peaceful protests
(c) purna Swaraj
(d) self-government under British rule

Ans. (c) Purna Swaraj

8. Ram Krishna Mission was established in the year by Swami Vivekananda.
(a) 1890 (b) 1897 (c) 1893 (d) 1896

Ans. (b) 1897

9. The slogan 'India for Indians' was given by
(a) Surendranath Banerjee (b) Dyananda Saraswati
(c) Dadabhai Naoroji (d) Rabindranath Tagore

Ans. (b) Dyananda Saraswati

10. Who was the founder of the Indian National Congress? **[Semester-I 2022]**
(a) AO Hume (b) WC Bonerjee
(c) Dadabhai Naoroji (d) Gopal Krishna Gokhale

Ans. (a) AO Hume

11. Complete the given analogy. **[Semester-I 2022]**
Brahmo Samaj : ? :: Arya Samaj : Dyananda Saraswati.
(a) Swami Vivekananda
(b) Ram Krishna Pramahamsa
(c) Raja Ram Mohan Roy
(d) Dwarkanath Tagore

Ans. (c) Raja Ram Mohan Roy

12. Complete the given analogy.
Indian Association of Calcutta :: Dadabhai Naoroji : East India Association :: ?
(a) Womesh Chandra Banerjee
(b) Bankim Chandra Chatterjee
(c) Dwarkanath Tagore
(d) Surendranath Banerjee

Ans. (d) Surendranath Banerjee

13. Complete the given analogy.
Bombay : First Session of INC :: .... : Second Session of INC
(a) Madras (b) Bombay
(c) Calcutta (d) Pune

Ans. (c) Calcutta

14. Replace the underlined word with the correct answer.
The Vernacular Press Act was passed in the year <u>1876</u>.
(a) 1878 (b) 1880
(c) 1875 (d) 1877

Ans. (a) 1878

15. Replace the underlined word and correct the statement **[Semester-I 2022]**
<u>Surendranath Banerjee</u> presided over the Second Session of the Indian National Congress.
(a) Dadabhai Naoroji (b) W.C. Bonerjee
(c) Rashbehari Bose (d) Badruddin Tyabji

Ans. (a) Dadabhai Naoroji

16. Replace the underlined word with the correct answer.
The Indian National Congress was founded by <u>Dadabhai Naoroji</u>.
(a) Surendranath Banerjee (b) Allan Octavian Hume
(c) Lord Dufferin (d) Dwarkanath Tagore

Ans. (b) Allan Octavian Hume

17. Complete the following table.

Indian Association of Calcutta	1876
?	1885

Ans. Indian National Congress

18. Complete the following table.

Gulamgiri	?
Gift to Monotheist	Raja Ram Mohan Roy

Ans. Jyotiba Phule

19. Choose the correct code from the following.

Which of the following is not a correct statement?

(i) British economic exploitation was the cause of growth of nationalism.

(ii) IIbert Bill was supported by Anglo- Indians.

(iii) Lord Rippon passed the Law of Abolition of Sati.

(iv) Arms Act was passed in 1878.

Codes

(a) Only (i) (b) Both (i) and (ii)

(c) Both (i) and (iv) (d) All are correct

Ans. (b) Both (i) and (ii)

20. What is the correct statement about the Indian National Congress (INC)?

(i) INC was formed in the year 1885.

(ii) The viceroy during the formation of INC was Lord Ripon.

(iii) It was a political association since its formation.

(iv) The Second Session of INC was presided by Dadabhai Naoroji.

Codes

(a) All are correct (b) Only (i)

(c) Both (i) and (iv) (d) Both (ii) and (iii)

Ans. (c) Both (i) and (iv)

21. Match the following.

List I	List II
A. Satyashodhak Samaj	1. Swami Vivekananda
B. Atmiya Sabha	2. Jyotiba Phule
C. Arya Samaj	3. Raja Ram Mohan Roy
D. Ram Krishna Mission	4. Dyananda Saraswati

Codes

	A	B	C	D		A	B	C	D
(a)	2	3	4	1	(b)	3	4	2	1
(c)	1	3	2	4	(d)	2	4	1	3

Ans. (a)

22. Match the following.

List I	List II
A. Landholder's Society	1. London
B. East India Association	2. Bombay
C. Arya Samaj	3. Belur
D. Ram Krishna Mission	4. Bengal and Orissa

Codes

	A	B	C	D		A	B	C	D
(a)	1	4	3	2	(b)	2	4	3	1
(c)	4	1	2	3	(d)	4	2	3	1

Ans. (c)

Picture Based Question

23. Look at the picture given below and answer the questions that follow.

(i) Identify the personality in given picture

(a) Dayananda Saraswati

(b) Jyotiba Phule

(c) Raja Ram Mohan Roy

(d) Surendranath Banerjee

Ans. (c) Raja Ram Mohan Roy

(ii) He founded an organisation to preach monotheism known as

(a) Arya Samaj

(b) Brahmo Samaj

(c) Dev Samaj

(d) Satya Shodhak Samaj

Ans. (b) Brahmo Samaj

(iii) It was due to his effort and contribution that was legalised in 1829.

(a) Widow remarriage

(b) Abolition of child marriage

(c) Abolition of polygamy

(d) Abolition of Sati

Ans. (d) Abolition of Sati

(iv) Which of the following is not a correct statement about him?

(a) He was against idol worship and meaningless rituals.

(b) He founded the Hindu college.

(c) He was against inter-caste marriages.

(d) He was against superstitions.

Ans. (c) He was against inter-caste marriages.

Passage Based Questions

1. Read the passage given below and answer the questions that follow.

From the second half of the 19th century the idea of nationalism started to originate in India. The ideas of democratic rights and liberty given by the French Revolution inspired the people of India. The memory of the revolt of 1857 also inspired Indians to go ahead with their struggle for freedom. These were several factors which were responsible for the rise and growth of the national movement. One of the most important factors was the influence of Western education. The British introduced, Western education in India to serve their own administrative and political ends.

They wanted trained clerks for their administration. However, the Western education broadened the views of Indians. India became aware of the ideals of French and American Revolution. In all parts of India, educated Indians could communicate with one another through English language. Further, Western Education encouraged Vernacular languages.

(i) Which of the following statement is true about Indian nationalism?
(a) It was largely influenced by the French Revolution.
(b) It was inspired by the ideal of liberty which was given by the American Revolution.
(c) Educated Indians played a great role in the nationalist movement.
(d) Both (a) and (c)

Ans. (d) Both (a) and (c)

(ii) Why was Western education introduced in India?
(a) British wanted every section of Indians to be educated.
(b) It was introduced after several protests held by Indians to introduce Western Education.
(c) British introduced Western education to serve their own administrative needs.
(d) It was introduced because of the Queen's order.

Ans. (c) British introduced Western education to serve their own administrative needs.

(iii) Which is true regarding the effect of Western Education in India?
(a) The Western education made people like British.
(b) The Western education made Indians realise the ideals of liberty and democracy.
(c) Both (a) and (b)
(d) None of the above

Ans. (b) The Western education made Indians realise the ideals of liberty and democracy.

(iv) In which year French Revolution took place?
(a) 1889 (b) 1789 (c) 1879 (d) 1679

Ans. (b) 1789

2. Read the passage given below and answer the questions that follow.

As a result of growing nationalism and political consciousness there was formation of various political associations. The earliest political organisation formed in India was the Landholder's Society founded in 1838 by Dwarkanath Tagore of Bengal. Its aim was to safeguard the interests of landlords of Bengal, Bihar and Orissa. The 'East India Association' was founded by Dadabhai Naoroji, the Grand Old Man of India. It was formed in London in 1866. The association voiced the grievances of Indians and suggested remedial measures. He thought that the British were basically just and fair but unaware of the situation of Indian people. Through his association he voiced the grievances of Indians so that the British could solve it and suggested remedial measures. The association demanded the withdrawal of Vernacular Press Act and abolition of cotton duties. The association had its branches in Bombay, Calcutta and Madras.

(i) Which of the following was the earliest formed political association of India?
(a) East India Association
(b) Landholder's Society
(c) Indian Association
(d) Association of Landholders

Ans. (b) Landholder's Society

(ii) Consider the following statements and choose the correct statement.
(a) Landholder's society worked for the causes of landlords of all the states of India.
(b) It was founded in 1836.
(c) It was founded in Bengal.
(d) It was formed by Devendranath Tagore.

Ans. (c) It was founded in Bengal.

(iii) Which of the following is not correct about Dadabhai Naoroji?
(a) He is known as the 'Grand Old Man' of India.
(b) He founded East India Association in 1864.
(c) He believed British to be fair and just at first.
(d) His organisation voiced out several grievances of Indian people.

Ans. (b) He founded East India Association in 1864.

(iv) Which of the following is a true fact about 'East India Association'?
(a) It was found by Dadabhai Naoroji.
(b) The association was in favour of the Vernacular Press Act.
(c) It had only one branch in India.
(d) It was formed in India in 1866.

Ans. (a) It was found by Dadabhai Naoroji.

Section-II

Short Questions

1. There were various factors that promoted the growth of nationalism in India in the 19th century. Give the meaning of 'nationalism' in this context. **[2011]**

Ans. Nationalism was the most successful political force of the 19th century. Nationalism is a feeling of oneness which the people feel about their nation. It was a result of a new social and economic force, which had put an end to feudalism.

2. Explain the reason of industrial stagnation in British India.

Ans. The British economic policy of exploitation brought about industrial stagnation in India. They hardly made any attempt to revive or promote Indian industries. But the government assisted the British industries. The Britishers established their monopoly in jute, tea, coffee industries with the help of cheap Indian labour.

3. Name the Act of Lord Lytton's regime which aimed at limiting the freedom of the press.

Ans. Lord Lytton passed the Vernacular Press Act in 1878 to suppress the freedom of the native press. According to this act, government could censor the reports of the Vernacular papers, which they thought as anti-British.

4. Mention two acts against which Surendranath Banerjee protested. **[2008]**

Ans. Surendranath Banerjee protested against the following acts
(i) The Indian Arms Act
(ii) The Vernacular Press Act

5. What do you mean by Gagging Act? When was it passed?

Ans. Vernacular Press Act is known as Gagging Act. This act provided the government with extensive rights to censor reports and editorials in the Vernacular newspapers which might incite feelings of dissatisfaction against the British Government.
This act was passed in 1878.

6. What was the Indian Arms Act?

Ans. Lord Lytton passed the Indian Arms Act in 1878 which compelled the Indian to acquire a license to keep, sell or purchase arms. But this law was not applicable to English, Anglo-Indians and government servants of some particular categories.

7. Mention any two economic factors responsible for the growth of nationalism in India. **[2018]**

Ans. (a) Two economic factors responsible for the growth of nationalism in India were
(i) Educated Indians were not appointed to high posts. High posts in civil and military services were only reserved for the British. As a result the Indian began to feel alienated by the British.
(ii) The government levied high taxes on land. Revenues were generally not reduced even during droughts, floods, etc. This led to growth of nationalism among Indian peasantry.

8. How did English language play a leading role in the growth of nationalism in India?

Ans. The spread and popularity of English language gave the educated Indians a common language, i.e. a lingua franca through which they could communicate and exchange their views.
In this way, English language played a leading role in the growth of nationalism in India.

9. Which were the two papers published by Raja Ram Mohan Roy?

Ans. Raja Ram Mohan Roy started two papers. i.e. 'Sambad Kaumudi in Bengali' and 'Miratul Akbar' in Persian. These two papers were devoted of propagating the case for social reforms.

10. Name the personality who set-up
(i) Brahmo Samaj (ii) Arya Samaj
(iii) Ramkrishna Mission

Ans. (i) Brahmo Samaj was set-up by Raja Ram Mohan Roy in 1828.
(ii) Arya Samaj was set-up by Swami Dyananda Saraswati in 1875 in Bombay.
(iii) Ramkrishna Mission was set-up by Swami Vivekananda in 1897 at Belur, West Bengal.

11. Mention any two contributions of Jyotiba Phule in preparing the ground for the national movement. **[2015]**

Ans. The two great contribution of Jyotiba Phule in preparing the ground for the national movement were
(i) In 1873, Jyotiba Phule founded Satya Shodhak Samaj to fight against the caste system.
(ii) He pioneered the widow remarriage movement in Maharashtra and worked for the education of women.

12. Who raised the slogan, 'India for the Indians'? Name the institution founded by him.

Ans. Social reformer Swami Dyananda Saraswati raised the slogan 'India for the Indians'.
He founded the Arya Samaj at Bombay in 1875 to spread his ideas and reforms. The Arya Samaj helped in the revival of the Vedas and the Vedic values.

13. State two factors responsible for the growth of nationalism in India. **[2011]**

Ans. Two important factors responsible for the growth of nationalism in India were
(i) The British introduced Western education in India which inspired Indians and made them politically conscious and disillusioned with the British policies.
(ii) Indian National Congress was founded in 1885 which helped in uniting the people of India.

14. Who founded the 'Landholder' Society and when? Name the organisation in which it was merged to form the 'British Indian Association of Bengal'.

Ans. Landholder's Society was founded by Dwarkanath Tagore in 1838.
The Landholder's Society and the Bengal British Indian Society (1843) were merged to form the British Indian Association of Bengal.

15. Name the two main associations that were the precursors of the Indian National Congress? **[2017]**

Or Name two forerunners of the Indian National Congress.

Ans. East India Association (1866) founded by Dadabhai Naoroji and Indian Association of Calcutta (1876) founded by Surendranath Banerjee, were two precursors or forerunners of the Indian National Congress.

16. Mention the regional association that Surendranath Banerjee was associated with.

Ans. The Indian Association of Calcutta was founded in 1876 by Surendranath Banerjee. This was the first organised political party to express people's disillusionment with British administration.

17. When and by whom was the Indian National Congress founded?

Or When was the Indian National Congress established? Who presided over its first session? **[2014]**

Ans. The Indian National Congress was established in 1885 by AO Hume.

WC Bonnerjee was the President of its first session. The first session of the Congress was attended by 72 delegates from all parts of India, including some eminent persons like Dadabhai Naoroji, Pherozeshah Mehta, Badruddin Tyabji etc.

18. Mention any two objectives of the Congress as enumerated by WC Bonnerjee. **[2011]**

Ans. The objectives of Indian National Congress, which were declared by the W. C Bonnerjee in December, 1885 were

(i) To promote friendly relations between nationalist political workers from various parts of the country.

(ii) To develop and consolidate the feelings of national unity, irrespective of caste, religion or province.

19. Name the Presidents who presided over the first two sessions of the Indian National Congress. **[2018]**

Ans. WC Bonnerjee presided over the first session of the Indian National Congress at Bombay in 1885. Dadabhai Naoroji presided over the second session of the Indian National Congress at Calcutta in 1886.

Structured Questions

1. The Second half of the 19th centrury witnessed the growth of a strong feeling of nationalism. With reference to the statement, answer the following.

(i) Write any four repressive colonial policies of the British.

(ii) State any three ways in which the Press played an important role in developing nationalism amongst Indians.

(iii) Explain the meaning of nationalism.

Ans. (i) Four repressive colonial policies of the British were

(a) Agricultural India was made an economic colony to serve the interests of Industrial England.

(b) India was made to accept readymade British goods either duty free or at nominal duty rates, while Indian products were subjected to high import duties in England.

(c) The British capital invested in Indian markets especially in railway, shipping, oil exploration, tea and coffee plantations etc. was used to get huge profits and were sent to England.

(d) In 1877, when India was faced by a severe famine, Lord Lytton organised a Grand Delhi Durbar to proclaim Queen Victoria as the Empress of India without thinking about the welfare of famine gripped Indians. This angered the Indian masses.

(ii) The role played by the Press in developing nationalism amongst Indians was

(a) It played an important role in carrying ideas to the people.

(b) During the later half of the 19th century, a large number of newspapers were started. These papers fostered patriotism and ideas of liberty and justice in our country.

(c) The press was a powerful factor in building and developing a strong nationalistic sentiment among the Indians.

(iii) Nationalism is a feeling of togetherness and common consciousness based on political, historical, religious, cultural, psychological and other factors in a state. It is a strong sentiment, a feeling of love and pride for one's own country. It is fundamental for a nation's progress and unity.

2. With reference to nationalism, explain each of the following.

(i) Impact of socio-religious reform movement in nationalism.

(ii) Role of the press.

(iii) How did the British react when the Indian National Congress was founded? Why did their attitude change later?

(iv) What was the opinion of Dadabhai Naoroji about British?

Ans. (i) This socio-religious reform movement impacted the growth of nationalism in following ways

(a) It showed the ways of reform to Indian masses.

(b) People started to believe in Indian leadership.

(c) It infused the sense of belongingness among Indian masses.

(ii) The press played an enormous role in fostering national unity and creating consciousness among the Indians. A large number of newspapers were started in the later half of the 18th century which promote patriotism. Some of the prominent newspapers were The Amrit Bazar Patrika, The Bengali, The Tribune, The Pioneer, The Times of India, The Hindu and The Statesman in English.

(iii) The Indian National Congress was founded by Allan Octavian Hume. He was supported by the Indian Nationalists. Many Britishers, including Viceroy Lord Dufferin encourged Hume to form such an organisation.

The aim of the organisation was to work for the material, moral and political advancement of the people in India.

This organisation wanted to provide legitimate outlets to the grievances of the educated Indians and try to satisfy their ambition.

Initially, the British Government was friendly with the Congress as the goal of the Congress was self-government within the British Empire, Lord Dufferin felt that the foundation of the Congress would act as a 'safety valve' for popular discontent. But gradually, the British Government began to distrust the Congress as the popularity of the Congress increased year by year.

(iv) In Dadabhai Naoroji's opinion British were basically just and fair. They were unaware of the grievance of Indian people. If they were informed about the grievances, they could solve them. For this purpose, he founded 'East India Association'.

3. After 1858, various factors led to the rise of Indian nationalism. In this context, describe the impact of the following

(i) Social reformers

(ii) Ilbert Bill Controversy

(iii) Literature

(iv) Impact of Jyotiba Phule in social reform movement.

Ans. (i) Refer to chapter theory page no. 100.

(ii) The Ilbert Bill was a measure to put Indian judges on the same footing as Europeans in dealing with all cases in the Bengal Presidency. It suggested the trials of Europeans by Indian Judges for criminal offences. This provoked a strong criticism among the Britishers.

A systematic campaign to criticise Indian character and culture was launched through press and public meetings. The purpose of the bill was to remove judicial inequalities in the powers of the Indian and the British Magistrates. It was hailed as a liberal and reasonable measures taken by Lord Ripon. Ultimately, the government withdraw the bill.

(iii) Literature became an important instrument for promoting social reforms, awareness of social problems and patriotism and nationalism. During this period, prose writing became important and new forms of literary writings such as novel, short story, drama and essay began to develop.

Writers like Bankim Chandra Chattopadhyay, Rabindranath Tagore, Bharatendu Harishchandra etc, played an important role in promoting consciousness among people.

Bankim Chandra's famous novel 'Anandamath' (1882) was considered as the 'Bible of modern patriotism'. 'Vande Mataram' written by Bankim Chandra and many patriotic songs written by Rabindranath Tagore, Dwijendralal Roy, Muhammad Iqbal inspired Indians and prepared them for the national struggle.

(iv) Jyotiba Phule was an activist, thinker, social reformer who belonged to a low caste family from Maharashtra. Jyotiba Phule and his wife established the first girls school at Poona in 1851. He founded the Satya Shodhak Samaj to fight against the caste system. He was the first leader who started the widow remarriage movement in Maharashtra.

4. With reference to the rise of national consciousness in India, explain the following. **[2017]**

(i) The influence of Western education.

(ii) Any three contributions of Raja Ram Mohan Roy.

(iii) The contribution of Swami Dayananda Saraswati.

(iv) Development of the means of communication and transportation.

Ans. (i) Refer to chapter theory page no. 100.

(ii) Refer to chapter theory page no. 101.

(iii) Refer to chapter theory page no. 101.

(iv) Refer to chapter theory page no. 100.

5. In the latter part of the 19th century, nationalism in India found an organisation of its own, the Indian National Congress. In this context, explain the following.

(i) The Indian Association of Calcutta and All India National Conference.

(ii) East India Association.

(iii) The gradual changes in the objectives of the Congress.

Ans. (i) Refer to chapter theory page no. 102.

(ii) Refer to chapter theory page no. 102.

(iii) The gradual changes in the objectives of the Congress were

- The Congress was founded as an organisation of educated persons such as teachers, professors, lawyers, medical men and businessmen. First, it was a non-political association which tried to get some concession from the British ruler. But gradually the Congress attracted wide membership.
- Then the aim of the Congress was to achieve self-government within the British Empire.
- The Britishers thought that the Congress would act as a safety valve for popular discontent. But with the arrival of new leadership within the Congress, the demands of the Congress changed.
- The early nationalist believed in petition, appeals and memorandum because they had faith in the goodness of the British. But the leaders of the Assertive nationalists started to demand total independence for India.

6. With reference to the growth of national consciousness in India. Explain each of the following. **[2015]**

(i) The immediate objectives of the Indian National Congress.

(ii) Two contributions of Dadabhai Naoroji.

(iii) The relationship between the British and the Congress become bitter.

Ans. (i) The immediate objectives of the Congress were

- To develop the friendly relations between nationalist political workers from different parts of the country.
- To promote and consolidate the feelings of national unity irrespective of caste, religion or province.
- To formulate popular demands and present them before the government.
- To train and organise the public opinion in the country.

(ii) Contributions of Dadabhai Naoroji are

(a) He founded the East Indian Association in London. The association demanded the withdrawal of Vernacular Press Act and abolition of cotton duties.

(b) He presided the second session of Indian National Congress held in Calcutta.

(iii) Initially, the relationship between the British and the Congress was friendly as the aim of the Congress was to achieve self-government within the British Empire. But gradually the British Government started to distrust the Congress for its growing popularity and changing demands.

The Congress started to hold its sessions annually in different cities to rouse public opinion in favour of them. Their increasing popularity worried the British Government and the relationship between the Congress and the British became bitter.

Picture Based Question

1. Look at the the picture given below and anwser the questions that follow.

(i) Identify the personality in the given picture.

(ii) His New Law for Civil Service Examination.

(iii) Write about his policies which heightened the resentment against the British rule.

Ans. (i) The above picture belongs to Viceroy Lord Lytton (1876-80). During his tenure the suppressive policies of the British encouraged the growth of nationalist movement in India.

(ii) Refer to chapter theory page no. 100.

(iii) Lord Lytton's policies the heightened the resentment against the British rule were

- He abolished import duties which crippled the local textile industry. It created a wave of anger throughout India.
- He organised a Grand Delhi Durbar in 1877 to proclaim Queen Victoria as the Empress of India. Lakhs of rupees were spent on the event but nothing was done for the people of South India who were suffering from the effects of a severe famine.
- In order to suppress public opinion, Lytton passed the Vernacular Press Act in 1878.

Chapter Assessment

Section-I

Multiple Choice Questions

1. The year in which the Congress was established
   (a) 1885 (b) 1856
   (c) 1898 (d) 1886
2. Who established Ramakrishna Mission?
   (a) Raja Ram Mohan Roy
   (b) Swami Dayananda Saraswati
   (c) Swami Vivekananda
   (d) Jyotibha Phule

Section-II

Short Questions

1. Give any two examples to indicate that the British followed the policy of economic exploitation in India.
2. In what way did the land revenue charge by the British affect the Indian peasants?
3. When and by whom the Indian Association of Calcutta was organised?
4. Mention two important ways in which the press aroused nationalism.
5. Mention any two demands of the Congress at the beginning.
6. Define the term industrial stagnation during the British period.
7. Name the social evils that were condemned by Raja Ram Mohan Roy.

Structured Questions

1. Explain the role of the following in the growth of nationalism in India.
   (i) Divide and Rule policy of the British rulers
   (ii) Rise of middle class
   (iii) Modern means of communication and transport
   (iv) Dayananda Saraswati
2. Many factors were responsible for the growth of nationalism in India. In this context explain the followings.
   (i) Repressive colonial policies
   (ii) Contribution of Raja Ram Mohan Roy
   (iii) Contribution of Jyotiba Phule
   (iv) Meaning of Nationalism
3. The establishment of the Indian National Congress led to the development of the national movement in India. In this context, explain the following.
   (i) When was the Indian National Congress established? Who presided over its first session?
   (ii) What are the main aims of the Congress?
   (iii) How the standpoint of the British about the National Congress was changed?
   (iv) Precursors of Indian National Congress
4. Explain these factors that promoted the growth of nationalism.
   (i) Industrial stagnation and British apathy to famines
   (ii) Influence of Western education
   (iii) Indian Arms Act, 1878

CHAPTER

03

First Phase of the Indian National Movement (1885-1907)

SYLLABUS

First Phase of the Indian National Movement (1885-1907) Objectives and methods of struggle of the Early Nationalists •Any two contributions of Dadabhai Naoroji, Surendranath Banerjee and Gopal Krishna Gokhale

The first phase of Indian National Movement include the role of the early nationalists in starting the protest against the British rule.

The Early Nationalists (or Moderates)

In the year from 1885 to 1907, the Congress was led by a group of leaders, who were called early **nationalists**[1] or moderates. The early nationalists included the educated middle class consisting of professionals like lawyers, barristers, teachers and officials.

The early nationalists were included from all parts of the country. It included

- Womesh Chandra Bonnerjee, Rash Behari Ghosh and Surendranath Banerjee from Bengal.
- Pandit Madan Mohan Malviya from Uttar Pradesh.
- PR Naidu, Subramania Iyer and Ananda Charlu from Andhra Pradesh and Tamil Nadu.
- Some other moderates were from Maharashtra and Gujarat like Dadabhai Naoroji, Gopal Krishna Gokhale, Justice Ranade, Pherozeshah Mehta, etc.
- There were also some Liberal Englishmen like Hume and William Wedderburn.

Beliefs of the Early Nationalists

- The early nationalist leaders believed in moderate politics and in loyalty to the British Crown. They asked for constitutional and other reforms within the framework of the British rule as they had faith in the British sense of justice and fair play.
- They thought that Englishmen are willing to put India on the path of democracy and self-governance.
- They relied on constitutional and peaceful methods to achieve their aims. They believed in patience and reconciliation rather than in violence and protest.
- The early nationalists wanted the 'Home Rule' thus, they believed that the British would grant 'Home Rule' to Indians. They also believed on the **solemn pledges**[2] made by the British Government.
- They believed that with help of the British rule they could clean the Indian society and eliminate all the social ills like sati, untouchability and child marriage.
- They believed that Indian society created many obstacles in the path of progress of the country.

1 **Nationalist** A person who wants his country to become independent.

2 **Solemn Pledges** A solemn promise or agreement to do or refrain from doing something.

The main obstacles were the social and economic backwardness of Indians and not the British colonial rule.

Demands of the Early Nationalists

The early nationalists worked on the lines of least resistance and also did not ask for immediate achievement of their demands. They feared that the British Government would suppress their activities and thus, they aimed at winning freedom through a gradual process. They made several demands or reforms

Constitutional Reforms

- The early nationalists demanded the expansion and reformation i.e. increase the membership of Indians, of the Legislative Council and Legislative Assemblies both at the centre and in the Provinces.
- They demanded for complete separation between the executive and judicial branches of administration.
- They also demanded to the British rule to provide Indian control over the **public purse**[3] and raised the slogan 'No taxation without representation', that had earlier been raised by the Americans during their War of Independence.
- By the beginning of the 20th century, they demanded for Swarajya or self- government within the British rule like the self-governing colonies of Canada and Australia.
- They also demanded an adequate representation of Indians in the Executive Council of the Viceroy and those of the Governors.

Administrative Reforms

- The early nationalists demanded that more educated Indians should be appointed to the higher posts which were completely occupied by the British officials.
- They demanded that there should be simultaneous examinations in England and India for recruitment to the Civil Service.
- They demanded to repeal the Arms Act and Licence Act.
- They wanted to spread primary education among the maximum population of India.
- They demanded to increase the powers of the local (municipal) bodies in India and reduce the official control over these bodies.
- They demanded for the improvement of the police system to make it honest, efficient and popular and to remove corruption.

Economic Reforms

- The early nationalists demanded reduction in land-revenue and protection of the rights of peasants against the unjust demands of the zamindars.
- They demanded eradication of poverty by increasing industrial production and by giving protection and encouragement to Indian industries.
- They demanded abolition of salt tax and the duty on sugar which was a burden on the poor and lower middle classes.
- They demanded to develop banking, irrigation, medical and health facilities for Indians. Peasants should get cheap credit through agricultural banks.
- They demanded trade protection for industrial growth. It means to imposed a heavy tax on imported goods and to give out loans for the development of iron, coal, paper and sugar industries in India by the government.
- They demanded for the reduction in expenditure on the army and wanted that it should be spent to improve the welfare activities in India, e.g. health and education.
- They also demanded that the British rule should enquire about the growing poverty and famines in India.

Reforms to Defend Civil Rights and Liberties

- The early nationalists demanded Right to Freedom of Speech and Expression.
- They demanded the right to assemble and to form association, to organise meeting and to educate the people.
- They demanded to repeal the Preventive Detention Act and the restoration of civil liberties.
- They demanded the right to circulate leaflets, pamphlets and the repeal of the laws imposing censor on the press i.e. the Vernacular Press Act.

Methods of the Early Nationalists

The early nationalists relied on constitutional and peaceful methods in order to achieve their objectives. The method which they used is popularly known as constitutional agitation method. Their methods were based on two objectives

3 **Public Purse** The funds raised by a government through taxation or other means.

First Objective

The first objective of the early nationalist was to educate people, arouse political consciousness and create public opinions which could change the destiny of the Indians. To achieve this, they used methods such as

- They arranged meetings and discussions. They also organised annual sessions. In these sessions, delegates from all over India participated. After prolonged discussions, resolutions were adopted and these resolutions were forwarded to the government, so that the government could take proper actions.
- They used the print media (e.g. press) to criticise the British policies.
- They sent memorandums and petitions to British Government officials and the British Parliament after having mutual consent.

  These petitions were carefully drafted with facts and arguments. Through these petitions, the early nationalists wanted to educate the Indian people.

Second Objective

The second objective of the early nationalists was to influence the British Government and the British public. To achieve this, they used methods such as

- They used three P's i.e. *Petitions*, *Prayers* and *Protests*. Petitions, requests and letters of protest were send by them to the British Government to consider the problems of the Indians.
- They adopted the method of sending delegation for the fulfilment of its programme and to divert the attention of the British Government towards Indians. Moreover, nationalist like Dadabhai Naoroji raised many issues in the British Parliament.
- In 1889, they formed a British Committee of the Indian National Congress in London. This committee published a weekly journal named, 'India' to present the events and case of Indian people before the British public.

Check Your LEARNING...

1. Write the name of two moderate leaders.
2. What are the two administrative reforms of early nationalists?
3. Write any one demand of the early nationalists which was associated with civil rights and liberties.
4. What was the first objective of early nationalists?

Prominent Early Nationalist Leaders

Some of the prominent early nationalist leaders were Dadabhai Naoroji, Surendranath Banerjee and Gopal Krishna Gokhale.

Dadabhai Naoroji

He was born on 4th September, 1825 in a Parsi family of Bombay. He was a Parsi intellectual and educator. He is popularly known as the **Grand Old Man of India**.

He was elected to two government bodies i.e. the Mumbai Municipal Corporation and the Town Council. He founded the Bombay Association.

He edited the newspaper 'Rast Goftar' (Speaker of Truth) and started a magazine known as **Dharma Marg Darshak**. He died on 30th June, 1917.

His main contributions as an early nationalist were

As India's Unofficial Ambassador

- In England, Dadabhai represented India and its situation before the British Government and thus, considered as the unofficial Ambassador of India who fought for the cause of his country.
- He founded the **London India Society** in 1865 with a joint effort of WC Bonnerjee. The aim of this society was to address the miseries of the Indian people before the British Government.
- He was the first Indian who was elected to the British House of Common in 1892 as Liberal Party candidate.
- After becoming a member of the British Parliament, he tried to present important matters related to India before the House.
- He opposed the discrimination policy of the British and was in favour of appointing educated Indians to high posts like other British officials.
- In the year 1893 due to his efforts, a resolution was passed by the House of Commons to hold the Imperial Civil Service (ICS) examination in England and India simultaneously.
- He started the **East India Association** in 1866 in order to win the sympathies of the British for Indians in England and India. The main aim of this association was to develop closer relations between the Indians and the British on a social level. Later, he opened the branches of this association in Calcutta, Bombay and Madras.
- Through East India association, Dadabhai opposed Vernacular Press Act and criticised atrocities committed by *zamindars* on the poor peasants.

Role in the Indian National Congress

- He took an active part in the formation of the Indian National Congress in 1885. He was elected its President three times, in 1886, 1893 and 1906.
- He is credited for demanding Swaraj for the first time from the Congress platform in 1906 when he was the President of the Congress.
- Under his presidentship, the resolutions of Swaraj, Swadeshi, Boycott and National Education were passed in the annual session of the Congress in 1906.

Exposed the Economic ills of India

Dadabhai's greatest contribution was the economic theory given by him. In his book, **Poverty and Un-British Rule in India,** he exposed the economic exploitation of India by the British. This book explained the fact that India could not progress because the British drained off its wealth. This was known as the famous 'Drain of Wealth' theory.

Surendranath Banerjee

He was born on 10th November, 1848 in Bengal in a Brahmin family. He was a nationalist leader, popular journalist and dedicated educationist. He is popularly known as **Rashtraguru** or the **Father of the Nationalist Movement in India.** He died in Bengal on 6th August, 1925.

His main achievements were

- He advocated constitutional means for attaining his political goals. He advocated for the establishment of self–government in India. He also advocated the idea of boycotting foreign goods and using Swadeshi as methods of anti-colonial protest.
- He set up his own school that later called **Ripon college.**
- He was the first Indian to qualify for Civil Service Examination.
- He was elected as the President of the Congress twice in 1895 and 1902.
- He was elected to the reformed Legislative Council of Bengal four times.
- He remained as a member of the Calcutta Corporation for nearly two decades.
- In 1921, he was appointed as minister of self-government and health by the Governor of Bengal and held from 1921 to 1924. He became the first Indian to hold this position.

His main contributions as an early nationalists were

As Founder of the Indian Association

In 1876, he founded the 'Indian Association' in order to fight against cruel policies of the British. The important aim of this Association was to promote the political, intellectual and material advancement of people through every legal means.

As Founder of All-India National Conference

Surendranath established an All India National Conference in 1883 in Kolkata. This was the first political organisation of an all-India character.

In 1886, the Indian National Conference merged with the Indian National Congress as both organisations had similar objectives.

His Political Ideas

- A newspaper named as 'Bengalee' was edited by him in the year 1879. It proved as a powerful medium for mobilising public opinion in the country.
- He gave his political concern and views about self-government in his book 'Nation in the Making'.
- He led agitation against many cruel policies and acts of the British such as against the 'License Act', 'Arms Act', 'Vernacular Press Act' and against lowering the age from 21 to 19 years to appear in the ICS Examination.
- He also showed his disapproval to the Morley-Minto Reforms of 1909 which introduced separate electorates for the Hindus and the Muslims.
- He opposed the division of Bengal in 1905 by Lord Curzon.

Gopal Krishna Gokhale

He was born at Kolhapur in Maharashtra on 9th May, 1866. He was greatly influenced by the ideals of Justice MG Ranade. As a result, he became a member of the **Deccan Education Society** founded by Justice Ranade.

The Society sent him to England to propagate Indian views before the Welby Commission. Gokhale was an idealist and at the same time he was a practical thinker. He favoured the use of constitutional means. He died on 19th February, 1915. His main achievements were

- Gokhale received the title of **Companion of the Indian Empire** (CIE).

- He became a member of the Congress in 1889. He became General-Secretary of the Congress in 1897. He was elected President of the Congress in 1905 and presided over the Varanasi session of Congress in the same year.
- He edited the quarterly journal, *'Sudharak'*.

His main contributions as an early nationalists were

As Founder of Servants of India Society

In 1905, Gokhale founded the 'Servants of India Society'. The aim of the society was to train national missionaries dedicated to the service of India.

Some important members of this society were Shrinivas Shastri, Pandit Hridaynath Kunzru, etc. The society organised many campaigns to promote education, especially women education, sanitation, healthcare and fought against the social evils like untouchability, discrimination, alcoholism, poverty, oppression of women, etc.

Persuaded the British for Reforms

- He requested the British Government to reduce the land revenue and repeal the production tax on cotton. These both taxes greatly affected the farming community.
- He requested the British Government for the reform of the Legislative Councils and separation of judiciary from the executive.
- He was the member of the Indian Public Service Commission. During this time period, he urged to the British Government to increase the share of Indians in higher services.
- During his visit to England, he tried his best to persuade the British Government not to give the assent to the partition of Bengal which took place in 1905.
- He opposed the policies of British regime whenever he found it faulty. He criticised the British Government for
  - adopting a policy of racial discrimination for the appointment at higher administrative posts.
  - imposing an exploitative economic policy.

Role as a Member of Imperial Legislative Council

- He became the member of the Imperial Legislative Council in the year 1902 and requested the Council for reduction in salt duty.
- He is credited for the reduction in toll-tax.
- He wanted to make primary education compulsory for Indians and tried to introduce a bill regarding this, but the British Government did not give its consent on this bill.
- He demanded radical changes in the fiscal policy and better jobs for the educated middle class.
- He wanted that the high land revenue should be reduced in India and forced the government to do so.

Gokhale and Gandhiji

- Gokhale helped Gandhiji in his fight against racial discrimination in South Africa.
- He is also credited to persuade Gandhiji to return to India and live a life like an Indian.
- In his autobiography, Gandhiji called Gokhale his mentor and guide due to which Gokhale is best known as the **Political Guru of Gandhiji**.

Check Your LEARNING...

1. Mention any one achievement of Dadabhai Naoroji.
2. Who was known as the Father fo the Nationalist Movement in India?
3. Who were the members of the 'Servants of India Society'?
4. What was the role of Gopal Krishna Gokhale in Gandhiji's life ?

Time Line

Year	Important Events
1825	Dadabhai Naoroji was born
1848	Surendranath Banerjee was born
1866	Gopal Krishna Gokhale was born
1876	Indian Association of Calcutta was founded by SN Banerjee
1879	Newspaper 'The Bengalee' was founded
1885-1905	The Indian National Congress was led by the Early Nationalists
1886	Public Service Commission established
1889	Gopal Krishna Gokhale became a member of the Congress
1892	The Indian Council Act
1895	Introduction of the Welby Commission on Indian Expenditure
1897	Gokhale became the General-Secretary of the Congress
1905	Gokhale became the President of the Congress and founded the 'Servants of India Society'
1906	Dadabhai Naoroji became the President of Congress
1915	Gopal Krishna Gokhale died
1921-1924	Surendranath Banerjee held office as minister for local self-government.
1925	Surendranath Banerjee died

QUiCK Revision

- The early nationalists class comprised of mainly the educated middle class, they trusted the British for their sense of justice, honesty and integrity.
- They demanded self-government within the British Empire and asked for constitutional and other reforms within the framework of the British rule.
- In order to achieve self-government, the early nationalists demanded some constitutional reforms, administrative reforms and economic reforms.
- They also demanded some civil rights and liberties, like Right to Freedom of Speech and Expression, right to assemble and form association, etc.
- To fulfil their aim, the early nationalists relied on constitutional and peaceful methods.
- The early nationalists tried to convince the British through petitions, prayers and protests.
- Dadabhai Naoroji established the East India Association in 1866. The famous 'Drain of Wealth' theory was given by Dadabhai Naoroji.
- In 1906, Dadabhai was elected as the President of Indian National Congress.
- Rashtraguru Surendranath Banerjee with the help of other leaders founded the Indian Association of Calcutta in 1876.
- The association strongly protested against the government decision of reducing the age limit in Civil Service Examination. The other demands were repeal of the Arms Act and Vernacular Act, etc.
- In 1883, Surendranath first established a political organisation 'All India National Conference'.
- He advocated the idea of boycotting foreign goods and swadeshi as methods of anti-colonial protest.
- Gopal Krishna Gokhale is best known as 'the Political Guru of Gandhiji.' He believed in harmonious co-operation of India with England.
- In 1905, Gokhale founded the 'Servants of India Society'. The society promoted women education, sanitation, health care and fighted against the social evils like untouchability, discrimination, alcoholism, poverty, oppression of women, etc.
- Gokhale criticised the policy of racial discrimination, exploitative economic policy of the British.
- Gokhale strongly opposed the partition of Bengal and government's control over universities.
- Gokhale forced the British Government to recognise the capabilities of the educated new generations and include them in governing process.

Chapter Practice

Section-I

Multiple Choice Questions

1. Which of the following was the feature of the early nationalists?
   (a) They were not loyal to the British.
   (b) They did not believe in the sense of justice, fair play, honesty and integrity of the British.
   (c) They wanted the 'Home Rule'.
   (d) They believed that the British would not grant 'Home Rule' to Indians.

Ans. (c) They wanted the 'Home Rule'.

2. Which of the following was the prevailing social evil in the Indian Society during the times of early nationalists?
   (a) Sati system
   (b) Untouchability
   (c) Child marriage
   (d) All of the above

Ans. (d) All of the above

3. What was the demand of the early nationalists, by the beginning of the 20th century?
   (a) Demand for Swarajya or self- government within the British rule.
   (b) An adequate representation of Indians in the Executive Council of the Viceroy and those of the Governors.
   (c) Separate electorate
   (d) Both (a) and (b)

Ans. (d) Both (a) and (b)

4. Which medium were used by early nationalists to criticise government policies?
   (a) Public meetings (b) Speeches
   (c) Press (d) All of these

Ans. (d) All of these

5. Who became widely known for his unfavourable opinion of the economic consequences of British rule in India?
   (a) Surendranath Banerjee
   (b) Madan Mohan Malviya
   (c) Dadabhai Naoroji
   (d) Gopal Krishna Gokhale

Ans. (c) Dadabhai Naoroji

6. Which of the following was the most effective contribution made by Dadabhai Naoroji to the cause of Indian National Movement?
   (a) Brought the problems of Indians to the notice of the British
   (b) Exposed the economic exploitation of Indians by the British
   (c) Interpreted the ancient Indian texts and restored the self-confidence of Indians
   (d) Stressed the need for eradication of all the social evils before anything else

Ans. (b) Exposed the economic exploitation of Indians by the British

7. When the Indian Council Act was passed?
   (a) 1892 (b) 1896
   (c) 1891 (d) 1899

Ans. (a) 1892

8. The first phase of Indian National Congress was called the phase of ....
   (a) Revolutions (b) Militants
   (c) Moderates (d) Extremists

Ans. (c) Moderates

9. The prominent members of the moderates were ....
   (a) Lala Lajpat Rai, Bipin Chandra Pal, Subhash Chandra Bose
   (b) Bipin Chandra Pal, Chandrashekar Azad, Dadabhai Naoroji
   (c) Chandrashekar Azad, Gopal Krishna Gokhale, Feroz Shah Mehta
   (d) SN Banerjee, Gopal Krishna Gokhale, Dadabhai Naoroji

Ans. (d) SN Banerjee, Gopal Krishna Gokhale, Dadabhai Naoroji

10. Which of the following statements about early nationalists is false? **[2021]**
    (a) The leaders were Dadabhai Naoroji and Gopal Krishna Gokhale.
    (b) They believed in constitutional means of protest.
    (c) They wanted to launch violent agitations against the British.
    (d) They wanted self-government under British rule.

Ans. (c) They wanted to launch violent agitations against the British.

11. Which of the following is a method of the early nationalists?
    (a) Swadeshi
    (b) Sending Petitions
    (c) Passive Resistance
    (d) Revivalism

Ans. (b) Sending Petitions

12. Formation of Congress : 1885 : : Formation of Muslim League : .... **[2023]**
    (a) 1905 (b) 1906
    (c) 1907 (d) 1908

Ans. (b) 1906

13. Complete the given analogy.
Dadabhai Naoroji : Bombay :: SN Banerjee : ?
(a) Uttar Pradesh (b) Bihar
(c) Assam (d) Bengal

Ans. (d) Bengal

14. Complete the given analogy.
? : Rashtra Guru :: Grand Old Man of Indian Politics : Dadabhai Naoroji
(a) Surendranath Banerjee
(b) Gopal Krishna Gokhale
(c) Madan Mohan Malviya
(d) Justice Ranade

Ans. (b) Gopal Krishna Gokhale

15. Replace the underlined word to correct the statement.
A person who wants his country to become independent is known as <u>Anti-nationalist</u>.
(a) Revolutionaries (b) Nationalist
(c) Inconstant (d) Perfidious

Ans. (b) Nationalist

16. To stop or abolish something by government or a person with authority is known as <u>Deputation</u>.
(a) Repeal (b) Restoration
(c) Vehement (d) None of these

Ans. (a) Repeal

17. Complete the following table.

Dadabhai Naoroji became the President of Congress.	1886
Gopal Krishna Gokhale became the President of Congress.	?

(a) 1905 (b) 1911 (c) 1925 (d) 1966

Ans. (a) 1905

18. Who among the following criticised the British Government for adopting a policy of racial discrimination?
(i) SN Banerjee
(ii) Madan Mohan Malviya
(iii) Justice Ranade
(iv) Gopal Krishna Gokhale

Codes
(a) Only (i) (b) Both (ii) and (iii)
(c) Only (iv) (d) All of these

Ans. (c) Only (iv)

19. Match the following.

	List I		List II
A.	1879	1.	The Indian Council Act
B.	1886	2.	Newspaper 'Bengalee' was founded
C.	1889	3.	Public Service Commission was established
D.	1892	4.	Gopal Krishna Gokhale became a member of Congress

Codes

	A	B	C	D		A	B	C	D
(a)	1	2	3	4	(b)	2	3	4	1
(c)	3	4	1	2	(d)	4	3	1	2

Ans. (b)

20. Match the following.

	List I		List II
A.	1895	1.	Foundation of Servants of India Society
B.	1897	2.	SN Banerjee died
C.	1906	3.	Introduction of Welby Commission on Indian Expenditure
D.	1915	4.	Gokhale became General- Secretary of Congress

Codes

	A	B	C	D		A	B	C	D
(a)	1	2	3	4	(b)	2	1	4	3
(c)	3	4	1	2	(d)	4	3	2	1

Ans. (c)

Picture Based Questions

21. Look at the picture given below and answer the questions that follow.

(i) Which of the following personalities is shown in the given picture?
(a) Gopal Krishna Gokhale
(b) Dadabhai Naoroji
(c) Madan Mohan Malviya
(d) Justice Ranade

Ans. (b) Dadabhai Naoroji

(ii) He is associated with which of the following organisations?
(a) Theosophical Society (b) East India Association
(c) Servants of India Society (d) All of these

Ans. (b) East India Association

(iii) In which places he opened the branch of his organisation in India?
(a) Calcutta (b) Bombay
(c) Madras (d) All of these

Ans. (d) All of these

(iv) Dadabhai Naoroji opposed which of the following 'Acts of British Government'?
(a) Simon Commission (b) Cripps India Mission
(c) Vernacular Press Act (d) All of these

Ans. (c) Vernacular Press Act

22. Look at the picture given below and answer the questions that follow.

(i) Which of the following personalities is shown in the given picture?
(a) Gopal Krishna Gokhale (b) Dadabhai Naoroji
(c) Surendranath Banerjee (d) Justice Ranade

Ans. (c) Surendranath Banerjee

(ii) He was regarded as which of the following title?
(a) Rashtra Guru
(b) Father of the National Movement in India
(c) Father of Nation (d) Both (a) and (b)

Ans. (d) Both (a) and (b)

(iii) He is associated with which of the following organisations?
(a) Indian Association of Calcutta
(b) East India Association
(c) Servants of India Society
(d) All of the above

Ans. (a)Indian Association of Calcutta

(iv) He protested against which of the following through the Association founded by him?
(a) Vernacular Press Act
(b) Arms Act
(c) Inhuman treatment towards the Indian workers in tea and Indigo plantations owned by the British
(d) All of the above

Ans. (d) All of the above

Passage Based Questions

23. Read the passage given below and answer the questions that follow.

The early nationalists were loyal to the British. They firmly believed in the sense of justice, fair play, honesty and integrity of the British. The early nationalists wanted the 'Home Rule' thus, they believed that the British would grant 'Home Rule' to Indians. They also believed on the solemn pledges made by the British Government.

They believed that with help of the British rule they could clean the Indian society and eliminate all the social ills like sati, untouchability and child marriage. They believed that the British would help Indians to govern themselves based on the norms of the Western standards. The early nationalists saw that Indian Society created many obstacles in the path of progress of the country. The main obstacle was the social and economic backwardness of Indians and not the British colonial rule.

(i) The phase of moderates is recorded from which of the following period?
(a) 1888-1899 (b) 1899-1905
(c) 1885-1907 (d) 1907-1920

Ans. (c) 1885-1907

(ii) Which among the following was the demand of moderates?
(a) Spread of primary education among the maximum population of India.
(b) Reduction of military expenditure.
(c) Separation of judiciary from Executive.
(d) All of the above

Ans. (d) All of the above

(iii) In which year the Radicals and the Moderates were divided?
(a) 1905 (b) 1907
(c) 1909 (d) 1911

Ans. (b) 1907

(iv) Which of the following is not among the moderate leaders?
(a) Rash Behari Ghosh (b) WC Bonnerjee
(c) Surendranath Banerjee (d) Bal Gangadhar Tilak

Ans. (d) Bal Gangadhar Tilak

24. Read the passage given below and answer the questions that follow.

When Dadabhai Naoroji was in England, he represented India and its situation before the British Government and thus, considered as the Unofficial Ambassador of India who fought for the cause of Indian people.

He founded the 'London India Society' in 1865 with a joint effort of WC Bonnerjee. The aim of this society was to address the miseries of the Indian people before the British Government. Dadabhai was the first Indian who was elected to the British House of Common in 1892 as Liberal Party candidate.

After becoming a member of the British Parliament, he tried to present important matters related to India before the House. He was opposed to the discrimination policy of the British and was in favour of appointing educated Indians to high posts like other British officials. In the year 1893 due to his great efforts, the House of Commons passed a resolution in favour of holding the Imperial Civil Service (ICS) Examination in England and India simultaneously.

(i) Dadabhai Naoroji was among which leaders of Congress?
(a) Revolutions (b) Militants
(c) Moderates (d) Extremists

Ans. (c) Moderates

(ii) Which of the following book was written by Dadabhai Naoroji ?
(a) Hind Swaraj
(b) Poverty and Un-British Rule in India
(c) India Divided (d) None of these

Ans. (b) Poverty and Un-British Rule in India

(iii) Dadabhai Naoroji was elected as the President of India for how many times?
(a) Two (b) Three (c) Four (d) Five

Ans. (b) Three

(iv) In which year Dadabhai was elected to the British House of Common as Liberal Party candidate and became the first Indian to be elected in the House?
(a) 1885 (b) 1892 (c) 1905 (d) 1910

Ans. (a) 1885

Section-II

Short Questions

1. Mention the period of India's freedom struggle, which is known as moderate phase.

Ans. The period between 1885 to 1907 is known as moderate phase in India's freedom struggle. This period was dominated by the early nationalists or moderates. WC Bonnerjee, Gopal K Gokhale and Dadabhai Naoroji etc are the examples of some moderate leaders.

2. Why were the early Congressmen called moderates? **[2013]**

Ans. The early Congressmen were called moderates because
- Early moderates believed in loyalty to the British Crown.
- They had faith in the British sense of justice and fair play. Their attitude was not anti-British.
- They believed that the British rule had many benefits, for example it aided in cleaning social ills like sati, untouchability and child marriage.

3. What did the early nationalists class think about the British?

Ans. The early nationalists class mainly comprised of the educated middle class. They trusted the British for their sense of justice, honesty and integrity. They believed that, if the British would know the grievances of Indians, they would do what was right for Indians.

4. How did the early nationalists try to convince the British?

Ans. To convince the British, the early nationalists used petitions, prayers and protests. They thought that the British Government could be persuaded by arguments and they would respond to Indian public opinion.

5. What kind of self-government did the early nationalists demand?

Ans. The early nationalists demanded self-government within the British Empire and hoped that the British Government would guide them. So, they asked for constitutional and other reforms within the framework of the British rule along with the self-government.

6. Explain the method of struggle of the early nationalists.

Ans. The method of struggle of the early nationalists was known as constitutional agitation. It included discussions, processions, speeches, peaceful propaganda through press, memorandum, sending delegations, holding annual sessions and passing resolutions.

7. Mention any two economic issue raised by the early nationalists.

Ans. The early nationalists blamed the colonial powers for all economic issues of India. They demanded
(i) reduction in land-revenue and protection of the rights of peasants against the unjust demands of the zamindars.
(ii) abolition of salt tax and the duty on sugar.

8. Mention two reasons for the faith of the moderates in the British sense of justice. **[2012]**

Ans. Two reasons for the faith of the moderates in the British sense of justice were
(i) The moderates thought that the Englishmen thought about progressing India and putting, it on the path of democracy and self-governance.
(ii) The moderates thought that English rule had conferred benefits upon them, especially the English language and the modern means of communication and transport.

9. Name the weekly journal which was published in England to create public opinion in favour of Indians at the period of the early nationalism.

Ans. A weekly journal called 'India' was published in England for circulation among the Britishers. It wanted to create public opinion in favour of Indians at the period of the early nationalism.

10. Write two methods of the early nationalists to influence the people in Britain.

Ans. The two methods adopted by the early nationalists to influence the people in Britain were
(i) They arranged lectures in different parts of England to create public opinion in favour of Indians.
(ii) A British committee of the Indian National Congress was set up in 1889.

11. State any two methods adopted by the early nationalists in the National Movement. **[2020]**

Ans. Two methods adopted by the early nationalists in the National Movement were
(i) Passing Resolution
(ii) Sending Petitions

12. Mention the regional association that each nationalist was associated with **[2010]**
(i) Surendranath Banerjee
(ii) Dadabhai Naoroji

Ans. (i) Surendranath Banerjee was associated with the Indian Association of Calcutta (1876).
(ii) Dadabhai Naoroji was associated with the East India Association (1866).

13. What did Dadabhai Naoroji do through his East India Association?

Ans. Through his East India Association, Dadabhai Naoroji opposed Vernacular Press Act, condemned atrocities committed by zamindars on the poor peasants and took an active part in the formation of the Indian National Congress in 1885.

14. Who exposed the economic exploitation of India through his book 'Poverty and Un-British Rule in India'? **[2013]**

Ans. Dadabhai Naoroji exposed the economic exploitation of India through his book 'Poverty and Un-British Rule in India.'

15. Name the two books that Dadabhai Naoroji authored explaining the Drain of India's Wealth. **[2019]**

Ans. Two books of Dadabhai Naoroji explaining the Drain of India's Wealth are

(i) Poverty of India

(ii) Poverty and Un-British Rule in India

16. Mention any two contributions of Dadabhai Naoroji in the Indian Movement. **[2006]**

Ans. Two contributions of Dadabhai Naoroji were

(i) He established the East India Association in 1866 in order to win the sympathies of the British for Indians.

(ii) He presented the economic theory, 'Drain Theory' in his book 'Poverty and Un-British Rule' in India.

17. Which session of the Indian National Congress was presided over by Dadabhai Naoroji? Which important resolutions were passed in this session?

Ans. Dadabhai Naoroji presided over the annual session of the Indian National Congress in 1906.
The resolutions of Swaraj, Swadeshi, Boycott and National Education were passed in this session.

18. Mention two acts against which Surendranath Banerjee protested. The ideas of Surendranath Banerjee was influenced by which person?

Ans. Surendranath Banerjee protested against the Arms Act and the Vernacular Press Act. The liberal progressive thinking of Surendranath Banerjee was deeply influenced by his father Durga Charan Banerjee.

19. Why was Surendranath Banerjee dismissed from the post of District Magistrate?

Ans. Surendranath Banerjee was dismissed from the post of District Magistrate because he opposed the racial discrimination policy of the British. He was the second Indian to qualify Indian Civil Service examination in 1869. But he was removed from it claiming that he was misrepresented his age.

20. Who is regarded as the Political Guru of Mahatma Gandhi? Give a reason for him being considered as Mahatma's Guru.

Ans. Gokhale helped Gandhiji in his fight against racial discrimination in South Africa. He is also credited to persuade Gandhiji to return to India. That is why he is regarded as the Political Guru of Gandhiji.

21. Name some important members of the 'Servants of India Society'.

Ans. The 'Servants of India Society' was founded by Gopal Krishna Gokhale in 1905. Some important members of this association were Shrinivas Shastri, Pandit Hridaynath Kunzru, etc.

22. What was the aim of 'Servants of India Society'?

Ans. The aim of the 'Servants of India Society.' was to train national missionaries dedicated to the service of India. The society worked for women education, sanitation, healthcare, untouchability etc.

Structured Questions

1. The period of National Movement from 1885-1907 is known as the moderate phase. In this context, explain the following questions.

(i) Why was this period called as the period of the moderates?

(ii) Methods of the moderates.

(iii) Main demands of the moderates.

(iv) Beliefs of the early nationalists.

Ans. (i) This period was called as the period of the moderates because it was dominated by the moderate leaders. The Indian National Congress was founded in 1885. Leaders of that time were – Dadabhai Naoroji, Gopal Krishna Gokhale, Justice Ranade and Pherozeshah Mehta etc.
Between 1885-1907 the moderates adopted the path of prayer and petition i.e. pleading with the British to fulfil their demands. That is why this phase is known as the period of moderates.

(ii) Refer to chapter theory page no. 110.

(iii) The main demands of the moderates were

- For constitutional reform they demanded expansion and reformation of the Legislative Council and an increase in membership and powers of the councils.
- The moderates demanded administrative reforms like wider employment for Indians in the higher services, simultaneous Civil Service Examinations in England and India, repeal of the Arms Act etc.
- They demanded some economic reforms like abolition of salt tax and duty on sugar, protection and encouragement for Indian industry, development of banking, irrigation and health facilities etc.

(iv) Refer to chapter theory page no. 112-113.

2. With reference to the early nationalists or the moderates answer the following questions. **[2014]**

(i) Criticism of the early nationalists.

(ii) Four achievements of the moderates.

(iii) Four basic beliefs of the early nationalists.

Ans. (i) The criticism about early nationalists was

- The moderates or the early nationalists failed to draw the maximum people into the mainstream of the National Movement.
- Their field of influence was very limited to the urban educated Indians.
- Their leadership was confined by the particular professional groups like lawyers, doctors, journalists and teachers, etc.

(ii) The achievements of the moderates were

- Early nationalists, like Dadabhai Naoroji wrote in his book, 'Poverty and Un-British Rule in India' about how the British were draining India's resources.
- The moderates like Govind Ranade and Gopal Krishna Gokhale raised their voice against social evils such as child marriage, sati system, etc. 'The Servants of India Society' established by Gokhale worked for the upliftment of the depressed classes.
- The efforts of moderate resulted in the appointment of a Public Service Commission in 1886 which pass a resolution (1893) in the House of commons for simultaneous Civil Service Examination in India and London.
- The Britishers passed the Indian Council Act of 1892. It was regarded as one of the achievements of the moderated.

(iii) The basic beliefs of the early nationalists were

- The early nationalists believed that the Britishers were just and reasonable. They thought the British Government could be persuaded by arguments and they would do justice to Indians.
- They expressed loyalty to the British Crown and believed that the British presence in India was a blessing to India.
- They thought that the British rule had done much good to Indian society by cleaning the Indian society evils, like custom of sati, untouchability, child marriage etc.
- They also recognised the benefits of the English rule, especially the English language and modern means of transport and communication.

3. With reference to the role of the moderates in arousing national awakening in India, answer the following questions.

(i) Name some moderate leaders. Why were they called so?

(ii) Who was known as 'India's Unofficial Ambassador in England'? Explain.

(iii) What were his views on the cause of poverty in India?

(iv) Mention about the associations formed by him.

Ans. (i) Dadabhai Naoroji, WC Bonnerjee, Madan Mohan Malviya, Gopal Krishna Gokhale, Justice Ranade and Pherozeshah Mehta were some major moderate leaders.

They were called moderate leaders because the nature of their demands were moderate along with their methods, which were constitutional as well.

(ii) Dadabhai Naoroji, the 'Grand Old Man of India,' was known as 'India's Unofficial Ambassador in England' and can be viewed as the architect who laid the foundation of the Indian Freedom Struggle. He sacrificed his career and his family for the country. In 1866, he founded the East India Association in London. The main aim of the association was to inform the British about the grievances of Indians.

In 1892, Dadabhai was elected to the British Parliament. Here, he delivered speeches about the sufferings of Indians and also about the cause of the people of Indian origin living in South Africa.

(iii) The views of Dadabhai Naoroji on the cause of poverty in India were

- He was a economic thinker. He said that British are responsible for poverty in India.
- He also explained that how the Britishers are draining wealth from India.
- His veiws on Indian economy are given in his work 'Poverty and Un-British Rule in India'.
- He wanted that Indians should be appointed to high posts.

(iv) Dadabhai Naoroji founded the 'London India Society' in 1865 with a joint effort of WC Bonnerjee.

He started the East India Association in 1866 in order to win the sympathies of the British for Indians in England and in India.

4. The moderates relied on constitutional and peaceful methods in order to achieve their aim. In this context, explain the following questions.

(i) The administrative reforms demanded by the early nationalists and the demands regarding civil rights and liberties.

(ii) The constitutional reforms demanded by the moderates.

(iii) The economic reforms demanded by the moderates.

Ans. (i) Refer to chapter theory page no. 113.

(ii) Refer to chapter theory page no. 113.

(iii) Refer to chapter theory page no. 113.

Picture Based Questions

1. Read the extract based on the pictures given below and answer the questions that follow. **[2007]**

(1)

(2)

"... the Indians who actively worked for the creation of an all-India political organisation represented new social forces that were increasingly opposed to the exploitation of India for British interests. They needed an organisation that would fight for India's political and economic advancement."

–From 'Freedom Struggle'

(i) (a) In the context of the above, identify the two individuals in Pictures 1 and 2, who were the early leaders of the organisation to be formed?

(b) How did the person in Picture 1, explain the economic exploitation of India for British interests?

(ii) Name the organisation which was to be formed. What were the objectives behind the formation of this political body?

(iii) Explain the major ideological differences which emerged amongst the leaders within the first 20 years of the foundation of this organisation.

Ans. (i) (a) Dadabhai Naoroji is in Picture 1 and Gopal Krishna Gokhale is in Picture 2.

(b) In his book, 'Poverty and Un-British Rule in India' Dadabhai Naoroji exposed the economic exploitation of India by the British. In this book, he pointed out the various ways India was being exploited and, explained robbed of its resources by the British. Dadabhai elaborated the 'Drain Theory' and explained how, it was adversely affecting India's economic development and resulting in economic impoverishment of the Indian masses.

(ii) Indian National Congress was to be formed. The objectives of Indian National Congress were

- Promotion of close relations between nationalistic workers from different parts of the country.
- Development and consolidation of a feeling of national unity, irrespective of caste, religion or province.
- Formulation of popular demands and their presentation before the government.
- To train and organise the public opinion in the country.

(iii) The views of moderates were different from the views of the radicals and this difference emerged within the first 20 years of the foundation of this organisation. The differences in their views were

- The moderates expressed their faith in the British rule and thought it as a blessing for India, but the radicals had no faith in the British.
- The moderates believed in the supremacy of European culture, but the radicals highlighted the supremacy of Indian culture.
- The moderates thought that people of India could not rule themselves, so they demanded for self-government within the British Empire. But the radicals thought that Indians could rule themselves. So, they demanded complete independence from the British.

2. Look at the picture given below and answer the questions that follow.

(i) Identify the personality in the picture. To which section of the Congress did he belong?

(ii) What was the ultimate objectives of the Congress of this section?

(iii) State his contribution as a part of this section of Congress.

Ans. (i) The personality in the above picture is Gopal Krishna Gokhale. He belongs to moderate section of the Indian National Congress. He had deep faith in British liberalism. He is a moderate leader believed in harmonious co-operation of India with England.

(ii) The objectives of moderates were

- The moderates believed in the sense of justice, honesty and integrity of the British. They wanted self-government within the British Empire.
- They asked for constitutional, administrative, economic reforms and also some civil rights and liberties within the British Empire.

(iii) The contributions of Gokhale as moderate were

- Gokhale became a member of the Indian National Congress in 1889. He became General-Secretary of the Congress in 1897 and was elected President of the Congress in 1905.
- He believed in harmonious co-operation of India with England. He declared that the goal of the Congress was to attain self-government like other British colonies.
- In 1905, Gokhale founded the 'Servants of India Society' for the upliftment of poor in our society. The members of the society served the country with a strong devotion.
- At the time of Bengal Partition (1905), he strongly condemned the action of the British Government and gave full support to Boycott Movement.

Chapter Assessment

Section-I

Multiple Choice Questions

1. The London India Society and East India Association were founded by whom?
   (a) Gopal Krishna Gokhale
   (b) Dadabhai Naoroji
   (c) WC Bonnerjee
   (d) Madan Mohan Malviya
2. All India National Conference was established in which year?
   (a) 1883 (b) 1899
   (c) 1906 (d) 1910
3. Early Nationalist's demand for Indianisation of services comes under ....
   (a) Legislative demands
   (b) Constitutional demands
   (c) Economic demands
   (d) Administrative demands
4. Complete the given analogy.
   Abolition of Salt Tax : Economic Reform :: Repeal of Arms Act : ?
   (a) Constitutional Reform
   (b) Administrative Reform
   (c) Cultural Reform
   (d) Social Reform

Section-II

Short Questions

1. Mention the period in which the early nationalists dominate the Indian National Congress.
2. List out any three important leaders of the moderates.
3. Name the person who started the East India Association in 1866.
4. What method did the moderates use to achieve their objectives?
5. Describe the attitude of the moderates towards the British ruler.
6. What did the moderates advocate in the field of Civil Rights?
7. What was the main aim of the East India Association?
8. Who was responsible to establish the first political organisation of an all-India character?

Structured Questions

1. The early nationalists dominated the Congress from 1885-1907. In this context, explain the following questions
   (i) The reasons for the early nationalists being called the moderates.
   (ii) Describe the attitude of the British towards them.
   (iii) State the methods of working of the early nationalists.
   (iv) Role of Dadabhai Naoroji.
2. The early nationalists were liberal in their views and outlook. In this context, explain the following questions
   (i) Mention three basic beliefs of the early nationalists.
   (ii) Demands of the early nationalists.
   (iii) Any two achievements of the early nationalists.
   (iv) Role of Gopal Krishna Gokhale.
3. State the role played by Surendranath Banerjee in National Movement and explain the following
   (i) His political ambition and opposition to the repressive methods adopted by the British.
   (ii) Establishment of new organisation.
   (iii) His achievements.

CHAPTER

04

Second Phase of the Indian National Movement (1905-1916)

SYLLABUS

Second Phase of the Indian National Movement (1905-1916) Brief mention of the causes of the Partition of Bengal and its perspective by the Nationalists. • Brief mention of Surat Split of 1907, objectives and methods of struggle of the Radicals. • Any two contributions of Bal Gangadhar Tilak, Bipin Chandra Pal and Lala Lajpat Rai.

The second phase of the Indian National Movement (1905-1916) witnessed the Partition of Bengal, Swadeshi Movement and the rise of assertive nationalism.

Partition of Bengal

It was the most important event during the tenure of Viceroy Lord Curzon (1899-1905). The Presidency of Bengal was the largest and the most populous state of British India. At that time, it included Bihar, Orissa, Chotanagpur, Assam and some other remote areas. Lord Curzon divided Bengal into two provinces which were

(i) **West Bengal** It included the Western districts of Bengal proper, Bihar and Orissa. Calcutta was made its capital.

(ii) **Eastern Bengal and Assam** It consisted of the Eastern districts of Bengal proper and Assam. Dacca was the capital of this province.

Western Bengal was dominated by Non-Bengali population and Eastern Bengal was dominated by Bengali Muslims. In both the provinces, Hindus-Bengali became a minority.

Partition of Bengal was made public in 1903 and was announced on 20th July, 1905. Curzon's proposal for the division of Bengal received royal assent on 1st September, 1905. Then, it was implemented on 16th October, 1905.

Causes of the Partition of Bengal

According to the British administration, the main reason behind the Partition of Bengal was administrative necessity. They explained that the province was very large, hence it was to be divided. However, there were other motives for partitioning Bengal. These were

- At that period, Bengal had become the main centre of the Indian politics and Indian nationalism. So, the British expected to regulate the rising tide of nationalism by the division of Bengal.
- Another reason of the Partition of Bengal was to destroy the political influence of the educated middle class, among whom the Bengali intellectuals was the most prominent.
- With this partition, Curzon hoped to achieve double advantages which were

  (i) To split up and thus weaken the Nationalist Movement.

(ii) To create a Mohammedan province where Islam and its followers could be pre-dominant.

- Hindu-Muslim unity demonstrated during the uprising of 1857 was a threat to British rule, so it had to be broken by the partition. East Bengal would have majority of Muslims and West Bengal would have majority of Hindus.

Perspectives of Nationalists for Partition of Bengal

Nationalist leaders realised that the Partition of Bengal was an attempt to divide the Bengalis that shared a common culture, language and tradition. Thus, they oppose the partition in the following ways

- The Indian National Congress, all national leaders and all sections of people, even zamindars and merchants protested against partition.
- Protest meetings and campaigns against the partition were organised all over the Bengal by eminent leaders like Surendranath Banerjee, Krishna Kumar Mitra, PC Ray, Bipin Chandra Pal, Ananda Mohan Bose, etc.
- Some Bengali newspapers like **Bengali, Hitabadi** and **Sanjibani** played an important role in opposing partition.
- On 7th August, 1905, Anti-Partition Movement was initiated in which a demonstration was organised against the partition in the Town Hall of Kolkata.

People's reaction to the Partition of Bengal

- On 16th October, 1905 when the Partition came into effect, was declared to be 'a day of mourning'. There was *hartal* in Kolkata. People fasted, walked bare-footed and bathed in Ganga.
- The Hindus and Muslims celebrated 'Raksha Bandhan' and tied *rakhis* on one another's wrist as a symbol of unity.
- People sang 'Vande Mataram' which became the theme song of the National Movement.
- Rabindranath Tagore composed the patriotic song 'Amar Sonar Bangla' which was sung by a huge number of people.
- Anand Mohan Bose laid the foundation of 'Federation Hall' where all people gathered to take the promise to follow Swadeshi.

Check Your LEARNING...

1. When did the Curzon's proposal for the division of Bengal received royal assent?
2. When was the Partition of Bengal implemented?
3. Name some leaders who protested against Partition of Bengal.
4. Which newspaper played important role in condemning the Partition of Bengal in 1905?

The Assertive Nationalists or Radicals

In the second phase of the National Movement, new and younger leaders emerged within the Congress who had a different ideology that advocated active resistance to British Imperialism. They were known as assertive nationalists or radicals.

They held the British responsible for the country's downfall. They criticised the peaceful protests held by the early nationalist leaders. These radical leaders wanted complete 'Swaraj' to be achieved by self-reliant methods and sacrifices. 'Swaraj' for them meant complete independence just as in the colonies of Australia, New Zealand, etc.

Bal Gangadhar Tilak, Lala Lajpat Rai & Bipin Chandra Pal were the three prominent leaders of this group, called as 'Lal, Bal, Pal'.

Causes for the Rise of Assertive Nationalism

- **Recognition of the True Nature of British Rule** The reactionary policies of Lord Lytton and Lord Curzon made it possible for the people to recognise the true nature of the British rule in India. It was recognised that British rule was responsible for the economic ruin and growing poverty of India. Besides, the British Government did nothing to provide welfare measures during the severe famine which lasted from 1896 to 1900.
- **Failure of Moderates** The moderates were loyal to the British Queen. However, the younger leaders of the Congress were dissatisfied with the methods of peaceful agitation followed by the early leaders which could not result into any substantial advantage. Thus, the younger elements of Congress wanted a more vigorous political action.
- **Impact of International Events** International events like the defeat of Russia by Japanese and the Boer's War which was fought against the British Empire in South Africa (1879-1902), inspired the assertive nationalists to get united and overthrow the British Empire from India.
- **Partition of Bengal** The Partition of Bengal provided an immediate cause for the rise of radical leaders into action. This was because the policy of petitions, prayers and protests of early nationalists did not produce any results.
- **Growth in Education and Unemployment** A large numbers of educated Indians were unemployed or employed on low salaries, because of the policies of British. Hence, these educated Indians became the follower of assertive nationalism.

Objective and Methods of Struggle of the Radicals

National freedom was the sole objective of the radicals. The objective and methods of struggle of the radicals were

Promotion of Swadeshi

The radicals asked the people to use only Swadeshi goods, i.e. goods produced in India. Use of Swadeshi goods was promoted to encourage Indian industries and provide the people with more opportunities for work and employment.

As a result of the Swadeshi Movement, a number of Indian textile, mills, national banks, hosiery units, soap factories, tanneries and Swadeshi stores were established throughout the country.

The radicals appealed for the total boycott of foreign goods. They also suggested to boycott government services, honours, titles and social boycott of persons trading in foreign goods. They realised that economic boycott might prove a powerful weapon against economic exploitation by the Britishers.

National Education

The radicals called upon students to boycott schools and colleges run by the government. Special schools and colleges like, Bengal National College was established in Kolkata and large number of national schools were established in East Bengal. In Chennai, a National College was established.

In Punjab, DAV (Dayanand Anglo Vedic) Movement started that spread education through various school and colleges. The National Council of Education was set up in 1906.

Co-operative Organisations

The radicals encouraged co-operative organisations. Voluntary associations were set-up for rural sanitation, preventive police duties, regulation of fairs and pilgrim gatherings, for providing relief during famines and other natural calamities.

Involvement of the Masses

The radicals involved the masses by organising festivals, boycott, Swadeshi and national education. They spoke and wrote in the vernacular language and were easily able to reach the masses.

They suggested that self-dependence and sacrifices of the patriots could help the welfare of the country.

Surat Split of Indian National Congress

In the year 1907, the Annual Session of the Congress was held in Surat. In this session, assertive nationalists or radicals wanted to adopt revolutionary methods as announced by them, but the early nationalists or moderates were not in favour of such methods. Thus, the Indian National Congress split into two groups at the Surat Session.

The radicals were led by Bal Gangadhar Tilak, Lala Lajpat Rai and Bipin Chandra Pal and the moderates were led by Gopal Krishna Gokhale. The radicals proposed the name of Lala Lajpat Rai as the President of the Surat Session, whereas the moderates proposed the name of Rash Behari Ghosh.

Finally, the moderates were expelled from the Congress. They remained out of the Congress for 9 years and finally at the Lucknow Session in 1916, the Congress regained its unity.

Prominent Assertive Nationalist Leaders

Some of the prominent assertive leaders were Bal Gangadhar Tilak, Bipin Chandra Pal and Lala Lajpat Rai.

Bal Gangadhar Tilak

He was born on 23rd July, 1856 in a Brahmin family of Maharashtra. He started his career as lawyer, but soon dedicated himself to serving the country. His ideas stimulated new spirit of assertive nationalism in the Congress. He died on 1st August, 1920.

Bal Gangadhar Tilak

His main contributions were

- In 1880, he started the Poona New English School with a view to educate Indians by charging small fees.
- He was one of the founder members of the Deccan Education Society and Fergusson College.
- He started two newspapers i.e. **the Mahratta** (English) and **Kesari** (Marathi) in order to spread the idea of nationalism.
- He revived **Ganapati** festival in 1893 and **Shivaji festival** in 1895 to promote national feeling among Indians.

- He organised many *akharas* and *lathi* clubs where physical training was given.
- He wrote two famous books i.e. the **Gita Rahasya** and the **Arctic Home of the Vedas**.
- He setup Home Rule League in 1916 at Pune to attain self-government under the British.

Bipin Chandra Pal

He was born on 7th November, 1858 in Sylhet district of the Assam. In 1876, he joined the Brahmo Samaj. In 1898, he was sent to Oxford by Brahmo Samaj to study theology. In his later life, he left Brahmo Samaj and became a total convert to orthodox Hinduism.

He is popularly known as the **Father of Revolutionary Thought in India.** In the beginning, he supported the early nationalists (moderates) but during the Anti-Partition Movement, he took active role in promote radical ideals. He died on 20th May, 1932.

His main contributions were

- He travelled to different parts of India spreading the message of Swaraj or freedom.
- He opposed the '**Arms Act**[1]' and like other radical leaders, he stressed on self-reliance and national pride.
- He started the newspaper 'New India' in 1901. His writings were regularly published in various newspapers like, 'The Englishman', 'The Statesman' and 'Modern Review'. Through his oratory and journalistic skills, he spread the message of Boycott, Swadeshi and National Education very effectively.
- He advocated widow remarriage and opposed the existing caste system. He provide all his support to the Age of Consent Bill in 1891.
- He emphasised on the development of indigenous industries in the country.
- He promoted the use of Swadeshi goods and boycott of foreign goods.
- He demanded an increase in wages and 48 hours of work in a week.

Bipin Chandra Pal

Lala Lajpat Rai

He was born in Jagraon in Ludhiana district of Punjab on 28th January, 1865. He was greatly influenced by his father Radha Krishna who was a follower of Dayananda Saraswati, founder of Arya Samaj.

Lala Lajpat Rai

He was popularly known as **Sher-e-Punjab** (The Lion of Punjab). In 1888, he joined the Congress and remained under it till the end of his life. He died on 17th November, 1928 few weeks after sustaining severe injuries during a baton charge.

His main contributions were

- He laid the foundation of DAV College at Lahore. He also opened orphanages, hospitals and schools.
- In 1914, he established an education trust and founded Radha Krishna High School at Jagraon.
- He started various newspapers, like 'Punjabi', 'Vande Mataram' (Urdu Daily) and 'People' (English weekly).
- He wrote various books like, 'Young India', 'England's Debt to India', 'Political Future of India' and 'Unhappy India'.
- He also wrote biographies of Mazzini, Garibaldi, Swami Dayanand Saraswati, Shivaji, etc. During his exile in Mandalay, he wrote his autobiography, **The Story of My Deportation.**
- He supported worker's movement, and became the first President of All India Trade Union Congress in 1920.
- He founded the 'Servants of the People Society' in 1921, which worked for the freedom movement as well as social reforms in the country.

Check Your LEARNING...

1. What was the radicals asked the students to boycott?
2. Mention any one contribution of Bal Gangadhar Tilak.
3. Who was known as the 'Father of Revolutionary Thought in India'?
4. Who wrote his autobiography as 'The Story of My Deportation' ?

1 **Arms Act** The Indian Arms Act, 1878 stipulated that no Indians will be allowed to bear arms without a proper permit. It was introduced by Lord Lytton.

Time Line

Years	Important Events
1885	Indian National Congress was founded.
1885-1905	The Period of early nationalists
1887	Bipin Chandra joined the Congress.
1888	Lajpat Rai joined the Congress
1899-1905	Tenure of Lord Curzon
1903	Scheme of Partition was made public.
1904	Indian Universities Act, Official Secrets Act passed by Lord Curzon.
20th July, 1905	The Partition of Bengal was announced.
1st Sep, 1905	The proposal for the division of Bengal received Royal assent
10th Oct, 1905	Carlyle Circular was implemented.
16th Oct, 1905	The Partition of Bengal was implemented.
1906	Calcutta Session of Indian National Congress, National Council of Education were established.
1907	The Prevention of Seditious Meetings Act
1907	Lajpat Rai and Sardar Ajit Singh led an agitation against the 'Colonisation Bill'.
1907	Surat split
1907	Bipin Chandra was sent to jail for not giving testimony in Aurobindo Ghosh's case
1908	The Explosive Substances Act, the Newspapers Act
1914	Lajpat Rai went to England as member of the Congress delegation.
1916	Tilak started Home Rule League in Maharashtra.
1919	Jallianwala Bagh Massacre
1920	Lajpat Rai became the first President of the Indian National Congress.
1926	Lajpat Rai went to Geneva to attend the 8th International Labour Conference.
1928	Lajpat Rai was severely wounded while leading a peaceful procession against the Simon Commission.
1928	Lajpat Rai died.

QUiCK Revision

- The Viceroy Lord Curzon (1899-1905) announced on 20th July, 1905 the Partition of Bengal, which was implemented on 16th October, 1905.
- The main reason behind the Partition of Bengal was administrative necessity. Beside this, there were several other reasons for the partition.
- After the implementation of the scheme of partition, the Anti-Partition Movement started and the day of partition (16th October, 1905) was observed as 'Day of Mourning'.
- In 1907, at the annual session of Indian National Congress at Surat, the Congress splitted into two groups i.e. moderates and radicals. This split was based on ideological differences.
- After 1907, the radical leaders criticised the methods of moderates and adopted aggressive mode to demand 'Swaraj'.
- Radicals promoted Swadeshi and boycotted foreign goods. They emphasised on involvement of the masses in freedom struggle.
- Bal Gangadhar Tilak started two newspapers the 'Marathi' and 'Kesari' to spread the idea of nationalism. In 1916, he setup the Home Rule League at Pune to attain self-government under the British.
- Bipin Chandra Pal emphasised on total socio-economic transformation. Due to his thought, he is known as the 'Father of Revolutionary Thought in India'.
- Lala Lajpat Rai also known as the Sher-e-Punjab was one of the greatest freedom fighter of India. He founded the 'Servants of People Society' in 1921, which worked for the freedom movement as well as social reforms in the country.

Chapter Practice

Section-I

Multiple Choice Questions

1. When did Lord Curzon become the Viceroy of India?
(a) 1899 (b) 1898
(c) 1901 (d) 1905

Ans. (a) 1899

2. When was Bengal Partitioned? **[Semester-I 2022]**
(a) 1905 (b) 1907
(c) 1906 (d) 1991

Ans. (a) 1905

3. Which of the following was a nationalist perspective of the Partition of Bengal? **[Semester-I 2022]**
(a) There were Hindus in West Bengal.
(b) To divide the Hindus and Muslims.
(c) There were many riots in Bengal.
(d) It was an administrative necessity as Bengal was a large territory.

Ans. (b) To divide the Hindus and Muslims.

4. .... was declared as the 'Day of Mourning'.
(a) 16th October, 1906 (b) 16th October, 1905
(c) 20th July, 1905 (d) 20th July, 1906

Ans. (b) 16th October, 1906

5. The theme song of the Anti-Partition Movement was
(a) Amar Sonar Bangia (b) Vande Mataram
(c) Both (a) and (b) (d) None of these

Ans. (b) Vande Mataram

6. The Lucknow Pact was signed between ..... . **[2023]**
(a) the British and the Congress
(b) the Congress and the Muslim League
(c) the Early and the Assertive Nationalists
(d) the Muslim League and the British

Ans. (b) the Congress and the Muslim League

7. National Council of Education was set up in
(a) 1905 (b) 1908
(c) 1906 (d) 1907

Ans. (c) 1906

8. When was the age of Consent Bill passed?
(a) 1891 (b) 1890 (c) 1889 (d) 1892

Ans. (a) 1891

9. Whose autobiography is 'The Story of My Deportation'?
(a) Bal Gangadhar Tilak (b) Bipin Chandra Pal
(c) Lala Lajpat Rai (d) Aurobindo Ghosh

Ans. (c) Lala Lajpat Rai

10. Who among the following was not a part of the famous 'Lal-Bal-Pal' Trio?
(a) Bal Gangadhar Tilak (b) Lal Bahadur Sashtri
(c) Lala Lajpat Rai (d) Bipin Chandra Pal

Ans. (b) Lal Bahadur Sashtri

11. Complete the given analogy.
Kesari : : ? : Punjabi : Lala Lajpat Rai
(a) Bipin Chandra Pal (b) Aurobindo Ghosh
(c) Bal Gangadhar Tilak (d) Gopal Krishna Gokhale

Ans. (c) Bal Gangadhar Tilak

12. Complete the given analogy.
Announcement of Partition of Bengal : ? :: Proposal of Partition received Royal Assent : 1st September, 1905
(a) 20th July, 1905 (b) 12th July, 1905
(c) 20th June, 1905 (d) 12th June, 1905

Ans. (a) 20th July, 1905

13. Complete the given analogy.
1907 : ? :: 1916 : Lucknow Session
(a) Partition came into effect
(b) Surat split
(c) Boycott Resolution
(d) National College, Kolkata

Ans. (b) Surat split

14. Replace the underlined word with the correct answer.
The Partition of Bengal came into effect on <u>20th July, 1905</u>.
(a) 20th June, 1905 (b) 16th October, 1905
(c) 1st September, 1905 (d) 16th October, 1906

Ans. (b) 16th October, 1905

15. Replace the underlined word with the correct answer.
The newspaper 'New India' was started by <u>Lala Lajpat Rai</u>.
(a) Bal Gangadhar Tilak (b) Krishna Kumar Mitra
(c) PC Ray (d) Bipin Chandra Pal

Ans. (d) Bipin Chandra Pal

16. Complete the following table.

?	Father of Revolutionary Thought in India
Lala Lajpat Rai	Lion of Punjab

(a) Bal Gangadhar Tilak
(b) Aurobindo Ghosh
(c) Rasbehari Ghosh
(d) Bipin Chandra Pal

Ans. (d) Bipin Chandra Pal

17. Complete the following table.

Fergusson College	Bal Gangadhar Tilak
National College of Kolkata	?

(a) Lala Lajpat Rai (b) Aurobindo Ghosh
(c) KK Mitra (d) Anand Mohan Bose

Ans. (b) Aurobindo Ghosh

18. Which of the following is true about the newspaper 'Mahratta'?
(i) It was written by Bal Gangadhar Tilak.
(ii) It was written in Marathi.

Codes
(a) Both (i) and (ii) (b) Only (i)
(c) Only (ii) (d) None of these

Ans. (b) Only (i)

19. Which of the following is not a true statement?
(i) Lord Curzon wanted to divide Bengal into West and East Bengal.
(ii) East Bengal was dominated by Bengali Hindus.
(iii) East Bengal consisted of Assam also.
(iv) Capital of East Bengal was declared to be Calcutta.

Codes
(a) Only (i) (b) Both (ii) and (iv)
(c) Only (iii) (d) Both (iii) and (iv)

Ans. (b) Both (ii) and (iv)

20. Which of the following is true about assertive nationalists radicals ?
(i) They wanted Swaraj, a form of self-government within the British Empire.
(ii) They were not loyal to the British Crown.
(iii) They wanted to protest within the Framework of Law.
(iv) They were supported by educated middle class only.

Codes
(a) Only (ii) (b) Only (i)
(c) Both (iii) and (iv) (d) Both (i) and (iv)

Ans. (a) Only (ii)

21. Match the following.

List-I	List-II
A. Gopal Krishna Gokhale	1. Brahmo Samaj
B. Lala Lajpat Rai	2. Moderate
C. Aurobindo Ghosh	3. Extremist
D. Bipin Chandra Pal	4. Principal of National College of Calcutta

Codes

	A	B	C	D		A	B	C	D
(a)	3	2	1	4	(b)	2	3	1	4
(c)	2	3	4	1	(d)	3	1	2	4

Ans. (c)

22. Match the following.

List-I	List-II
A. Partition of Bengal	1. 1905
B. Surat Split	2. 1907
C. INC founded	3. 1885
D. The Newspaper Act	4. 1908

Codes

	A	B	C	D		A	B	C	D
(a)	1	2	3	4	(b)	4	3	2	1
(c)	3	1	4	2	(d)	2	4	1	3

Ans. (a)

Picture Based Questions

23. Look at the picture given below and answer the questions that follow.

(i) Identify the person given in the picture.
(a) Lord Lytton
(b) Lord Rippon
(c) Lord Curzon
(d) None of the above

Ans. (c) Lord Curzon

(ii) Which of the following is not true regarding the person in the picture?
(a) He was a reactionary Viceroy.
(b) He had proposed the Partition of Bengal.
(c) He was compassionate towards Indians.
(d) He wanted to weaken the Nationalist Movement of Bengal.

Ans. (c) He was compassionate towards Indians.

(iii) He was the Viceroy of India till ....
(a) 1905 (b) 1906
(c) 1907 (d) 1904

Ans. (a) 1905

(iv) Which of the following events happened during his tenure?
(a) The Surat split
(b) Partition of Bengal
(c) Calcutta Session of INC
(d) All of the above

Ans. (b) Partition of Bengal

24. Look at the picture given below and answer the questions that follow.

(i) Identify the person given in the picture.
(a) Rajguru (b) Batukeswar Dutt
(c) Rash Behari Ghosh (d) Bal Gangadhar Tilak

Ans. (d) Bal Gangadhar Tilak

(ii) Which of the following was his famous newspaper?
(a) New India (b) People
(c) Kesari (d) Sanjibanee

Ans. (c) Kesari

(iii) Which of the following is true about his contribution?
(a) He was the founding member of Deccan Education Society.
(b) He organised Ganapati festivals.
(c) He organised many akhara clubs
(d) All of the above

Ans. (d) All of the above

(iv) Which of the following is not true about him?
(a) He started Poona New English School in 1880.
(b) His English newspaper was 'The Statesman'.
(c) He was from Maharashtra.
(d) He was a part of the famous 'Lal-Bal-Pal' trio.

Ans. (b) His English newspaper was 'The Statesman'.

25. Look at the picture given below and answer the questions that follow. **[Semester-I 2022]**

(i) Identify the leaders in the picture
(a) Surendranath Banerjee, Dadabhai Naoroji, Gopal Krishna Gokhale
(b) Dadabhai Naoroji, Lala Lajpat Rai, Bipin Chandra Pal
(c) Gopal Krishna Gokhale, Bal Gangadhar Tilak, Dadabhai Naoroji
(d) Lala Lajpat Rai, Bal Gangadhar Tilak, Bipin Chandra Pal

Ans. (d) Lala Lajpat Rai, Bal Gangadhar Tilak, Bipin Chandra Pal

(ii) Which group of Congress did they belong to?
(a) Early Nationalists (b) Assertive Nationalists
(c) Revolutionaries (d) Swarajists

Ans. (b) Assertive Nationalists

(iii) What was their main objective?
(a) Attainment of Poorna Swaraj
(b) Self-Government under British Rule
(c) Abolition of India Council
(d) Demand for Provincial Government for Indians

Ans. (a) Attainment of Poorna Swaraj

(iv) What are the methods associated with them?
(a) Prayers and Protests.
(b) Swadeshi and boycott.
(c) Sending deputations of Indian leaders to Britain.
(d) Sending petitions to the British Government.

Ans. (b) Swadeshi and boycott

Passage Based Questions

26. Read the passage given and answer the questions that follow.

He was born in Punjab in 1865. He laid the foundation of DAV College at Lahore. He was greatly influenced by his father Radha Krishna, who was a follower of Swami Dayananda Saraswati, founder of Arya Samaj. In 1914, he established an education trust and founded Radha Krishna High School at Jagraon. He started newspapers like 'Punjabi', 'Vande Mataram' (Urdu Daily) and 'People' (English Daily). He wrote biographies of Mazzini, Garibaldio etc. His autobiography is 'The Story of My Deportation.' He founded the 'Servants of the People Society.' He supported worker's movement and became the first President of All India Trade Union Congress in 1920.

(i) The passage describes about whom?
(a) Bal Gangadhar Tilak (b) Bhagat Singh
(c) Rajguru (d) Lala Lajpat Rai

Ans. (d) Lala Lajpat Rai

(ii) He has been given a very famous title. Which of the following is that title?
(a) Father of Revolutionary Thought in India
(b) Lion of Punjab
(c) Father of Extremism
(d) Tiger of Punjab

Ans.(b) Lion of Punjab

(iii) According to the passage, he founded the Servant's of India Society. When was it founded?
(a) 1920 (b) 1924
(c) 1921 (d) 1922

Ans. (c) 1921

(iv) Which of the following is his famous book?
(a) Young India
(b) England's Debt to India
(c) Political Future of India and Unhappy India
(d) All of the above

Ans. (d) All of the above

27. Read the passage given below and answer the questions that follow.

In one of the annual sessions of the Congress, the Indian National Congress was divided into groups. The groups were Extremists led by Bal Gangadhar Tilak and others. Another group was the moderates who were led by Gopal Krishna Gokhale.

The Extremists wanted to adopt revolutionary methods but the moderates were not in favour of such methods. Besides, the Extremists wanted Lala Lajpat Rai as the President of the session and moderates wanted their own leader to be the President of the session. Finally, the extremists were expelled out from the Congress. They remained out of the Congress for 9 years until they were re-admitted.

(i) The following passage refers to which session of the Congress?

(a) Calcutta (b) Lucknow (c) Surat (d) None of these

Ans. (c) Surat

(ii) When did this session of Congress take place?

(a) 1906 (b) 1905 (c) 1907 (d) 1911

Ans. (c) 1907

(iii) What were the causes of the split among Congress Leaders?

1. Moderates did not like the Extremist Leaders.
2. Extremists wanted Bal Gangadhar Tilak to be President of the session.
3. Moderates wanted Rashbehari Ghosh as the President.
4. Extremists remained away from Congress for next 9 years.

Codes

(a) Both 1 and 2 (b) Both 2 and 3
(c) Both 3 and 4 (d) Both 1 and 4

Ans. (c) Both 3 and 4

(iv) In which session were the Extremists re-admitted to the Congress?

(a) Surat Session 1911 (b) Lucknow Session 1916
(c) Calcutta Session 1911 (d) Lucknow Session 1912

Ans. (c) Lucknow Session 1916

Section-II

Short Questions

1. When was Bengal Partitioned? Name the viceroy responsible for it. **[2011]**

Ans. The plan about the Partition of Bengal was first made known on 20th July, 1905. 'Partition of Bengal' was effected on 16th October, 1905. Viceroy Lord Curzon was responsible for it.

2. What were Curzon's two real motives behind the Partition of Bengal? **[2009]**

Ans. Curzon's two real motive behind the Partition of Bengal were as follows

(i) Bengal was the main centre of Indian nationalism at that time.
Thus, to weaken the Nationalist Movement, Curzon wanted to divide Bengal,

(ii) It was the step to apply 'Divide and Rule Policy' among the Hindus and the Muslims.

3. Why is 16th October, 1905 regarded as an important day in the history of Indian National Movement? **[2020]**

Ans. 16th October, 1905 is regarded as an important day in the history of Indian National Movement because on this day, Bengal was partitioned which separated Eastern parts of Bengal from the rest of the Bengal. It was announced on 19th July, 1905 by Viceroy of India, Lord Curzon. This Day was observed as 'Day of Mourning' throughout Bengal.

4. In which areas except Bengal, Swadeshi Movement was spread?

Ans. Besides Bengal, Swadeshi Movement was spread in Uttar Pradesh, Central Provinces, Bombay, Punjab and Madras. The entire country followed Bengal and soon the Swadeshi Movement acquired national dimensions.

5. Name some leaders who were deported during the Swadeshi and Boycott Movements.

Ans. Some leaders were deported during the Swadeshi and Boycott Movements. They were Bal Gangadhar Tilak, Lala Lajpat Rai and Ajit Singh. After that, the movement lost its strength.

6. Suggest some new lessons brought by the Swadeshi Movement.

Ans. The Swadeshi Movement gave some new lessons such as

- It taught the press to be fearless.
- It inspired Hindus and Muslims to co-operate.
- It also taught students to defy unjust authority and to make sacrifices even of their lives for the sake of their country.

7. State two impacts of the Swadeshi and Boycott Movements.

Ans. Two impacts of the Swadeshi and Boycott Movements were

(i) Indian industries received a great stimulus.
(ii) It enhanced the differences between the early nationalist and the assertive nationalists.

8. The Swadeshi and Boycott Movements had an adverse impact on the Indian National Congress. What was the adverse impact? What was the main difference between the two groups of Congressmen?

Ans. The Swadeshi and Boycott Movements had an adverse impact on the Indian National Congress. There was a split in the Surat Session of Indian National Congress.

In this session, the main difference between the two groups of congressmen was that the assertive nationalists wanted to adopt revolutionary method, but the moderates were not in favour of such methods.

9. Name some acts enacted by the government to suppress the Anti-Partition Movement.

Ans. The acts enacted by the government to suppress the Anti-Partition Movement were
- Prevention of Seditious Meeting Act, 1907
- Explosive Substances Act, 1908
- Criminal Law Amendment Act, 1908
- Newspaper Act, 1908

10. What did the radicals of the Congress mean by the 'boycott'?

Ans. The radicals of the Congress appealed for total boycott of foreign goods. They meant boycott of foreign goods, services, honours, titles and also social boycott of those person who were trading in foreign goods.

11. When did Surat split take place? Who became the Congress President after this?

Ans. Surat split is mainly known for 'Separation of Congress' partymen into moderates and radicals at the Surat Session of Congress on 26th December, 1907. Dr Rash Behari Ghosh became the President after this split.

12. What were two basic reasons responsible for the Surat split in 1907 between the early nationalists and the assertive nationalists? **[2014]**

Ans. The reasons behind Surat split were

(i) There were much debate and disagreement between the moderates and the radicals in the Indian National Congress. The moderates wanted to achieve Swaraj through constitutional means and radicals believed that unless they put a stronger pressure on the government, they would never achieve their objectives.

(ii) The moderates proposed the name of Rash Behari Ghosh for the post of the Congress Presidentship, but the radicals proposed the name of Lala Lajpat Rai. The ideology conflict between the two groups led to the split of the Congress.

13. Mention two international events that influenced the radical groups of the Congress.

Ans. Two International events that influenced the radical groups of the Congress were

(i) The Boer's War which was fought against the British Empire in South Africa (1879-1902).

(ii) The defeat of the Russians by the Japanese in 1905.

14. State any three methods adopted by the early nationalists in the National Movement. **[2020]**

Ans. The three methods adopted by the early nationalists in the National Movement were

(i) They arranged lectures in different parts of England to create public opinion in favour of Indians.

(ii) A British committee of the Indian National Congress was set-up in 1889.

(iii) They used Swadeshi goods and promoted to encourage Indian industries.

15. What were the two methods adopted by the radical nationalists in the freedom struggle? **[2010]**

Ans. Swadeshi and Boycott were the two methods, which were adopted by the radical nationalists in the freedom struggle. They urged to use only Swadeshi products and followed the methods of non-cooperation with the British Government by boycotting government service, courts, school, colleges and British goods.

16. What methods were used by radicals for attaining independence in the field of education?

Ans. The radicals suggested two methods for attaining independence in the field of education.

(i) The radicals asked the students to boycott schools and colleges set-up by the British Government.

(ii) Special schools and colleges like Bengal National College and many National Schools were established to impart national education on the education according to the needs of the nation.

17. Name the nationalist who said 'Swaraj is my birth-right'. Mention one contribution of his to the National Movement. **[2018]**

Ans. Bal Gangadhar Tilak said 'Swaraj is my birth-right'. The contribution of Bal Gangadhar Tilak was that he revived Ganapati and Shivaji festivals to instill national feeling among Indians. Both these festivals inspired the Indians and infused new spirit of nationalism in them.

18. (i) Name any two methods used by Bal Gangadhar Tilak to enthuse the youth.

(ii) Give the names of two leaders who led the 'Home Rule Movement in India'?

Ans. (i) Bal Gangadhar used some methods to enthuse the youth. Two of these methods were

(a) Celebrating Ganapati and Shivaji festivals.

(b) Setting up *akharas* and *lathi* clubs.

(ii) Two leaders who led the Home Rule Movement in India were Bal Gangadhar Tilak and Annie Besant.

19. Name two newspapers started by Bal Gangadhar Tilak in order to spread the ideals of nationalism. Also name two books written by him.

Ans. Bal Gangadhar Tilak started two newspapers i.e. The Mahratta (English) and The Kesari (Marathi), in order to spread the ideals of nationalism. Two famous books written by Bal Gangadhar Tilak were

(i) Gita Rahasya

(ii) Arctic Home in the Vedas

20. Mention two important contributions of Lala Lajpat Rai. **[2019, 2014]**

Ans. Two important contributions of Lala Lajpat Rai were

(i) Lala Lajpat Rai was popularly known as 'Punjab Kesari' or 'Sher-e-Punjab' He founded newspapers like 'Punjabi', 'Vande Mataram' (Urdu Daily) and 'People' (English Weekly).

(ii) In 1914, he established an education trust and founded Radha Krishna High School at Jagraon.

Structured Questions

1. To some extent, Lord Curzon was responsible for the transformation of the anti-partition agitation into a mass movement. In this context, answer the following questions. **[2006]**
   (i) What was Lord Curzon's argument in favour of the Partition of Bengal?
   (ii) How did the nationalists interpret Lord Curzon's motives?
   (iii) How did the people express their unhappiness against the Partition of Bengal.
   (iv) Explain the terms Swadeshi and boycott in the context of the National Movement in India.

Ans. (i) Curzon's arguments in favour of the Partition of Bengal was that the area of Bengal was very large and it was also the most thickly populated province in British India. It was difficult for the British to administer the same efficiently. Hence, according to Lord Curzon, Partition of Bengal was administrative necessity.

(ii) The Indian nationalists interpreted the motive of Lord Curzon's as
   (a) The Partition of Bengal intended to curb Bengali influence by not only placing Bengalis under two administration but by reducing them to a minority in Bengal itself.
   (b) Bengal was the centre of the Indian nationalism, so the British hoped to stop the rising tide of nationalism by partitioning Bengal.
   (c) The partition was meant to foster division on the basis of religion. East Bengal would be predominantly a Muslim majority state and West Bengal a Hindu majority state.
   (d) It was considered as a price for Muslim League's loyalty towards British.

(iii) People's reactions to the Partition of Bengal were
- On 16th October, 1905, the Partition of Bengal came into effect. The leaders of the protest movement declared it a 'Day of Mourning' throughout Bengal. It was also observed as a 'day of fasting'.
- The streets of Calcutta were full of the cries of Vande Mataram, which became the theme song of the National Movement.
- People showed their anger by boycotting foreign goods. They observed fasts and pledged support to the nationalists for forcing the government to cancel the partition.

(iv) In the year 1905, the Swadeshi and Boycott Movements started as a part of the agitation against the Partition of Bengal.
'Swadeshi' literally means 'one's own country'. The aim of the Swadeshi Movement was the promotion of indigenous industries for strengthening the nation. It was a weapon forged by the people to achieve industrial and economic regeneration. Boycott Movement meant 'abstaining from the purchase of British goods'. It includes the following conditions
- Boycott of English goods like clothes, salt and sugar, etc.
- Rejection of English speech.
- Rejection of government posts and seats in Legislative Council.
- Social boycott of people, who purchased foreign goods.

2. Bengal was partitioned in the year 1905 by Lord Curzon. In the light of this, describe briefly.
   (i) The motives of Lord Curzon behind the partition.
   (ii) The measures taken by the British to crush the Anti-Partition Movement.
   (iii) The reasons given by the British to justify the Partition of Bengal.
   (iv) The perspectives of nationalists on Partition of Bengal and their opposition.

Ans. (i) The motives of Lord Curzon behind the Partition were
- The partition was intended to curb Bengali influence by not only placing Bengalis under two administrations, but by reducing them to a minority in Bengal itself.
- Curzon's real motive behind the partition was to break 'the growing solidarity of Bengali nationalism.' Another motive was to drive a wedge between the Hindus and the Muslims.
- The partition was meant to foster divisions on the basis of religion. East Bengal would be predominantly a Muslim majority state and West Bengal would have a Hindu majority.

(ii) The measures taken by the British were
- The government banned processions and meetings, curbed the newspapers by rigorous press laws and imprisoned the leaders of the movement without trial.
- The government made use of several repressive measure's such-as Prevention of Seditious Meeting Act, Explosive Substances Act, Criminal Law Amendment Act and Newspapers Act.
- The singing of Vande Mataram was forbidden in the streets of Bengal. The leaders of the movement were ill-treated. Some leaders were tried for seditious writing in various papers.
- The educational institutions were warned that, if they did not prevent their students from participating in the Boycott Movement, their grants-in-aid would be stopped.

(iii) The reasons given by the British to justify the Partition of Bengal
- Bengal was a huge territory which originally comprised the whole of Bihar, Orissa, Assam, Western and Eastern Bengal.
- Lord Curzon stated that it was too large a state to be effectively administered by a single provincial government. Therefore, to provide good administration, it should be divided into two provinces.

(iv) The perspective of nationalist leaders was that they realised that the Partition of Bengal was an attempt to divide the Bengalis that shared a common culture, language and tradition. Thus, they oppose the partition in the following ways
- The Indian National Congress, all national leaders and all sections of people, even zamindars and merchants protested against partition.
- Protest meetings and campaigns against the partition were organised all over the Bengal by eminent leaders like Surendranath Banerjee, Krishna Kumar Mitra, PC Ray, Bipin Chandra Pal, Ananda Mohan Bose, etc.

3. From 1905 to 1918, there emerged a new and a younger group of leaders within the Congress who did not agree with the old leadership. In this context, answer the following questions. **[2010]**

(i) Differentiate between the moderates and the radical nationalists in their objectives and achievements stating one objective and two achievements of each wing of the Congress.

(ii) Name the radical leader known as the forerunner of Gandhiji. Why is the person known as the forerunner of Gandhiji?

(iii) Explain how the repressive policies of Lord Curzon and influence of international events led to radical nationalism.

(iv) Describe the role of Bipin Chandra Pal in Indian National Movement.

Ans. Differences between Moderates and Radical Nnationalists in their objectives were

Moderates	Radical Nationalists
The moderates agitated only for certain administrative and economic reforms.	The radicals demanded 'Purna Swaraj' or complete Independence of India.
They wanted that the Indians should have some role in the government and administration of the country.	They thought that 'Swaraj' was the only solution to all problems being faced by the Indians.

Differences between Moderates and Radical Nationalists in their achivements were

Moderates	Radical Nationalists
The moderates were successful in inspiring the common masses of India.	The social base of the movement was broadened under the leadership of the radicals.
They sowed the seed of nationalism and developed the spirit of national unity among Indians.	They instilled self-confidence and self-reliance among people.

(ii) Bal Gangadhar Tilak was regarded as the forerunner of Mahatma Gandhi. Gandhiji's ideal of complete independence was similar to Tilak's ideal of Swaraj. Moreover, no-rent campaign, Boycott and Swadeshi preached and practiced by Tilak was also accepted by Gandhiji. Thus, it can be said that Gandhiji's ideals were moulded by Tilak's thought and Tilak was the forerunner of Gandhiji.

(iii) Lord Curzon adopted many repressive policies toward Indians. Lord Curzon passed the 'Calcutta Corporation Act' (1899), Indian Universities Act (1904), Official Secrets Act (1904) etc. All these measures outraged Indians against British rule. Some international events also greatly inspired radicals. The defeat of the Italians by the Ethiopians in 1896 and of the Russians by the Japanese in 1905 encouraged them to fight against foreign rulers. Moreover, the Boers War (1899-1902) against the British power in South Africa, Home Rule agitation in Ireland and the revolutionary movements in Russia, China, etc. influenced the radical nationalism.

(iv) Refer to chapter theory page no. 129.

4. With reference to the effect of the Swadeshi and Boycott Movements, describe the following.

(i) Involvement of the masses.

(ii) Decline in import of foreign goods and the role of Co-operative organisations in extremist movement.

(iii) Growth of national literature and culture.

Ans. (i) The Swadeshi and Boycott movements were undertaken by the Indian nationalist leaders to remove the British from power and improve India's economic conditions. The radicals emphasised to involve the masses in the movement. The day of partition was observed as 'Day of Mourning'. On the call of Rabindranath Tagore the people observed the day of partition as rakshabandhan and tied *rakhis* on each other's hand. Both Hindus and Muslims enthusiastically participated in this movement. Beside this, women, peasants, children, students all participated in this movement.

(ii) Swadeshi and Boycott movements led to the decline of import of foreign goods in the following ways
- Though Manchester cloth was the chief target of attack, the movement was extended to other British manufacturers also, such as salt and sugar as well as luxury goods in general.
- Foreign cigarettes and clothes were bought and burnt on the streets.
- Some people refused to assist any religious ceremonies in houses where European salt and sugar in houses were used and traders were warned from importing foreign articles.

The radicals encouraged co-operative organisations. Voluntary associations were set up for rural sanitation, preventives, police duties, regulation of fairs and pilgrim gatherings for providing relief during famines and other natural calamities.

(iii) Swadeshi and Boycott movements led to the growth of national literature and culture in the following ways
- As a result of the spread of modern Western education and thought during the 19th century, a large number of Indians imbibed a modern rational, secular, democratic, and nationalist

political outlook. The educated Indians were the first to feel the humiliation of foreign subjection.

- The writings of authors like, Bankim Chandra Chattopadhyay, Rabindranath Tagore, Fakir Mohan Senapati inspired people to develop self-confidence and self-respect.
- Teaching of social reformers led to cultural growth. In Bengal, the worship of godesses Kai and Durga was revived to inspire the people to take up arms against the evil powers.

Picture Based Questions

1. Look at the picture given below and answer the questions that follow.

(i) Identify the person given in picture. To which section of the Congress did he belong and what was its ultimate objective?

(ii) State the contributions of the person in freedom struggle.

(iii) Highlight three different methods of struggle adopted by the moderates and the radicals.

Ans. (i) Person in this picture is Lala Lajpat Rai, one of the assertive leaders of the Congress.

The main objective of the assertive nationalists was the immediate attainment of 'Swaraj'. This meant complete independence and not just self-government, as was in the colonies of Australia, New Zealand, etc.

(ii) The contributions of Lala Lajpat Rai in the freedom struggle were

- He wrote a book 'The Young India', to spread the message of the right of India to attain Swaraj.
- He opened orphanages, hospitals and schools. He set-up 'Servants of the People Society' for the welfare of the downtrodden and outcastes.
- He inspired Indians to take action against the British rulers rather than following the three P's- Prayers, Petitions and Protests for this purpose.

(iii) The methods of struggle adopted by each section of the Congress were

Methods of the Moderates

- The moderates relied on constitutional and peaceful methods and avoided violence and confrontation.
- They believed in the prayers, petitions and protests to achieve their objectives.
- They had full faith in the British sense of justice and fair play and believed that India needed a balanced representation of its demands before the British rulers.
- They sent memorandums and petitions to the government officials and to the British Parliament.

Methods of the Assertives

- The methods of the assertive nationalists included Swadeshi, Boycott, National Education and co-operative organisations.
- They favoured use of force and revolutionary methods for achieving their aims.
- They mainly relied on the strength of their masses. They converted the National Movement into a mass movement. They aroused the masses by influencing them with their sacrifices and sufferings.

2. Look at the picture given below and answer the questions that follow.

(i) (a) What were the three personalities popularly known as?

(b) Which section of the Congress did they represent?

(c) Mention two of their popular beliefs.

(ii) State any four methods that they advocated for the achievement of their aims.

(iii) The split in the Congress in 1907.

Ans. (i) (a) The three personalities were popularly known as 'Lal-Bal-Pal'.

(b) They represent the assertive nationalist section of the Congress.

(c) Their two popular beliefs were

- They had no faith in the British sense of justice.
- They believed that the British had ruined our civilisation.

(ii) Four methods that they advocated for the achievement of their aims are following

(a) They asked the people to use only Swadeshi goods and boycott the foreign goods.

(b) They emphasised on national education and called upon students to boycott schools and colleges run by the British Government.

(c) They encouraged co-operative organisations.

(d) They also emphasised on involvement of masses in the National Movement.

(ii) Refer to chapter theory page no. 128.

Chapter Assessment

Section-I

Multiple Choice Questions

1. The nationalists felt that Bengal was Partitioned ..... .
   (a) to divide Hindus and Muslims.
   (b) for effective administration.
   (c) to stop the spread of Swadeshi.
   (d) to help the Muslims.
2. Surat split took place in
   (a) 1905 (b) 1906
   (c) 1907 (d) 1908
3. Who started the newspaper 'Kesari' in Marathi?
   (a) Bal Gangadhar Tilak
   (b) Bipin Chandra Pal
   (c) Lala Lajpat Rai
   (d) Gopal Krishna Gokhale
4. Which of the following is a method of the assertive nationalists?
   (i) Swadeshi (ii) Boycott
   (iii) Passive Resistance (iv) Revivalism
   Codes
   (a) Only (i)
   (b) Only (ii)
   (c) Both (iii) and (iv)
   (d) All of the above

Short Questions

1. State the real motives for the Partition of Bengal.
2. In what unique way did Bengali's observe partition day?
3. How did the Swadeshi Movement promote national education?
4. State the territorial reorganisation in the Partition of Bengal.
5. In what way did the Swadeshi Movement achieve success?
6. When was the Partition of Bengal revoked?
7. What was the main aim of the radical nationalists?
8. Mention two important anti-Indian policy adopted by Lord Curzon which brought about aggressive nationalism in India.
9. What was the contribution of Bal Gangadhar Tilak in the field of education in our country?

Structured Questions

1. With reference to Partition of Bengal, explain the following questions
   (i) Why was Bengal Partitioned?
   (ii) How did the Partition of Bengal affected national movement?
   (iii) What did people do to make this movement a success?
   (iv) Who were the prominent leaders of Anti-Partition Movement?
2. With reference to the Swadeshi and Boycott Movements, answer the following questions.
   (i) Give the objectives of this movement.
   (ii) How did these movements spread and become popular?
   (iii) How did these movements help to strengthen the national movement?

CHAPTER

05

The Muslim League and Lucknow Pact

SYLLABUS

The Muslim League Factors leading to the formation of the Muslim League and its objectives

Lucknow Pact Brief mention of the significance of the Lucknow Pact-1916.

India is known for the Hindu-Muslim unity for centuries. They together have fought for the injustice rule of the British during the First War of Independence in 1857. Thus, the British realised that, if they want to rule India, they have to divide both these communities which posed great threat to the British imperialism. When the National Movement started in India, the British encouraged the communal forces to suppress the movement. They started the 'Divide and Rule policy' and encouraged the Muslims to set up their own separate political organisation. This policy of British led to the rise of communal riots and **Muslim League** came into existence in 1906.

Factors/Events Leading to the Formation of the Muslim League

The British Policy of Divide and Rule

After the revolt of 1857, the British started to **discriminate**[1] between the Hindus and the Muslims. The British rulers thought that the movement might unite the people and cause a problem to the British Empire. So, they applied 'Divide and Rule policy' and encouraged **separatist**[2] and communal politics in India in the following ways

- To use the 'Divide and Rule' policy, Lord Mayo's government adopted a resolution in 1871 which made Urdu the medium of instruction for Muslims in primary and secondary schools. The government also increased its aid to Muslim educational institutions.
- They used foul words about both the communities' rulers and tried to create hatred among them. The British stated that Muslim rulers are plunderers and Hindu rulers are cruel kings to their Muslim subjects.
- The British Government justified itself on the question of the Partition of Bengal. They tried to convince the Muslims that Bengal was being partitioned to create a new Muslim majority province where they can dominate and no Hindus would be able to interfere in their internal matters.
- They tried to create hatred among the different castes of Indian society and tried to turn the non-Brahmins and the lower castes against high castes Hindus.

1 **Discriminate** To show a difference between people or things.

2 **Separatist** A group of people within a country who want to separate from the rest of the country and form their own government.

- They tried to spread communal hatred through the press, posters, literature and public platform.

Educational and Economic Backwardness of the Muslims

The thought of a separate institution for Muslims was provoked by the educational and economic backwardness of the Muslims as

- The Muslims considered that the Britishers were responsible for the end of Mughal rule. They felt humiliated after the last Emperor Bahadur Shah Zafar was dethroned and deprived of power, titles and privileges. Muslims, zamindars, aristocrates were considered as upper class Muslims who became anti-British, conservative and opposed Western education. Thus, there were very few Muslims who were educated in Western system of education. This resulted in economic and educational backwardness of Muslims. On the other hand, Hindu who received Western education easily got government jobs.
- Muslims also remained backward in the field of commerce and industry. They did not much involve in the growth of any organised industry. Thus, they lagged behind in the economic front.
- After 1858, a discrimination policy was adopted towards the Muslims by the British Government which considered that the Muslims were responsible for the uprising of 1857. The British use this policy of discrimination at the time of recruitment in civil and military services.
- The ordinary Muslim population was under the influence of their zamindars. These zamindars class were loyal to the British ruler class who found it easy to make difference between Hindu-Muslim communities.

Loss of Sovereignty by Mughal Rulers

Before the British period, many rulers of India were followers of Islam. The British established its rule in India after defeating Mughal ruler. This resented the Muslim community against the British rulers and they participated in the **Wahabi movement**. This movement aimed to end the British rule in India. Muslims also took part in the revolt of 1857. This made the British suspicious about Muslim community. So, they took a policy of indifference towards Muslims and started to **appease**[3] Hindus.

However, after the 1870s, the British Government changed its attitude and tried to appease the Muslims in order to undermine the National Movement. The British spread a feeling of hatred between the two communities and encouraged communal tendencies.

Role of Sir Syed Ahmad Khan

Sir Syed Ahmad Khan was a renowned educationist and social reformer in India. According to him, Hindus and Muslims were one *Quam* (nation). The Mohammedan Anglo-Oriental College was founded by him at Aligarh in 1875, which had both Hindu and Muslim patrons.

Under British influence, Sir Syed gradually became more conservative and communal in his political views in the following ways

- By 1889, he gave up his earlier political views and declared that the interests of Hindus and Muslims were completely different.
- When the Indian National Congress was founded, Sir Syed Ahmad Khan opposed it.
- In 1888, he founded the **United Indian Patriotic Association** which was a political organisation and had aims to oppose the Congress and develop close ties between the Muslim community and the British Raj. Mr. Beck, the British Principal of Mohammedan Anglo-Oriental (MAO) College (Aligarh) supported this effort. Beck gave his idea that Anglo-Muslim unity was possible but there was no possibility of Hindu-Muslim unity.
- In 1893, Sir Syed founded the **Mohammedan Anglo-Oriental Defence Association** to keep the Muslims away from the Congress, to promote loyalty towards the rulers and to prevent Muslims from participating in any political movement.
- Sir Syed Ahmad Khan was one of the earliest advocates of the 'Two-Nation Theory' that Hindu and Muslim should have separate nations. His philosophy guided the creation of the **All India Muslim League** in 1906, as a political party separate from the Congress. British took his idea of separatism and used it to separate Hindu and Muslims.

The Hindi-Urdu Controversy

In the United Provinces (present Uttar Pradesh), Urdu was the court language. All the petitions to the offices and courts were submitted in Urdu. But some sections of the society protested against this practice.

On 8th April, 1900, the government issued a decree granting equal status to both Hindi and Urdu languages. All the petitions were to be submitted in Hindi, in Devanagri Script and the official announcements of the court to be issued in Hindi as well as in Urdu.

3 **Appease** To make somebody calmer by giving them what they want.

This was opposed by the Muslims. Sir Syed Ahmed Khan promoted the adoption of Urdu as the **lingua franca**[4] of all Indian Muslims. He strongly opposed the adoption of Hindi as a second official language of the United Provinces.

The Aligarh Politics

After the death of Sir Syed in 1898, Nawab Mohsin-ul- Mulk led the **Aligarh Movement** in India. The Aligarh Movement was started to make the Muslims loyal towards the British Government and to keep them away from the Indian political life.

On the Hindi-Urdu controversy of 1900, Mohsin-ul-Mulk opposed the order of the British Government because this order granted equal status to both Hindi and Urdu in Uttar Pradesh.

After this opposition, Macdonnel the Lt. Governor of Uttar Pradesh, demanded that the Nawab should either resign from the Secretaryship of the Trust or separate himself from the agitation against the government order. This made the Muslim leaders angry and they wanted a separate political organisation of the Muslims to raise their voice.

Incorrect Interpretation of History

The British and some communal Indian historians were also responsible for creating communal hatred among Hindus-Muslims in the country by interpreting incorrect history. For example

- These communal historians divided the Indian history into the Hindu and the Muslim periods. They stated that the rule of Turks, Afghans and Mughals was the Muslim rule. They also stated that these Muslim rulers were the followers of Islam and their subjects were the followers of other religions.
- According to these communal historians in the so-called Hindu period, the Muslim rulers were considered the foreign invaders who came from outside in India. They portrayed Rana Pratap and Shivaji as national heroes and Akbar and Aurangzeb as foreign invaders. This started to increase the communal feelings in Indians.
- These communal historians and British people ignored the theme of united India which was based on composite culture. They tried to create a wedge between the two important communities.
- They spread the communal bias through their poetry, drama, novels, short stories, newspapers, etc.
- Some communal historians did not give much importance to the medieval period, which was dominated by the Mughal rulers in the development of Indian economy, culture and society.

According to Mahatma Gandhi, communal harmony could not be permanently established in India as long as incorrect interpretation of history were taught in its schools.

Rise of Assertive Nationalism

The Indian history marked the great contribution of the assertive nationalists in the National Movement. But every action of them was not adopted by all the Indians. They used some communal actions which resented some sections of Indian society.

For example, promotion of Shivaji and Ganapati festivals by Tilak, the concept of Aurobindo Ghosh of India as mother and nationalism as religion and the relation of anti-partition agitation to dips in the Ganga did not liked by some of the Muslims.

Economic Backwardness of the Country

One of the main reasons of the growth of communalism in India was the economic backwardness of the country. The British applied their colonial policies in India due to which India lacked in modern industrial development. So, acute educated unemployment grown in the country.

It started a fierce competition among the educated youth to secure the few available jobs. It ultimately led the demand of reservation in government jobs on the basis of caste, creed or religion. This provided an opportunity to the British who increased the communal rift among the educated Indians.

The Partition of Bengal

The Partition of Bengal, 1905, by Lord Curzon further **aggravated**[5] the conflict between the Hindus and Muslims. The new province of Eastern Bengal and Assam with Dacca as its capital **demarcated**[6], it as a predominantly Muslim area. Its creation satisfied the Muslim's dream for a separate region and also ensured their loyalty to the British. It affect the National Movement led by the Indian Congress.

The Congress started Swadeshi and Boycott Movements in protest against government's decision of dividing Bengal. Many Muslim leaders did not support this movement, as they thought that this newly developed province would become the centre of their political activity.

---

4 **Lingua Franca** A language that is adopted as a common language between speakers whose mother tounges are different.

5 **Aggravated** To make a bad or unpleasant situation worse.

6 **Demarcated** To mark or establish the limits of something.

On 16th October, 1905, the **Mohammedan Provincial Union** was founded. All the existing societies and organisations were invited to join with it. Nawab Salimullah Khan was chosen as its patron who was a supporter of the Partition of Bengal.

Muslim Delegation to Lord Minto

Viceroy **Lord Minto** wanted to use Muslims against the Hindus. So, he invited Muslim delegations to meet their demands. Some of the Muslim leaders decided to address to the Viceroy. Archibald who was the new principal of Mohammedan Anglo-Oriental (MAO) College, gave some suggestions on content of this address on the basis of which it was prepared. These suggestions were

- The address should contain the proclamation of loyalty to the British rulers.
- The Muslims should clearly express their fear about the general system of elections because it would harm the interests of the Muslims minority group in the country.
- The Muslim leaders should ask for some system of nomination or representation in the political system on the basis of religious lines.

For this address, a **delegation**[7] was organised by Mohsin-ul-Mulk, the Secretary of MAO college. On, 1st October, 1906, 35 influential Muslims from all over the country led by Agha Khan met the Viceroy in Shimla. They submitted the following demands to the Viceroy

- Representation of Muslims in elected bodies on the basis of its political importance and not on numerical strength of the community.
- Separate electoral constituency for the Muslims both in the Provincial Council and the Imperial Legislative Council.
- Reservation of seats for Muslims in the state services.
- More state aids for promoting new Muslim Universities.
- While nominating members of the Viceroy's Council, preference to be given to Muslims.

The Viceroy gave a favourable reply to the Muslim delegation and declared separate electorates for the Muslim. This was a part of the Indian Council Act of 1909, popularly known as the **Morley-Minto Reforms.**

Separate **electorate**[8] meant that elections were to be held on the basis of communal representation. It meant that the Muslims could vote for a Muslim candidate and the Hindus for a Hindu candidate. Thus, the Muslim community would be represented as a community in the councils.

Check Your LEARNING...

1. Who founded the Anglo Mohammedan Oriental College?
2. When was the Mohammedan Provincial Union founded?
3. Which act is known as 'Morley-Minto Reforms'?
4. Who was the leader of Aligarh Movement after the death of Sir Syed Ahmad Khan?

Formation of Muslim League

The success of the Muslim delegation to the Viceroy on 1st October, 1906 inspired and motivated the Muslim to start a new political organisation. In December, 1906, **Nawab Salimullah** arranged the meeting at Dacca and under his leadership on 30th December, 1906, the All-India Muslim League was founded.

Muslim League's original political goal was to define and advance the Indian Muslim's civil rights and to provide protection to the Muslims. Its constitution was framed in 1907 at Karachi.

Sir Sultan Muhammad Shah (Agha Khan III) was elected as permanent President of Muslim League. Its headquarters was at Aligarh, but its central office was shifted to Lucknow in 1910. A committee framed its rules and regulations. The **First Regular Session** of the Muslim League was held in December, 1908 at Amritsar. Its Chairman was **Syed Ali Imam.**

Objectives of the Muslim League

- To promote the feelings of loyalty towards the British Government amongst the Indian Muslims and to remove any misconception regarding the intentions of the government in relation to the Indian Muslims.
- To protect and advance the political rights and other interests of the Muslims of India.
- To place their needs and aspirations before the government in mild and moderate language.
- To promote friendly relations between the Muslims and other communities of India and to prevent the rise of any opposition between them.
- To promote social and economic interests of the Muslims.
- To secure a rightful place for the Muslims in the Indian society and economy.

7 **Delegation** A group of people who represents the views of an organisation.
8 **Electorate** The people in a country or an area who have the right to vote.

Impact of the Muslim League on the National Movement

The British supported the formation of the Muslim League in order to provide an opposition to the Congress. They told the Muslims that their interests were different from those of the Hindus. Thus, the policies of the Muslim League have an impact on the nationalist sentiments in the following ways

League's Role in the Beginning

Initially, the Muslim League did not support the National Movement, opposed the Anti-Partition Movement and the Swadeshi and Boycott Movements. The Muslim League wanted more seats in Assemblies than its numerical representation.

It was much move against the Congress as compared to the British. As the leaders of the Muslim League belonged to the elite class, they did not work from ground level in order to remove the grievances of the Muslim masses.

Support of Government to the League

The League demanded separate electorates and reservation of posts in the services to protect the rights of the Muslims. The British gave full support to their demands. As per the demand, the Morley-Minto Reforms of 1909 provided separate electorates for Muslim. Thus, seats were reserved for the Muslims and they now could vote for the Muslim candidates. Thus, the Britishers were successful in starting conflict between the Hindus and Muslims.

Demand for Self-Government

From 1910 to 1913, a group of young men started to promote radical and nationalist ideas. The most prominent among them were Maulana Abul Kalam Azad, Habib-ur-Rahman, Hakim Ajmal Khan and Mazhar-ul-Haq.

In 1913, the Muslim League adopted the goal of self-government for India. In 1913, Muhammad Ali Jinnah joined the Muslim League. He also supported the progressive and national aims of the Congress. This change in attitude took place due to various factors

- Britain's cruel policy towards Turkey in the Turko-Italian War (1911-12) and the Balkan Wars (1912-13) which Muslim leaders aggressive against such cruel policies of the British.
- In 1911, when the Partition of Bengal was rejected, it was considered as harmful for the interests of the Muslims in India.
- The younger Muslim leaders did not want to please the British Government and also did not like the leadership of big nawabs and zamindars.
- The Deoband school of Muslim studies inspired some young scholars and filled nationalist sentiments in them.

Growth of Nationalism

In the First World War, when the safety of Turkey was threatened, Indians reacted and anti-British sentiments started to grow among the Muslims. As a result, many more radical young Muslims joined the nationalists towards the common cause.

On the advice of Abul Kalam Azad, Habib-ur-Rahman founded **Masjlis-i-Ahrar** (The society of freeman). The emergent section of nationalist Muslims, changed the attitude of the Muslim League towards the Congress.

Congress and the League

When the British Government supported the cause of the Balkan countries and ignored the Turkish interests, the Indian Muslims launched the Khilafat Movement against them. The Congress supported the movement and this movement also included the demand of the Non-Cooperation Movement. Thus, a pact which is known as the Lucknow Pact was signed between Congress and the Muslim League.

Partition of the Country on Communal Basis

Despite having the nationalist feelings and combine struggle of both the Muslims and Hindus, the communal divide continued in India. In 1930, the situation further aggravated when the idea of 'Two Nation- States' originated. Jinnah put forward his 'Two-Nation Theory' in the Lahore session of the Muslim League in 1940. Despite a severe opposition from Gandhiji and many other leaders, the country had to face the partition. The communal riots took place in all over the country and Pakistan came into existence as a separate nation in 1947.

Check Your LEARNING...

1. When was the Muslim League founded?
2. Where was the Constitution of Muslim League framed?
3. Where was the first regular session of the Muslim League held?
4. In which year Muhammad Ali Jinnah joined the Muslim League?

The Lucknow Pact

It was the outcome of the events which took place during the First World War (1914-1918). The Lucknow Pact was signed in 1916 between the Indian National Congress and the Muslim League. It refers to the joint scheme of political reforms agreed by both the Congress and the Muslim League. It was based on the principle to form a structure of government in India and make the strong relationship between the Hindus and the Muslims.

According to this Pact, the Congress agreed to the concept of **communal electorate**[9] which the communal bitterness in the country.

Events/Circumstances Leading to the Lucknow Pact

International Events

During the war between Turkey and Italy and during the Balkan Wars between 1912 and 1913, Britain maintained indifference towards Turkey. The Muslims regarded the Sultan of Turkey as their Caliph or the religious head.

Moreover, the British occupation of Egypt and Anglo-Russian Convention of 1907, dividing Persia and bringing it, under control were not accepted by the Muslims.

This annoyed the sentiments of the Muslims as they believed that the British were pro-Christian and anti-Muslim. Thus, Muslims gradually began to support the Congress' aim of self-government.

National Events

When the Partition of Bengal was cancelled, some prominent nationalist Muslims like Abul Kalam Azad and Ali Brothers (Maulana Mohammad Ali and Shaukat Ali) took this as an opportunity to spread nationalist ideas among the Muslims.

Azad started the Urdu newspaper *Al-Hilal* and Ali brothers started *Hamdard* in Urdu and *Comrade* in English to mobilise public opinion in favour of self-government.

Relations between the Muslim League and the Congress

In 1913, Mohammad Ali Jinnah joined the Muslim League and passed a resolution adopting self-government as its goal. Since the aim of the Congress and the Muslim League was identical, i.e. self- government, both the parties started to co-operate with each other. The arrest of prominent Muslim leaders under the **Seditious**[10] Meetings Act brought the Muslim League even closer to the Congress.

Annie Besant and Bal Gangadhar Tilak played a significant role in bringing the two organisations together. Annie Besant reunite the two parts of the Congress i.e. the early nationalists (moderates) and the assertive nationalists (extremists).

In 1916, when Bal Gangadhar Tilak rejoined the Congress, he played a key role in resolving the differences between the Congress and the Muslim League.

Efforts were made by the leaders of both parties to reach an agreement on the scheme of political reforms in India. In 1915, both the party leaders met at Bombay, where they made a joint plan of post war constitutional reform.

In 1916, both the Indian National Congress and the Muslim League again held simultaneous sessions at Lucknow. The joint scheme of political reforms was put forward and passed by both parties in 1916 which came to be known as the Lucknow Pact.

Main Terms of the Lucknow Pact

- **India as Dependant and Self-Governing State** It declared that India must cease to be dependent. It must be raised to the status of self governing state as an equal party with equal rights and responsibilities as an independent unit of the empire.
- **Members of the Imperial Legislative Council** The council should consist of 150 members of these, 4/5th were to be elected and 1/5th were to be nominated. 1/3rd of the members were to be Muslims. The elected members of the Imperial Legislative Council were to be elected by elected members of the Provincial Legislative Council.
- **Non-Interference of Imperial Legislature** The imperial legislature would not have control over defence, foreign affairs and political relations in India (relating to war, treaties or peace).
- **Representation of Minorities** The minorities should be given adequate separate representation in elected bodies.
- **Religious Interests** No bill would be introduced by a non-official member, if it affected the interest of any community. Such a bill would not be passed, if it was opposed by three-fourth of that community.

9 **Communal electorate** Only the representative of a particular community contest the election.

10 **Seditious** The use of words or actions that are intended to encourage people to oppose a government.

- **Power of the Legislative Council** All bills passed by the legislature should be effective unless voted by the Governor-General in council. If the same bill was passed again by the Legislative Council within a year, the government would be obliged to pass it. Extensive power was to be given to the legislature for control over financial matters.
- **Members of Executive Council** Atleast half of the members of the Viceroy's Executive Council were to be given to Indians, nominated by the elected members of the Central Legislature.
- **Autonomy in Provinces** The provinces should be given a large measure of autonomy. For each Province the number of Muslim members was decided and they were to be elected through separate electorates.
- **Separation of Judiciary from Executive** The Executive officers should not have judicial powers. Highest court of a province would control the members of the judiciary in that particular Province.
- **Abolition of Indian Council** India Council of Secretary of State operated from England should be replaced by two permanent members under secretaries out of which one should be an Indian.

Significance of the Lucknow Pact

- **Hindu-Muslim Unity** The Lucknow Pact symbolised Hindu-Muslim unity as both the Congress and the Muslim League worked together from 1916 to 1922. It is considered important, as for the first time the Congress and the Muslim League had come up with a joint programme, which was difficult for the British to ignore.

  The Congress compromised on its secular character by accepting the scheme of a Muslim electorate while the Muslim League accepted the principles of election and the majority rule.
- **Unity Within the Congress** The Lucknow Pact was symbol of the unity between two sections of the Congress i.e. extremists and moderates. The extremists, who were expelled from the Congress in 1907 were welcomed back within the fold of the Congress in 1916.
- **Pressure on the Government** The British Government was pressurised by the unity of the Congress and the Muslim League. It could not easily reject the demand for constitutional reforms.
- **Demand for Self-Government** Both the Congress and the League demanded self-government. The leaders of both the parties did not want to give the British Government any excuse for delaying political reforms. Thus, the Government tried to pacify the Indians by the 'Declaration of 20th August, 1917' which promised a policy of gradual development of self-government institutions in India.

Limitations of the Lucknow Pact

- Some people criticised that compromise between the Hindus and the Muslims in Lucknow Pact demanded more sacrifice on the part of the Hindus. They thought that, it marked the beginning of the appeasement of Muslims by the Congress.
- The pact did not involve the masses, either of Hindu or of Muslim community.
- The pact provided for Muslim representation in the council in excess of their proportion in the total population.
- The Congress failed to retain its secular character by agreeing to a pact of communal electorate. By accepting the separate electorates for Muslims, the Congress opened the scope for future communal tension.
- The pact introduced a new type of communal veto. It declared that no legislature could enact a law, if it was opposed by 3/4th of the members of a particular community.
- Even after this pact, the leaders of both the Hindu and Muslim community could not formulate any means to bring the masses of both communities closer to each other. This pact failed to deliver any responsible government for India.

Check Your LEARNING...

1. Who started the Urdu newspaper Al-Hilal?
2. In which year Mohammad Ali Jinnah joined the Muslim League?
3. Which leaders played a significant role in bringing the Muslim League and Congress together?
4. On what basis, the Lucknow Pact was criticised?

Time Line

Year	Important Events
1867	Hindi-Urdu Controversy
1875	Mohammedan Anglo-Oriental College was founded by Sir Syed Ahmed Khan.
1893	Mohammedan Anglo-Oriental Defence Association was founded.
16th October, 1905	Mohammedan Provincial Union was founded.
1st October, 1906	Muslim delegations met Viceroy Lord Minto at Shimla.
30th December, 1906	All-India Muslim League was founded.
1908	The First Session of the Muslim League was held at Amritsar.
1909	Indian Council Act/Morley–Minto Reforms
1913	Muhammad Ali Jinnah joined the Muslim League. The Muslim League adopted the goal of self-government.
1916	The Lucknow Pact
1915	Both the party's leaders met at Bombay

QUiCK Revision

- The Britishers applied 'Divide and Rule policy' and encouraged separatist and communal politics in India.
- Lord Curzon divided the country on communal lines by announcing the Partition of Bengal (1905).
- Muslims were anti-British, conservative and hostile to Western education. It resulted in economic and educational backwardness of Muslims.
- The British became the ruler after defeating Mughal ruler. This made the Muslims enemies towards them.
- In 1875, Sir Syed founded Mohammedan Anglo-Oriental College, which later developed into 'Aligarh Muslim University'.
- Muslim intellectuals started Aligarh Movement to secure the future of Indian Muslims.
- In 1893, Sir Syed founded the Mohammedan Anglo-Oriental Defence Association to keep the Muslims away from the Congress.
- Sir Syed was one of the earliest advocates of the 'Two-Nation Theory' i.e. Hindus and Muslims should have separate nations.
- The Partition of Bengal aggravated the conflict between the Hindus and Muslims.
- A Muslim delegation led by Sir Sultan Muhammad Shah (Agha Khan III) met Viceroy Minto in Shimla. They demanded more representation of Muslims, separate electorate constituency, etc. Viceroy gave a favourable reply to the delegation and declared separate electorates for the Muslims.
- On 30th December, 1906, the All India Muslim League was founded under the leadership of Nawab Salimullah of Dacca.
- The main objectives of the Muslim League was to promote loyalty among the Indian Muslims towards the British, to protect the political rights and interests of Muslims, to promote friendly relation between the Muslims and other communities, etc.
- Initially, Muslim League opposed the Nationalist Movement but later, some prominent radical leaders like, Maulana Abul Kalam Azad, Habib-ur-Rahman, etc changed the attitude of the Muslim League towards the Congress.
- In 1916, both the Congress and the Muslim League signed an agreement which was known as the Lucknow Pact. It claimed self-government for India. According to this pact, atleast half of the members of the Governor should be Indians and the provinces should be given a large measure of autonomy.
- The Lucknow Pact is considered important as for the first time, the Indian National Congress and the Muslim League had come up with a joint programme.
- Some scholars criticised that the Lucknow Pact marked the beginning of the appeasement of Muslims by the Congress. By accepting the separate electorates for Muslims, the Congress paved the way for future communal tension.

Chapter Practice

Section-I

Multiple Choice Questions

1. After which war the British started to discriminate between Hindus and Muslims in India?
   (a) Battle of Buxar
   (b) Battle of Plassey
   (c) First War of Independence in 1857
   (d) None of the above

Ans. (c) First War of Independence in 1857

2. Which of the following was the favourable policy of the British to create a rift between two important communities in India?
   (a) Declaration of 1942 (b) Divide and Rule
   (c) Morley Minto Reform (d) Seditious Meeting Act

Ans. (b) Divide and Rule

3. Whose government adopted a resolution in 1871 which made Urdu the medium of instruction for Muslims in primary and secondary schools?
   (a) Lord Ripon's Government
   (b) Lord Curzon's Government
   (c) Lord Mayo's Government
   (d) Lord Hastings' Government

Ans. (c) Lord Mayo's Government

4. After the year .... a discrimination policy was adopted towards the Muslims by the British Government which considered that the Muslims were responsible for the uprising of 1857.
   (a) 1855 (b) 1858
   (c) 1890 (d) 1900

Ans. (b) 1858

5. .... was one of the causes of the Quit India Movement. **[2023]**
   (a) Failure of the Second Round Table Conference
   (b) Rowlatt Act
   (c) Mountbatten Plan
   (d) Failure of the Cripps Mission

Ans. (d) Failure of the Cripps Mission

6. The Mohammedan Anglo-Oriental College was founded in which year?
   (a) 1875 (b) 1880
   (c) 1890 (d) 1899

Ans. (a) 1875

7. When the Indian National Congress was founded, ... opposed it.
   (a) Hakim Ajmal Khan (b) Sir Syed Ahmad Khan
   (c) Agha khan (d) Mazhar-ul-Haq

Ans. (b) Sir Syed Ahmad Khan

8. From the given list, identify the objective of the Muslim League. **[Semester-I 2021]**
   (a) To train and organise public opinion in the country.
   (b) To promote friendly relations between nationalists political workers.
   (c) To promote among Muslims of Indian support for the British Government.
   (d) To agitate through constitutional means.

Ans. (c) To promote among Muslims of Indian support for the British Government.

9. Which of the following was not the aim of the Muslim League?
   (a) To develop and consolidate the feelings of national unity among Muslims.
   (b) To protect and advance the political rights of Muslims.
   (c) To promote support for the British Government among Muslims of India.
   (d) To prevent hostilities between Muslims and other communities.

Ans. (a) To develop and consolidate the feelings of national unity among Muslims.

10. Khilafat Movement was the result of which of the following events
   (a) Support of the British Government to the cause of the Balkan countries.
   (b) Ignorance of the British towards the Turkish interests.
   (c) First War of Independence of 1857.
   (d) Both (a) and (b)

Ans. (d) Both (a) and (b)

11. Complete the given analogy.
   Mr Beck : Mohammedan Anglo-Oriental College : : Agha Khan : ?
   (a) Non-Aligned Movement
   (b) Quit India Movement
   (c) Lucknow Pact
   (d) INA

Ans. (c) Lucknow Pact

12. Complete the given analogy.
   Muslim League : 1906 : : Constitution of Muslim League : ?
   (a) 1907 (b) 1909 (c) 1911 (d) 1915

Ans. (a) 1907

13. Complete the given analogy.
   Dacca : ? :: Karachi : Pakistan
   (a) Bhutan (b) Bangladesh
   (c) Myanmar (d) Afghanistan

Ans. (b) Bangladesh

14. Replace the underlined word to correct the statement.
A language that is adopted as a common language between speakers whose mother tongues are different is known as Local language.
(a) National Language
(b) Lingua Franca
(c) Official Language
(d) Regional Language

Ans. (b) Lingua Franca

15. Replace the underlined word to correct the statement.
According to Hakim Ajmal Khan Hindus and Muslims were one Quam (nation).
(a) Lord Minto
(b) Agha Khan
(c) Sir Syed Ahmed Khan
(d) None of the above

Ans. (c) Sir Syed Ahmed Khan

16. Complete the following table.

Mohsin-ul-Haq	Secretary of Mohammedan Anglo-Oriental College
Sir Syed Ahmed Khan	?

(a) Founder of Muslim League
(b) Founder of Mohammedan Anglo-Oriental College (MAO)
(c) Secretary of Mohammedan Anglo-Oriental College (MAO)
(d) Principal of Mohammedan Anglo-Oriental College (MAO)

Ans. (b) Founder of Mohammedan Anglo-Oriental College (MAO)

17. The Lucknow Pact was signed between which of the following
(i) Agha Khan and Mahatma Gandhi
(ii) Mahatma Gandhi and Jawaharlal Nehru
(iii) Bal Gangadhar Tilak and Mohammad Ali Jinnah
(iv) Bal Gangadhar Tilak and Agha Khan

Codes
(a) Only (i) (b) Both (ii) and (iv)
(c) Only (iii) (d) All of these

Ans. (c) Only (iii)

18. Who among the following played a key role to reunite the two parts of the Congress i.e. the early nationalists (moderates) and the assertive nationalists (extremists)?
(i) Bal Gangadhar Tilak (ii) Annie Besant
(iii) AO Hume (iv) Mahatma Gandhi

Codes
(a) Only (i) (b) Only (ii)
(c) Both (iii) and (iv) (d) All of these

Ans. (b) Only (ii)

19. Match the following

	List I		List II
A.	1867	1.	Mohammedan Anglo-Oriental Defence Association was founded
B.	1875	2.	Mohammedan Provincial Union was founded
C.	1893	3.	Hindi-Urdu Controversy
D.	1905	4.	Mohammedan Anglo-Oriental College was founded

Codes

	A	B	C	D		A	B	C	D
(a)	1	2	3	4	(b)	2	1	4	3
(c)	3	4	1	2	(d)	4	3	2	1

Ans. (a)

20. Match the following

	List I		List II
A.	1908	1.	The First Session of the Muslim League was held at Amritsar
B.	1909	2.	Balkan Wars
C.	1913	3.	Mohammad Ali Jinnah joined the Muslim League
D.	1912-13	4.	Indian Council Act

Codes

	A	B	C	D		A	B	C	D
(a)	1	2	3	4	(b)	2	1	4	3
(c)	1	4	3	2	(d)	4	3	2	1

Ans. (c)

Picture Based Question

21. Look at the picture given below and answer the questions that follow.

(i) Which of the following personalities is shown in the given picture?
(a) Nawab Salimullah (b) Mohammad Ali Jinnah
(c) Madan Mohan Malviya (d) Justice Ranade

Ans. (b) Mohammad Ali Jinnah

(ii) He is associated with which of the following political parties?
(a) Theosophical Society (b) Muslim League
(c) Servants of India Society
(d) Indian National Congress

Ans. (b) Muslim League

(iii) He joined a popular muslim political party in which of the following years.

(a) 1903 (b) 1908

(c) 1910 (d) 1913

Ans. (d) 1913

(iv) He put forward his 'Two-Nation Theory' in which session of the Muslim League in 1940.

(a) Lucknow (b) Lahore

(c) Bombay (d) Madras

Ans. (b) Lahore

Passage Based Questions

22. Read the passage given below and answer the questions that follow.

The British and some communal Indian historians were also responsible for creating communal hatred among Hindus-Muslims in the country.

These historians divided the Indian history into the Hindu and the Muslim periods. They said that the rule of Turks, Afghans and Mughals was the Muslim rule. They also said that these Muslim rulers were the followers of Islam and their subjects were the followers of other religions. Whereas according to these communal historians, in the so-called Hindu period, the Muslim rulers were the foreign invaders who came from outside in India. They created a portrait and fit Rana Pratap and Shivaji into it as national heroes and Akbar and Aurangzeb as foreign invaders. This started to increase the communal feelings in Indians.

These communal historians and British people ignored the theme of united India which was based on composite culture. They tried to create a wedge between the two important communities.

These communal historians misinterpreted the historical facts and spread the myth that the ancient period was the golden era of Indian society and culture but it declined during the medieval period when Mughal rulers came to India. They did not highlight the contribution of Mughals in the development of Indian economy, religion, art, literature, culture and society.

(i) The events of communal hatred increased after which event in India?

(a) Partition of Bengal

(b) 1857 Revolt

(c) Queen Victoria's Proclamation of 1858

(d) Formation of Congress

Ans. (b) 1857 Revolt

(ii) Who among the following is responsible for the communal division of Indian history?

(a) Scholars

(b) Extremists

(c) Communal historians and the British

(d) All of the above

Ans. (c) Communal historians and the British

(iii) What was the main aim of the communal historians and the British?

(a) To create communal harmony

(b) To misguide the masses

(c) To sow the seed of communal hatred among Hindus-Muslims

(d) Both (a) and (b)

Ans. (d) Both (a) and (b)

(iv) Which among the following rulers gave their contributions in the development of economy, religion, art, literature and society in India?

(a) Mughals (b) Turks

(c) Afghans (d) None of these

Ans. (a) Mughals

23. Read the passage given below and answer the questions that follow.

The British rulers used many dirty politics for example, to use the Divide and Rule' policy Lord Mayo's government adopted a resolution in 1871 which made Urdu the medium of instruction for Muslims in primary and secondary schools. The government also increased its aid to Muslim educational institutions. They used foul words about both the communities rulers and tried to create hatred among them.

The British Government justified itself on the question of the Partition of Bengal and tried to convince the Muslims that Bengal was being partitioned to create a new Muslim majority province where, they can dominate and no Hindus would be able to interfere in their internal matters.

They tried to create hatred among the different castes of Indian society and also to turn the non-Brahmins and the lower castes against high castes Hindus. They tried to spread communal hatred through the press, posters, literature and public platform.

(i) What frightened the British after the revolt of 1857?

(a) The Hindu- Muslim Unity

(b) The Nationalist feeling of the Indian masses

(c) The culture of India

(d) Both (a) and (b)

Ans. (d) Both (a) and (b)

(ii) Why the British Government increased its aid to Muslim educational institutions after the revolt of 1857?

(a) To encourage Muslim education

(b) To show its bias behavior

(c) To promote education in India

(d) To popularise the feeling of nationalism in India

Ans. (b) To show its bias behavior

(iii) The Partition of Bengal took place in which year?

(a) 1902 (b) 1905 (c) 1911 (d) 1916

Ans. (b) 1905

(iv) Which of the following was the feature of Indian society during the British period?
(a) The Indian masses were loyal to the British.
(b) The Indian society was divided into many caste system.
(c) The Indian masses wanted to Partition of Bengal.
(d) None of these

Ans. (b) The Indian society was divided into many caste system.

Section-II

Short Questions

1. When did the communal politics develop in India and why?

Ans. In the early 20th century, the communal politics developed in India.

It developed as a result of wrong policies taken by the British rulers.

2. State any two ways through which the Britishers encouraged separatist politics in India.

Ans. The two ways taken by the Britishers to encourage separatist politics in India were
(i) They started favouring Muslims against the Hindus.
(ii) They branded the Congress as a Hindu organisation.

3. Why the Muslims were hostile to Western education?

Ans. The Muslims considered the British responsible for the end of Mughal rule. They felt humiliated after the last Emperor Bahadur Shah Zafar was dethroned, deprived of power, titles and privileges. So, the Muslims became hostile to Western education given by the Britishers.

4. What was the view of Sir Syed Ahmad Khan regarding education?

Ans. Sir Syed Ahmad Khan realised that the lack of scientific education forced the Muslim community towards backwardness. Thus, he founded many national schools and Mohammedan Anglo-Oriental College to educate the Muslim community.

5. Sir Syed Ahmad Khan thought Indian National Congress was a Hindu organisation. Was it correct or not?

Ans. Sir Syed Ahmad Khan's view regarding Indian National Congress was not correct. It was a secular organisation and had many eminent Muslim leaders like Badruddin Tyabji, Abdul Rasul, Hasrat Mohani, etc.

6. State any two aims of Mohammedan Anglo-Oriental College.

Ans. The two aims of Mohammedan Anglo-Oriental College were
(i) To provide a centre of Western learning for the Muslims.
(ii) To promote loyalty towards the rulers and solicit their favours.

7. Write the name of any two associations founded by Sir Syed Ahmad Khan to safeguard the rights of the Muslims.

Ans. Sir Syed Ahmad Khan founded the following two associations to safeguard the rights of the Muslims
(i) Mohammedan Anglo-Oriental Defence Association.
(ii) United Indian Patriotic Association.

8. Why did Sir Syed Ahmad Khan oppose the policies of the Indian National Congress?

Ans. Sir Syed Ahmad Khan opposed the policies of the Indian National Congress as he preached complete obedience to British rule. When the Indian National Congress was formed, he decided to oppose it because he feared that since most of the prominent leaders of the Congress were Hindus, they would dominate the Muslims. So, he urged the Muslims not to join the Indian National Congress.

9. Why did the imperial regime encourage separatist tendencies among the minority community?

Ans. The imperial regime encouraged separatist tendencies among the minority community as they wanted to check the growth of a united national feeling in India. The British knew that the united people could not be subjugated or suppressed for a long time.

10. Give any two demands forwarded by the delegation led by Agha Khan III.

Ans. Two demands forwarded by the delegation led by Agha Khan III were
(i) Separate electoral constituency for the Muslims.
(ii) More state aids for promoting new Muslim Universities.

11. What was the meaning of separate electorate?

Ans. Separate electorate meant that elections were to be held on the basis of communal representation. It meant that the Muslims could vote for a Muslim candidate and the Hindus for a Hindu candidate.

12. Give two examples to show that the British encouraged communal and separatist attitude in Indian politics.

Ans. The British encouraged communal and separatist attitude in Indian politics. For example
(i) Lord Curzon partitioned Bengal to weaken the Hindu-Muslim unity.
(ii) Morley-Minto Reforms of 1909 provided for separate representation to the Muslim community in the Imperial Legislative Council.

13. What did the British do to foster the policy of Divide and Rule, which gave rise to the formation of the Muslim League?

Ans. The British did the following to foster the policy of Divide and Rule
- The British Government started favouring Muslims against the Hindus.
- They branded the Congress as Hindu organisation and encouraged the upper class Muslim to form their own organisation.

14. When was the Muslim League formally founded? Who presided over its session at Dacca?

Ans. The Muslim League was formally founded on 30th December, 1906. Nawab Salimullah presided over its session at Dacca.

15. Name the Muslim leader who welcomed the Partition of Bengal.

Ans. Nawab Salimullah of Dacca welcomed the Partition of Bengal. He took the initiative to form a political organisation for the Muslim. His proposal was accepted and the Muslim League was formally founded.

16. Under whose chairmanship was the First Regular session of the Muslim League held? Name the city.

Ans. The First Regular session of the Muslim League was held in 1905 at Amritsar under the leadership of Syed Ali Imam.

17. Name the organisation founded by Habib-ur-Rahman.

Ans. On the advice of Abul Kalam Azad, Habib-ur-Rahman founded Masjlis-i-Ahrar (The society of freeman). The organisation made great sacrifices for the cause of India's freedom.

18. How did the British apply 'Divide and Rule policy' in the Government of India Act, 1919?

Ans. According to the Government of India Act, 1919, the electorates to elect the members of the legislature were arranged under the communal and sectional bases. In this way, the Britishers applied the 'Divide and Rule policy' in the Government of India Act.

19. Which decision of the Britishers were not acceptable to the Muslims?

Ans. The British occupation of Egypt and Anglo-Russian Convention of 1907, dividing Persia and bringing it under control were not acceptable to the Muslims.

20. Why did the Indians help the British during the First World War?

Ans. Indians helped the British during the First World War with men, money and material in the hope that the British Government would grant India self-government as soon as the war ended.

21. Name the founders of newspapers like 'Al- Hilal', 'Hamdard' and 'Comrade'.

Ans. Maulana Abul Kalam Azad started the Urdu newspaper 'Al-Hilal' and Ali brothers (Maulana Mohammad Ali and Shaukat Ali) started 'Hamdard' in Urdu and 'Comrade' in English to mobilise public opinion in favour of self-government.

22. Why was there an important change in the attitude of the Muslims towards the British rulers?

Ans. There was an important change in the attitude of the Muslims towards the British rulers because Britain was fighting the First World War against Turkey, whose ruler, Caliph was the temporal and spiritual head of all the Muslims. This annoyed the sentiments of the Muslims and gradually they began to support the Congress aim of self-government.

23. Name the famous pact that demonstrated the unity between the Congress and the Muslim League. When was it signed? **[2016]**

Ans. Lucknow Pact demonstrated the unity between the Congress and the Muslim League.

It was signed in 1916.

24. Which incidence brought Muslim League closer to the Congress?

Ans. Arrest of prominent Muslim leaders under the Seditious Meetings Act, brought the Muslim League closer to the Congress.

25. What was the importance of the Lucknow Pact of 1916 ? **[2013]**

Ans. Lucknow Pact played an important role, as it brought about a unity between the Hindus and the Muslims. Both the communities agreed to compromise on some areas for their common good. Congress compromised on its secular character by accepting the scheme of separate electorates for Muslims while the Muslim League accepted the principles of election and the majority rule.

26. What were the provisions regarding bills in Lucknow Pact?

Ans. There was a provision in the Lucknow Pact that no bill would be introduced by a non-official member, if it affected the interest of any community. Such a bill would not be passed, if it was opposed by 3/4th of that community.

27. What was the main demand of the Lucknow Pact?

Ans. The main demand of the Lucknow Pact was self-government at all levels of administration. This Pact declared that India must cease to a dependency and be raised to the status of self-governing state as an equal party with equal rights and responsibilities as an independent unit of the empire.

28. What was the demand of Lucknow Pact, regarding reform of secretariat?

Ans. The Lucknow Pact demanded that India Council of Secretary of State should be replaced by two permanent under secretaries out of which one should be an Indian.

29. Which communal veto was introduced in Lucknow Pact?

Ans. The Lucknow Pact introduced a new type of communal veto which declared that no legislature could enact a law. If it was opposed by 3/4th of the members of a particular community.

Structured Questions

1. With reference to nationalism and the birth of the Indian National Congress, explain each of the following. **[2012]**
   (i) Political views of Sir Syed Ahmad Khan towards Congress.
   (ii) The demand of Muslim delegations to Viceroy Lord Minto.
   (iii) Three main objectives of the Muslim League.

Ans. (i) Refer to chapter theory page no. 141.
(ii) Refer to chapter theory page no. 143.
(iii) Refer to chapter theory page no. 143.

2. The reasons for the formation of the Muslim League were many. In this context, explain the following questions. **[2013]**
   (i) Any three factors that led to the formation of the Muslim League in India.
   (ii) Any three demands made by the Muslim Deputation in 1906 to the Viceroy Lord Minto.
   (iii) What were the aims and objectives of the Muslim League?

Ans. (i) Refer to chapter theory page nos. 140-141.
(ii) They demands of Muslim delegations to viceroy Lord Minto were
- Representation of Muslims in elected bodies on the basis of its political importance and not on numerical strength of the community.
- Separate electoral constituencies for the Muslims.
- Special favours granted to the Muslims in appointment to government services and to the membership of Central and Provincial Councils.

(iii) Refer to chapter theory page no. 143.

4. The British Policy of Divide and Rule gave rise to the formation of the Muslim League. In this context, state the following.
   (i) The British Policy of Divide and Rule.
   (ii) The objectives of the Muslim League.
   Or State any two objectives of the Muslim League. **[2023]**
   (iii) Two direct impacts of the formation of the Muslim League.
   (iv) The Hindi-Urdu controversy.

Ans. (i) Refer to chapter theory page no. 140-141.
(ii) Refer to chapter theory page no. 143.
(iii) Refer to chapter theory page no. 144.
(iv) Refer to chapter theory page nos. 141-142.

5. With reference to the formation of Muslim League explain the following questions.
   (i) Whose ideas led to the formation of the Muslim League?
   (ii) What was the reaction of the nationalist Muslim?
   (iii) Hindi-Urdu controversy made conflict between two communities.

Ans. (i) The ideas of Nawab Salimullah Khan led to the formation of the Muslim League. In December, 1906, the delegates from various provinces assembled for the Muslim Educational Conference at Dacca. They felt the need to establish a political organisation and they were encouraged by the British to do so. Nawab Salimullah Khan of Dacca took the initiative to form a political organisation of the Muslims. His proposal was accepted by all and the Muslim League was formally founded on 30th December, 1906. Sir Syed Ahmed Khan was the pioneer of Two-Nation Theory. His philosophy guided the path to create separate organisation i.e. Muslim League which was founded later by the Nawab of Dacca.
(ii) The reactions of the nationalist Muslim to the Muslim League were
- Some nationalist Muslims believed in active co-operation with the Congress. Leaders like Maulana Abul Kalam Azad, Habib-ur-Rahman, Hakim Ajmal Khan, Mazhar-ul-Haq etc joined the Nationalist Movement.
- On the advice of Abul Kalam Azad, Habib-ur-Rahman founded Masjlis-i-Ahrar (The society of freemen). The Ahrar made great sacrifices for the cause of India's freedom.

(iii) Refer to chapter theory page no. 141-142.

6. With reference to the Lucknow Pact of 1916, answer the following questions. **[2013]**
   (i) Mention two terms of the Lucknow Pact.
   (ii) What is the significance of this Pact?
   (iii) On what grounds this Pact was criticised?

Ans. (i) Refer to chapter theory page nos. 145.
(ii) Significance of the Lucknow Pact were
- The Lucknow Pact is considered important as for the first time, the Congress and the Muslim League had come up with a joint programme which the British found difficult to ignore.
- Both the parties demanded for self-government.
- The moderates and the extremists faction of the Congress were reconciled at Lucknow Session.
- At that time, Home Rule Movement intensified the National Movement, thus the British rulers could not easily ignore the constitutional reforms demanded by this Pact.

(iii) Lucknow Pact was criticised in the following ways
- Critics thought that this pact demanded more sacrifice on the part of the Hindus and it marked the beginning of the appeasement of Muslims by the Congress.
- The scheme did not involve the masses from both the communities.
- It provided for Muslim representation in the council in excess of their proportion in the total population.
- The Congress failed to maintain its secular character by accepting separate electorates for Muslims.

7. Lucknow Pact of 1916 is considered as landmark in the history of Indian National Movement. Answer the following questions in this regard. [2013]
   (i) Changes in the relations between the Congress and Muslim League.
   (ii) The main significance of the Pact.
   (iii) Impact of the Pact on National Movement.

Ans. (i) Following changes were seen in the relations between the Congress and Muslim League
- After Lucknow Pact Muslims began to support the Congress aim of self-government.
- Both the parties compromised with each other and the Pact symbolised Hindu-Muslim unity to both parties.
- The leaders of both the parties did not want to give the British Government and excuse for delaying political reforms.

(ii) Refer to chapter theory page no. 146.

(iii) Following were the impacts of Lucknow Pact on National Movement
- It discouraged the British Policy of 'Divide and Rule'.
- The pace of the movement increased as both the parties at all India level successfully mobilised the masses.
- The Congress which was divided between moderates and radicals, now united and strengthened in position.
- The Congress acknowledged the 'Separate Electrorate' concept of the Muslim League. This proved very problematic in later period.

Picture Based Question

1. Answer the following questions based on the picture given below.

   (i) Identify the person given in the picture.
   (ii) When and why Mohammedan Anglo-Oriental Defence Association was founded?
   (iii) What was his contribution in respect of 'Two-Nation Theory'?

Ans. (i) The person given in the picture is Sir Syed Ahmad Khan. He was a great reformer and educationalist of Muslim Community. He founded the Mohammedan Anglo-Oriental College at Aligarh in 1875 with the aim of spreading Western education and modernising the Muslim community.

(ii) In 1893, under the influence of Principal of the Mohammedan Anglo-Oriental College, Aligarh, Sir Syed Ahmad Khan founded the Mohammedan Anglo-Oriental Defence Association.
This organisation was founded in order to keep away the Muslims from the Congress, to promote loyalty towards the rulers and to prevent Muslims from participating in any political movement. Sir Syed feared that the Muslim community would be dominated by the Hindus, if the Congress were to come power. The British through this association, wanted to dissuade Muslims from joining the Congress.

(iii) Sir Syed Ahmad Khan opposed the policies of Indian National Congress. He declared that the interests of Muslims and Hindus were different. He advised the Muslims not to identify themselves with the Hindus and the Congress. Sir Syed was one of the earliest advocates of the 'Two-Nation Theory', that Hindus and Muslims should have separate nations.
British took his idea of separatism and used it to separate Hindus and Muslims. In 1909, the British Government passed the Indian Council Act or Morley-Minto Reform. This cut off the Muslim masses from the National Movement. This new communal politics in India gave birth to the 'Two-Nation Theory', which was a development of Sir Syed Ahmad Khan's separatist ideology.

Chapter Assessment

Section-I

Multiple Choice Questions

1. Who among the following is associated with the Mohammedan Anglo-Oriental College?
   (a) Maulana Azad
   (b) Hakim Ajmal Khan
   (c) Annie Besant
   (d) Sir Syed Ahmed Khan
2. The First World War took place in which year?
   (a) 1914-18
   (b) 1916-18
   (c) 1918-20
   (d) 1920-22
3. In which year Bal Gangadhar Tilak rejoined the Indian National Congress?
   (a) 1907 (b) 1910
   (c) 1912 (d) 1916
4. Complete the given analogy.
   Arundale Committee : ? : : Muslim Deputation : Agha Khan
   (a) Lord Minto
   (b) Lord Dalhousie
   (c) Lord Lytton
   (d) Lord Linlithgow

Section-II

Short Questions

1. Why did the British treat the Muslims badly immediately after the uprising of 1857?
2. What were the reasons for the educational and economic backwardness of the Muslims in India?
3. Give two examples to show that the British incited the Muslims against the Hindus.
4. How did the principal of Mohammedan Anglo-Oriental College encourage the Muslim communalism?
5. When was separate electorate granted to the Muslims?
6. What was the belief of the nationalist Muslims?
7. Give reasons for the establishment of the Mohammedan Anglo-Oriental Defence Association in 1893.
8. Why did Sir Syed Ahmed Khan advise the Muslims not to join the Indian National Congress?

Structured Questions

1. There were many events that led to the formation of the Muslim League in 1906. In this context, explain the following questions.
   (i) The British Policy of Divide and Rule.
   (ii) Loss of sovereignty by the Muslims.
   (iii) Muslim deputation sent to Viceroy Lord Minto.
   (iv) Impact of Partition of Bengal
2. With reference to the factors responsible for the growth of separatist trend among the Muslims, briefly explain the following questions.
   (i) Economic backwardness of India.
   (ii) Communal bias of Muslim society against Western education.
   (iii) Many Muslims supported the Partition of Bengal.
   (iv) The Aligarh Politics
3. A Muslim delegation under the Leadership of Agha Khan III was received by Lord Minto in 1906. In the context to this, answer the following.
   (i) The demands given by the delegation.
   (ii) Assurance given by the Viceroy to the delegation.
   (iii) Morley-Minto Reforms of 1909.

CHAPTER

06

Mahatma Gandhi and the National Movement (1915-1947)

SYLLABUS

Mahatma Gandhi • Non-Cooperation Movement : causes (Khilafat Movement, Rowlatt Act, Jallianwala Bagh Tragedy), programme and suspension-Chauri Chaura incident and impact of the movement.
• The Civil Disobedience Movement : causes (reaction to the Simon Commission, declaration of Poorna Swaraj at the Lahore Session of 1929), Dandi March, programme and impact of the movement, Gandhi-Irwin Pact and Second Round Table Conference.
• The Quit India Movement : causes (failure of the Cripps Mission, Japanese threat), Quit India Resolution and the significance of the Movement.

In India, the period from 1915 to 1947 is regarded as the Mass Phase of National Movement in which Mahatma Gandhi played a significant role. In this phase, various movements were organised against the British which include Non-Cooperation Movement, the Civil Disobedience Movement and the Quit India Movement.

Mahatma Gandhi

Mohandas Karamchand Gandhi (popularly known as Bapu or Mahatma Gandhi) was born on 2nd October, 1869 in Porbandar, a coastal town at Gujarat. His father was the Diwan (Chief-Minister) of Porbandar. In 1883, Gandhiji was married to Kasturba at the age of 13. In 1888, he went to London for higher studies in Law. He came back to India after completing his studies and started practicing Law at Rajkot.

In 1893, he went to South Africa and spent the next 21 years living in South Africa. At that time, the system of 'Apartheid' or racial segregation was very much present in South Africa. Gandhiji founded a political movement, against this racial injustice and discrimination to Indians. This movement was known as **Natal Indian Congress.**

Due to this movement, the Government of South Africa repealed most of the unfair acts against the Indians. It was during this movement that Gandhiji revolved the method of Satyagraha or non-violent resistance.

In 1915, Gandhiji returned to India and involved in the Indian freedom movement. He organised **Satyagraha Movements** in Champaran (1917), Kheda and Ahmedabad (1918). The success of these movements encouraged him to launch a nationwide Satyagraha against the British Raj which started with the Non-Cooperation Movement in 1920.

Non-Cooperation Movement

The Non-Cooperation Movement was the first mass based political movement under Gandhiji. In his famous book **Hind Swaraj** (1909), Mahatma Gandhi declared that British rule was established in India with the cooperation of Indians and had survived only because of this cooperation of Indians. If Indians refuse to cooperate, British rule in India would collapse within 1 year and Swaraj would come as a result.

The resolution of the Non-Cooperation Movement was adopted in the session of the Congress held at Calcutta in September, 1920. It was approved in the regular session of the Congress at Nagpur in December, 1920.

Causes of the Non-Cooperation Movement

The Rowlatt Act

In 1919, the Rowlatt Act was passed through the Imperial Legislative Council in spite of unanimous opposition of the Indian members. This act was introduced by the Sedition committee headed by **Justice Rowlattus** in February, 1919 and passed in March 1919. This act gave unlimited powers to the government to arrest and imprison suspects without trial for maximum 2 years.

Through the Rowlatt Act, the British Government

- Arrest of a person without warrant.
- In camera trial (trial in seclusion).
- Restrict the movements of individuals.
- Suspension of the Right of **Habeas Corpus**[1].

Gandhiji opposed this act and started a non-violent civil disobedience against it with a *hartal* or strike on 6th April, 1919. Rallies were organised in various cities, workers went on strike in railway workshops and shops were closed down. 6th April, 1919, was observed as **Satyagraha Day** when people all over the country observed fast and *hartal.* It was the first countrywide agitation by Gandhiji and it marked the foundation of the Non-Cooperation Movement.

Jallianwala Bagh Massacre

On 13th April, 1919, a large crowd gathered in the enclosed ground of Jallianwala Bagh in Amritsar to protest against the arrest of leaders like Saifuddin Kitchlew and Satya Pal under the provisions of Rowlatt Act. The **martial laws**[2] were already imposed in Amritsar.

As a result, **General Dyer**, the military commander of Amritsar surrounded the area and opened fire on the crowd, killing thousands of innocent demonstrators. Dyer did this with an aim to create a feeling of terror and awe in the minds of Satyagrahis. This led to the events like strikes or *hartals,* conflict with the police and attacks on government buildings.

The government responded to these events with brutal repression seeking to humiliate and terrorise people. Satyagrahis were forced to rub their noses on the ground, crawl on the streets and do *salaam* (salute) to all Sahibs. People were beaten and villages were bombed. Rabindranath Tagore returned his **Knighthood**[3] after this massacre to express the pain and anger of the country.

Entrance to Jallianwala Bagh

Hunter Commission

The Hunter Commission under the Chairmanship of Lord Hunter was appointed in 1920 to enquire the Jallianwala Bagh Massacre. The Commission criticised Dyer's action and stated that though Dyer had acted in a harsh and ruthless way, military or legal charge would not be possible on him due to political reasons.

Khilafat Movement

In the First World War, the Ottoman Turkey was defeated. There were rumours that a harsh peace treaty was going to be imposed on the Ottoman emperor, who was the spiritual head (Khalifa) of the Islamic world. Thus, the Muslims of India decided to force Britain to change its Turkish policy and a Khilafat Committee was formed under the leadership of Maulana Azad, Hakim Ajmal Khan and Hasrat Mohani.

Some young Muslim leaders like the brothers Muhammad Ali and Shaukat Ali also started discussing with Mahatma Gandhi about the possibility of a united mass action on the Khilafat issue. Gandhiji saw this as an opportunity of uniting Hindus and Muslims together.

1 **Habeas Corpus** It is a writ in the Constitution against unlawful and indefinite imprisonment.

2 **Martial Laws** It was an imposition of direct military control over the civilians.

3 **Knighthood** It is a title given to a man by British King or Queen for achievements or his service to his country.

On October 17th, 1919 **Khilafat Day** was observed. The Khilafatists formed a three-point programme

(i) The Ottoman Caliph should retain his empire.

(ii) The Caliph must be left with sufficient territory to enable him to defend the Islamic faith.

(iii) The Arab lands (Arabia, Syria, Iraq and Palestine) must remain under the Muslim rule.

In November, 1919, Gandhiji was elected as the President of the **All-India Khilafat Conference** and gave advice to the Khilafat Committee to adopt a policy of Non-Cooperation with the Government. On this advice, the Khilafat Non-Cooperation Movement began from 31st August, 1920. Many activities took place during this movement such as

- People resigned from government services.
- Students boycotted schools and colleges
- Shops selling foreign goods were picketed.
- Hartals and demonstrations were held all over the country.
- In 1921, all the Muslims were appealed not to join police and armed forces and not to pay any taxes to the British government.

The British Government was enraged by these acts of Khilafatists and arrested the Ali Brothers on charges of sedition.

Objectives of the Non-Cooperation Movement

- The first objective was to attain self-government within the British Government, if possible and outside if necessary.
- The British Government should express its regret on the happenings in Punjab, particularly in Amritsar.
- The British should adopt a just attitude towards Turkey, and restore its power and old status of the Sultan of Turkey.

Programmes of Non-Cooperation Movement

The following programmes of resistance were adopted in the Non-Cooperation Movement

Boycott Programmes

- Surrendering of titles and offices and resignation from nominated posts in the local bodies.
- Boycott of legislatures, law courts, schools, colleges and all institutions having connection with the British.
- Boycott of foreign goods and adoption of Swadeshi.
- Boycott of election of 1919 and other government functions.

Swadeshi Programmes

- Adoption of Swadeshi and Khadi by reviving hand-spinning and hand-weaving clothes in the country.
- Establishment of national schools and colleges and panchayats (private arbitration courts) all over the country.
- Revive the Hindu-Muslim unity.
- Removal of untouchability for the welfare of Harijan.
- Empowerment of women in the country.

Supression of the Non-Cooperation Movement

Non-Cooperation Movement was started with full enthusiasm but due to government's strict action and some violent incidence, it collapsed abruptly. All important leaders except Gandhiji were arrested and sent to prison. Any processions or public meetings were prohibitted. One of the important reason due to which the Non-Cooperation Movement ended was the Chauri Chaura incident.

Chauri Chaura Incident

This incident occured on 5th February, 1922 in Chauri Chaura village in Gorakhpur district of Uttar Pradesh. In this incident, a procession of 3,000 peasants was marched to the police station to protest against a police officer who had beaten some volunteers picketing a liquor shop. However, they were fired upon by the police due to which some demonstrators set the nearby police station on fire, killing many policemen. Gandhiji who was a firm believer of non-violence, was shocked by this incident and decided to call off the movement immediately. Thus, on 12th February, 1922, Gandhiji withdraw the Non-Cooperation Movement. This withdrawal of movement was criticised by many leaders like Motilal Nehru and Lala Lajpat Rai. Subhash Chandra Bose called it a 'National Calamity'. He felt that people were not yet ready for a non-violent struggle. He thought that violence would breed violence and British could easily suppress it.

Gandhiji was arrested on 10th March, 1922 and was sentenced to 6 years' imprisonment on the charge of sedition, but after two years he was released due to his ill health.

Impact of the Non-Cooperation Movement

Though the Non-Cooperation Movement ended in apparent failure and was unable to achieve its immediate goals, but it had great historical importance. Its impacts were

- **Becoming an All India Movement** Earlier the National Movement had remained the concern of the middle class and intelligentsia. But later, it became an all India Movement and Gandhiji became the symbol of the poor and the downtrodden. It spread nationalism to every part of the country.
- **Uniting Hindu-Muslim Community** By supporting the Khilafat Movement and later involving Muslim masses, Gandhiji was able to unite Hindu and Muslim community. The Non-Cooperation Movement tried to remove caste distinctions and bound the whole nation in a common bond, i.e. to achieve Swaraj.
- **Congress became a Nationalist organisation** This movement made the Congress as a nationalist organisation by adopting new, revolutionary method which was supported by the masses. The Congress became a continuous political organisation and its Constitution was amended in the Nagpur session in December, 1920. Provincial Congress Committees were established and reorganised on the basis of linguistic areas. A Working Committee of 15 members, including the President and the secretaries was set up in the Congress which was responsible for implementing resolutions. The Congress also added members from Indian villages.
- **Effect on British Industries** The economic boycott during Non-Cooperation Movement affected British industries. There was a decline in the import of cotton goods from England in 1920-22. As a consequence, the Indian textile industry flourished. It promoted Indian handicrafts and Khadi became a symbol of the National Movement.
- **Instilled Confidence Among People** The Non-Cooperation Movement gave political lesson to Indians. It instilled confidence in Indians. The myth of invincibility of British power no longer dominated them.
- **Promoted Social Reforms** The movement led many social reforms in the Indian society, e.g. prohibition and removal of untouchability. Due to this movement, many Indian schools and colleges were opened in the country.

Check Your LEARNING...

1. When and where was Gandhiji born?
2. Name the act which gave the government power to suppress political activity and detain political prisoners without trial.
3. Mention the event which seemed as an opportunity of uniting Hindus and Muslims in our country to Mahatma Gandhi.
4. For what purpose the Hunter Commission was appointed?

Civil Disobedience Movement

This movement was started by Gandhiji in 1930. This movement was an attempt to weaken the administration of British by breaking some specific rules and regulations.

Causes of the Civil Disobedience Movement

Reaction to the Simon Commission

Simon Commission was constituted in November, 1927 under John Simon to review the functioning of the constitutional system in India and suggest changes. Indian leaders opposed the Commission as there were only 7 British members of Parliament in the commission and no Indians in it.

The National Congress in its Madras session in 1927, presided by Dr. Ansari, decided to boycott the Simon Commission. Its decision was supported by the Muslim League and Hindu Mahasabha. When Simon Commission arrived Bombay on 3rd February, 1928, the leaders organised an All India *Hartal*.

This Commission was greeted with the slogan 'Simon Go Back' along with black flags. As a result, the British Government tried to brutally suppress this opposition. Lala Lajpat Rai was seriously injured in a police Lathi charge on 30th October, 1928 while leading a demonstration, due to which he died.

Recommendations of the Simon Commission

- It was recommended that **Dyarchy**[4] should be abolished and there should be complete autonomy in the Provinces including the department of law and order. But the Governor should be given overriding powers in certain matters, e.g. the internal security.
- Provincial Legislative Councils should be enlarged.
- Federal Government at the centre should support not only British India but also the Princely States.

4 **Dyarchy** A system of double government introduced by the Government of India Act (1919) for the provinces of British India

- The Governor-General should select and appoint members of his Cabinet.
- British troops and British officers should continue to stay in Indian regiments for many more years.
- High Courts should be controlled by the British Government of India.
- The Communal representation was to be continued.

Declaration of Purna Swaraj

In Lahore session of December 1929, under the Presidency of Jawaharlal Nehru, the Congress formalised the demand of Purna Swaraj for India. The Purna Swaraj resolution meant Complete Independence, which was set forth as the goal of the National Movement. For this, the Congress Working Committee met in January 1930 and decided the following programmes

- Preparation for Civil Disobedience Movement.
- It was proposed that 26th January, 1930 would be celebrated as the 'Purna Swaraj Day' or Independence Day all over the country with the hoisting of the tricolour flag.
- Resignations by members of the legislature.
- Withdrawal from all possible association with the British Government. A pledge was drawn up, which was to be read and solemnly taken, while celebrating the day.

Programmes of the Civil Disobedience Movement

- The movement included violation of salt laws, non-payment of taxes and revenues, boycott of foreign cloth, British goods and liquor.
- The movement was followed by violation of forest laws in Maharashtra, Karnataka and the Central Provinces.
- People refused to pay the rural Chaukidari tax in Eastern India.
- People joined *hartals*, demonstrations and the campaign to boycott foreign goods and refused to pay taxes.
- Satyagraha was adopted by many Indians.
- The North-West Frontiers of India also experienced the Civil Disobedience Movement. The Pathans organised the society of 'Khudai Khidmatgars, known as 'Red Shirts' under the leadership of Khan Abdul Ghaffar Khan, (popularly known as 'The Frontier Gandhi'). They adopted non-violence for the freedom struggle.

Events of the Civil Disobedience Movement

Dandi or Salt March

On 31st January, 1930, Gandhiji sent a letter to **Viceroy Irwin** stating eleven demand, i.e. **Eleven Points Ultimatum**. Some demands were of general interest and some were specific demands of different classes from industrialists to peasants.

The most strong among all the demands was to abolish the salt tax. Salt was one of the most essential food item and was consumed by both rich and poor. After getting no response from the British Government, Gandhiji started a March on 12th March, 1930 along with 78 followers from Sabarmati Ashram to Dandi, the coastal town of Gujarat. On 6th April, he reached Dandi and ceremonially violated the Salt Law, by manufacturing salt by boiling sea water. This marked the beginning of the Civil Disobedience Movement.

The Salt March

First Round Table Conference

The Round Table Conferences were a series of peace conferences organised by the British Government and Indian political leaders to discuss constitutional reforms in India. Three Round Table Conference were held from 1930 to 1932.

The First Round Table Conference was held in 1930 in London. However the Congress boycotted it due to the following reasons

- The Congress was convinced that the Indian princes and representatives of communal parties would not support the demand of the Congress for complete Independence and a joint electorate.
- The Congress wanted the summoning of a Constituent Assembly to draft a Constitution for India but the British Government refused to accept this demand of the Congress.

Gandhi-Irwin Pact

On 5th March, 1931, Viceroy Lord Irwin and Gandhiji signed an agreement on 5th March, 1931. This agreement is known as Gandhi-Irwin Pact. This agreement led to the end of the Civil Disobedience Movement. The provisions of the Gandhi-Irwin Pact were

- According to this Pact, the Viceroy agreed to release all political prisoners except those convicted of violence and killing.
- The government agreed to withdraw all ordinances and end prosecution.
- The Viceroy agreed to permit peaceful picketing of liquor as well as opium shops and to allow people living within some distance of the sea shore to collect or manufacture salt free from any tax.
- The British Government agreed to restore the confiscated properties of the Satyagrahis. They also agreed not to force police investigation in the past events.
- The Congress and Gandhiji on their part agreed to discontinue the Civil Disobedience Movement and agreed to participate in the Second Round Table Conference.

Events after the Civil Disobedience Movement

Second Round Table Conference

It was held from 7th September to 1st December, 1931 in London. Mahatma Gandhi was appointed as the sole representative of the Congress to this conference. In this conference, the representatives of other groups like Muslims, Sikhs, Christians, Princes and planters were more interested to safeguard their narrow interests than fighting for the country's interest. The conference focussed on communal problems like separate electorates demanded by Muslims, depressed classes, Indian Christians, Anglo-Indians, etc. However there was no agreement regarding communal representation in this conference.

The lack of agreement among many delegate groups led to no substantial results regarding India's constitutional future. The session ended with Mac Donald's announcement of

- Two Muslim provinces (North-West Frontier province and Sindh).
- Setting up of an Indian consultative committee.
- Setting up three expert committees i.e. Finances, Franchise and State Committees.
- The prospect of unilateral British Communal Award if Indian fail to agree.

Second Round Table Conference

Renewal of Civil Disobedience Movement

After the failure of the Second Round Table Conference and due to the great depression of 1930s in the world, Gandhiji sought an interview with Viceroy Willington, but the interview was refused. Then Congress passed a resolution for the renewal of the Civil Disobedience Movement. After this event, Gandhiji was arrested on January 4th, 1932.

The British Government started to repress the movement and assumed special powers. It declared Congress as an illegal organisation and arrested many Congress leaders. It also seized their properties. Communalism was spread everywhere. Soon the Civil Disobedience Movement became weak and finally Congress called it off in 1934.

Third Round Table Conference

It was held on 17th November, 1932 to December 24th, 1932 in London in which only 46 delegates were present. The Indian National Congress and the Labour Party decided not to attend it. Dr. Bhimrao Ambedkar attended this conference and demanded separate electorate for the depressed classes.

On this request, Ramsay Macdonald, the Prime Minister of Britain, announced an award known as the **Communal Award** which provided separate representation to the Muslims, Buddhists, Sikhs, Indian Christians, Anglo-Indians, Europeans and the Depressed Classes. This award was strongly opposed by Mahatma Gandhi. He believed that this award would disintegrate Indian society so, he started a fast in protest against it.

As a result, 'Poona Pact' was signed between Dr. Bhimrao Ambedkar and the Congress (Mahatma Gandhi) on 25th September, 1932. As per this pact, reservation of seats were provided for the depressed classes in the Provisional legislatures, within the general electorate without any separate electorate. Thus, the depressed classes received 148 seats in the legislature, instead of the 71 seats as per the Communal Award.

Impact of the Civil-Disobedience Movement

- It created political consciousness and a deep sense of patriotism in the minds of the people.
- It brought women out of their homes and made them equal partners in the freedom struggle.
- It made the British Government to realise the need for constitutional reform. As a consequence, the Government of India Act, 1935 was passed which introduced the principle of a Federation and the principle of Provincial Autonomy i.e. responsible government in the Province.
- In June 1934, the government withdrew the ban on the Congress. Even after the suspension of the movement, people did not abandon their struggle for freedom. For example, merchants and shopkeepers, peasants, tribals and workers in different parts of the country were mobilised for the Indian National Movement.
- People adopted the idea of non-violence. People in towns and villages popularised the patriotic songs like 'Prabhat Pheris' and handwritten Patrikas or news-sheets were issued in large numbers.
- The movement improved the condition of depressed classes. They were now allowed to perform prayer in temples and could access to wells. The Birla and the **'Harijan Sevak Sangh'**[5] played a significant role in this regard.
- Indian leaders now wanted to contest Assembly elections. In 1937, the Congress won many seats in the elections of the Central Legislative Assembly and Provincial Legislative Assemblies.

Check Your LEARNING...

1. Who founded 'Swaraj Party'?
2. When did Simon Commission arrive in India?
3. When was the Gandhi-Irwin Pact signed?
4. Where was the Third Round Table held?

Events Leading to Quit India Movement

Resignation of the Congress Ministries and Demand for Pakistan

When the Second World War started, the British Government of India immediately joined the war to support Poland in September, 1939, without consulting the National Congress or the elected members of the Central Legislature.

The Congress opposed this action as India itself was enslaved by the British. The Congress leaders, therefore, demanded that India must be declared free or at least have effective power, before it could actively participate in the war. But the Viceroy Lord Linlithgow did not give any assurance on this demand. He declared **Dominion Status**[6] as the goal of the British Policy in India.

The British Government tried to make the religious minorities and Indian Princes against the Congress. Thus, the Congress asked its ministries to resign from the United Provinces, Central Provinces, Orissa, Bihar, Madras, Bombay, Assam and the North-West Frontier.

The Ministries resigned on 22nd December, 1939. The Muslim League was happy over this resignation and celebrated this day as a **day of deliverance** and **thanks-giving**.

The Muslim League passed a resolution in 1940 in which it demanded the Partition of India and the creation of a state called Pakistan which would include Punjab, Afghan (North-West Frontier Province), Kashmir, Sind and Baluchistan in it.

August Offer (1940)

During the Second World War, the situation in Europe got worse. The international pressure forced the British Government to settle issues with the Congress. On August 8th, 1940 Lord Linlithgow, the Viceroy, made a new offer known as the **August Offer**. As per this offer, the British Government was ready to give Dominion Status to India after the war. But the Muslim League rejected the offer, as it did not give a clear assurance for the establishment of Pakistan.

Quit India Resolution

It was adopted by the Congress Working Committee at Wardha on 14th July, 1942. According to the resolution, it was proposed that the congress would start a non-voilent movement under the leadership of Gandhiji if its demand of complete independence was not accepted by the British.

Quit India Movement

The Quit India Resolution was formally passed on 8th August, 1942 at the Bombay session of the Congress. However, before the movement started, the British Government imprisoned the entire Congress leadership without trial.

5 **Harijan Sevak Sangh** It was a NGO founded by Mahatma Gandhi in 1932 to eradicate untouchability in India.

6 **Dominion Status** It implied giving autonomous status to India and not full independence where India would still accept the British sovereignty and the British Monarch remain as the head of the state.

The Congress was banned as an illegal organisation and the press was censored. The news of the arrest of all leaders shocked the entire nation due to which following events happened

- The people expressed anger and resentment through numerous agitations, *hartals*, processions and demonstrations in all over the country.
- People burnt government building, post offices, police stations, etc. They disconnected railway, telegram and telephone lines.
- Students, peasants, workers and women all took part in this movement.

The British took this situation as a challenge and used force to suppress it. As a result of brutal oppression and to avoid getting arrested many leaders were forced to go underground like Achyutrao Patwardhan, Sucheta Kripalani, Aruna Asaf Ali, Ram Manohar Lohia, Biju Patnaik, Jayaprakash Narayan, etc. and started the underground movement. The other leaders were arrested and the British Government succeeded in suppressing the movement.

Causes of Quit India Movement

Cripps Mission (1942)

During the Second World War, when the Japanese Army was rapidly approaching towards India, the British Government tried to resolve the political issues in India. Prime Minister Winston Churchill sent Sir Stafford Cripps, a seasoned diplomat with some proposals of constitutional reforms. This mission is known as Cripps Mission. These constitutional reforms were

- Promise of dominion status after the Second World War.
- An elected Constituent Assembly for framing the Constitution of free India. Its members would be elected by the Lower House of the Indian Legislature and the representatives of the Princely States nominated by their rulers.
- Proposals of an interim government during the war.
- Indian leaders would invited to participate in the council of their country and the common wealth.
- There would be a federation of British India and Indian States. Any province that was not prepared to accept the Constitution would be allowed to obtain Dominion Status separately and would formulate their own Constitution.
- The matters related to the complete transfer of responsibilities would be discussed between the British Government and the Constituent Assembly.
- Provisions would also be formulated. for the protection of the racial and religious minorities.
- If any British Province did not wish to join the federation, it could retain its present position and the British Government would give it the same status as the rest of the Indian Union.
- During the war times, the powers of the Viceroy would remain as earlier and he would be responsible for the defence of the country.

Failure of the Cripps Mission

The Cripps Mission failed due to the following reasons

- There was no clarity in the mission of the independence in the near future.
- It had a plan of Partition of India. The Hindu Mahasabha rejected the proposals because it feared the partition of the country.
- The Muslim League opposed the creation of a single nation. There was no proposals of creation of Pakistan.
- The mission did not provide sufficient safeguards for the interests of the Sikhs, the Anglo-Indians, the Indian Christians and labour, thus they also opposed it.
- As per the mission, the people of the Princely States had no right to send their representatives to the proposed Constitution making body.
- Gandhiji opposed this mission and urged the Working Committee to reject it. He called this proposal a 'post-dated cheque in a fast failing bank'.

Failures of Cripps Mission led to disappointment and bitterness among Indians. Gandhiji felt that it was the correct time to launch the final struggle for freedom.

Japanese Threat

In 1942, the Japanese Army attacked Myanmar and marched towards India. This threat (of a Japanese invasion) convinced the Indian leaders of the need to eliminate the Britishers from India immediately. So, they decided to launch a movement that force the British to Quit India. On 9th August, 1942, all prominent leaders like Gandhiji, Nehru, Patel, etc were arrested but the others like JP Lohiya, Aruna Asaf Ali, Usha Mehta, etc continued the revolution for struggle. Violence spread throughout the country. Several government offices were destroyed and damaged, the telegraph wires were cut and communication was stopped.

Significance of the Quit India Movement

The Quit India Movement though short-lived and suppressed by the British, but it is one of the greatest mass movements of historical significance.

Its significance can be explained through its following impacts

- This movement was a mass movement joined by all walks of life like the Hindus, Muslims, Sikhs, Christians, Parsis, etc. This movement clearly indicated the capacity of the Indian people for sacrifice and determined struggle. It displayed the depth of national feelings.
- This movement attracted world attention. The pressure of public opinion in USA and Britain in favour of India's independence was so strong that Britain found it difficult to with hold the Independence of India after the Second World War was over.
- The mass upsurge in this movement weakened the basic foundations of the British Raj in India. It was evident that the British would no longer find it to rule India against the wishes of Indians.
- This movement developed the feelings of political awakening and consciousness among masses. It showed Indian's anger and hatred against imperialism.
- This movement strengthened the Congress Socialist Party which continued underground movement till 1944.
- The suppression of this movement resulted to a temporary set back to the national movement and there was hardly any political activity till the end of the Second World War in 1945.

Check Your LEARNING...

1. Where was the 'Quit India Resolution' passed?
2. Who gave the slogan 'Do or Die'?
3. In which year the Japanese Army attacked Myanmar?
4. Mention any one significance of the Quit India Movement?

Time Line

Year	Important Events
1915	Mahatma Gandhi returned to India.
1917	Gandhiji travelled to Champaran in Bihar to inspire the peasants against oppressive plantation system,
1918	Gandhiji organised Satyagraha in Kheda district, Gujarat. Gandhiji went to Ahmedabad to organise Satyagraha among cotton mill workers.
March, 1919	Rowlatt Act
1919	Khilafat Committee was formed in Bombay, *hartal* against Rowlatt Act.
19th April, 1919	Jallianwalla Bagh Massacre
17 October, 1919	Khilafat Day
September 1920	Gandhiji convinced other leaders of the need to start a Non-Cooperation Movement in support of Khilafat as well as for Swaraj in Calcutta Congress Session, Non-Cooperation Movement launched.
31st August, 1920	Non-Cooperation and Khilafat Movement launched.
5th February, 1922	Incident of Chauri Chaura 12th February, 1922 Gandhiji withdraw Non-Cooperation Movement.
3rd February, 1928	The Simon Commission arrived in India.
October, 1929	Lord Irwin announced a vague offer of 'dominion status' for India.
1929	Congress adopted the demand for 'Purna Swaraj'.
26 January, 1930	Purna Swaraj Day.
6th April, 1930	Gandhiji begins Civil Disobedience Movement by breaking Salt Law at Dandi.
12th March to 6th April, 1930	Dandi March
12th November, 1930	First Round Table *Conference*
19th January, 1931	
1931	Gandhiji ends Civil Disobedience Movement.
5th March, 1931	Gandhi-Irwin Pact
7th Sep-1st Dec, 1931	Second Round Table Conference.
1932	Poona Pact signed between Dr. Babasaheb Ambedkar and Mahatma Gandhi. Civil Disobedience Movement relaunched.
17th Nov.-24 Dec, 1932	Third Round Table Conference
1935	Government of India Act.
September, 1939	Second World War started.
8th August, 1940	August offer
1942	Cripps Mission
8th August, 1942	Quit India Movement resolution was passed in the Bombay Session.
1945	The end of Second World War.

QUiCK Revision

- In India, the growth of modern nationalism developed through the struggle against British colonialism.
- Mahatma Gandhi was the person who first united the people of India under the banner of Indian National Movement.
- Gandhiji returned to India in 1915 from South Africa. After arriving India, he successfully organised Satyagraha Movements in Champaran, Kheda and Ahmedabad (1916-1917).
- Gandhiji wanted non-violent Civil Disobedience against Rowlatt Act (1919). Under this unjust law, government could arrest and imprison suspects without trial for maximum 2 years.
- On 13th April, 1919 Jallainwala Massacre was happened. Rabindranath Tagore rejected his 'Knighthood' in protest of this killing.
- In 1920, at the Calcutta Session, the Congress passed the resolution to start the Non-Cooperation Movement in support of Khilafat Movement. It was the first mass based on political movement under Gandhiji.
- In 1920, Indian National Congress started the Non-Cooperation Movement under the leadership of Mahatma Gandhi.
- The Non-Cooperation Khilafat Movement began in 1920. The movement started with middle class participation in the cities which included students, headmasters, teachers, lawyers, etc.
- By supporting the Khilafat Movement, Gandhiji was able to unite Hindus and Muslims. This movement gave political lesson to Indians.
- In the Non-Cooperation Movement people surrendered their titles and honorary offices, boycott of civil services, army, police, courts and legislative councils, schools and foreign goods.
- A violent incident at Chauri Chaura on 5th February, 1922 made Gandhiji to call-off the movement. Gandhiji was a firm believer of non-violence and believed that violence would breed violence and the British could easily suppress it.
- The Non-Cooperation Movement was a great success. *Strikes*, *hartals* and demonstrations spread all over the country. In December, 1921 at Ahmedabad Session, the Congress decided to continue the Non-Cooperation Movement.
- Simon Commission (1928) was rejected by all, as it had no Indian members in it. In October, 1929 Lord Irwin announced a vague offer of dominion status for India.
- In December, 1929 under the Presidency of Jawaharlal Nehru, the Lahore Congress formalised the demand of 'Purna Swaraj' or full independence for India.
- On 12th March, 1930 Gandhiji with his followers started his March from Sabarmati Ashram for Dandi, the coastal town of Gujarat. This marked the beginning of the Civil Disobedience Movement.
- The Civil Disobedience Movement spread all over the country. Everywhere , demonstrations and picketing of foreign goods were organised on a large scale.
- The Congress boycotted the First Round Table Conference (1930) as the British Government refused to accept its demands of complete independence and a joint electorate.
- Lord Irwin and Gandhiji signed Gandhi-Irwin Pact on 5th March, 1931.
- Second Round Table Conference was held from 7th September to 1st December, 1931. The conference sidelined the major issues and focussed communal problems.
- The Quit India Movement began in August, 1942. All the prominent leaders were arrested. The movement spread all over India. Due to brutal oppression many leaders were forced to go underground.
- The mass upsurge of this movement shook the basic foundations of the British Raj. It developed the feelings of political awakening and consciousness among masses.

Chapter Practice

Section-I

Multiple Choice Questions

1. Which of the following statements on Gandhian Movement is not correct?
   (a) Mahatma Gandhi was in favour of mass movement.
   (b) In Gandhian Movements, leadership had no role.
   (c) Gandhian Movements were non-violent in nature.
   (d) Mahatma Gandhi was in favour of passive resistance.

Ans. (b) In Gandhian Movements, leadership had no role.

2. Who among the following was the author of 'Hind Swaraj' book?
   (a) Jawaharlal Nehru (b) Indira Gandhi
   (c) Khan Abdul Ghaffar Khan (d) Mahatma Gandhi

Ans. (d) Mahatma Gandhi

3. During the Non-Cooperation Movement the Congress became a continuous political organisation and its Constitution was amended in the .... session in December 1920.
   (a) Nagpur (b) Lahore
   (c) Madras (d) Kolkata

Ans. (a) Nagpur

4. What was the cause for the sudden suspension of the Non-Cooperation Movement? **[Semester-I 2022]**
   (a) Repressive measures of the British
   (b) The Chauri-Chaura incident
   (c) The Gandhi-Irwin Pact
   (d) The Jallianwala Bagh massacre

Ans. (b) The Chauri-Chaura incident

5. Identify the clauses of the Rowlatt Act. **[Specimen Paper Semester-I 2022]**
   (a) In camera trial
   (b) Arrest people with a warrant
   (c) Vernacular Press must not publish anything against the British
   (d) Compulsory License for arms

Ans. (a) In camera trial

6. Which of these statements is not associated with the Jallianwala Bagh massacre? **[Semester-I 2022]**
   (a) It happened in the year 1919.
   (b) General Dyer was responsible for this massacre.
   (c) It became a cause for the Non-Cooperation Movement.
   (d) It became a cause for the Civil Disobedience Movement.

Ans. (d) It became a cause for the Civil Disobedience Movement.

7. Which of the following was the reason of Khilafat Movement?
   (a) To unite Hindus and Muslims together through a mass struggle
   (b) Injustice done to Turkey and Caliph by the British
   (c) To end the First World War
   (d) Both (a) and (b)

Ans. (d) Both (a) and (b)

8. The Khilafat Movement was started under the leadership of .... **[Semester-I 2022]**
   (a) Ali Brothers
   (b) Dr. Saifuddin Kitchulu
   (c) Khan Abdul Ghaffar Khan
   (d) Sir Sayyid Ahmad Khan

Ans. (a) Ali Brothers

9. Which of the following activities took place during Khilafat Movement?
   (a) People resigned from government services.
   (b) Students boycotted schools and colleges.
   (c) Shops selling foreign goods were picketed.
   (d) All of the above

Ans. (d) All of the above

10. The Civil Disobedience Movement was launched in .... **[Specimen Paper Semester-I 2022]**
    (a) 1929 (b) 1920 (c) 1930 (d) 1942

Ans. (c) 1930

11. Mahatma Gandhi signed a pact with .... to end the Civil Disobedience Movement. **[Specimen Paper Semester-I 2022]**
    (a) Lord Mountbatten (b) Lord Irwin
    (c) Lord Wavell (d) Stafford Cripps

Ans. (b) Lord Irwin

12. Which of the following was the feature of Ramsay MacDonald's Communal Award?
    (a) Privy-purses to native princes
    (b) Communal representation to Muslim
    (c) Reservations to Sikhs in election.
    (d) Separate electorates for depressed classes.

Ans. (d) Separate electorates for depressed classes.

13. The Poona Pact which was signed between the Dr. Bhimrao Ambedkar and Mahatma Gandhi in 1934 provided for
    (a) creation of dominion status for India
    (b) separate electorates for the Muslims
    (c) the separate electorate for the Harijans
    (d) a joint electorate with the reservation for Harijans

Ans. (d) a joint electorate with the reservation for Harijans

15. What were the causes of the Quit India Movement? **[Semester-I 2022]**
(a) Failure of Simon Commission and Rowlatt Act.
(b) Failure of the Cripps Mission and Declaration of Poorna Swaraj.
(c) Growing Unemployment and Jallianwala Bagh massacre.
(d) Failure of Cripps Mission and Japanese threat.

Ans. (b) Failure of the Cripps Mission and Declaration of Poorna Swaraj.

16. Complete the given analogy. **[Specimen Paper Semester-I 2022]**
Simon Commission: Civil Disobedience Movement:: Cripps Mission :?
(a) Non-Cooperation Movement
(b) Anti Partition Movement
(c) Quit India Movement
(d) Khilafat Movement

Ans. (c) Quit India Movement

17. Complete the given analogy.
Government of India Act : 1919 : : Hunter Commission : ?
(a) 1918 (b) 1920 (c) 1930 (d) 1942

Ans. (b) 1920

18. Complete the given analogy.
Non-Cooperation Movement : 1920 : : Civil Disobedience Movement ?
(a) 1919 (b) 1932 (c) 1931 (d) 1930

Ans. (d) 1930

19. Complete the given analogy.
Salt March: Gujarat : : Chauri- Chaura : ?
(a) Maharashtra (b) Punjab
(c) Uttar Pradesh (d) Bengal

Ans. (c) Uttar Pradesh

20. Replace the underlined word to correct the statement.
The system of racial segregation was prevalent in South Africa during 20th Century which was known as <u>Discrimination Policy</u>.
(a) Apartheid (b) Rowlatt Act
(c) No Entry Act (d) Untouchability Act

Ans. (a) Apartheid

21. Replace the underlined word to correct the statement.
Khan Abdul Ghaffar Khan was popularly known as '<u>Father of Nation</u>'.
(a) Massiah of Indians (b) The Frontier Gandhi
(c) Father of Indian National Movement
(d) None of the above

Ans. (b) The Frontier Gandhi

22. Complete the following table.

Day of Deliverance	22nd December, 1939
Chauri- Chaura Incidence	?

(a) 5th February, 1922 (b) 8th March, 1925
(c) 10th April, 1930 (d) 2nd October, 1935

Ans. (a) 5th February, 1922

23. Which of the following was the objective of the Non-Cooperation Movement?
(i) To attain self-government within the British Government if possible and outside if necessary.
(ii) Eliminate the Rowlatt Act and improving the 'Punjab wrong'.
(iii) Improve the 'Khilafat wrong'.

Codes
(a) Only (i) (b) Only (ii)
(c) Only (iii) (d) All of these

Ans. (d) All of these

24. Which of the following was the major cause of the failure of the Quit India Movement?
(i) Lack of Coordination among people
(ii) Lack of clear cut programme
(iii) No use of Satyagraha
(iv) Inappropriate leadership

Codes
(a) Both (i) and (ii) (b) Only (ii)
(c) Only (iii) (d) All of these

Ans. (a) Both (i) and (ii)

25. Match the following.

List-I		List-II	
A.	1915	1.	Mahatma Gandhi returned to India
B.	1917	2.	Champaran Satyagraha
C.	1918	3.	Khed Satyagraha
D.	1919	4.	Rowlatt Act

Codes

	A	B	C	D		A	B	C	D
(a)	1	2	3	4	(b)	2	1	4	3
(c)	3	4	1	2	(d)	4	3	2	1

Ans. (a)

26. Match the following.

List-I		List-II	
A.	September, 1920	1.	Withdrawal of Non-Cooperation Movement
B.	February, 1922	2.	Non-Cooperation Movement
C.	1929	3.	Gandhiji ended Civil Disobedience Movement
D.	1919	4.	Demand of Purna Swaraj

Codes

	A	B	C	D		A	B	C	D
(a)	1	2	3	4	(b)	2	1	4	3
(c)	3	4	1	2	(d)	4	3	2	1

Ans. (b)

Picture Based Question

27. Look at the picture given below and answer the questions that follow.

(i) Which of the following event is shown in the given picture?
(a) Non-Cooperation Movement
(b) Opposition of Simon Commission
(c) Welcome of Simon Commission
(d) Civil Disobedience Movement

Ans. (b) Opposition of Simon Commission

(ii) In which year this Commission came in India?
(a) 1922 (b) 1915
(c) 1928 (d) 1940

Ans. (c) 1928

(iii) Which organisation was against this Commission?
(a) Muslim League (b) Congress
(c) Hindu Mahasabha (d) All of these

Ans. (d) All of these

(iv) What was the reason of its failure?
(a) It proposed a resolution of separate nation
(b) It proposed to grant India freedom but after the First World War
(c) It supported minoritiesonly
(d) It had no Indian in its meeting

Ans. (d) It had no Indian in its meeting

Passage Based Questions

28. Read the passage given below and answer the questions that follow.
[Specimen Paper Semester-I 2021]

On February 4th, 1922 a large group of nationalist volunteers had gathered on the streets of a small, obscure hamlet. More than a year had passed since Mahatma Gandhi had launched the movement with the aim of attaining 'Purna Swaraj' (full independence). The volunteers marched through the streets shouting slogans of Gandhi and the Khilafat. Soon they walked into the police. Sticks and stones were thrown from one end in return for bullets from the other. As the crowd grew larger and fiercer, the cops retreated inside the police station.

The protestors do used the building in kerosene and set it on fire. Twenty-three policemen perished. A total of 228 people were brought to trial in the incident, out of which 19 were sentenced to death.

(i) Where did this incident take place?
(a) Lahore (b) Chauri-Chaura
(c) Dandi (d) Awadh

Ans.(b) Chauri-Chaura

(ii) Which movement did Gandhiji withdraw because of this incident?
(a) Non-Cooperation Movement
(b) Civil Disobedience Movement
(c) Quit India Movement
(d) Anti-Partition Movement

Ans. (a) Non-Cooperation Movement

(iii) Identify the programmes which were adopted during this movement.
(a) Swadeshi and Boycott
(b) Violent agitations
(c) Walked barefoot and bathed in the Ganga
(d) Established many British schools

Ans. (a) Swadeshi and Boycott

(iv) Identify the impact of the movement that was suspended due to this event.
(a) Instilled confidence in people
(b) Led to large scale communal riots
(c) Promoted Social reforms
(d) Led to the First Round Table Conference

Ans. (a) Instilled confidence in people

29. Read the passage given below and answer the questions that follow.

In June, 1934 the British Government withdrew the ban on the Congress. Even after the suspension of the Movement people did not abandon their struggle for freedom. For example, merchants and shopkeepers, peasants, tribals and workers in different parts of the country were mobilised for the Indian National Movement. People adopted the idea of non-violence. People in towns and villages were popularised the patriotic songs like 'Prabhat Pheris' and handwritten Patrikas or news-sheets were issued in large numbers. The Movement also improved the condition of depressed classes. They were now allowed to perform prayer in temples and could access to wells. The Birla and the 'Harijan Sevak Sangh' played a significant role in this regard.

Indian leaders now wanted to contest Assembly elections. In 1937, the Congress won many seats in the elections of the Central Legislative Assembly and Provincial Legislative Assemblies.

(i) This movement was started from which place?
(a) Dandi (b) Chauri-Chaura
(c) Lucknow (d) Lahore

Ans. (a) Dandi

(ii) What was the main achievement of this movement?
(a) Participation of Women in the National Movement
(b) The Government of India Act, 1935
(c) Created political consciousness among masses
(d) All of the above

Ans. (d) All of the above

(iii) On the social grounds what was the main feature of this movement?
(a) End of untouchability
(b) Equal participation of both men and women in the freedom struggle
(c) Removal of ban on the Congress
(d) Both (a) and (b)

Ans. (d) Both (a) and (b)

(iv) Which programme was adopted during this movement?
(a) Violence of Salt law
(b) Non- payment of taxes
(c) Boycott of foreign goods
(d) All of the above

Ans. (d) All of the above

Section-II

Short Questions

1. Against which policy of the British Government Mahatma Gandhi did his struggle in South Africa?

Ans. Gandhiji's struggle in South Africa was against the policy of racial discrimination followed by the British Government.

2. When did Gandhiji return to his homeland and from where?

Ans. Mahatma Gandhi returned to his homeland in January, 1915. He came back from South Africa where he fought for the Indian community against racial discrimination imposed by the British Government.

3. State the two methods of political struggle evolved by Mahatma Gandhi as a part of the National Movement.

Ans. The two methods of political struggle evolved by Mahatma Gandhi were as follows
(i) Gandhiji promoted the use of Satyagraha which emphasised the power of truth and the need to search for truth.
(ii) Gandhiji advocated the non-violence movement. According to him, non-violence is not a negative, but a positive and active force.

4. What do you mean by Satyagraha?

Ans. The idea of Satyagraha emphasised the power of truth and the need to search for truth. This idea developed during Gandhiji's struggle against racial discrimination in South Africa.

5. When 'Satyagraha day' was observed?

Ans. 6th April, 1919 was observed as 'Satyagraha day' when people all over the country observed fast and *hartal*. It marked the foundation of Non-Cooperation Movement.

6. State any two causes for the Non-Cooperation Movement. **[2019]**

Ans. The causes that led to the Non-Cooperation Movement were
(i) Rowlatt Act was introduced in the Central Legislature in February, 1919. This act authorised the Government to imprison any person without trial and convict him in a court.
(ii) A peaceful crowd gathered at the Jallianwala Bagh in Amritsar on 13th April, 1919 to protest against the arrest of leaders like Dr. Saifuddin Kitchlu and Dr. Satyapal. Without any warning, General Dyer ordered the army to open fire at this crowd. This event shocked Gandhiji and he decided to stop every cooperation with the British Government at every level.

7. What was the Khilafat Movement? **[2017]**

Ans. The Khilafat Movement (1919-20) was a movement to express Muslim support for the Caliph of Turkey against the Allied Powers particularly Britain. The Muslims demanded that the Caliph Sultan must retain sufficient territories, so that he would be able to defend the Islamic faith.

8. Name the leaders of the Khilafat Movement that was launched in India to champion the cause of the Caliph of Turkey. **[2019, 2013]**

Ans. Mohammed Ali and Shaukat Ali were the leaders of the Khilafat Movement.

9. Why was the Rowlatt Act (1919) passed?

Ans. The Rowlatt Act was passed to curb the growing upsurge in the country. In spite of opposition from the Indians, the Rowlatt Act was passed in March, 1919.

10. State any two provisions of the Rowlatt Act passed by the Government in 1919? **[2017]**

Ans. Following were the provisions of the Rowlatt Act
(i) The Government could arrest any person without a warrant.
(ii) The Governor-General was empowered to give effect the Act to any area.

11. What was Hunter Commission?

Ans. The Hunter Commission under the Chairmanship of Lord Hunter was appointed to enquire about the Jallianwala Bagh Massacre. The Commission criticised Dyer's action, but mentioned that legal prosecution against Dyer would not be possible due to political reasons.

12. When and where was the resolution of Non-Cooperation Movement passed by the Congress?

Ans. The resolution of Non-Cooperation Movement was passed by the Congress at Nagpur Session in December 1920.

13. Mention two methods of resistance adopted in the Non-Cooperation Movement.

Ans. Two methods of resistance adopted in the Non-Cooperation Movement were as follows:
(i) Surrendering of titles and offices and resignation from nominated posts in the local bodies.
(ii) Boycott of foreign goods and adoption of Swadeshi.

14. Name some institutions which were set up during the Non-Cooperation Movement.

Ans. Some institutions which were set up during the Non-Cooperation Movement were as follows
(i) Jamia Millia Islamia of Aligarh
(ii) Bihar Vidyapeeth
(iii) Kashi Vidyapeeth
(iv) Gujarat Vidyapeeth

15. Name some famous personalities who renounced their titles during the Non-Cooperation Movement.

Ans. Rabindranath Tagore, Mahatma Gandhi, Subramania Iyer and Jamnalal Bajaj renounced the titles and honours conferred upon them by the British.

16. Suggest an important feature of the Non- Cooperation Movement.

Ans. Important feature of the Non-Cooperation Movement was that earlier National Movement had remained the concern of the middle class and intelligentsia but the Non-Cooperation Movement became an all India Movement and Gandhiji became the symbol of the poor and downtrodden.

17. Why was the Simon Commission rejected by the Congress? **[2015]**

Ans. The Simon Commission was rejected by the Congress on the following basis
(i) All members of this Commission were Europeans (Whites) and no Indian was associated with it.
(ii) This was seen by the Congress as a violation of the principle of self-determination and a deliberate insult to the self-respect of the Indians.

19. Why was the Simon Commission boycotted by the Indians? **[2013]**

Ans. The Simon Commission was boycotted by the Indians because
(i) It was boycotted everywhere because all its members were Englishmen.
(ii) The government showed no inclination towards accepting the demand for Swaraj.

20. Why was the Congress session held at Lahore in 1929 significant to the National Movement?

Ans. The Congress session held at Lahore in 1929 was significant to the National Movement because the resolution of 'Purna Swaraj' was passed here.

21. Mention any two events which led to the Civil Disobedience Movement of 1930. **[2018]**

Ans. The two events which led to the Civil Disobedience Movement of 1930 were
(i) A resolution was passed in the Lahore Session of Congress in 1929, which declared Poorna Swaraj to become the objective of the Congress.
(ii) An 'Eleven Points Ultimatum' was served by Gandhiji to the British Government. After the government's failure to negotiate, Gandhiji started the Civil Disobedience Movement.

22. Why did Mahatma Gandhi start his historic March to Dandi? **[2017]**

Ans. Mahatma Gandhi started his historic Dandi March to break the salt law and start the Civil Disobedience Movement.

23. On what assurances did Gandhiji withdraw the Civil Disobedience Movement?

Ans. Gandhiji's withdrawal of the Civil Disobedience Movement was on the basis of the following assurances from the British Government
(i) Withdrawal of all the ordinances and the prosecutions.
(ii) Releasing the political prisoners, except those guilty of violence and killing.

24. Mention any one provision of the Gandhi-Irwin Pact signed in 1931. **[2014]**

Ans. One of the provisions of the Gandhi-Irwin Pact 1931 was that the Viceroy agreed to release all political prisoners except those convicted of violence and killing.

25. Mention atleast two proposals given by Cripps Mission.

Ans. The proposals given by Cripps Mission (1942) were
(i) Promise of dominion status after the Second World War.
(ii) Proposals of an interim government during the war.

26. What was the most significant feature of the Quit India Movement?

Ans. The most significant feature of the Quit India Movement was that it was a mass movement joined by all walks of life like the Hindus, Muslims, Sikhs, Christians, Parsis etc. It displayed the depth of national feelings.

27. Name some leaders who were forced to go underground during the Quit India Movement.

Ans. Some prominent leaders like Achyutrao Patwardhan, Sucheta Kripalani, Aruna Asaf Ali, Biju Patnaik, Jayaprakash Narayan were forced to go underground during the Quit India Movement.

Structured Questions

1. Gandhiji introduced new ideas in politics and adopted new methods to give a new direction to the Political Movement. In this context, answer the following questions. **[2012]**
   (i) Gandhiji's Doctrine of Satyagraha.
   (ii) Gandhiji's social ideas.
   (iii) Which mass struggle was launched by him on non-violent lines in 1920? Explain in brief the programmes of such a campaign.

Ans. (i) Gandhiji introduced the Satyagraha, which was a method of agitation and protest based on truth and non-violence. It suggested that if the cause was true, if the struggle was against injustice, then physical force was not necessary. A Satyagrahi could win the battle through non-violence. It was a passive resistance consisting of defiance of laws, non-payment of taxes, boycott of government institutions etc.
Gandhiji's Satyagraha Movement was directed against the British system of exploitation and not against the British people individually or collectively. These experiments in Satyagraha brought Gandhiji into a close touch with the masses, with both the peasants in the rural areas and the workers in the urban areas. In course of time, he became the symbol of the poor and the downtrodden, whose authenticity could not be questioned or doubted.

(ii) The social ideas of Gandhiji were based on non-violence. According to Gandhiji, 'Truth and non-violence is the weapon of strong, mighty and powerful individual'. Gandhiji always used mass movements as weapon of protest. He realised that movement which involved rural, urban, men, women, educated, uneducated are more liable to have an effect.
He launched many movements like Non-Cooperation, Civil Disobedience, Quit India Movement for gaining freedom, but none of them was violent. During the Non-Cooperation Movement, he suspended the movement, when it was on its zenith just because of the Chauri-Chaura incident, in which 22 policemen were burnt alive. The movements under his leadership shook the basic foundation of British Raj in our country.
The British Government realised that it would not be possible to rule India against the wishes of Indians.

(iii) In the year 1920, Non-Cooperation Movement was started by Gandhiji on the basis of non-violence. The programmes of Non-Cooperation Movement were
- Surrendering of titles and offices and resignation from nominated posts in the local bodies.
- Boycott of legislatures, law courts, schools, colleges and all institutions having connection with the British.
- Boycott of foreign goods and adoption of Swadeshi.
- Boycott of election of 1919 and other government functions.
- Adoption of Swadeshi and Khadi by reviving hand-spinning and hand-weaving clothes in the country.
- Establishment of national schools and colleges and panchayats (private arbitration courts) all over the country.
- Revive the Hindu-Muslim unity and removal of untouchability for the welfare of Harijan.

2. In 1919, Gandhiji plunged into India's struggle for freedom. He guided the affairs of the Indian National Congress with new techniques. Through various National Movements, he got the public support to win freedom for India. In this context, explain the following. **[2009]**
   (i) Which resolution was passed on 8th August, 1942 leading to a mass struggle on non-violent lines? State any two reasons behind the launching of this movement.
   (ii) The impact of the Non-Cooperation Movement in India's struggle for freedom.
   (iii) The reasons leading to the Non-Cooperation Movement.

Ans. (i) On 8th August, 1942, the All India Congress Committee passed the Quit India Resolution. The proposal of Quit India Movement was adopted at Wardha in July, 1942.
The reasons behind the launching of Quit India Movement were
- Japan declared war against Britain and America on 7th December, 1941. Its sensational victories in the opening months of 1942 obliged the British Government to resolve the political deadlock in India.
- On the night of 9th August, the British Government arrested many prominent leaders like Gandhiji, Maulana Azad, Sardar Patel, Jawaharlal Nehru and other members of the Congress working committee and sent them to Pune. This hasty action of the government led to the movement immediately.

(ii) The Impacts of Non-Cooperation Movement in India were
- It generated a desire for freedom and inspired people to challenge the colonial rule.
- It fostered Hindu-Muslim unity, which could be seen in the merge of Khilafat issue with this movement.
- This movement gave a new boost to nationalism in India at its annual session in Nagpur in December, 1920.
- The demand for Swaraj became much popular.
- It transformed the Indian National Congress from a deliberative assembly into an organisation for action.

(iii) The reasons that led to the Non-Cooperation Movement were
- In the year of 1918-1919, the mill workers of Ahmedabad were on a strike and received the support of Gandhiji.
- On receiving a report of Sedition Committee headed by Justice Rowlatt, the Anarchical and Revolutionary Crimes Act was introduced in the Central Legislature in February, 1919. The purpose of the bill, was to curb the growing upsurge in the country. This act authorised the government to imprison any person without trial and convict him in a court.
- A peaceful crowd gathered at the Jallianwala Bagh in Amritsar On 13th April, 1919 to protest against the arrest of leaders like Dr Saifuddin Kitchlu and Dr Satyapal. Without any warning, General Dyer ordered the army to open fire at the crowd. This event shocked Gandhiji and he decided to stop every cooperation with the British Government at every level.
- The Muslims of India decided to force Britain to change its Turkish policy and a Khilafat Committee was formed. Gandhiji saw this as an opportunity i.e to unite Hindu-Muslim Community. So, he decided to start a Non-Cooperation Movement in support to Khilafat Movement.

3. In the Nagpur Session (1920), the Congress ratified the resolution to launch the Non-Cooperation Movement under the leadership of Gandhiji. In this context, answer the following questions. **[2014]**

(i) What were the objectives which the Non-Cooperation Movement sought to achieve?

(ii) What do you understand by the term Non-Cooperation?

(iii) Explain the impact of the Non-Cooperation Movement in India's struggle for freedom.

Ans. (i) Mahatma Gandhi urged the Indian National Congress to launch a Non-Cooperation Movement on three issues (objectives).
These were

(a) Redressal of the wrongs committed in Punjab that entailed the Jallianwala Bagh Massacre and the atrocities related to the Martial Law.

(b) Supporting the Khilafat issue by restoring the old status of the Sultan of Turkey.

(c) Accomplishment of Swaraj by boycotting election and other government functions and organisations and foreign goods.

(ii) Non-Cooperation is a way of protesting, in which one does not cooperate with the evil-doer, Gandhiji asked the people not to assist the Foreign Government to rule over them. In his book, 'Hind Swaraj' Mahatma Gandhi declared that the British Rule was established in India with the cooperation of Indians and had survived only because of this cooperation. If Indians refused to cooperate, British rule in India would collapse within one year and Swaraj would come.

(iii) Refer to chapter theory page no. 159.

4. Through various National Movements, Gandhiji mobilised public support to win freedom for India. In this context, state the following. **[2016]**

(i) Any three causes for Gandhiji to launch the Non-Cooperation Movement.

(ii) The name given to the uprising of 1942. Two reasons for launching this mass uprising.

(iii) The impact of the Non-Cooperation Movement in India's freedom struggle.

Ans. (i) Refer chapter theory page no. 157.

(ii) The name given to the uprising of 1942 was 'Quit India Movement'. Two reasons for launching this mass uprising were following

(a) Failure and rejection of the Cripps proposals.

(b) There was a general demoralisation of the congress leaders. Gandhiji was desperate and wanted to call for "do-or-die" after the failure of the individual Satyagraha.

(iii) Refer to chapter theory page no. 159.

5. The Simon Commission was appointed in November, 1927 by the British Government. Subsequently, the Civil Disobedience Movement began. In this context, answer the following questions. **[2010]**

(i) Why was the Simon Commission appointed by the British Government? Why did the Congress boycott the Commission?

(ii) The Civil Disobedience Movement was launched by Gandhiji with his famous Dandi March on 12th March, 1930. Mention the significance of this historic event.

(iii) Why did Gandhiji call off the Civil Disobedience Movement and later renew it?

Ans. (i) In November, 1927, the British Government appointed the Indian Statutory Commission, which was popularly known as the Simon Commission (after the name of its Chairman Sir John Simon) to investigate the need for further constitutional reforms. This commission was composed by the seven British members of Parliament.
Simon Commission was boycotted by the Congress on the following basis
- All members of this commission were Europeans (whites) and no Indian was associated with it. This was seen as a violation of the principle of self-determination and a deliberate insult to the self-respect of the Indians.
- The position of Governor-General remained unaffected.
- No provision to abolish separate electorate but rather extended to other communities as well.

(ii) Significance of the Dandi March was
- The movement spread rapidly. Violation of Salt Laws over the country was soon followed by defiance of forest laws in Maharashtra, Karnataka and the Central Provinces and the refusal to pay the rural Chaukidari tax in Eastern India.
- In the North-West Frontier Province, the Pathans adopted the policy of Non-Cooperation under the leadership of Khan Abdul Ghaffar Khan.
- The British Government was put out of gear in many places example, Midnapore in Bengal.
- The monopoly of the British over the salt was abolished by this movement.

(iii) The Civil Disobedience Movement was called off by Gandhiji because of the Gandhi-Irwin Pact, signed between Gandhiji and Viceroy Lord Irwin. In this pact, Irwin agreed to some of the demands of Gandhiji, like the abolition of salt tax, release of political prisoners, permit peaceful picketing of liquor etc. After this, Gandhiji agreed to call off the Civil Disobedience Movement and attend the Second Round Table Conference in London. When Gandhiji came back from London, he renewed the movement again because of the failure of the Second Round Table Conference. The British Government refused to consider the basic nationalist demand of freedom on the basis of immediate grant of dominion status. There was no agreement regarding communal representation. Disgusted Gandhiji returned back to India empty handed and called for the Civil Disobedience Movement.

6. The Civil Disobedience Movement was significant in the history of the National Movement. In this context, write briefly on the following points. **[2011]**

(i) The circumstances leading to the Civil Disobedience Movement.

(ii) The Second Round Table Conference.

(iii) The Gandhi-Irwin Pact.

Ans. (i) Following circumstances led to the Civil-Disobedience Movement
- Simon Commission arrived in India in 1928 to review the functioning of the constitutional system in India and suggest changes. This commission was opposed by Indians because no Indians were included in it.
- At Lahore Session of Indian National Congress in 1929, the Congress formally demanded 'Purna Swaraj'.
- Gandhiji started Dandi March on 12th March, 1930 and violated salt laws on 6th April, 1930 by manufacturing salt.

(ii) Refer to chapter theory page no. 161.

(iii) Gandhi-Irwin Pact was an agreement signed between Viceroy Lord Irwin and Gandhiji on 5th March, 1931. Following were the provisions of this pact
- The Viceroy agreed to release all political prisoners except those convicted of violence and killing.
- The Government agreed to withdraw all ordinances and end prosecution.
- The Viceroy agreed to permit peaceful picketing of liquor as well as opium shops and to allow people living within some distance of the sea shore to collect or manufacture salt free from any tax.
- Gandhiji on his part agreed to discontinue the Civil Disobedience Movement and agreed to participate in the Second Round Table Conference.

7. The Congress Working Committee passed the famous Quit India Resolution at Wardha in July, 1942. With reference to this, answer the following questions. **[2013]**

(i) What were the reasons for the passing of this resolution?

(ii) What was the British Government's reaction to the Quit India Movement?

(iii) What was the impact and significance of this movement?

Ans. (i) Following were the factors for the passing of this resolution
- **Failure of the Cripps Mission** The Cripps Mission did not bring with its promise of Independence in the near future. The Muslim League opposed the creation of a single union. The proposals did not accept Pakistan specifically. The Indians were also not happy at the proposals of the Cripps Mission because proposals contained such provisions which could divide India into hundreds of independent provinces. Gandhiji opposed the declaration and described the Cripps proposals as a Post-dated cheque in a fast failing bank.
- **The Threat of Japanese** In the year of 1942, the Japanese Army attacked Myanmar and marched towards India. The threat of Japanese invasion on India convinced the Indian leaders that for India's safety, the British should withdraw from India immediately, Gandhiji asked the British to quit India because with an orderly and peaceful withdrawal the British could save India both from the internal anarchy and also external aggression.

(ii) The Reaction of the British Government to the Quit India Movement was
- The Government resorted to severe measures to crush the Quit India Movement. The press was completely puzzled. The demonstrating crowds were machine gunned and even bombed from the air. Prisoners were tortured. The police and

secret police reigned. Over 1,00,000 people were arrested by the end of 1942. The military took over many towns and cities. Rebellious villages had to pay huge sum as punitive fines and the villagers had to undergo mass floggings.

- India had not witnessed such intense repression since the First War of Independence, 1857. Gandhiji was detained at the Agha Khan Palace in Pune and other prominent leaders were sent to jail in Ahmednagar Fort. In the end, the government succeeded in crushing the movement.

(iii) Impact and significance of the Quit India Movement was

- It demonstrated the depth of the nationalist feelings in India and the great capacity for struggle and sacrifice that the people had developed.
- It was obvious that the British would no longer found it possible to rule India against the wishes of the people.
- It was a mass uprising before attaining Independence. People from all the parts of India took part in the processions and demonstrations. The Hindus, Muslims, Sikhs, Christians and Parsis and even people from the Princely States participated.
- The emergence of Parallel Government in various places of India like Ballia in Uttar Pradesh. Midnapur in Bengal and Satara in Maharashtra took place.
- The Quit India Movement led to the strengthening of the Congress Socialist Party because of its magnificent and heroic role in the movement. Its socialist ideas had an impact on the Indian National Congress.

8. The Quit India Resolution in 1942 was one of the final calls given by Gandhiji for the British to leave India. Moving towards Independence, Lord Mountbatten's Plan was significant. In this context, answer the following questions. **[2018]**

(i) State two reasons for the launching of the Quit India Movement.

(ii) Give any three effects of the Quit India Movement launched by Gandhiji in 1942 that was significant to the last phase of the National Movement of India.

(iii) Give any four clauses of the Mountbatten Plan of 1947.

Ans. (i) Refer to chapter theory page no. 163.

(b) Three effects of the Quit India Movement launched by Gandhiji in 1942 that was significant to the last phase of the National Movement of India were

(a) This movement developed the feelings of political awakening and consciousness among masses. It showed Indian's anger and hatred against imperialism.

(b) The mass upsurge in this movement shook the basic foundations of the British Raj . It was evident that the British would no longer be able to rule India against the wishes of Indians.

(c) This movement clearly indicated the capacity of the Indian people for sacrifice and determined struggle. It displayed the depth of national feelings.

(iii) Four clauses of the Mountbatten Plan of 1947 were

(a) India would be divided into two dominions i.e. India and Pakistan.

(b) The Princely State would have the choice of joining either of the two dominions or to remain Independent.

(c) A plebiscite would be held in the North-West Frontier Province to ascertain whether the people in the area wanted to join India or not.

(d) The Provinces of Assam, Bengal and Punjab were also to be divided.

9. The period between 1920 and 1947 was marked with major events and reforms that finally led us to our Independence. In this context, answer the following questions.

(i) Three provisions of the Gandhi-Irwin Pact as a result of the Civil Disobedience Movement.

(ii) Reasons for the protest of Rowlatt Act.

(iii) Chauri-Chaura Incident.

(iv) Khilafat Movement

Ans. (i) Refer to chapter theory page no. 161.

(ii) Following were the reasons for the protest of Rowlatt Act

- It was implemented to restrict fundamental rights like freedom of expression by giving more privileges to police.
- This act authorised the Government to imprison for a maximum period of two years, without trial, any person suspected of terrorism.

(iii) Refer to chapter theory page no. 158.

(iv) Refer to chapter theory page no. 157-158.

10. With reference to the National Movement from 1930 to 1947, answer the following. **[2019]**

(i) State any three features of the programme of the Civil Disobedience Movement launched in 1930.

(ii) What was the significance of the Second Round Table Conference held in 1931?

(iii) State any four clauses of the Cabinet Mission Plan of 1946.

Ans. (i) The three features of the programme of Civil Disobedience Movement were

(a) It shattered people's faith in the British Government. It received the will to fight the elections.

(b) It laid the social roots for the freedom struggle and popularised the new methods of propaganda like the Prabhat pheris, pamphlets, etc.

(c) Violation of the salt laws was soon followed by the defiance of forest laws in Maharashtra, Karnataka and the Central Provinces and the refusal to pay the rural 'chaukidari tax' in Eastern India. It ended the monopoly of the British over salt manufacturing.

(ii) The Second Round Table Conference was organised in 1931 in London by Lord Irwin. The significance of Second Round Table was

- This was the sole Round Table Conference in which Gandhiji participated, the only representative on behalf of the Congress.
- In this conference, Congress raised the communal question and minority representations in the legislature.

The Conference, however, failed as Gandhiji could not agree with British Prime Minister Ramsay Mac Donald on his policy of Communal Representation and the refusal of the British Government for the basic Indian demand for freedom. The Conference closed on 1st December, 1931 without any concrete results.

(iii) Four main clauses of the Cabinet Mission Plan were

(a) There will be a Federal Union of the British provinces and of the Princely States.

(b) The Union Government would control Defence, Foreign Affairs and Communications.

(c) The provinces would enjoy full autonomy for all subjects other than the union subjects.

(d) The British provinces would be divided into three groups i.e. Group A, Group B and Group C on the basis of religion.

11. With reference to the Mass Phase of the National Movement under the leadership of Gandhi, answer the following.

(i) Briefly explain the Dandi March of 1930.

(ii) State reasons for the launching of the Quit India Movement.

(iii) Explain any three significant effects of the Quit India Movement.

Ans. (i) 'Dandi March' was undertaken by Gandhiji in response to British disapproval of his 'Eleven Point Ultimatum'. He began this march from Sabarmati Ashram to Dandi, the coastal town of Gujarat.

The two features of 'Dandi March' were

(a) It marked the beginning of the Civil Disobedience Movement.

(b) By Dandi March, Gandhiji broke the salt laws because the salt-tax affected all sections of society especially poor.

(ii) Refer to chapter theory page no. 163.

(iii) Refer to chapter theory page no. 163-164.

Picture Based Questions

1. Answer the following questions based on the picture given below.

(i) Identify the two male personalities in the above picture. Mention the ideological tenets of the Indian leader.

(ii) Explain the reason behind the merging of Khilafat Movement with Non-Cooperation Movement.

(iii) What was the consequence of the withdrawal of Non-Cooperation Movement within the Congress Party?

Ans. (i) The two male personalities in the above picture are Lord Mountbatten and Mahatma Gandhi.

The main ideological tenets of Indian leader i.e. Gandhi were

- **Satyagraha** It is a method of agitation and protest based on truth and non-violence. Gandhiji believed that the dharma of non-violence could unite all Indians.
- **Non-violence** Gandhiji's whole philosophy was based on non-violence. According to him, non-violence was the weapon of strong, mighty and powerful individual.
- **Swadeshi** This literally means one's own country. Gandhiji was in favour of using 'Swadeshi' goods and boycott of foreign goods to harm English trade and to boost up cottage industries of our country.

(ii) The reason behind merging the Khilafat and Non-Cooperation Movement was to bring Muslims and Hindus under a unified National Movement.

The Khilafat Movement (1919-1924), was a pan-Islamic, political protest campaign launched by Muslims in British India to influence the British Government and to protect the Ottoman empire during the aftermath of First World War. The First World War had ended with the defeat of Ottoman Turkey. There was a fear that the power of the spiritual head of the Islamic world (Khalifa) would be curtailed. To defend his power, a Khilafat Committee was formed in Bombay in 1919. The Khilafat leaders put pressure upon the British Government give better treatment to Turkey.

The Khilafat Movement was launched by Muhammad Ali and Shaukat Ali. Gandhiji saw this as an opportunity to bring Muslims under the umbrella of a unified National Movement.

At the Calcutta Session of the Congress in September 1920, he convinced other leaders to start a Non- Cooperation Movement in support of Khilafat Movement.

(iii) The Non-Cooperation Movement led so a division within the Congress. A section of the Congress led by Deshbandhu Chitta Ranjan Das and Motilal Nehru organised a separate party known as the 'Swaraj Party' within the Congress in December, 1922.

It started a new line of political activity and returned to the constitutional mode of agitation. Its leaders believed that the Congress should contest elections to the legislatures and oppose the British Government from within the council.

The other section of leaders including Jawaharalal Nehru, Sardar Vallabhbhai Patel, Dr Rajendra Prasad etc strongly opposed the idea of council entry. They were known as No-Changers.

The Congress allowed the Swarajists to function as a political party in the legislature and carry out its programmes. The Swarajists contested elections to the imperial and provincial legislatures and won many seats. They disapprove the British claim that the reforms were acceptable to a large section of the people. The Swaraj party opposed the government and on many occasions the Viceroy and the Governors had to use their special powers to keep up the administration. The year 1925-27 saw demoralisation and decline of the Swarajists.

2. Look at the picture given below and answer the following questions. **[2023]**

(i) Name the march being led by Gandhiji in the above picture. Which movement did this march launch ?

(ii) What were the three causes of the Non-Cooperation Movement? Name the incident which led to the suspension of this movement.

(iii) Mahatma Gandhi and Lord lrwin signed a pact in 1931. Mention any two conditions that the Congress agreed to and two conditions that the British Government agreed to according to this pact.

Ans. (i) Dandi March was led by Gandhiji. This march marked the beginning of the Civil Disobedience Movement.

(ii) Causes that led to the Non-Cooperation Movement were

(a) Crimes Act was introduced in the Central Legislature in February, 1919. This act authorised the government to imprison any person without trial and convict him in a court.

(b) A peaceful crowd gathered at the Jallianwala Bagh in Amritsar on 13th April, 1919 to protest against the arrest of leaders like Dr Saifuddin Kitchlu and Dr Satyapal. The crowd was fired upon on the order of General Dyer.

(c) Economic hardship due to World War I caused a lot of economic hardships to the people. Prices of goods increase leads to resentment against the government.

Suspension of the Non-Cooperation Movement

The incident at Chauri Chaura, a village of Gorakhpur district in Uttar Pradesh occurred on 5th February, 1922. Gandhiji, a believer in Ahimsa was greatly shocked at these incidents and he withdrew the Non-Cooperation Movement on 12th February, 1922.

(iii) Mahatma Gandhi and Lord Irwin concluded an agreement at Delhi on 5th March, 1931 known as the Gandhi Irwin Pact.

The pact made the British Government to agree some demands, which were

(i) To release all the political prisoners.

(ii) To permit the free collection or manufacture of salt.

Under this pact, the Congress agreed to

(i) suspend the Civil Disobedience Movement.

(ii) take part in the Second Round Table Conference.

3. With reference to the picture given below, answer the following questions. **[2019]**

(i) (a) Identify the Memorial built for those who were killed in this incident.

(b) Where did this incident take place ?

(c) Name the movement launched by Gandhiji in 1920 as a consequence.

(ii) Explain briefly the reason for the suspension of this particular movement by Gandhi in 1922.

(iii) State any four impacts of the movement.

Ans. (i) (a) This monument was established in 1951 by the Government of India in Amritsar, to commemorate the Jallianwala Bagh massacre.

(b) The incident took place in the Jallianwala Bagh on 13th April, 1919 where a large number of people assembled on the day of Baisakhi.

(c) Mahatma Gandhi started Non-Cooperation Movement in 1920 as a consequence of this incident.

(ii) Gandhiji suspend the Non-Cooperation Movement because of a violence incident happened at Chauri-Chaura, a village of Gorakhpur district in Uttar Pradesh on 5th February, 1922. In this incident, a procession of 3,000 peasants was marched to the police station to protest against a police officer who had beaten some volunteers picketing a liquor shop. However, they were fired upon by the police due to which some demonstrators set the nearby police station on fire, killing many policemen. Gandhiji, a believer in Ahimsa was greatly shocked at these incidents due to which he withdraw the Non-Cooperation Movement on 12th February, 1922.

(iii) Refer to chapter theory page no. 159.

Chapter Assessment

Section-I

Multiple Choice Questions

1. The term Satyagraha was coined by Gandhiji when he was in
   (a) England
   (b) Sabarmati Ashram
   (c) Agha Khan Palace
   (d) South Africa

2. Gandhi-Irwin Pact was signed in which year?
   (a) 1920 (b) 1930
   (c) 1931 (d) 1940

3. Gandhiji returned to India in ______.
   (a) 1915 (b) 1920
   (c) 1921 (d) 1930

4. Complete the given analogy.
   Non- Cooperation and Khilafat Movement : ? : : Simon Commission : 1928
   (a) 1922 (b) 1920
   (c) 1929 (d) 1940

Short Questions

1. Gandhiji's struggle in South Africa was against which policy of the British Colonial Power?
2. What would a Satyagrahi do against injustice?
3. Define the term Swadeshi.
4. Mention any two positive aspects of the Non-Cooperation Movement.
5. What was the importance of Chauri-Chaura incident?
6. How can you justify the reaction of the Indians to the Simon Commission?
7. Why was the Rowlatt Act passed?

Section-II

Structured Questions

1. Various circumstances were responsible for the Non-Cooperation Movement started by Gandhiji. In this context, write the short notes on the following.
   (i) Rowlatt Act
   (ii) Jallianwala Bagh Tragedy
   (iii) Khilafat Movement
   (iv) Chauri Chaura

2. Trace the programme and progress of the Civil Disobedience Movement under the leadership of Mahatma Gandhi with reference, to the following.
   (i) Demand of Purna Swaraj
   (ii) Salt March
   (iii) Gandhi-Irwin Pact
   (iii) The Third Round Table

3. State the importance of the following.
   (i) The Communal Award, 1932
   (ii) Value based politics of Gandhiji
   (iii) The spread of the Civil Disobedience Movement

CHAPTER 07

Forward Bloc and Indian National Army (INA)

SYLLABUS

Forward Bloc Objectives
INA Objectives and contribution of Subhas Chandra Bose

Forward Bloc was an organised left-wing party within the Congress formed as a result of conflict of views within the Congress. On the other hand, Indian National Army was an armed force formed in South-East Asia during the Second World War. In both of these, Subhash Chandra Bose, an Indian nationalist played an important role.

Formation of Forward Bloc

Subhash Chandra Bose was elected as the President of the Congress in two sesions (Haripur Session in 1938 and Tripuri session in 1939). At Tripuri Sesssion on 29th April, 1939, he resigned from the presidentship due to having different views from Gandhiji (as Gandhiji supported Pattabhi Sitaramayya). After that, he formed the Forward Bloc, on 3rd May, 1939.

The major cause for the formation of this party was difference in the views of Bose and Congress (Gandhiji) which were

- Gandhiji opposed the presidentship of Subhash Chandra Bose as he favoured the policy of large scale industrialisation. Whereas Gandhiji favoured the idea of small scale industries to make the villages self-reliant.
- In Tripuri session, Bose wanted that Congress should help the people of the Princely states in their struggle for freedom whereas Gandhiji criticised this demand.
- When the Britain was facing difficulties because of German threat, Gandhiji wanted to adopt a compromising attitude towards the British and also opposed to organise any national movement during the war. But Bose wanted to take this opportunity to eliminate the British from India.

Composition and First Conference of Forward Bloc

In July 1939, Subhash Chandra announced the committee of the Forward Bloc. It had Subhash Chandra as President, SS Cavesheer from Punjab as its Vice-President, Lal Shankarlal from Delhi as its General-Secretary and many more prominent members. In August, 1939, Bose started publishing a newspaper titled 'Forward Bloc'. He travelled around the country for gaining support for his new political party.

On 20th-22nd June, 1940 the Forward Bloc held its first All India Conference in Nagpur. In this conference, the Forward Bloc was declared as a **socialist**[1] political party.

1 **Socialist** Believes in or supports socialism.

The date of 22nd June was considered as the founding date of the party by the Forward Bloc itself. The conference passed a resolution that declared 'All Power to the Indian People' that urged for militant action for struggle against the British colonial rule.

Objectives of the Forward Bloc

- The main objective of the Forward Bloc was to unite all the left-wing sections within the Congress and to develop an alternative leadership.
- Its immediate objective was the liberation of India with the support of workers, peasants, youths and all radical organisations.
- It aimed to establish a socialist society. For this, it adopted some measures, which were
  - State-planning for the reorganisation of agriculture and industry on socialist lines.
  - Abolition of landlordism, i.e. *Zamindari* System. Making the 'Right to Work' as a fundamental right of the citizens.
  - Providing workers several kinds of benefits.
  - A new monetary and credit system.
  - World peace, disarmament and friendly relations with socialist nations like Russia.

Formation of the Indian National Army (INA)

The Indian National Army was the idea of Mohan Singh, an Indian Officer in the British Indian Army, who was in Malaya and decided not to join the retreating British army.

He went to Japanese for help, who at that time encouraged Indians to join anti-British organisations. Japanese handed over Indian Prisoners of War (POWs) to Mohan Singh. He inducted these soldiers into Indian National Army.

On 1st September, 1942, the Indian National Army was formally established. Around 45,000 Indian Prisoners of War joined the INA by the end of 1942.

It was decided that the army would come into action only after the invitation of the Congress and the Indian masses.

The formation of the INA was the result of an important role played by the following conferences

Tokyo Conference

It was held at Tokyo by South-East Asian Indian Nationalist groups between 28th and 31st March, 1942. This conference was organised by the efforts of **Rash Behari Bose**. The Indian Independence League, the Indian Council and other small local Indian associations and clubs joined the conference to meet the Japanese High Command.

Some decisions taken in this conference were

- To form an Indian National Army (INA).
- To expand and strengthen Indian Independence league in all Asian countries controlled by Japan.
- To hold a conference of the representatives of Indians at Bangkok in June 1942.

Bangkok Conference

It was held from 15th June to 23rd June, 1942. Rash Behari Bose was elected as President of the conference. It was attended by more than 150 representatives from East-Asian countries like Malaya, Singapore, Burma, Thailand, Hongkong, Manila and Java.

In this Conference, Indian Prisoners Of War (POWs) under Japan, volunteered to fight for the freedom of India. Rash Behari hoisted the tricolour flag and formally inaugurated the Indian Independence League. It aimed to fight for the attainment of complete and immediate Independence of India.

Some decisions taken in this conference were

- It was decided that the Indian Independence League (IIL) would make arrangement for the supply of men, material and money required by the Indian National Army.
- Subhash Chandra Bose was invited to lead the Indian National Army.
- Mohan Singh was appointed as the Commander-in- Chief of the Indian National Army.
- A council of action was founded for carrying out all necessary actions in connection with the Independence Movement.

Subhash Chandra Bose and INA

On 4th July, 1943 he assumed the leadership of the Indian Independence League (IIL).

He took charge of Indian National Army (INA) and became its Supreme Commander in August 1943. He set up its headquarters in **Yangon** and **Singapore** and started to reorganise Indian National Army.

He set up recruitment and training departments to strengthen the army. Fighting brigades or regiments were established which had names like Gandhiji, Azad, Nehru, Subhash and Rani Jhansi (regiment of women which was led by Captain Lakshmi Sahgal).

Subhash Chandra Bose was fondly called **Netaji** by the soldiers and the civilians. He gave the call to his soldiers, 'Give me blood and I shall give you freedom'. His **battle cry**[2] were, 'Dilli Chalo' and 'Jai Hind'.

Objectives of INA under Subhash Chandra Bose

- To mobilise all the forces effectively to lead Indian people to regain their freedom.
- To prepare the Indian people inside and outside India for a modern armed struggle against the British.
- To organise a Provisional Government of free India.
- Total mobilisation of Indian man-power and money for a total war.
- 'Unity, Faith, Sacrifice' was the motto of the Indian National Army (INA).

Contribution of Subhash Chandra Bose in INA

Setting up Provisional Government of Free India

Netaji Subhash Chandra Bose founded the Provisional or Interim Government of Free India (Arzi Hukumat-e-Azad Hind) at Singapore on 21st October, 1943.

The government was recognised by the world powers like Axis powers and their satellites including Germany, Italy, Japan, Thailand and Burma. As the head of the Provisional Government, Netaji declared War against Britain.

The objective of the Provisional Government of Free India was to establish a permanent national government of Azad Hind. Netaji transferred the headquarters of the Provisional Government to Rangoon which had a strategic importance as Myanmar was close to India's Eastern Border where INA would reach easily. Netaji's Provisional Government got its first independent territory when Japan handed over Andaman and Nicobar Islands to Netaji on 6th November, 1943. He named them **Shaheed** and **Swaraj Islands**, respectively.

Declaration of War

On 23rd October, 1943, the cabinet of the Provisional Government called a meeting where it was decided to start war against Britain and USA. Netaji himself broadcast this decision on radio.

By March 1944, the INA 'Azad Hind Fauj' with the Japanese army had reached the very frontier of India.

They entered Indian territory and captured Mowdok, a place near Chittagong. Then it marched towards Kohima in Nagaland and captured it.

They hoisted tricolour flag for the first time in India on 19th March, 1944.

The Surrender of the INA

In 1944, INA became victorious but the further incidents forced the INA to surrender. These incidents were

- Japanese had to withdraw their forces from the Indo-Burma border because of their war with the USA in the pacific regions.
- The early arrival of monsoon hampered the supply of ration and ammunition to the army and the INA failed to seize Imphal.
- Rangoon was recaptured by the British.
- The bombardment on Hiroshima and Nagasaki (6th and 9th August, 1945) forced Japan to surrender on 15th August, 1945.

As a result of this surrender, Netaji went to Bangkok and then to Tokyo. It was supposed that Netaji died in an plane accident on his way to Tokyo on 18th August, 1945.

The INA Trials

After the surrender of the INA, the British Government in India decided to prosecute some INA officers like Colonel Prem Sehgal, Colonel Gurbaksh Singh Dhillon and Major General Shah Nawaz Khan for **treason**[3]. These INA trials held in a public trial at **Red Fort**.

This gave rise to a wave of anger and protests among Indians. These trials attracted much publicity and public sympathy for the defendants who were perceived as patriots in India.

The trials was defended by the INA Defence Committee formed by the Congress. This Committee had legal experts like Jawaharlal Nehru, Bhullabhai Desai, Kailashnath Katju and others. As a result of this defendence, the British Government release the INA officers.

Impact of INA

- The Indian National Army did not succeed fully in achieving its objective, but it set an inspiring example of patriotism and sacrifice before the Indian people.
- The heroic deeds and sacrifices of the soldiers of INA stimulated political consciousness among the Indian forces.
- INA marked the last major campaign when the Congress and the Muslim League worked together. The battle of the INA was not affected

2 **Battle Cry** A shout that soldiers used to give in battle to encourage their own army or to frighten the enemy.

3 **Treason** It is the action of betraying one's country.

by communal divisions. There were Hindus, Muslims, Sikhs in the INA who fought together as Indians. This promote unity among the nation.

- The battle of INA inspired uprisings in the Armed Forces of the country. The Indian Navy rose in revolt at Bombay, Calcutta, Madras and Karachi in February 1946. These revolts destroyed the very foundation of the British Raj.
- Historians believed that the INA trials and its effects brought a decisive change in British policy.

Check Your LEARNING...

1. When was the Forward Bloc formed?
2. Mention any one objective of the INA.
3. Who gave the call of 'Dilli Chalo'?
4. Who were prosecuted in INA trials?

Time Line

Year	Important Events
23rd Jan, 1897	Subhash Chandra Bose was born.
1920	Subhash Chandra passed Indian Civil Service Examination.
1938	Subhash Chandra was elected as the President of the Congress at Haripura Session.
1939	Subhash Chandra was elected as the President of the Congress at Tripuri Session.
3rd May, 1939	Forward Bloc was formed by Subhash Chandra Bose.
20th-22nd June, 1940	First All India Conference of the Forward Bloc held in Nagpur.
22nd June,1940	Considered as the founding date of the Forward Bloc by itself.
July, 1940	Subhash Chandra was arrested under the 'Defence of Indian Rules'.
17th Jan, 1941	Subhash Chandra escaped from house arrest and went to Peshawar.
1942	Japan had occupied the British colonies of Singapore, Malaya and Burma.
28th-31st March, 1942	Tokyo Conference
15th-28th Jan, 1942	Bangkok Conference
1st Sep, 1942	Indian National Army was established.
1943	Subhash Chandra left for Japan.
4th July, 1943	Subhash Chandra assumed the leadership of INA and IIL.
21st Oct,1943	Subhash Chandra founded the Provisional Government of free India at Singapore.
23rd Oct, 1943	Provisional Government called meeting where it was decided to start war against Britain and USA.
6th-9th Aug, 1945	Bombardment on Hiroshima and Nagasaki.
18th Aug, 1945	Netaji was killed in a plane crash.
Feb, 1946	Indian Navy revolted in Bombay, Calcutta, Madras and Karachi.

QUiCK Revision

- On 3rd May, 1939, Netaji Subhash Chandra Bose founded the new political party, Forward Bloc.
- In its first conference at Nagpur (1940), the Forward Bloc passed the resolution 'All Power to the Indian People' and adopted militant action for struggle against the British.
- The initial aim of the Forward Bloc was to unite all the left-wing sections within the Congress and to develop an alternative leadership.
- The Forward Bloc wanted to reorganise agriculture and industry, abolish landlordism, introduce new monetary and credit system , achieve world peace, etc.
- In the Tokyo Conference of IIL, decision about the formation of Indian National Army was taken.
- In Bangkok Conference of IIL, Rash Behari Bose was elected as President of the Conference. He hoisted the tricolour flag and inaugurated the IIL.
- On 1st September, 1942, the Indian National Army (INA) was established and captain Mohan Singh became its Commander-in-Chief.
- On 4th July, 1943, Subhash Chandra assumed the leadership of IIL and INA.
- Netaji set up recruitment and training departments to strengthen the army. Fighting brigades were named after Gandhi, Azad, Nehru, Subhash and Rani of Jhansi.
- Subhash Chandra founded the Provisional or Interim Government of free India at Singapore on 21st October, 1943.
- On 23rd October, 1943, the Cabinet of the Provisional Government decided to start war against Britain and USA. With the help of Japanese Army, INA captured Mowdok, a place near Chittagong.
- After that INA marched towards Kohima and hoisted tricolour flag on the hilltops of Kohima. But Japan had to withdraw their troops at that time as they became busy to struggle with USA in the Pacific regions.
- The bombardment on Hiroshima and Nagasaki forced Japan to surrender and the Second World War came to an end.
- The public trials of INA officers gave rise to a wave of anger and protest in all over India. The British Government had no option but to release them.
- The great contribution of the INA to our freedom struggle was to inspire patriotism and to stimulate political consciousness among the Indians.

Chapter Practice

Section-I

Multiple Choice Questions

1. For how many times Subhash Chandra Bose was elected as the President of the Congress?
(a) One time (b) Two times
(c) Three times (d) Four times

Ans. (b) Two times

2. In which year the Tripuri Session of Indian National Congress took place?
(a) 1905 (b) 1907 (c) 1938 (d) 1939

Ans. (d) 1939

3. Why did Subhash Chandra Bose give resign from the presidentship of the Congress?
(a) Due to establish a new political party.
(b) Due to ill- health.
(c) Due to having different views from Gandhiji.
(d) Due to having no support from anyone.

Ans. (c) Due to having different views from Gandhiji.

4. In which year Subhash Chandra Bose gave resign from the presidentship of Congress?
(a) 1942 (b) 1939
(c) 1932 (d) 1920

Ans. (b) 1939

5. In which year Forward Block was founded?
(a) 1939 (b) 1942 (c) 1944 (d) 1943

Ans. (a) 1939

6. To reorganise agriculture and industry on socialist lines was an aim of **[Specimen Paper Semester-I 2022]**
(a) Indian National Congress
(b) The Indian National Army
(c) The Forward Bloc
(d) The Muslim League

Ans. (c) The Forward Bloc

7. The Supreme Commander of the Indian National Army **[Specimen Paper Semester-I 2022]**
(a) Subhash Chandra Bose
(b) Rash Behari Ghosh
(c) Jawaharlal Nehru
(d) Lord Wavell

Ans. (a) Subhash Chandra Bose

8. The Indian National Army was the idea of .... , an Indian Officer in the British Indian Army.
(a) Mohan Singh (b) Rash Behari Bose
(c) Subhash Chandra Bose
(d) Mahatma Gandhi

Ans. (a) Mohan Singh

9. The immediate cause of the First World War was ....
(a) Imperialism (b) Alliance System **[2023]**
(c) Sarajevo Crisis (d) Arms Race

Ans. (c) Sarajevo Crisis

10. Identify the famous slogan of Subhash Chandra Bose **[Semester-I 2022]**
(a) Give me blood and I shall give you freedom
(b) Swaraj is my birth right and I shall have it.
(c) Do or Die
(d) Vande Mataram

Ans. (a) Give me blood and I shall give you freedom

11. The title 'Father of Nation' was given to Gandhiji by
(a) Bal Gangadhar Tilak
(b) Subhash Chandra Bose
(c) Jawaharlal Nehru
(d) Khan Abdul Ghaffar Khan

Ans. (b) Subhash Chandra Bose

12. Complete the given analogy.
Haripura Session of Congress : 1938 : : Tripuri Session of Congress : ?
(a) 1939 (b) 1941 (c) 1943 (d) 1945

Ans. (a) 1939

13. Complete the given analogy.
Headquarters of the Provisional Government : Rangoon : : Headquarters of the INA : ?
(a) Java (b) Sumatra
(c) Malaya (d) Rangoon

Ans. (d) Rangoon

14. Complete the given analogy.
Birth anniversary of Subhash Chandra Bose : ? : : Death of Subhash Chandra Bose : 1945
(a) 1888 (b) 1891 (c) 1897 (d) 1910

Ans. (c) 1897

15. Replace the underlined word to correct the statement. **[Specimen Paper Semester-I 2022]**
Unity, Faith, Sacrifice was the motto of the <u>Forward Bloc</u>.
(a) Indian National Congress (b) Indian National Army
(c) East India Association (d) The Muslim League

Ans. (b) Indian National Army

16. Replace the underlined word to correct the statement.
Subhash Chandra Bose started a newspaper in August 1939 with the name of '<u>The India Times</u>'.
(a) New India (b) Free India
(c) Forward Bloc (d) New Nation

Ans. (c) Forward Bloc

17. Complete the following table

Establishment of the Provisional Government of free India	Singapore
Establishment of the INA	?

(a) Malaysia (b) Singapore
(c) Japan (d) Java

Ans. (b) Singapore

18. Which of the following countries gave military aid to Subhash Chandra Bose?
(i) Germany (ii) Italy
(iii) France (iv) Afghanistan

Codes
(a) Only (i)
(b) Only (ii)
(c) Both (iii) and (iv)
(d) All of the above

Ans. (a) Both (i)

19. Which of the following countries recognised the 'Arzi Hukumat-e- Azad Hind'?
(i) Italy (ii) Japan
(iii) Thailand (iv) Germany

Codes
(a) Only (i) (b) Only (ii)
(c) Both (iii) and (iv) (d) All of these

Ans. (d) All of these

20. Match the following

	List-I		List-II
A.	20th to 22nd June, 1940	1.	Tokyo Conference
B.	22nd June, 1940	2.	Subhash Chandra Bose was arrested under the Defence of Indian Rules
C.	July, 1940	3.	Founding date of Forward Bloc
D.	1942	4.	First all India Conference of Forward Bloc

Codes

	A	B	C	D		A	B	C	D
(a)	1	2	3	4	(b)	2	1	4	3
(c)	3	4	1	2	(d)	4	3	2	1

Ans. (d)

21. Match the following.

	List-I		List-II
A.	1942	1.	Subhash Chandra Bose assumed leadership of INA and IIL
B.	14th July, 1943	2.	INA was established
C.	6th to 9th August, 1945	3.	Indian Navy revolted in Bombay, Calcutta, Madras and Karachi
D.	1946	4.	Bombardment on Hiroshima and Nagasaki

Codes

	A	B	C	D		A	B	C	D
(a)	1	2	3	4	(b)	2	1	4	3
(c)	3	4	1	2	(d)	4	3	2	1

Ans. (b)

Picture Based Question

22. Look at the picture given below and answer the questions that follow

(i) Which of the following personalities is shown in the given picture?
(a) Rash Behari Bose (b) Nawab Salimullah
(c) Madan Mohan Malviya (d) Justice Ranade

Ans.(a) Rash Behari Bose

(ii) The person in the picture was associated with which of the following?
(a) INA (b) Forward Bloc
(c) Congress (d) Both (a) and (b)

Ans. (a) INA

(iii) He was elected as the President of which of the following conferences?
(a) Tokyo Conference (b) Japan Conference
(c) Bangkok Conference (d) Rio de Janeiro Conference

Ans.(c) Bangkok Conference

(iv) 'To form an Indian National Army' was the motive of which of the following conferences for which he made great efforts?
(a) Bangkok Conference (b) Tokyo Conference
(c) Berlin Conference (d) Hiroshima Conference

Ans.(b) Tokyo Conference

Passage Based Questions

23. Read the passage given below and answer the questions that follow.

After resigning from the presidentship of Indian National Congress on 29th April, 1939, Subhash Chandra Bose felt the urgent need to establish an organised left-wing party within the Congress. Gandhiji was opposed to his presidentship as Subhash Chandra Bose favoured the policy of large-scale industrialisation. Whereas Gandhiji favoured the idea of small- scale industries to make the Indian villages self- reliant. Bose also wanted that Congress should help the people of the Princely states in their struggle for freedom whereas Gandhiji criticized his demand. When the Britain was facing difficulties because of German threat Gandhiji wanted to adopt a compromising attitude towards the British and also opposed to organise any national movement during the war. But Bose wanted to take this opportunity to eliminate the British from India.

Due to these different views of Bose and the Congress (Gandhiji), Subhash Chandra Bose formed the Forward Bloc on 3rd May, 1939.

(i) In the Congress Subhash Chandra Bose had different views which led to the formation of which of the following?
(a) A socialist party
(b) A political party
(c) A communist party
(d) None of the above

Ans. (b) A political party

(ii) At which place the session of Congress was held in 1939 after which Subhash Chandra Bose resigned from its presidentship?
(a) Haripura (b) Kolkata
(c) Madras (d) Tripuri

Ans. (d) Tripuri

(iii) Who was Mahatma Gandhi's preferred presidential candidate in 1939 at Indian National Congress Tripuri Session?
(a) Jawaharlal Nehru
(b) Subhash Chandra Bose
(c) Maulana Azad
(d) Pattabhi Sitaramayya

Ans. (d) Pattabhi Sitaramayya

(iv) What was the main aim of establishing the new party by Subhash Chandra Bose?
(a) Liberation of India
(b) To unite all the left-wing sections within the Congress
(c) Reorganisation of agriculture and industry on socialist lines
(d) All of the above

Ans. (d) All of the above

24. Read the passage given below and answer the questions that follow.

The Indian National Army (INA) did not succeed fully in achieving its objective, but it set an inspiring example of patriotism and sacrifice before the Indian people. The heroic deeds and sacrifices of the soldiers of INA infused political consciousness among the Indian forces. INA marked the last major campaign when the Congress and the Muslim League worked together. The battle of the INA was not affected by communal divisions. There were Hindus, Muslims, Sikhs in the INA who fought together as Indians.

The battle of INA inspired uprisings in the Armed forces of the country. The Indian Navy rose in revolt at Bombay, Calcutta, Madras and Karachi in February 1946. These revolts destroyed the very foundation of the British Raj. Historians believed that the INA trials and its effects brought a decisive change in British policy. So, INA played a significant role in the final decision of the British Government to Quit India.

(i) INA was established with the aim to
(a) mobilise all the forces effectively to lead Indian people to regain their freedom.
(b) total mobilisation of Indian man-power and money for a total war.
(c) organise a Provisional Government of free India.
(d) All of the above

Ans. (d) All of the above

(ii) What was the battle cry for INA?
(a) Dilli Chalo
(b) Jai Hind
(c) Swaraj is my Birth right
(d) Both (a) and (b)

Ans. (d) Both (a) and (b)

(iii) What was the positive feature of INA?
(a) It united all the communities of India.
(b) It infused political consciousness among the Indian forces.
(c) It inspired uprisings in the Armed forces of the country.
(d) All of the above

Ans. (d) All of the above

(iv) Name the Brigade of INA which was exclusively formed for women.
(a) Durga Shakti (b) Rani of Jhansi
(c) Pride of India (d) Naari Shakti

Ans. (b) Rani of Jhansi

Section-II

Short Questions

1. By which name Subhash Chandra Bose was popularly known and why?

Ans. Subhash Chandra Bose was popularly known as 'Netaji' which means 'respected leader'. Due to his fearless spirit and endeavour to liberate India, people called him 'Netaji'.

2. Mention any two objectives of the Forward Bloc. **[2020]**

Ans. The objectives of the Forward Bloc were
(i) To unite all the left-wing sections within the Congress under one head and to develop an alternative leadership.
(ii) To liberate India with the support of workers, peasant, youths and all radical organisations.

3. How was the Indian Independence League formed? Who was its President?

Ans. The Indian Independence League was formed with the help of different associations of South-East Asia, who were sympathetic about India's freedom struggle, Rash Behari Bose was its President.

4. Mention any two objectives of the Indian National Army. [2014, 2017]

Ans. The two important objectives of the Indian National Army were as follows
(i) To organise an armed revolution and to fight the British army with modern arms.
(ii) To organise a Provisional Government of Free India in order to mobilise all the forces effectively.

5. How were the prisoners reorganised as Indian National Army after the capture of British Indian Soldiers by Japanese?

Ans. Japanese captured Indian soldiers in South-East Asia. During this time, Britain's defeats aroused great hopes among Indian soldiers, which led to the formation of the Indian Independence League by Rash Behari Bose. A conference which was held in Tokyo, where decision was taken to form an Indian National Army.

6. Who was elected the President of the Bangkok conference? Which organisation was formally inaugurated at this conference?

Ans. Rash Behari Bose was elected the President of Bangkok Conference.
In this conference, Rash Behari Bose hoisted the tricolour flag and formally inaugurated the Indian Independence League.

7. Mention two contributions of INA (Indian National Army) to the Indian National Movement. [2016]

Ans. Two contributions of INA to the Indian National Movement
(i) The INA inspired uprisings in the armed forces of the country. The Indian Navy rebelled in February, 1946 at Bombay, Calcutta, Madras and Karachi.
(ii) The struggle of INA officers took the form of a massive movement against the trial of the soldiers and officers of the INA.

8. Name the military organisation revamped by Subhash Chandra Bose.

Ans. Indian National Army (INA) was the military organisation revamped by Subhash Chandra Bose with Japanese Support. The INA under Bose was a model of diversity by region, ethnicity, religion and even gender.

9. Where and when the Provisional Government of free India was set up?

Ans. The Provisional Government of free India was set-up at Singapore on 21st October, 1943 by Netaji Subhash Chandra Bose.

10. When did Netaji Subhash Chandra Bose declared war against the British?

Ans. On 23rd October, 1943, the Cabinet of the Provisional Government decided to start a war against Britain and USA. Netaji himself broadcast this decision on radio.

11. Name some prominent legal experts who defended the trials of INA officers at Red Fort.

Ans. Some prominent legal experts like Jawaharlal Nehru, Bhullabhai Desai, Kailashnath Katju defended the trials of INA officers at Red Fort. These trials attracted much publicity and public sympathy for the defendants who were perceived as patriots in India.

Structured Questions

1. In the political scenario of 1939, important developments took place in India and abroad. In this context, answer the following questions.
(i) Who was the founder of the 'Forward Bloc'? Why was this organisation formed?
(ii) Forward Block held its first All India Conference in which place and what was its significance?
(iii) How the Indian National League and Indian National Army were formed?
(iv) Describe in brief about Tokyo Declaration Conference.

Ans. (i) Netaji Subhash Chandra Bose was the founder of the Forward Bloc.
The Forward Bloc was formed for the liberation of India with the support of workers, peasants, youths and other organisations.
(ii) Forward Block held its first All India conference in Nagpur on 20th-22nd June, 1940. In this conference, the forward Block was declared as a socialist political party. and 22nd June was considered as the founding date of the party.
(iii) Indian Independence League (IIL) was formed as a result of associations started by people living in South-Asia territories with the objective of working for the liberation of India.
People living in the South-East Asia territories were free from European domination and sympathetic about Indian National Movement. Rash Behari Ghosh was the leader of IIL. It aimed to fight for the attainment of complete and immediate independence of India.
In the Tokyo conference (28th and 31st March, 1942) of the Indian Independence League, decision about the formation of an Indian National Army (INA) was taken. Then, the Indian National Army (INA) or Azad Hind Fauj was formed by Indian Nationalists on 1st September, 1942 in South-East Asia during the Second World War. It became the military army of Indian Independence League.
(iv) Refer to chapter theory page no. 179.

2. The heroism of the Indians was revealed by the courage of Subash Chandra Bose and the Indian National Army. With reference to this, answer the following questions. [2023]
(i) Mention any three objectives of the Forward Bloc.
(ii) Mention any three contributions of Subash Chandra Bose.
(iii) Who was the founder of the Indian National Army ? Mention any three of its objectives.

Ans. (i) The objectives of the Forward Bloc were

(a) To unite all the left-wing sections within the Congress under one head and to develop an alternative leadership.

(b) To liberate India with the support of workers, peasant, youths and all radical organisations.

(c) Abolition of landlordism, i.e. *Zamindari* System. Making the 'Right to Work' as a fundamental right.

(ii) The three contribution of Subhash Chandra Bose are

(a) Netaji Subhash Chandra Bose founded the Provisional or Interim Government of Free India (Arzi Hukumat-e-Azad Hind) at Singapore on 21st October, 1943. The objective of the Provisional Government of Free India was to establish a permanent national government of Azad Hind.

(b) He took the charge of Indian National Army and became its Supreme Commander in August 1943.

(c) He set up training and recruitment departments to strengthen the army.

(iii) Subhash Chandra Bose was the founder of the Indian National Army. The main objectives of the Indian National Army are as follows

(i) To organise an armed revolution and to fight the British army of occupation with modern arms.

(ii) To organise a provisional government of free India in order to mobilise all forces effectively.

(iii) Total mobilisation of India's manpower and money for a total war was one of the main objectives of INA.

Picture Based Question

1. With reference to the picture given below answer the following. **[2018]**

(i) Identify the personality.

(ii) Where and when the Provisional Government of Free India was set up? Who was the head of this government?

(iii) Explain the contribution of Subhash Chandra Bose in INA.

Or (i) Identify the leader given in the picture. Name the political party and the Military Organisation that he formed.

(ii) State any three objectives of the political party that he founded.

(iii) Mention any four objectives of the Military Organisation that he formed.

Ans. (i) The picture belongs to Subhash Chandra Bose, one of the most respected and prominent leaders of Indian Freedom Movement. He is popularly known as 'Netaji'. He was elected President of the Indian National Congress twice, but due to difference with Mahatma Gandhi, he had to resign. He founded a new political party, the Forward Bloc in 1939. It was a socialist party and wanted to consolidate the left-wing, within the Congress.

(ii) Subhash Chandra Bose founded the Provisional Government of Free India at Singapore on 21st October, 1943. He proclaimed the formation of the Arzi Hukumat-e-Azad Hind on the Provisional Government of Free India (Azad Hind). The Indian National Army was declared the Army of Azad Hind, which was to fight for independence of India from Britain. Subhash Chandra Bose was the head of this government.

(iii) Refer to chapter theory page no. 180.

Or (i) The given picture belongs to Subhash Chandra Bose, one of the most respected and prominent leader of Indian Freedom Movement. Forward Bloc was a political party and the Indian National Army was a Military Organisation formed by him.

(ii) Three objectives of the political party Forward Bloc were

(a) The main objective of the Forward Bloc was to unite all the left-wing sections within the Congress and to develop an alternative leadership.

(b) Immediate objective was the liberation of India with the support of workers, peasants, youths and all radical organisation.

(c) It aimed to establish a socialist society.

(iii) Four objectives of the Indian National Army were

(a) To mobilise all the forces effectively to lead Indian people to regain their freedom.

(b) To prepare the Indian people inside and outside India for a modern armed struggle against the British.

(c) To organise a provisional government of free India.

(d) To fight the British army with modern arms and weapons.

Chapter Assessment

Section-I

Multiple Choice Questions

1. In which year did the INA trials begin?
   (a) 1940 (b) 1942
   (c) 1945 (d) 1947
2. Bangkok Conference was associated with which of the following
   (a) Congress (b) INA
   (c) Forward Bloc (d) None of these
3. Tripuri Session was associated with ....
   (a) INA
   (b) Forward Bloc
   (c) Congress
   (d) Indian National Movement
4. Which of the following territories was handed over by Japan to Provisional Government of Free India?
   (a) Lakshadweep Island
   (b) Andaman and Nicobar islands
   (c) Pondicherry
   (d) Tripura

Short Questions

1. Mention any one irreconcilable difference between Gandhiji and Subhash Chandra Bose.
2. Give one reason which led to a split in the Congress in 1939.
3. State two important objectives of the Forward Bloc.
4. What standpoint was taken regarding the Indian Independence League in Tokyo Conference?
5. Who was the first Commander-in-Chief of the INA?
6. When and by whom was 'Provisional Government of Free India' proclaimed?
7. Name any two top ranking officers of the INA who stood upon the historic trial as traitors in the Red Fort at Delhi.

Section-II

Structured Questions

1. The differences between Gandhiji and Subhash Chandra Bose led to the formation of the Forward Bloc. In this context explain the following questions.
   (i) The main difference between Subhash Chandra Bose and Mahatma Gandhi.
   (ii) The formation of the Forward Bloc the INA.
   (iii) The main objectives of the Forward Bloc.
2. The Bangkok conference was held in June, 1942. In context of this, answer the following questions.
   (i) Who was elected as the President of the Conference?
   (ii) Which organisation was formally inaugurated at this conference?
   (iii) Why did Subhash Chandra take the responsibility of both INA and IIL?
   (iv) What were INA trails? Explain in brief.
3. Netaji Subhash Chandra Bose and the INA occupy a high position in the history of India's National Movement. In this context, answer the following questions.
   (i) What were the objectives of the INA?
   (ii) What were the INA's major achievements and victories?
   (iii) What is the significance of INA's heroic struggle against the British Raj?
   (iv) Why did INA surrender to British?
4. With reference to the Indian National Army, answer the following questions.
   (i) Explain three measures taken by Netaji Subhash Chandra Bose to establish a socialist society.
   (ii) What were the three decisions taken at the Tokyo conference?
   (iii) Explain any two contributions of Subhash Chandra Bose to the National Movement.
   (iv) Describe how and when Netaji declared war against British.

CHAPTER

08

Independence and Partition of India

SYLLABUS

Independence and Partition of India Cabinet Mission Plan (clauses only) •Mountbatten Plan (clauses and its acceptance) •The Indian Independence Act of 1947 (clauses only)

The period after the Second World War (May, 1945) was extremely difficult for India's freedom struggle. This was because of the disturbances during Quit India Movement, the failure of the INA and the demand of Muslim League for partition of India.

There was also a constitutional **deadlock**[1] in India which existed since the resignation of Congress Ministries in 1939. In order to break this deadlock, Lord Wavell who became the Viceroy of India in October 1943, announced a plan popularly known as Wavell Plan.

Wavell Plan

Lord Wavell announced the Wavell Plan in a conference at Shimla on 25th June, 1945.

The main proposals of Wavell's Plan were

- To grant the Dominion status to India in the long-run.
- To draft the Constitution of India by the Indians.

The Wavell Plan was not accepted by the Muslim League as they claimed that the right to appoint Muslim members should be enjoyed by the Muslim League only. On the other hand, the plan did not accept the demand for Pakistan.

The Congress also rejected this plan because it did not accept the total independence of India from the foreign rule. Thus, the non-compromising attitude of Congress and the Muslim League led to the failure of the Wavells Plan.

The Cabinet Mission of India

On 26th July, 1945, after 3 weeks of the Shimla Conference, Mr Clement Attlee became Prime Minister of Britain by replacing Mr Churchill. On 15th March, 1946, Mr Clement Attlee, announced in the House of Commons that a Cabinet Mission would be sent to India to facilitate the process of transfer of power and to help the Indian leaders to decide the form of government that would suit them.

The Cabinet Mission which arrived on 24th March, 1946 consisted of three Cabinet members. They were

(i) Mr Pethic Lawrence (the Secretary of State).
(ii) Sir Stafford Cripps (President of the Board of Trade).
(iii) Mr AV Alexander (the First Lord of Admiralty).

They discussed with different Indian leaders representing all sections and parties. Most of the leaders favoured a United India, whereas Mr Jinnah

1 **Deadlock** A complete failure to reach agreement or settle an argument.

and the members of the Muslim League stuck to their demand for a separate nation 'Pakistan'.

The mission submitted a proposal on 16th May, 1946 popularly known as the **Cabinet Mission Plan.** However, this plan also failed due to the conflicting goals of the Congress and the Muslim League.

Clauses of the Cabinet Mission Plan

Provisions for Federal Union

- India should be a union or a federation of all the British Provinces and Indian States.
- The Union Government would deal with foreign affairs, defence and communications.
- All subjects other than union subjects and all residuary powers would **vest**[2] in the provinces.
- The union would have its own executive and legislature composed of members elected by and sent by all provinces.

Provisions for British Provinces

- The British Provinces would be divided into three groups which were
  - (i) **Group 'A'** It would consist of Madras, Bombay, Uttar Pradesh, Central Provinces, Bihar and Orissa.
  - (ii) **Group 'B'** It would consist Punjab, North-West Frontier Province and Sindh.
  - (iii) **Group 'C'** It would have Bengal and Assam.

  The provinces would be free to decide the provisional subjects to be taken in common. Of the Chief Commissioner's Provinces, Delhi, Ajmer-Marwar and Coorgs were to join Group A and Baluchistan was to join Group B.
- Each group would draft their own Constitutions in consultation with other provinces included in each group.
- A province could opt out of any group and join another group by a majority decision of its legislature.

Provision for Constituent Assembly

- A Constituent Assembly would be set up to frame the new Constitution of the Indian Union. It would consist of 389 members of which 296 members would be elected from the British Provinces and 93 members from the Indian States.
- The Provincial Legislative Assemblies would elect the members of the Constituent Assembly. It would eliminate Adult suffrage (all eligible voters voting) to avoid delay in the making of the Constitution.
- The Constituent Assembly would sign a treaty with Britain to provide for certain matters arising out for the transfer of power.

Other Provisions

- An **interim government** at the centre with 14 members representing all communities would be formed on the basis of equality between the representatives of the Hindus, Sikhs and Muslims. All portfolios including that of War Minister would be held by Indian Ministers.
- It was proposed that for the time being, the Viceroy would reconstitute his Executive Council consisting of representatives of all communities.
- India would be free to remain within the British Commonwealth or separate from it.

Check Your LEARNING...

1. When did the Cabinet Mission arrive in India?
2. In how many groups the British Provinces were divided as per Cabinet Mission Plan?
3. When was the elections held for the Constituent Assembly?
4. What was the composition of Constituent Assembly as per Cabinet Mission Plan?

The Mountbatten Plan

Lord Mountbatten succeeded Lord Wavell and became new Viceroy and Governor-General in 1947. After coming to India, Lord Mountbatten began to hold consultations with leaders of different parties and communities.

He discussed with the leaders of both the Congress and the Muslim League to resolve the conflict between them. However, he could not unite these major parties, thus he realised that partition of the country was inevitable.

He discussed his plan for the Partition of India, also known as Mountbatten Plan, with 'big seven' leaders. These were Jawaharlal Nehru, Sardar Vallabhbhai Patel, Kripalani, Jinnah, Liaquat Ali, Abdul Rab Nishtar and Baldev Singh. This plan was announced on 3rd June, 1947.

Clauses of the Mountbatten Plan

- India would be divided into two dominions, i.e. India and Pakistan.
- It was up to the two Dominions, i.e. India and Pakistan, to decide what relations they would have with the British Commonwealth and with each other.

2 **Vest** To give somebody the legal rights or power to do something.

- A boundary commission was to be set up to determine the boundaries of the two nations.
- A referendum or **plebiscite**[3] would be held in the North-West Frontier Province and in Sylhet district (Muslim majority are) to ascertain whether the people in the area wanted to join India or not.
- The Princely states would have the choice of joining either of the two dominions or to remain independent.
- The provinces of Assam, Bengal and Punjab were also to be divided.
- The existing Constituent Assembly would continue to work and draft the Constitution of free India. Pakistan would have a separate Assembly.
- The date of British withdrawl from India was to be preponed to 15th August, 1947 which was earlier decided in June 1948. The British Parliament would pass an act for the transfer of power before this date.
- The Legislative Assembly of Sindh would take its own decision at a special meeting.
- The Muslim majority district of Sylhet would decide by referendum whether it would join East Bengal or remain in Assam.

Acceptance of the Mountbatten Plan

The Mountbatten Plan had a mixed reaction for its acceptance by both the Muslim League and the Congress.

Reaction of the Muslim League

The Muslim League accepted the plan on 10th June, 1947. But Jinnah complained that they got a small and underdeveloped Pakistan referring to the division of Punjab and Bengal. Sikh leaders accepted and welcomed the plan.

Reaction of the Congress

The Congress was committed to a United India, but had to accept the partition as a 'necessary evil'. The Congress formally accepted the Mountbatten Plan on 15th June, 1947. Gandhiji was still opposed to partition. He was persuaded by other leaders to accept the plan.

Patel believed that partition was the only alternative left to make the country safe and strong and the unification of the rest of the country was the immediate necessity.

Maulana Azad and many more nationalist Muslim leaders opposed partition, but they had to accept it as inevitable.

Reasons behind the Acceptance by the Congress

- The most important reason for this acceptance was the safety of the Indians. The Congress leaders realised that the large-scale communal riots and mass killing could be prevented only by accepting the Muslim League's demand for Pakistan.
- The Congress believed that it could not have the joint administration with the Muslim League as it had bitter experience in interim government of 1946.
- Sardar Patel thought that a United India even if it was smaller in size was better than a disorganised, troubled and weak bigger India.
- The Congress leaders realised that the extension of the British rule would be harmful to India. By applying the 'Divide and Rule Policy' the Britishers not only divided Hindu and Muslim community in India but they instigated the native rulers of the Indian States to remain independent.
- They felt that further delay in the transfer of power could lead Civil War in India.
- They also thought that partition would rid the Constitution of separate electorates and other undemocratic procedures. India could then evolve a truly secular and democratic polity.

The Indian Independence Act, 1947

After the Mountbatten Plan was accepted by the Indian leaders, the British Prime Minister Clement Attlee introduced the Indian Independence Bill in the House of Commons on 4th July, 1947.

This bill was passed by both Houses of the British Parliament on 18th July, 1947. The Indian Independence Act was a short document, consisting of less than 20 sections and 3 schedules.

The Indian Independence Act marked the end of the British rule in India. The Dominions of India and Pakistan came into existence.

Muhammad Ali Jinnah became the Governor-General of Pakistan. Lord Mountbatten remained in office as Governor-General of India up to June 1948 and **C Rajagopalachari** became the first and last Indian Governor-General.

On 26th January, 1950 India became a Republic. **Dr Rajendra Prasad** took over as the first President of the Indian Republic and the Constituent Assembly became the Parliament of India.

3 **Plebiscite** A vote by the people of a country or a region on an issue that is very important.

Clauses of the Indian Independence Act

Provisions for Two Dominions

- India would be partitioned and two independent dominions i.e. India and Pakistan would be created from 15th August, 1947. The act provided the legislative supremacy of both the dominions.
- The territories of the two dominions were divided in such terms that Pakistan would comprise of Sindh, British Baluchistan, North-West Frontier Province, the West Punjab and East Bengal. The exact boundaries of the dominions would be determined by a Boundary Commission.
- For each of the two dominions, there would be a Governor-General who would be appointed by the British King and who would represent the king for the purposes of the government of the dominions. He was to function as a constitutional head. Similarly, the provincial Governors were to act on the advice of the elected ministers.
- Each of the Dominions and all Provinces were to be governed in accordance with the Act of 1935 till the new Constitution was formed.
- The Constituent Assemblies of both the dominions were to act as the Central Legislatures and would have full powers to make laws for the respective dominion. They would act as sovereign bodies for legislative purposes.

Provisions for Secretary of the State and Division of Army and Assets

- The office of the Secretary of the State for India was abolished.
- Provisions were made for safeguarding the interests of the existing officers appointed by the Secretary of the State. The Secretary of the State however lost his power for future appointments.
- Provisions were made for the division of the Indian army between the two dominions and steps were to be taken to share the assets and liabilities between the two dominions.

Provisions for Partition

- Both Bengal and Punjab would be divided if so desired by the people. The Provincial Assemblies of the two parts would meet separately representing Hindu majority districts and Muslim majority districts and would decide through a majority vote whether they wanted the division of the province or not.
- A plebiscite would be held in North-West Frontier Province (NWFP) and in Sylhet district which was a Muslim majority area in East Bengal to determine whether they would join Pakistan or India. After partition, both these provinces joined West and East Pakistan, respectively.

Provision regarding End of Jurisdiction of the British Parliament

- The legislative authority of the British Parliament would cease from 15th August, 1947. It would not have any responsibility for the Government of India and all treaties and agreements between the British Government and the rulers of Indian States or any authority in tribal areas would lapse.
- The Governor-General was vested with necessary powers for bringing Indian independence into effective operation. He was given the powers to modify or adopt the Government of India Act, 1935 by 31st March, 1948.
- The title of the 'Emperor of India' was dropped from the royal style.
- The right of the King to veto laws was abolished and it was given to the Governor-General.

Check Your LEARNING...

1. When did Lord Mountbatten announce his plan?
2. When did the Congress formally accept the Mountbatten Plan?
3. When was the Indian Independence Act passed by the both Houses of the British Parliament?
4. How many schedules were there in Indian Independence Act?

Time Line

Year	Important Events
May, 1945	Second World War ended.
26th July, 1945	Clement Attlee became the Prime Minister of Britain
February, 1946	Revolt of navy in Bombay.
24th March, 1946	The Cabinet Mission arrived at India.
16th May, 1946	The Cabinet Mission submitted the Cabinet Mission Plan.
July, 1946	Elections of Constituent Assembly were held.
29th July, 1946	The Muslim League passed a Direct Action Resolution.
16th August, 1946	Direct Action Day
26th October, 1946	Representatives of the Muslim League were inducted in interim government.
9th December, 1946	The Constituent Assembly met and Dr Rajendra Prasad was elected its President.
31st January, 1947	League demanded the dissolution of the Constituent Assembly.
24th March, 1947	Lord Mountbatten became the Viceroy of India.
3rd June, 1947	The Mountbatten Plan was announced.
10th June, 1947	The Muslim accepted the Mountbatten Plan.
15th June, 1947	The Congress accepted the Mountbatten Plan.
4th July, 1947	Attlee introduced the Indian Independence Act in the House of Commons.
18th July, 1947	The Indian Independence Act was passed by both the Houses of the British Parliament.
15th August, 1947	Country divided into two independent nations.
20th June, 1948	C Rajagopalachari became the first Indian Governor-General.
26th January, 1950	New Constitution was adopted and India became Republic.

QUiCK Revision

- The Second World War ended in May, 1945. Prime Minister of Britain, Mr Winston Churchill invited Lord Wavell, the Viceroy of India to discuss the problems of India.
- Lord Wavell's Plan was not accepted by the Muslim League. They claimed that right to appoint Muslim members should be only enjoyed by the Muslim League, but the Congress did not support this.
- The Cabinet Mission was sent to India on 24th March, 1946. The mission tried to bring about a formula which would be acceptable to both the Congress and the Muslim League.
- The Cabinet Mission rejected the Muslim League's demand for a separate nation. It divided the British provinces into three groups i.e. Group A, Group B and Group C. Each group would draft their own Constitution.
- On June, 1947, Lord Mountbatten announced his plan. The main clauses of the plan were the country would be divided into two nations. North-West Frontier Province and Princely States had the option to join according to their will and two countries would have different Constituent Assemblies.
- The Muslim League accepted the Mountbatten Plan. The Congress accepted the plan for the safety of the Indians. The Congress leaders believed that the extension of the British rule would be harmful to India.
- On 18th July, 1947, the Indian Independence Act was passed by both Houses of the British Parliament.
- According to this Act, India would be partitioned and two independent dominions i.e. India and Pakistan would be created from 15th August, 1947.
- The exact boundaries of the two dominions should be determined by the Boundary Commission.
- The Constituent Assemblies of both the dominions would have full powers to make laws for the respective dominion.
- The office of the Secretary of the State for India was abolished. Indian army, assets and liabilities would be divided between the two dominions.

Chapter Practice

Section-I

Multiple Choice Questions

1. During the period of the 'Second World War' the Prime Minister of Britain was ....
   (a) Sir Stafford Cripps
   (b) Mr Winston Churchill
   (c) Mr Clement Attlee
   (d) Mr AV Alexander

Ans. (b) Mr Winston Churchill

2. The Cabinet Mission Plan led to ....
   (a) the Interim government
   (b) the transfer of power
   (c) elections to provincial assemblies
   (d) integration of princely states

Ans. (b) the transfer of power

3. What was decided about Indian Independence?
   (a) Prime Minister Attlee announced that the British would leave India by 15th August, 1947.
   (b) Lord Mountbatten would replace Lord Wavell.
   (c) Power would be handed over to the Muslim League.
   (d) The Princely States would continue to be under British control.

Ans. (b) Lord Mountbatten would replace Lord Wavell.

4. According to the Mountbatten Plan, where would a referendum take place?
   (a) Bengal
   (b) Punjab
   (c) North-West Frontier Province
   (d) Assam

Ans. (c) North-West Frontier Province

5. Provincial autonomy means
   (a) Independence of the provinces.
   (b) Independence of the Princely States.
   (c) Elected legislatures in the provinces.
   (d) Elected legislatures in the Princely States

Ans. (a) Independence of the provinces.

6. Congress agreed to Mountbatten's proposal for partition because
   (a) they wanted to avoid communal strife.
   (b) they had finally accepted the Two-Nation Theory.
   (c) they realised that extension of the British rule would be harmful to India.
   (d) Both (a) and (c)

Ans. (d) Both (a) and (c)

7. Which of the following was a reason for the acceptance of the Mountbatten Plan? **[Semester-I 2022]**
   (a) The British forced the Congress to accept the plan.
   (b) The Muslim League would cooperate in the governance.
   (c) The only alternative to partition was a federation with a weak centre.
   (d) The Princely States wanted to accept the plan.

Ans. (c) The only alternative to partition was federation with a weak centre

8. Indian Independence Act 1947 came after ....
   (a) Cabinet Mission
   (b) the Mountbatten Plan
   (c) Second World War
   (d) All of the above

Ans. (d) All of the above

9. Which of the following is not a clause of the Indian Independence Act of 1947? **[Semester-I 2022]**
   (a) All treaties made with the British would lapse.
   (b) The army and assets would belong only to India.
   (c) The Constituent Assemblies would serve as Central Legislatures.
   (d) The Princely States were free to associate themselves with either dominion.

Ans. (b) The army and assets would belong only to India

10. Which of these was not a provision of the Indian Independence Act, 1947? **[Specimen Paper Semester-I 2022]**
    (a) There would be a Governor-General for each dominion.
    (b) There would be no division of the army.
    (c) The office of the Secretary of State was abolished.
    (d) The jurisdiction of the British Parliament would end.

Ans. (b) There would be no division of the army.

11. Complete the given analogy.
    Group 'A' Province : Madras : : Group 'B' Province : ?
    (a) Uttar Pradesh (b) Bihar
    (c) Punjab (d) Assam

Ans. (c) Punjab

12. Complete the given analogy.
    Approval of the Mountbatten Plan : ? : : Wavell Plan : Shimla
    (a) India (b) England (c) USA (d) USSR

Ans. (b) England

13. Complete the given analogy.
Acceptance of Mountbatten Plan by the Muslim League : 10th June, 1947 : : Acceptance of Mountbatten Plan by the Congress : ?
(a) 15th June, 1947
(b) 1st August, 1947
(c) 1st January, 1948
(d) 15th August, 1949

Ans. (a) 15th June, 1947

14. Replace the underlined word to correct the statement.
The Prime Minister of Britain, Mr Mountbatten introduced the Indian Independence Bill 1947 in the House of Commons in London.
(a) Mr Churchill (b) Mr Clement Attlee
(c) Mr Ripon (d) Mr Pethic Lawrence

Ans. (b) Mr. Clement Attlee

15. Replace the underlined word to correct the statement.
As per the Indian Independence Act 1947, the office of the Governor-General for India was abolished.
(a) Viceroy
(b) Secretary of State
(c) Member of Parliament
(d) Member of Legislative Assembly

Ans. (b) Secretary of State

16. Complete the following table.

Lord Wavell's Plan	25th June, 1945
Cabinet Mission	?

(a) 23rd June, 1945
(b) 22nd april, 1943
(c) 24th March, 1946
(d) 25th October, 1944

Ans. (c) 24th March, 1946

17. Which of the following was the reason of the failure of Wavell's Plan?
(i) It did not accept the demand for a separate nation.
(ii) It did not accept the total independence of India from the foreign rule.
(iii) It proposed to give partial independence to India.

Codes
(a) Only (i) (b) Only (ii)
(c) Only (iii) (d) All of these

Ans. (d) All of these

18. Who among the following was not the member of the Cabinet Mission Plan?
(i) Mr Winston Churchill (ii) Mr Pethic Lawrence
(iii) Mr MV Alexander (iv) Sir Cripps

Codes
(a) Only (i) (b) Only (ii)
(c) Both (iii) and (iv) (d) All of these

Ans. (a) Only (i)

19. Match the following.

List-I	List-II
A. May 1945	1. The Cabinet Mission submitted the Cabinet Mission plan
B. 26th July, 1945	2. The Muslim League passed a Direct Action Resolution
C. 16th May, 1946	3. The Second World War ended
D. 29th July, 1946	4. Clement Attlee became the Prime Minister of Britain

Codes

	A	B	C	D		A	B	C	D
(a)	1	2	3	4	(b)	2	1	4	3
(c)	3	4	1	2	(d)	4	3	2	1

Ans. (c)

20. Match the following.

List-I	List-II
A. 16th August, 1946	1. Lord Mountbatten became Viceroy of India
B. 9th December, 1946	2. The Constituent Assembly meet
C. 31st January, 1947	3. The Muslim League demanded to end the Constituent Assembly
D. 24th March, 1947	4. Direct Action Day

Codes

	A	B	C	D		A	B	C	D
(a)	1	2	3	4	(b)	2	1	4	3
(c)	3	4	1	2	(d)	4	3	2	1

Ans. (d)

Picture Based Question

21. Look at the picture given below and answer the questions that follow.

[Specimen Paper Semester-I 2022]

(i) Identify the man with Mahatma Gandhi.
(a) Lord Mountbatten (b) Lord Curzon
(c) Lord Wavell (d) Lord Dalhousie

Ans. (a) Lord Mountbatten

(ii) He was deputed to India for the following reason.
(a) To implement Lord Wavell Plan
(b) For effective administration
(c) For peaceful transfer of power
(d) To delay the partition of India

Ans. (c) For peaceful transfer of power

(iii) Identify from the list the proposal of the plan formulated by him.
(a) The country would be divided into two dominions
(b) Formation of a Constituent Assembly
(c) There would be grouping of provinces
(d) Setting up of a Boundary Commission

Ans. (a) The country would be divided into two dominions

(iv) Which of the following clauses about the Princely States was not part of the plan proposed by him?
(a) Princely States had to join only India
(b) All treaties with the Princely States would come to an end
(c) Princely states could remain independent
(d) The States could join either India or Pakistan

Ans. (a) Princely States had to join only India

Passage Based Questions

22. Read the passage given below and answer the questions that follow.

According to the Cabinet Mission Plan, India should be a union or a federation of all the British Provinces and Indian States. The Union Government would deal with foreign affairs, defence and communications. All subjects other than union subjects and all residuary powers would vest in the provinces. The union would have its own executive and legislature composed of members elected by and sent by all provinces.

The British Provinces would be divided into three Groups. Group 'A' consist of Madras, Bombay, Uttar Pradesh, Central Provinces, Bihar and Orissa; Group 'B' would consist Punjab, North-West Frontier Province and Sindh and Group 'C' would have Bengal and Assam. The provinces would be free to decide the provisional subjects to be taken in common.

(i) The Cabinet Mission Plan was proposed during which Prime Minister of England?
(a) Mr Winston Churchill (b) Mr Clement Attlee
(c) Mr Pethic Lawrence (d) Mr Ripon

Ans. (b) Mr Clement Attlee

(ii) Which of the following was not a clause of the Cabinet Mission Plan?
(a) Two Nations-Theory
(b) Approval of a Union Government
(c) Dealing of Foreign Affairs
(d) Communication would be a part of the Union Government

Ans. (a) Two Nations-Theory

(iii) Which of the following was not included in the Treaty to be negotiated as provided in the Cabinet Mission Plan?
(a) The Indian Union
(b) Constituent Assembly
(c) Indian National Congress
(d) The United Kingdom

Ans. (c) Indian National Congress

(iv) The Group 'C' of the British Provinces was mainly a
(a) Hindu majority region
(b) Muslim majority region
(c) Sikh majority region
(d) None of the above

Ans. (d) None of the above

23. Read the passage given below and answer the questions that follow.

Both Bengal and Punjab would be divided if so desired by the people. The Provincial Assemblies of the two parts would meet separately representing Hindu majority districts and Muslim majority districts and would decide through a majority vote whether they wanted the division of the province or not.

A plebiscite would be held in North-West Frontier Province (NWFP) and in Sylhet district which was a Muslim majority area in East Bengal to determine whether they would join Pakistan or India.

It was proposed in the plan that the legislative authority of the British Parliament would cease from 15th August, 1947. The title of the 'Emperor of India' was dropped from the royal style.

Till the new Constitution was framed, each of the Dominions and all Provinces were to be governed in accordance with the Act of 1935. The Governor-General was given the powers to modify or adopt the Government of India Act 1935 by 31st March, 1948. The right of the King to Veto laws was given up. This right was given to the Governor-General.

(i) Indian Independence Act was the outcome of which of the following plans?
(a) Wavell's Plan
(b) Shimla Conference
(c) Cabinet Mission Plan
(d) Mountbatten Plan

Ans. (d) Mountbatten Plan

(ii) Indian Independence Bill was passed in which year?
(a) 4th August, 1946 (b) 18th July, 1947
(c) 15th August, 1948 (d) 16th September, 1948

Ans. (b) 18th July, 1947

(iii) North-West Frontier Province became a part of which of the following dominions?
(a) Pakistan
(b) India
(c) Remained Independent
(d) Bangladesh

Ans. (a) Pakistan

(iv) Who became the first and last Indian Governor-General?
(a) Jawaharlal Nehru (b) Dr Rajendra Prasad
(c) Abul Kalam Azad (d) C Rajagopalachari

Ans. (d) C Rajagopalachari

Section-II

Short Questions

1. When did the Second World War ended? Who was the Prime Minister of Britain at that time?

Ans. In Europe, the Second World War ended in May 1945.

At that time Mr Winston Churchill was the Prime Minister of Britain.

2. Why Lord Wavell's Plan was not acceptable to the Muslim League? On what grounds Congress rejected the proposals of the Muslim League?

Ans. Lord Wavell's Plan was rejected by the Muslim League as they claimed that the right to appoint Muslim members should be enjoyed by the Muslim League only. But in Wavell's Plan the Executive Council should have equal representation of Hindus and Muslims.

The Congress did not support the claim of the Muslim League. The Congress represented both the Hindus and Muslims. Thus, the proposals of the Muslim League was rejected by the Congress.

3. How did the change of power in Britain became beneficial for India?

Ans. The change of power in Britain become beneficial for India as Mr Clement Attlee, leader of the Labour Party became the Prime Minister of Britain on 26th July, 1945, replacing Winston Churchill. Labour Party had always favoured self-rule for India. Thus, it became beneficial for India's Freedom Movement.

4. When was the Cabinet Mission sent to India? Write an international event that led to the Cabinet Mission.

Ans. The Cabinet Mission was sent to India on 24th March, 1946.

The International event that led to the Cabinet Mission was that the end of the Second World War had changed the balance of power. The USA and the Soviet Union emerged as the superpowers and both supported India's demand for freedom.

5. Name the three members of the Cabinet Mission. **[2014]**

Ans. Lord Pethick Lawrence, Sir Stafford Cripps and AV Alexander were the members of Cabinet Mission.

6. What was mentioned in the Cabinet Mission Plan regarding provisional autonomy? **[2012]**

Ans. The Cabinet Mission Plan proposed that the British Provinces would be divided into three Groups A, B and C. Each group would draft a Constitution for regional union. The provinces would enjoy full autonomy for all subjects other than the union subjects.

7. What was suggested about the power of interim government in the Cabinet Mission?

Ans. According to the Cabinet Mission, an interim government at the centre representing all communities would be installed on the basis of parity between the representatives of the Hindus and the Muslims. All portfolios including that of War Minister would be held by Indian Ministers.

8. In what way did the Cabinet Mission Plan try to preserve the unity of India?

Ans. The Cabinet Mission Plan tried to preserve the unity of India by giving the clause that India should be a union or a federation of British Provinces and Indian states.

9. What were the two proposals related to the Princely States in the Mountbatten Plan? **[2013, 2006]**

Ans. The two proposals related to the Princely States in the Mountbatten Plan were

(i) All treaties and agreements made by the British with reference to states would lapse from 15th August, 1947.

(ii) They would be free to associate themselves with either of the two dominions or to remain independent.

10. What was the Muslim League's reaction about the Mountbatten Plan?

Ans. On 10th June, 1947 the Muslim League accepted the Mountbatten Plan. But Mr Jinnah complained that they got a 'truncated and moth-eaten' Pakistan referring to the division of Punjab and Bengal Provinces.

11. Who was Clement Attlee?

Ans. Clement Attlee of Labour Party was the Prime Minister of Britain when India became independent. He was the person who declared on 20th February, 1947 that the British would quit India by 30th June, 1948.

12. Why was Mountbatten's Plan finally accepted by the Congress? **[2016]**

Or Write any two reasons for the acceptance of the Mountbatten Plan by the Congress. **[2019]**

Or Give two reasons for the acceptance of the Mountbatten Plan by the Congress. **[2023]**

Ans. The Mountbatten Plan was accepted by the Congress because

(i) The large-scale of communal riots that engulfed the whole country convinced all that the only solution to the communal problem lay in the partition of India.

(ii) The League had joined the Interim Government to obstruct and not to cooperate. Experience of working with the League had convinced the Congress that it could not have a joint administration with the League.

13. When was the Bill of Indian Independence Act introduced in the House of Commons of Britain and by whom?

Ans. British Prime Minister Clement Attlee introduced the Bill of Indian Independence Act on 4th July, 1947 in the House of Commons. This Bill passed by the both houses of the Parliament on 18th July, 1947.

14. State any two provisions of the Indian Independence Act, 1947 that was to decide the fate of Princely States. **[2019]**

Ans. The provisions of the Indian Independence Act, 1947 for the Princely States were
(i) India would be partitioned and two independent dominions India and Pakistan would be created on 15th August, 1947.
(ii) The territories of the two dominions were divided in such terms that Pakistan would comprise Sindh, British Baluchistan, North-West Frontier Province, the West Punjab and East Bengal.

15. Name the last Viceroy of India. State any one of the provisions of the Indian Independence Act of 1947. **[2018]**

Ans. Lord Mountbatten was the last British Viceroy of India. One of the provisions of the Indian Independence Act, 1947, was the partition of British India into two independent nations, India and Pakistan.

16. Name the last Viceroy of India. State one of his proposals in regard to the Princely States. **[2008]**

Ans. Lord Mountbatten was the last Viceroy of India. The proposal of Mountbatten with regard to the Princely States was that they would be free to associate themselves with either of the dominions (i.e. with India or Pakistan) or to remain independent.

Structured Questions

1. The period between 1920 to 1947 was marked with major events and reforms that finally led us to our Independence. In this context, answer the following questions. **[2017]**
(i) Any three proposals of the Lord Wavell's Plan.
(ii) How did the Congress and the Muslim League respond to the Mountbatten Plan?
(iii) Mention any four clauses of the Cabinet Mission Plan.

Ans. (i) Proposals of the Lord Wavell's Plan were
- Except for the post of Viceroy and Commander-in-Chief, all members of the Council would be Indians, with balanced representation of all communities.
- Hindus and Muslims would be represented equally in the Viceroy's Council.
- India would be given dominion status in the long-run.

(ii) Refer to chapter theory page no. 190.
(iii) Refer to chapter theory page no. 189.

2. With reference to the transfer of power to India, answer the following questions. **[2015]**
(i) Explain the Cabinet Mission's proposals regarding the setting up of a Constitution making body.
(ii) Mention any two clauses of the India Independence Act, 1947.
(iii) Why Muslim League had accepted the Mountbatten Plan?

Ans. (i) According to the Cabinet Mission, a Constituent Assembly would be set up to frame the new Constitution of the Indian Union. It would consist of 389 members, 296 members would be elected from the British Provinces and 93 members from the Indian states. After the election, the Constituent Assembly would meet at New Delhi and elect a Chairman, then the members would be divided into three groups representing A, B and C to frame their respective Constitution.
(ii) Refer to chapter theory page no. 191.
(iii) Refer to chapter theory page no. 190.

3. The Mountbatten Plan was the final proposal put forward by the British to solve the deadlock between the main political parties in India. In this context, answer the following questions.
(i) Any three developments which paved the way for Mountbatten Plan.
(ii) Three long-term impacts of Mountbatten Plan on Indian Politics.
(iii) Any two clauses of the Mountbatten Plan.
(iv) The reasons for the acceptance of Mountbatten Plan.

Ans. (i) Three developments which paved the way for Mountbatten Plan were
- On 26th October, 1946, representatives of the Muslim League were inducted into the interim government. The government seemed to be helpless by non-cooperation of the members of the Muslim League.
- After consultation with Indian leaders, Mountbatten concluded that he would not unite the major parties.
- Lord Mountbatten personally went to England to inform the British Government about the situation of India and get his plan approved by them.

(ii) Three long-term impacts of Mountbatten Plan on Indian Politics were
- It gave birth to unended communal dispute between Hindus and Muslims.
- The demarcation of boundaries were not clearly defined.
- It left Kashmir issue unsettled.

(iii) Refer to chapter theory page no. 189-190.
(iv) Refer to chapter theory page no. 190.

Picture Based Questions

1. Answer the questions based on the picture given below. **[2011]**

(i) Identify the event in the above picture. Name the lady seen in the given picture. Mention the year when the event took place.
(ii) What were the main provisions of the Indian Independence Act?
(iii) Mention the reasons that made the Congress accept the partition proposals under Mountbatten Plan.

Ans. (i) The event is the transfer of power ceremony. Here, Jawaharlal Nehru took the oath as the first Prime Minister of India. The lady shown in the picture is Edwina Mountbatten, wife of Viceroy Lord Mountbatten.
This event took place in the year 1947.
(ii) Refer to chapter theory page no. 191.
(iii) Refer to chapter theory page no. 190.

2. In the given below historic photograph of Pandit Jawaharlal Nehru, is seen giving his famous speech in the Constituent Assembly on 14th August, 1947. In this context, answer the following questions.

(i) Mention the provisions of the Indian Independence Act of 1947 regarding the Constituent Assemblies.
(ii) Discuss three basic reasons why the Cabinet Mission Plan rejected the demand for Pakistan.
(iii) Mention four important reasons for the All-Indian Congress Committee accepting the Mountbatten Plan.

Ans. (i) The provisions of the Indian Independence Act of 1947 regarding the Constituent Assemblies were
- The Constituent Assemblies of both the dominions (India and Pakistan) were to act as the Central Legislatures and would have 'full powers' to make laws for the respective dominion.
- The Constituent Assemblies would act as sovereign bodies for legislative purpose. The legislative authority of the British Parliament would cease from 15th August, 1947.

(ii) The Cabinet Mission Plan rejected the demand for Pakistan because
- The demand for a separate nation was not viable.
- Areas in Eastern part of Bengal demanded by the Muslim League were separated from the Western part they demanded, by thousands of miles.
- In Sindh and Punjab, Hindus and Muslims constituted the population almost in equal numbers. Moreover, there was no justification for keeping large Hindu districts in Bengal, Assam and Punjab in Pakistan.

(iii) Refer to chapter theory page no. 190.

Chapter Assessment

Section-I

Multiple Choice Questions

1. Who was elected as the President of the Constituent Assembly in 1946?
   (a) Jawaharlal Nehru
   (b) Ram Manohar Lohia
   (c) Mahatma Gandhi
   (d) Dr Rajendra Prasad
2. On February 20th, 1947, what was the deadline announced by the British Prime Minister, Mr Clement Attlee to solve issues for granting of Independence to India?
   (a) June 1947 (b) August 1947
   (c) June 1948 (d) December 1949
3. Who was the last British Viceroy of India?
   (a) Lord Mountbatten (b) Lord Ripon
   (c) Lord Clement (d) None of these

Section-II

Short Questions

1. What was the purpose of sending Cabinet Mission to India in 1946?
2. What was the Congress's view point regarding grouping of the provinces under the Cabinet Mission Plan?
3. What did the Mountbatten Plan provide in regard to the Princely States?
4. Why was Attlee's announcement welcomed by the Muslim League?
5. What did the stand point of the Indian Independence Act of 1947 regarding the Secretary of State for India?

Structured Questions

1. With reference to the Indian Independence Act of 1947, explain the following questions.
   (i) Areas included in Pakistan and reasons for such inclusion.
   (ii) Position of his Majesty's government regarding India.
   (iii) The power of the Constituent Assembly.
   (iv) Impact on the office of 'Secretary of State' & 'Governor-General?
2. The Cabinet Mission Plan proposed a two- tiered federal union of British Provinces and Princely States. With reference to this describe the following.
   (i) The federal structure proposed by the Cabinet Mission Plan.
   (ii) 'Grouping of Provinces' that was recommended by the plan.
   (iii) Clauses of the Cabinet Mission Plan.

CHAPTER

09

The First World War

SYLLABUS

The First World War Causes (Nationalism and Imperialism, Armament Race, Division of Europe and Sarajevo crisis).
• Results (Treaty of Versailles, territorial rearrangements, formation of League of Nations).

In 1914, a war started between the great powers of Europe in 1914, which is known as the **First World War.** It started on 28th July, 1914 and lasted until 11th November, 1918. The First World War was fought between Allied Powers (Britain, France, Russia and their Allies) and Central Powers (Germany, Austria and their Allies). It was fought in different areas known as Fronts such as **Western Front** between Germany and Northern France and **Eastern Front** between Germany and the Russian forces.

The outbreak of the First World War was the result of the numerous political tensions and rivalry that existed among the European powers. It was one of the deadliest conflicts in the world. This war was fought not only by soldiers but also by civilians. Many soldiers and civilians died in this war. Initially, the war began in Europe, but soon it spread to Asia and Africa. It marked an end to a long period of peace which was maintained after Franco–Prussian War of 1871.

Causes of the First World War

Nationalism

Nationalism is an ideology in which the people of a nation who are common in terms of their history, language and culture, feel a sense of unity. The 19th century became an era of narrow and militant nationalism and patriotism which means love for one's own nation and hatred towards other nations. Each nation thought about its own national interests which resulted into aggressive nationalism in Europe.

There were many nations which wanted their territories back. For example,

- France wanted to get back its provinces of Alsace and Lorraine from Germany.
- Italy wanted to get back the territory of Trentino Trieste from Austria.
- Balkan States like Serbia wanted that their inhabitants who lived in other states, should come together to form a greater Balkan State.
  The Balkans was a region of geographical and ethnic variation comprising modern-day Romania, Bulgaria, Albania, Greece, Macedonia, Croatia, Bosnia- Herzegovina, Slovenia, Serbia and Montenegro.

Fierce competition in economic and defence areas were the causes of growing nationalistic feelings. Aggressive nationalism and fierce economic competition gave rise to fear, confusion, insecurity and mutual hatred in whole of Europe.

Imperialism

The expansionist policies in the name of nationalism led to the rise of imperialism. Imperialism occurs when a strong nation takes over a weaker nation or region and dominates its economic, political and cultural life.

When a nation was conquered, it was claimed as a **colony**. These types of colonies were governed and administered by the imperial nation through its **puppet government**[1]. These colonies were exploited on the grounds of their natural resources, raw material, cheap labour, agricultural lands, trading ports, etc.

England and France built up a huge colonial empire in Asia and Africa by the end of the 19th century. The main focus of the British imperialism was to expand its trade by exploiting the resources of its colonies such as India, Sri Lanka, Myanmar, South Africa, Egypt, Caribbean Islands and many parts of Africa.

Germany, Italy, Russia and Japan worked to increase their influence and increase their colonies in the least developed countries like Asia and Africa.

Armament Race

The use of arms and spreading of new types of weapons by every nation made the situation unfavourable for peace. Every nation started research and development in defence sector in the name of self–defence. e.g.

- Germany acquired colonies in Africa and few islands in the Pacific Ocean. In order to protect these, Germany developed its naval power. In 1912, Germany manufactured the largest ship of that period namely **Imperator**. It also made the Kiel Canal deeper so that battleships could enter its waters.
- Britain also launched its new battleship. It resulted into the naval rivalry between Britain and Germany.
- France also entered this **armament**[2] race for its own safety.

This created an atmosphere of fear, insecurity and mutual hatred. The defence expenditure of every country increased massively during 1908 to 1914.

Division of Europe in Two Groups

In the early 20th century, there were two kinds of states in Europe

(i) **Single Nation-States** It include states like France, Holland and Germany. Their national identities were based on common language and tradition.

(ii) **Imperial States** It include states like the Austria-Hungarian Empire and Russian Empire. Hapsburg dynasty of Austria ruled over the Austria-Hungarian Empire. Its territory included Hungarian, Serb, Bosnian and Croat people who had different cultures and languages.

In order to secure their interests, these states entered into alliances. Formation of these alliances divided Europe into two groups which were

(i) **Triple Alliance** Germany, Austria–Hungary and Italy had formed Triple Alliance in 1882. Before it, there was Dual Alliance formed between Germany and Austria in 1879. Italy left the Alliance after the out break of the First World War but two other powers, i.e. Bulgaria and Ottoman Empire joined it. Then, they were known as **Central Powers.**

(ii) **Triple Entente** This include Russia, France and Britain. France established friendly relations with Russia and Britain after the death of Bismarck (German statesman and diplomat) and they together formed the Triple Entente in 1907 against the Triple Alliance.

The Russian Empire had a mixed population of Polish, Ukrainian, Mongol and Turkish which had different cultures. During the First World War, Canada, Australia, Italy, Japan and the United States also joined the Triple Entente. These were also known as **Allied Powers.**

Balkan Tension as a Cause of First World War

In the 19th century, a large part of the Balkans started disintegrating from the Ottoman Empire. One by one, nation broke away from its control and declared independence. All European powers, viz Russia, Germany, England, Austria were interested to extend their control on the Balkans.

Within the Austrian Empire, the most restive nationality was the Southern slavs. They wanted to join the independent kingdom of Serbia and the provinces of Bosnia-Herzegovina to form a United South Slav State. However, Austria annexed the provinces of Bosnia-Herzegovina.

Russia was the largest slav nation, thus it considered itself to be the protector of the Balkan slavs. It wanted the Bosnia-Herzegovina issue to be settled in international conference, but Germany supported Austria and Russia was forced to give in. This tension led to series of war and ultimately the First World War.

Sarajevo Crisis

This crisis was the immediate cause of the First World War. This crisis started when the Archduke or emperor of Austria, Francis Ferdinand was murdered along with his wife at the Bosnian capital of Sarajevo on 28th June, 1914.

1 **Puppet Government** A government that is appointed and whose affairs are directed by an outside authority.

2 **Armament** Rush to aquire arms and ammunitions.

This dual murder was planned by a secret society **Union of Death** or popularly known as **Black Hand**. The assassin Gavrilo Princep was a 19 years old Bosnian.

The group aimed at uniting all the South Slavs in Serbia. Thus, they killed the Prince who was the heir of Austria-Hungarian Empire.

On 23rd July, 1914, Austria sent an ultimatum to Serbia and made 11 demands. Some of these were

- Austria wanted the conspirators to be caught and handed over to the Austrian Government.
- It demanded that all anti–Austrian publications, meetings and educational institutions should be banned.
- All revolutionary movements aimed against Austria were to be suppressed.

Serbia agreed to fulfill most of the demands except those that would have led to the loss of its sovereignty.

As a result of this Austria declared war against Serbia on 28th July, 1914. Russia supported Serbia in the war. Thus, on 1st August, Germany declared war on Russia and on 3rd August on France.

Germany's plan for fighting France and Russia was called the **Schlieffen Plan**. Germany demanded free passage through Belgium to invade France. But Britain asked Germany to show respect for Belgian neutrality. Germany failed to respond to this so, Britain declared war on midnight of 4th August, 1914.

In this way all the major European powers i.e. Austria, Germany, Russia, France and Britain became involved in the war. Turkey and Bulgaria supported Germany in the war. Many other countries gradually became involved in the war, like Japan declared war against Germany as it wanted to capture German colonies in the far East.

Europe Before the First World War

Results of the First World War

The Allied powers were victorious in the First World War. The Treaty of Versailles, territorial arrangement and formation of League of Nations were the significant results of the First World War.

The Treaty of Versailles

On 28th June, 1919, the Treaty of Versailles was signed in Versailles in Paris between Allied powers and Germany. It was designed to prevent further war. The terms of the peace treaties were mainly decided by **Woodrow Wilson,** the then President of the United States, **Lloyd George,** the Prime Minister of Britain and **George Clemenceau** the then Prime Minister of France.

The main **terms** of the treaty were

- Germany was held responsible for the war and was to pay 33 billion dollars as war compensation to the Allies.
- The fertile and mineral rich land of Rhine valley was to be taken by Allied powers for 15 years.
- Germany was forced to give up her colonies and other acquired areas in Africa and Europe.
- Germany was made to return Alsace Lorraine to France, Eupen-et-Malmedy to Belgium and Schleswig to Denmark.
- The Saar valley (coal mines in German area) was given to France for 15 years. This area was governed by the League of Nations.
- Danzig became a Free port in the Polish territory. Most of the Polish territory held by Germany were returned to the new Republic of Poland.
- A restriction was forced on Germany to keep its military. It was allowed to keep only a small army of 1 lakh soldiers, 15,000 navy men and 24 ships. Airforce and Sabmarines were banned.
- Countries like Belgium, Poland, Czechoslovakia, Yugoslavia, Estonia, Latvia and Lithuania were declared as independent countries.
- Germany gave up parts of its pre-war territory to Denmark, Belgium, Poland, Czechoslovakia and France.
- Germany had give up its merchant ships to the Allied Powers as compensation. It had to supply huge quantity of coal to France, Italy and Belgium for 10 years.
- Germany lost its colonies which were in the Pacific and China regions to Japan. Though China was aligned with the Allied Powers in times of the First World War, but its German- occupied regions were given to Japan.

Territorial Rearrangements

The peace treaties led to rearrangement of territories and transformed the political map of the world, particularly Europe in the following ways

- Three ruling dynasties, *viz* the Romanov in Russia, the Hohenzollern in Germany and the Hapsburg in Austria–Hungary were destroyed.
- In Turkey, the Ottoman Empire came to an end.
- Czechoslovakia, Yugoslavia, Finland, Estonia, Latvia and Lithuania emerged as Independent states.
- Austria and Hungary became separate independent states in Europe. This led to the end of autocratic monarchial system and emergence of democracy in European states.
- Alsace- Lorraine was restored to France and Schleswig – Holstein was restored to Denmark.

Formation of League of Nations

The unexpected outcomes of the First World War convinced the world leaders to have such a mechanism that could prevent war. Thus, a world level institution was formed known as **League of Nations**. The League of Nations was established on 10th January, 1920 having headquarters at Geneva in Switzerland.

It had 42 members during its formation. The League had four permanent members i.e. Britain, France, Italy and Japan.

Germany and the Soviet Union were not allowed to become member of the League of Nations for many years due to guilty of war. Later, Germany joined it as permanent member in 1926. In 1935, it had 58 members.

Italy and Germany saw the rise of **dictatorships**[3] which disturbed the world peace once again and further, led to the weakening of the League of Nations. Unfortunately, the League came to an end on 20th April, 1946.

Aims and Objectives of League of Nations

- The primary goals of League of Nations included preventing wars through collective security and disarmament and settling international disputes through negotiations.
- As per its aim all the nations of the world were prohibited from entering into any secret alliances.

3 **Dictatorship** A political leadership in which a person possesses absolute power, or a form of government characterised by a single leader or group of leaders.

- The member-states were not supposed to maintain huge armies, warships and destructive armaments.
- All states were to respect each other's independence.
- The member-states were to take necessary action as directed by the League against any state which tried to disturb world peace and order.
- Other important objectives were proper labour conditions, just treatment of native inhabitants, prohibition of human and drug trafficking, arms trade, maintaining global health, protection of prisoners of war and minorities in Europe.

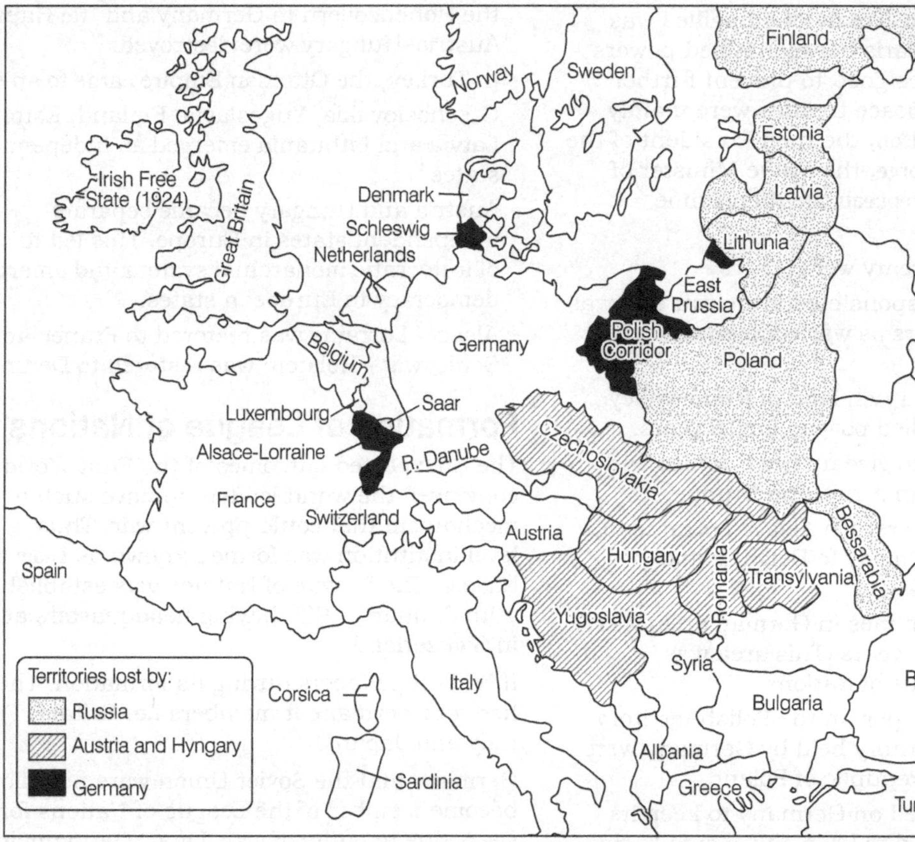

Europe After the First World War

Check Your LEARNING...

1. Name an Asian country that was involved in militant nationalism.
2. What were two blocs dividing Europe before the First World War?
3. When was the Treaty of Versailles signed?
4. Which two nations were formed from the Austria–Hungarian Empire after the Treaty of Versailles?

Time Line

Year	Important Events
1882	Triple Alliance between Germany, Austria-Hungary and Italy.
1907	Triple Entente between Britain, France and Russia.
1914	Beginning of the First World War.
1915	Italy deserted Triple Alliance and joined Triple Entente.
1916	Romania joined the First World War on the side of the Allied Powers.
6th April,	America declares war on Germany thereby joining the
1917	Allies.
1917	The Russian revolution known as 'October Revolution' or 'Bolshevik Revolution'. Exit of Russia.
1918	End of the First World War.
28th June, 1919	Signing of the Treaty of Versailles.
10th September,1919	Signing of the Treaty of Germany.
10th January, 1919	Formation of the League of Nations.
10th August, 1920	Signing of the League of Nations.

QUiCK Revision

- The First World War (1914-1918) was fought between the Allied Powers and the Central Powers.
- Aggressive/Narrow Nationalism followed by arms race was responsible for the war.
- The whole of Europe except some nations got divided into two hostile camps i.e. Triple Entente and Triple Alliance.
- Immediate cause was the murder of Austrian Prince Archduke Ferdinand in Sarajevo town.
- Austria attacked Serbia on 28th July, 1914 which culminated into the World War.
- In the First World War, on Allies side, there were Serbia, Russia, England, France, Japan, Italy, America, etc. On the Central Powers side, there were Germany, Austria, Turkey, Bulgaria, etc.
- Results of the First World War included the after effect of the Treaty of Versailles, Territorial rearrangement, the huge loss of life, costliest war, emergence of the USA as a world power, the rise of Nazi and Facist dictatorship, etc.
- After the First World War Germany was compelled to return Saar Ruhr to France and was forced to curtail her military power.
- Countries like Belgium, Poland, Czechoslovakia, Yugoslavia, became independent.
- League of Nations was formed on 10th January, 1920 with its headquarters at Geneva in Switzerland. All member states were asked to refer any international disputes to it.

Chapter Practice

Section-I

Multiple Choice Questions

1. Which country made the first declaration of war?
   (a) Germany (b) Serbia
   (c) Russia (d) Austria-Hungary

Ans. (d) Austria-Hungary

2. the International Court of Justice has....... judges. [2023]
   (a) 5 (b) 10
   (c) 12 (d) 15

Ans. (d) 15

3. In what city was Archduke Francis Ferdinand assassinated?
   (a) Zagreb (b) Sarajevo (c) Belgrade (d) Vienna

Ans. (b) Sarajevo

4. Germany's attack upon which country directly provoked Britain to go to war?
   (a) France (b) Russia
   (c) Belgium (d) Holland

Ans. (c) Belgium

5. Germany's plan for fighting France and Russia was called
   (a) the Hindenburg Plan (b) the Schlieffen Plan
   (c) Operation Barbarossa (d) None of these

Ans. (b) the Schlieffen Plan

6. Italy's action in the war was primarily against
   (a) Germany (b) Greece
   (c) Austria-Hungary (d) France

Ans. (c) Austria-Hungary

7. .... country joined the war on the side of the Allied Powers in 1916.
   (a) Bulgaria (b) Greece
   (c) Serbia (d) Romania

Ans. (d) Romania

8. On .... the United States declared war on Germany.
   (a) December 7, 1914 (b) April 6, 1917
   (c) January 29, 1918 (d) November 4, 1917

Ans. (b) April 6, 1917

9. The Treaty of Versailles mandated Germany to pay a war reparation of ....
   (a) 35 billion dollars
   (b) 40 billion dollars
   (c) 33 billion dollars
   (d) 50 million pounds

Ans. (c) 33 billion dollars

10. Complete the given analogy.
    Triple Alliance : Central Powers : : Triple Entente : ?
    (a) Allied Friends (b) Allied Powers
    (c) Supreme Powers (d) World Powers

Ans. (b) Allied Powers

11. Complete the given analogy.
    Black Hand : Bosnia : : Slavs : ?
    (a) Italy (b) Balkan State
    (c) Ottoman Empire (d) None of these

Ans. (b) Balkan State

12. Replace the underlined word to correct the statement.
    After declaring war, the United States was at war only with <u>Austria-Hungary</u>.
    (a) Australia (b) Germany
    (c) Japan (d) Italy

Ans. (b) Germany

13. Replace the underlined word to correct the statement.
    When a strong nation takes over a weaker nation and dominates its economic, political and cultural life it is known as <u>dictatorship</u>.
    (a) Secularism (b) Imperialism
    (c) Monarchy system (d) Democratic system

Ans. (b) Imperialism

14. Complete the following table.

Triple Alliance	Austria- Hungary
Triple Entente	?

   (a) Italy (b) Germany
   (c) Bulgaria (d) Ottoman Empire

Ans. (a) Italy

15. Which of the following joined the First World War taking the side of the Allied Powers in 1916?
    (i) Romania (ii) Serbia
    (iii) Greece (iv) USA
    Codes
    (a) Only (i) (b) Only (ii) (c) Only (iii) (d) All of these

Ans. (a) Only (i)

16. Which of the following nations was not part of the central powers?
    (i) Bulgaria (ii) Austria-Hungary
    (iii) Russia (iv) None of these
    Codes
    (a) Both (i) and (ii) (b) Only (iii)
    (c) Only (iv) (d) All of these

Ans. (b) Only (iii)

17. Match the following

	List I	List II
A.	1907	1. Italy deserted Triple Alliance and joined Triple Entente
B.	1915	2. Triple Entente between Britain, France and Russia
C.	1916	3. Russian Revolution
D.	1917	4. Romania joined the Allied Powers

Codes

	A	B	C	D		A	B	C	D
(a)	1	2	3	4	(b)	2	1	4	3
(c)	3	4	1	2	(d)	4	3	2	1

Ans. (b)

18. Match the following

	List I	List II
A.	1918	1. Signing of Treaty of Germany
B.	1919	2. Signing of League of Nations
C.	10th September, 1919	3. End of First World War
D.	1920	4. Treaty of Versailles

Codes

	A	B	C	D		A	B	C	D
(a)	1	2	3	4	(b)	2	1	4	3
(c)	3	4	1	2	(d)	4	3	2	1

Ans. (c)

Picture Based Question

19. Look at the picture given below and answer the questions that follow.

(i) The given map represents which of the following continents?
(a) Australia (b) Asia (c) Europe (d) Africa

Ans. (c) Europe

(ii) Alsace Lorraine was handed over to which of the following nations after the First World War?
(a) Russia (b) USA (c) France (d) Germany

Ans. (c) France

(iii) Which of the following nations became separate independent states in Europe after the First World War?
(a) Austria- Hungary (b) France- Germany
(c) Ottoman Empire and Russia (d) Serbia- Bosnia

Ans. (a) Austria- Hungary

(iv) After the War Schleswig-Holstein was restored to which of the following nations?
(a) Denmark (b) Germany
(c) USA (d) Russia

Ans. (a) Denmark

Passage Based Question

20. Read the passage given below and answer the questions that follow.

The Archduke or emperor of Austria Francis Ferdinand was murdered along with his wife at the Bosnian capital of Sarajevo on 28th June, 1914. This dual murder was planned by a terrorist outfit 'Union of Death' or popularly known as Black Hand. The assassin Gavrilo Princep was a 19 years old Bosnian. The group aimed at uniting all the South Slavs in Serbia. Thus, they killed the Prince who was the heir of Austria-Hungarian Empire. On 23rd July, 1914, Austria sent an ultimatum to Serbia and made 11 demands. Austria wanted the conspirators to be caught and handed over to the Austrian Government. It also demanded that all anti-Austrian publications, meetings institutions should be banned. All revolutionary movements aimed against Austria were to be suppressed. The German Government pressurised Austria for an immediate declaration of war. On 28th July, 1914 Austria declared war against Serbia. Russia began to mobilise her troops to defend Serbia. On 1st August Germany declared war on Russia and on 3rd August on France.

(i) First World War was a global war originating in Europe that lasted from ....
(a) 1914 to 1918 (b) 1924 to 1928
(c) 1933 to 1944 (d) None of these

Ans. (a) 1914 to 1918

(ii) Which among the following was not a part of Allied powers?
(a) Britain (b) France
(c) Russia (d) Hungary

Ans. (c) Russia

(iii) Which country was involved in the First World War?
(a) Belgium (b) Italy
(c) United Kingdom (d) All of these

Ans. (d) All of these

(iv) The First World War took place between which Groups?
(a) Triple Alliance and Super Powers
(b) Triple Entente and Group of Supremes
(c) Triple Alliance and Triple Entente
(d) All of the above

Ans. (c) Triple Alliance and Triple Entente

Section-II

Short Answer Questions

1. What was meant by the term 'imperialism', as a cause for First World War?

Ans. Imperialism occurs when a strong nation takes over a weaker nation or region and dominates its economic, political and cultural life. In 19th century, aggressive and fierce economic competition gave rise to fear, confusion, insecurity and mutual hatred in Europe. This was follwed by expansionist policies which led to rise of imperialism and further led to First World War.

2. How did militant nationalism added to the causes of the First World War?

Ans. Militant nationalism increased rivalry and competitiveness among nations. This resulted in gaining military strength by acquiring or developing more weapons. Thus, it added to the causes of the First World War.

3. Why military strength among nations grew in 19th century?

Ans. Military strength among nations grew because of its comparison with national prestige. National prestige was counted on its military strength, so each nation went after it.

4. How did the race for armaments divided Europe?

Ans. The race for armaments divide Europe in the following ways

- The use of arms and spending new weapons by every nation made the situation unfavourable for peace.
- Every nation started research and development in defence sector.
- Race for armaments fueled rivalry and competition.
- Race for arms created alliances that divided Europe.

5. Why major European nations were interested in creating colonies in least developed nation?

Ans. Major European nations were interested in creating colonies in least developed nations as they were in need of raw materials and natural resources and they can get them easily from the least developed nation.

6. How did the division of Europe resulted in the First World War?

Ans. Europe was divided into rival blocs known as 'Triple Alliance' and 'Triple Entente'. As these blocs showed rivalry by initiating arms race and capturing colonies of Asia and Africa, it resulted in the First World War.

7. Why was the place Sarajevo got highlighted?

Ans. The place Sarajevo was highlighted because here the Archduke or Emperor of Austria, Francis Ferdinand was murdered along with his wife on 28th June, 1914.

The dual murder was planned by a Secret Society, Union of Death popularly known as Black hand.

8. What was the immediate cause of the First World War? **[2013]**

Ans. The Sarajevo crisis was the immediate cause of the First World War. It was related to the assassination of the heir to throne of Austria, Archduke Francis Ferdinand and his wife on 28th June, 1914, in Sarajevo, the capital of Bosnia.

9. Name the countries of the Triple Alliance (1882). State the rival bloc that was formed. **[2020, 19]**

Ans. Triple Alliance was formed by Germany, Austria-Hungary and Italy.

The rival bloc was Triple Entente which was formed by Russia, France and Britain.

10. Why Italy attacked Germany?

Ans. When Bulgaria and Turkey joined Germany in the war, Italy broke the Triple Alliance and joined in Triple Entente and then attacked Germany after some time of neutrality.

11. State any two objections imposed by the Treaty of Versailles on the German military power. **[2019]**

Ans. The two objections imposed by the Treaty of Versailles on the German military power were

(i) German colonies were forcibly taken away and divided among the victors.
(ii) Germany was burdened with huge war indemnities and her military power also got reduced.

12. Mention any two terms of the Treaty of Versailles signed on 28th June, 1919. **[2014]**

Ans. The main terms of the Treaty of Versailles were as follows

(i) The Treaty declared Germany guilty of aggression.
(ii) The area of the Rhine valley was to be demilitarised and the German Territory West of Rhine was to be occupied by the Allied Troops for 15 years.

13. How much Germany have to pay as war reparation in the charge according to the Treaty of Versailles? **[2010]**

Ans. Germany was asked to pay to the victorious nations a war indemnity of 33 billion dollars for reparations, according to the Treaty of Versailles.

14. Mention any two important consequences of the First World War. [2009]

Ans. The two important consequences of the First World War were

(i) Establishment of the League of Nations.

(ii) Saar valley was returned to France from Germany for 15 years.

15. Why was the League of Nations established? [2019]

Ans. The unexpected outcomes of the First World War convinced the world leaders to have such a mechanism that could prevent war. Thus, League of Nations was established on 10th January, 1920 having headquarters at Geneva in Switzerland.

Structured Questions

1. There were many causes that culminated into the First World War. Explain the following questions.

(i) Militant/Aggressive Nationalism.

(ii) Formation of two blocs in Europe.

(iii) Expansionist policies of European nations.

(iv) Imperialism

Ans. (i) Refer to chapter theory page no. 200.

(ii) The formation of two blocs in Europe was an important cause of the First World War. With the greed of colonies in least developed parts of the world, the European nations started groupism and faction politics to gain foreign lands. Many nations were in need of raw materials and foreign markets. So, the nations started taking interest in the formation of blocs. Triple Alliance (Germany, Austria, Italy) and Triple Entente (Russia, France, Britain) were formed as two blocs which finally fought against each other in 1914.

(iii) All European nations started expansionist policies to gain grounds in foreign lands. They tried to grab colonies in least developed countries through political tactics (ideas). They made colonies in African and Asian nations for market and raw materials.

In the 19th century energised by the Industrial Revolution and under pressure from a rapidly growing population, Europe launched a new period of colonial expansion, inspired by the discovery of new markets. Necessity of new areas for the settlement of Europe's poor migrants and the desire to civilise the barbarian nations motivated Europeans to adopt expansionist policies.

(iv) Imperialism occurs when a strong nation takes over a weaker nation or region and dominates its economic, political and cultural life.

When a nation was conquered, it was claimed as a colony. These types of colonies were governed and administered by the imperial nation through its puppet (dependant) government. These colonies were exploited on the grounds of their natural resources, raw material, cheap labour, agricultural lands, trading ports.

2. The world witnessed a 'Great War' in the year between 1914-1918. In this context answer the following questions.

(i) Discuss any three reasons which led to the war in 1914.

(ii) Mention three clauses of the Treaty of Versailles.

(iii) Explain the territorial rearrangement happened after the Treaty of Versailles.

Ans. (i) Reasons for the war in 1914 were

(a) Militant nationalism which aggravated the mechanism of keeping armies and navies and also the establishment of a class of military and naval officers.

(b) Division of Europe into two hostile powers was equally responsible for the war.

(c) There was a mad race for armaments in the name of self-defence and preservation of place.

(ii) Three clauses of the Treaty of Versailles were

(a) Germany was to pay 33 billion dollars as a fine to the Allies.

(b) Its coal mines were ceded to France for 15 years.

(c) The Germany army and navy were dramatically reduced.

(iii) Refer to chapter theory page no. 203.

3. The war that broke out in 1914 was different from the previous wars in many ways. In this context, explain the following points briefly. [2015]

(i) Militant Nationalism as a cause of the war.

(ii) How did the Treaty of Versailles seek to cripple Germany's military strength?

(iii) What was the territorial rearrangement of Europe as a result of this war?

Ans. (i) Refer to chapter theory page no. 200.

(ii) The Treaty of Versailles seek to cripple Germany's strength through its terms which were

- The German army was disbanded. It was allowed to keep only 1 lakh soldiers. The airforce and submarines were also banned. Its navy was limited to 15,000 navy men and 24 ships.
- Germany had to pay a war indemnity of 33 billion dollars to the Allies, to be paid in yearly installments for 42 years. This heavy debt crippled Germany and made it impossible to maintain its military strength.

(iii) Refer to theory page no. 203.

4. The 1914 and 1939 Wars the engulfed almost the entire world, known as World Wars due to its unprecedented impact and damage. In this context, answer the following: **[2017]**

(i) Explain the immediate cause of the First World War.

(ii) Explain the consequences of the First World War.

(iii) Mention any four terms of the Treaty of Versailles which affected Germany after First World War.

Ans. (i) The immediate cause of the First World War was the Sarajevo Crisis. The crisis took place on 28th June, 1914, when the crown prince of Austria, Archduke Francis Ferdinand and his wife were assassinated at Sarajevo (Capital city of Bosnia). It was traced that the assassination was planned by the 'Black Hand' because they wanted to unite all Serbians under a single Serbian state. However, Austria sent them an ultimatum. The Serbian government refused to accept some of the demands, resulting in Austria declaring war against Serbia.

(ii) Following were the consequences of the First World War

- First World War cost the participating countries a lot of money. Germany and the Great Britain spent about 60% of the money, their economy produced. Countries had to raise taxes and borrow money from their citizens.
- First World War brought an end to four monarchies that were Czar Nicholas II of Russia, Kaiser Wilhelm of Germany, Emperor Charles of Austria and the Sultan of Ottoman Empire had to step down.
- First World War changed society completely. Birth rates went down because millions of young men died. Civilians lost their homes and fled to other countries.

(iii) Refer to chapter theory page no. 203.

5. With reference to the First World War, answer the following questions: **[Specimen Paper Semester-II 2021]**

(i) Name the two alliances formed in Europe during the First World War.

(ii) Name the two countries which came under dictatorship after the First World War. Name the dictators.

(iii) Explain the Sarajevo Crisis.

(iv) Mention any three ways in which the Treaty of Versailles benefitted France.

Ans (i) The two alliances formed in Europe during the First World War were

- **Triple Alliance** Germany, Austria-Hungary and Italy had formed Triple Alliance in 1882. Before it, there was Dual Alliance formed between Germany and Austria in 1879. Italy left the Alliance after the out break of the First World War but two other powers, i.e. Bulgaria and Ottoman Empire joined it. Then, they were known as Central Powers.
- **Triple Entente** This include Russia, France and Britain. France established friendly relations with Russia and Britain after the death of Bismarck and they together formed the Triple Entente in 1907 against the Triple Alliance. The Russian Empire had a mixed population of Polish, Ukrainian, Mongol and Turkish which had different cultures. During the First World War, Canada, Australia, Italy, Japan and the United States also joined the Triple Entente. These were also known as Allied Powers.

(ii) The two countries which came under dictatorship after the First World War are Italy and Germany.

The two dictators are Benito Mussolini (ruler of Italy) and Adolf Hitler (ruler of Germany).

(iii) Refer to chapter theory page no. 201-202.

(iv) Three ways through which the Treaty of Versailles benefited France were

- Through the Treaty of Versailles got France more colonies as all the German colonies were taken and given to Britain and France.
- As per the demand made by France, the Rhineland, the area between France and Germany was demilitarised. The Germany army could no longer get into this territory.
- On the security ground also. France was at the gaining end to some extent. It was because as per the treaty, German could only have 1,00,000 men in the army and six battleships. No submarines and air force was allowed.

Picture Based Questions

1. The murder of prince of Austria in Sarajevo brought the war near. Explain the following with reference to the picture given below.

(i) Describe the picture.

(ii) The Allies and the objection against alliances by Germany.

(iii) The Central powers

Ans. (i) The picture shows the murder of the Austrian Archduke Francis Ferdinand. The Austrian prince Archduke Francis Ferdinand was assassinated in the Sarajevo city capital of Bosnia on 28th June, 1914.

As a result of this event, Austria blamed Serbia and declared war on Serbia on 28th July, 1914. Serbia was supported by Russia.

(ii) The Allies were the bloc that was led by France, Serbia, Russia, England, Japan, Italy and America against the Central powers of Germany, Austria-Hungary, the Ottoman Empire, Bulgaria and their colonies. The Allies provided military support to any members whenever it was required.

Germany was afraid that Britain would attempt to destroy the German fleet which was posing a challenge to the British Navy. Thus, Germany objected strongly against the policy of alliances.

(iii) The Central powers were headed by Germany. Austria blamed Serbia for the death of its prince. When Austria attacked Serbia, Russia gave the support to Serbia.

The Central powers included Germany, Austria, Turkey and Bulgaria. All four were located between the Russian Empire in the East and France and US in the West. The alliances made between these four nations were a result of Germany's inability to gain power on the 'World Stage'.

2. Study the picture given below and answer the questions that follow.

(i) Why Germany and France fought?

(ii) Why England attacked Germany over the attack of Germany on Belgium?

(iii) How the 'Allies' fought?

Ans. (i) France fought the war as it wanted to get back the provinces of Alsace and Lorraine which were famous for its iron deposits.

Germany fought the war as it did not wanted to return Alsa and Lorraine to France.

Both the countries also wanted to make its hold on Morocco in Africa. Germany wanted Morocco as an independent state but France wanted to control it. Morocco crisis also became a reason for the tension between the two countries.

(ii) Germany came across Belgium and entered the Southern parts of France. The French army along with the British Army met the German forces in the Battle of Marne which was only 15 miles far off Paris. However, after it the German forces were unable to go.

On this pretext, Britain also waged war on Germany and first time used tanks to destroy German army.

(iii) The Allies were more powerful than the Central powers. Many of the countries of the Central powers bloc were not well equipped with modern weapons and huge naval warships.

Many nations of the Allies had large standing army with huge amount of arms. The Allied Powers launch a huge military offensive against the Central Powers.

All Allies' War aims changed over the course of the conflict in response to military and diplomatic developments and to pressure from the US to make them clear as a basis for negotiating peace.

Chapter Assessment

Section-I

Multiple Choice Questions

1. The geographical exploration in Africa was directly linked to
   (a) search for scientific information
   (b) imperial projects
   (c) vast land with rich resources
   (d) labour to work for plantations in America
2. During the First World War, which country signed the Peace Treaty (1917) with Germany?
   (a) England (b) USA (c) Russia (d) Austria
3. Which Treaty set up the League of Nations?
   (a) Versailles (b) Trianon
   (c) Sevres (d) St. Germaine

Short Questions

1. Name the two alliances which divided Europe into two hostile blocs.
2. How militant nationalism became a cause for the First World War?
3. What was the immediate cause of the First World War?
4. Why was the League of Nations formed?
5. What was the effect of Treaty of Versailles on Austria-Hungary?
6. Define armament race in the year 19th century.
7. Name five major powers that were involved in the First World War.
8. Which country declared war on Serbia and when?
9. Name any two Balkan countries.

Section-II

Structured Questions

1. With reference to the Treaty of Versailles, explain the following.
   (i) How much Germany had to pay?
   (ii) How was Germany destroyed after the war?
   (iii) What were the outcome of the Treaty of Versailles?
2. With reference to the First World War, answer the following questions.
   (i) The three causes of it.
   (ii) Changes in the political map of the world.
   (iii) Formation of the League of Nations and its objectives.
   (iv) Territorial rearrangement after the Treaty of Versailles.
3. The Sarajevo crisis became the immediate cause that initiated the First World War. In this context, answer the following.
   (i) Explain the Sarajevo crisis.
   (ii) Austria's reaction to the crisis.
   (iii) Reactionary steps taken by major European powers like Germany and Russia.
   (iv) Schlieffen Plan
4. The division of Europe created rivalry among the nations. In this context, explain the following.
   (i) The two power blocs in Europe before the First World War.
   (ii) Race for the armaments.
   (iii) Aggressive nationalism shown by European nations.

CHAPTER

10

Rise of Dictatorships: Fascism and Nazism

SYLLABUS

Rise of Dictatorships Causes for the rise of Fascism in Italy and the rise of Nazism in Germany. A comparative study of Mussolini's Fascist and Hitler's Nazi Ideologies.

A dictatorship is a form of government in which a single leader (dictator) or a small group of leaders have absolute executive power. The massive destruction brought by the First World War affected social, political and economic life of Europe. European countries suffered from unemployment, social unrest and different nationalists aspiration, etc. These led to emergence of parties with extreme ideologies like Socialist, Communist, Fascist and Nazi parties.

In Italy and Germany, leaders like Benito Mussolini and Adolf Hitler established dictatorship. The authoritarian rule in Italy was known as **Fascism** and in Germany, it was known as **Nazism**. Many intellectuals and people were not satisfied with the democratic set-up, so they started favouring the authoritarian rule.

Fascism

The word 'Fascism' derives from the Italian word *Fascio* which means union or league. Fascism means an anti-democratic type of government, where one man have all the powers of the state. It is compulsory for all to accept his policies and actions. Facism was established in Italy by **Benito Mussolini.**

Rise of Mussolini

Mussolini was born in a small town named Predappio in Italy. His father was a blacksmith, socialist and his mother was a catholic school teacher.

He was a leading member of the Italian Socialist Party. However, he was expelled from the Party due to his opposition of the neutral standpoint taken by the Socialist Party during First World War. He denounced the Party and later founded the Facist Movement in Italy.

Mussolini formed different groups in Italy namely **Fascios** i.e. groups or bands. This group used to organise violence against socialists and communists. They wore a black uniform and were known as **Black-Shirts**. The 'fasces' (a bundle of rods with a projecting axe blade) was their symbol.

These volunteers believed in violence and took over factories, municipalities and police stations. Later this group was organised into the 'Fascist Party'. Then onwards, he became anti-socialist and advocated dictatorship.

Benito Mussolini

Rise of Fascism in Italy

Italy was ruled by King Victor Emmanuel III at the beginning of the First World War. In 1919, democracy was introduced in Italy. There was total instability and disorder between 1919 to 1922 as no single party gained clear majority.

In October 1922, a conference of the Fascist Party was held at Naples. In this conference, Mussolini announced that if the demands of fascists were not fulfilled, he would attack Rome with his volunteers. Mussolini put forward the following demands

- Five members of the Fascist Party to be included in the Cabinet.
- New elections to be announced.
- The Government should act firmly on its foreign policy.
- Economic reforms to be implemented as early as possible.

However, the Italian Government did not show any interest towards these demands. Thus, Mussolini marched and captured Rome in October 1922.

Emperor Victor Emmanuel III who was a weak ruler of Italy, invited Mussolini and offered him to form a new Government. Mussolini accepted the offer and on 30th October, 1922 he became the Prime Minister of Italy. He established his one-party dictatorship i.e. Fascism in Italy. He was called **Duce** i.e. the Leader.

In 1945, Italy was defeated in the Second World War and Mussolini was executed which ended Fascism in Italy.

Causes Behind the Rise of Fascism in Italy

Fascism emerged as a national movement in Italy after First World War to provide solutions to the continuing problems of the time. The important causes for the rise of Fascism in Italy were

Dissatisfaction after the Treaty of Versailles

Italy joined the Allies in the First World War to gain territories of Turkey and Germany. However, according to the Treaty of Versailles Italy only gained Southern Tyrol, Trentino and coastal areas of Dalmatia and Albania. It could not get any port of German and Turkish Colonial empire.

Economy of Italy

First World War made Italy weak in economic field. The war disturbed the life of common people including the soldiers. Trade and business also got disturbed that led to large-scale unemployment. There was also shortage of foodgrains that led to price rise and war debts increased. All these conditions made the situation worst.

Inefficient Government

Between 1919 and 1922, more than 6 coalition governments were formed in Italy. The governments adopted different policies but could not find any solutions for unemployment, strikes and riots which took place during 1921-22. People wanted bold and efficient government which led to the birth of Fascism.

Threat of Communism

In Italy, the socialists included the Anarchists, the Communists and the Social Democrats. They created conditions which led to the rise of Fascism such as

- The communists inspired people with their revolutionary ideas.
- The peasants extorted the land of the landlords and the workmen organised strikes, broke machines and captured factories.
- Lawlessness and uncertainty spread everywhere.

People became tired of these things and they wanted a stable government which would establish peace and prosperity for them. This social scenario supported Mussolini and his Fascist Party.

Failure of League of Nations

The League of Nations was formed according to the Treaty of Versailles, to minimise the possibility of the future wars in Europe. However, it failed to achieve its aims. It failed to check the rise of dictatorships. Many nations were unhappy with this world organisation. For example,

- Many nations which were crushed and was asked to pay huge war **indemnity**[1], so never gave importance to the League of Nation.
- Russia did not participate in its formation.
- The victorious nations like Italy were not happy in redistribution of areas and colonies among each other.

1 **Indemnity** It means protection against damage or loss.

Class Conflicts

After the First World War, class conflict increased in many countries. The real issue in many countries of Europe was whether the control of government and economic systems would be given to aristocracies or less privileged majorities. During the First World War, the common man had been promised that he would be rewarded by greater attention to his economic needs but after the war, no promises were fulfilled.

Check Your LEARNING...

1. What do you mean by Facism ?
2. With what name the authoritarian rule was known in Germany?
3. Italy joined the Allies in the First World War to gain which territories?
4. Which title was assummed by Mussolini?

Nazism

Nazism is the ideology and practices associated with Adolf Hitler and the Nazi Party in Germany. Germany fought the First World War alongside the Austrian Empire and against the Allies (England, France and Russia). The Allies strengthened by the US entry in 1917 defeated Germany and the Central Powers in November 1918.

As a result of economic and psychological impacts due to this defeat the Germans revolted against their King Kaiser Wilhelm-II and forced him to resign. This gave the parliamentary parties an opportunity to recast German polity. The Constitution Assembly was formed to frame the new Constitution which was introduced on 10th August, 1919 at Weimar. It set up a democratic republic, Weimar Republic.

Rise of Hitler

Hitler was born in Austria in 1899. In the First World War, he joined the army and earned medal for bravery. In 1919, Germany's defeat and the humiliating Versailles Treaty made him join the German Worker's Party which was based in Munich.

He took over the organisation and renamed it as National Socialist German Workers Party, which was later known as **Nazi Party** (1920). The Nazi Party had its own army which was divided into two groups

(i) **First Group** The main function of the first group was to save its party members and to break up the meetings of the opposition parties. It used to wear brown shirts.

(ii) **Second Group** The main function of the second group was to save the Nazi party leaders. It used to wear black shirts.

Adolf Hitler

Rise of Nazism in Germany

When elections were held in 1932, no party gained majority in the Reichstag (Lower House of the Legislature) and Hitler also failed to get majority. As a result, there were around 21 Ministries headed by 12 Chancellors (Prime Ministers) between 1919 and 1933.

However, these coalition cabinets were unable to face the problems of the country. Weimar Republic was unable to pursue consistent policies of recovery or stop riots. Thus, people lost confidence in the democratic parliamentary system, which seemed to offer no solutions.

As a result, President of Germany, Hindenburg offered Chancellorship to Hitler. Hitler then formed his **first Nazi Government** on January 30th, 1933.

General Elections were again took place but in spite of the terror of the Nazis, the Nazi Party did not gain the majority in the Parliament. Then Hitler assumed dictatorial powers.

When President Hindenburg died, Hitler became President and Chancellor of Germany. He adopted the designation of **Fuhrer** i.e. the Leader. When Hitler became the Dictator of Germany, he abolished the Constitution.

Hitler sought lebensraum (living space) for the German people. Under his leadership and racially motivated ideology, the Nazi regime was responsible for the **genocide**[2] of at least 5.5 million Jews (Jewish people) and millions of other victims whom he and his followers thought as socially undersiable.

In 1945, Hitler committed suicide after the defeat of Germany in the Second World War by the Allied powers. This marked the end of Nazism in Germany.

2 **Genocide** It refers to the deliberate killing of a large group of people.

Autobiography of Hitler

Mein Kampf (My struggle) was the autobiography of Hitler which laid out Hitler's plan for transforming German society into one based on race. In this book, Hitler expressed the aims of the Nazi Movement such as

- To praise nationalism.
- To advocate the rule by a great leader from a single party.
- To hate internationalism, peace and democracy.
- To use force and brutality.
- To praise war.
- To uphold the racial supremacy of the Germans and to hate Jews.

Causes behind the Rise of Nazism in Germany

Treaty of Versailles

The signing of Treaty of Versailles was one of the main cause of rise of Nazism in the following ways

- The Weimar Republic signed this disgraceful treaty. According to this treaty, Germany was forced to gave large part of its important territory to France, Belgium, Poland and Denmark.
- Its overseas colonies were shared by the victorious nations.
- It had to paid reparations and war indemnity worth 33 billion dollars.
- Its army was minimised to one lakh only.

These conditions gave an opportunity to Hitler to encourage the people, disobey the signed treaty and rose to power.

Poor Economic Condition

With the end of the First World War, all nations involved in the war became weak economically. For example,

- Agricultural production, foreign investments, colonies, trade contracts, etc. were destroyed.
- The foreign nations raised tariffs on the entry of German goods.
- The rate of unemployment increased considerably.

These conditions also led to rise of Nazism and Hitler. Hitler promised to the industrialists that if they support him, he would stop communists and the nationalisation of industries.

He also exploited the people and assured them that if they adopted Nazi ideology, their economic hardships would come to an end and Germany would regain its lost glory.

Fear of Communism in Western Europe

After the Bolshevik or October Revolution in Russia (8th March, 1917 to 16th June, 1923), the influence of Communists increased in Germany as it captured a number of seats in the Reichstag. This gave Hitler a chance to persuade people that he would stop the communist influence in Germany.

Anti-Semitic Propaganda

Hitler adopted an **anti-semitic propaganda**[3] that the Jews had conspired with the Allies during the First World War. The Jews were dominant in the German economy. He persuaded the German people that he could free them from the exploitation at the hands of the Jews.

In Nazi Germany, Jews remained the worst sufferers. Jews had been stereotyped as killers of Christ and **usurers**[4]. Until medieval times, they were not allowed to own land. Their main occupations were trade and moneylending. Jews lived in separately marked areas called **ghettos**.

Hitler's hatred of Jews was based on **pseudoscientific**[5] theories of race, which could be solved only through their total elimination. From 1933 to 1938, the Nazis terrorised, pauperised and segregated the Jews.

Resurgence of Militant Nationalism

The Germans did not appreciate the functions of the democratic parliamentary system. They wanted their past prestige and glory back and felt that only a strong leader could do this. They also wanted to check the rising popularity of Communism in Germany. When Hitler promised to bring back this glory, they accepted him as their leader.

Absence of Strong Opposition

There was no strong opposition party in Germany that could rise against the Nazi Party. Thus, it became easy for the Nazi Party to gain popularity in Germany as it did not have to encounter any effective resistance against it.

Establishment of Volunteer Corps

As per the harsh terms of the Treaty of Versailles, the military force of Germany was reduced considerably. It rendered a large number of German soldiers unemployed. Hitler used this opportunity and established the Volunteer Corps. He influenced all these soldiers to join the Volunteer Corps, which served as the Nazi Party Army. The members of Volunteer Corps worked for safeguarding the interests of the Party.

---

3 **Anti-semitic Propaganda** It refers to discrimination against Jewish people.

4 **Usurers** A person who lends money at unreasonably high rates of interest.

5 **Pseudoscientific** It means something falsely or mistakenly claimed or regarded as being based on scientific method.

Personality of Hitler

Hitler's personality was also a cause for his rise in Germany. Hitler was a powerful orator. His passionate speech influenced the people. He promised to build a strong nation, undo the injustice of the Versailles Treaty and restore the dignity of the German people. He promised a secure future for youth, to eliminate all foreign influences and resist all foreign conspiracies against Germany.

Further, Nazi **propaganda**[6] projected Hitler as **Messiah**, who had arrived to rescue people from their distress. People attracted towards Hitler as their dignity and pride had been shattered and they were living in a time of acute economic and political crisis.

Comparative Study between the Ideology of Nazism and Fascism

- Fascism was in **vogue**[7] between 1919 and 1945, while Nazism became popular between 1933 to 1945.
- Fascism is a term that was originally referred to the fascists of Italy under Mussolini, while Nazism is an ideological concept of the Nazi party of Hitler.
- Fascism believes in the **Corporatism**[8] of all elements in the society to form an organic state, while Nazism emphasised on racism.
- Fascism gave more importance to the state, while Nazism considered **Aryanism**[9] as more important.

Similarity between the Ideologies of Fascism and Nazism

- Both favoured totalitarian rule.
- They both were against democratic political system.
- Both believed in state supremacy, which could suppress Fundamental Rights and individual freedom.
- Both wanted to uphold one party and one leader.
- Both believe in aggressive nationalism and imperialism.
- Both regarded war as an instrument of national interests.
- Both wanted to uphold intensely nationalistic, anti- communist and anti-democratic rule.

Similarity between the Causes of Fascism and Nazism

- Both had discontentment after the Treaty of Versailles.
- Both had hatred for democratic principles and preference for totalitarian system and one party rule.
- Both had fear of the spread of Communism in their country.
- Both the countries i.e. Italy and Germany, faced economic crisis like decline in production in agriculture and unemployment and trade.
- Both the countries were facing a situation of political instability and class conflict between the aristocrats and the common people.

Check Your LEARNING...

1. When did Hitler become the dictator of Germany?
2. Name the leader associated with Fascism and Nazism.
3. Which ideology believed in mass killings?
4. Why Hitler was considered as Messiah by German people?

Time Line

Year	Important Events
1919	Treaty of Versailles by Germany and Italy.
1920	Formation of the Nazi party in Germany.
1922	Mussolini became the Prime Minister of Italy.
1923	Hitler wrote his autobiography 'Mein Kampf'.
1932	The Nazi party failed to get majority.
1933	Hitler formed Nazi government.

6 **Propaganda** It means information which a political organisation publishes in order to influence people.

7 **Vogue** It refers to the prevailing fashion or style at a particular time.

8 **Corporatism** It means the control of a state or organisation by large interest groups.

9 **Aryanism** It is an ideology of racial supremacy which views the supposed Aryan race as a distinct and superior racial group which is entitled to rule the rest of humanity.

QUiCK Revision

- After the First World War dictatorship was established in Germany and Italy.
- Economic and social conditions of Italy helped the Fascists to grow.
- Fascism means the rule of a supreme leader.
- Benito Mussolini captured supreme power in Italy.
- The different causes of rise of Fascism were dissatisfaction after the Treaty of Versailles, economy of Italy, inefficient government, threat of communism and failure of the League of Nation.
- Germans faced humiliation at the hands of the Allies during the signing of the Treaty of Versailles.
- Huge war indemnity followed by reparation of war was levied upon Germany.
- Communism started gaining ground in Germany and there was fear of its spread in the whole of Europe. To stop communism, Hitler was chosen by the German and also by the foreign people.
- Hitler convinced the people that all problems were due to lack of powerful government at the top. He urged the people to support him to regain the lost glory of Germany.
- Hitler came to power in 1933. He combined the post of Chancellor and President.
- The causes behind the rise of Nazism were the affect of Treaty of Versailles, poor economic conditions, fear of communism, anti-semitic propaganda and personality of Hitler.
- Facism was a trend between 1919 to 1945, while Nazism became popular between 1933 to 1945.
- There were many similarities between the views of Hitler and Mussolini regarding their foreign policies like aggressive foreign policy, opposition to Britain and France, etc.
- Both the ideologies of Fascism and Nazism had similarities, *viz* both supported 'One party, One Leader', both ignored the importance of the League of Nations, both opposed Communism and adopted Imperialism and Capitalism, etc.

Chapter Practice

Section-I

Multiple Choice Questions

1. Which of the following was not a common ideology of the dictators? **[Specimen Paper Semester-II 2022]**
   (a) Faith in totalitarian rule
   (b) One party and One Leader
   (c) Faith in Communism
   (d) Aggressive Nationalism and Imperialism

Ans. (c) Faith in Communism

2. Many Italians supported the Fascist party because it
   (a) promised to improve the economy.
   (b) was the only political party.
   (c) pledged to unite Italy and Germany.
   (d) ended the influence of the Church.

Ans. (a) promised to improve the economy.

3. Under Mussolini's rule in Italy ....
   (a) a democracy was put in place.
   (b) the socialists came into power.
   (c) there was a one-party dictatorship.
   (d) free speech was encouraged.

Ans. (c) there was a one-party dictatorship.

4. The appeal of Mussolini's Fascist Government to Italians was that ....
   (a) the Fascists supported democratic ideals
   (b) the Fascists supported a classless society
   (c) the Fascists ended political feuding in government
   (d) the Fascists worked for socialist change

Ans. (c) the Fascists ended political feuding in government

5. Which of the following helped Adolf Hitler to gain power in Germany?
   (a) The promise of a new democracy
   (b) The great depression
   (c) Big business and labour
   (d) The support of the Weimar Government

Ans. (b) The great depression

6. Which of the following statements regarding Germany under Hitler is true?
   (a) Most Germans were barely affected by Nazism.
   (b) The Nazis controlled all aspects of German life.
   (c) The Nazis controlled the government but had little influence on other German institutions.
   (d) The Nazis kept firm control over Germany but followed moderate and tolerant policies.

Ans. (b) The Nazis controlled all aspects of German life.

7. 'One people, one state, one leader' was the policy of which of the following leaders.
   (a) Lenin (b) Stalin
   (c) Hitler (d) Mussolini

Ans. (c) Hitler

8. What measure did the Nazis take to reject the Treaty of Versailles?
   (a) They launched large public works projects.
   (b) They rearmed Germany.
   (c) They passed the Nuremberg Laws.
   (d) They established the Gestapo.

Ans. (b) They rearmed Germany.

9. Which of these leaders was an architect of the Non-Aligned Movement ? **[2023]**
   (a) Joseph Stalin (b) Abdel Nasser
   (c) Winston Churchill (d) Franklin Roosevelt

Ans. (b) Abdel Nasser

10. Complete the given analogy.
    Nazism : Germany : : Fascism: ?
    (a) Poland (b) Italy
    (c) France (d) USSR

Ans. (b) Italy

11. Complete the given analogy.
    Mussolini : ? : : Hitler : Germany
    (a) Poland (b) USSR (c) Japan (d) Italy

Ans. (d) Italy

12. Complete the given analogy.
    'Fuhrer': Hitler : : 'Duce' : ?
    (a) Stalin (b) Mussolini
    (c) Hindenburg (d) None of these

Ans. (b) Mussolini

13. Replace the underlined word to correct the statement.
    In the First World War the Allied Powers was consisted England, France and <u>Germany</u>.
    (a) Russia (b) Belgium
    (c) Austria-Hungary (d) Bulgaria

Ans. (a) Russia

14. Replace the underlined word to correct the statement.
    'Facsio' is an Italian word which means <u>'Strong Army'</u>.
    (a) A bundle of lay (b) Union of League
    (c) Democratic Republic (d) Both (a) and (b)

Ans. (d) Both (a) and (b)

15. Complete the following table.

Hitler joined German's Worker Party	1919
Hitler formed Nazi Party	?

(a) 1920 (b) 1921 (c) 1922 (d) 1923

Ans. (a) 1920

16. Which of the following was a method of the Nazi party?

(i) War (ii) Boycott
(iii) Passive Resistance (iv) Revivalism

Codes
(a) Only (i) (b) Only (ii)
(c) Only (iii) (d) All of these

Ans. (a) Only (i)

17. Which of the following was not a major cause of the fall of the Weimar Republic?

(i) The inability of successive Chancellors to gain a majority in the Reichstag.
(ii) Economic woes attributed to the great depression.
(iii) The failure of coalition governments to control the Nazi Party.
(iv) President Hindenburg's repeated use of the "rule by decree" powers.

Codes
(a) (i) and (ii) (b) (iii) (c) (iv) (d) All of these

Ans. (b) (iii)

18. Match the following.

	List I	List II
A.	1914	1. Beginning of the First World War
B.	1917	2. USA joined the First World War
C.	1918	3. End of First World War
D.	1919	4. Treaty of Versailles

Codes

	A	B	C	D
(a)	1	2	3	4
(b)	2	1	4	3
(c)	3	4	1	2
(d)	4	3	2	1

Ans. (a)

19. Match the following.

	List I	List II
A.	1945	1. Mussolini became the Prime Minister
B.	1922	2. The Second World War ended
C.	1933	3. Beginning of Second World War
D.	1939	4. Hitler formed Nazi Government

Codes

	A	B	C	D
(a)	1	2	3	4
(b)	2	1	4	3
(c)	3	4	1	2
(d)	4	3	2	1

Ans. (b)

Picture Based Question

20. Look at the picture given below and answer the questions that follow.

(i) Identify the personality on the left side shown in the given picture.
(a) Lord Mountbatten (b) Hitler
(c) Mussolini (d) Lord Dalhousie

Ans. (c) Mussolini

(ii) He was responsible to form which party in Italy?
(a) Nazism (b) Fascist (c) Democratic (d) Communist

Ans. (b) Fascist

(iii) He formed different groups in Italy namely 'Fascios' which was also known as
(a) white shirts (b) black shirts
(c) brown shirts (d) blue shirts

Ans. (b) black shirts

(iv) Which of the following was the ideology of this personality?
(a) Totalitarian rule (b) Aggressive nationalism
(c) Hatred for communism (d) All of these

Ans. (d) All of these

Passage Based Questions

21. Read the passage given below and answer the questions that follow.

Mussolini formed different groups in Italy namely 'Fascios' i.e. groups or bands. This group used to organise violence against socialists and communists. They wore a black uniform and, were known as 'Black-Shirts'. The 'fasces' (a bundle of rods with a projecting axe blade) was their symbol. These volunteers believed in violence and took over factories, municipalities and police stations. Later this group was organised into the 'Fascist Party'.

A conference of the Fascist Party was held at Naples in October 1922. In this conference, he announced that if the demands of fascists were not fulfilled, he would attack Rome with his volunteers.

(i) Mussolini participated in which of the following wars?
(a) Napoleonic Wars (b) First World War
(c) Second World War (d) Both (b) and (c)

Ans. (d) Both (b) and (c)

(ii) Who offered Mussolini to be the Prime Minister of Italy?
(a) Victor Emmanuel II (b) Victor Emmanuel III
(c) Felipe VI (d) Elizabeth II

Ans. (b) Victor Emmanuel III

(iii) Mussolini was against which of the following ideologies?
(a) Socialist (b) Communist
(c) Democratic (d) All of these

Ans. (d) All of these

(iv) In which conference Mussolini asked the Italian Government to fulfill the demands of the Fascist Party?
(a) Rome (b) Milan (c) Naples (d) Genoa

Ans. (c) Naples

22. Read the passage given below and answer the questions that follow.

The Nazi Party had its own army which was divided into two groups. The main function of the First group was to save its party members and to break up the meetings of the opposition parties.

It used to wear brown shirts. On the other hand, the second group used to wear black shirts and its main function was to save the Nazi party leaders.

When elections were held in 1932, Hitler failed to get majority in the Reichstag. Later on, President Hindenburg offered Chancellorship to Hitler. He then formed his first Nazi government on January 30th, 1933. General Elections were again took place but in spite of the terror of the Nazis, the Nazi Party did not gain the majority in the Parliament. Then Hitler assumed dictatorial powers. When President Hindenburg died Hitler became President and Chancellor of Germany. He adopted the designation of 'Fuhrer' i.e. the Leader. When Hitler became the Dictator of Germany he abolished the Constitution.

After the defeat of Germany in the Second World War by the Allied powers, Hitler committed suicide in 1945. His death marked the end of Nazism in Germany.

(i) When did Hitler join German Worker's Party?
(a) 1918 (b) 1920 (c) 1919 (d) 1921

Ans. (c) 1919

(ii) Hitler was a member of which of the following parties?
(a) Social Reformers (b) Communist Group
(c) German Worker's Party (d) None of these

Ans. (c) German Worker's Party

(iii) Reichstag was associated with which of the following?
(a) Upper House of the Legislature
(b) Lower House of the Legislature
(c) Senate (d) White House

Ans. (b) Lower House of the Legislature

(iv) The book 'Mein Kampf' is the autobiography of
(a) Mussolini (b) Hitler
(c) Hindenburg (d) Victor Emmanuel II

Ans. (b) Hitler

Section-II

Short Questions

1. Name the two alliances formed in Europe before the beginning of the First World War. **[2023]**

Ans. In Europe, there were two kinds of states, first was single nation states like France, Holland and Germany, which were based on common languages and common traditions that they shared.

The other kind were the imperial states consisting Austria-Hungarian empire and the Russian empire, who spoke different languages and had different cultural traditions.

2. What is the meaning of 'Fascism'? **[2015]**

Ans. Fascism means an anti-democratic type of government, where one man have all the powers of the state. It is compulsory for all to accept his policies and actions.

3. State two underlying principles of Fascism. **[2011]**

Ans. The two underlying principles of Fascism were
(i) Opposition has no space in government.
(ii) It highlighted that 'Italy got nothing from the colonial dinner' at the Treaty of Versailles.

4. Why Fascism was prevalent in Italy?

Ans. Fascism was prevalent in Italy because it did not get its worth in the Treaty of Versailles and on the other hand, it was economically ruined after the losses in the war. There was total instability and disorders.

6. Give any two reasons for the rise of Fascism. **(2020)**

Ans. The reasons for the rise of Fascism were
(i) Italy joined the Allies in the First World War to gain territories of Turkey and Germany. However, according to the Treaty of Versailles Italy only gained Southern Tyrol, Trentino and coastal areas of Dalmatia and Albania. It could not get any port of German and Turkish Colonial empire.
(ii) First World War made Italy weak in economic field. The war ruined the life of common people, trade, business, etc.

7. Why was a conference held by Fascists at Naples?

Ans. A conference was held by Fascist at Naples because Mussolini announced that if the demands of the Facists were not fulfilled, they would attack Rome. In October, 1922, over 40,000 armed volunteer gathered in Naples.

8. What was the standpoint taken by the League of Nations towards Italy?

Ans. League of Nations declared Italy to be an aggressive nation and the member states agreed to impose restriction on economic sanction of Italy, except coal and oil.

9. Describe any two features of Fascism.

Ans. The two features of Fascism were

(i) Fascism was the supporter of one leader.

(ii) Fascism supported the expansionist and agressive nationalism.

10. List any two features of Nazism.

Ans. The two features of Nazism were

(i) The Nazists were the follower of Nazism and thought that the Aryans race was superior among all.

(ii) The Nazists followed its own policies and flouted openly the signed 'Treaty of Versailles'.

11. How was Nazi party formed?

Ans. The formation of Nazi party was led by the disintegration of Weimer Republic after the First World War. Adolf Hitler who fought in German army in 1919, joined a small group called 'The German Workers Party' based in Munich. Soon, he became its leader and changed its name to the Nationalist Socialist German Workers Party' or Nazi Party.

12. Mention the underlying similarities between Fascism and Nazism. **[2010]**

Or State the similarities between Nazism and Fascism. **[2018, 2007]**

Ans. Similarities between Nazism and Fascism were

(i) Both were anti-people and anti-democratic.

(ii) Both advocated aggressive nationalism and imperialism.

Structured Questions

1. 'Dictatorship established in two nations of Europe.' Explain the following questions.

(i) Failure of the League of Nations.

(ii) Treaty of Versailles (1919).

(iii) Economic crisis after the First World War.

(iv) Threat of Communism as a cause behind the Rise of Fascism in Italy.

Ans. (i) League of Nations was formed while signing the Treaty of Versailles in 1919. Many victorious nations signed it along with defeated ones. League of Nations did not had universal acceptance as Russia did not accept the treaty. Many clauses of the League of Nations were not practical and many unjust clauses became wound for some weak and victorious nations. Germany openly flouted the treaty and followed expansionist policies.

(ii) Treaty of Versailles (1919) was signed to 'make the world safe for democracy.' After the war, monarchical governments were abolished and republics were formed. This treaty was not based on justice as per Germany and Italy. Both nations thought that they were cheated due to the greed of the victorious nations. Many of the provisions were humiliating to Germany.

(iii) After the First World War, economics of many nations were badly hit in the following ways

- Whole Europe fell into the economic crisis. Germany came under the grip of unemployment and poverty.
- Inflation, price-rise, ruin of German trade and industry coupled with world depression created an economic disaster of the worst form in Germany.
- America's factories and countrysides were unharmed and performed better than ever.
- In the late 1920s, the German economy stabilised somewhat, but after the American stock market crash in 1929, the Great depression spread to Germany.
- From 1929 into the early 1930s, depression again wreaked havoc (to cause great damage) in German Society.

(iv) Refer to chapter theory page no. 214.

2. Fascism was the supporter of anti-democratic policies. Answer the following questions.

(i) Thinking of a Fascist

(ii) Attitude of Fascism towards democracy

(iii) Mussolini.

(iv) Economy of Italy as a cause behind the Rise of Fascism in Italy

Ans. (i) The thinking of Fascists were

- Many people who belived in Fascism were fascinated by their supreme leader.
- Many of them were eager to listen to the speeches of Mussolini. Their motto was "everything for the state, everything within the state and nothing outside the state."
- Many people were against the rising communism and so they gave their support openly so as to get rid of communistic influence.

(ii) Democracy was established in 1919 in Italy after the First World War and no one in Italy was happy due to the weak leadership. Italy was badly hit due to the First World War and unemployment and poor economy made them believe that they would be good only under strong leadership. Many Italians believed that if Fascists would rule they would control the capitalists, industrialists, labourers, landlords, peasants and artisans. Weak leaders were responsible for their conditions. Italy got nothing from the Versailles Treaty even if it emerged victorious.

(iii) Mussolini was born in a small town named Predappio in Italy. His father was a blacksmith, socialist and his mother was a catholic school teacher. He was a leading member of the Italian Socialist Party. However, he was expelled from the Party due to his opposition of the neutral standpoint taken by the Socialist Party during First World War. He denounced the Party and later founded the Facist Movement in Italy.

Mussolini formed different groups in Italy namely Fascios i.e. groups or bands. This group used to organise violence against socialists and communists.

(iv) Refer to chapter theory page no. 214.

3. 'Nazism was formed to regain the last glory of Germany.' Answer the following questions.
(i) Treaty of Versailles and its effect on Germany.
(ii) State the condition of post war Germany.
(iii) Weak Government in post war Germany.
(iv) The Resurgence of Militant Nationalism as a cause behind the Rise of Nazism in Germany.

Ans. (i) Treaty of Versailles proved very humiliating and was badly incorporated by the unjust terms and conditions. Its effects were
- According to this treaty, Germany was forced to gave large part of its important territory to France, Belgium, Poland and Denmark.
- Its overseas colonies were shared by the victorious nations.
- Reparations and war indemnity worth 33 billion dollars were fetched from it.
- Its army was minimised to one lakh only.

(ii) After the First World War, Germany was not allowed to trade with other foreign European nations. If some allowed, then high tariffs were levied upon it for the import of goods. Huge loss of men and money devastated Germany. Important mines of iron and coal was taken by other nations, so losses in natural resources made production of machine made goods quite impossible. Unemployment was emerging swiftly in Germany after the war.

(iii) Germany had to face many economic problems after the First World War. The Government of Germany, Kaiser William II could not able to control the condition and was forced to resign. Then, the Constituent Assembly was formed on 19th January, 1919 to frame the Constitution, it was introduced on 10th August, 1919. However, this Constitution established a Democratic Republic in Germany, which faced massive problems and as a result of its failure gave birth to dictatorship or Nazism in Germany, under the leadership of Adolf Hitler from 1920s.

(iv) Refer to chapter theory page no. 216.

4. Germany and Italy was ruled by dictators in the post First World War. Explain the following questions.
(i) Economic reforms of Hitler.
(ii) Comparative study between Nazism and Fascism.
(iii) Similarity between the ideologies of Fascism and Nazism and the similarities between the causes of Fascism and Nazism.

Ans. (i) Hitler launched the First Five Plan to increase production and improve the economy.

Following steps taken in this regard were
- Factories were set up to provide work to the labourers.
- Industrial and agricultural production and trade were encouraged.
- Strikes were banned.
- A food corporation was created.
- Imports and exports were controlled to maintain favourable trade balance.

(ii) Refer to chapter theory page no. 217.
(iii) Refer to chapter theory page no. 217.

Picture Based Questions

1. Answer the questions that follow based on the picture given below. **[2016]**

(i) Identify the leader in the picture. Give two examples to state that the leader followed an expansoinist policy.
(ii) State three factors that led to the rise of Fascism.
(iii) State four similarities between the ideologies of Nazism and Fascism.

Ans. (i) Benito Mussolini has been depicted in the given picture.
Two examples to state that the leader followed an expansionist policy are
- He used to say 'Italy must expand or Perish'. He regained the Island of Rhodes, Dodecanese as well as the city of Fiume.
- He turned Albania into a protectorate of Italy and entered into commercial and diplomatic treaties with France and Russia. He captured Abyssinia in 1936.

(ii) Refer to chapter theory page no. 214.
(iii) Refer to chapter theory page no. 217.

2. Study the picture given below and answer the following questions. **[2013]**

(i) Identify the leader in the picture.
(ii) Study any four factors that led to the rise of dictatorships in Germany.
(iii) Why did he invaded Poland?

Ans. (i) The above picture belongs to Adolf Hitler, the German Chancellor. He became the Chancellor of Germany in 1933. Acquiring power, he set out to dismantle the structures of democratic rule. The Nazi party controlled Germany under the leadership of Hitler and adopted the slogan 'One person, one empire and one leader'.

(ii) Four factors that led to the rise of dictatorship in Germany were

(a) Treaty of Versailles was unjust to Germany. Many leaders at the time of signing the treaty also believed this.

(b) Political instability followed by poor economic condition during the post war period, made the citizens ready for a rule of dictators.

(c) Threat of communism, the rising power of the communism in Russia made every nation of Europe fearful.

(d) Hitler promised to restore the dignity of the German people and create opportunities for the unemployed people in Germany.

(iii) Hitler invaded Poland because he thought the Polish state is persecuting those Germans, who lived in Poland. The series of border violations proved that the polish no longer were willing to respect the German frontier. Further the demand of Danzig for roadways to connect East Prussia with Germany was rejected by Poland. Poland made a military alliance with UK and France. All these factors agitated Hitler and he attacked Poland in August 1939.

Chapter Assessment

Section-I

Multiple Choice Questions

1. Which of the following crisis formed the background for the rise of Hitler in Germany?
   (a) Economic crisis (b) Political crisis
   (c) Crisis in the society (d) All of these
2. Which policy of Hitler was considered to be the primary cause of the Second World War?
   (a) Colonial Policy (b) Aggressive Foreign Policy
   (c) Democratic Policy
   (d) Non-payment of reparation amount
3. Who was assigned the task of economic recovery in Germany by Hitler?
   (a) Emperor Victor Emmanuel III (b) Hindenburg
   (c) Mussolini (d) Hjalmar Schacht
4. Germany was forced to cede its large and important territories to which of the following nations?
   (a) France (b) Belgium
   (c) Poland (d) All of these

Section-II

Short Questions

1. Name the two countries in Europe where dictatorship was established.
2. Why Germany faced economic problems due to Treaty of Versailles?
3. Who invited Mussolini in Italy to form a new government?
4. Where was Hitler born? Where he first formed his party?
5. State two dissimilarities between the Nazism and Fascism.
6. State two similarities between the Nazism and Fascism.
7. What was the result of the rise of the two dictators in Europe?

Structured Questions

1. Nazism and Fascism were against the rising support of communism. Explain the following questions.
   (i) Why European nations were against the communism and socialism?
   (ii) Why people of Italy and Germany liked supreme leader's rule?
   (iii) What were the political condition of both the nation?
   (iv) Why 'Anti-Semitic' propaganda was a prominent reason for the growth of Nazism in Germany?
2. Both Hitler and Mussolini gained power by violence. Explain the following questions.
   (i) March on Rome by Fascists.
   (ii) March on Berlin and its effects.
   (iii) Humiliating treaty terms and fear of communism in Western Europe.

CHAPTER

11

The Second World War

SYLLABUS

The Second World War Causes (Dissatisfaction with the Treaty of Versailles, Rise of Fascism and Nazism, Policy of Appeasement, Japanese invasion of China , Failure of League of Nations and Hitler's invasion of Poland).
- Brief mention of the attack on Pearl Harbour and bombing of Hiroshima and Nagasaki.
- Consequences (Defeat of Axis Powers, Formation of the United Nations and Cold War).

A lot of events throughout the world led to the beginning of Second World War. In various ways, Second World War was a direct result of the **turmoil**[1] left behind by First World War. The use of two atomic bombs in two cities of Japan and its disastrous effect proved Second World War more fatal than the First World War.

Causes Behind the Second World War

The Second World War started in 1939 and lasted upto 1945. The main causes of the Second World War were

Dissatisfaction with the Treaty of Versailles

The Treaty of Versailles was a peace treaty, which was signed at the end of the First World War. But it led to dissatisfaction among the countries, especially, Germany and Italy.

Germany had been forced to sign this treaty and had to pay heavy war compensation which it could never pay. All Germany colonies were forcibly taken away and divided into two parts for benefits of Poland. German military power was reduced. This humiliation gave rise to the spirit of revenge.

On the other hand, Italy was not favoured by Allies for the compensation of war. So, the Italians felt that they had won the war but lost the peace. The Treaty of Versailles was a dictated and imposed treaty by the victorious countries on the defeated countries. Thus, the frustrated people started turning towards **totalitarian**[2] ideas and **authoritarian**[3] regimes.

Rise of Fascism and Nazism

Fascism was a political ideology and mass movement that dominated many parts of Central, Southern and Eastern Europe. Italy joined the First World War from the side of the Allies to capture its wishful regions but got nothing out of the Treaty of Versailles. Dictatorship got established in Italy under the powerful leadership of **Benito Mussolini**.

Mussolini focussed on recovering the lost glory of the old Roman Empire. He joined the Anti-Comintern Pact in 1937 and formed a ten years alliance with Germany in 1939, to strength

1 **Turmoil** A state of great disturbance, confusion or uncertainity.
2 **Totalitarian** Relating to a system of government that is centralised and dictatorial.
3 **Authoritarian** Favouring complete obedience to authority as opposed to individual freedom.

their position. He introduced changes in administration and followed an aggressive policy. Under him, Italy captured Abyssinia and Albania. The League of Nations declared Italy aggressor and imposed economic sanctions on it but Italy did not respond and created enemity in the world.

Nazism was a political ideology of **Adolf Hitler**. In 1933, Hitler came into power. Soon in 1934, he was proclaimed the leader and became dictator of Germany. He violated the military clauses of the Treaty of Versailles and declared rearmament. He wanted to restore Germany's power by expanding his empire. He captured Austria in 1938 and then Czechoslovakia.

In this way, rise of both the Fascism and Nazism forced the countries of the world towards another World War.

Policy of Appeasement

It is a diplomatic policy of making political or material compromise with enemy power, in order to avoid conflict. Britain and France followed this policy and tried to appease Germany and Hitler. They hoped that by meeting Hitler's demand, he would be satisfied and there would not be any war. However, this only made Hitler bolder and gave him time to build up his army.

Japanese Invasion of China

Japan and China fought the First World War on the side of the Allies. After the war, Japan became ambitious and started developing its army. In 1931, Japan attacked over China, seized Manchuria and renamed it as Manchukuo, an independent state. China appealed to the League of Nations to declare sanctions against Japan but leading members of League i.e. Britain and France did not pay any attention to it.

Japan joined the Berlin-Rome Axis to form the Berlin-Rome-Tokyo Axis to further expand its territory. In 1933, Japan left the League of Nations and started occupying the British and American territories in China. These circumstances led to the situation of another world war.

Failure of the League of Nations

The League of Nations was created after the First World War to maintain peace in the world. However, the League suffered an initial failure when the USA did not joint the League.

The causes for the failure of the League were

- It was intended that all countries would be members of the League and that if there were disputes between countries, they could be settled by negotiation rather than by force. However, there was a lack of cooperation among the member-nations and they wanted to use the League for their own benefits. Even those who joined the League were not interested in the principle of collective security.
- In 1920, the League did nothing when Poland, with the support of France seized a part of Luthuania.
- In 1923, there was a threat of war between Italy and Greece. The dispute was settled by direct mediation of England and France because Italy refused the League's intervention.
- When Italy annexed Abyssinia, Japan annexed Manchuria and Germany annexed Austria and Czechoslovakia, the League of Nations could not take any action against them.
- In December, 1939, Soviet Union was declared guilty of aggression against Finland and expelled from the League of Nations.

As a result of these causes, member-nations lost their faith in the League and started preparing the war materials on a large scale.

Hitler's Invasion of Poland

The invasion of Poland by the Hitler led to the beginning of the Second World War. Hitler invaded Poland for the following reasons

- Under the Treaty of Versailles, Germany was divided into two parts. In order to give a land-route to Poland up to the sea, the port of Danzig was handed over to Poland.
- Danzig city was inhabited mainly by the Germans and by occupying Danzig corridor, German could connect with East Prussia.
- In August 1939, Germany signed a Non-Aggression Pact with Russia, but Poland was accused of committing atrocities against Germans who were living there.

Due to these reasons, Hitler attacked Poland on 1st September, 1939. As a result, France and Britain gave an ultimatum to Germany but in reaction, Germany attacked France. Thus, on 3rd September, 1939, Britain and France declared war against Germany and this started the Second World War.

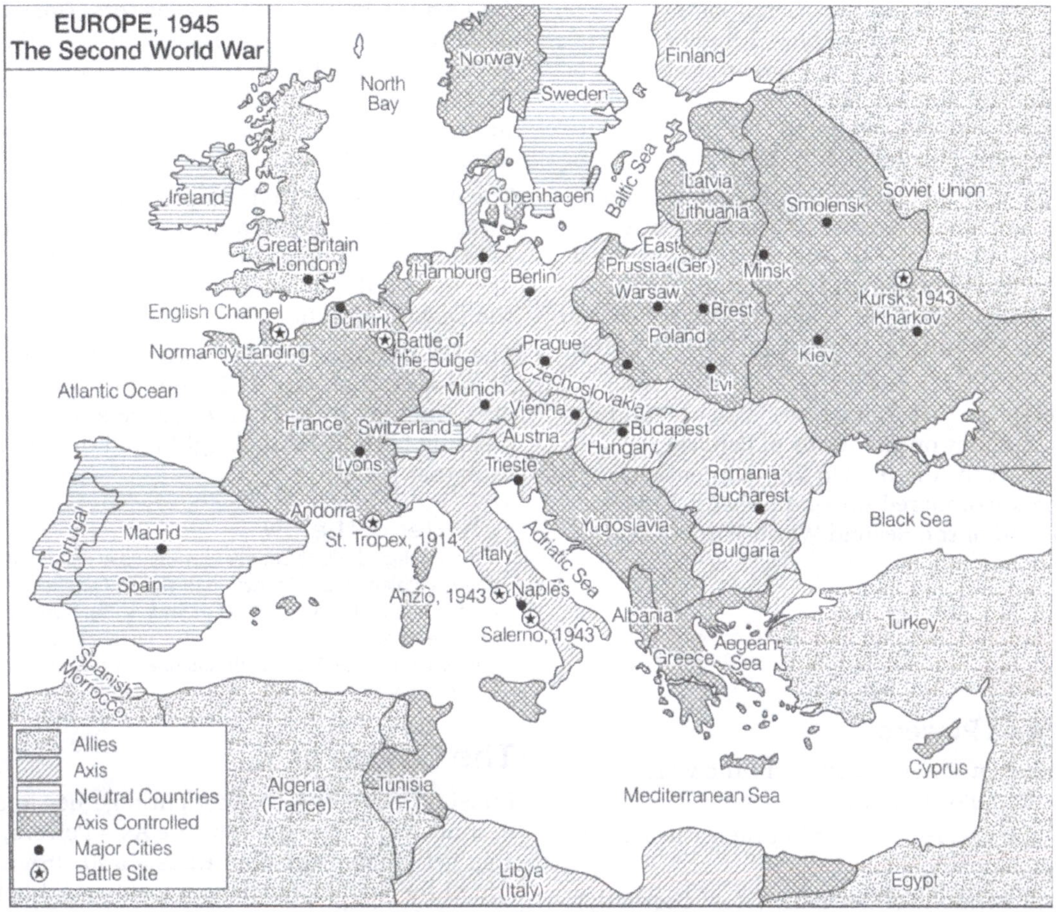

Map of the Europe during Second World War

Check Your LEARNING...

1. In 1938, Britain signed 'A Gentleman's Pact' with which country?
2. With what purpose, 'The League of Nations' was formed?
3. When did Japan attack on China?
4. In which year Hitler invaded Poland?

Major Events of the Second World War

Attack on Pearl Harbour

America followed a policy of strict neutrality during the Second World War. The Congress of America decided to gave armaments to Britain and Cliva, because their defence was significant for the defence of the United States.

Pearl Harbour (Hawaii) was a US naval base near Honolulu, Hawaii. On 7th December, 1941, Japan under the premiership of General Tojo, ordered a surprise aerial attack on the Pearl Harbour. Hundreds of Japanese fighter planes descended on the base and destroy nearly 20 American naval vessels, including 8 enormous battleships and over 300 airplanes. Around 3,700 people were killed.

The day after this assault, President Franklin D Roosevelt asked Congress to declare war on Japan. Thus, on 8th December, 1941 USA joined the war against Japan.

The Americans campaigned against Japan to free the islands in the South West Pacific. A number of Japanese ships were destroyed by the American Navy and Air force, but Japan was still firm and strong in Manchuria (China) and other places.

Bombings of Hiroshima and Nagasaki

In 1945, a special force called the **Kamikaze** (the suicide air corps) was formed by the Japanese in the Philippines. The young pilots of Japan moved a plane carrying explosives into the side or deck (floor of ship) of Americanship.

Japan had occupied Hong Kong, Philippines, Singapore, Myanmar, parts of new Guinea and Indonesia. Before the invasion of Japan, scientists of USA developed the most powerful weapon i.e. the 'Atom Bomb'. The first such bomb was detonated in a desert near New Mexico in July 1945.

On 26th July, 1945, Potsdam Conference was held, the Allied Power asked Japan to surrender, but Japan refused. Thus, on 6th August, 1945, the first atomic bomb was dropped on Hiroshima. Despite the terrible destruction, the Japanese still refused to surrender. As a result, on 9th August 1945, another bomb was dropped on Nagasaki.

After bombings on Hiroshima and Nagasaki, Japan offered to surrender on the terms of **Potsdam declaration**[4] on 10th August. On 2nd September, 1945, Japan surrendered unconditionally. This marked the end of the Second World War.

Consequences of the Second World War

Defeat of Axis Powers

After the defeat of the Axis Powers in the war, they had to face the following consequences

- Germany was divided into zones under the army of each of the Allied Powers.
- The Federal Republic of Germany (West Germany) was administered by UK, France and the USA with Bonn as the capital. It came under the Capitalist bloc.
- German Democratic Republic (East Germany) was administered by the Soviet Union with East Berlin as the capital. It came under the Communist bloc.
- Japan and Italy became very weak. American army occupy Japan in 1952. All the lands acquired or captured by Japan since 1895 were taken away.

Formation of the United Nations

The Second World War led to the formation of the United Nations (UN). The immense loss of man and money in the Second World War made every nation serious to prevent any future wars.

They did not want further involvement and emergences of such kinds of wars.

Consequently, the three big leaders, **Frank D Roosevelt** (US President), **Winston Churchill** (Prime Minister of Britain) and **Josef Stalin** (Premier of Russia) met at Yalta in Crimea in February, 1945 to discuss about international peace. This meeting further led to the formation of United Nations on 24th October, 1945.

The Allies made sure to improve the UN, especially by splitting the power among five major countries i.e. United Kingdom (Britain), USA, China, France and Russia (USSR) instead of just two or three as in the League of Nations.

The UN headquarters is located at New York, USA. At present, there are 193 members. Its basic objectives are international peace and security, creating faith in human rights and dignity of the humans.

Charter of the UN

In June 1945, the UN Charter was signed at San Francisco by 50 nations. Poland was 51st nation to sign in October, 1945. The charter was ratified by founder members (Big Five), who became its permanent members. The charter came into force on 24th October, 1945. So, 24th October, is celebrated as UN Day every year.

The Cold War

Russia (USSR) and USA fought together in the Second World War against the Axis Powers, but a split get created between Russia and USA after the end of the war. Both these countries did not engage in actual fight against each other but an extreme political tension developed between them.

As a result of this political tension, each of them adopted policies to strengthen themselves and weaken the other with armed conflict. This was known as the Cold War. Some of the policies of the Cold War induded formation of the military alliances, arms race by gathering nuclear and conventional weapons, economic warfare and **proxy wars**[5].

Thus, two new powerful blocs emerged in the world which were

(i) **The Democratic and Capitalist Bloc** It is led by USA called Western bloc or American bloc. They believed in liberal democracy based on capitalism.This bloc comprised of Britain, France, Belgium, Italy, Canada, Australia, Netherlands, Greece, Pakistan, Turkey, etc.

4 **Potsdam Declaration** It was an ultimatum issued by the USA, UK and China on 26th July, 1945, calling for the unconditional surrender of Japan.

5 **Proxy War** A war fought between two smaller countries.

(ii) **The Communist Bloc** It is led by the USSR, called as Easter bloc or Soviet bloc. They believed in communism based on **Marxist theory**[6].

The Soviet bloc countries considered the Western style democracy as a force, means only for rich and upper middle class. The USSR was determined to maintain political, economic and military control of the countries in Eastern Europe which were liberated from Nazi control. Thus, by 1948 governments which were loyal to Moscow were established in Hungry, Poland, Bulgaria, Romania and Czechoslovakia.

These two blocs openly propagated against each other, but at a same time, they made every effort to avoid direct conflict.

Check Your LEARNING...

1. Mention any one consequence of the Second World War.
2. On which two Japanese cities, atom bomb were dropped during Second World War?
3. Why do we celebrate 24th October as UN Day every year?
4. The Cold War fought between which country?

Time Line

Year	Important Events
1922	Mussolini formed the government in Italy.
1933	Adolf Hitler came into power.
1939	Hitler invaded Poland.
1940	Hitler invaded Norway and Denmark.
1940	Paris captured by Germany.
1941	Japan attacked on Pearl Harbour.
1943	Italy surrendered.
1944	Rome was conquered.
1945	Atom bombed on Hiroshima and Nagasaki.
1945	United nations formed.

QUiCK Revision

- The Second World War was the direct result of the turmoil created by the First World War.
- Italy and Germany were unhappy over the unjust or humiliating treatments at the hands of the Allied Powers.
- The Treaty of Versailles was a peace treaty which signed at the end of the First World War. But it lead to gross dissatisfaction among the countries, especially Germany and Italy.
- Benito Mussolini formed dictatorship in Italy by the Fascists party's help.
- Mussolini focussed on recovering the lost glory of the old Roman Empire. He captured Abyssinia and Albania and changed the administrative policies of Italy.
- Adolf Hitler became the Chancellor of Germany in 1933 and grabbed the status of Supreme Leader.
- Appeasement policy was practiced by England and France to forgive Germany over small faults.
- League of Nations failed to address the problems of nations and each nations tried to solve disputes in their own way.
- When Italy annexed Abyssinia, Japan annexed Manchuria and Germany annexed Austria and Czechoslovakia, the League of Nations would not take any action against them.
- Japan followed expansion policy to grab Manchuria Island from China.
- Germany attacked Poland without proper ultimatum and in reply Britain and France attacked Germany. Therefore, the attack over Poland is considered as the start of the Second World War.
- In reply of air attack over Pearl Harbour America dropped first atomic bomb over Hiroshima.
- Second bomb was dropped in Nagasaki which made Japan surrender.
- United Nation was set-up for world peace in 24th October, 1945.
- Cold War began in the world between the USA and the USSR.

6 **Marxist Theory** It was given by Karl Marx based on the struggle between capitalists and the working class.

Chapter Practice

Section-I

Multiple Choice Questions

1. The First World War come to an end in ....

(a) 1915 (b) 1916
(c) 1917 (d) 1918

Ans. (d) 1918

2. In which year the World War II was started?

(a) 1935 (b) 1936
(c) 1937 (d) 1939

Ans. (d) 1939

3. The Treaty of Versailles mandated Germany to pay a war compensation of **[Specimen Paper Semester-II 2022]**

(a) 35 billion dollars (b) 40 billion dollars
(c) 33 billion dollars (d) 50 million pounds

Ans. (c) 33 billion dollars

4. Benito Mussolini was the leader of

(a) Italy (b) France
(c) Germany (d) USSR

Ans. (a) Italy

5. Who captured Abyssinia and Albania?

(a) Germany (b) Japan
(c) USSR (d) Italy

Ans. (d) Italy

6. Adolf Hitler came into power in ....

(a) 1923 (b) 1929 (c) 1933 (d) 1934

Ans. (c) 1933

7. In April, 1938, Britain signed 'A Gentleman's Pact' with ....

(a) Germany (b) USA
(c) USSR (d) Italy

Ans. (d) Italy

8. Which of the following is a cause of failure of the League of the Nations?

(a) Lack of cooperation among the member nations.
(b) Some countries wanted to use the League for their own benefits.
(c) There was threat of war between Italy and Greece.
(d) All of the above

Ans. (d) All of the above

9. In which year Potsdam Conference was held?

(a) 26th July, 1945 (b) 26th July, 1946
(c) 18th Aug, 1942 (d) 7th April, 1948

Ans. (a) 26th July, 1945

10. Complete the analogy.
Hiroshima : 6 Aug, 1945 : : Nagasaki : ?

(a) 7th August, 1945
(b) 8th August, 1945
(c) 9th August, 1945
(d) 10th August, 1945

Ans. (c) 9th August, 1945

11. Complete the analogy.
World War II started : 1939 : : World War II ended : ?

(a) 1942 (b) 1943
(c) 1944 (d) 1945

Ans. (d) 1945

12. Complete the analogy.
Democratic bloc : America : : Communist bloc : ?

(a) England (b) France
(c) Belgium (d) USSR

Ans. (d) USSR

13. Replace the underlined word to correct the statement?
On 3rd Sept, 1939, Britain and France declared war against <u>Japan</u> .

(a) Italy (b) Germany
(c) USSR (d) China

Ans. (b) Germany

14. Replace the underlined word to correct the statement.
<u>England</u> dropped the atom bomb on Hiroshima and Nagasaki.

(a) USA (b) USSR
(c) China (d) Germany

Ans. (a) USA

15. Complete the following table.

Japan attacked China	1931
Japan attacked Pearl Harbour	?

(a) 1935 (b) 1939
(c) 1940 (d) 1941

Ans. (d) 1941

16. Complete the following table.

Axis Power	German, Italy and ?
Allied Power	Britain, France, USA and USSR

(a) China
(b) Japan
(c) Hungary
(d) Austria

Ans. (b) Japan

17. Which of the following were the consequences faced by Axis Power?
(i) Germany was divided into two zones.
(ii) The federal Republic of Germany was administered by UK, France and USA.
(iii) Japan and Italy became very weak.

Codes
(a) Only (i) (b) Only (ii)
(c) Both (i) and (ii) (d) All of these

Ans. (d) All of these

18. Match the following.

	Column I		Column II
A.	1922	1.	Mussolini formed the Government in Italy
B.	1933	2.	Hitler came into power
C.	1939	3.	Hitler invaded Poland
D.	1940	4.	Paris captured by Germany

Codes

	A	B	C	D		A	B	C	D
(a)	1	2	3	4	(b)	4	3	2	1
(c)	3	1	4	2	(d)	2	4	1	3

Ans. (a)

19. Match the following.

	Column I		Column II
A.	1941	1.	United Nations was formed
B.	1943	2.	Rome was conquered
C.	1944	3.	Italy surrenderd
D.	1945	4.	Japan attacked on Pearl Harbour

Codes

	A	B	C	D		A	B	C	D
(a)	1	2	3	4	(b)	4	3	2	1
(c)	2	4	1	3	(d)	3	1	4	2

Ans. (b)

Picture Based Question

20. Look at the picture given below and answer the questions that follow.

(i) Identify the man in the given picture.
(a) Mussolini (b) Hitler
(c) Roosevolt (d) None of these

Ans. (b) Hitler

(ii) He became the Chancellor of Germany in
(a) 1933 (b) 1935
(c) 1936 (d) 1938

Ans. (a) 1933

(iii) During his reign, the Germany faced
(a) Germany was divided into two zones.
(b) Federal Republic of Germany was administered by other country.
(c) Germany lost their wealth, soldiers, etc.
(d) All of the above

Ans. (d) All of the above

(iv) He shoot himself because
(a) he lost the Second World War
(b) he violated the military clauses of the treaty of Versailles
(c) Both (a) and (b)
(d) he was unable to invade Poland.

Ans. (a) He lost the Second World War

Passage Based Questions

21. Read the passage given below and answer the questions that follow.

The Americans started their offensive against Japan to liberate the Islands in the South West Pacific. Long before the invasion, scientists were working on the most powerful weapon ever conceived–the 'Atom Bomb'. The first such bomb was detonated in a desert near New Mexico.

In 1945, days before the first bomb was dropped on Japan, American planes dropped leaflets warning about the deadly weapon and urging the Japanese people and the government to end the fighting. On 6th August, 1945, the first atomic bomb ever to be used on humans, was dropped on Hiroshima. Despite the terrible destruction, the Japanese still refused to surrender.

(i) America entered into war because
(a) Pearl Harbour was attacked.
(b) they wanted to support Germany.
(c) America wanted to shown her power.
(d) None of the above

Ans. (a) Pearl Harbour was attacked.

(ii) Who was the President of America when atom bomb was dropped on Japan?
(a) FD Roosevelt (b) Harry S Truman
(c) Warren Harding (d) Herbert Hoover

Ans. (a) FD Roosevelt

(iii) The second atom bomb was dropped on
(a) Nagasaki (b) Hiroshima
(c) Tokyo (d) None of these

Ans. (a) Nagasaki

(iv) Name the bomb which was dropped on Hiroshima.
(a) Little Boy (b) Fat Man
(c) Big Boy (d) Thin Boy

Ans. (a) Little Boy

22. Read the passage given below and answer the questions that follow.

Another consequence of the Second World War was the formation of the United Nations (UN). After the First World War, the League of Nations was formed but it had several problems which led to Second World War. The immense loss of man and money made every nation serious to prevent any future wars. They did not want further involvement and emergences of such kinds of wars.

Consequently, the three big leaders, Frank D Roosevelt (US, President), Winston Churchill (Britain, Prime Minister) and Josef Stalin (Russia, Premier) met at Yalta in Crimea in February, 1945 to discuss about international peace. This meeting further led to the formation of United Nations on 24th October, 1945.

(i) The objective of United Nations was
(a) to maintain peace
(b) to create faith in human rights
(c) to maintain international security
(d) All of the above

Ans. (d) All of the above

(ii) UN day is celebrated every year on
(a) 27th April (b) 24th October
(c) 30th December (d) 1st January

Ans. (b) 24th October

(iii) The headquarters of the United Nations is located in
(a) Paris (b) London (c) Berlin (d) New York

Ans.(d) New York

(iv) How many member countries are there in UN?
(a) 191 (b) 192 (c) 193 (d) 194

Ans. (c) 193

Section-II

Short Questions

1. Which two countries were mainly dissatisfied over the Treaty of Versailles? Why Germany became aggressive after the Treaty of Versailles?

Ans. Germany and Italy were mainly dissatisfied over the Treaty of Versailles. Germany became aggressive due to the humiliation at the hands of the Allies. So, it started to get rid of this treaty.

2. State the factors of Policy of Appeasement. **[2011]**

Or State the significance of the Policy of Appeasement as a cause for the Second World War. **[2017]**

Ans. Policy of Appeasement is a diplomatic policy of making political or material compromise with enemy power in order to avoid conflict. Britain and France followed this policy and tried to appease Germany and Hitler. They hoped that by meeting Hitler's demand, he would be satisfied and there would not be any war.

3. State two reasons why Britain and France followed the appeasement towards Germany in 1930s. **[2007]**

Ans. Britain and France followed the appeasement towards Germany in 1930s because
(i) Britain and France felt that the Germany had a real cause of grievances and if their grievances were removed they would not disturb others.
(ii) Both wanted to check the communist ideology of Russia. So, that they appeased Germany by ignoring its imperialist attitude.

4. State two factors which were responsible for the failure of the League of Nations. **[2014]**

Ans. The two factors which were responsible for failure of this League were
(i) Lack of cooperation among the member-nations and they used League as grinding their own axis.
(ii) The League had no army to depend upon.

5. Give the reason as to why Japan invaded China? **[2017]**

Ans. Japan invaded China due to its ambitiousness. In 1931, Japan attacked over China and captured Manchuria. Japan also captured many nations of the South-East regions such as Malaya (British tin miner), Burma, Singapore, Philippines etc.

6. What was the immediate cause of the Second World War?

Ans. The invasion of Poland by Germany became the immediate cause of the Second World War. On 1st September, 1939, German troops attacked due to which Poland on 3rd September, Britain and France declared war on Germany.

7. What was the issue between Germany and Poland that was a cause of Second World War?

Ans. Following were the major issue between Poland and Germany that caused Second World War II
- Many Germans were living in Poland and Hitler wanted to free them by annexing Poland.
- Part of Danzig was demanded back by Germany but Poland refused to give which was taken after the First World War.

8. Name the countries that formed the Axis bloc, during the World War II. **[2018]**

Ans. Germany, Italy and Japan formed the Axis bloc, during the Second World War.

9. How did USA enter the Second World War and why?

Ans. America (USA) remained neutral even during the Second World War but on 7th December, 1941, Japan surprisingly attacked the Pearl Harbour of Hawaii Island through aircrafts. This made USA to join the war.

10. How did Germany surrendered to the Allies?

Ans. Germany conquered many nations, so that it attacked on Russia, but Hitler's forces were trapped due to cold weather of Russia. Germany fought on two fronts at same time, Britain and USA on one side and Russia on the other side. Seeing his defeat, Hitler committed suicide. Thus, the German forces surrendered to the Allies unconditionally on 7th May, 1945.

11. Why did America drop the atom bombs on the cities of Hiroshima and Nagasaki? [2006]

Ans. America dropped the atoms bomb on two cities of Japan, Hiroshima and Nagasaki because America was surprisingly attacked by Japan on Pearl Harbour, in the Pacific ocean on 7th December, 1941.

12. What made Japan surrender to the Allies in August, 1945? [2016]

Ans. Bombing at Hiroshima and Nagasaki, made Japan surrender to the Allies in August, 1945.

13. What was the positive effect of the Second World War?

Ans. The formation of United Nations is considered by many scholars to be the positive effect of the Second World War. It is a world organisation which works for maintaining world peace and also for world's cultural development.

14. Why United Nations was set-up?

Ans. United Nations was set-up to bring an end to the wars and to establish peace in the world as the world saw two World Wars and every nations lost more than they have gained out of it.

15. How did the United Nations form?

Ans. On 24th October, 1945, the United Nations came into existence when three big leaders of Allied Powers, Roosevelt, Churchill and Stalin met at Yalta in Crimea to discuss international peace.

16. How the world got divided again after the Second World War?

Ans. The world got divided after the Second World War into two blocs

(i) **The Democratic and Capitalist Bloc** It is led by USA called Western bloc or American bloc. They believed in liberal democracy based on capitalism.This bloc comprised of Britain, France, Belgium, Italy, Canada, Australia, Netherlands, Greece, Pakistan, Turkey, etc.

(ii) **The Communist Bloc** It is led by the USSR, called as Easter bloc or Soviet bloc. They believed in communism based on Marxist theory. The Soviet bloc countries considered the Western style democracy as a force, means only for rich and upper middle class.

17. How many divisions were faced by the Germany after defeat in the Second World War?

Ans. As a result of the defeat of Germany in the Second World War, Germany was divided into four zones and its capital Berlin was divided into four sectors. The sectors assigned to the British, American and French joined together to form the West Berlin thereby leaving the Eastern Germany all alone under Russia. Berlin lay deep influence in Eastern Germany but it fail in Russian occupation zone. So, Russian influence was much greater than the three Western power zones.

18. What is meant by the term Cold War? [2013]

Ans. Cold War is a war where the two groups fight over policies, their influences, ideas, types of public administration and their areas of influence. It is neither a war nor is a peaceful situation.

19. Why the Cold War emerged after the Second World War? Which two superpowers were the main opponents?

Ans. The Cold War emerged after the Second World War due to the differences in the policies of the countries. The USA and the USSR were the two opponents of the Cold War.

Structured Questions

1. Second World War took place in Europe after 20 years since the end of the First World War. Explain the following questions.
   (i) Humiliating Treaty of Versailles.
   (ii) Clash of Interests.
   (iii) Drawbacks in the League of Nations.
   (iv) Hitler's invasion of Poland.

Ans. (i) The Treaty of Versailles was a peace treaty, which was signed at the end of the First World War. But it led to dissatisfaction among the countries, especially, Germany and Italy. Germany had been forced to sign this treaty and had to pay heavy war compensation which it could never pay. All Germany colonies were forcibly taken away and divided into two parts for benefits of Poland. German military power was reduced. This humiliation gave rise to the spirit of revenge.

(ii) The clash of interests different nations was an important cause of the Second World War. For example, many nations followed aggressive nationalism and it became a race to win over foreign lands in Europe. Germany and Japan waged war to grab areas which were lost from them during the First World War. Japan attacked Manchuria and many cities fell into the hands of the Japanese.

(iii) League of Nations was set-up to make peace over the world. But it failed in its objective due to the following reasons

- The League lacked universal representation. The permanent members opposed decision which were against their own interests.
- It has no military force to act against any wrong actions, Germany and Italy started foreign aggression to regain the lost regions and the world followed it later.

(iv) Refer to chapter theory page no. 226.

2. Axis Powers and Allied Powers were the two blocs that were against each other in Europe. Explain the following.
(i) Hitler's invasion of Poland
(ii) Significance of Appeasement Policy
(iii) Japanese invasion of China and the Attack on the Pearl Harbour.

Ans. (i) Refer to chapter theory page no. 226.
(ii) Following were the significance of Appeasement Policy
- The Appeasement Policy caused Second World War because it allowed Hitler and the Nazis to build Germany's military power untill it was strong enough to fight a major war.
- Appeasement encourage Germany, making it think the Allies would never have the will to fight.
- It made Germany much more aggressive and encourages it to take the steps that eventually led to war.

(iii) Refer to chapter theory page no. 226 for Japanese invasion of China.
Pearl Harbour (Hawaii) was a US naval base near Honolulu, Hawaii. On 7th December, 1941, Japan under the premiership of General Tojo, ordered a surprise aerial attack on the Pearl Harbour. Hundreds of Japanese fighter planes descended on the base and destroy or damage nearly 20 American naval vessels, including 8 enormous battleships and over 300 airplanes. Around 3,700 people were killed.

3. State how each of the following factors were the causes of the Second World War. **[2011]**
(i) The Failure of the League of Nations.
(ii) The Aggressive Nationalism of Germany.
(iii) The Policy of Appeasement.

Ans. (i) Refer to chapter theory page no. 226.
(ii) The aggressive nationalism of Germany was one of main causes of the Second World War. Germany, under the Nazi's Government of Hitler wanted to revive its past glory and also to avenge the humiliating Treaty of Versailles. Hitler declared re-armament in 1936 and started regaining its lost territories on all frontiers.
He annexed Austria, occupied Rhineland and dismembered Czechoslovakia. He also set his eyes on Danzig and Poland. This aggressive policy of Germany was the main cause of the Second World War. When it attacked Poland to stop Germany, Britain and France declared a war on Germany.
(iii) Refer to chapter theory page no. 226.

4. With the surrender of Japan, the Second World War was finally over. The war had far reaching consequences, against this background, write short notes on
(i) Effect of Second World War on Japan.
(ii) The Division of Germany.
(iii) Formation of the United Nations.
(iv) Emergence of two new super powers of the world.

Ans. (i) The effects of Second World War on Japan were
- After Second World War, Japan became very weak and was decided to be governed by conquering forces.
- It was to be occupied by America till 1952 and after that Japan was to resume managing their own affairs.
- The Emperor Hirohito was left on the throne, though some of its power was retained by the Japanese Parliament.
- Japan was reduced to the pre-1895 territorial extent and the lands acquired after that were taken away from her.

(ii) The last German armies surrendered on 7th May, 1945 and the next day was celebrated as the day of celebration of victory. The victorious nations divided Germany into two zones each under the army of allied nations. These zones were
(a) Federal Republic of Germany (FRG), commonly known as the West Germany, was administered by United Kingdom, France and the USA with Bonn as the capital.
(b) German Democratic Republic (GDR), known as East Germany, was administered by the Soviet Union with East Berlin as the capital.

(iii) Refer to chapter theory page no. 228.
(iv) After the Second World War British and France declined as superpowers and two new powerful blocs emerged which were
(a) **The Democratic and Capitalist Bloc** It is led by USA called Western bloc or American bloc. They believed in liberal democracy based on capitalism. This bloc comprised–Britain, France, Belgium, Italy, Canada, Australia, Netherlands, Greece, Pakistan and Turkey, etc.
The Communist Bloc It is led by the USSR, called as Easter bloc or Soviet bloc. They believed in communism based on Marxist theory. The Soviet bloc countries considered the Western style democracy as a force, means only for rich and upper middle class.

5. With reference to the causes of the Second World War, answer the following questions. **[2014]**
(i) Explain how the ideologies of Fascism and Nazism led to the Second World War.
(ii) How did the Japanese invasion on China create conditions for the outbreak of the war?
(iii) Explain the consequences of the Second World War with reference to the formation of the United Nations.

Ans. (i) The ideologies of Fascism and Nazism led to Second World War in following ways
- Fascism and Nazism developed out of a general crisis of the European Political System connected with the rise of the mass participation.

- The Fascist-Nazi Political revolutions stemmed from profound anxieties about the disintegration of the social order and of the national or racial unit.
- Both the ideologies believed in the leadership of one party, one man.

(ii) The Japanese invasion on China created conditions for the outbreak of the war in the following ways

- Japan's ambition to control far East was one of the causes of the war. It intervened in Manchuria in 1931 and in spite of the League's opposition, occupied it. This marked the beginning of undeclared war on China by Japan.
- Japan joined Berlin-Rome Axis to form the Berlin-Rome-Tokyo Axis to further its policy of expansion. In 1933, it left the League and started occupying the British and American properties in China.

(iii) Refer to chapter theory page no. 228.

Picture Based Questions

1. Study the map given below carefully and answer the following questions.

(i) Why Germany faced strong fight in Western front?

(ii) Why Russia was attacked by Germany?

(iii) What was the immediate cause of the Second World War?

Ans. (i) Germany and France were old rivals as they had also fought against each other in the First World War. Many nations were against the harsh terms of the Treaty of Versailles and no one came against Germany except France and Britain. So, Germany faced strong fight from France and Britain on the Western side of itself during the war.

(ii) Russia was attacked by Germany because

- In August 1939, Germany signed a Non-Aggression Pact with Russia, but Poland was accused of committing atrocities against German who were living there.
- It is considered that Hitler wanted to win whole of Europe and in its mission he attacked Russia.
- In August 1939, Germany signed a Non-Aggression Pact with Russia but Poland was accused of committing atrocities against German who were living there.

(iii) The immediate cause of the Second World War was the invasion of Poland. Hitler invaded Poland for the following reasons

- Under the Treaty of Versailles, Germany was divided into two parts. In order to give a land-route to Poland up to the sea, the port of Danzig was handed over to Poland.
- Danzig city was inhabited mainly by the Germans and by occupying Dansig corridor, German could connect with East Prussia.
- In August 1939, Germany signed a Non-Aggression Pact with Russia, but Poland was accused of committing atrocities against German who were living there.

Chapter Assessment

Section-I

Multiple Choice Questions

1. United Nations was formed on .... 1945.
   (a) 23th April
   (b) 24th October
   (c) 30th December
   (d) 5th January
2. Replace the underlined word to correct statement
   Japan annexed Austria and Czechoslovakia.
   (a) Germany (b) France
   (c) USA (d) Britain
3. Complete the analogy.
   Hitler came to power : 1933 : : Hitler invaded Poland : ?
   (a) 1934 (b) 1935
   (c) 1936 (d) 1939

Section-II

Short Questions

1. How did Italy get disappointed with the signing of the Treaty of Versailles?
2. How did Germany react against the unjust terms of the Treaty of Versailles?
3. How dictatorship in Europe became a major cause of the Second World War?
4. How Germany transformed itself in Hitler's rule?
5. Why did Britain follow appeasement policy?
6. Why did Poland become important nation to win over by Germany?
7. How Germany got earlier Victory in the Second World War?
8. Why did Manchuria become famous?
9. What is the Cold War and how did it affect over world politics?
10. Why United Nations was set-up after the Second World War?
11. Why was Pearl Harbour was important and for whom?
12. Why was Japan attacked by America?

Structured Questions

1. Germany was badly hit by the Treaty of Versailles. Explain the following questions.
   (i) Why it is said that Germany was hit hard in Treaty of 1919?
   (ii) Why Italy went against the Allies?
   (iii) Why Japan followed imperialism?
   (iv) Why Japan attacked on China?
2. Attack on Poland by Germany is known as the immediate cause of the Second World War. Explain the following questions.
   (i) Effects of war on Germany.
   (ii) Effects of war over Japan.
   (iii) Use of weapons in this war and rise of USSR as a superpower.

CHAPTER 12

United Nations and its Major Agencies

SYLLABUS

United Nations
- The objectives of the UN
- The composition and functions of the General Assembly, the Security Council and the International Court of Justice

Major Agencies of the United Nations UNICEF, WHO and UNESCO-functions only

The two world wars happened between the period from 1914 to 1945. The Second World War was more disastrous and had more widespread destruction than that of the First World War. In order to check such destruction, the world leaders like US President Roosevelt and the British Prime Minister Winston Churchill realised the importance of peaceful existence for all nations. Thus, to avoid future war and to promote world peace, they realised that there should be a world organisation, more powerful than the League of Nations. This led to the formation of **United Nations.**

United Nations

United Nations was set-up on 24th October, 1945 at San Francisco when the Charter was ratified by 29 Nations including the five permanent members of the Security Council. The organisation works for the world peace and cultural and economic development for all. The headquarters of United Nations is situated at New York City in the USA.

Reasons for the Establishment of the United Nations

- Failure of the League of Nations to establish peace and prevent another World War', demanded the formation of a more powerful organisation.
- As the Second World War was the result of events associated with the First World War, people feared that the Second World War would similarly culminate into a Third World War.
- The division of the world into two power blocs led by the USA and USSR needed a transparent and balanced organisation for the resolution of issues.
- The massive use of weapons of mass destruction in the Second World War made it necessary to form an organisation which could keep a check on the use of such destructive weapons.

Objectives of the United Nations

The objectives of the United Nations have been outlined in the Preamble to the UN Charter. The objectives of the UN can be divided into four groups i.e. Security, Justice, Welfare and Human Rights.

The objectives of the United Nations are
- To maintain international peace and security.
- To take effective collective measures for the prevention and removal of threats to the peace.
- To bring about by peaceful means in conformity with the principles of justice and international law, adjustment or settlement of international disputes or situations which might lead to a breach of the peace.
- To develop friendly relations among nations, based on respect for the principle of equal rights and self-determination of people.
- To take other appropriate measures to strengthen universal peace.
- To achieve international co-operation in solving international problems of economic, social, cultural or humanitarian character.
- To promote and encourage respect for human rights and for fundamental freedoms for all, without any distinction in race, sex, language or religion.
- To be a centre for combining the actions of nations in the attainment of these common objectives.
- Apart from these, three new objectives are set by the UN which are disarm, decolonise and develop.

Flag and Official Language of the UN

The UN Flag was adopted on October 20th, 1947. The UN flag is light blue in colour and at its centre is the white coloured emblem of the UN. The UN emblem consists of a polar map of the world embraced by twin Olive branches.

The official languages of the UN are Arabic, Chinese, English, French, Russian and Spanish.The documents are however written only in the working languages that are English and French.

UN Emblem

Membership of the UN

All peace-loving nations who believe in the principles of the UN and abide by the UN charter can become the member of the UN. There were 50 members who took part in San Francisco Conference and approved the UN charter and became the founding members of the UN.

They were the original members. Other countries are admitted by the General Assembly upon the recommendation of the Security Council by a 2/3rd majority of votes. India was one of the 50 members which took part in San Francisco Conference. India was represented at this conference by Jawaharlal Nehru. India has sent troops to Africa and other parts of the world as a part of UN Peace-keeping Missions.

At present, 193 countries are the members of the UN. South Sudan became the last member of the UN in 2011.

Check Your LEARNING...

1. When and where does the UN was set-up?
2. How many countries are the member of the UN?
3. Mention any one objective of the UN.
4. In which year the flag of UN was adopted?

Composition and Functions of Important Organs of UN

The United Nations has 6 organs which are the General Assembly, the United Nations Security Council, the International Court of Justice, the Secretariat, the Trusteeship Council and the Economic and Social Council.

1. The General Assembly

It is one of the important organs of the United Nations. It is known as **the Parliament of the United Nations** because all the member nations are member of it and therefore, it represents all nations of the world.

All the members of the United Nations are the members of the General Assembly. There are five representatives of each member in the General Assembly, but each member has one vote.

Composition and Session

Each year, the regular session of the General Assembly begins on the third Tuesday in September and continues until the third week of December. At every new regular session, the assembly elects a new President, 21 Vice-Presidents and the Chairman of each of the 6 main committees of the General Assembly.

Special Sessions are organised at the request of the Security Counsellor or at the special request by a majority of members. Important decisions like the election of non-permanent members of the security council, admission or suspension of members, budgetary issues, etc are taken by 2/3rd majority while simple decisions are taken by a simple majority.

Powers and Functions

- It consider and make recommendations on the general principles of co-operation, for maintaining international peace and security including disarmament.
- It discuss any question relating to international peace and security make recommendations on it, except where a dispute or situation is currently being discussed by the Security Council.
- It discuss and make recommendations on any questions within the scope of the charter or affecting the powers and functions of any organ of the United Nations.
- It initiate studies and make recommendations on the following
  - to promote international political co-operation .
  - the development and **codification**[1] of international law the realisation of human rights and fundamental freedoms.
  - international collaboration in the economic, social, humanitarian, cultural, educational and health fields.
- It make recommendations for the peaceful settlement of any situation that might impair friendly relations among nations.
- It receive and consider reports from the Security Council and other United Nations organs.
- It consider and approve the United Nations budget and establish the financial assessments of member states.
- It elect the members of other principal organs of the United Nations, namely; the non-permanent members of the Security Council, members of the Economic and Social Council and Judges of the International Court of Justice. It also elects members to its subsidiary organs and to the executive boards and governing councils of the United Nations agencies, funds and programmes.
- It appoints the Secretary-General on the recommendation of the Security Council.
- According to the 'Uniting for Peace' resolution adopted in November 1950 by the General Assembly, it may take action if the Security Council fails to act in a case which may led to a threat to the International peace.

2. United Nations Security Council (UNSC)

It is the executive body of the United Nations. It was founded on 24th October, 1945. Its headquarters is located at New York, USA. A representative of each member of the Security Council has to remain in the headquarters of the UN.

Composition

It consists of 15 members. It has 5 permanent members i.e. China, France, Russia, Britain and the United States of America and 10 non-permanent members i.e. 5 members from Afro-Asian nations, 2 members from Latin American nations, 2 members from West European nation and 1 member from East European nation.

These non-permanent members get elected by a 2/3rd majority for a 2 years term by the General Assembly. Any member who is retiring, is not eligible to be re-elected.

Veto power can be exercised only by permanent members and any decision is taken by the affirmative votes of all permanent members.

Veto Power

Each of the 5 permanent members of the Security Council has the power to veto a decision. The negative vote of a permanent member is called a veto. By application of this right, a permanent member may reject any decision at the Security Council. The Council is unable to act further if any of the permanent member uses the veto power. However, if a member refused to vote, then it will not be counted as a negative vote.

Powers and Functions

- It maintain international peace and security in accordance with the principles and purposes of the United Nations.
- It investigate any dispute or situation which might lead to international friction.
- It recommend methods of adjusting such disputes or the terms of settlement.
- It formulate plans for the establishment of a system to regulate armaments.
- It determine the existence of a threat to the peace or act of aggression and recommend the action that should be taken.
- It call on members to apply economic sanctions and other measures not involving the use of force to prevent or stop aggression.
- It take military action against an aggressor.
- It recommend the admission of new members.
- It exercise the trusteeship functions of the United Nations in **strategic areas**[2].

1 **Codification** The action or process of arranging laws or rules according to a system or plan.

2 **Strategic areas** Area of importance of any nation in respect to others.

- It recommend to the General Assembly for the appointment of the Secretary-General. Along with the General Assembly, it elect the Judges of the International Court of Justice.

3. The International Court of Justice

It is the principal judicial organ of the UN. It was established in June 1945 by the Charter of the UN and began to work in April 1946.

Its headquarters is located at the Hague (Netherlands). It is the only organ of the UN among the 6 organs which is not located in New York in USA. Its official languages are English and French.

Composition and Qualifications

The court comprises of 15 Judges. They are elected for a term of 9 years by the UN General Assembly and Security Council sitting independently of each other. Elections are held every 3 years for 1/3rd of the seats. A retired Judge may be re-elected. The President and Vice-President of the court are elected for a term of 3 years.

The Judges must have the qualifications required in their respective countries for appointment to the highest judicial offices or should be a jurist of recognised competence in international law. Any Judge can be impeached only by unanimous votes of all the other Judges.

Powers and Functions

- The court decides cases according to the international treaties and conventions in force and is capable to take a case into consideration if the parties so involved agree for it.
- It settle the legal disputes submitted to it by the states in accordance with international law.
- It give advisory opinions on legal questions referred to it by authorised International agencies and organs.
- The advisory procedure of the court is open only to its 5 organs of the United Nations and 16 other authorised agencies of the UN family or affiliated organisation.
- The court plays a significant role in the codification of international laws.
- The court may recommend appropriate procedures/ methods of settlement during or at the end of the case.

4. The Secretariat

It was formed in 1945. It carries out the day-to-day work of the UN as mandated by the General Assembly and the other main organs. The Secretary General is the head of the Secretariat as well as the Chief Administrative Officer of the UN. Its headquarters is located at New York. Its main function is to supervise the activities of the UN.

5. The Trusteeship Council

It was established in 1945 to supervise the administration of trust territories as they transitioned from colonies to sovereign nations. The council suspended its activities in 1994, when Palau, the last among the 11 trust territories gained its independence. Its headquarters was located at New York.

6. The Economic and Social Council (ECOSOC)

It was formed on 26th June, 1945. It acts as a central forum for discussing international economic and social issues as well as for formulating policy recommendations. The Council plays a key role in fostering international cooperation for development. The Council has 54 members, elected by the General Assembly for term of 3 years. Its headquarters is located at New York, United States and Geneva, Switzerland.

Check Your LEARNING...

1. Name the important organs of the UN.
2. Which are the official languages of the International Court of Justice?
3. What is the term of a Judge of the International Court of Justice?
4. The ECOSOC has how many members?

Major Agencies of the UN

There are some specialised agencies that carry out various functions of UN. The major agencies of the UN are

The United Nations International Children's Emergency Fund (UNICEF)

It was created by the General Assembly during its first session in 1946, to help the emergency needs of the children. In 1950, its aim extended. Thus, its name also changed United Nations Children's Fund to provide long range benefits to the children of all developing countries. It is governed by a 36 members executive board. Its headquarters is located at New York.

To finance its projects the agency depends on voluntary contributions made by different governments, by private agencies, through sale of greeting cards and *via* other fund raising campaigns.

UNICEF was awarded the **Nobel Prize** for Peace in 1965 and the **Indira Gandhi Prize** for Peace in 1989.

UNICEF Logo

Functions of UNICEF

- It works for the protection of children in respect of their survival, health and well being. It also supports child-immunisation programmes.
- It provides funds for training the personnel, including health and sanitation workers, teachers and nutritionists, etc.
- It provides technical supplies, equipments and other aids to villages.
- It assists governments to plan, develop and extend community services.
- It provides help to children and mothers in case of emergencies.
- It makes efforts to prevent diseases like tuberculosis, malaria, eye diseases, skin diseases, etc.

World Health Organisation (WHO)

It was established on 7th April, 1948 with the objective of achieving the highest possible level of health for all. Its headquarters is located at Geneva in Switzerland. Its main aim is to help the government raise the standards of public health and medical research. 7th April is celebrated as the World Health Day every year.

WHO Logo

Functions of WHO

- It helps countries to improve their health system by building up infrastructure.
- It gives important drugs needed for medical care.
- It launches programmes to immunise children against 6 major diseases such as measles, diphtheria, tetanus, tuberculosis, polio and whooping cough.
- It promotes research to cure and prevent diseases.
- It works towards providing safe drinking water and adequate waste disposal.
- It organises conferences, seminars and training activities for health care personnel.
- It aims at fighting diseases and preventing them from spreading.
- It publishes health journals to create health consciousness among people.

United Nations Educational, Scientific and Cultural Organisation (UNESCO)

It was established on 4th November, 1946 with the main objective to contribute the peace and security in the world, by promoting collaboration among nations through education, science, culture and communication. Its headquarters is located at Paris. All the members of the UN are automatically entitled to the membership of UNESCO.

UNESCO Logo

Functions of UNESCO

- Removal of illiteracy by encouraging adult education, distance education and open school education.
- It provide financial assistance for the education of disabled children. It also lays special emphasis on the education of women and girls.
- It encourage scientific education by providing regional training centres.
- It advices about the production of textbooks, syllabus and teacher-training.
- It helps to set-up library systems and also gives fellowships.
- It organises book fairs and festivals at both national and international levels.

Functions in Scientific Activities

- It promotes research in the fields like Geology, Mathematics, Physics and Oceanography.
- It helps in correcting the existing imbalances in scientific and technological manpower.
- It encourages the study of Social Sciences in order to focus attention on combating all forms of discrimination, improving the status of women and helping the youth in solving their problems.

- It organises conferences to bring scientists together.
- It circulates information through journals. 'Courier' is the official monthly magazine of UNESCO.

Functions for Preservation of Cultural Heritage

- It provides technical advice and assistance, equipments and funds for the preservation of monuments like Taj Mahal and other works of art.
- It aims to protect the world inheritance of books, works of art and rare manuscripts. It also helps in translating rare manuscripts.
- It promotes cultural exchange between people of different countries by sponsoring travelling, art exhibitions and similar activities.
- It gives encouragement to artistic creations in Literature and Fine Arts.

Check Your LEARNING...

1. How many members are there in the executive board of UNICEF?
2. When was the WHO established?
3. Where is the headquarters of UNESCO?
4. Mention any two scientific activities of UNESCO .

Timeline

Years	Important Events
1945	UN established
1945	UNSC established
1945	International Court of Justice established
1945	The Trusteeship founded
1945	The Secretariat founded
1945	ECOSOC established
1946	UNESCO established
1946	UNICEF founded
1947	UN flag was adopted
1948	WHO established

QUiCK Revision

- Second World War, failure of League of Nations, rise of dictatorships in European nations, invention of deadly weapons led to the set-up of the world body i.e. the United Nations.
- The purposes of the United Nations are to maintain international peace and security, to develop friendly relations among nations, to achieve international co-operation, etc.
- The 6 organs of United Nations are the General Assembly, Security Council, the International Court of Justice, the Secretariat, the Trusteeship Council and the Economic and Social Council.
- The General Assembly is also known as the 'Parliament of the United Nations'. All Members to the UN are automatically the part of the General Assembly and each member has one vote.
- Important functions of the General Assembly are to make recommendations on the general principles of co-operation for maintaining international peace and security, discuss any question relating to international peace and security, make recommendations for peaceful settlement of disputes, etc.
- The Security Council is the executive body of the United Nations. It has 15 members. All permanent members are its all time members. Other non-permanent members are chosen among members of the General Assembly for 2 years.
- Different types of functions performed by the Security Council are to maintain international peace and security, to investigate any dispute or situation which can cause friction, to formulate system to regulate armaments, to take military action against an aggressor, to recommend new member's entry, to recommend to the General Assembly, the appointment of the Secretary-General, to elect Judges of the International Court of Justice, etc.
- The International Court of Justice works for the settlement of disputes which are submitted to it by the member states. It has 15 judges elected for a term of 9 years. They are chosen from all nations by merit.
- UNICEF stands for United Nations International Children's Emergency Fund. Later its name changed into United Nations Children's Fund, but its acronym continued.
- The functions of UNICEF are to work for the protection of children in respect of survival, health and well being, provides technical supplies, equipments and other aids to villages, etc. Its headquarters is at New York.
- WHO stands for 'World Health Organisation'. Its headquarters is at Geneva in Switzerland. Its main aim is to help the government to raise the standards of public health and medical research.
- UNESCO stands for United Nations Educational, Scientific and Cultural Organisation. Its headquarters is at Paris in France.
- UNESCO aims for the promotion of collaboration among nations through education, science, culture and communication, removal of illiteracy by encouraging adult education, establishing library systems, etc.

Chapter Practice

Section-I

Multiple Choice Questions

1. When was the United Nations set up?
(a) 24th October, 1946
(b) 24th October, 1945
(c) 24th September, 1945
(d) 24th September, 1946

Ans. (b) 24th October, 1945

2. What were the reasons for the establishment of the United Nations?
(a) Failure of League of Nations
(b) Fear of Third World War
(c) First and Second World War
(d) All of the above

Ans. (d) All of the above

3. The UN flag is .... in colour.
(a) navy blue (b) light blue
(c) dark green (d) light green

Ans. (b) light blue

4. Which one of the following is not an official language of the United Nations?
(a) Arabic (b) Chinese
(c) Russian (d) Italian

Ans. (d) Italian

5. .... is the executive body of the United Nations.
(a) United Nations General Assembly
(b) The Trusteeship Council
(c) The Secretariat
(d) The Security Council

Ans. (d) The Security Council

6. Who elects the non-permanent members of the United Nations Security Council?
(a) United Nations Security Council
(b) United Nations General Assembly
(c) The Secretariat
(d) The Secretary General

Ans. (d) The Secretary General

7. The non-permanent members of the Security Council are elected for a term of ....
(a) 1 year (b) 5 years
(c) 2 years (d) 3 years

Ans. (c) 2 years

8. When was the UNESCO established?
(a) 4th November, 1946 (b) 4th October, 1946
(c) 14th November, 1945 (d) 14th October, 1945

Ans. (a) 4th November, 1946

9. Complete the given analogy.
The General Assembly : New York : : International Court of Justice : ?
(a) Paris (b) Geneva (c) Hague (d) New York

Ans. (c) Hague

10. Complete the given analogy.
ECOSOC : ? : : UNSC : 15 Members
(a) 193 Members (b) 54 Members
(c) 60 Members (d) 53 Members

Ans. (b) 54 Members

11. Complete the given analogy.
Afro-Asia Nations : 5 Members : : East European Nations : ?
(a) 2 Members (b) 3 Members
(c) 4 Members (d) 1 Member

Ans. (d) 1 Member

12. Replace the underlined words with the correct answer.
Secretary General is the head of the <u>Trusteeship Council</u>.
(a) Secretariat (b) General Assembly
(c) Security Council (d) None of these

Ans. (a) Secretariat

13. Important decisions of the General Assembly is taken by a <u>1/3 rd majority</u>.
(a) simple majority (b) 2/3 rd majority
(c) absolute majority (d) 1/4th majority

Ans. (b) 2/3 rd majority

14. Complete the following table.

UNGA	Policy making organ
?	Forum for discussing economic issues

(a) The ECOSOC (b) UNESCO
(c) UNGA (d) UNICEF

Ans. (a) The ECOSOC

15. Complete the following table.

WHO	Prevention of spreading of diseases
?	Removal of illiteracy

(a) UNICEF (b) UNESCO
(c) ECOSOC (d) General Assembly

Ans. (b)UNESCO

16. Which of the following is not true about the International Court of Justice?
(i) It's head-quarter is not located in New York.
(ii) It is composed of 20 Judges.
(iii) Judges are elected for a term of 9 years.

17. Which is/are the correct statement(s) about UNESCO?
 (i) Its headquarter is situated at Geneva.
 (ii) It publishes Health Journals.
 (iii) It encourages scientific education.
 (iv) All members of the UN becomes the member of UNESCO automatically.

Codes
(a) Only (i) (b) Both (i) and (ii)
(c) Both (iii) and (iv) (d) All of these

Ans. (c) Both (iii) and (iv)

18. Match the following.

	List I		List II
A.	WHO	1.	New York
B.	UNICEF	2.	Hague, Netherland
C.	UNESCO	3.	Geneva
D.	ICJ	4.	Paris

Codes

	A	B	C	D		A	B	C	D
(a)	1	4	3	2	(b)	3	1	4	2
(c)	1	3	4	2	(d)	3	2	3	1

Ans. (b)

Picture Based Question

19. Study the picture and answer the questions that follows. **[2012]**

 (i) Name the organisation associated with the above emblem from the options given below.
 (a) International Court of Justice (b) WHO
 (c) United Nations (d) UNESCO

Ans. (c) United Nations

 (ii) Which of the following organs suspended its activities in 1994?
 (a) The ECOSOC (b) The Trusteeship Council
 (c) The Secretariat (d) UNICEF

Ans. (b) The Trusteeship Council

 (iii) Which of the following countries is not a permanent member of the executive body of the UN (The Security Council)?
 (a) Russia (b) China (c) Italy (d) France

Ans. (c) Italy

 (iv) Which of the following statements are true about UN?
 (i) India was not a founding member of the UN.
 (ii) The documents are written only in English and French.
 (iii) The contributions made by the member countries to the UN is decided by the General Assembly.
 (iv) Membership of the UN is not open to all nations.

Codes
(a) Only (i) (b) Both (ii) and (iii)
(c) Both (i) and (iv) (d) Only (iv)

Ans. (b) Both (ii) and (iii)

Passage Based Questions

20. Read the passage given below and answer the questions that follow.
It is the main policy-making organ of the United Nations. It comprises of all member states and provides a unique forum for multi-lateral discussion of international issues. Its headquarter is situated at New York. The body meets from September to December each year and thereafter from January to September as per the requirement. The body elects a President, some Vice-Presidents and the Chairman of the committees. Important decisions are taken by 2/3rd majority. Each member nation gets to vote. The powers of the body comprise discussing issues relating to international peace, establishing the financial assessment of member states, considering the UN budget etc.

 (i) Identify the body of the UN which the passage is describing about.
 (a) The Security Council (b) The General Assembly
 (c) The Secretariat (d) UNESCO

Ans. (b) The General Assembly

 (ii) Which of the following is not true about this organ of UN?
 (a) All members of the UN are members of this body.
 (b) Each states has 4 representatives.
 (c) Each state has one vote.
 (d) All are not true

Ans. (b) Each states has 4 representatives

 (iii) The body elects how many Vice-Presidents?
 (a) 20 (b) 1 (c) 21 (d) 10

Ans. (c) 21

 (iv) Which of the following are the functions of this body?
 (a) Appoint Secretary General on the recommendation of the Security Council.
 (b) Considers reports from the other organs of UN.
 (c) Approves the budget of the UN.
 (d) All of the above

Ans. (d) All of the above

21. Read the passage given below and answer the questions that follow.
It is the principle judicial organ of the UN established in June 1945. The headquarter of this organ is the only one which is situated outside New York. It has two official languages. It settles the legal disputes submitted to it by the states and also gives advisory opinions. It comprises of 15 Judges elected for a term of 9 years. Elections are held every 3 years for 1/3rd of the seats. Any Judge can be impeached only by unanimous votes of all other Judges.

The body also elects a President and a Vice-President. Only the member states of UN may apply and appear before the body.

(i) The passage describes about which of the following organ of the United Nations?
(a) ECOSOC (b) UNESCO
(c) Trusteeship Council
(d) International Court of Justice

Ans. (d) International Court of Justice

(ii) What are the official languages of this organ?
(a) English and French (b) English and Spanish
(c) English and Italian (d) English and Russian

Ans. (a) English and French

(iii) The President and Vice-President of this organ are elected for a term of
(a) 2 years (b) 3 years (c) 5 years (d) 1 year

Ans. (b) 3 years

(iv) Which of the following is true regarding this body of UN?
(a) Every Judge is of different nationality.
(b) Judges cannot be impeached.
(c) A retired Judge cannot be re-elected.
(d) A nation, not a member of the UN can appear before this body.

Ans. (a) Every Judge is of different nationality.

Section-II

Short Questions

1. Describe briefly the need to have a world level body after the Second World War.

Ans. The world saw two disastrous World Wars and its impact on the world. Loss of men and money made world leaders convinced that peace was highly needed. Thus, for the peaceful existence of all nations, a world body was needed which would reduce the threat of war and could prevent future wars.

2. When and where was the United Nations formed?

Ans. United Nations was formed at San Francisco in USA on 24th October, 1945. It was set-up to give peace a chance in solving world's disputes.

3. What are the official languages of the UN and explain the flag of the United Nation?

Ans. Arabic, Chinese, English, French, Russian and Spanish are the official languages of the UNO.

The UN flag is light blue in colour and is portrayed in white. At its centre is UN Emblem, a polar map of the world, embraced by twin Olive branches.

4. What is meant by the General Assembly of the United Nation?

Ans. The General Assembly of the United Nations is known as 'the Parliament of the United Nations'.

All the member of nations are member of the General Assembly and have one vote each.

5. Mention the big five countries that constitute the permanent members of the Security Council (USA).

Ans. The five permanent members of the Security Council are Britain, France, Russia, China and the United States of America (USA).

6. Name the principal judicial organ of UN. Explain briefly its composition.

Ans. The International Court of Justice is the principal judicial organ of the UN. The court consists of 15 Judges elected for a period of 9 years and can get re-elected. The court elects its President and Vice-President for a term of 3 years.

7. What is meant by the term 'Veto Power'? **[2019]**

Ans. Veto Power can be exercised by the permanent members of the Security Council. By application of this right, a permanent member may reject any decision at the Security Council. A negative vote which is cast by any of the permanent body of the Security Council is called 'Veto'. The Council is unable to act further if any of the permanent member uses the veto power. However, if a member refused to vote, then it will not be counted as a negative vote.

8. Who appoints the Secretary General of the United Nations?

Ans. The Secretary General of the United Nations is appointed by the General Assembly on the recommendation of the Security Council for 5 years. He may be re-elected also.

9. Which agency of the UN looks after the interests of the children in the world? What was the original purpose of setting up this agency?

Ans. United Nations International Children's Emergency Fund (UNICEF) looks after the interests of the children's in the world. The original purpose of setting up this agency is to protect children from adversity and by preparing them for life.

10. State the full forms of the following agencies of the United Nations, UNICEF and UNESCO. **[2018, 2016]**

Ans. UNICEF stands for United Nations International Children's Emergency Fund.

UNESCO stands for United Nations Educational, Scientific and Cultural Organisation.

11. Explain the three vital roles that the WHO plays in combating diseases. **[2010]**

Ans. The vital roles that the WHO plays in combating diseases are

(i) It helps the countries to build up infrastructure in the health sectors.
(ii) It promotes research to cure and prevent diseases.
(iii) It gives important drugs needed for medical care. For example, it launched a programme to immunise children against six major diseases.

12. Where is the headquarters of the WHO located? Mention any one function of the Security Council.

Ans. The headquarters of the WHO is located at Geneva in Switzerland.

A function of the Security Council is that it formulates plans for the establishment of a system to regulate armaments.

13. Write the expanded form of UNESCO. Mention two of its functions in the field of education.

Or Mention any two functions of UNESCO in the field of education. **[2017]**

Ans. UNESCO stands for United Nations Educational, Scientific and Cultural Organisation. The functions of UNESCO in the field of education are

(i) It provides financial assistance for the education of disabled children.

(ii) It works for the removal of illiteracy by encouraging adult education, distance education and the open school system.

14. Mention any two scientific activities of UNESCO.

Ans. Two scientific activities of UNESCO are

- It promotes research in the fields like Geology, Mathematics, Physics and Oceanography.
- It helps in correcting the imbalance in scientific and technological manpower, so existing.

Structured Questions

1. The United Nations was established to be an effective peace keeping international organisation. In this context, explain the following questions.

(i) Its objectives and purposes. **[2015]**

(ii) The meaning of human rights as incorporated in the human charter.

(iii) Name the agency that the UN set-up to deliver relief to children and mothers after Second World War. State any three of its functions.

Ans. (i) Refer to chapter theory page no. 237-238.

(ii) The meaning of human rights as incorporated in the human charter is

- **Article 1** All human beings are born free and equal in dignity and rights. They are endowed with reason and conscience and should act towards one another with spirit of brotherhood.
- **Article 2** Everyone is entitled to all the rights and freedom a set forth in this declaration, without distinction of any kind, such as race, colour, sex, language, religion, political or other opinion, national or social origin, property, birth or other status. Furthermore, no distinction should be made on the basis of the political, jurisdiction or international status of the country or territory to which a person belongs, whether it be independent, trust, non-self governing or under any other limitation of sovereignity.

(iii) United Nations Children's Emergency Fund (UNICEF) is the agencies that the UN set-up to deliver relief to childrens and mothers after the Second World War. Its functions are

- It provide funds to strengthen the training and study of national personnel, who are giving service in health and sanitation, teaching fields, nutrition experts and child welfare specialists.
- It assists governments to plan, develop and extend in both rural and urban environment the low cost community based services in maternal and child health care.
- It provide assistance for long-term programme for children and meeting needs of mothers and children in emergencies arising due to natural disasters, epidemics or civil strife.

2. The United Nations Organisation was established to maintain peace and 'promote social progress and better standards of life in larger freedom'. With reference to this, explain the following questions. **[2013]**

(i) The composition of the Security Council.

(ii) The functions of the Security Council related to maintaining world peace.

(iii) The role of UNESCO in the development of science and technology.

Ans. (i) Refer to chapter theory page no. 238.

(ii) The functions of the Security Council related to maintaining world peace are

- The Security Council investigates, any dispute or situation which might lead to International friction.
- It recommends methods of adjusting any such dispute and the terms of settlement.
- The Council can call on members to apply economic sanctions and other measures not involving the use of force to prevent or stop aggression.

(iii) The role of UNESCO in the development of science and technology are

- It organises seminars and conferences of scientists of various countries and circulates information through journals, press and exhibition.
- It promotes research in the fields of Geology, Mathematics, Physics and Oceanography.
- It helps in correcting the imbalance in scientific and technological manpower that exists.
- It encourages the study of Social Science in order to focus attention on combatting all forms of discrimination.

3. With reference to the United Nations and its related agencies, answer the following questions. **[2016]**

(i) Explain any three functions of the WHO.

(ii) State the composition of the International Court of Justice.

(iii) State any four functions of the General Assembly.

Ans. (i) The functions of WHO are

(a) It helps countries to improve their health system by building up infrastructure.

(b) It gives important drugs needed for medical care.

(c) It launches programmes to immunise children against 6 major diseases such as measles, diphtheria, tetanus, tuberculosis, polio and whooping cough.

(ii) The International Court of Justice comprises of 15 Judges. They are elected for a term of 9 years by the UN General Assembly and Security Council sitting independently of each other. Elections are held every 3 years for 1/3rd of the seats. A retired Judge may be re-elected. The President and Vice-President of the court are elected for a term of 3 years.

(iii) The functions of General Assembly are

(a) It consider and make recommendations on the general principles of co-operation, for maintaining international peace and security including disarmament.

(b) It discuss any question relating to international peace and security make recommendations on it, except where a dispute or situation is currently being discussed by the Security Council.

(c) It discuss and make recommendations on any questions within the scope of the charter or affecting the powers and functions of any organ of the United Nations.

(d) It make recommendations for the peaceful settlement of any situation that might impair friendly relations among nations.

4. The United Nations Organisation aims to maintain international peace. With reference to its organs and agencies, answer the following. **[2023]**

(i) What is the composition of the Security Council ? What is the term of the non-permanent members?

(ii) Mention any three functions of the General Assembly.

(iii) Give the full form of UNESCO. Mention any three of its function.

Ans. (i) The Security Council comprises of 5 permanent members and 10 non-permanent members elected for a term of 2 years. It is the executive body of the United Nations.

Non-Permanent members are elected from various groups, which are as follows

(i) Afro-Asian Countries-5

(ii) Latin American Countries-2

(iii) West European and other Countries-2

(iv) Eastern European Countries-1

(ii) Refer to Structured Question 3 (iii).

(iii) The full form of UNESCO is The United Nations Educational, Scientific and Cultural Organisation. UNESCO is a United Nation specialist organisation established in 1945.

5. The horrors of the two World Wars, led to the formation of the United Nations Organisations, while the formation of the Non-Aligned Movement followed later. In this context, answer the following. **[2017]**

(i) Mention any three aims and objectives of the United Nations Organisation.

(ii) Explain any three functions of the Security Council.

(iii) What do you mean by veto power?

Ans. (i) Refer to chapter theory page no. 237-238.

(ii) Refer to chapter theory page no. 239.

(iii) Refer to chapter theory page no. 239.

6. With reference to the United Nations and its specialised Agencies, answer the following questions. **[2018]**

(i) Mention any three functions of the International Court of Justice.

(ii) State the composition of the General Assembly.

(iii) State any two functions of the UNICEF and any two functions of WHO.

Ans. (i) Three functions of the International Court of Justice are

(a) The court decides cases according to the international treaties and conventions in force and is capable to take a case into consideration if the parties so involved agree for it.

(b) It settle the legal disputes submitted to it by the states in accordance with international law.

(c) It give advisory opinions on legal questions referred to it by authorised International agencies and organs.

(ii) Refer to chapter theory page no. 238.

(iii) Two functions of UNICEF are

(a) It works for the protection of children in respect of their survival, health and well beings. It also supports child immunisation programmes.

(b) It provides technical supplies, equipments and other aids to villages.

Two functions of WHO are

(a) It helps countries to improve their health system by building up infrastructure.

(b) It gives important drugs needed for medical care.

Picture Based Question

1. Look at the picture given below and answer the following questions.
   (i) Mention three scientific activities undertaken by UNESCO.
   (ii) What measures are taken by UNESCO to preserve the cultural heritage?
   (iii) Explain the functions of UNESCO.

Ans. (i) Refer to chapter theory page no. 241-242.

(ii) The measures taken by UNESCO to preserve the cultural heritage are
- It provides technical advice and assistance, equipments and funds for the preservation of monuments like Taj Mahal and other works of art.
- It aims to protect the world inheritance of books, works of art and rare manuscripts. It also helps in translating rare manuscripts.
- It promotes cultural exchange between people of different countries by sponsoring travelling, art exhibitions and similar activities.

(iii) Refer to chapter theory page no. 241.

Chapter Assessment

Section-I

Multiple Choice Questions

1. When did the International Court of Justice begin to work?
   (a) June, 1945 (b) July, 1945
   (c) August, 1946 (d) April, 1948
2. Which among the following is a part of UN flag?
   (a) Olives (b) Rose Petals
   (c) Dolphines (d) Light torch
3. How many Non-permanent members are there in UN Security Council?
   (a) 5 (b) 10 (c) 4 (d) 15

Section-II

Short Questions

1. Name the international organisation which was set-up after First World War.
2. How many nations are there in the General Assembly? Are they form part of the Security Council?
3. Mention the functions which are performed by the Security Council.
4. Why did the UNESCO came into existence?
5. Give the main functions of the UN General Assembly.
6. How do UNESCO work for the good of the children?
7. What is the main aim of WHO?

Structured Questions

1. UN works through major agencies and organs. In this context, explain the following.
   (i) Functions of UNICEF
   (ii) Functions of WHO
   (iii) Functions of UNESCO
   (iv) Functions of International Court of Justice
2. UN works for World Heritage. In this context, explain the following questions.
   (i) Describe the growing need of the preservation of culture of the world.
   (ii) How important is the work of UNESCO?
   (iii) Describe the scientific activities undertaken by UNESCO.
   (iv) Any two functions of UNESCO.
3. In the absence of UN the world would not have been so peaceful. With reference to this context, explain the following.
   (i) Importance of UN (ii) Powers of UN
   (iii) Reasons for the establishment of UN

CHAPTER

13

The Non-Aligned Movement

SYLLABUS

Non-Aligned Movement Brief meaning and objectives
• Panchsheel • Role of Jawaharlal Nehru • Name of the architects of NAM

The concept of Non-Aligned Movement emerged as a result of the Second World War (1939-45) which divided the world into two rival power blocs. One was led by the USA and the other by the USSR or the erstwhile Soviet Union. During this period, many newly independent countries in Asia and Africa decided not to join any of the two blocs and remain neutral and non-aligned.

Meaning of Non-Aligned Movement (NAM)

NAM is an assembly of developing world states or newly independent nations that are not formally aligned with or against any major power bloc.

The main features of NAM are

- It is against military alliances like NATO (North-Atlantic Treaty Organisation), SEATO (South-East Asia Treaty Organisation), Warsaw Pact, etc.
- It is the belief that each country has the complete freedom to take independent Foreign Policy decisions.
- It stands for action rather than **passivism**[1] and it judges an issue on merit. It is for the freedom and justice of people.
- It actively participates in the politics among nations.

1 **Passivism** It refers to the state of being inactive or not participating.

Objectives of NAM

At the beginning, the main objective of NAM was keep away the newly independent nations of Asia and Africa from the rivalry of the two power blocs and preserve their newly acquired national independence. The other objectives of NAM are

- To remove all those factors and tendencies that could lead to war.
- To protect the growing freedom of the newly independent Asian and African countries and help them to keep away from colonial domination.
- To protect human rights and the environment.
- To strengthen the United Nations Organisation as an organ of world peace.
- To oppose colonialism, imperialism and racial discrimination.
- To encourage friendly relations among countries.
- To advocate peaceful settlement of international disputes.
- To oppose the use of force and nuclear weapons.
- To advocate sovereign equality of all States.

Non-Aligned Movement Summit

The first ever, Non-Aligned Movement Summit was held in September, 1961 at Belgrade in Yugoslavia. It was attended by 25 Afro-Asian nations and one European nation. In this summit, several issues related to world peace were discussed.

The second summit of the NAM took place in Cairo in 1964 where the number of Non-Aligned countries increased to 47. They all discussed the matters which were the problems of newly independent countries of Asia, Africa and Latin America.

The Main Architects of Non-Aligned Movement

Non-Alignment as a movement originated when the first Prime Minister of India, Pandit Jawaharlal Nehru, gave the idea of an organisation of newly independent states of Africa and Asia in a radio speech in 1946.

The main architects of Non-Aligned Movement were

(i) Prime Minister Pandit Jawaharlal Nehru of India.
(ii) President Sukarno of Indonesia.
(iii) President Josip Broz Tito of Yugoslavia.
(iv) President Colonel Gamal Abdel Nasser of Egypt.
(v) President Kwame Nkrumah of Ghana.

Role of Jawaharlal Nehru in Non-Aligned Movement

- Under the leadership of Jawaharlal Nehru, India became the first country to initiate the policy of non-alignment. It played a major role for world peace and supported the rights of all those people who were fighting against exploitation and imperialism.
- He highlighted the dangers arising out of the tension between the two power blocs at the Asian Relations Conference in New Delhi in March 1947 and advised all the newly independent countries to stay away from the power blocs.
- He advised all the newly independent countries to adopt the policy of non-alignment and focus on self-development with mutual cooperation.
- He opposed the military or economic alliances like NATO, SEATO, etc initiated by USA and the Warsaw Pact, Cominform, etc initiated by USSR, as he believed that they encouraged colonialism and imperialism.
- He advocated the principles of democratic socialism. His policy of non-alignment did not meant to promote a third bloc, but it was meant to ensure freedom of decision making of the newly independent countries.
- He also organised the Bandung Conference of 1955 along with other leaders like Ho-Chi-Minh of Vietnam, Chou-En-Lai of China, etc. In this conference, it was decided to form an organisation of the newly independent countries.

Principles of Panchsheel

In 1954, India and China signed an agreement of peaceful co-existence known as Panchsheel Agreement. The five principles of Panchsheel concept was given by Pandit Nehru to save sovereignty and territorial integrity of the newly independent nations from foreign powers.

These five principles were of Panchsheel Agreement

(i) Mutual non-interference in each other's internal affairs.
(ii) Mutual non-aggression.
(iii) Equality for mutual benefit.
(iv) Mutual respect for each other's territorial integrity and sovereignty.
(v) Peaceful co-existence.

Achievements of NAM

- It helped in solving tensions between the two power blocs and brought an end to the Cold War.
- It acted against the arms race of the superpowers during the Cold War era.
- It supported the cause of international peace, justice and freedom.
- NAM countries emphasised on the **New International Economic Order**[2] (NIEO). The first UN Conference on Trade and Development (UNCTA) was organised in 1964 due to the efforts of the NAM countries.

Check Your LEARNING...

1. What does NATO stand for?
2. In which year Bandung Conference held?
3. The Panchsheel Agreement was signed between which countries?
4. What does NIEO stand for?

2 **New International Economic Order** It is a set of proposals advocated by developing countries to end economic colonialism and dependency through a new interdependent economy.

QUiCK Revision

- With the help of all other nations, the NAM led nations solved the tensions between the two power blocs and brought an end to the Cold War.
- The strategy to follow a Non-Aligned policy and to protect the independence of the self is known as the Non-Aligned Movement.
- All NAM supports the cause of International peace, justice and freedom.
- All NAM nations remained away from the arms race and have full faith in co-operation and peaceful existence.
- NAM began a political movement against imperialism and racialism of Western countries.
- All the non-aligned countries condemned the social discrimination of South Africa i.e. apartheid.
- Jawaharlal Nehru met Marshal Tito of Yugoslavia, President Nasser of Egypt at Belgrade, in 1956 and gave the practical shape to Non-Aligned Movement.
- The First Summit of NAM took place at Belgrade in September, 1961. It was participated by 25 countries of the world.
- Second Summit took place in Ciaro, in 1964 and number of countries rose to 47.
- Bandung Conference was held in 1955, in Indonesia, which led to the foundation of the Non-Aligned Movement.
- India along with China formed the Panchsheel policy which puts pressure on peaceful existence of all nations.

Chapter Practice

Section-I

Multiple Choice Questions

1. The first Non-Aligned Movement Summit was held on ....
(a) September, 1960 (b) September, 1961
(c) October, 1961 (d) October, 1960

Ans. (b) September, 1961

2. The first Non-Aligned Summit was attended by .... Afro-Asian nations.
(a) 30 (b) 35
(c) 25 (d) 20

Ans. (c) 25

3. Who of the following gave idea of the Non-Aligned Movement?
(a) Josip Brot Tito
(b) Gamal Abdel Nasser
(c) Jawaharlal Nehru
(d) None of the above

Ans. (c) Jawaharlal Nehru

4. Who became the first Secretary-General of the NAM?
(a) Jawaharlal Nehru of India
(b) Sukarno of Indonesia
(c) Kwame Nkurmah of Ghana
(d) Josip Brot Tito of Yugoslavia

Ans. (d) Josip Brot Tito of Yugoslavia

5. Complete the given analogy.
Belgrade : 1st NAM Summit : : ? : 2nd NAM Summit
(a) India (b) Indonesia
(c) Cairo (d) Ghana

Ans. (c) Cairo

6. Complete the given analogy.
NAM : Non-Aligned Movement : : NIEO : ?
(a) New International Economic Order
(b) New International Economic Organisation
(c) New International Environmental Order
(d) New International Environmental Organisation

Ans. (a) New International Economic Order

7. Replace the underlined word with the correct answer.
In the Second Summit of the NAM, the number of Non-aligned countries increased to <u>50</u>.
(a) 48 (b) 47 (c) 45 (d) 40

Ans. (b) 47

8. Replace the underlined word with the correct answer.
The nations which led to the beginning of NAM were mostly from the countries of the <u>1st world</u>.
(a) 2nd world (b) 3rd world
(c) 4th world (d) None of these

Ans. (b) 3rd world

9. Complete the following table.

1961	1st NAM Summit
?	2nd NAM Summit

(a) 1962 (b) 1965 (c) 1966 (d) 1964

Ans. (d) 1964

10. Complete the following table.

NATO	?
SEATO	South-East Asia Treaty Organisation

(a) North-American Treaty Organisation
(b) North-Asian Treaty Organisation
(c) North-Atlantic Treaty Organisation
(d) None of the above

Ans. (c) North-Atlantic Treaty Organisation

11. Which of the following is not an objective of NAM?
(i) To oppose the use of force and nuclear weapons in the international arena.
(ii) To protect human rights.
(iii) To serve as a forum of political co-ordination of the developed countries.
(iv) To promote sovereign equality of all states.

Codes
(a) Only (i) (b) Only (iii)
(c) (i),(ii) and (iv) (d) Only (iv)

Ans. (c) (i), (ii) and (iv)

12. Which of the following statements is true?
(i) The Bandung Conference gave a practical shape to the 'Panchsheel' Agreement.
(ii) Bandung Conference was held in 1954.
(iii) Panchsheel was signed between India and China.
(iv) Panchsheel became guidelines for the NAM.

Codes
(a) Only (i)
(b) (i) and (ii)
(c) (i), (ii) and (iii)
(d) (i), (iii) and (iv)

Ans. (d) (i), (iii) and (iv)

13. Match the following.

	Architects of NAM	Countries
A.	Josip Broz Tito	1. Ghana
B.	Gamal Abdel Nasser	2. Yugoslavia
C.	Kwame Nkrumah	3. Egypt
D.	Sukarno	4. Indonesia

Codes

	A	B	C	D		A	B	C	D
(a)	1	3	2	4	(b)	1	2	3	4
(c)	2	3	1	4	(d)	2	1	3	4

Ans. (c)

Picture Based Question

1. Study the picture carefully and answer the questions with respect to him.

(i) Identify the personality in the given picture.
(a) Lal Bahadur Sashtri
(b) Sardar Vallabhbhai Patel
(c) Jawaharlal Nehru
(d) Maulana Azad

Ans. (c) Jawaharlal Nehru

(ii) The movement founded by this personality brought an end of the ....
(a) II World War (b) I World War
(c) India-Pakistan War (d) Cold War

Ans. (d) Cold War

(iii) What were the factors responsible for the establishment of a movement by this personality?
(a) Global tension caused by the Cold War
(b) Struggle against imperialism
(c) The newly independent states wanted to solve their problems without outside interference.
(d) All of the above

Ans. (d) All of the above

(iv) Which of the following statement is true about this personality?
(a) He talked about neutrality of Asian and African states.
(b) He opposed alliances which could encourage imperialism.
(c) He believed in disarmament
(d) All of the above

Ans. (d) All of the above

Passage Based Question

1. Read the passage given below and answer the questions that follow.

Non-alignment is the policy of a sovereign state according to which it does not join or align itself with any of the power blocs. After the Second World War, the World War divided into two powers one led by the USA and the other by the Soviet Union (USSR). However, the newly independent countries in Africa and Asia decided not to join any of these blocs and hence led to the beginning of the Non-Aligned Movements (NAM). The idea of the organisation was first given by the Indian Prime Minister Jawaharlal Nehru in 1946. The first NAM Summit was held in September, 1961 at Belgrade in Yugoslavia.

(i) Which of the following factors led to the formation of the Non-Aligned Movement (NAM)?
(a) Struggling against the imperialism and new-colonialism
(b) Poverty of newly independent nations
(c) Formation of collective forces
(d) All of the above

Ans. (d) All of the above

(ii) Who among the following was not the architect of the NAM?
(a) President Sukarno (b) Winston Churchill
(c) Jawaharlal Nehru (d) None of these

Ans. (b) Winston Churchill

(iii) Which of the following is/are the achievements of NAM?
(a) It helped to bring an end to the Cold War.
(b) It could not help in solving tensions between the two power blocs.
(c) It supported the cause of international peace.
(d) NAM emphasised on NIEO.

Ans. (b) It could not help in solving tensions between the two power blocs.

(iv) Which of the following statements about NAM is not true?
(a) NAM supports the Warsaw Pact.
(b) The Belgrade Conference was attended by one European nation.
(c) The Panchsheel was given a practical shape at the Bandung Conference.
(d) All of the above

Ans. (a) NAM supports the Warsaw Pact.

Section-II

Short Questions

1. What is meant by the term 'Non-Alignment'? [2015]

Ans. Non-Alignment refers to the international policy of a sovereign state on the basis of which it does not align itself with any of the power blocs.

2. Explain briefly the emergence of Non-Aligned Movement.

Ans. The concept of Non-Aligned Movement emerged as a result of the Second World War (1939-45) which divided the world into two rival power blocs. One was led by the USA and the other by the USSR or the Soviet Union. During this period, many newly independent countries in Asia and Africa decided not to join any of the two blocs and remain neutral and non-aligned.

3. What are the features of Non-Aligned Movement? Explain any two.

Ans. Two features of Non-Aligned Movement are
(i) It is not aligned to any power blocs.
(ii) It is against military alliances like NATO, Warsaw Pact etc.

4. What were the factors responsible for NAM? State any three of them.

Ans. Factors responsible for NAM were
(i) Global tension caused by the Cold War.
(ii) Restructuring of the international economic order.
(iii) Struggle against imperialism and neo-colonisation.

5. Name the two architects of NAM. [2013]

Ans. The two architects of NAM were
(i) Marshall Joseph Bronze Tito
(ii) Pandit Jawaharlal Nehru

6. Mention any two social objectives of NAM.

Ans. The social objectives of NAM are
- NAM led to end of imperialism
- helping the United Nations
- supporting peace and actions against Human Rights violations.

7. Why the two superpowers tried to influence other weak nations?

Ans. The two superpowers tried to influence other weak nations because.
- America and Russia both wanted to show the world their respective dominance. They tried to attract them by aids and ideas.
- They wanted to polarise all weak nations into their favour.

8. Why did Nehru give more emphasis on not to join the power blocs?

Ans. Jawaharlal Nehru gave more emphasis on not to join either of the two power blocs and focus on self-development with mutual co-operation because all the newly independent nations had a very painful experience of colonial rule and after independence they were influenced by self-reliant policies.

9. What are the basic principles of the Non-Aligned Movement or Panchsheel? [2018, 2011]

Ans. The basic principles of Non-Aligned Movement are
(i) Mutual non-interference in each other's internal affairs.
(ii) Mutual non-aggression.
(iii) Equality for mutual benefit.
(iv) Mutual respect for each other's territorial integrity and sovereignty.
(v) Peaceful co-existence.

10. Who proclaimed the principle of 'Panchsheel'?

Ans. Panchsheel was proclaimed by the Chinese premier Chou-En-Lai and Jawaharlal Nehru of India.

11. When and where were the first and second summit of Non-Aligned Movement held?

Ans. The first Non-Aligned Movement summit was held in September, 1961 at Belgrade, in Yugoslavia.
The second Non-Aligned Movement summit of the NAM took place in Cairo in 1964 where the number of Non-Aligned countries increased to 47.

12. State any three achievements of NAM.

Ans. Three achievements of NAM are
(i) It helped in solving tensions between the two power blocs and brought an end to the Cold War.
(ii) It acted against the arms race of the superpowers.
(iii) It supported the cause of international peace, justice and freedom.

Structured Questions

1. With reference to the Non-Aligned Movement, explain the following. [2014]
(i) 'Non-Alignment'.
(ii) Two factors responsible for its formation.
(iii) Role of Pandit Jawaharlal Nehru.

Ans. (i) Non-Alignment is the policy through which the developing world states or newly independent nations are not formally aligned with or against any major power bloc. It is against military alliances like NATO (North-Atlantic Treaty Organisation), SEATO (South-East Asia Treaty Organisation), Warsaw Pact, etc. It is the belief that each country has the complete freedom to take independent Foreign Policy decisions. It stands for action rather than passivism and it judges an issue on merit. It is for the freedom and justice of people.
(ii) Two factors responsible for the formation of Non-Aligned Movement were
(a) **Asian Relations Conference (1947)** Asian Relations Conference was held in Delhi in March, 1947 by the world leaders. Its aim was to show the world that Asian nations are not the puppet in the hands of the superpowers and that they would exist independently in the maintenance of peace.

(b) **Arms Race** America showed its dominancy by dropping of the two atomic bombs over Japan. This was unexpected and many countries were worried about the lack of arms in comparison to America and other superpowers. Newly independent nations were influenced by the fear of arms so they too participated in the arms race. The race of armaments made the Non-Aligned Movement as a mass movement.

(iii) The role of Jawaharlal Nehru in Non-Aligned Movement was

- Under the leadership of Jawaharlal Nehru, India became the first country to initiate the policy of non- alignment. It played a major role for world peace and supported the rights of all those people who were fighting against exploitation and imperialism.
- He highlighted the dangers arising out of the tension between the two power blocs at the Asian Relations Conference in New Delhi in March 1947 and advised all the newly independent countries to stay away from the power blocs.
- He advised all the newly independent countries to adopt the policy of non-alignment and focus on self-development with mutual cooperation.
- He opposed the military or economic alliances like NATO, SEATO, etc initiated by USA and the Warsaw Pact, Cominform, etc initiated by USSR, as he believed that they encouraged colonialism and imperialism.

2. With reference to the Non-Aligned Movement, state.

(i) Write the names of the architects of the Non-Aligned Movement. What is meant by Non-Alignment?

(ii) What was the role of Nehru in the Non-Aligned Movement?

(iii) Mention any three objectives of the Non-Aligned Movement.

(iv) How the concept of Non-Aligned Movement emerged?

Ans. (i) The names of the artchitects of the Non-Aligned Movement are

- Prime Minister Pandit Jawaharlal Nehru of India.
- President Sukarno of Indonesia.
- President Josip Broz Tito of Yugoslavia.
- President Colonel Gamal Abdel Nasser of Egypt.
- President Kwame Nkrumah of Ghana.

Non-Alignment is the policy through which the developing world states or newly independent nations are not formally aligned with or against any major power bloc.

(ii) Refer to chapter theory page no. 250.

(iii) The objectives of Non-Aligned Movement are

(a) To remove all those factors and tendencies that could lead to war.

(b) To protect the growing freedom of the newly independent Asian and African countries and help them to keep away from colonial domination.

(c) To protect human rights and the environment.

(iv) The concept of Non-Aligned Movement emerged as a result of the Second World War which divided the world into two rival power blocs. One was led by the USA and the other by the USSR or the Soviet Union. During this period, many newly independent countries in Asia and Africa decided not to join any of the two blocs and remain neutral and non-aligned.

Picture Based Question

1. Look at the picture and answer the following questions.

(i) The picture given is related to which conference? Why the leaders of the least developed nations had gathered at this conference?

(ii) Why the people of the developing countries are against the imperialism of the superpowers?

(iii) What was the result of the gathering of these people?

Ans. (i) The picture is related to the Bandung Conference. The leaders of the least developed nations have gathered at Bandung to form the Non-Aligned Movement. They have planned to form a world body which would be away from the power blocs of the two superpowers (America and Russia). Many became independent from the imperialist nations, so they were anxious for free governance. A world body was important as it would a collection of nations having common motive and common purpose. The new independent nations wanted to detach from the influences of the two superpowers. Many new policies of self-development and respect for fellow nations were initiated under it.

(ii) The developing countries were once the colonies of the colonial powers of the world. Many were convinced that the imperialists were the synonyms of exploitation and humiliation. The people wanted to get governed by self chosen leaders and not by the sayings of any of the superpower.

(iii) The result of the gathering of these leaders was that they had shaped the foreign policy of their nations in a new way. It was asserted that development could be done in a way which suited their land and people. So, they made a world body i.e. NAM and remained un-influenced by the superpowers and withheld their sovereignty.

Chapter Assessment

Section-I

Multiple Choice Questions

1. Panchsheel Agreement was signed in the year 1954, between India and ......
   (a) Egypt (b) USSR
   (c) China (d) Bangladesh
2. Where did the second summit of NAM take place?
   (a) Cairo (b) New Delhi
   (c) Jakarta (d) Bejing
3. Which of the following are considered among five principles of Panchsheel?
   (i) Mutual non-agression
   (ii) Not to take part in any war
   (iii) Peaceful co-existence

   Codes
   (a) Only (ii) (b) Only (i)
   (c) Both (i) and (ii) (d) All of these

Short Questions

1. What do you mean by Non-Aligned Movement?
2. Which all factors contributed to the rise of Non-Aligned Movement?
3. Which all nations came forward to form the NAM?
4. When and where was Panchsheel formed?
5. What are the prime objectives of NAM?
6. When was the first NAM Summit held and where?
7. How Pandit Jawaharlal Nehru played an important role in NAM?

Section-II

Structured Questions

1. Self development was the prime motive of the formation of Non-Aligned Movement. Answer the following in relation to this.
   (i) Why did development become the prime importance of the newly independent nation?
   (ii) How was the objective of the Non-Aligned Movement fulfilled? Who were the architects of NAM?
   (iii) Explain the affects of joining any superpowers.
2. Jawaharlal Nehru and other leaders wanted to practice self rule in world politics. Answer the following questions in relation to this.
   (i) Why the motto of the newly independent nations was self rule through NAM?
   (ii) Many joined the superpowers. Why did they do so? How India benefitted due to following its own policies?
   (iii) How world politics changed after the formation of NAM?
   (iv) Describe in brief about Bandung Conference.

SAMPLE
QUESTION PAPERS (1–5)

SAMPLE QUESTION PAPER 1

A HIGHLY SIMULATED Sample Question Paper for ICSE Class X

History & Civics (Unsolved)

General Instructions

1. Answers to this paper must be written on the paper provided separately.
2. You will not be allowed to write during the first 15 minutes.This time is to be spent in reading the question paper.
3. The time given at the head of this Paper is the time allowed for writing the answers.
4. Attempt all questions from Part I (Compulsory).
5. A total of five questions are to be attempted from Part II, two out of three questions from Section A and three out of five questions from Section B.
6. The intended marks for questions or parts of questions are given in brackets ( ).`

Time : 2 Hrs **Max. Marks : 80**

Part - I

(30 Marks)

Attempt all questions from this Part

Question 1

(i) In a significant constitutional development, the President of India recently exercised the power to return a bill for reconsideration. The bill, initially passed by both Houses of Parliament, was sent to the President for approval. However, due to concerns over certain provisions, the President chose to withhold assent and returned the bill for further deliberation. *XYZ News , 25th May, 2023*

Which power of the President of India is highlighted in the above case? **(1)**

(a) Pocket Veto

(b) Suspensive Veto power

(c) Ordinance Veto

(d) Power to appoint the Prime Minister

(ii) When a deadlock occurs between the two Houses of Parliament over a bill, a joint sitting is convened. Who presides over the joint sitting of Parliament? **(1)**

(a) The President of India (b) The Vice President of India

(c) The Speaker of the Lok Sabha (d) The Chief Justice of India

(iii) Identify the meaning of the writ mentioned in the news below. (1)

(a) You shall have the body (b) Command

(c) FORBID (d) By what authority

(iv) Given below are the details of few Indian citizens.

Candidate	Age	Other Details
A	25	Has a name in electoral roll
B	21	Just graduated
C	40	Bankrupt
D	75	Retired judge

Select the person who fulfils the eligibility criteria to become the member of Lok Sabha? (1)

(a) A (b) B (c) C (d) D

(v) Read the two statements given below about the Nationalism and select the option that shows the correct relationship between (A) and (R).

Assertion (A) In India the rise of nationalism is associated with anti-colonial movement.

Reason (R) The sense of being oppressed under colonialism connected many groups together.

Codes

(a) (R) contradicts (A) (b) (R) is the reason for (A)

(c) (A) is true but (R) is false (d) (A) and (R) are independent of each other

(vi) Identify the correct statement related to the Prime Minister's role in relation to the President? (1)

P. The Prime Minister is the main advisor to the President.

Q. The Prime Minister can directly appoint ministers without the President's approval.

R. The Prime Minister advises the President regarding the appointment of important officials like the CAG and members of UPSC.

S. The Prime Minister has no role in communicating the decisions of the Council of Ministers to the president.

(a) P and R are correct (b) P and Q are correct

(c) P and S are correct (d) Q and R are correct

(vii) Identify the odd one out from the following objective of the Non-cooperation? (1)

(a) The attainment of Swaraj.

(b) Measures to promote Hindu-Muslim unity.

(c) End the monopoly of the British over salt manufacturing.

(d) Removal of untouchability and Harijan welfare.

(viii) Rina a 26, year old women lived at the time when India was struggling against the British rule. She read the history of Britishers wars. She read that the British army suffered disappointment in first Afghan war (1838-42), Punjab wars (1845-49) and in the Crimean war (1854-56).

Which of the following conclusion is most likely that can be drawn according to Rina's thinking? (1)

(a) Britishers can also be defeated (b) Britishers can never be defeated

(c) India can never get the freedom from Britishers (d) Britishers are very powerful

(ix) Which of the following territories in France wanted to retrieve from Germany during the First World War? (1)

(a) Saint Pierre and Miquelon (b) Alsace and Lorraine

(c) Wallis and Futuna (d) Reunion and Lorraine

(x) Bipin Chandra Pal : English Weekly :: Lala Lajpat Rai : .... (1)

(a) The Kesari (b) The Maratha

(c) New India (d) Young India

(xi) Read the description and identify the person.
He was the soldier whose defiance against the British in 1857 marked the beginning of the uprising. (1)

(a) Mangal Pandey (b) Tatya Tope

(c) Rani Lakshmibai (d) Bahadur Shah Zafar

(xii) Which of the following was not the demands of Moderates? (1)

(a) More Indians should be appointed in higher posts.

(b) To make Indians aware about their self-respect and rights to freedom of speech and right of property, etc.

(c) A larger share in the government of the country.

(d) Reduction in land revenue extracted by Zamindars.

(xiii) Identify the country or countries emerged as independent states after the First World War? (1)

(a) Finland (b) Yugoslavia (c) Both (a) and (b) (d) Japan

(xiv) Identify the personality who founded the Satya Shodhak Samaj in 1873. (1)

(a) Jyotiba Phule (b) Raja Rammohan Roy

(c) Surendernath Banerjee (d) Dadabhai Naoroji

(xv) Which of the following is not correct about Treaty of Versailles? (1)

(a) Germany was held responsible for the war. (b) Rhine Valley was given to the Allied Powers.

(c) League of Nations was created. (d) It was signed on 28th July, 1919.

(xvi) Who was the Editor of below depicted newspaper? (1)

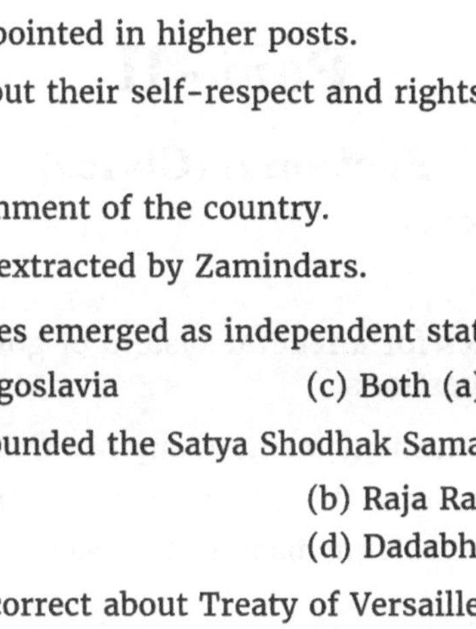
केसरी.

वर्ष १. पुणे—मंगळवार तारीख ४ जानेवारी १८८१. अंक १.

(a) RC Dutt (b) Lala Lajpat Rai (c) Lokmanya Tilak (d) Surendranath Bannerjee

Question 2

(i) Mention any two exclusive powers of the Lok Sabha. (2)

(ii) Read the given news carefully.

Headline 9 States Assemblies Dissolved, President signs proclamation after late cabinet talks, Government dissolved the assemblies of as many as nine states ruled by non-Congress (I) parties .

Source Indian Express

Name and briefly discuss the article using which above action is taken. (2)

(iii) Name any two leaders of the freedom movement, which were associated with assertive nationalism in India. (2)

(iv) Give two reason for the passage of the Indian Independence Act, 1947, which make it historically significant? (2)

(v) Mention any two major contributions of Swami Dayanand Saraswati. (2)

(vi) In the history of Indian National Movement 'Surat Split' is considered as one of the landmarks. In the light of the statement answer the following. (2)

(i) Who headed the Surat split congress session?

(ii) When did Surat split took place?

(vii) Imagine you were a freedom fighter in India, mention any two effects that emerged due to change of power in Britain which influenced India. (2)

Part - II

(50 Marks)

Section A (Civics)

Attempt any two questions from this Section

Question 3

The Constitution of India provides for a federal system of government in the country. In this context, explain the following questions.

(i) What do you understand by federation? Mention any two unitary features of Indian Constitution. (3)

(ii) Mention any three federal features of the Indian Constitution? (3)

(iii) Justify the role of President in resolving disputes between the Central and State Governments in a federal system. (4)

Question 4

In the parliamentary form of government, the President is the nominal executive head and Prime Minister is the real executive head. In respect to this, answer the following questions.

(i) The Prime Minister of India is the real executive head of the government. Mention any three legislative powers that justifies his position. (3)

(ii) Mention any three swears of the oath to the office of the Prime Minister. (3)

(iii) Describe about the financial powers of Council of Ministers. (4)

Question 5

The Supreme Court is the highest court in India and its powers and jurisdictions are extensive. With reference to this, answer the following questions.

(i) (a) From where the Supreme Court gets its powers? (3)

(b) Mention any two of its writ jurisdiction.

(ii) How can the Supreme Court invalidate the Legislative enactment and executive order? (3)

(iii) Explain the original jurisdiction of the Supreme Court. Mention any three types of cases that comes under this jurisdiction. (4)

Section B (History)

Attempt any three questions from this Section

Question 6

Read the excerpt given below and answer the questions that follows.

The great Revolt of 1857 was a momentous struggle against colonial rule in the Indian subcontinent-the most widespread anti-colonial struggle during the nineteenth century. It began in the second week of May and soon encompassed large parts of Northern, Central and Eastern India. Several hundred thousand subjects of the British Indian empire were killed during the revolt. Whereas the British managed to restore their authority in most of the areas where the uprising took place, the final operations continued till the beginning of 1859. The upheaval of 1857-59 was not an isolated event. It was part of a long tradition of resistance to the East India Company (EIC). *Source* Daily Star

(i) Explain any three immediate cause of this revolt. (3)

(ii) Mention any three revolutionary fighters and their contribution. (3)

(iii) Discuss any four impacts of this revolt. (4)

Question 7

Study the picture and answer the questions that follow.

(i) Who is the person shown in the picture? Mention any two socio-religious changes brought by him. (3)

(ii) Mention any three contribution of him in Indian nationalism. (3)

(iii) Highlight any four contribution of his social reform institution into contemporary society. (4)

Question 8

There were clash of interests and many other issues which finally ended into First World War. In this context, answer the following questions.

(i) Name the Person, who was killed in Sara Jevo. Mention any two impact of the incident. (3)

(ii) Justify the role of European powers such as Russia and Hungary in Balkan crises. (3)

(iii) Mention any four factor that led the military nationalism. (4)

Question 9

'Great war' is witnessed by world in the year 1914-1918. In this context, answer the following questions.

(i) Analyse how the Treaty of Versailles was responsible for the beginning of the second World War. (3)

(ii) The treaty imposed several significant clauses on Germany and reshaped Europe. Justify this statement by mentioning any three points. (3)

(iii) Explain how the dissolution of the Austro-Hungarian and Ottoman Empires, as a result of the Treaty of Versailles contributed to the creation of new countries. (4)

Question 10

United Nations is the world body in governance of world nations. In this respect, answer the following questions.

(i) Mention any three major aims or objectives of the United Nations. (3)

(ii) Explain the importance of International Court of Justice (ICJ) and the Economic and Social Council (ECOSOC) in maintaining of global peace and development. (3)

(iii) Describe the role of the UN Security Council in maintaining world peace. (4)

Answers

1 (i) (b) Suspensive Veto power
(ii) (c) The Speaker of the Lok Sabha
(iii) (a) You shall have the body
(iv) (a) A
(v) (b) (R) is the reason for (A)
(vi) (a) P and R are correct
(vii) (c) End the monopoly of the British over salt manufacturing.
(viii) (a) Britishers can also be defeated
(ix) (b) Alsace and Lorraine
(x) (d) Young India
(xi) (a) Mangal Pandey
(xii) (b) To make Indians aware about their self-respect and right to freedom of speech and right of property, etc.
(xiii) (c) Both (a) and (b)
(xiv) (a) Jyotiba Phule
(xv) (d) It was signed on 28th July, 1919.
(xvi) (c) Lokmanya Tilak

SAMPLE QUESTION PAPER 2

A HIGHLY SIMULATED Sample Question Paper for ICSE Class X

History & Civics (Unsolved)

General Instructions : See Sample Paper 1

Part - I

(30 Marks)

Attempt all questions from this Part

Question 1

(i) Complete the given analogy.
Lok Sabha maximum strength : 550 :: Rajya Sabha maximum strength: ?

(a) 238 (b) 250 (c) 240 (d) 200 (1)

(ii) Which of the following article deals with the President's Rule in a state? (1)

(a) Article 352 and Article 353
(b) Article 356 and Article 365
(c) Article 360 and Article 361
(d) Article 354 and Article 355

(iii) Given below are the details of few Indian citizens. (1)

Candidate	Age	Other Details
A	32	Member of Lok Sabha
B	27	Doctor
C	36	Eligible for election to Rajya Sabha
D	45	Bankrupt

Which of the above candidate fulfills the eligibility criteria to become Vice-President of India?

(a) A (b) B (c) C (d) D

(iv) Identify the type of cases the Lok Adalat basically deals with? (1)

(a) Land disputes
(b) Matrimonial disputes
(c) Partition disputes
(d) All of these

(v) The person below has held which of the following offices? (1)

(a) Vice-President
(b) Chairman of Rajya Sabha
(c) Prime Minister
(d) Both (a) and (b)

(vi) Identify the qualifications for a High Court judge in India. (1)

P. Must have been an advocate in a High Court or equivalent court for at least 10 years.

Q. Must have been a Judge of a lower court for at least 5 years.

R. Must be a citizen of India.

S. Must have completed 40 years of age.

(a) P and R
(b) P and Q
(c) R and S
(d) Q and S

(vii) Read the two statements given below about aspects of freedom and select the option that shows the correct relationship between (A) and (R). (1)

Assertion (A) The notions of freedom were different for every social groups.

Reason (R) Every class are group felt the effects of colonialism differently.

Codes

(a) (R) contradicts (A)
(b) (R) is the reason for A
(c) (A) is true but (R) is false
(d) (A) and (R) are independent of each other

(viii) Swati lived at the time when Indians were fighting against Britishers to get the freedom. In the year 1905, she saw that many shops were getting closed near by her home. She wanted to by some foreign products but none of the shops had the stocks of foreigner's product.

Which of the following event is most likely occurred in the year 1905?

(a) Swadeshi Movement
(b) Civil Disobedience Movement
(c) Quit India Movement
(d) Anti-partition Movement

(ix) Read the following description and identify the person
He was associated with the policy of "One people, one state, one leader".

(a) Lenin
(b) Hitler
(c) Stalin
(d) Mussolini

(x) Your school has organised a poster making competition on the topic "1857 Revolt and its impact on Indian Nationalism." Which of the following leaders would most likely be part of the poster? (1)

(a) Mangal Pandey
(b) Digambar Biswas
(c) Haidar Ali
(d) Jawaharlal Nehru

(xi) The government of Country Y has passed a law similar to the Rowlatt Act of 1919. Who will be most directly impacted by this law? (1)

(a) The Students
(b) The Farmers
(c) The Political Leaders
(d) The Working Class

(xii) World War II, also known as WWII, WW2, or Second World War, was the second largest global war that lasted from 1939 to 1945. World War II was one of the deadliest conflicts in human history, marked by 70 to 85 million fatalities, most of whom were civilians in the Soviet Union and China.

(The Times of India)

Identify the event which triggered World War II? (1)

(a) Attack on South Dakota
(b) The invasion of Poland
(c) The Cuba crisis
(d) The bombing of Hiroshima

(xiii) Which of the following is a feature of Non-Aligned Movement? (1)

(a) It remained against military alliances like NATO, SEATO and Warsaw Pact.

(b) It stands for passivism.

(c) It actively participates in the politics among nations.

(d) Both (a) and (c)

(xiv) Which of the following movement was launched after the incident held at below place? (1)

(a) Civil Disobedience Movement (b) Non-Cooperation Movement
(c) Kheda Satyagraha (d) Quit India Movement

(xv) Identify the odd one out of the following about the Cold War? (1)
(a) Increased harmony between US and USSR.
(b) A state of extreme political tension between US and USSR.
(c) USA believed in democracy and capitalism.
(d) USSR believed in Communism based on Marxist Theory.

(xvi) Identify the countries which were part of the Axis Power in the Second World War. (1)
(a) Poland, Germany and Japan (b) France, Japan and Britain
(c) Germany, Italy and Japan (d) Italy, Japan and Britain

Question 2

(i) Imagine you are a member of the Indian National Congress (INC) in the late 19th century. You have just returned from a meeting where you discussed the growing dissatisfaction among Indians under British rule. What steps would you take to address these concerns and rally support for the cause? (2)

(ii) M Venkaiah Naidu writes: Lessons from Emergency we must not forget.
The Emergency serves as a reminder of the importance of upholding democratic principles and protecting the rights and freedoms of individuals. As the maxim goes, 'Eternal vigilance is the price of liberty'. *Source Indian Express 24th June, 2023*
Briefly discuss about declaration of emergency. (2)

(iii) Give two reasons why Balgangadhar Tilak is known as 'Lokmanya'. (2)

(iv) Name the two main leaders who were associated with the movement against the Partition of Bengal in 1905. (2)

(v) Lord Curzon was the Viceroy of India from 1899 to 1905, in this regard answer the following. (2)
(a) When did the Viceroy of India make the proclamation for the partition of Bengal?
(b) Which two provinces were created after the partition of Bengal?

(vi) Mention the two major aims of Mohammedan Anglo-Oriental College. (2)

(vii) Mention two methods of resistance adopted in the Non-Cooperation Movement. (2)

Part - II

(50 Marks)

Section A (Civics)

Attempt any two questions from this Section

Question 3

The subordinate courts are so called because of their subordination to High Court. With reference to this, answer the following questions.

(i) Mention the three qualifications needed for a person to be appointed as a District Judge. (3)

(ii) Who administers the appointment of District Judge? Mention any two roles district judge plays in district judiciary. (3)

(iii) List any four types of cases that are dealt by the High Court which are exclusively part of it. (4)

Question 4

The office of the Vice-President is the second highest office of our country. In this regard, answer the following questions.

(i) Mention any three qualifications for the office of the Vice-President. (3)

(ii) When does the Vice-President act as the President? Mention any two differences between the powers of Vice President and President. (3)

(iii) Discuss the term of the office of the Vice-President. (4)

Question 5

With relation to the President, answer the following questions.

(i) The President takes special powers during an emergency to protect the nation and maintain order. Justify the statement. (3)

(ii) Explain the objectives of conferring the veto powers of the President? (3)

(iii) In what circumstances does the office of the President of India became vacant? Explain briefly. (4)

Section B (History)

Attempt any three questions from this Section.

Question 6

With reference to photograph of Pandit Jawaharlal Nehru, 'famous speech in the Constituent Assembly on 14th August, 1947', answer the following questions.

(i) Mention any four reasons why All Indian Congress Committee is accepting the Mountbatten Plan. (3)

(ii) Highlight the provisions of the Indian Independence Act of 1947 regarding the Constituent Assemblies? (3)

(iii) The Cabinet Mission plan aimed to unite India while answering fair representation for all communities. (4)

Question 7

Read the excerpt given below and answer the questions that follow.

The Swadeshi Movement has been the core of the Independence movement as well and has contributed a lot to the development of Indian nationalism. This Swadeshi Movement has got much wider support from the masses since 1906 against the erstwhile Partition of Bengal and ultimately turned into a full-blown independence movement in the early 20th century till we attained Independence.

(i) Name the major cause of this movement. Give any two reasons for partition of Bengal. (3)

(ii) The Swadeshi Movement opened a new chapter in history for common people in national struggle. Analyse this statement with suitable points. (3)

(iii) Mention any four impacts of Swadeshi Movement. (4)

Question 8

Emergence of Fascism and Nazism were the indirect outcome of First World War. In this context, answer the following questions.

(i) The rise of Hitler in Italy was a major cause for the World War II. Mention any three points which were responsible for the emergence of Nazism. (3)

(ii) The Treaty of Versailles was responsible for the totalitarian rule among the world. Justify this statement with suitable points. (3)

(iii) Fascissm is an authoritarian political ideology characterised by dictatorial power and extreme nationalism. Analyse this statement by mentioning any four points. (4)

Question 9

Second World War was the outcome of failure of the League of Nations which was meant to check the aggression of member countries. In this regard, answer the following questions.

(i) The Second World War reshape global politics and international relations. Justify the statement with suitable examples. (3)

(ii) Analyse the consequences of the Second World War with reference to the formation of the United Nations. (3)

(iii) 'The Defeat of the Axis powers' led to the birth of New world. Justify the statement by mentioning any three point. (4)

Question 10

The United Nations played a key constructive role in maintaining global peace and dynamic relations among its members. In this respect, answer the following questions.

(i) Mention any three powers of the International Court of Justice (ICJ). (3)

(ii) What is the composition of the UNICEF? Analyse the major functions of the UNICEF in protection of children rights across the world. (3)

(iii) A momentous achievement for India as Santiniketan, West Bengal, has been officially inscribed on UNESCO's World Heritage List. *(The Indian Express)*
Explain any four functions of the UNESCO in preservation of the Cultural Heritage. (4)

Answers

1. (i) (b) 250
(ii) (b) Article 356 and Article 365
(iii) (c) C
(iv) (d) All of these
(v) (d) Both (a) and (b)
(vi) (a) P and R
(vii) (b) (R) is the reason for (A)
(viii) (a) Swadeshi Movement
(ix) (b) Hitler
(x) (a) Mangal Pandey
(xi) (c) The Political leaders
(xii) (b) The invasion of Poland
(xiii) (a) It remained against military alliances like NATO, SEATO and Warsaw Pact.
(xiv) (b) Non-cooperation Movement
(xv) (a) Increased harmony between the US and USSR.
(xvi) (c) Germany, Italy and Japan

SAMPLE QUESTION PAPER 3

A HIGHLY SIMULATED Sample Question Paper for ICSE Class X

History & Civics (Unsolved)

General Instructions : See Sample Paper 1

Part - I

(30 Marks)

Attempt all questions from this Part

Question 1

(i) Identify the appointments made by the below body through the President.

(a) Judge of Supreme Court
(b) Governors of State
(c) Attorney General of India
(d) All of these

(ii) Which of the following statement is correct about the formation of government in India? (1)

(a) Majority of the members of the Lower House of Parliament.
(b) Minority of members of the Upper House of Parliament.
(c) Majority of the members of the Upper House of the Parliament.
(d) Minority of members of the Lower House of Parliament.

(iii) Which of the following is also known as the ex-officio chairperson of the Rajya Sabha? (1)

(a) President of India
(b) Speaker of the Lok Sabha
(c) Vice-President of India
(d) Chief Justice of India

(iv) Given below are details of a few Indian citizens

Person	Age [in years]	Description
P	50	Is a practicing lawyer in the High Court for 10 years
Q	45	Has held an administrative position in the government
R	55	Is a retired judge of a lower court
S	60	Has been a professor of Political Science at a university

Select the person who fulfills the eligibility criteria to become a judge of the Supreme Court of India.

(a) P (b) Q (c) R (d) S

(v) In 2020, Member of Parliament (MP) X from Rajasthan and MP Y from Uttar Pradesh raised concerns about the lack of infrastructure development in rural areas during a Parliamentary session. Both MPs, along with other concerned members, participated in a committee discussion where they shared their grievances and debated over policy measures to improve rural infrastructure. After several rounds of discussions and suggestions, the MPs, along with the committee, proposed a comprehensive rural development plan that was later passed in the Parliament with bipartisan support. (1)

Which advantage of Parliament is highlighted in the above case?

(a) Encourages debates and discussions (b) Ensures transparency in decision-making
(c) Promotes cooperative decision-making (d) Strengthens regional development

(vi) On 15th June, 2023, the Supreme Court of India delivered a landmark judgement in a case related to the Right to Privacy, interpreting it as a Fundamental Right under Article 21 of the Constitution. The judgement reaffirmed that the Right to Privacy is intrinsic to individual liberty. *-The Hindu*

What information about the Supreme Court's judgement can we obtain from the above passage? (1)

(a) The judgement relates to the interpretation of the Fundamental Rights.
(b) The judgement was delivered by the President of India.
(c) The Supreme Court can only deal with privacy-related cases.
(d) The judgement was related to a case under Article 18.

(vii) Read the two statements given below about the Early Nationalists and select the option that shows the correct relationship between (A) and (R). (1)

Assertion (A) The Early Nationalists focused on achieving political reforms through Constitutional means.

Reason (R) The Early Nationalists believed that cooperation with the British government would lead to gradual reforms.

Codes

(a) (R) contradicts (A)
(b) (R) is the reason for (A)
(c) (A) is true but (R) is false
(d) (A) and (R) are independent of each other

(viii) Identify the country which emerged as a world power, militarily and economically after the First World War. (1)

(a) Great Britain (b) United States of America
(c) France (d) Italy

(ix) The British Government introduced the The Permanent Settlement Act of 1793 in Bengal. Who was most directly affected by this act? (1)

(a) The Farmers (b) The Zamindars
(c) The Artisans (d) The British Officers

(x) Sonali, a student of class 10th, had a project on history, so she started collecting news and books of the history. She read that between 1939 to 1945 many events occurred in the Europe, USA and Japan. For example, European Nations Declare War, Hitlers attacks, Germany invaded Poland, etc.

Which of the following event is most likely occurred in the year 1941? (1)

(a) Hitler attacked on Poland (b) Kamikaze was formed
(c) USA joined the war against Japan (d) World War II started

(xi) Which of the following was not an objective of the Muslim League? (1)

(a) To keep the Muslim intelligentsia away from the mainstream of the National Movement.
(b) To protect the political and other rights of Muslims.
(c) To promote a feeling of loyalty among the Indian Muslims towards the British Government.
(d) To expose the true character of the British Rule.

(xii) Identify the provisions of the Indian Independence Act of 1947.

P. It provided for the partition of British India into two independent dominions - India and Pakistan.

Q. It gave the British Parliament the authority to control Indian affairs for the next 10 years.

R. It ended British control over India and granted full independence to India and Pakistan.

S. It created the post of Prime Minister in India.

Which of the above provisions are correct?

(a) P and Q (b) P and R (c) R and S (d) Q and S

(xiii) Read the description and identify the person.

He was a political Guru of M.K. Gandhi. (1)

(a) Gopal Krishna Gokhale (b) Subhash Chandra Bose
(c) Bipin Chandra Pal (d) Bal Gangadhar Tilak

(xiv) Identify the odd one out from the following states of Bengal province of British India? (1)

(a) Bihar and Orissa (b) Chotanagpur and Assam
(c) Manipur and Nagaland (d) None of these

(xv) The below book is said to be written by who amongst the following? (1)

(a) Woodrow Wilson (b) Archeduke Ferdinand
(c) Mussolini (d) Hitler

(xvi) Complete the given analogy.
Gandhi: Quit India Movement:: Nelson Mandela : (1)

(a) The Russian Revolution
(b) The Apartheid Resistance Movement
(c) The Meiji Restoration
(d) The Industrial Revolution

Question 2

(i) **Headline PM Modi to chair meeting of Council of Ministers on 3rd, July amid talk of Union Cabinet reshuffle, Prime Minister Narendra Modi will chair a meeting of the Union Council of Ministers on 3rd July, amid talk of a possible Union Cabinet reshuffle ahead of the 2024 Lok Sabha elections.**

Source Times of India 29th June, 2023

Who can approve or disapprove bill before it is laid into Parliament by any minister. Who is the head of the cabinet? (2)

(ii) State any two differences between the Council of Ministers and the Cabinet. (2)

(iii) Mention any two principles of the Parliamentary structure of government. (2)

(iv) Mention any two terms of the 'Treaty of Versailles'. (2)

(v) "Imagine you were a weaver in the year 1850. Mention any two ways in which the British trade policies would have affected your livelihood".

(vi) Who headed the following committees of the Constitutional Assembly? (2)
a. Drafting committee b. Union Power Committee (2)

(vii) Name any two states which were affected by the Doctrine of Lapse. (2)

Part - II

(50 Marks)

Section A (Civics)

Attempt any two questions from this Section

Question 3

The Cabinet holds a pivotal position in the working of the Indian Parliamentary Government. In this context, discuss the following questions.

(i) Who appoints the cabinet ministers in India? Mention any two important role of the cabinet in working of the government. (3)

(ii) Cabinet is also called as the powerhouse of the government. Justify this statement with suitable points. (3)

(iii) Mention any four Executive Powers of the Cabinet. (4)

Question 4

With reference to the Union Parliament, answer the following questions.

(i) What is the maximum strength of the Lok Sabha provided by the Constitution? How many members does the President nominate to the Lok Sabha? How the members of the Lok Sabha are elected? (3)

(ii) The two Houses of the Parliament enjoy co-equal power in many spheres, Justify the statement by giving any three examples. (3)

(iii) Explain any four of the Rajya Sabha's exclusive powers in India's federal set-up. (4)

Question 5

With reference to the judiciary, answer the following questions.

(i) How does the President appoint an acting Chief Justice and ad hoc judge of the Supreme Court? (3)

(ii) The Constitution has made various provisions to safeguard and ensure the independent and impartial functioning of the Supreme Court. Analyse this statement by mentioning of any three points in favour of the statement. (3)

(iii) State the four aspects of the appeal by special level power of the Supreme Court. (4)

Section B (History)

Attempt any three questions from this Section

Question 6

Read the excerpt given below and answer the questions that follow.

Around the same time, in 1913, Jinnah had finally joined the Muslim League. Remarkably, he continued to be a member, simultaneously, of the Congress, which he had joined in 1906. He was held in high esteem in both Congress and Muslim League circles and was popularly known as an "ambassador of Hindu-Muslim unity". Tilak and Jinnah had already worked together in the previous decade. Hence, a confluence of India's two main political streams led to the historic Lucknow Pact in 1916.

(i) Mention three national events that led to signing of Lucknow Pact. (3)

(ii) Name the President of the Lucknow Congress Session and also mention any two features of the Lucknow Pact. (3)

(iii) The Lucknow Congress Session was a significant session, which united and dissolved the strife of moderates and extremists in India. Justify this statement with suitable arguments. (4)

Question 7

There were many factors which finally led to the outbreak of 1857 Revolt, with this reference, answer the following questions.

(i) Mention any three reasons of resentment of the rulers of the native states against the British. (3)

(ii) Analyse the factors responsible for dissatisfaction among Indian artisans and Craftman. (3)

(iii) Mention any four points to highlight the impact of the introduction of the Enfield Rifles. (4)

Question 8

During entire colonial rule, India witnessed a number of repressive measures by the British Government. With this reference, answer the following questions.

(i) The British introduced the Vernacular Press Act to control the Indian press. Mention any three reasons for the introduction of this act. (3)

(ii) The Vernacular Press Act affected the Freedom of Speech and the press in India? Analyse this statement with suitable examples. (3)

(iii) The Vernacular Press Act was a significant step in curbing nationalistic sentiments. Mention any four consequences of this act on Indian society. (4)

Question 9

Answer the following questions based on the picture given below.

(i) Identify the picture of this person. Mention any two contributions of him to the Indian national movement. **(3)**

(ii) Mention any three contributions in the field of economy of his time? **(3)**

(iii) Analyse how Dadabhai Naoroji's contributions helped in raising awareness about British economic exploitation of India during the National movement. **(4)**

Question 10

(i) Who were the founding members of the Non-Aligned Movement (NAM)? Mention any two objectives of the NAM. **(3)**

(ii) The Non-Aligned Movement played a significant role during the Cold War. Justify this statement with any three points. **(3)**

(iii) Explain the following terms **(4)**

(a) Bandung Conference **(b) Peaceful Coexistence of countries**

Answers

1. (i) (d) All of these
(ii) (a) Majority of the members of the Lower House of Parliament
(iii) (a) President of India
(iv) (a) P
(v) (c) Promates cooperative decision making
(vi) (a) The judgement relates to the interpretation of the Fundamental Rights.
(vii) (b) (R) is the reason for (A)
(viii) (b) United States of America
(ix) (a) The Farmers
(x) (c) USA joined the war against Japan
(xi) (d) To expose the true character of the British Rule.
(xii) (b) P and R
(xiii) (a) Gopal Krishna Gokhale
(xiv) (c) Manipur and Nagaland
(xv) (d) Hitler
(xvi) (b) The Apartheid Resistance Movement

SAMPLE QUESTION PAPER 4

A HIGHLY SIMULATED Sample Question Paper for ICSE Class X

History & Civics (Unsolved)

General Instructions : See Sample Paper 1

Part - I

(30 Marks)

Attempt all questions from this Part

Question 1

(i) Which of the following motions can be brought up during the budget session to disapprove any monetary policy of the government by the Parliament? (1)

(a) Adjournment Motion
(b) Cut Motion
(c) No-Confidence Motion
(d) Censure Motion

(ii) Your school has organised a discussion on the topic - Role of the Court in Indian Federalism. Which of the following leaders would most likely be part of the discussion? (1)

(a) K.K. Aziz
(b) Justice V.R. Krishna Iyer
(c) P.V. Narsimha Rao
(d) Fazl Ali

(iii) Identify the act which led to the establishment of the institution as shown in the picture below.

(a) Morley Minto Reforms
(b) Montagu Chelmsford Reforms
(c) Government of India Act, 1935
(d) Pitts India Act

(iv) Given below are details of few Indian citizens.

Candidate	Age	Other Details
A	25	Post Graduate in Law
B	56	Judge in High Court for 7 years
C	41	Retired Civil Servant
D	32	Retired Police Officer

Select the person who fulfills the criteria to become Judge of Supreme Court. (1)

(a) A (b) B (c) C (d) D

(v) On 1st July, 2023, the President of India exercised his powers under Article 72 of the Constitution to grant a pardon to a person convicted of a criminal offense. The decision was made after careful review of the case. *XYZ News , 5th July, 2024*

What information about the President's power can we obtain from the above passage? (1)

(a) The President has the power to reduce prison sentences only.

(b) The President can grant pardons in cases of criminal offences only.

(c) The President can only grant pardons for political offences.

(d) The President's power to grant a pardon must be approved by the Cabinet.

(vi) Read the two statements given below about President and select the options that shows the correct relationship between (A) and (R).

Assertion (A) Indian President is the head of the State.

Reason (R) Indian Parliament consists of the President, Lok Sabha and Rajya Sabha. (1)

Codes

(a) (R) contradicts (A) (b) (R) is the reason for (A)

(c) (A) is true (R) is false (d) (A) and (R) are independent of each other

(vii) Identify the exclusive powers of the International Court of Justice. (1)

P. Can give advisory opinions on legal questions

Q. Can hear disputes between states

R. Can impose sanctions on countries

S. Can create international laws

Codes

(a) P and Q (b) R and S

(c) P and R (d) Q and S

(viii) The Government of Country B has introduced a law similar to the Salt Tax Act of 1882. Who will be impacted by this law? (1)

(a) The Traders (b) The Farmers and common people

(c) The British officials (d) The Indian soldiers

(ix) Which of the following is a drawback of the Lucknow Pact? (1)

(a) The Congress lost its secular character by accepting separate electorates for Muslims and hence paved the way for communal tensions.

(b) It emphasised separate political existence for the Hindus and Muslims.

(c) Communal Veto in legislation was provided by this pact.

(d) All of the above

(x) Lala Lajpat Rai who is also known as the 'Lion of Punjab,' was a prominent freedom fighter who fought against British colonial rule. He played a significant role in the non-violent struggle for Indian independence and was known for his advocacy for the rights of Indians under British oppression.

Which aspect of Lala Lajpat Rai's contributions is highlighted in the above passage?

(a) He was involved in the political struggle for independence.

(b) He focused on economic development for the country.

(c) He never promoted social reforms.

(d) He was the leader of peaceful agitation method of resistance against British rule.

(xi) A student named Rohan is doing a research on a personality who led the Revolt of 1857 from Kanpur. Whom is he doing a research on? (1)

(a) Nana Sahib (b) Tantia Tope

(c) General Bakht Khan (d) Kunwar Singh

(xii) Identify the odd one out from the following, which is not correct about Subhash Chandra Bose? (1)

(a) He inaugurated the Indian National Planning Committee.

(b) He became an active worker of the Freedom Movement during Non-Cooperation.

(c) He was unanimously selected as the President of the Congress in 1938.

(d) He did not supported Gandhiji when Non-Cooperation Movement was withdrawn.

(xiii) Which of the following were part of the Mahatma Gandhi's Civil Disobedience movement? (1)

(a) Non-violent satyagraha (b) Boycott of schools, colleges, courts, foreign goods

(c) No tax campaigns (d) All of these

(xiv) Complete the given analogy. (1)

Fascism : Mussolini :: Nazism : ?

Options

(a) Stalin (b) Hitler (c) Churchill (d) Roosevelt

(xv) The below picture depicts Germany's invasion on a country that led to beginning of World War II. Name the country. (1)

(a) Poland (b) Cuba (c) Japan (d) China

(xvi) Read the description and identify the person.

He was a prominent freedom fighter, known for his slogan, 'Swaraj is my birthright, and I shall have it,' (1)

(a) Lala Lajpat Rai (b) Bal Gangadhar Tilak

(c) Subhas Chandra Bose (d) Mahatma Gandhi

Question 2

(i) Read the Questions given below and answer the following.

a. Who were the architects of NAM? b. When was the Panchsheel Agreement signed? (2)

(ii) Read the given news carefully.

Aren't you accountable, My Lord?......

In the past few days, there has been a striking development which is not of much public interest yet intellectual interest. The Union Government and the Supreme Court have locked horns on the matter of the appointment of judges in various courts...... *Source Organiser; 27th June, 2023*

Give two reasons why did Constitution makers emphasised more on independence of judiciary.

(iii) Mention any two reasons for the growth of Nationalism in India. (2)

(iv) Mention the provisions of the Government of India Act, 1919 which throw light on the 'Divide and Rule' policy of the British Government? (2)

(v) Imagine you were a political leader in 1919. Mention any two ways in which the Government of India Act, 1919, would have affected you. (2)

(vi) Mention any two reasons for the acceptance of Mountbatten Plan by the Muslim League. (2)

(vii) Name the two dictators who rose to power in Europe before World War II. (2)

Part - II

(50 Marks)

Section A (Civics)

Attempt any two questions from this Section

Question 3

The President is the Executive Head of the Union of India. In this regard, answer the following questions.

(i) Mention any three qualifications for the President. (3)

(ii) Explain the impeachment procedure of the President. (3)

(iii) Explain the following terms.

(a) Pardonery powers (b) Emergency powers (4)

Question 4

The Supreme Court of India is the apex judicial authority and the final court of appeal in the country. With reference to the Supreme Court, answer the following questions.

(i) Who appoints the Chief Justice of India? Mention any two powers of the Supreme Court. (3)

(ii) Under Article 142, the Supreme Court of India can pass any order to do complete justice. Justify this statement with any three points. (3)

(iii) What is meant by the Revisory jurisdiction? Why it is important in the judicial system? How does it function in the Indian judiciary? (4)

Question 5

The Rajya Sabha is the Upper House of Parliament and plays a vital role in the legislative process. With reference to this, answer the following questions.

(i) The Rajya Sabha is a Revising Chamber and cannot initiate Money Bills. Mention any three powers of the Rajya Sabha that justify its role as a revising body. (3)

(ii) Mention any three qualifications required for a person to be elected as a member of the Rajya Sabha. (3)

(iii) Describe the process of election of members to the Rajya Sabha. (4)

Section B (History)

Attempt any three questions from this Section

Question 6

The Swadeshi Movement was a key part of the Indian independence struggle, focusing on self-reliance and boycott of foreign goods. With reference to this, answer the following questions.

(i) The Swadeshi Movement was based on promoting indigenous industries. Mention any three strategies adopted during the movement to achieve this. **(3)**

(ii) Analyse the impact of Swadeshi Movement on the British economic interests in India? **(3)**

(iii) The Swadeshi Movement led to the rise of strong nationalist sentiments. Justify this statement by stating any four outcomes of the movement in India. **(4)**

Question 7

Read the excerpt given below and answer the questions that follow.

After a book on the history of non-violent resistance in the Indian nationalist movement, historian David Hardiman's latest work takes his study forward to examine the culmination of the first surge of struggle from its launch in 1920 to its end with Mahatma Gandhi's arrest two years later.

The book, "Non-Cooperation in India: Non-Violent Strategy and Protest", was released on Monday. It is published by Westland Books. The Non-Cooperation Movement by the Indian National Congress (INC), organised and led by Gandhi, was the first mass movement organised nationwide during India's struggle for freedom.

(i) Who was the Viceroy of India during this movement? Mention any two causes of this movement. **(3)**

(ii) Mention any three activities under this movement. **(3)**

(iii) Analyse any four impacts of this movement. **(4)**

Question 8

Lucknow Pact of 1916 has historical significance due to a number of reasons. With the reference of this pact, answer the following questions.

(i) Mention three changes were observed in the relations between the Indian National Congress and the Muslim League? **(3)**

(ii) In what ways it influenced the Indian National Movement? Mention the importance of Lucknow Pact in consolidating the demand of Independence. **(3)**

(iii) The Lucknow Pact marked a new phase in Indian politics. Analyse this statement by stating any four outcomes of the pact for Indian politics. **(4)**

Question 9

The United Nations (UN) is an international organisation aimed at promoting peace, security and cooperation among nations. With reference to this, answer the following questions

(i) The UN was established to address global challenges. Mention any three primary objectives of the United Nations. **(3)**

(ii) The United Nations ensure the representation of all countries in its decision-making processes? Justify this statement with any four points. **(3)**

(iii) The United Nations plays a significant role in addressing human rights issues. Analyse this statement by stating any four major contributions of the UN in promoting human rights worldwide. **(4)**

Question 10

Study the picture given below and answer the following questions.

(i) Identify the leader in the picture and mention any two components of his ideology. (3)

(ii) Mention three reasons for his popularity in the world politics? (3)

(iii) Hitler implemented several policies to consolidate power. Mention any four policies that led to the beginning of World War II. (4)

Answers

1. (i) (b) Cut Motion
(ii) (b) Justice V.R. Krishna Iyer
(iii) (c) Government of India Act, 1935
(iv) (b) B
(v) (d) The President's power to grant a pardon must be approved by the Cabinet.
(vi) (b) (R) is the reason for (A)
(vii) (a) P and Q
(viii) (b) The Farmers and common people.
(ix) (d) All of the above
(x) (a) He was involved in the political struggle for independence.
(xi) (a) Nana Sahib
(xii) (c) He was unanimously selected as the President of the Congress in 1938.
(xiii) (d) All of the above
(xiv) (b) Hitler
(xv) (a) Poland
(xvi) (b) Bal Gangadhar Tilak

SAMPLE QUESTION PAPER 5

A HIGHLY SIMULATED Sample Question Paper for ICSE Class X

History & Civics (Unsolved)

General Instructions : See Sample Paper 1

Part - I

(30 Marks)

Attempt all questions from this Part

Question 1

(i) On 20th July, 2023, the President of India nominated four eminent persons to the Rajya Sabha under Article 80 of the Constitution, recognising their contributions in the fields of arts, literature, and science. - *The Express, July 21, 2023* **(1)**

What information about presidential nominations can we obtain from the above passage?

(a) The President can nominate members to the Lok Sabha.

(b) The President nominates members to the Rajya Sabha based on their expertise.

(c) The President's nominations require approval from the Prime Minister.

(d) The nominated members have a tenure of three years.

(ii) A landmark case was brought before the Supreme Court, where a long-pending land dispute was resolved through a constitutional bench ruling. The judgement set a precedent, ensuring uniform interpretation of property laws across states. *Case Study, Supreme Court of India* **(1)**

Which function of the Supreme Court is highlighted in the above case?

(a) Judicial Review (b) Guardian of the Constitution

(c) Court of Record (d) Final Court of Appeal

(iii) Identify the exclusive powers of the Lok Sabha. **(1)**

P. Can introduce a Money Bill.

Q. Can remove the Vice President through a resolution.

R. Can initiate a motion of no confidence against the government.

S. Can recommend the creation of a new All India Service.

(a) P and Q (b) R and S

(c) P and R (d) Q and S

(iv) Identify the person to whom the below depicted institution should advise while appointing any person to judicial service of the state. (1)

(a) Governor
(b) Chief Minister
(c) President
(d) Prime Minister

(v) Given below are details of few Indian citizens.

Candidate	Age	Other Details
A	57	Metropolitan city Judge for 14 years
B	66	Lawyer
C	35	Member of Lok Sabha
D	52	Magistrate for four years

Choose the person who fulfills the criteria to become the judge of High Court. (1)

(a) A (b) B (c) C (d) D

(vi) Read the two statements given below about jurisdiction of Supreme Court and select the option that shows the correct relationship between (A) and (R). (1)

Assertion (A) The Supreme Court of India has exclusive jurisdiction regarding the constitutional validity of law.

Reason (R) The Supreme Court is the Guardian of the Indian Constitution.

Codes

(a) (R) contradicts (A)
(b) (R) is the reason for (A)
(c) (A) is true, but (R) is false
(d) (A) and (R) are independent of each other

(vii) Complete the given analogy

Simon Commission: 1927 :: Gandhi-Irwin Pact: .... (1)

(a) 1928 (b) 1929 (c) 1930 (d) 1931

(viii) Which of the following aspect is not correct with respect to Simon Commission? (1)

(a) The commission was constituted under Sir John Simon.
(b) It was constituted to review the functioning of the Constitutional system in India.
(c) A vague offer for Dominion status was offered by this commission.
(d) This commission was opposed by the Indians as there were no Indians in it.

(ix) The headquarters of the below depicted organ of UN is located in which city? (1)

(a) Hague (b) New York (c) Paris (d) London

(x) Identify the odd one out from the following which is not correct about the Early Nationalists (Moderates)? (1)

(a) They fought against unfavourable policies of the British Government.

(b) They relied on constitutional and peaceful methods.

(c) They believed in expansion of Legislative Council and Legislative Assembly.

(d) They had faith in British sense of Justice and fairness.

(xi) Country X has been forced to sign a treaty similar to the Treaty of Versailles (1919) after losing a major war. Which of the following is likely to be impacted the most by this treaty? (1)

(a) The territorial boundaries of the country (b) The agricultural policies of the country

(c) The cultural heritage of the country (d) The education system of the country

(xii) Your school has organised a poster-making competition on the topic - Economic Exploitation of India during British Rule. Which of the following leaders would most likely be part of the poster? (1)

(a) Bal Gangadhar Tilak (b) Dadabhai Naoroji

(c) Lala Lajpat Rai (d) Bipin Chandra Pal

(xiii) Identify the main principle for which the Second World War was fought?

(a) Protecting the national interests. (b) Maintaining military alliances.

(c) To make the world safe for democracy. (d) Removal of aggressive policies.

(xiv) Read the description and identify the person.

He was a prominent Indian leader, a social reformer and a key figure in the Indian Renaissance, known for his contributions to education and the promotion of Indian languages. (1)

(a) Surendranath Banerjee (b) Raja Ram Mohan Roy

(c) Lala Lajpat Rai (d) Bipin Chandra Pal

(xv) Which of the following was a common ideology of the dictators? (1)

(a) Faith in Totalitarian rule (b) One Party One Leader

(c) Aggressive Nationalism and Imperialism (d) All of these

(xvi) Which of the following scenarios describes the principle of Panchsheel? (1)

(a) A country forms a military alliance with neighbouring countries.

(b) A country respects the sovereignty and territorial integrity of other nations.

(c) A country advocates for armed conflict as a means of resolving disputes.

(d) A country seeks to dominate other nations economically.

Question 2

(i) Mention any two exclusive powers of the Rajya Sabha. (2)

(ii) Read the extract given below and answer the question which follows.

Telangana National Lok Adalat to be held on 10th June. All kinds of civil, compoundable criminal cases, matrimonial disputes, maintenance cases, harassment cases, domestic violence, cases under Sec 138 of negotiable instruments act, motor vehicle accident claims, etc pending before High Court and lower courts can be settled through the Adalat.

Source The Siyasat Daily 6th June, 2023

Give information about the role of Lok Adalat in Indian Judicial System. (2)

(iii) Name any two impacts of the Swadeshi and Boycott Movements. (2)

(iv) Mention any two provision of the 'Panchsheel'. (2)

(v) Which category of action was taken during the Freedom Struggle in the following scenarios

(a) Introduction of the Rowlatt Act

(b) Formation of the Quit India Movement (2)

(vi) Mention any two points by which the Cabinet Mission Plan try to preserve the unity of India? (2)

(vii) Imagine you were a farmer during the First World War. Mention any two ways in which the war would have affected you. (2)

Part - II

(50 marks)

Section A (Civics)

Attempt any two questions from this Section

Question 3

With reference to the power of the High Court, answer the following questions.

(i) Mention any three powers of the criminal appellate jurisdiction of High Court? (3)

(ii) Who supervise the lower court in a state? Mention any two powers given under original jurisdiction to High Court. (3)

(iii) Analyse the powers of High Court related to the exercises of the Subordinate Courts? (4)

Question 4

The Parliament of India is the supreme legislative body, responsible for making laws and overseeing the functioning of the government. With reference to the Parliament, answer the following questions.

(i) The Rajya Sabha has certain unique functions. Justify this by mentioning any three distinct powers of the Rajya Sabha. (3)

(ii) The Lok Sabha recently passed a bill with a majority vote. Who can dissolve the Lok Sabha? Mention any two provisions related to the composition of the Lok Sabha. (3)

(iii) Describe any four functions of the Parliament apart from lawmaking. (4)

Question 5

The Prime Minister of India is the head of the government and plays a crucial role in the functioning of the executive. With reference to the Prime Minister, answer the following questions.

(i) The Prime Minister holds significant powers in the Cabinet. Justify this by mentioning any three powers of the Prime Minister. (3)

(ii) The Prime Minister recently appointed new ministers in the Cabinet. Who approves these appointments? Explain the role of the Prime Minister in forming the Cabinet. (3)

(iii) Mention any four responsibilities of the Prime Minister in the functioning of the government. (4)

Section B (History)

Attempt any three questions from this Section

Question 6

Read the excerpt given below and answer the questions that follow.

The Indian National Army trial was a historic event that took place between November 1945 and May 1946 at Delhi's Red Fort. The trial was a court martial of a number of INA officers on the charges of torture, treason, murder and abetment to murder during the World War II, with all Indians cutting across their differences supporting the freedom fighters. Virtually refreshing the memory of today's generation about this event was the play 'Lal Quile Ka Aakhri Muqadma' staged by Pierrot's Troupe and directed by M. Sayeed Alam at New Delhi's LTG Auditorium recently.

Source India Narrative June, 2023

(i) Name any two conferences that led to the formation of above organisation. Mention about any two personalities that were associated with this. (3)

(ii) Mention the three objectives of above organisation. (3)

(iii) Analyse any four achievements of this organisation. (4)

Question 7

The League of Nations was an international organisation established after World War I to promote peace and cooperation among countries. With reference to the League of Nations, answer the following questions.

(i) The League of Nations aimed to prevent future conflicts. Mention any three key objectives of the League of Nations. (3)

(ii) How did the failure of the League of Nations impact global politics and the subsequent formation of the United Nations? (3)

(iii) The League of Nations faced challenges in maintaining peace and resolving conflicts. Analyse this statement by stating any four limitations of the League of Nations. (4)

Question 8

Dictatorship refers to a form of government where power is concentrated in the hands of one individual or a small group. With reference to the rise of dictatorship in Italy, answer the following.

(i) Name the dictator who rose to power in Italy in the 1920s. Mention any two key factors that led to the establishment of a dictatorship in Italy. (3)

(ii) The media and propaganda played an important role in the rise of dictatorship. Thus, the dictatorship leaders used propaganda to control public opinion. Mention any three ways propaganda that was used to support the regime. (3)

(iii) The dictatorship of the 1930s and 1940s led to the suppression of many rights. Mention any four policies or actions enforced by the dictator to consolidate power. (4)

Question 9

Look at the picture given and answer the following questions.

REDS BOMB INDIAN LEGISLATURE

BLAST FOLLOWING SHARP PARLIAMENTARY CRISIS CAUSES INJURY TO MANY

(i) Describe the incident depicted in the image. Mention any two effects of it on nationalism. (3)

(ii) Mention any three points to analyse how the growth of nationalism led to changes in political boundaries and social structures. (3)

(iii) Nationalist movements were often met with opposition. Analyse this statement with any four reasons that explain why some countries resisted nationalist movements during the 19th and 20th centuries. (4)

Question 10

The United Nations Children's Fund (UNICEF) works to protect the rights and well-being of children worldwide. With reference to UNICEF, answer the following.

(i) Who heads the UNICEF? Mention any two important roles of UNICEF in global child welfare. (3)

(ii) Mention any three major programs or initiatives led by UNICEF to improve children's lives worldwide. (3)

(iii) UNICEF's work is essential for global development, Justify the statement with four suitable examples. (4)

Answers

1. (i) (b) The President nominates members to the Rajya Sabha based on their expertise.

(ii) (d) Final Court of Appeal

(iii) (c) P and R

(iv) (a) Governor

(v) (a) A

(vi) (a) (R) contradicts (A)

(vii) (d) 1931

(viii (c) A vague offer for Dominion status was offered by this commission.

(ix) (a) Hague

(x) (a) They fought against unfavourable policies of the British Government.

(xi) (a) The territorial boundaries of the country

(xii) (b) Dadabhai Naoroji

(xiii) (a) Protecting the national interests.

(xiv) (b) Raja Ram Mohan Roy

(xv) (d) All of these

(xvi) (b) A country respects the sovereignty and territorial integrity of other nations.

ICSE
LATEST SPECIMEN PAPER

ICSE Latest Specimen Paper

History & Civics (Fully Solved)

General Instructions

1. Attempt all questions from Part I (Compulsory). A total of 5 questions are to be attempted from Part II, 2 out of 3 questions from Section A and 3 out of 5 questions from Section B.
2. The intended marks for questions or parts of questions are given in brackets ( ).

Time : 2 Hrs **Max. Marks : 80**

Part - I

(30 Marks)

Attempt all questions from this Part.

1. Choose the correct answers to the questions from the given options. **(16)**

(Do not copy the question, write the correct answers only.)

(i) On 19th May, 2023, the President of India exercised legislative power under Article 123 of the Constitution, during the period Parliament was in recess, to promulgate The Government of National Capital Territory of Delhi Ordinance, 2023. *–The Hindu, 26th May, 2023*

What information about an ordinance can be obtain from the above passage? **(1)**

(a) The ordinance must be approved within six weeks.

(b) Only the Cabinet can prepare an ordinance.

(c) It is issued when the Parliament is not functioning.

(d) If the Parliament does not approve it within six weeks it becomes inoperative. **[Application]**

(ii) Given below are details of few Indian citizens.

Person	Age [In years]	Description
W	34	Is a Professor in the Government College
X	35	Has taken up the citizenship of the United States of America
Y	27	Is a reputed sportsperson
Z	36	Is a scientist

Select the person who fulfils the eligibility criteria to become the President of India. **[Understanding] (1)**

(a) W (b) X

(c) Y (d) Z

(iii) Who made the amendment which resulted in the below headline? **[Application] (1)**

THE TIMES OF INDIA

In Historic Move Within 100 Days Of Modi-2, Govt Bifurcates State Into 2 UTs, Defangs Article 370 & Scraps 35A

KASHMIR IS NOW UNION'S TERRITORY

J&K To Lose Special Status, Centre To Directly Rule Ladakh

INDIA'S NORTH POLE SHIFTS TO CENTRE

Why now? PM, Shah felt political tide and timing favoured action

(a) The Supreme Court (b) The President
(c) The Parliament (d) The Prime Minister

(iv) Residents of Jodhpur, X and Y got married in the year 2014 and after 4 months of wedlock, petty family issues and arguments resulted in their separation for 6 years. The matter was placed before the Bench of Lok Adalat Family Court, Jodhpur wherein all efforts were made to reunite the family again. With constant efforts of counselling parties agreed to live together and withdraw their Divorce Petition

Case Study, Lok Adalat, District - Jodhpur.

Which advantage of the Lok Adalat is highlighted in the above case? **[Application] (1)**

(a) Saves money
(b) Speedy justice
(c) Works on the spirit of compromise
(d) Reduces the burden on High Courts

(v) District Judge : Cases :: Sessions Judge : Criminal Cases **[Recall] (1)**

(a) Advisory (b) Civil
(c) Constitutional (d) Appellate

(vi) Identify the exclusive powers of the Rajya Sabha.

P : Can introduce a new All India Service

Q : Can impeach the President

R : Can never be dissolved as a whole

S : Can introduce a Money Bill **[Recall] (1)**

(a) P and Q (b) R and S
(c) P and R (d) Q and S

(vii) Read the two statements given below about the Civil Disobedience Movement and select the option that shows the correct relationship between (A) and (R).

Assertion (A) The Civil Disobedience Movement was renewed by Mahatma Gandhi.

Reason (R) The Second Round Table Conference was a failure. **[Analysis] (1)**

(a) R contradicts A
(b) R is the reason for A
(c) A is true but R is false
(d) A and R are independent of each other

(viii) The government of Country X has introduced a law similar to Ilbert Bill introduced in 1883. Who will be impacted by this Bill? **[Understanding] (1)**

(a) The Farmers
(b) The Artisans
(c) The Soldiers
(d) The Judges

(ix) The area in which Anand stays has had no water supply for three days in spite of repeated complaints. The residents have a meeting and discuss a few methods to resolve this problem. Being a follower of the beliefs and methods of the Early Nationalists, which of the following methods is Anand not likely to approve? **[Application] (1)**

(a) Peaceful procession by the residents
(b) Follow the method of boycott
(c) Write a petition to the government
(d) Write an article in the newspaper highlighting the problem.

(x) Which of the given policies is not aligned with the ideologies of the leader seen in the picture? **[Understanding] (1)**

(a) Prioritising military expansion
(b) Promoting racist policies
(c) Hosting an anti-communist seminar
(d) Holding pro-democracy rallies

(xi) Identify the odd one out of the following objectives of the Muslim League. **[Analysis] (1)**

(a) To promote among Muslims of India, support for the British.
(b) To promote cultural and socio-economic cooperation among Muslims.
(c) To protect and advance political rights and interests of the Muslims.
(d) To present the needs and demands of the Muslims to the government.

(xii) Your school has organised a poster making competition on the topic - Education empowerment for girls in India. Which of the following leaders would most likely be part of the poster? **[Understanding] (1)**

(a) Surendranath Banerjee
(b) Pherozeshah Mehta
(c) Dadabhai Naoroji
(d) Jyotiba Phule

(xiii) Read the description and identify the person–

He established the Forward Bloc and coined the slogan, 'Delhi Chalo'. **[Recall] (1)**

(a) Mahatma Gandhi
(b) Subhash Chandra Bose
(c) Bal Gangadhar Tilak
(d) Dadabhai Naoroji

(xiv) Which of the following countries will not be part of this cartoon? **[Application] (1)**

(a) China (b) Japan (c) Russia (d) Britain

(xv) Identify the cities most affected by American action in World War II. **[Recall] (1)**

(a) Rome, Berlin (b) Tokyo, Berlin (c) Hiroshima, Nagasaki (d) Tokyo, Rome

(xvi) Which of the following scenarios describes the Non-Alignment Policy (NAM)? **[Understanding] (1)**

(a) A country forms a military alliance only with the United States.
(b) A country maintains relations with both factions during the Cold War and does not take sides.
(c) A country is part of a religious movement advocating non-violence.
(d) A country aligns with Soviet Union and receives military aid.

2. Read the extract given below and answer the question which follows.

Congress member's adjournment motion disallowed. The notice, along with another moved demanding a discussion on China, was disallowed in the Lok Sabha. *The Times of India, 10th Feb, 2023*

(i) Who can allow or disallow the above motion? What does this motion mean? **[Understanding] (2)**

(ii) Which category of power is being exercised by the President in the following. **[Recall] (2)**

(a) Approval of Bills
(b) Appointment of the Supreme Court judges

(iii) Imagine you were an artisan, in the year 1856. Mention any two ways in which the economic policies of the British would have affected you. **[Understanding] (2)**

(iv) Give two reasons for the acceptance of the Mountbatten Plan by the Congress. **[Recall] (2)**

(v) Mention any two leaders of the Assertive Nationalists. **[Recall] (2)**

(vi) Mention any two objectives of the League of Nations. **[Recall] (2)**

(vii) Name the two alliances formed in Europe before the beginning of the First World War. **[Recall] (2)**

PART-II

SECTION - A

(20 marks)

Attempt any two questions from this Section.

3. The Union Legislature of India is not only the law-making body, but the center of all democratic political process. With reference to the Parliament, answer the following questions.

(i) The Lok Sabha is more powerful than the Rajya Sabha. Justify this by mentioning any three points. **[Analysis] (3)**

(ii) Rajya Sabha adjourned sine die, overall productivity at 79 percent. *–Deccan Herald, 21st December, 2023*

Who can adjourn the above session? Explain the composition of this house. **[Recall] (3)**

(iii) Mention any four legislative powers of the Parliament. **[Recall] (4)**

4. The President is the nominal head of the executive, the first citizen of the country, as well as the commander-in-chief of the Indian Armed Forces. With reference to this, answer the following questions.
   (i) The President is the nominal head of the country and cannot act independently.
   Mention any three legislative powers of the President which justifies the nominal position. **[Understanding] (3)**
   (ii) Mention any three financial powers of the President. **[Recall] (3)**
   (iii) Describe the procedure of impeachment of the President. **[Recall] (4)**

5. The Supreme Court of India is the supreme judicial authority and the highest court of the Republic of India. It is the final court of appeal for all civil and criminal cases. With reference to the Supreme Court, answer the following questions.
   (i) Who appoints the judges of the Supreme Court?
   Mention any two qualifications required for a person to be appointed as a judge of the Supreme Court. **[Recall] (3)**
   (ii) Under Article 129, the Supreme Court of India is called a Court of Record.
   Justify this statement with any three points. **[Analysis] (3)**
   (iii) Explain the following terms.
   (a) Revisory Jurisdiction
   (b) Advisory Jurisdiction **[Recall] (4)**

SECTION-B

(30 Marks)

Attempt any three questions from this Section.

6. The Indian Rebellion of 1857 was a major uprising against the rule of the British East India Company, which functioned as a sovereign power on behalf of the British Crown. With reference to this, answer the following questions.
   (i) The British used many policies of expansion. Mention any three such policies. **[Recall] (3)**
   (ii) How did the failure of this Revolt impact the Mughals and the Peshwas? **[Recall] (3)**
   (iii) The India army was reorganised after 1858,
   to prevent the reoccurrence of another uprising. Analyse this statement by stating any four changes made in the army after the Revolt. **[Analysis] (4)**

7. Nationalism refers to the feeling of oneness that emerges when people consider themselves as one nation. With reference to
   the growth of nationalism, answer the following.
   (i) Name the first President of Congress. Mention any two of its objectives. **[Recall] (3)**
   (ii) The press played an important role in the growth of Indian Nationalism. Thus, the British saw the need for curbs on the press. Mention any three points to analyse the role of the press in the growth of nationalism. **[Analysis] (3)**
   (iii) Lord Lytton's repressive policies led to the growth of Nationalism. Mention any four policies enforced by him. **[Recall] (4)**

8. Read the excerpt given below and answer the questions that follow

   The March, which took place in India, was led by Mohandas Gandhi to protest British rule in India. During the march, thousands of Indians followed Gandhi from his religious retreat near Ahmedabad to the Arabian Sea coast, a distance of some 240 miles. The march resulted in the arrest of nearly 60,000 people, including Gandhi himself. *–The Marion (Ohio) Star [Edited]*

(i) Name the march being discussed above. Which movement did this march lead to? In which year was that movement launched? **[Recall] (3)**

(ii) The movement which began with this march made a considerable impact on the social and political surroundings of the country. Analyse this statement by mentioning any three impacts. **[Analysis] (3)**

(iii) Mention any four clauses of the Gandhi Irwin Pact. **[Recall] (4)**

9. Look at the picture given and answer the following questions. **[Recall] (3)**

(i) Describe the incident depicted in the cartoon.

(ii) Mention any three points to analyse how Europe was rearranged as a consequence of the war caused by this incident. Consequence of the war caused by this incident. **[Recall] (3)**

(iii) The Germans described the Treaty of Versailles as harsh and humiliating.

Give any four reasons that justify this statement. **[Analysis] (4)**

10. The United Nations Organisation aims to maintain international peace. With reference to its organs and agencies, answer the following.

(i) What is the composition of the International Court of Justice? **[Recall] (3)**

(ii) Mention any three functions of the General Assembly. **[Recall] (3)**

(iii) Gujarat's famed garba dance received the intangible heritage tag. Which agency of the United Nations is authorized to give this tag? Mention any three other contributions of that agency in the preservation of culture. **[Application & Recall] (4)**

Answers

1. (i) (c) It is issued when the Parliament is not functioning.

(ii) (d) Z

(iii) (c) The Parliament

(iv) (c) Works on the spirit of compromise

(v) (b) Civil

(vi) (c) P and R

(vii) (b) R is the reason for A

(viii) (d) The Judges

(ix) (b) Follow the method of boycott

(x) (d) Holding pro-democracy rallies

(xi) (a) To promote among Muslims of India, support for the British.

(xii) (d) Jyotiba Phule

(xiii) (b) Subhash Chandra Bose

(xiv) (b) Japan

(xv) (c) Hiroshima, Nagasaki

(xvi) (b) A country maintains relations with both factions during the Cold War and does not take sides.

2. (i) The Speaker of the Lok Sabha has the authority to allow or disallow an adjournment motion. This power is crucial for maintaining order and focusing the discussion in the house.

An adjournment motion is used to temporarily stop proceedings to discuss a matter of urgent public importance. The discussion must be specific and is intended to draw the government's attention to a particular issue that needs immediate attention.

(ii) (a) The President of India exercises legislative powers under Article 111 of the Constitution to approve bills passed by both houses of Parliament.

(b) The President exercises executive power to appoints judges to the Supreme Court of India under Article 124 of the Constitution.

(iii) An artisan in the year 1856 would have been affected by the British policies in the following ways

- **Reduced demand for local goods** As an artisan in 1856, British economic policies such as the promotion of British-made goods would have severely affected his/her livelihood by reducing the demand for locally made products.
- **Taxation and raw material supply** One would likely face heavy taxes imposed by the British, which would diminish their earnings. Additionally, the colonial focus on raw material exportation would limit his/her access to necessary resources, further impacting his/her ability to produce and sell.

(iv) Two reasons for the acceptance of the Mountbatten Plan by the Congress were

(a) **Immediate Transfer of Power** One of the primary reasons Congress accepted the Mountbatten Plan was the provision for immediate transfer of power from British to Indian hands, which promised a quicker end to British rule.

(b) **Avoidance of Civil War** The plan proposed the partition of India into two dominions, which, despite being a painful decision, was seen by Congress leaders as a necessary compromise to prevent a civil war between different communal groups.

(v) Two leaders of the Assertive Nationalists were

(a) **Bal Gangadhar Tilak** Often referred to as 'Lokmanya, Tilak' was a prominent leader of the Assertive Nationalists, advocating for Swaraj as a birthright of Indians. He initiated the Shivaji festival in 1896 to inspire nationalism in addition to the Ganesh festival.

(b) **Lala Lajpat Rai** He was also called 'Punjab Kesari' and 'Lion of Punjab' and was instrumental in the freedom struggle and was known for his advocacy of aggressive policies against British rule. Along with Bipin Chandra Pal and Bal Gangadhar Tilak, he formed the Lal-Bal-Pal trio of extremist leaders.

(vi) Following are the two main objectives of League of Nations.

(a) **Prevention of wars** The League of Nations aimed to maintain peace and prevent wars through collective security and disarmament and settling international disputes through negotiation and arbitration.

(b) **Promotion of international cooperation** The league of Nations aimed to foster cooperation among nations in solving international problems of an economic, social, or humanitarian nature and to achieve international peace and security.

(vii) Before the beginning of the First World War, two major alliances were formed in Europe. These were

(a) **The Triple Entente** This alliance, established in the early 20th century, included France, Russia and the United Kingdom. It was formed through a series of agreements that aimed to counterbalance the growing strength of the Triple Alliance and provide mutual support and cooperation among the member nations.

(b) **The Triple Alliance** This alliance was formed in 1882 and comprised and Germany, Austria-Hungary and Italy. It was intended primarily as a defensive pact, where each member promised to support the others in case of an attack by two or more powers, or in case of aggression by France against Germany or Italy.

3. (i) The Lok Sabha is more powerful than the Rajya Sabha because it has

- **Legislative Power over Money Bills** The Lok Sabha holds exclusive powers to introduce and make decisions on money bills.
  While the Rajya Sabha can suggest amendments, it cannot reject or indefinitely withhold its approval of money bills, which must be returned within 14 days.
- **Major Role in Government Formation** The Lok Sabha is directly involved in the formation of the government, as the Prime Minister and the majority of the cabinet ministers are typically from the Lok Sabha. This house reflects the direct choice of the electorate.
- **Motion of No-Confidence** Only the Lok Sabha has the power to move and pass a motion of no confidence against the sitting government.
  If such a motion passes, it necessitates the resignation of the entire cabinet, underscoring the greater political power of the Lok Sabha.

(ii) The session of the Rajya Sabha can be adjourned sine die by the Chairman of the Rajya Sabha, who is the Vice-President of India. This type of adjournment marks the end of a session without any definite date for resumption.

The Rajya Sabha, or the Upper House of Parliament, is composed of representatives from the states and union territories. 238 members are elected by the state legislative assemblies, and 12 members are nominated by the President of India.

The total membership is limited by the Constitution, which allocates seats based on the population of each state and territory.

(iii) The four legislative powers of the Parliament are as follows

(a) **Amendment of the Constitution** Parliament can amend the Constitution, subject to the provisions of Article 368.

(b) **Passing Laws** Parliament can legislate on subjects listed in the Union List and, under certain circumstances, on the Concurrent List shared with states.

(c) **National Emergency** During a national emergency, Parliament assumes the power to make laws on any subject, including those normally reserved for states.

(d) **Creation or Abolition of States** Parliament can pass laws changing the boundaries of states or creating new ones.

4. (i) The three legislative powers of the President that justify the nominal position are as follows

- **Bill Assent** The President has the power to give assent to bills passed by Parliament, which is required for a bill to become law. This role is largely ceremonial as refusal to assent is rare and usually done on the advice of the cabinet.
- **Ordinance Issuance** The President can issue ordinances under article 123, when Parliament or any of the two houses are not in session, which have the same force as laws passed by Parliament.
- **Summoning and Proroguing Parliament** The President summons and prorogues the sessions of Parliament, but these actions are typically performed on the advice of the Prime Minister and the cabinet.

(ii) The three financial powers of the President are as follows

(a) **Budget Presentation** The budget is presented in the Parliament with the President's prior recommendation, necessary for any proposals involving expenditure from the Consolidated Fund of India.

(b) **Financial Bills** No financial bills involving expenditure can be introduced in Parliament without the President's recommendation.

(c) **Contingency Fund** The President is the custodian of the Contingency Fund of India (Article 267(1) of the Indian Constitution), allowing him to make advances to meet unforeseen expenses.

(iii) Impeachment procedure of the President is discussed below

- **Initiation** The process can be initiated by either house of Parliament i.e Rajya Sabha or Lok Sabha. The motion to impeach must be supported by at least one-fourth of the total number of members of that house.
- **Investigation** The charges are investigated, and the President has the right to appear and to be represented at the investigation.

- **Decision** For the impeachment to succeed, it must be passed by a two-thirds majority of the total membership of each house of the Parliament.

This rigorous procedure emphasises the stability of the executive head and ensures that impeachment is a measure of last resort based on substantial misdeeds or incapacity.

5. (i) Appointment and Qualifications of Supreme Court Judges.

The Judges of the Supreme Court are appointed by the President of India after consulting the Chief Justice of the Supreme Court.

The qualifications required for being a Supreme Court Judge are

(a) **Experience in the Judiciary** A person must have been a judge of one or more high courts for at least five years, or an advocate there for at least ten years.

(b) **Distinguished Jurist** Alternatively, a person must be a distinguished jurist in the opinion of the President, recognised for their expertise and contributions to the legal field.

(ii) Under Article 129, the Supreme Court of India is called a Court of Record. This statement can be justified the rough the following points

(a) **Permanent Record Keeping** As a Court of Record, all judgments, proceedings, and acts of the Supreme Court are recorded for perpetual memory and testimony.
These records are recognised as legal precedents and authoritative references.

(b) **Power to Punish for Contempt** The Court of Record status grants the Supreme Court the authority to punish for contempt of itself. This power helps maintain the respect and authority of the court.

(c) **Precedential Value** Decisions made by the Supreme Court as a Court of Record are binding on all lower courts within the territory of India. This ensures consistency and predictability in the application of the law across the country.

(iii) (a) Revisory jurisdiction refers to the power of the Supreme Court to review, revisit and possibly overturn its own decisions or those of lower courts. This jurisdiction is exercised to correct errors or injustices in judgments and to ensure that justice is served in accordance with law and evolving legal standards.

(b) Under Article 143 of the Constitution, the President of India can seek the advice of the Supreme Court on any question of law or fact that is of public importance or that which involves interpretation of the Constitution. This is known as the Advisory Jurisdiction. While the advice provided by the Supreme Court is generally respected, it is not binding on the President. This jurisdiction helps in clarifying legal issues and aiding executive decisions with judicial insight.

6. (i) The three British Policies of expansion were as follows

(a) **Doctrine of Lapse** Introduced by Lord Dalhousie, this policy allowed the British to annex any princely state where the ruler died without a direct heir.

(b) **Subsidiary Alliance** This strategy, pioneered by Lord Wellesley, involved placing British forces in a princely state and making it a protectorate of the British Empire, effectively controlling its external affairs.

(c) **Direct Conquest** Several regions of India were directly conquered through military force, expanding British territorial holdings and control over resources.

(ii) The impacts of the failure of Revolt of 1857 on the Mughals and Peshwas were

- **End of the Mughal Empire** The failure of the Revolt marked the end of the Mughal Empire, with Emperor Bahadur Shah II being deposed and exiled. This effectively eliminated the Mughal Empire as a political entity and symbol of authority in India.
- **Decline of the Peshwas** The Peshwas, who were leaders of the Maratha Empire, also faced decline as their power had been waning through earlier defeats. After the Revolt, any remaining influence or claims to authority by the Peshwas were further diminished, consolidating British dominance.

(iii) The Indian army was reorganised after the Revolt of 1857 in the following ways

- **Reduction of Indian Troops** The proportion of Indian soldiers in the army was reduced, and the number of European troops was increased to prevent future revolts.
- **Strategic Placement of Troops** The artillery units, which were crucial in any military engagement, were placed under direct British control and Indians were largely removed from these key positions.
- **Enhanced Segregation** The troops were reorganised based on ethnicity and religion to divide and rule by fostering distrust among different groups.

- **Improved Communication** The British improved infrastructure, like roads and telegraphs, to facilitate faster movement and communication of their forces across the country.

7. (i) The first President of the Indian National Congress was Womesh Chunder Bonnerjee.

The Objectives of Congress were

(a) **Promote Political Education and Unity** One of the main objectives was to promote political education among Indians and to foster a sense of unity against colonial rule.

(b) **Formulate and Present Demands** The Congress aimed to provide a platform for all Indians to discuss public matters and to formulate demands for greater civil and political rights from the British administration.

(ii) The role of the Press in the Growth of Nationalism was

(a) **Educating the Masses** Newspapers and periodicals played a critical role in educating the masses about political ideas and the impacts of colonial policies.

(b) **Fostering Unity** The press helped in creating a shared sense of identity and purpose among diverse linguistic and cultural groups across India.

(c) **Exposing Injustices** The press was instrumental in exposing the injustices and exploitation under British rule, which galvanised support for nationalist movements.

(iii) The four policies enforced by Lord Lytton's were

(a) **Vernacular Press Act (1878)** This act aimed to curb the freedom of the Indian press, particularly vernacular newspapers, to prevent the spread of nationalist ideas.

(b) **Arms Act (1878)** This law prohibited Indians from possessing arms without a licence.

(c) **Reduction of Maximum Age for Civil Service Examinations** Lord Lytton reduced the maximum age for appearing in civil service exams, making it difficult for Indians to enter the service.

(d) **Imperial Assemblies** Lord Lytton hosted luxurious assemblies and durbar to reinforce the might of the British Empire, even during famines and hardships faced by Indians, showing a stark disconnect and fueling resentment.

8. (i) The Salt March, also known as the Dandi March, is one of the most iconic events in the history of India's struggle for independence.

This march was a key part of the Civil Disobedience Movement, where Indians were encouraged to disobey British laws non-violently to press for independence.

The Civil Disobedience Movement was officially launched in 1930 following the culmination of the Salt March. The march itself began on 12th March, 1930.

(ii) The impacts of the Civil Disobedience Movement were as follows

- **Increased National Unity** The Civil Disobedience Movement, sparked by the Salt March, played a crucial role in bringing together Indians from different backgrounds. It transcended regional, caste and religious boundaries, creating a widespread collective consciousness against British rule.
  This unity was pivotal in strengthening the national movement and making it a mass movement rather than being limited to the intellectuals and the elite.
- **Economic Impact** By boycotting British goods, refusing to pay taxes, and halting other economic activities that benefited the British economically, the movement delivered a blow to the British economy in India.
  These boycotts were effective in reducing the revenue the British could extract from India.
- **International Attention** The non-violent nature of the protest drew widespread international attention, particularly from the Western world. Reports of British repression during the movement helped gain sympathy for the Indian cause, boosting support for Indian independence on an international level.

(iii) The four clauses of the Gandhi-Irwin Pact were

(a) **Release of Political Prisoners** A significant achievement of the pact was the release of thousands of political prisoners who were imprisoned for participating in the Civil Disobedience Movement. However, those convicted of violence were not included in this amnesty, which was a point of contention among some nationalists.

(b) **Salt Manufacture** The agreement allowed the collection and manufacture of salt by the coastal communities, which was crucial since the Salt March was specifically initiated against the salt tax imposed by the British.

(c) **Return of Confiscated Properties** Under the pact, the British agreed to return the confiscated lands and properties of the satyagrahis, although properties seized directly by the government were not returned. This clause aimed at alleviating some of the financial strains on the protesters who had sacrificed much in their fight against British laws.

(d) **Right to Peaceful Protests** The pact acknowledged the right of Indians to conduct peaceful protests. It also allowed Gandhi to represent the Indian National Congress at the Round Table Conference in London, marking a significant step toward negotiations for Indian self-rule.

9. (i) The cartoon likely illustrates the assassination of Archduke Franz Ferdinand of Austria in Sarajevo.

This event occurred on 28th June, 1914, when the heir to the Austro-Hungarian throne was assassinated by Gavrilo Princip, a Bosnian Serb nationalist.

This assassination is widely acknowledged as the spark that ignited the First World War I, leading to the mobilisation of allied and central powers into one of the deadliest conflicts in human history.

(ii) Europe was rearranged as a consequence of the first world war in the following ways

(a) **New Nations Formed** The map of Europe was dramatically redrawn with several new nations emerging, such as Czechoslovakia, Poland and Yugoslavia, as multi-ethnic empires like Austro-Hungarian and Ottoman were dismantled.

(b) **Territorial Losses for Central Powers** Countries like Germany and Austria-Hungary lost significant territories to neighbouring states and new nations, altering the political landscape of Europe.

(c) **New Blocks Formed** There were formation of new blocks in Europe along with other non-European countries for example; UK sided with USA etc.

(iii) The Treaty of Versailles was viewed as Harsh and humiliating by Germans due to the following reasons

(a) **Territorial Losses** Germany lost significant territories, such as Alsace-Lorraine to France and parts of Prussia to the new Polish state, reducing its size and economic power.

(b) **War Guilt Clause** Article 231, known as the War Guilt Clause, forced Germany to accept sole responsibility for starting the war, a point of national humiliation.

(c) **Reparations** Germany was required to pay huge reparations, which strained its economy and contributed to severe economic hardships during the interwar period.

(d) **Military Restrictions** The treaty drastically limited the size and capability of the German military, undermining national defence and pride.

10. (i) The International Court of Justice (ICJ) is composed of 15 judges elected to nine-year terms by the United Nations General Assembly and the Security Council. These judges represent the principal legal systems of the world and no two judges may be from the same country, ensuring a diversity of legal traditions.

(ii) The three functions of the General Assembly are

(a) **Legislative Functions** The General Assembly passes resolutions that influence international law and practices.

(b) **Budgetary Functions** It approves the budget of the United Nations and determines the financial contributions of member states.

(c) **Electoral Functions** The General Assembly elects non-permanent members of the Security Council, judges of the International Court of Justice and other key officials within the UN system.

(iii) UNESCO (United Nations Educational, Scientific and Cultural Organisation) is authorised to give the intangible heritage tag.

The contributions of UNESCO in the preservation of culture are as follows

(a) **World Heritage Sites** It identifies and preserves cultural sites and natural wonders around the world that are of outstanding value to humanity.

(b) **Preserves Heritage** It aims at preserving the rich cultural heritage of the countries and focuses on preserving its significance.

(c) **Intangible Heritage** It also maintains a list of Intangible heritage for example, Garba, Vedic Chanting etc from India to preserve their cultural significance.

ICSE
SOLVED PAPER 2024

ICSE Solved Paper 2024

History & Civics (Fully Solved)

General Instructions

1. Answers to this paper must be written on the paper provided separately.
2. You will not be allowed to write during the first 15 minutes.This time is to be spent in reading the question paper.
3. The time given at the head of this Paper is the time allowed for writing the answers.
4. Attempt all questions from Part I (Compulsory). A total of 5 questions are to be attempted from Part II, 2 out of 3 questions from Section A and 3 out of 5 questions from Section B.
5. The intended marks for questions or parts of questions are given in brackets [].

Time : 2 Hrs **Max. Marks : 80**

Part - I

(30 Marks)

Attempt all questions from this Part

1. Select the correct answers to the questions from the given options. [16 ×1]

(i) The salaries and allowances of the ministers are decided by the

(a) Parliament (b) Finance Minister (c) President (d) Prime Minister

(ii) Civil Cases: Court of District Judge: : Criminal Cases:

(a) Revenue Court (b) Family Court (c) Sessions Court (d) Commissioner's Court

(iii)

The Lok Adalat has many advantages. Which of the following statements about the advantages of the Lok Adalat is best described in the picture given above?

(a) It is inexpensive (b) It is organised in various parts of the country

(c) It works on the spirit of compromise (d) It reduces the burden of the higher courts

(iv) Given below are details of Indian citizens. Select the ones who are eligible for appointment as a High Court Judge

Candidate	Age	Details
P	65	Is a distinguished jurist
Q	61	Has been a High Court Advocate for 10 years
R	67	Has been a High Court Advocate for 5 years
S	56	Has held a judicial office for at least 10 years

(a) P and R (b) Q and S (c) R and P (d) Q and R

(v) The strength of the house is 550. On a particular day 50 members are present. The speaker decides to adjourn the house. Identify the most likely reason for the adjournment.
(a) Disorder in the house (b) Lack of quorum
(c) Breach of privilege (d) Contempt of the House

(vi) During a hung assembly when no party gets the majority, the President appoints the Prime Minister. What power is the President exercising?
(a) Legislative (b) Executive (c) Discretionary (d) Judicial

(vii) Read the two statements given below and select the option that shows the correct relationship between (A) and (R)
Assertion (A) Forward Bloc had the objective of abolishing Zamindari System.
Reason (R) Subhash Chandra Bose wanted to establish a socialist state.
Codes
(a) A is true but R is false (b) R is the reason for A
(c) Both A and R are false (d) Only R is true, A is false

(viii) The ...... aimed to introduce equality between British and Indian Judges.
(a) Vernacular Press Act (b) Gagging Act
(c) Indian Universities Act (d) Ilbert Bill

(ix) The Rowlatt Act was called the Black Act because the Indians
(a) could not possess any arms (b) could not export any goods
(c) could be arrested without a warrant (d) could be sent overseas on duty

(x) Who organised the Grand Delhi Durbar?
(a) Lord Curzon (b) Lord Canning (c) Lord Lytton (d) Lord Dalhousie

(xi) Tina is inspired by the methods of the Early Nationalists and wants to follow them. She notices that the road leading to her school is damaged and has many potholes. Which of the following methods is she most likely to follow, to solve this problem?
(a) Boycott the civic authorities
(b) Gather a group of students and protest
(c) Write a petition to the authorities highlighting the problem
(d) Block the entrance to the road

(xii) Given below are the objectives of the Indian National Army. Identify the odd one out of the following.
(a) To organise a provisional government of Free India (b) Total mobilisation of Indian manpower and money
(c) Unity, faith and sacrifice (d) To train and organise public opinion in the country

(xiii) Tahir is preparing to give a speech about the Sati system in India. Which of the following Indian leader's contribution must he mentions in his speech?
(a) Raja Rammohan Roy (b) WC Bonerjee
(c) Bipin Chandra Pal (d) Jyotiba Phule

(xiv) Which of the following is not a consequence of the Second World War?
(a) Austria and Hungary became separate states (b) Defeat of the Axis powers
(c) Beginning of the Cold War (d) Formation of the United Nations

(xv) Identify the principle of Panchsheel.
(a) Mutual non-aggression (b) Regulate armaments
(c) Take action against aggressor (d) Recommend admission of members

(xvi)

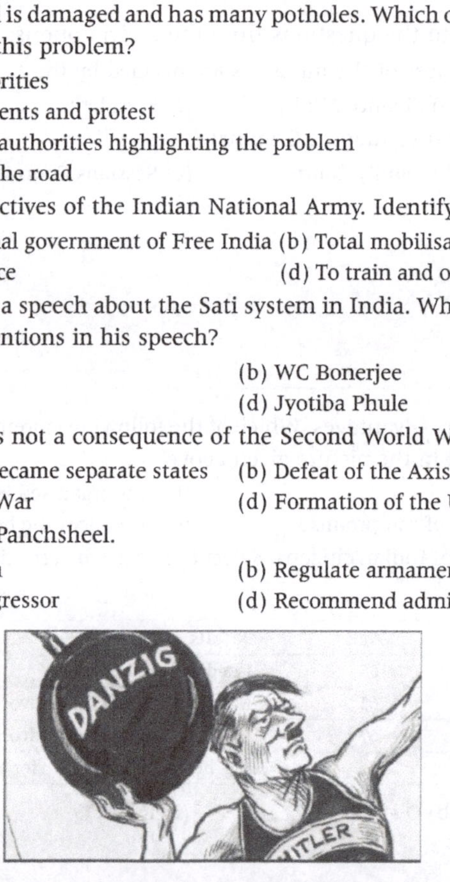

Which incident depicted in the above cartoon led to the beginning of the Second World War?

(a) Hitler's policy of Imperialism
(b) Hitler's attack on Poland
(c) Hitler's annexation of Austria
(d) Hitler's attack on Czechoslovakia

2. (i) Mention any two writs issued by the High Court. [2]

(ii) Imagine you are an Indian ruler who has signed the Subsidiary Alliance. Mention any two conditions of this agreement which will affect you. [2]

(iii) Mention any two causes of the Quit India Movement. [2]

(iv) In which year did the *Surat Split* happen? What was the result of this split? [2]

(v) Mention any two common ideologies of Fascism and Nazism. [2]

(vi) Name the two cities of Japan which were bombed by America in the year 1945. [2]

(vii) Read the given news carefully and answer the question that follows:

Govt's power to promulgate, repromulgate Ordinances _ why and how

An Ordinance "shall have the same force and effect as an Act of Parliament". But the government is required to bring an Ordinance before Parliament for ratification - and failure to do so will lead to its lapsing "at the expiration of six weeks from the reassembly of Parliament". *The Indian Express - 25th May, 2023*

Mention any two points regarding an ordinance that can be deduced from the above news. [2]

Part - II

SECTION - A (20 Marks)

Attempt any two questions from this Section

3. The Union Parliament is the supreme legislative body in the country. With reference to the Indian Parliament answer the following questions.

(i) The Rajya Sabha is called a Permanent House. Explain this statement. [3]

(ii) Explain the composition of the Rajya Sabha. [3]

(iii) Mention any two exclusive powers of the Lok Sabha and two powers exclusive to the Rajya Sabha. [4]

4. The Council of Ministers headed by the Prime Minister aids and advises the President. In this context, answer the following questions.

(i) Mention any three points to distinguish between the Council of Ministers and the Cabinet [3]

(ii) Who appoints the Cabinet Ministers? Mention any two administrative powers of the Cabinet. [3]

(iii) The President is the nominal head of the Indian Union. Mention any four functions of the Prime Minister with reference to the President. [4]

5. The judiciary is the system of courts that interprets and guards the Indian Constitution. With reference to the Supreme Court of India, answer the following:

(i) What is the composition of the Supreme Court? Why is it called the Court of Record? [3]

(ii) Explain the power of Judicial Review. [3]

(iii) What is meant by the term Original Jurisdiction? Mention any three cases which come under this jurisdiction. [4]

SECTION - B

(30 Marks)

Attempt any three questions from this Section.

6. The Revolt of 1857 was the beginning of the independence struggle against the colonial rule of the British. With reference to the consequences of the Revolt, answer the following:
   - (i) Mention any three changes made in the administration with the end of the Company's Rule. [3]
   - (ii) State any three policies promised to Indians in Queen Victoria's Proclamation. [3]
   - (iii) Mention any four changes made in the army after the Revolt. [4]

7. The Indian National Movement is divided into three phases. With reference to the Second Phase of the Indian National Movement, answer the following questions:
   - (i) Who partitioned Bengal? Mention any two points to explain the perspective of the Nationalists regarding the actual motive behind the decision of Partition. [3]
   - (ii) What was the objective of the Assertive Nationalists? Mention any two contributions of Bal Gangadhar Tilak. [3]
   - (iii) In which year was the Muslim League formed? Mention any three objectives of the Muslim League. [4]

8. Look at the picture given and answer the following questions.

The Times of India

WAY OUT OF INDIAN DEADLOCK

BRITAIN'S PLAN FOR SMOOTH TRANSFER OF POWER

Immediate Dominion Status Granted

PEOPLE ASKED TO DECIDE PARTITION QUESTION

Present Constituent Assembly Not Disturbed

"UNITED INDIA BEST SOLUTION"

Viceroy's Appeal

Only Practical Method

PREMIER'S VIEW

Plan Commended To Commons

MR. NEHRU COMMENDS PLAN TO NATION

Mr. Jinnah Hopeful Of League's Acceptance

SARDAR BALDEV SINGH CALLS IT "SETTLEMENT"

   - (i) Name the Viceroy who announced the plan for smooth transfer of power. Mention any two clauses of his plan with reference to the Princely States. [3]
   - (ii) Mention any three reasons for the acceptance of his plan by the Congress. [3]
   - (iii) Mention any four provisions of the Indian Independence Act of 1947. [4]

9. The final act of the long-drawn-out negotiations took place at Versailles on Saturday afternoon, and to-day Germany and the Allies - always with the exception of America - are at peace. Peace is a blessed word, and both the word and the fact are welcome to-day. So far as Germany is concerned there is for the present an end of strife, and at least a formal return to the decent relations of civilised states.

   Editorial : Peace in force (12th January, 1920)

   The Guardian
   - (i) Mention any three causes of the World War which ended with the signing of the treaty being discussed in the passage above. [3]
   - (ii) Name the organisation which was established in 1920 to maintain peace after this war. Mention any two of its objectives. [3]
   - (iii) Mention any four clauses of the Treaty which affected Germany. [4]

10. Both the United Nations Organisation and the Non-Aligned Movement aim to achieve international peace and security. In this context, answer the following:
    - (i) Mention any three functions of the Security Council. [3]
    - (ii) Mention any three functions of the World Health Organisation. [3]
    - (iii) Name any two founders of the Non-Aligned Movement. Mention any two of its objectives. [4]

Answers

1. (i) (a) Parliament
(ii) (c) Sessions Court
(iii) (c) It works on the spirit of compromise
(iv) (b) Q and S
(v) (b) Lack of quorum
(vi) (c) Discretionary
(vii) (b) R is the reason for A
(viii) (d) Ilbert Bill
(ix) (c) could be arrested without a warrant
(x) (a) Lord Curzon
(xi) (c) Write a petition to the authorities highlighting the problem
(xii) (b) Total mobilisation of Indian manpower and money
(xiii) (a) Raja Rammohan Roy
(xiv) (a) Austria and Hungary became separate states
(xv) (a) Mutual non-aggression
(xvi) (b) Hitler's attack on Poland

2. (i) The writs issued by the High Court are Habeas Corpus, Mandamus, Certiorari, Prohibitions and Quo-Warranto.

(ii) As an Indian ruler who has signed the Subsidiary Alliance, two conditions of this agreement that would significantly affect me are

(a) Military control and presence (b) Financial burden

(iii) The two causes of the Quit India Movement were

(a) Failure of Cripps Mission (b) Hardships caused during World War II

(iv) The Surat split happened on December 26, 1907.

The result of this split was the division of the Indian National Congress into Moderates and Radicals (extremists).

(v) The two common ideologies of Fascism and Nazism are as follows

(a) Both Mussolini and Hitler aimed at restoring the status and dignity of their nations by making them strong powers.

(b) Both aimed at providing strong, stable and efficient Governments.

(vi) Hiroshima and Nagasaki were the cities of Japan which were bombed by America in 1945.

(vii) The two points regarding an ordinance that can be deduced from the given news are

- Ordinance are temporary in nature
- Parliamentary Approval is necessary for an ordinance to remain in effect.

3. (i) The Rajya Sabha is called a Permanent House as it is the upper house of the Indian Parliament. Since, it is a permanent assembly, it cannot be dissolved. The Lok Sabha is the only body that can be dissolved. One-third members of Rajya Sabha retire every two years.

(ii) The composition of Rajya Sabha at present includes 245 members. Out of which 233 members are elected from States and Union Territories of Delhi and Puducherry and 12 are nominated by the President. These 12 members are distinguished people in the field of Literature, Science, Art and Social Sciences.

(iii) The two exclusive powers of the Lok Sabha are

(a) Only the Lok Sabha can vote on the demands for grants in the budget.

(b) The Council of Ministers is collectively responsible only to the Lok Sabha. Thus, the Lok Sabha alone can vote a minister out of office.

The two exclusive powers of Rajya Sabha are

(a) The Parliament can assume temporary power to legislate on State List subjects (Article 249) only if Rajya Sabha passes a resolution, which is supported by two-third (2/3rd) majority of its members present and voting.

(b) The All-India Services can be established only if the Rajya Sabha passes a resolution for it, which is supported by two-third (2/3rd) majority of its members present and voting.

4. (i) The three points to distinguish between the Councils of Ministers and the Cabinet are

Council of Ministers	Cabinet Ministers
(a) It is a wider body.	It is a smaller body.
(b) It includes all three categories of ministers, Cabinet members, ministers of state and deputy ministers.	It includes the ministers holding important ministries.
(c) It does not meet, as a body,to transact government business.It has no collective functions.	It meets as a body usually once a week to take decisions regarding the transactions of government business.

(ii) The Cabinet Ministers are appointed by the President on the advice of the Prime Minister.

The two administrative powers of the cabinet are

(a) **Policy Making** The Council of Ministers is mainly a policy formulating body. It formulates both external and domestic policies of the government on important matters.

(b) **Implementation of Policies** When the policy decision on any subject is taken by the Cabinet, then, the Minister of State and the Deputy Minister of the concerned ministry examine the policies.

(iii) The President is the nominal head of the Indian Union. The four functions of the Prime Ministers with reference to the President are as follows

(a) The Prime Minister is the principal advisor to the President.

(b) The Prime Minister chooses the ministers and on his advice the President appoints them.

(c) The Prime Minister acts as a link between the President and the Council of Ministers as it communicates all the decisions of the Council of Ministers to the President on administration of the Union.

(d) The Prime Minister advises the President with regard to the appointment of important officials, such as CAG, members of UPSC, ECs, etc.

5. (i) The Composition of the Supreme Court consists of 34 judges including 1 Chief Justice and 33 other Judges. Originally the strength was fixed at 8 (1 Chief Justice and 7 other Judges).

The Supreme Court is called the Court of Record because the judgments, proceedings and acts of the Supreme Court are recorded for perpetual memory and testimony. These records cannot be questioned when produced before any court.

(ii) Judicial Review is a power given to the courts of India to examine the actions of the legislatures, executive and administrative arms of the centre and state government. It is to ensure that such actions comply with the provisions of the Constitution.

If the enactments and orders are found to be violative of the Constitution, they can be declared as illegal, unconstitutional and invalid (null and void) by the judiciary.

(iii) The term Original Jurisdiction refers to the power to hear and determine a dispute in the first instance. It happens in those cases, which cannot be transferred in any court other than the Supreme Court.

Three cases which come under this jurisdiction include

(a) Centre-State or Inter-State Disputes

(b) Transfer of cases

(c) Protection of Fundamental Rights

6. (i) Three changes made in the administration with the end of the Company's Rule.

(a) **Establishment of the British Raj** The British government took direct control over India, replacing the rule of the East India Company.

(b) **Centralisation of Power** Authority was concentrated in the hands of British administrators appointed by the Crown.

(c) **Implementation of British Policies** New policies were introduced to impose British dominance.

(ii) The three policies promised to Indians in Queen Victoria's Proclamation are as follows

(a) Treat all subjects i.e. Indians and Europeans as equal (education and ability would be the basis of all appointments).

(b) Follow a policy of non-intervention in social and religious matters of Indians.

(c) A general pardon was granted to all those who laid down arms by 2nd January, 1859, except those who were found guilty of murder of British subjects.

(iii) The four changes made in the army after the Revolt were

(a) The proportion of the Europeans to Indians in the army was raised.

(b) Artillery and other effective weapons of war were placed exclusively under the charge of the Europeans.

(c) To curb nationalism, Indian soldiers of different communities, castes and religions were all mixed up and they were kept away in remote places.

(d) Indian soldiers were not provided newspapers, journals and nationalist publications to keep them separated from the life of the rest of the population.

7. (i) Bengal was partitioned by the Viceroy Lord Curzon.

The two major points to explain the perspective of the Nationalists regarding the actual motive behind the decision of partition were as follows

(a) At that period, Bengal had become the main centre of the Indian politics and Indian nationalism. So, the British expected to regulate the rising tide of nationalism by the division of Bengal.

(b) Another reason of the Partition of Bengal was to destroy the political influence of the educated middle class, among whom the Bengali intellectuals was the most prominent.

(ii) The objectives of Assertive Nationalists were to achieve 'Swaraj' by self-reliant methods and sacrifices.

The major contributions of Bal Gangadhar Tilak were

(a) In 1880, he started the Poona New English School with a view to educate Indians by charging small fees.

(b) He started two newspapers i.e. Maratha (English) and Kesari (Marathi) in order to spread the idea of nationalism.

(iii) The Muslim League was formed on 1st October, 1906.

The three objectives of the Muslim League were

(a) To promote the feelings of loyalty towards the British Government amongst the Indian Muslims.

(b) To remove any misconception regarding the intentions of the government in relation to the Indian Muslim.

(c) To protect and advance the political rights and other interests of the Muslims of India.

8. (i) Lord Mountbatten was the Viceroy who announced the plan for smooth transfer of power. The two clauses of his plan with reference to the Princely states were as follows

(a) India would be divided into two dominions, i.e. India and Pakistan.

(b) It was up to the two Dominions, i.e. India and Pakistan, to decide what relations they would have with the British Commonwealth and with each other.

(ii) The three reasons for the acceptance of his plan by the Congress were

(a) The Congress leaders realised that the large-scale communal riots and mass killing could be prevented only by accepting the Muslim League's demand for Pakistan.

(b) The Congress believed that it could not have the joint administration with the Muslim League as it had bitter experience in interim government of 1946.

(c) The Congress leaders realised that the extension of the British rule would be harmful to India. By applying the 'Divide and Rule Policy' the Britishers divided Hindu and Muslim community in India.

(iii) The four major provisions of Indian Independence Act of 1947 were

(a) India would be partitioned and two independent dominions i.e. India and Pakistan would be created from 15th August, 1947. The act provided the legislative supremacy of both the dominions.

(b) The territories of the two dominions were divided in such terms that Pakistan would comprise of Sindh, British Baluchistan, North-West Frontier Province, the West Punjab and East Bengal. The exact boundaries of the dominions would be determined by a Boundary Commission.

(c) For each of the two dominions, there would be a Governor-General who would be appointed by the British King and who would represent the king for the purposes of the government of the dominions.

(d) Each of the Dominions and all Provinces were to be governed in accordance with the Act of 1935 till the new Constitution was formed.

9. (i) The three main causes of the World War which ended with the signing of the treaty being discussed in the passage are

(a) **Military** The First World War was fought not only by the soldiers but also by the civilians. The use of arms and the spreading of new types of weapons by every nation made the situation unfavourable for peace. To protect their colonies the European powers developed their defence system in the colonies. This created an atmosphere of fear, insecurity and mutual hatred.

(b) **Alliance System** The war was fought between allied powers (Britain, France, Russia and their allies) and central powers (Germany, Austria and their allies). These alliances have their benefits for which they allied together and fought on different fronts.

(c) **Imperialism** Germany, Italy, Russia and Japan worked to increase their influence over the colonies in the least developed continents like Asia and Africa. Competition between European powers for colonies and resources around the world exacerbated tensions.

(ii) In 1920, the League of Nations was established.

The main objectives of this organisation were

(a) To ensure disarmament, war prevention through collective security.

(b) It also focuses on international conflict resolution through conversation and diplomacy and global well-being.

(iii) The four clauses of the Treaty which affected Germany were

(a) **War Guilt Clause** This clause assigned full responsibility for the war and its damages to Germany and its allies.

(b) **Territorial Losses** The mineral-rich land of Ruhr was given to France, which further deteriorated the conditions for Germany.

(c) **Reparations** A huge sum of money was signed to give as the war guilt by the winning parties. It put an additional pressure on the economy of Germany.

(d) **Demilitarisation and Military Restrictions** Germany was demilitarised and only a small number of the police force was allowed to be formed. This condition was given to reduce the chance of war initiation by Germany.

10. (i) The three main functions of the Security Council are

(a) It maintains international peace and security in accordance with the principles and purposes of the United Nations.

(b) It investigates any dispute or situation which might lead to international friction.

(c) It recommends methods of adjusting such disputes or the terms of settlement.

(ii) The three main functions of World Health Organisation are as follows

(a) It helps countries to improve their health system by building up infrastructure.

(b) It gives important drugs needed for medical care.

(c) It launches programmes to immunise children against 6 major diseases such as measles, diphtheria, tetanus, tuberculosis, polio and whooping cough.

(iii) The two founders of the Non-Aligned Movement were Jawaharlal Nehru of India and Kwame Nkrumah of Ghana.

The two main objectives of Non-Aligned Movement are

(a) To remove all those factors and tendencies that could lead to war.

(b) To project the growing freedom of the newly independent Asian and African countries and help them to keep away from colonial domination.

ICSE
SOLVED PAPER 2025

ICSE Solved Paper 2025

History & Civics (Fully Solved)

General Instructions

1. Attempt all questions from Part I (Compulsory). A total of 5 questions are to be attempted from Part II, 2 out of 3 questions from Section A and 3 out of 5 questions from Section B.
2. The intended marks for questions or parts of questions are given in brackets ( ).

Time : 2 Hrs **Max. Marks : 80**

Part - I

(30 Marks)

Attempt all questions from this Part.

1. Select the correct answers to the questions from the given options. **[1]**

(i) The Council of Ministers is collectively responsible to the.............. .

(a) Lok Sabha (b) President
(c) Rajya Sabha (d) Prime Minister

(ii) Given below are details of a few Indian Citizens. **[1]**

Person	Age (In years)	Description
W	25	Is a famous journalist
X	45	Is an industrialist
Y	35	Has declared insolvency
Z	50	Has taken citizenship of another country

Select the one who is eligible to be a member of the Rajya Sabha.

(a) X (b) W
(c) Y (d) Z

(iii) With reference to the Supreme Court of India, complete the following **[1]**

Advisory Jurisdiction : Advice the President :: Judicial Review : ....

(a) Review its own judgements.
(b) Review the judgements of the High Court.
(c) Review the laws passed by the Parliament.
(d) Review the administration of the Government.

(iv) Observe the given picture. In case of a similar unruly situation in the Lok Sabha, choose the action that may be taken by the Speaker. [1]

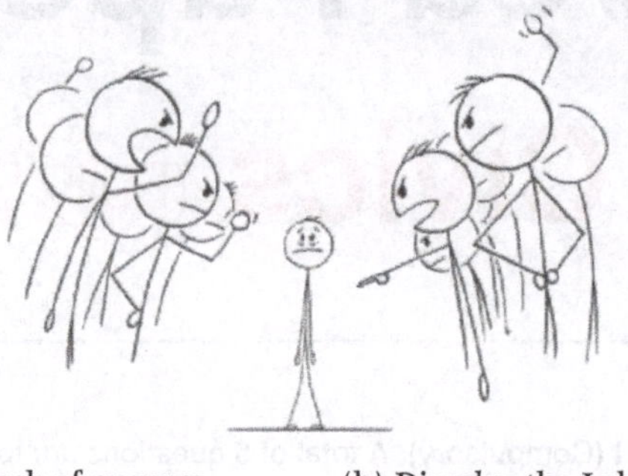

(a) Adjourn the House for lack of quorum. (b) Dissolve the Lok Sabha.
(c) Adjourn the House for lack of discipline. (d) Disqualify the members under Anti-defection law.

(v) If an Adjournment Motion is passed in the Lok Sabha .... [1]
(a) the Lok Sabha will be dissolved.
(b) the House will discuss a matter of urgent public importance.
(c) the President ends the session.
(d) the Government will fall.

(vi) Which emergency will be declared by the President if the security of the Nation is under threat? [1]
(a) General Emergency (b) Financial Emergency
(c) Constitutional Emergency (d) President's Rule

(vii) Read the statements given below and select the option that shows the correct relationship between (A) and (R). [1]

Assertion (A) Lord Curzon partitioned Bengal in 1905.

Reason (R) The Nationalists felt that the British wanted to divide the Hindus and the Muslims.

(a) (A) is true and (R) is false. (b) (R) is true but (A) is false.
(c) Both (A) and (R) are independent of each other. (d) (A) is the reason for (R).

(viii) Read the description and identify the person. [1]
He introduced the Subsidiary Alliance to expand the British control over India.
(a) Lord Dalhousie (b) Lord Canning
(c) Lord Wellesley (d) Lord Curzon

(ix) Identify the odd one out of the following Assertive Nationalists Leaders. [1]
(a) Bipin Chandra Pal (b) Lala Lajpat Rai
(c) Dadabhai Naoroji (d) Bal Gangadhar Tilak

(x) Who among the following is most associated with this picture? [1]

(a) Jyotiba Phule
(b) Raja Ram Mohan Roy
(c) Swami Dayanand Saraswati
(d) Aurobindo Ghosh

(xi) Identify the contributions of Subhash Chandra Bose [1]

P. Was the Supreme Commander of INA
Q. Signed the Lucknow Pact
R. Led the Quit India Movement
S. Founded the Forward Bloc

(a) P and Q (b) Q and R
(c) P and S (d) R and S

(xii) The market of a small industrial town *X* has been dominated by many products of foreign companies. The local residents decide to save the Indian industries by helping them increase their sales. Which method of the Assertive Nationalists must they follow to become self-reliant? [1]

(a) Passive Resistance (b) National Education
(c) Swadeshi (d) Revivalism

(xiii) Which of the following is not an objective of the United Nations Organisation? [1]

(a) Disarm (b) Disengage
(c) Decolonise (d) Develop

(xiv) Which agency of the United Nations Organisation is associated with this picture? [1]

(a) UNESCO (b) UNICEF
(c) WHO (d) ILO

(xv) Which of the following is a common cause for the rise of dictatorship? [1]

(a) Faith in Democracy (b) Economic Crisis
(c) Freedom of Press (d) Political Stability

(xvi) Which of the following causes of the First World War is connected to this headline? [1]

Weather Forecast: Showers Tonight; Fair Monday

The Washington Times

SUNDAY EVENING EDITION

SERB STUDENT ASSASSINATES ARCHDUKE AND HIS DUCHESS

(a) Imperialism (b) Aggressive Nationalism
(c) Armament Race (d) Sarajevo Crisis

2. (i) Mention any two powers of the Prime Minister with reference to the Cabinet. [2]

(ii) Imagine you are an Early Nationalist leader. Mention any two methods you would follow to fight against the British. [2]

(iii) Mention any two factors that led to the formation of the Muslim League. [2]

(iv) Mention any two objectives of the Forward Bloc. [2]

(v) Mention any two ways in which the Treaty of Versailles affected the German Miliary Force. [2]

(vi) What is meant by the term Non-Alignment? [2]

(vii) When a judicial system is correctly calibrated, the law is applied by judges fearlessly, without favour or fear and with respect. That is why judicial security of tenure is so fundamental. It is also why judges must be properly paid without any interference from the Executive or Legislature.

-(The Need for Independent Judiciary) UNODC

From the passage, deduce and mention any two ways in which the Constitution ensures the independence of the Judiciary. **[2]**

PART-II

SECTION - A

(20 Marks)

Attempt any two questions from this Section.

3. The Parliament of India comprises the President and the two houses. With reference to the Indian Parliament, answer the following questions

(i) Mention any three circumstances under which the Parliament can make laws on subjects in the State List. **[3]**

(ii) Explain the following terms **[3]**

(a) Question Hour (b) Quorum

(c) No-confidence Motion

(iii) When can the term of the Lok Sabha be extended? **[4]**

Mention any three powers of the Lok Sabha which show its superiority over the Rajya Sabha.

4. The Executive Power of the country is in the President and Vice President. With reference to this, answer the following questions

(i) Explain the impeachment process through which the Parliament can remove the President from power. **[3]**

(ii) Mention any three powers of the Vice President in her/his role as the Chairman of the Rajya Sabha. **[3]**

(iii) With reference to the powers of President, mention **[4]**

(a) any two Financial Powers (b) any two Executive Powers

5. The High Courts of India are the highest courts of appeal in each state. With reference to the High Courts of India, answer the following questions

(i) What is meant by the term Original Jurisdiction of the High Court? Mention any two cases which fall under this jurisdiction. **[3]**

(ii) Mention any two advantages of the Lok Adalat. Mention any one difference between the Sessions Court and the Court of the District Judge. **[3]**

(iii) Explain the following with reference to the High Court. **[4]**

(a) Revisory Jurisdiction (b) Court of Record

SECTION-B

(30 Marks)

Attempt any three questions from this Section.

6. The Revolt of 1857 was conscious beginning of the independence struggle against the British. With reference to this, answer the following questions

(i) What was the Doctrine of Lapse? Who introduced it? **[3]**

(ii) The British Government interfered in the social and religious matters of the Indians. Mention any three socio religious causes to justify this statement. **[3]**

(iii) Mention any four military causes which led to this revolt. **[4]**

7. The oppressive British colonial rule led to the growth of nationalism in India. With reference to this answer the following questions

(i) The repressive policies of Lord Lytton became a catalyst to the growth of nationalism. Mention any three of his repressive policies to justify this statement. **[3]**

(ii) Mention any three ways in which the Press promoted nationalism. **[3]**

(iii) Who presided over the second session of the Indian National Congress? Mention any three objectives of the Congress. **[4]**

8. Look at the given picture and answer the questions that follows.

Tears of Blood : When 1,650 Bullets Changed India Forever

—The Times of India, April 2019

(i) Identify the above incident. Which Gandhian movement did it lead to? Which incident led to the suspension of that movement? **[3]**

(ii) Mention any three repressive provisions of the Rowlatt Act. **[3]**

(iii) Mention the following. **[4]**

(a) Any two causes of the Quit India Movement.

(b) Any two causes of the Civil Disobedience Movement.

9. Read the passage given and answer the following questions.

In an effort to secure resources for its expanding industries, Japan invaded the Northern Chinese province of Manchuria. Although many Western nations protested the Japanese action, most members of the League of Nations, including Canada, opposed any form of military intervention to defend Chinese sovereignty. A League of Nations commission, headed by the British diplomat Lord Lytton, was dispatched to Manchuria to investigate. *—Loyal Edmonton Regiment Museum*

(i) How did the incident being described above become a cause for the Second World War? **[3]**

(ii) Mention any three reasons for Hitler's attack on Poland. **[3]**

(iii) Mention any four reasons for the failure of the League of Nations. **[4]**

10. The organs and the agencies of the United Nation Organisation work towards the development of the world. With reference to this, answer the following questions.

(i) What is the composition of the General Assembly? **[3]**

(ii) Mention any three functions of the International Court of Justice. **[3]**

(iii) Give the full form of UNICEF. Mention any three of its functions. **[4]**

Answers

1. (i) (a) (ii) (a) (iii) (c)
(iv) (c) (v) (b) (vi) (a)
(vii) (d) (viii) (a) (ix) (c)
(x) (a) (xi) (c) (xii) (c)
(xiii) (b) (xiv) (a) (xv) (b)
(xvi) (d)

2. (i) Two powers of the Prime Minister with reference to the cabinet are

- **Appointment and Allocation of Portfolios** The Prime Minister selects ministers and assigns them specific departments.
- **Presiding Over Cabinet Meetings** The Prime Minister leads discussions and ensures decisions align with government policies.

(ii) Two methods I would follow to fight against the British are

- **Petitions and Appeals** I submit petitions and requests to the British government to demand reforms and justice.
- **Public Meetings and Speeches** I organise meetings to raise awareness and encourage Indians to demand their rights peacefully.

(iii) Two factors that led to the formation of the Muslim League are

- **British Policy of Divide and Rule** The British encouraged communal divisions to weaken the nationalist movement.
- **Muslim Fear of Hindu Domination** Some Muslim leaders felt that their political and economic interests needed separate representation.

(iv) Two objectives of the Forward Bloc were

- **Complete Independence** To achieve full and immediate independence from British rule.
- **Radical, Social and Economic Reforms** To work for the upliftment of the poor through socialist policies and economic equality.

(v) Two ways in which the Treaty of Versailles affected the German military force were

- **Reduction in Army Size** The German army was limited to 100,000 soldiers, with no conscription allowed.
- **Ban on Heavy Weapons** Germany was prohibited from having tanks, submarines and an air force, weakening its military strength.

(vi) Non-Alignment refers to the foreign policy adopted by countries that chose to remain independent and not align with any major power blocs (USA or USSR) during the Cold War. It aimed at peaceful coexistence, economic development, and protecting national sovereignty.

(vii) Two ways in which the Constitution ensures the independence of the Judiciary are

- **Security of Tenure** Judges cannot be removed arbitrarily; they can only be removed through impeachment on grounds of proven misconduct.
- **Financial Independence** Judges' salaries and allowances are charged on the Consolidated Fund of India, ensuring they are not controlled by the Executive or Legislature.

3. (i) Three circumstances under which Parliament can make laws on subjects in the State List are

- **During a National Emergency**Under Article 249, Parliament can legislate on State List subjects when an emergency is declared.
- **When Rajya Sabha Passes a Resolution** If the Rajya Sabha declares, by a two-thirds majority, that a subject in the State List is of national importance, Parliament can legislate on it.
- **When States Request Parliament** If two or more states pass resolutions requesting Parliament to make a law on a State List subject, Parliament can legislate on it.

(ii) (a) **Question Hour** The first hour of a Parliamentary sitting where members ask questions to ministers regarding government policies and decisions.

(b) **Quorum** The minimum number of members required to be present in either House for proceedings to take place. In Lok Sabha, it is 1/10th of total number of members.

(c) **No-confidence Motion** A motion moved in Lok Sabha to test if the government still has majority support. If passed, the government must resign.

(iii) The term of the Lok Sabha can be extended by one year at a time during a National Emergency under Article 352.

Three powers of Lok Sabha that show its superiority over Rajya Sabha are

- **Control Over the Executive** The Council of Ministers is responsible to the Lok Sabha and it can be removed through a No-confidence Motion.
- **Financial Supremacy** Money Bills can only be introduced in the Lok Sabha and the Rajya Sabha cannot amend or reject them.
- **Final Decision in Case of Disagreements** In case of a disagreement over an Ordinary Bill, a joint session is held, where the Lok Sabha's larger strength ensures its dominance.

4. (i) The President of India can be removed through impeachment under Article 61 for violating the Constitution. The process involves

- **A charge** is initiated in either House of Parliament with one-fourth of the members signing a notice.
- **Investigation** The charges are investigated and the President is given an opportunity to defend.
- **Two-thirds Majority Required** If both Houses pass the resolution with a two-thirds majority, the President is removed from office.

(ii) Three powers of the Vice President as Chairman of the Rajya Sabha are

- **Presiding Over Sessions** The Vice President conducts and maintains order in the Rajya Sabha.
- **Deciding on Points of Order** The Vice President interprets rules of procedure and ensures smooth functioning of debates.
- **Casting Vote in Case of a Tie** If there is a tie in voting, the Vice President (as Chairman) casts the deciding vote.

These powers make the Vice President an important figure in the parliamentary system, ensuring efficiency and impartiality.

(iii) (a) Two financial powers of the President are

- **Money Bills Require Presidential Recommendation** No Money Bill can be introduced in Parliament without the President's approval.
- **Control Over the Contingency Fund** The President authorises emergency expenditures from the Contingency Fund of India.

(b) Two executive powers of the President are

- **Appointment Powers** The President appoints the Prime Minister, Governors, Chief Justice, Judges and other key officials.
- **Administration of Union Territories** The President directly administers Union Territories through Lieutenant Governors or Administrators.

5. (i) The Original Jurisdiction of a High Court refers to cases that can be directly filed in the High Court, rather than coming through an appeal from lower courts.

Two cases under this jurisdiction are

- **Disputes involving Fundamental Rights** The High Court can issue writs under Article 226 to protect citizens' rights.
- **Cases involving State Government and Individuals** The High Court can hear cases between the state government and private parties.

(ii) Two advantages of Lok Adalat are

- **Speedy and Low-Cost Justice** Cases are resolved quickly without expensive court procedures.
- **Binding Decisions with No Appeal** The decision of Lok Adalat is final, preventing unnecessary delays.

The difference between Sessions Court and the Court of the District Judge can be seen as

Session Court	Court of the District Judge
It deals with criminal cases like murder, robbery and serious offenses.	It handles civil cases like property disputes and contracts.

(iii) (a) **Revisory Jurisdiction** The High Court has the power of Revisory Jurisdiction, which allows it to review and correct decisions made by lower courts if they contain legal errors. If a subordinate court exceeds its authority or fails to follow proper legal procedures, the High Court can call for records, examine the case and make necessary corrections. This ensures that justice is administered fairly and that lower courts function within their prescribed limits. However, the High Court does not re-examine evidence but only checks for procedural and legal correctness.

(b) **Court of Record** The High Court is a Court of Record, meaning its judgements, decisions and legal proceedings are permanently recorded and can be used as legal precedents in future cases. These records hold binding authority over lower courts. Additionally, as a Court of Record, the High Court has the power to punish for contempt of court if someone disrespects or disobeys its rulings, ensuring the dignity of the judiciary.

6. (i) The Doctrine of Lapse was a policy introduced by Lord Dalhousie, the Governor-General of India. According to this doctrine, if a ruling king died without a biological heir, his kingdom would automatically be annexed by the British East India Company. Adopted sons were not recognised as legitimate heirs. Using this policy, the British annexed several princely states, including Satara, Jhansi, Nagpur and Awadh. This caused widespread resentment among Indian rulers and was one of the major political causes of the Revolt of 1857.

(ii) The British government interfered in the social and religious matters of Indians, which led to widespread dissatisfaction. The three socio-religious causes to justify this statement are

- **Interference in Religious Practices** The British banned Sati (1829) and discouraged child marriage, which was seen as an attack on Hindu customs and traditions.
- **Promotion of Christian Missionaries** The British encouraged Christian conversions, making Indians fear that their religion and cultural practices were under threat.
- **Social Discrimination** Indians were treated as inferior to the British, facing racial discrimination in jobs and administration, which created resentment among the people.

(iii) Four military causes which led to this revolt were

- **Discontent Among Sepoys** Indian soldiers (sepoys) were paid less, treated unfairly and had fewer promotion opportunities compared to British soldiers.
- **General Service Enlistment Act (1856)** This act forced sepoys to serve overseas, which was against Hindu religious beliefs, as crossing the sea (Kala Pani) was considered impure.
- **Greased Cartridge Incident** The new Enfield rifle cartridges were rumored to be greased with cow and pig fat, offending both Hindus and Muslims. Sepoys who refused to use them were punished, increasing their anger.
- **Annexation of Awadh** Many sepoys were from Awadh, which was annexed under the Doctrine of Lapse, leading to resentment among soldiers who had family ties to the region.

7. (i) Lord Lytton's repressive policies fueled nationalist sentiments in India. The three policies that became a catalyst for the growth of nationalism are

- **Vernacular Press Act (1878)** This act restricted the Indian press from publishing material against British rule, suppressing freedom of speech and limiting nationalist expressions.
- **Arms Act (1878)** This law prohibited Indians from possessing weapons without British permission, while Europeans were exempted, creating a sense of discrimination and weakening Indian resistance.
- **Extravagant Expenditure on Delhi Durbar** (1877) Despite a severe famine, Lytton hosted a lavish Delhi Durbar to celebrate Queen Victoria's title as Empress of India, showing British insensitivity toward the suffering of Indians.

(ii) Three ways in which the Indian press promoted nationalism were

- **Exposing British Policies** Newspapers like Kesari and The Hindu criticised British exploitation and called for reforms.
- **Uniting Indians** The press spread awareness about freedom movements, inspiring people across India to fight for independence.
- **Encouraging Political Participation** Nationalist leaders used newspapers to mobilise public opinion and urge Indians to join protests, boycotts and the Swadeshi movement.

(iii) The second session of the Indian National Congress (INC) was presided over by Dadabhai Naoroji in 1886 in Calcutta.

The Indian National Congress (INC) was formed in 1885 by A.O. Hume with the goal of achieving political rights and self-governance for Indians. Its three key objectives were

- **Promoting National Unity** The INC aimed to bring together Indians from different regions, religions and communities to develop a common national identity.

- **Political Awareness and Representation** It worked to educate Indians about their rights and demanded greater representation in government through constitutional means.
- **Social and Economic Reforms** The Congress sought to address issues like poverty, taxation and economic exploitation caused by British rule while promoting Indian industries and education.

8. (i) The incident described is the Jallianwala Bagh Massacre on 13th April, 1919, when General Dyer ordered troops to fire on a peaceful gathering in Amritsar, killing thousands. This incident led to nationwide outrage and was a major cause of the Non-Cooperation Movement (1920-1922) launched by Mahatma Gandhi.

The movement was later suspended due to the Chauri Chaura Incident (1922), where violent protesters burned a police station, killing policemen. Gandhiji, being a strong advocate of non-violence, called off the movement to prevent further bloodshed.

(ii) The Rowlatt Act was passed by the Imperial Legislative Council in March 1919 and was strongly opposed by Indian leaders. Three repressive provisions of the Rowlatt Act were

- **Arrest without Warrant** The government could arrest and detain any person suspected of anti-British activities without a trial for up to two years.
- **In Camera Trials** Trials could be conducted in secret (closed-door hearings) without allowing the accused to know the evidence against them.
- **Curb on Freedoms** The Act restricted freedom of speech, press, and movement and protests against the government were considered illegal.

(iii) (a) Two causes of the Quit India Movement were

- **Failure of the Cripps Mission** (1942) The British government sent the Cripps Mission to offer Dominion Status after World War II, but Congress rejected it as it did not promise full independence.
- **Japanese Threat** The Japanese Army was advancing towards India, increasing fears of an invasion. Indian leaders saw this as a chance to force the British to leave India immediately.

(b) Two causes of the Civil Disobedience Movement were

- **Simon Commission Boycott** (1927) The Simon Commission was sent to review India's political situation, but no Indian members were included. This angered Indian leaders, leading to widespread protests.
- **Declaration of Purna Swaraj** (1929) The Lahore Session of Congress (1929), under Jawaharlal Nehru's presidency, declared Complete Independence (Purna Swaraj) as India's goal, leading to mass protests against British rule.

9. (i) The Manchurian Incident (1931) exposed the weakness of the League of Nations, as it failed to take strong action against Japan. Despite investigations, no military intervention was made, encouraging aggressive expansionism. This emboldened other axis powers like Germany and Italy, showing that international bodies would not stop territorial invasions. Hitler and Mussolini saw this as a green light for their own ambitions, leading to further aggression in Europe and Africa. The failure of diplomacy and unchecked invasions ultimately escalated tensions, contributing to World War II.

(ii) Three reasons for Hitler's attack on Poland were

- **Reclaiming Lost Territory** Hitler wanted to take back Polish lands that Germany lost after World War I under the Treaty of Versailles.
- **Lebensraum** (Living Space) He aimed to expand German territory for its growing population.
- **Weak Western Response** Britain and France followed a policy of appeasement, making Hitler believe they would not intervene.

(iii) Four reasons for the failure of the League of Nations were

- **Lack of Cooperation Among Member Nations** Countries prioritised their own interests rather than supporting the League's principles of collective security. Even member nations ignored League decisions when it did not suit them.
- **Failure to Prevent Aggression**The League remained inactive when Poland seised Lithuania (1920) and Italy refused intervention in the Greece-Italy conflict (1923). This weakened its authority.
- **Ineffectiveness Against Expansionist Powers** The League failed to act when Italy annexed Abyssinia, Japan took Manchuria and Germany took Austria and Czechoslovakia. This encouraged further aggression.
- **Loss of Faith in the League** The League's inability to stop conflicts led nations to lose trust in it. Instead of maintaining peace, countries started preparing for war, leading to World War II.

10 (i) The General Assembly is the main deliberative body of the United Nations, where all member countries are represented. It consists of 193 member nations, with each nation having one vote, regardless of size or power. Every member country can send five representatives, but they still hold only one vote. The General Assembly meets annually and can hold special sessions in case of urgent matters. Important decisions, such as electing non-permanent members of the Security Council or approving the UN budget, require a two-thirds majority, while others are decided by a simple majority.

(ii) The International Court of Justice (ICJ) is the judicial organ of the UN, headquartered in The Hague, Netherlands. Its three main functions are

- **Settling Legal Disputes** It resolves disputes between member nations based on international law.
- **Advisory Opinions** It provides legal advice to the General Assembly, Security Council and UN agencies.
- **Interpreting International Treaties** The ICJ interprets treaties and agreements, ensuring their proper implementation.

(iii) The full form of UNICEF is United Nations International Children's Emergency Fund. Although its name later changed to United Nations Children's Fund, the acronym UNICEF remains the same.

Three major functions of UNICEF are

- **Child Healthcare and Immunisation** It provides vaccines to protect children against diseases like polio, measles and tuberculosis.
- **Education and Literacy Programs** It promotes education for underprivileged children, especially girls and disabled children.
- **Emergency Relief** UNICEF provides food, clean water and medical aid during natural disasters, wars and crises.